Information Security Management

Concepts and Practice

Information Security Management

Concepts and Practice

BEL G. RAGGAD

CRC Press
Taylor & Francis Group
Boca Raton   London   New York

CRC Press is an imprint of the
Taylor & Francis Group, an **informa** business
AN AUERBACH BOOK

CRC Press
Taylor & Francis Group
6000 Broken Sound Parkway NW, Suite 300
Boca Raton, FL 33487-2742

International Standard Book Number: 978-1-4200-7854-1 (Hardback)

Library of Congress Cataloging-in-Publication Data

Raggad, Bel G.
   Information security management : concepts and practice / Bel G. Raggad.
      p. cm.
   Includes bibliographical references and index.
   ISBN 978-1-4200-7854-1 (hardcover : alk. paper)
   1. Computer security--Management. 2. Data protection. I. Title.

QA76.9.A25R337 2010
005.8--dc22
                                                                  2009043226

Visit the Taylor & Francis Web site at
http://www.taylorandfrancis.com

and the CRC Press Web site at
http://www.crcpress.com

I am pleased and very proud to dedicate this book to

Zine El Abidine Ben Ali

You are a hero to me.

You are a savior for Tunisia.

You are a model for other world leaders and you are a friend to the States.

Our world is experiencing economic challenges. Tunisia's homeland is surrounded by unstable neighbors and continents filled with civil wars and conflicts. Even with Tunisia's limited resources, you defeated terrorism, succeeded in creating a peaceful and friendly people, established a secure nation, maintained your cultural identity, and brought peace to all of us wherever we are.

Your contributions to global security are unmatched.

God bless you.

Belgacem Raggad

To Tunisia, country of my birth, and her people.

May they live forever in peace, prosperity, and freedom.

Belgacem Raggad

Contents

SECTION II SECURITY PLAN

SECTION III   SECURITY ANALYSIS

SECTION IV   SECURITY DESIGN

SECTION VI SECURITY REVIEW

SECTION VII   CONTINUAL SECURITY

Preface

You cannot manage information security by championing one security activity in the security life cycle and neglect another. If this happens, then your security management success will just be as good as the weakest activity in your security life cycle. Effective security management rests on effective security activities throughout the security life cycle and their effective integration.

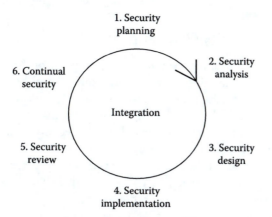

Information Security Life Cycle

Information security management defines a comprehensive framework to protect an organization's computing environment, including its people, activities, data, technology, and network. This includes the continual review and enhancements of current information security programs, subject to maintaining risks at or below acceptable levels in a cost-effective, timely, and efficient manner.

Information security management, as defined earlier, can only be realized throughout an integrated information security life cycle as defined above. We, therefore, have organized the book into seven sections: The first section presents a simple introduction of information security and management concepts. The next six sections of the book are reserved for the security life cycle phases, one section per phase.

Section I: Introduction

This section of the book presents an introduction to information security concepts, the focus of Chapter 1. Chapter 2 is reserved to introduce useful management concepts. Some of those concepts are redefined to ease their adoption in information security management. Chapter 3 presents the information security life cycle. This is probably the most important chapter of the book because it is used to organize its contents and define a coherent learning structure for it.

Section II: Security Planning

Security planning is obviously the most important phase of the information security cycle because it plans all security activities throughout the security life cycle. In addition to this, security planning also aims at defining and revising all information security requirements of the organization. In this book, we are primarily concerned with the development of two plans: the security plan (Chapter 4) and the business continuity plan (Chapter 6). However, because the security policy of a system is its acceptable computing behavior, those two chapters will not mean much if the organization does not have its security policy well defined before initiating such projects. In closing this section of the book on security planning we must add a very rich chapter on security policy (Chapter 5).

Section III: Security Analysis

This section is concerned with all security analysis activities needed in the security life cycle to devise a risk-driven security program. This constitutes a bridge to the security solutions produced at the design phase of the security life cycle. The design of those security solutions depends on the information security requirements produced by the security analysis phase. Security analysis acquires information on the valuation of information assets, their business impacts given identified threats, their security exposure levels, their vulnerability levels, the effectiveness of their current security controls, and their risk levels. All this information has to be assembled and used in defining current security requirements.

In order to bring together all the information we just listed, this section reserves Chapter 7 for security risk management, Chapter 8 for the integrated system fault-event analysis, Chapter 9 for active security assessment, and Chapter 10 for system availability requirements.

Section IV: Security Design

The security design section aims at devising security programs needed for effective information security management. We propose two security enhancement approaches. The first security enhancement approach is based on the ISO/IEC 27002 and is called nominal security enhancement based on ISO/IEC 27002. The term *nominal* is used to indicate that we are limited to a nominal security audit since the ISO/IEC 27002 does not provide the needed specifications of an information security management system, but only security best practices. The second security enhancement approach is based on technical security audit as specified in the ISO/IEC 27001 and produces an ISMS based on the specifications defined by this standard. This section presents two chapters, Chapter 11 on nominal security enhancement and Chapter 12 on technical security enhancement, using as its foundation ISO/IEC 27002 and ISO/IEC 27001.

Section V: Security Implementation

This section is reserved for all implementation aspects of current security programs. Usually, there are security activities that are in operation, under revision, or planned in the future. The most visible aspects of implemented information security are associated with the enforcement of security policies for various assets constituting the computing environment, or they implement the recommended security controls, security program, or security solutions imposed by the corporate security strategy or policies. Chapter 13 proposes a simple taxonomy of information security solutions, and Chapter 14 presents ISO/IEC 15408, which proposes the Common Criteria and its Common Evaluation Methodology.

Section VI: Security Review

This part presents useful knowledge on security review in an organization. Usually, security review is concerned with security auditing. Earlier, at the design phase, we introduced the nominal security audit based on ISO/IEC 27002 and the technical security audit based on ISO/IEC 27001. An organization is usually interested in three main achievements: certification against the right security standard required by the organization's security policy, accreditation of its information systems, and authorization of processing of critical systems.

The most useful security standards for effective security management are NIST SP 800-18, NIST SP 800-53, ISO/IEC 27002 (identical to ISO/IEC 17799), and ISO 27001. We intend to discuss the first two standards in Section II, reserved for security planning, and ISO/IEC 27002 and ISO 27001 in Section IV, reserved for security design.

This section presents and discusses general introduction to security audit in privacy rights, IT, and HIPAA.

Section VII: Continual Security

This section is concerned with the continual security phase. While this phase is usually approached by security review activities, it is important to note that those security review activities are not the same security review activities discussed in Section VI. The main differences between them are related to the way those activities are initiated and the way their security objectives are defined. For example, the security review activities in the continual security phase are triggered by signals of undesired incidents while those included in the security review phase are initiated by the security policy requirements.

Moreover, while the security review phase embraces the clear security objectives of certification, accreditation, and authorization, the continual security phase intends to analyze signals indicating negative changes and undesired incidents, and assess risks, and reiterate the security life cycle for the purpose of enhancing the organization security posture.

At this point there are still several areas that may be covered in Section VII that are related to continual security, but the ISMS studied in Chapter 12 and the ISO/IEC 27001 both produce required risk-driven security programs that assure continual security. The statements of applicability accompanying both systems assert its achievement. Early reviewers of some of the chapters indicated that it would be useful to talk about the Sarbanes–Oxley Act, cyberterrorism, and homeland security in the final part of the book dealing with continual security. We thought that given what we see around these days, with the intensification of the economic recession and the rise of cyberterrorism, there will be no harm done if we talk about SOX, cyberterrorism, and homeland security, as recommended. In fact, I thought that after the Enron scandal, corporate arrogance, executives' insensitivity and bad intentions, their greed, pervasive conflict of interest, and accountants' malicious games, all had gone. Unfortunately, when I hear of Citigroup spending $50 million of taxpayers' bailout money buying a French-made Dassault Falcon 7X jet for its executives, and when I see John Thain, the former Merrill Lynch CEO, just ousted, spending $1.2 million of taxpayers' bailout money redecorating his downtown

Manhattan office (as the company was firing employees), then discussing SOX and its evolution, is a chapter that imposes itself.

In this area, I invited Dr. Roy Girasa to help me writing the chapters on HIPAA, SOX, and cyberterrorism. I am very grateful to his contributions that discussed those areas that combine concepts relating to business, law, and IT security. Dr. Girasa is a professor of law in the Department of Legal Studies and Taxation, Lubin School of Business at Pace University, New York. He was a trial attorney for four decades and has appeared on a number of television shows. His specialties are international business law and cyberlaw. In addition to his great publications, both in quality and in number, he has written an especially excellent book, *Cyberlaw: National and International Perspectives*.

Who Needs to Read This Book?

If you are a security manager, with any title, you need to read this book.

If you are an IT manager, a manager in any functional unit, or a general manager, this book will provide the knowledge you need to participate in any organizational decisions related to information security management.

If you are an undergraduate or graduate student in any business-, computing-, IT-, or telecommunication-related program, majoring or minoring in any information security area, this book will provide a comprehensive recap of all information security activities of the information security life cycle and methodologies on how to perform them.

For undergraduate students, this book assumes that students have taken courses in information security concepts, information security solutions (at least three of the following security areas: security administration, cryptography, access control, security analysis, security monitoring, and physical security), security risk assessment, and information security standards. This volume can be a great textbook for a capstone course designed to be offered in the final semester of a student majoring in the area of information security or any related area of computing.

General readers who attended workshops or seminars in information security concepts, some of the security solutions above, and security risk assessment will have no problems reading this book.

This book provides great information and knowledge support for any person interested in learning information security management.

As explained earlier, this book adopts the security life cycle, discussed in Chapter 3, in defining the contents of the book and organizing it in a sequence parallel to the sequence of steps constituting the security life cycle. We reserved a special part for every phase in the security life cycle. Each part of the book is divided into two or more chapters as shown in the following diagram which depicts the parts and the chapters constituting this book.

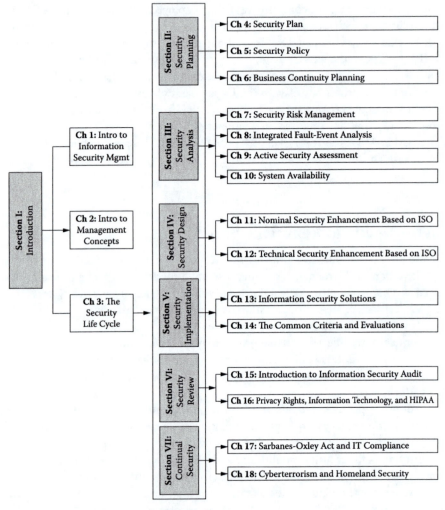

Book Structure

About the Author

Bel G. Raggad, Ph.D., is a professor of IT Security in the Seidenberg School of Computer Science and Information Systems, an NSA Center of Excellence in IA Education, at Pace University, New York. Dr. Raggad is Executive Chairman of the International Group of e-Systems Research and Applications (TIGERA).

Dr. Raggad obtained his Ph.D. in Information Systems from the Smeal School of Business at The Pennsylvania State University, University Park, PA, in 1989. His research interests include global computing, IT management, intelligent decision support, and information security. Dr. Raggad has written several books in the information security discipline.

Dr. Raggad is an international consultant in information security planning and auditing who actively advises governments in securing their computer networks. He was awarded a Gold Medal by the President of Tunisia in November 2001 for his advice and support in planning the security of public agencies against cyber crimes. Dr. Raggad is currently a member of the Fulbright Board of Directors and Secretary of the Philadelphia/Delaware Chapter.

INTRODUCTION

Chapter 1

Introduction to Information Security Management

Learning Objectives

After reading this chapter, students are expected to achieve an understanding of:

Why information security matters

Information sensitivity classification

Information security governance

How to secure a computing environment

That a goal-driven security model based on the CIA triad is not sufficient

That achieving security goals does necessarily achieve business goals

Parkerian hexad security model

Main classes of security controls: managerial, operational, and technical

National Security Agency (NSA) triad for security assessment

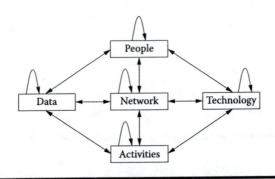

Figure 1.1   Computing environment with interacting components.

1.1 Introduction

This chapter gives a simple introduction to some of the security concepts needed to discuss effective security management. An organization is viewed, throughout this book, as a composite computing environment made of smaller computing environments and information systems. A computing environment, as in Raggad's taxonomy of information security, is made up of five continuously interacting components: activities, people, data, technology, and networks [8]. Figure 1.1 depicts a computing environment in which each component interacts with itself and the rest of the components in the same environment. People interact with people, for example, when an information owner hires a security administrator to manage the security of a given information resource. People interact with other components in the same environment, for example, when an information owner authorizes a given activity to be performed on a given data resource using a given technology. An information system is also viewed as a smaller computing environment made up of activities, people, data, technology, and networks that continuously interact to efficiently achieve information system objectives.

This chapter will then discuss the importance of security interdependence, and emphasize that all information system components have to be secured in order to achieve information system security. We will define each information system component and discuss how to protect it subject to its security policy and toward achieving comprehensive security for the entirety of the computing environment enclosing the information system. We then define and discuss the importance of information security governance in terms of corporate governance and IT governance.

In order to better discuss effective information security management, we present the CIA triad, and criticize this goal-driven security model because of its failure to incorporate the organization's business goals into this model. In order to balance security goals and business goals in a target organization, we propose the security star model, which introduces a risk-driven security model that proposes to achieve business objectives through the implementation of the security star. We additionally present the Parker's Hexad security model as an alternative security model to the CIA triad and the security star [6]. We also provide a brief description of information security management and introduce some useful concepts, for example, Defense-In-Depth, security risk, and the NSA triad for security assessment.

Information security is now better understood by organizations because most of them have experienced, one way or another, some harm produced by malware, intruders, or even by their own employees. There is not a single enterprise that has not seen some undesired events that affected its computing environment and its information systems. Several types of harm may have been inflicted on those organizations:

Theft, damage, or destruction of computer systems
Corruption or destruction of corporate data
Leakage of sensitive information to rivals
Stealing private information for employees, customers, or partners
Damage to the reputation of an organization
Denial of service that caused business loss

The methods employed by intruders to conduct the foregoing malicious activities are varied, and they are often available, for fee or at a low cost, on the Internet depending on their specifications. This book does not deal directly with specific countermeasures for specific attacks but will discuss effective security management methods that if followed thoroughly will lead to the mitigation of security risks associated with those attacks.

We have nowadays started seeing more and more attacks on enterprise information systems by insiders, hackers, and all types of viruses. The true number of security breaches is unknown as companies do not report their incidents, fearing negative publicity.

Despite all these threats, companies still fail to give the needed attention to information security. Information security management requires a great deal of management support in order to plan effective enterprise security. Effective information security management cannot be achieved without involving all people interacting with information resources, including information owners, security administrators, security technicians, and operators. Figure 1.2 depicts the layers of personnel around an information asset.

1.2 Why Information Security Matters

Enterprise business value generation capability is driven by information. If this information is accurate, complete, and timely, then there is business value; otherwise, there will be weak business value generation. This information is also the basis of competitive advantage. If a rival gets hold of some of this information, the consequences will be catastrophic. If a competitor intercepts the cost and price

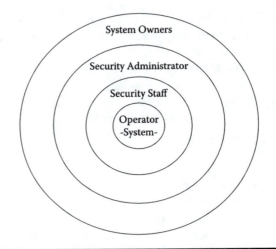

Figure 1.2   Layers of personnel around an information resource.

information exchanged with a major partner, you and your partners may suffer great business losses.

Moreover, assets are very interdependent, and one cannot value or protect a single asset without securing the rest of the assets constituting the information system, including people, activities, data, technology, and networks. Information security management emphasizes a comprehensive study of the computing environment rather than acquiring off-the-shelf solutions. Off-the-shelf solutions will not work in security management simply because (1) security requirements vary depending on the vulnerabilities and threats associated with the organization's computing environment, and (2) the effects and consequences of similar security incidents vary from one organization to another.

Information security cannot just be devised based on the specifications of security solutions; a thorough study of the organization business value generation model and its computing environment is needed before prescribing any security programs. Any information security investigation has to be risk driven.

1.3 Information Sensitivity Classification

Information should, however, be classified in terms of the value added to the organization and its sensitivity level. The sensitivity level and value of the asset will determine how much security will be deployed to protect it. A sensitivity taxonomy should, however, be simple to understand and easy to apply. It should also be effective in classifying assets in terms of their level of sensitivity. Information can, however, be organized as in Figure 1.3, where at the root, we only distinguish between two root classes of information sensitivity: public and confidential.

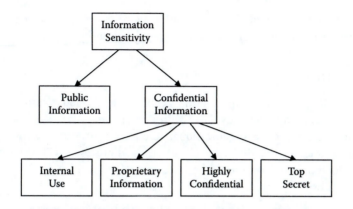

Figure 1.3 Information sensitivity taxonomy.

Public information is set to be public, and it may be shared by all. Confidential information should be shared with recipients who are explicitly authorized to obtain it. Information owners define agents who are authorized to access confidential information. This is often accomplished using the information resource's security policy.

We provide here the information sensitivity taxonomy proposed by the ISO/ IEC 17799 or ISO/IEC 27002 [4], which are as follows: public, internal use, proprietary, highly confidential, and top secret.

1.3.1 Top Secret

This is highly sensitive internal data. Any data of this type, if divulged to an unauthorized person, can produce catastrophic consequences to owners. This is the highest sensitivity level possible. Military information is an example of top secret information that if leaked could compromise national security. For a business, strategic plans, acquisition information, and R&D processes are all examples of top secret information.

1.3.2 Highly Confidential

Highly confidential information is highly critical information that is not top secret, but is considered critical to the organization's ongoing operations and could vitally hinder the organization's capability of business continuity. Losses are very high, but the company can absorb the damages and can, at higher cost, resume business. Such information includes accounting information, information about new business plans, new products, and new technology; these are examples of highly confidential information that if divulged to rivals will lead to major losses that may be offset at higher cost. Information about customers may be highly confidential if there are risks that law suits may take place if confidentiality is compromised.

Highly confidential information should not be copied or removed from the organization's operational control without specific authority.

1.3.3 Proprietary

Proprietary information is information produced by in-house resources, hardware, software, or methodology. If this proprietary information is lost or made public, information about organizational resources is also lost or made public. Operational information, design specifications, and processes will be lost to competitors. Such information should be restricted to proprietary use by authorized personnel only.

1.3.4 Internal Use Only

Internal information is confidential, but is not authorized to become public. If this type of information is made public, it may lead to unapproved general circulation outside the organization, where its disclosure would be a nuisance value to the organization's management, but risks of financial loss would be negligible.

Internal correspondence, announcements and minutes, and periodic activity reports are examples of internal use information.

1.3.5 Public Information

This refers to public information that can be made public without undesirable consequences. Examples are free-access Web site information, annual reports, ads, and commercials.

1.4 Information Security Governance

Before we discuss information security governance, let us first introduce corporate and IT governance, as the three concepts are related. Searchsecurity.com (August 17, 2006) published an article written by Shon Harris entitled "Information Security Governance Guide" on information security governance (http://search-security.techtarget.com/generic/0,295582,sid14_gci1211236,00.html) [7]. In this guide, information security governance is described as being similar in nature to corporate governance and IT governance because they share functionality and goals. Even though they have different focuses, all the three concepts work within an organizational structure of a company and they aim at ensuring, in their own way, that the company grows and prospers.

While corporate governance is concerned with how the board of directors and executive management run and control a company, IT governance is more concerned with how technology is used and managed to support business needs. The guide adopts the following definition of information security governance given by the IT Governance Institute in its Board Briefing on IT Governance, 2nd Edition:

> Security governance is the set of responsibilities and practices exercised by the board and executive management with the goal of providing strategic direction, ensuring that objectives are achieved, ascertaining that risks are managed appropriately and verifying that the enterprise's resources are used responsibly.

The guide criticizes the preceding definition as being too abstract to be useful. The definition is a simple strategic policy statement that will stay ineffective unless it is properly interpreted and transformed into meaningful tactical and operational functions and practices. That is, information security governance should consists of all of the tools, personnel, and business processes that ensure that security is carried out to meet an organization's specific needs. Additionally, the guide requires that ISG should provide for a favorable organizational structure, roles and responsibilities, performance measurement, defined tasks, and oversight mechanisms.

Shon Harris succeeded in demonstrating the effects of ISG by comparing the security-relevant managerial profiles of an organization that is adopting ISG and another without it. An organization with an ISG will have the following desirable features:

1. Board members understand that information security is critical to the company and demand to be updated quarterly on security performance and breaches.
2. CEO, CFO, CIO, and business unit managers participate in a risk management committee that meets each month, and information security is always one topic on the agenda to review.
3. Executive management set an acceptable risk level that is the basis for the company's security policies and all security activities.
4. Executive management holds business unit managers responsible for carrying out risk management activities for their specific business units.
5. Critical business processes are documented along with the risks that are inherent in the various steps within the business processes.
6. Employees are held accountable for any security breaches they participate in, either maliciously or accidentally.
7. Security products, managed services, and consultants are purchased (or hired) and deployed in an informed manner. They are also constantly reviewed to ensure they are cost-effective.
8. The organization is continuing to review its business processes, including security, with the goal of continuous improvement.

On the other hand, an organization that has not adopted ISG will demonstrate the following negative features:

1. Board members do not understand that information security is in their realm of responsibility, and focus solely on corporate governance and profits.
2. CEO, CFO, and business unit managers feel that information security is the responsibility of the CIO, chief information security officer (CISO), and IT department, and do not get involved.
3. The CISO employs boilerplate security policies, inserts his or her company's name, and has the CEO sign them.
4. All security activity takes place within the security department; thus, security works within a silo and is not integrated throughout the organization.
5. Business processes are not documented and analyzed for potential risks that can affect operations, productivity, and profitability.
6. Policies and standards are developed, but no enforcement or accountability practices have been envisioned or deployed.
7. Security products, managed services, and consultants are purchased (or hired) and deployed without any real research or performance metrics to be able to determine their ROI or effectiveness. Company has a false sense of security because it is using products, consultants, or managed services.
8. The organization does not analyze its performance for improvement, but continually marches forward and repeatedly makes the same mistakes.

A simple definition of ISG is provided by the same author at the end of her article as follows:

Information security governance is a coherent system of integrated security components (products, personnel, training, processes, policies, etc.) that exist to ensure that the organization survives and, hopefully, thrives.

1.5 The Computing Environment

We often talk about security without specifying the resource to be secured. The definition of security will vary when the resource is defined. For example, the definition of information security is not necessarily identical to the definitions of network security or personnel security.

Before we define security, let us define the resources in a computing environment that need to be protected. As stated earlier, in a computing environment we identify five main resources: people, activities, data, technology, and network. Securing the enterprise is achieved by securing its computing environment. An information system is a well-defined computing environment where information is generated for a specific group of users. Also, in order to protect information, we need to protect all information system components that jointly produce the information. That is, whether we are protecting the computing environment, the information systems, or information, we need to protect people, system activities, data resources, technology, and networks.

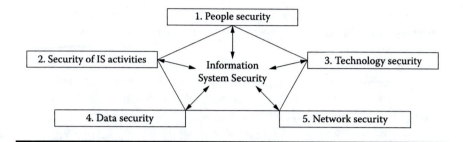

Figure 1.4 Security of an information system.

As shown in Figure 1.4, an information system consists of five components: people, activities, technology, data, and network. The security of information systems should be understood in terms of the security of all its components: the security of its people, the security of its activities, the security of its data, the security of its technology, and the security of its network.

Usually, however, we talk about information security to mean the security of an information system or one of its components. However we use it, information security is often expressed in terms of information confidentiality (C), information integrity (I), and information availability (A). We will later explain that these information security components, often denoted as CIA components, are the most common in the literature.

Essentially, activities—for example, procedures or policies—are implemented to explain to people and define to computers how to interact with the rest of the components in the computing environment in order to achieve its security objectives.

In most of the literature, authors use the terms *information security, information system security, computer security,* and *information assurance* interchangeably. Even though information assurance may be defined differently, as we will see later, often there is no harm in using those terms interchangeably as long as they aim at protecting the confidentiality, integrity, and availability of information in your computing environment.

Information security means protecting information from unauthorized interactions. The only authorized interactions are the ones defined in the security policy of the information resource containing the information. Interactions include access to the information and its use, disclosure, disruption, modification, or destruction.

Each organization defines its own security policies for all its information systems. Those organizations, public or private, store, process, and transmit large amounts of confidential information about their products, R&D, financial reports, customers, employees, and partners. The leakage of this information, its corruption, or its unavailability when needed can produce great financial losses, lawsuits, and undesired consequences for the organization. The protection of enterprise information is a vital business requirement that should not be overlooked when its information security is considered.

Information security is achieved by implementing managerial, operational, and technical controls that deliver information confidentiality, information integrity, and information availability.

Information confidentiality is the protection of information from unauthorized access or disclosure. Information integrity is the protection of information from unauthorized modification. Information availability is realized when a user who needs to know obtains the required information from the appropriate resource. The notion of information availability does not apply to the following situations:

The user does not satisfy the need-to-know requirement.
The resource is not designed to produce the intended information.

The need-to-know policy is a rule that restricts an information holder, a person or an information resource, to only present the held information to the user who without it cannot perform his or her authorized tasks as prescribed in his or her approved task specifications.

For example, a human resource manager may need to access some private fields in an employee record to perform certain managerial tasks required for affirmative action, while a project manager can only access the information field stored in the same employee record in order to schedule certain project activities to be performed by the employee.

The terms *need to know* and *least privilege* are sometimes used interchangeably even though the former is generally applied to people, while the latter is often applied to processes.

1.5.1 People

People depend on other people, activities, technology, data, and networks to perform their tasks. Their output depends on the security of all those components. Compromised components, due to information leakage, information corruption, or unavailability, will prevent people from attaining their work objectives and hence lower their productivity. People have to think of a defense system to protect their assets and, with time, they will develop a culture of secure behavior. For example, they will be able to recognize malicious components, without any testing activities; report security incidents, and behave as specified in the relevant security policy. On the other hand, people without such a security culture may unintentionally compromise the security of their computing environment by, for example, compromising their assigned roles, violating the relevant security policy, denying information to the need-to-know user, corrupting or leaking information, and so on.

The enforcement of security policy should begin by training and educating people before communicating the security policy to them. Often, a security policy is very long and hence very difficult to retain. People tend to forget things and take the easy way out even if some policy is violated. That is, the simple presentation and communication of the security policy without adequate training and testing may not result in good retention and, hence, we will see poor enforcement of security policy, and an insecure computing environment.

People should play a collaborative role in enhancing security through vigilance and the sharing of ideas and comments that lead to the development of new rules of thumb on how to enhance security. The security officer should work closely with people to share information with them at the need-to-know levels. This information sharing will allow the security officer to appropriately investigate all levels of security breaches and plan timely responses.

1.5.2 System Activities

Examples of activities are policies, procedures, standards, and guidelines. Policies describe how the organization plans to protect its computing environment, including people, activities, data, technology, and networks.

A security policy for an information system defines acceptable behavior of this system. A security policy is a formal statement of the rules that system components, people, data, activities, technology, and networks, all of which constitute the system, must adhere to. The policy defines the security goals for all system components, including users, administrators, managers, and owners. Even though the security policy defines the acceptable behavior of the information system, those agents have to understand their obligations, that is, their acceptable behavior, to protect the information system according to the security policy defined for the system. Those agents not only have obligations to define the appropriate security policy for their information system but also obligations to enforce this security policy. A good security policy is one that is easy to revise, communicate, and enforce.

An information system also depends on processes that owners develop, document, and review. Processes define how to manage all types of interactions among various components of the information system.

For a given information resource, its security policy defines its acceptable computing behavior. Security policies include comprehensive security requirements defined by systems owners that indicate certain behaviors for all the components of the computing environment. Those policies should be periodically reviewed.

Procedures define the methods and instructions by which policies are developed, communicated, reviewed, and enforced. Procedures are adapted to the security policy enforcement needs, and they differ from one information resource to another, depending on the role and placement of the resource in the computing environment.

Guidelines are suggestions for accomplishing a certain task. The organization, for example, has guidelines on how to develop security policies, how to develop security plans, and how to conduct security auditing.

It is important that the organization keep full documentation for the policies, standards, procedures, and guidelines for the purpose of easy reference when audit takes place. This documentation is also used for training and periodic review when changes to processes occur.

1.5.3 Data Resources

The data components in an information system or in a computing environment, in general, constitute all the conceptual resources that are transformed by people or computer programs to produce information that is used in making all system decisions. When we talk about conceptual resources, we usually mean those resources in a company's computing environment that are not tangible but add significant value. There are essentially four conceptual resources: noise, data, information, and knowledge.

1.5.3.1 Noise Facts

Noise is any raw fact with an unknown code system. For example, the raw fact "11," itself, is 11 if the code system is the decimal base, or 3 if the code system is the binary base. If we do not know the code system of the raw fact "11," then we cannot know for sure what it means.

For example, the raw fact "9$6#/12/%/15/0" is noise if the code system described in the following text is not known to the user. If the user knows this code system, this raw fact is no longer noise. In this case, it will have the meaning "Hello."

Code system: The code language is made of numbers and the special characters $, #, and %, which serve as separators. Each letter of the alphabet is coded as M(a) = rank(a). If this rank has two digits, it should be delimited inserted between two slashes.

On the Internet, there is an abundance of raw facts that is shared among users in a cryptographic manner. If intercepted, the transmitted raw facts are considered noise because the interceptor does not know the code system of cryptography and cannot hence read those facts. Noise of this kind is a very important resource for the users sharing the data because its meaning will be generated when the raw facts are decrypted. These raw facts can only be of great value to users, otherwise they would not have bothered to encrypt them to secure them when they are transmitted on the Internet.

1.5.3.2 Data Facts

Data consists of any raw facts with a known code system. In the foregoing example, "9$6#/12/%/15/0," this raw fact is not noise but becomes data after applying the code system.

1.5.3.3 Information

In most of the literature, information is defined as processed data. In a more technical sense, and for a more useful meaning, however, information should be defined as follows:

Information consists of a network of data facts that generate both cognition and surprise. Usually, information cannot be one piece of raw facts unless other pieces are implied. Even though the raw facts are data facts and hence of known code system, not all users can capture the meaning of those facts. For example, the raw facts "My first daughter was born on ٧/٢٩/١٩٩٣ in Ruston, Louisiana" are a mix of English words and Indian numbers written in the decimal base that may be of no meaning to you. This is not information to you as long as it does not generate any cognitivity to you. For somebody, however, who is familiar with Indian numbers, those raw facts mean "My first daughter was born on 7/29/1993 in Ruston, Louisiana."

At this point, the raw facts "My first daughter was born on ٧/٢٩/١٩٩٣ in Ruston, Louisiana" satisfy the first two definitional conditions for information but these raw facts become information only when they generate a surprise, that is, real news. For my wife and I, these raw facts are not information because we both know our daughter's birth date. For other people, these raw facts are information because they generate news to them.

As explained earlier, facts are only information for people who have no prior knowledge of them. This means that intruders seeking this type of information gain great value from unauthorizedly capturing information. This also means that information owners should invest more to protect new information.

1.5.3.4 Knowledge Facts

Knowledge consists of accepted facts, principles, or rules of thumb that are useful for specific domains. Knowledge can be the result of inferences and implications produced from simple information facts [2].

All those conceptual resources are referred to as data throughout this book. Data resources, as meant here, can contain data facts, encrypted data facts, information, or knowledge. These conceptual resources become useful when a transformation process is applied to produce the information needed to add business value.

1.5.4 Technology

Over time, the term *technology* has taken several meanings: Objects such as tools, machines, electronic devices, and so on; knowledge describing the know-how associated with innovations; methodologies describing the tasks, approaches, and methods invented to gain competitive advantage; processes defined to enhance productivity; etc.

In this context, we limit technology to the hardware and software tools needed to perform various computing activities required by the computing environment.

1.5.5 Network

In the context of a computing environment, the network component consists of all physical resources constituting the computing environment, including the network infrastructure, buildings, and equipment.

1.6 Security of Various Components in the Computing Environment

Because the organization may be assimilated to a large computing environment, and because an information system may be assimilated to a small computing environment, they may be both protected the same way, that is, the way a computing environment is protected. Because a computing environment consists of activities, people, data, technology, and networks, it can be protected by protecting all its components. That is, we can protect the organization, an information system, or any computing environment by providing for the following:

Personnel security to protect people
Procedural security to protect activities
Information security to protect data resources
Software and hardware security to protect technology
Network security to protect networks

1.6.1 Personnel Security

Information security is the result of the work of people, processes, and activities. If a security staff member employs the wrong security mechanism or fails to perform the activities prescribed to provide the planned security, then there will be no security. If the trusted staff member selected for a security task is not well trained to deliver, then the planned security will not be in place.

That is, employees can be a source of insecurity. Some of them may unintentionally harm the system by making mistakes; some will maliciously compromise the system.

What can be done to prevent the aforementioned security problems? We need what we call *personnel security*, which refers to those practices and tools adopted by the human resources unit to ensure that personnel security safeguards are applied.

Personnel security safeguards may be organized into several categories:

1. Qualification assurance: A person is only hired if he or she matches both the specifications of the job and the security clearance for the job. While a candidate's qualification for the job can be easily verified after technical testing and after reviewing his or her work experience, the security clearance task is not an easy process.
2. Screening assurance: Screening and background checks of candidates have to be conducted very thoroughly to make sure that candidates with a history of poor behavior cannot infiltrate into the system. The stringency of the security clearance associated with a position depends on the sensitivity/confidentiality of information accessible to this position.
3. Authorizing of process: This consists of granting or taking away any physical or system access privileges at the time of hiring of an employee, his or her transfer elsewhere, or at the termination of his or her duties. All privileges of an employee's system access may be granted, modified, or revoked following a formal and auditable process.
4. Security training: Security training programs are made available to employees in accordance with the security requirements of their position.
5. Nondisclosure agreements: All employees who are involved in security matters have to sign nondisclosure agreements appropriate to their positions. The nondisclosure agreements have to be signed by all individuals who need access to sensitive/confidential information, prior to granting access to that information.

1.6.2 Activity Security

Activities of an information system consist of all procedures, regulations, policies, standards, and protocols governing all interactions between all the components of the information system, and between these components and the information system and its environment.

Any weakness in any activity of the information system can produce undesired events that can compromise the security of the information system. Any corruption in those activities can damage the information system in unpredictable ways.

1.6.3 Information Security

Data is understood as all the facts that are processed into information. Information, however, describes the meanings and interpretations that users associate with those facts. The value of information stems from the ways it is interpreted and applied to make decisions that affect the organization's business-value-generation capabilities. A successful model that can more accurately define the generation of business value in an organization should probably incorporate a new approach to identify and redefine all information assets the organization owns and without whose efficient performance this business model would not work as planned. This new approach would define all the conceptual resources that can be transformed into information of great value that is capable of generating great business value.

All the conceptual resources we identified earlier are part of the computing environment and have to be adequately secured in order to ensure the security of the computing environment. In Raggad's taxonomy, those conceptual resources are reduced to activities, data, and the software part of technology. The physical resources are reduced to people, network, and the hardware part of technology.

Conceptual resources are physically secured to prevent unauthorized disclosure or unauthorized modification of their content as well as destruction of information technology resources. Moreover, equipment used to process conceptual resources, and buildings and office space housing information technology resources have to meet organizational physical security requirements. Security safeguards are acquired and maintained to ensure the continued availability and security of each facility's information technology equipment.

Unless it is specifically noted otherwise, we will use the terms *data* and *information* to mean the same thing throughout this book.

Information security is the protection of information resources against unauthorized access. Conceptual resources, such as programs, data, and information, can be secured by requiring users to supply passwords and digital certificates. While passwords prove that a correct code has been entered, we are still unsure who the supposed user is, in fact, the real one who entered the password. We can obviously employ digital certificates and biometric techniques to authenticate the user and control access to information resources, but security can still be compromised because many other violations such as eavesdropping can take place.

At the same time, users who have been authenticated and admitted into the system may dangerous. Those users may in fact, once admitted inside, initiate unauthorized activities or even intentionally perform malicious actions that could compromise the security of the system.

1.6.4 Technology Security

Technology may be soft or hard. They are both used to support enterprise operations and their security. If software or hardware is compromised, then their functions will be compromised. This will weaken enterprise operations and compromise their security. Imagine that an intrusion detection system, hardware or software, fails to perform as intended. As a result, the real-time alert system and any actionable visibility that provides actionable information to the security administrator about the detected intrusions will not work. Such a situation may produce dangerous consequences.

1.6.5 Network Security

A network is any set of interconnected resources. A computer network is simply a system of interconnected computers.

Network security is the protection of company networks and their services from unauthorized modification, destruction, or disclosure. It aims at providing assurance that the network is performing critical security-related functions and has not been compromised in any way.

In network security, the enterprise should secure all aspect of its network resources without taking any host-based security of those resources for granted. Once those resources are connected to the network, all host-based security attributes have to be reviewed to understand how they are affected by the network environment. Servers on the network may contain useful data and information on how to access internal resources.

Workstations on the network may contain malicious data and can be used to attack other computers. Routers, switches, bridges, hubs, and any other network equipment may be used as an access point to your network. Your network wiring and media may be exploited by intruders to access your network or to initiate a wireless access point to your internal network. You should also make sure that all laptops taken by company workers outside the company to conduct off-site work are reviewed for malicious content that can potentially harm the company when the laptops are connected to the internal network.

1.7 Security Interdependence

We have earlier defined information system security in terms of people security, activity security, data security, technology security, and network security. We do not intend to persuade you that those information system components are independent and that the security of each component can be addressed independently. That is not the case; on the contrary, all components are interrelated. For example, you cannot secure a network without securing its resources, which can be data, technology, people, or activities. But the taxonomy adopted to organize an information system into the foregoing components is very useful when stand-alone security is achieved before those resources are connected to the network. Security aspects of a network may be network based or host based. Personnel security, for example, requires adequate security clearance of a network administrator before he or she is assigned to the network. Also, a computer should be secured by checking its hardware and operating system before it is connected to the network. In fact, all information system components should be inspected for stand-alone or host-based security before they are connected to the network. This can be achieved, for example, by removing all known vulnerabilities, such as untrustworthy people, defective infrastructure, known malware and viruses in computers, or corrupted data in databases.

1.8 CIA Triad

Almost all the literature [5], and most companies, have accepted that security goals are what matters, and the only security goals they adopted are those constituting the CIA triad: confidentiality, integrity, and availability.

1.8.1 Confidentiality

Confidentiality aims at preventing information leakage to unauthorized recipients. For example, in order to protect the confidentiality of my social security number in an online session, the transmission of my social security number has to be encrypted. In fact, any data store where my social security number may end up in has to be encrypted and adequately secured. Confidentiality may be violated, for example, if my social security number is given over the phone or on a fax line to an unauthorized recipient. The inappropriate disposal of a document containing my social security number is another type of confidentiality breach.

1.8.2 Integrity

Data integrity aims at preventing information corruption. Corruption is the unauthorized modification of information by an agent. This agent can be a person, a virus, or a system. For example, a student obtains access to his or her instructor's grade file and modify his or her grade. A virus infection can also lead to information corruption if a file or one of its records is modified or deleted.

1.8.3 Availability

Availability aims at making information available to users as stated in the security policy of the information resource where it resides. In an information system, this requires that all the components needed to produce this information be functional.

1.9 Security Goals versus Business Goals

Along with the CIA triad, the community of security consumers found out they could not do much without security requirements such as authentication (needed for access control) and non-repudiation (needed to validate the origin of transmissions). Here is an example.

If I am managing a sales point, what good does confidentiality do for me if the online orders that are encrypted to ensure their confidentiality are intercepted on their way to me. A missing patch may be to blame, but I just lost sales despite confidentiality. What good does integrity do for me if the online orders that are encrypted to ensure their integrity get lost on their way to me? A computer virus may be to blame, but I just lost sales despite data integrity. What good does availability do for me if all servers connected to my sales point are 100% available but the online orders get eaten up before they get to me? Faulty software may be to blame, but I just lost sales despite availability. Well, what good has all those security goals of the CIA triad done for me when I continue to lose business despite meeting all those security goals?

This example should be sufficient to show that achieving security goals may not necessarily lead to achievement of business objectives. There is certainly a faulty connection somewhere between security goals and business goals. Maybe risk has to be incorporated somewhere or perhaps the security goals in the CIA triad have to be rewritten in terms of business goals.

Adopting this goal-driven security model may be bothersome because achievement of your security goals may not always be compatible with achievement of your business goals.

A firewall, as any other software or hardware tool, has vulnerabilities and flaws that may be exploited. When this occurs, the firewall may not function as configured or may even crash, and in this case, the internal network will be at the mercy of intruders.

What would happen if the CIA triad security goals were achieved as prescribed but other incidents with catastrophic consequences occurred due to threats such as viruses, keystroke loggers, Trojan horse viruses, spyware, and other malicious tools?

Moreover, this goal-driven security model stops after achieving those security goals, and those security goals may remain unchanged. The computing environment and its information systems, however, keep changing in terms of new vulnerabilities, new threats, new technology, new data, new people, new activities, and new networks while the old security goals retain their same states. What could happen when one of the foregoing computing environment components has changed and produced risks that are just too high for many critical services to operate? The goal-driven security model does not know how to manage information security in the organization after all prescribed security goals have been achieved. There is still a need to value all assets, identify all threats, review existing security controls, identify asset vulnerabilities, assess all risks, mitigate risks, and devise a risk-driven security management program that could work at the top of all security goals prescribed by system owners and asset security policies.

Even if there is a way to manage the prescribed security goals and minimize their idle time periods, that is, when they are not fully satisfied, there is still a great deal of uncertainty associated with changes in the computing environment that require the setting of new security goals, or some old security goals may need to be dropped. However, no matter where we are, nothing can be done without assessing security risks. The CIA triad may be revised by adding more security goals and the risk security requirement. Security goals tend to encourage the acquisition of on-the-shelf security solutions capable of solving very detailed security situations, despite all the vulnerabilities that come with them.

1.10 The Security Star

As shown earlier, the CIA triad suffers from at least two drawbacks:

1. The three security goals, confidentiality, integrity, and availability, are not sufficient, and more security goals have to be added.
2. Even if all the required security goals are added, a risk-driven model based on the extended CIA triad is not sufficient to achieve security as long as security management is not incorporated in the security model.

With simplicity as an objective, we extend the CIA triad by adding two security goals and a sound security management foundation. The two security goals to be added are authentication and non-repudiation. The security management foundation to be added is the risk concept. The extended CIA triad model is transformed into a five-angle star with a nucleus. As depicted in Figure 1.5, each angle represents a security goal, and the nucleus represents risk.

1.10.1 Authentication

Authentication is a mechanism designed to verify the identity of an agent, human, or system before access is granted. Usually, this process requests a user ID and password. Authentication is necessary for effective security management. It may also

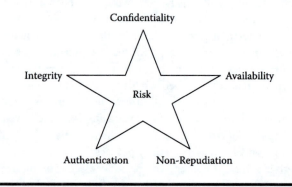

Figure 1.5   Security star model.

be implemented using smart cards, public key infrastructure, or biometrics. On a network with many resources, authentication tickets may be issued once so that if a new resource on the same network decides to authenticate you, the access control of this system will not request new authentication information.

1.10.2 Non-Repudiation

In legal matters, the term *non-repudiation* refers to a party's intention to fulfill accepted obligations. In information security, non-repudiation implies that both ends of a transmission cannot deny their involvement in this transmission. The sender cannot deny sending the information and the recipient cannot deny receiving it if in fact received. On the Internet, digital signature may be used to enforce non-repudiation.

1.10.3 Risk Management

Risk is the chance that some undesired events, usually information leakage, information corruption, or denial of service, would take place and produce bad consequences associated with financial losses. Usually, risks are linked to opportunities threat agents may see in exploiting asset vulnerabilities. A security program should be devised based on risks. For a given asset, if its security risk is smaller than its tolerated risk, no security controls will be adopted to protect it. For an asset with a security risk higher than its tolerated risk, you should not invest in more security controls than are needed to reduce current risks down to the asset's tolerated risk. Risks have to be identified, assessed, and mitigated by a group of people including information owners, business experts, and security experts. Studying risk involves studying the existing threats, vulnerabilities, and security controls and their capabilities to counter existing threats, consequences of the effects of threats on vulnerabilities and possible business losses, and ways to mitigate risks.

Let us borrow, from the 2006 *CISA Review Manual* [1], a simple but powerful definition of risk management:

> Risk management is the process of identifying vulnerabilities and threats to the information resources used by an organization in achieving business objectives, and deciding what countermeasures, if any, to take in reducing risk to an acceptable level, based on the value of the information resource to the organization.

Well, risk management is a sequential process that starts with the identification of risks, then risk assessment and, finally, risk mitigation by selecting the appropriate security controls. Risk is identified by identifying threats and asset vulnerabilities; it is assessed by studying the effects of the threats on those assets; and it is mitigated by recommending security controls that can reduce current risks to acceptable levels.

Some of the steps needed to manage risks include the following:

1. Identify and value assets in your computing environment.
2. Assess asset vulnerabilities and their probabilities of being exploited.
3. Assess threats and their probabilities of occurrence.
4. Estimate each threat impact on each asset.
5. Estimate basic risk, before adopting any security controls.
6. Select the security controls that can reduce risks to acceptable levels.
7. Mitigate risks by adopting the risk-driven security program devised in step 6.
8. Evaluate the effectiveness of the risk-driven program to make sure it is reducing risks to acceptable levels.

1.11 Parker's View of Information Security

In 2002, Donn Parker proposed an additional three components to information security: possession, utility, and authenticity. The resulting new group of six components constituting information security is referred to, in the literature, as the Parkerian hexad.

The Parkerian hexad components of information security are the following:

1. Confidentiality
2. Integrity
3. Availability
4. Possession
5. Authenticity
6. Utility

The literature claims that the foregoing components are atomic and cannot be broken down into further elements. It is also accepted that any information security breach can be traced back to affecting one or more of these fundamental attributes of information.

1.11.1 Authenticity

Authenticity aims at ensuring that the origin of the transmission is correct and that the authorship of the transmitted documents is valid.

1.11.2 Possession Envelope

Possession defines ownership or control of information. Even if the information is securely encrypted in a packet, just losing the packet is a breach of possession.

1.11.3 Utility

Utility emphasizes the usefulness of the information in possession. If this information is available to you in an encrypted form but you have no way to decrypt it, this information is not useful to you as is. Receiving a message or a warning written in a foreign language that you cannot read is a breach of utility.

1.12 What Is Information Security Management?

Information security management is a process that is capable of (1) accurately identifying an organization's computing environment, defining its criticality, and prioritizing its contributions to the organization's business-value-generation capabilities; (2) accurately identifying all security risks, assessing them, and then mitigating them by devising a comprehensive risk-driven security program; and (3) providing for the continual improvement of the organization's risk position by automatically revising the risk-driven security program as security requirements change with changes in the computing environment.

Achieving an effective security management program is only possible if the organization's assets are valued and the risk to them studied in terms of the vulnerabilities, existing threats, effects of the threats on the assets, and the evaluation of the consequences when undesired incidents take place.

1.13 Defense-In-Depth Security

It is too cold; you need to bundle up. Those layers that are wrapping your body will prevent the cold from getting to your bones. In the same way, you can apply many security layers to further secure your assets. The main idea is to use multiple barriers to make sure that if an intruder penetrates one layer, the next layer will hopefully prevent him or her from getting through. For example, the external layer may be a good security awareness program. The second layer may be a restrictive filtering program. The third layer may be a current antivirus program. And so on.

Defense-In-Depth strategy employs successive layers of defense capable of stopping an intruder who succeeds breaking through one layer from penetrating the next encountered security layer, and if this latter layer is infiltrated, the next one will provide extra defense. Those security layers may be security awareness programs, security technology, security policy, security staff, etc.

1.14 Security Controls

There are thousands of different attacks, and there are thousands of ways we can counter such attacks. Usually, those attacks remain undetected and uncountered, but there are many known countermeasures that can be deployed to secure the target assets. We provide a table (see Table 1.1) showing examples of countermeasures to specific attacks.

A risk-driven security program is usually written in terms of three different sets of security controls:

Managerial security controls, operational security controls, and technical security controls.

Managerial controls focus on the management of the information system and the management of risk for a system. They are techniques and concerns that are normally addressed by management. The following are managerial security controls:

Risk assessment
Planning
System and services acquisition
Certification, accreditation, and security assessments

Operational controls address security methods focusing on mechanisms primarily implemented and executed by people (as opposed to systems). These controls are put in place to improve the security of a particular system (or group of systems). They often require technical or specialized expertise and often rely on management activities as well as technical controls. The following are operational security controls:

Personnel security
Physical and environmental protection
Contingency planning
Configuration management
Maintenance
System and information integrity
Media protection
Incident response
Awareness and training

Technical controls focus on security controls that the computer system executes. The controls can provide automated protection for unauthorized access or misuse, facilitate detection of security violations, and support security requirements for applications and data. Technical controls use software and data to monitor and control access to information and computing systems; for example, passwords, network- and host-based firewalls, network intrusion detection systems, access control lists, and data encryption are logical controls. The following are examples of technical controls:

Personnel security
Physical and environmental protection

Table 1.1   Example of Security Controls to Counter Some Known Threats

Security Goals	Threat Sources	Countermeasures
Confidentiality		
Objective: Ensures that the necessary level of secrecy is enforced at each junction of data processing and prevents unauthorized disclosure. This level of confidentiality should prevail while data resides on systems and devices within the network, as it is transmitted, and once it reaches its destination.	Network monitoring	Encrypting data as it is stored and transmitted
	Shoulder surfing: monitoring key strokes or screen	Network padding
	Stealing password files	Implementing strict access control mechanisms and data classification
	Social engineering: one person posing as another	Training personnel on proper procedures
Integrity		
Objective: Integrity of data is protected when the assurance of accuracy and reliability of information and system is provided, and unauthorized modification is prevented.	Viruses	Strict access control
	Logic bombs	Intrusion detection
	Backdoors	Hashing
Availability		
Objective: Availability ensures reliability and timely access to data and resources to authorized individuals.	Device or software failure	Maintaining backups to replace the failed system
	Environmental issues such as heat, cold, humidity, static electricity, and contaminants can also affect system availability	IDS to monitor network traffic and host system activities
	Denial-of-service (DoS) attacks	Use of certain firewall and router configurations

Contingency planning
Configuration management

1.15 The NSA Triad for Security Assessment

As seen earlier, there are at least five security goals that we have to achieve in a feasible manner. Feasibility is modeled as a balance between cost and residual risks. That is, a security program should not do more than reduce risks to their acceptable levels. No money should be spent to mitigate risks beyond the tolerated risk levels. Hence, there is a great deal of security assessment before a risk-driven program can be devised.

In an effort to help public agencies enhance their security posture, and to comply with the Presidential Decision Directive (PDD)-63 requirements for vulnerability assessments, the NSA developed an information security training program called Information Assurance Training and Ratings Program (IATRP) [3].

NSA's security assessment triad is a top-down approach to studying the security posture of an organization. It consists of a sequential process made up of three phases: assessment, evaluation, and penetration testing [9].

1.15.1 Assessment

In a first phase, the agency starts with a high-level review of the organization's critical assets. This is part of security planning, where potential security incidents are studied to understand their effects on business over the next 3 years. The security objective is to recommend long-term directions about how to improve the overall information security posture of the organization.

1.15.2 Evaluation

In the second phase, the agency initiates evaluation activity. This is a detailed review of the organization's information systems in terms of their strengths in enforcing their security policies. The security objective of the evaluation phase is to recommend medium-term directions on how to use technology to support information security. The evaluation activity is conducted internally with the collaboration of all relevant players, such as information owners, users, and customers.

The evaluation report should show where policy cannot be effectively implemented, where policy was not effectively implemented, and whether the agency is achieving its security expectations. In addition to this evaluation report, the evaluation phase can also result in certification and accreditation of the systems evaluated.

The NSA has developed a methodology for system evaluation called the NSA's INFOSEC Assessment Methodology (IAM). The evaluation also provide assurance that the systems are enforcing relevant policy, that configurations in place are working, and that potential undesired events are ranked and prioritized.

1.15.3 Penetration Testing

Penetration testing activity is a technical activity that goes deeper in the computing environment to identify vulnerabilities that are ready to be exploited by existing threats to harm the organization. It searches for short-term weaknesses that can result in undesired incidents. This is a noncooperative activity in which the testers simulate real hackers to compromise the security of an organization's computing environment.

The assessment phase remains a preliminary study that is characterized by the following characteristics:

Not technical, often qualitative
Does not involve any testing
Collaborative, often shared by users, managers, and owners

The evaluation phase remains preliminary but involves intensive testing. It has the following attributes:

Technical but not invasive
Passive testing required for self-study
Collaborative to some extent
Involves diagnostic tools
Involves internal auditors

The penetration testing phase is invasive in nature, and has the following characteristics:

Noncollaborative
Technical in nature
Invasive in nature
Involves external auditors
Active penetration tests
Risk to compromise the target system exists but has to be avoided
Active assessment expertise is required

Usually, the NSA security assessment triad is conducted in the context of a certification and accreditation process. In this process, the certifier or accrediter evaluates an organization's system against a well-defined set of prescribed security controls defined in terms of the criticality and sensitivity of the system security requirements. Because the NSA triad was originally developed for the government and public agencies, risks in public agencies are always assessed in terms of what effects any potential incidents would have on national security.

1.16 Summary

This chapter gave a simple introduction to some of the security concepts needed to discuss effective security management. We proposed that an organization be viewed as a computing environment in which people, activities, data, technology, and networks are combined for the purpose of generating business value.

We discussed that securing the enterprise cannot be achieved without adequately protecting its components. We discussed personnel security, procedural security, information security, software and hardware security, and network security.

An information system is also viewed as a smaller computing environment made up of activities, people, data, technology, and networks that continuously interact to efficiently achieve information system objectives. That is, an information system may be secured in the same way that a computing environment is secured.

We also discussed how information sensitivity is classified, and defined information security governance. We argued that a goal-driven security model based on the CIA triad is not sufficient and proposed that it be replaced by our star security model. We also presented the Parkerian hexad security model and left it to students, as an exercise, to discuss its usefulness in security management. We concluded the chapter by presenting the NSA security assessment triad and examples of security controls.

1.17 Review Questions

1. Explain security interdependence among components in a computing environment. Give three examples demonstrating security interdependence in an information system.
2. Explain, in your own way, the importance of the information security governance concept in securing an enterprise. Suggest steps to implement it.
3. This chapter provides alternative definitions for noise, data, information, and knowledge. Give an example for each conceptual resource. Explain how those alternative definitions are useful in assessing information value.
4. Demonstrate, using an example for each class, the utility of information sensitivity classification in a small enterprise.
5. Explain, using a simple real example, the non-repudiation concept.
6. Give an example of a security policy for managing a password.
7. This chapter defined security policy for an information resource as its acceptable computing behavior. Apply this definition to the development of a

security policy for an information system. Hint: Use the components constituting the information system: people, activities, data, technology, and network.

8. Suggest your own steps to achieve personnel security in a small enterprise.
9. Suggest your own steps to achieve network security in a small enterprise with an online presence.
10. Explain, your own way, why a goal-driven security model such as the CIA triad is not sufficient to achieve enterprise security. Give a counterexample to support your answer.
11. Explain, using a simple example, how the security star works.
12. Demonstrate the utility of the Parkerian hexad using simple examples.
13. Demonstrate, using a simple example, how a Defense-In-Depth strategy needed to enhance the security of an information resource.
14. Demonstrate how the NSA triad is useful in information security management.
15. Give examples of managerial, operational, and technical security controls.
16. Consider a small business with an online presence. Using the concepts you learned in this chapter, suggest steps for securing this enterprise.

1.18 Workshops

Workshop 1

Consider a small e-business enterprise with its Web site hosted at a secure ISP company. Customers buy online on the company Web site. Assume that the enterprise has a computing environment consisting of two LANs: a private LAN for the administration of the computing environment and a public LAN for employees. How can you best devise a security program based on the concepts you learned in this chapter?

Workshop 2

Consider your home computing environment. Assume that your home has a wireless router connected to a local Internet service provider. Assume that you family has three computers and a printer connected to the router. Using the concepts you learned in this chapter, devise a security program that maximizes your home security. Show sufficient details when presenting your security program steps.

References

1. CISA, *CISA Review Manual 2006*, ISACA (Certified Information Systems Auditor), 2006.
2. Davenport, T. H., and L. Prusak, *Working Knowledge: How Organizations Manage What They Know*, Boston, MA: Harvard Business School Press, 2000.
3. INFOSEC Assurance Training and Rating Program, IATRP, www.iatrp.com.
4. ISO/IEC 27002:2005 (ISO/IEC 17799:2005)—Information Technology Security Techniques—Code of Practice for Information Security Management. International Standards Organization, June 2005. (Source: http://www.iso.org.)
5. Layton, T. P., *Information security: Design, Implementation, Measurement, and Compliance*, Boca Raton, FL: Auerbach Publications, 2007.
6. Bosworth, S., and M. E. Kabay, *The Computer Security Handbook, 4th ed.*, New York: John Wiley & Sons, 2002.
7. Harris, S., Information Security Governance Guide, August, 2006, [http://searchsecurity.techtarget.com/generic/0,295582,sid14_gci1211236,00.html].
8. Raggad, B., Corporate Vital Defense Strategy: A Framework for Information Assurance, 23rd National Information Systems Security Conference, NIST/NSA, Baltimore, 2000.
9. Rogers, R., G. Miles, E. Fuller, T. Dykstra, and M. Hoagberg, *Security Assessment: Case Studies for Implementing the NSA IAM*, Rockland, MA: Syngress Publishing, 2004.

Chapter 2

Introduction to Management Concepts

Learning Objectives

After reading this chapter, students are expected to achieve an understanding of:

Review selected management concepts
Understand how managers should be computer, information, and security literate
Understand required managerial skills
Understand the redefinition of Mintzberg's managerial roles that incorporates security management requirements
Understand strategic management concepts
Understand IS security management activities
Understand the information security management cycle
Relate the information security management cycle to management concepts
Differentiate IS security management from functional management
Understand roles and responsibilities of an IS security manager
Understand ISO personality traits for effective IS security management

2.1 Introduction

We will first briefly review some management concepts that we may need throughout this book. In order to better understand information security management, we have to relate it to the general foundation and practices of management. We will therefore review some of the principles of management that we think are most relevant to the information security field.

We introduce some useful management concepts, and we show how to adapt them to information security management. For example, we redefine Mintzberg managerial roles, and we extend them to include the information security management roles that apply to effective security management. We relate information security management concepts to management theory, showing that traditional management concepts still apply to information security management. Information security managers are defined in terms of the traditional organizational structure found in both the public and private sectors. We defined information security managers' roles and responsibilities based on the same organizational structure.

2.2 Brief History of Management

Late in the 19th century and earlier in the 20th century, management theory was represented by mainly two independent schools of management theory that were studied and advocated in Europe, particularly France, and the United States.

Henri Fayol, a French engineer, belonged to the classical school of management theory. Frederick Taylor, in the United States, developed scientific management theory, which emphasized the idea of specification and measurement of all organizational tasks. According to this theory, tasks were standardized as much as possible. In contrast to Mintzberg' ideas, which are discussed later, both Fayol and Taylor had task-oriented theories, but had developed two different management approaches. While Fayol emphasized authority and its implementation, Taylor emphasized work organization.

Later, but still in the middle of the 20th century, Max Weber extended scientific management theory with his ideas about bureaucracy. Weber focused on dividing organizations into hierarchies, establishing strong lines of authority and control [2]. He suggested that organizations develop comprehensive and detailed standard operating procedures for all routine tasks.

Given its authoritarian nature, and given the strict discipline imposed in security management, Weber's theory seems to fit the information security management concept better. We, however, have no proof that this is the case, but I believe it is worthy of consideration by the reader.

At about the same time, the human relations movement started. Unions and government regulations reacted to what they thought were the rather dehumanizing effects of Fayol's, Taylor's, and Weber's theories. The new theories, which are still prevalent, emphasized individuals and their unique capabilities in the organization. Organizations' health and wealth were linked to workers' health and wealth. The idea of creating human resource departments to represent their workers was implemented in organizations. Many other management theories have emerged since then, but the principles of management coined in the late 19th century and later still apply.

Management is a process that is used to accomplish organizational goals. Managers are the people who are in charge of achieving those goals. Managers perform the four main managerial functions that are agreed upon in most of the literature: (1) planning, (2) organizing, (3) directing, and (4) controlling. These managerial functions are performed throughout an organization independently of the type of service offered.

Planning: Planning is determining what the organization should achieve in the future. For example, while functional planning sets goals for the mid and short terms, strategic planning is concerned with goals for the next 3 to 5 years. A manager also develops strategies for achieving the goals of the organization, and acquires all the resources that are needed for the implementation of those strategies in order to achieve the goals.

In addition to strategic planning and functional planning, a manager is also responsible for contingency planning and business continuity. Contingency plans will replace the original functional plans if something goes wrong.

Organizing: A manager performs the organizing function when he or she allocates resources, assigns tasks, and evaluates the progress of achieving organizational goals. In order to do so, however, the manager needs to develop a framework, often called organizational structure or network, that connects workers, tasks, and resources together for the purpose of achieving those goals.

Directing: The directing function consists of supervising and leading workers to accomplish the goals of the organization. Directing often involves making assignments, assisting workers to carry out assignments, interpreting organizational policies, and evaluating workers' performance. Some studies add leadership as a managerial function in defining what managers do, because directing is also concerned with leading, so managers should have leadership skills to guide workers to perform effectively.

Controlling: Managers perform this function by evaluating workers' performance in terms of how effectively those goals are being achieved. This function applies management by exceptions; it detects undesired situations and corrects them. Management by exception requires that standards, indicating accepted levels of performance, be defined and communicated to workers and their supervisors. The manager is then concerned with monitoring workers' performance to ensure that the standards are met. If there are problems, the manager has to determine the reasons before recommending corrective actions.

2.3 Traditional Management Skills and Security Literacy

Traditional management theory emphasized the importance of computer literacy and information literacy in management. Managers who are not computer literate and information literate cannot provide effective management. We will argue that, in global computing, even managers who are computer literate and information literate cannot be effective managers if they are not security literate. We are not here talking about information security managers; of course, those managers have to be a lot more than security literate, and they have to be trained and educated in information security. Rather, we are talking about general mangers who cannot provide for effective management if they are not security literate, because everything they do nowadays involves some security aspect.

Many management skills have been studied in the literature, and they are all applicable to security managers. In the last three decades, managerial skills evolved to include computer literacy, and then information literacy. Due to the Internet and global computing, managerial skills also evolved to embrace security literacy. While we do not intend to discuss all those skills that concern all types of management, we will here only discuss computer literacy, information literacy, and security literacy.

Managers belong to different ranks depending on their positions in the organizational hierarchy; and even when they are at the same managerial level, they can perform different managerial activities because they belong to different functional units or divisions. Any functional area specializes in a specific managerial function, such as human resources, finance, marketing, manufacturing, and information services. Of course, management skills also distinguish managers at different organizational levels. Technical skills are often associated with operational managers. Interpersonal and human skills are found with managers who are involved in managing human resources. Creativity is an important skill that is found in managers at a higher level, where more intelligent, more abstracted, and more valuable strategic information is needed. The value of information goes up as we go up the organizational hierarchy.

2.3.1 Computer Literacy

Computer literacy, which is the ability to use computers to perform a variety of tasks, is becoming fundamental to the learning process. There are many computer skills that are useful and, in some cases required, as an essential part of managerial activities. Usually, organizations offer many opportunities for learning these skills.

McLeod (1996) defined computer literacy as the knowledge of the computer that is necessary to function in today's world. This knowledge consists of a good understanding of computer terminology, a sufficient awareness about computers' strengths and weaknesses, and the ability to perform end-user computing.

Computer literacy also includes knowledge of a working vocabulary of computers and information system components, and the fundamental principles of information technology (IT). To be a computer-literate manager, you must be able to define information requirements effectively and have an understanding of decision support tools such as the Internet, database managers, report writers, spreadsheets, and financial planning systems.

2.3.2 *Information Literacy*

Information Literacy is defined as the ability to know when there is a need for information, to be able to identify, locate, evaluate, and effectively use that information for the issue or problem at hand.

National Forum on Information Literacy (http://www.infolit.org/)

The manager should be able to recognize any need for information and be able to find it, evaluate it, and combine it with the available information in the decision process. The manager encounters a great deal of information while performing his or her managerial activities. Those activities could go far beyond the manager's purview and involve many other projects or systems elsewhere in the organization or its computing environment.

The computer-literate manager should also be information literate. He or she should know how to acquire information, how to organize it, and how to communicate it. The manager should also understand how information is used in decision making. Information literacy is independent of computer literacy and a person can hence be computer literate but information illiterate; however, a manager has to be both computer literate and information literate.

The American Library Association (1989) explained that information-literate people are those who have learned how to learn. They know how knowledge is organized, how to find information, and how to use it so that others can learn from them. Security managers, for example, should be ready for continuous learning as they have to, at any time, find the information needed for any task or decision at hand (ALA, 2000).

The information-literate security manager will know how to effectively and efficiently access the information needed to evaluate any business disruptions detected. The information acquired has to be accurate and complete and its source thoroughly validated. The manager has to ensure the feasibility of the information to be used, including its economical feasibility, operational feasibility, ethical/legal feasibility, and social feasibility.

Successful information literacy conduct is generally tied to continuous training and exercise of general accountability, and outcomes measurement or assessment. Usually, these forms of assessment are required by the organization or its accrediting agency. The relationship between security management outcomes and information literacy should be recognized as an important condition for effective security management.

The Information Literacy Competency Standards for Higher Education by the Association of College and Research Libraries (ACRL) (http://www.ala.org/acrl/ilstandardlo.html) [1] defined five standards, recognizing performance indicators and measurable outcomes, as follows:

1. The information-literate individual determines the extent of the information needed.
2. The information-literate individual accesses needed information effectively and efficiently.
3. The information-literate individual evaluates information and its sources critically and incorporates selected information into his or her knowledge base and value system.
4. The information-literate individual uses information effectively to accomplish a specific purpose.
5. The information-literate individual understands the economic, legal, and social issues surrounding the use of information, and accesses and uses information ethically and legally.

Created in 1990, the National Forum on Information Literacy (http://www.infolit.org) promoted activities in the following four areas [8,9]:

Examining the role of information literacy in the organization and ensuring its effective integration in various security projects or departments of the security division.

Examining any evidence for supporting, initiating, and monitoring information literacy projects in the security division and other IT departments.

Examining whether or not conditions are favorable for the creation and adoption of information literacy guidelines in the division.

Examining the existence of information literacy programs to make sure that security managers are able to incorporate information literacy into their managerial activities.

2.3.3 Security Literacy

NIST 800-16 defines the term *security literacy* as the transitional learning activity between security awareness and security training [9]. Security literacy guarantees that the security-literate manager is familiar with relatively generic security concepts such as confidentiality, integrity, and availability, common information assurance terms, and associated learning modules.

Security literacy must not be confused with computer literacy, which refers to a manager's familiarity with a basic set of knowledge needed to use a computer.

IT security literacy refers to an individual's ability to apply security basics needed to protect electronic information and systems. And, as in the case of computer literacy, where this term is generic and not associated with any specific computer technology, similarly, information literacy is generic and is not associated with any particular information technology. This also applies to security literacy; this term too is generic and is not associated with any security specific technology. In fact, all managers have to have, regardless of their functional unit, or their specific job responsibilities, know IT security basics and be able to apply them.

2.4 Managerial Skills

In addition to the foregoing summarized management steps, effective management also requires at least three skills for effective managers:

Technical skill
Human skill
Creativity skill

Technical skills give the ability to handle the technical side of the assigned task. Many bright managers perceive some weaknesses when it comes to the technical side of their tasks. Even though all the technical support they need may be available to them as needed, some managers may still feel crippled when they find themselves dependent on others to complete their tasks. Proficiency in the technical knowledge of your job and company is critical for most managerial jobs.

Human skills give the power to communicate effectively with your colleagues and employees. In one of his studies, Mintzberg showed that 80% of what people do in their offices is communication. Usually, managers are even more involved in communications than other workers. Learning to effectively communicate with people is a key skill that is needed to become a successful manager.

Creativity skills involve the formulation of innovative ideas and concepts. Managers with great conceptual skills often have the power to create innovative proposals that can lead to alternate ways of generating business value.

The skills we just discussed, when applied to the basic managerial functions of planning, organizing, directing, and controlling, will guarantee at least the minimal requirements for effective management.

We now provide a brief discussion of managerial concepts and, in some cases, redefine them to adapt them to the area of information security management.

2.5 Redefining Mintzberg's Managerial Roles

While Fayol viewed managerial activities as managerial functions, Mintzberg looked at them as managerial roles. We are not redefining them in this chapter but discussing them in terms of what they lack for application to information security management. We also extend them to make them useful in information security management.

Fayol's management concepts have been around for more than a century, and they are still valid. Most organizations are now, however, connected to the Internet and are open to online services. With the Internet, the organization will be exposed to many threats that can potentially produce great security disruptions capable of causing major economical and social losses to the organization. These threats are present at, and can menace, any aspect of organizational function. Managerial functions or roles, at various levels of management, in any area of the organization, have to be studied. The traditional Fayol's managerial functions and Mintzberg's managerial roles may need to be revised.

2.5.1 Redefining Interpersonal Roles

Mintzberg's interpersonal roles are figurehead, leader, and liaison:

Figurehead: Usually, it is the manager who performs ceremonial duties, such as giving tours of the facilities. This role is still valid for today's managers, but the type of ceremonies and the facilities to be visited must be compatible with the organization's security policy. For example, large gatherings in facilities that are exposed to the public may be a risky event to plan, especially if the organization has aggressive rivals who may be tempted to ruin the image of the organization.

Leader: Usually, the manager maintains the unit by hiring and training the staff, and provides motivation and encouragement. This managerial role is becoming even more important for today's managers. The activities associated with the leader role will, however, be very different and very costly at times. The activity of hiring, when performed by a leader manager, has to conform to all the rules and regulations specified in the personnel security policy document.

The training activity also has to be in compliance with the security policy applicable to the category of staff to be trained. Training programs in security are necessary for any manager to learn how to identify, assess, and manage security risks. Managers have to be familiar with basic security concepts such as how to maintain confidentiality, integrity, and availability in their work units.

Liaison: Usually, the manager has to meet people outside the organization to support the organizational business mission.

Supporting the business mission by playing a liaison role requires a stringent security clearance. The corporate security policy will restrict the liaison role to be limited to that allowed by the business mission.

2.5.2 Redefining Informational Roles

Mintzberg's informational roles consist of three roles: monitor, disseminator, and spokesperson:

Monitor: Usually, the manager regularly collects information and processes it for the purpose of identifying areas of low performance. This role involves a great deal of information sensitivity and has to be studied in terms of the sensitivity level of the information resources being monitored and the clearance level assigned to the manager. Information sensitivity classes are introduced in Chapter 2, but they are also discussed in later chapters.

Disseminator: Usually, the manager is a source of valuable information to others in his or her unit. This role also involves a great deal of information sensitivity and has to be studied in terms of the sensitivity level of the information being disseminated and the clearance level assigned to the manager.

Spokesperson: Often, the manager is a source of valuable information to others outside the unit. This role involves a great deal of information sensitivity and has to be studied in terms of the sensitivity level of the information being transferred and the clearance level assigned to the manager.

2.5.3 Redefining Decisional Roles

Mintzberg's decisional roles consist of four roles: entrepreneur, resource allocator, negotiator, and disturbance handler roles:

Entrepreneur: Often, the manager improves the structure of the unit in a permanent way for better efficiency. There should be a security policy designed to control all system activities, including any improvement in the business structure. Imagine how much physical security will be added when closed-circuit television (CCTV) monitors and video cameras are installed all around company facilities.

Disturbance handler: It is the manager who is called upon to react to an unexpected event. All aspects of the manager's reaction, in this case, have to be in conformity with the security policy. Intrusion detection systems have the capability to detect changes in the computing environment and generate reports based on which managers can plan recovery and corrective actions.

Resource allocator: One of the manager's functions is to allocate available resources to people working on projects. The resource allocation activity is now conducted according to security policies specifically designed for them.

Negotiator: Usually, the manager resolves conflicts within the unit or outside it. The negotiation activity is now conducted in accordance with security policies specifically designed for all involved components.

2.6 Strategic Management Concepts

Managers are organized into three levels of managerial activities: upper management, who are concerned with strategic planning; middle management, who are concerned with functional management; and lower management, who are concerned with operational management. Figure 2.1 shows a generic organizational structure that depicts the hierarchy among managerial units. With respect to information security management, we can think of senior management and upper levels of management who are involved with the vision of the company, the business goals, and the objectives. Underneath upper management, we recognize functional management, whose members understand how their individual functional units or divisions work, what functional roles individuals play within the company, and how security affects their unit directly. Operational managers and staff are at a lower layer, where they are closer to the actual operations of the company. They have detailed information

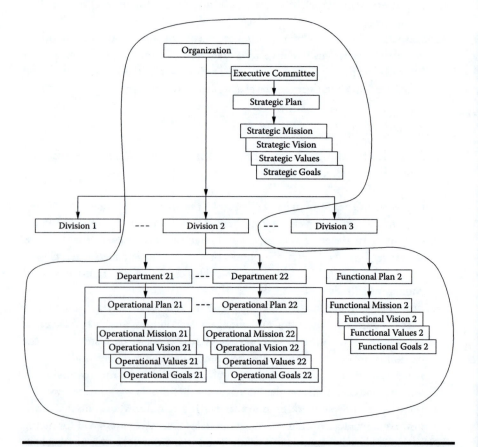

Figure 2.1 Generic organizational structure that shows managerial functional units and operational departments.

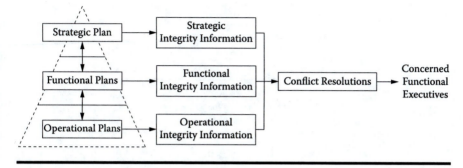

Figure 2.2   Integrated managerial environment.

about the technical and procedural requirements, the systems, and how the systems are used. The employees at these layers understand how security mechanisms integrate into systems, how to configure them, and how they affect daily productivity.

In general, however, management refers to activities performed by managers for the purpose of achieving predefined objectives that return both economic and noneconomic benefits to the organization and its environment. The manager is the individual who is in charge of orienting those activities toward an efficient realization of those objectives. Taylor (1911), Fayol (1949), and Mintzberg (1973) are recognized as the founders, in chronological order, of most of the management theory we see in education and in practice.

The information security unit is often included in the organizational IT functional unit. In this case, a security manager should first fully understand the strategic plan of the IT functional unit and obtain his or her CIO's support in defining a realistic mission for the security division. This vision should be consistent with the IT unit's strategic plan and its mission. At the same time, the IT unit's strategic plan and its mission should also be consistent with the organizational strategic plan and its mission. At least in theory, one may think of an integrated scheme in which all strategic plans, missions, visions, values, goals, objectives, and operational programs are fully consistent with one another. Figure 2.2 shows a model of such a strategic scheme.

Every strategic plan has its strategic mission, strategic vision, strategic goals, strategic values, and strategic programs. Every functional plan has its functional mission, functional vision, functional goals, functional values, and functional programs. Also, every operational plan has its operational mission, operational vision, operational goals, operational values, and operational programs. While the strategic plan tends to span from 3 to 5 years, functional planned activities are concerned with shorter terms. Operational planned activities are immediate actions that have well-defined goals. Figure 2.3 shows how all strategic plans interact and that those interactions traverse the strategic plan for information security. This embodies the idea that all managerial units are concerned with security because they host

Figure 2.3 Interaction among all strategic plans in an organization with the information security until is a separate functional unit in the organization.

people, data, and computers, and all those resources are susceptible to security risks. Figure 2.4 depicts a functional plan for the information security unit.

The foregoing integrity scheme is a theoretical framework where functional management can enforce consistency over time and through the organizational functional units, by communicating with both their operational managers at a lower management level and with the executive committee at an upper management level. In this framework, operational managers can ensure that their operational units do not violate their operational plans' missions, goals, and values. Additionally, the operational unit has to align with its functional division to achieve consistent integrity.

The organizational strategic mission, vision, goals, and values have to be sufficiently realistic for functional management to be able to translate them into functional missions, visions, goals, and values. Functional management is responsible for defining the conditions under which, and functional settings in which, strategic agendas can be implemented. The functional plan will define a network of resources and controls to translate the functional missions, vision, goals, and programs into operational programs. Operational management will be then responsible for translating the functional plan into an operational plan that defines the necessary operations to be immediately carried out.

The integrity scheme aims at resolving all conflicts that can arise across managerial levels for the purpose of maintaining efficiency in realizing the main mission of the organization.

The strategic values are of no value if customers do not benefit by them. Customers, however, do not care much about the values stated in the strategic plan, but they would rather see those values translated into tangible outcomes

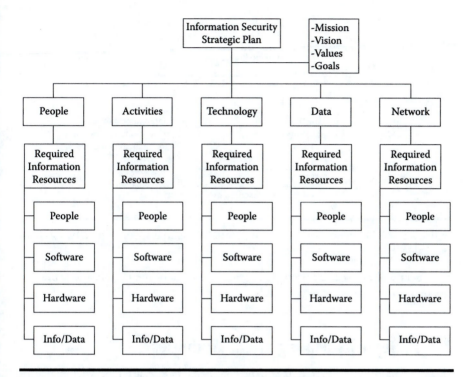

Figure 2.4 A generic information security strategic plan.

they can benefit from. These outcomes should be spelled out clearly in operational plans and perceived by customers when they acquire services or goods from the organization.

The levels of implementations of various plans, when you come down from strategic heights to the lower operational level, cannot preserve all the information when it is transformed from its strategic significance, to its functional scheme, to its operational detailed formats. There is no easy way to synchronize all the strategic managers, functional managers, and operational mangers involved in achieving their defined set of activities. This idea is depicted in Figure 2.5, which shows that a lot can be easily lost at the several implementation layers needed for planned activities.

A strategic plan has no utility if its mission, vision, goals, and values cannot be transformed into outcomes valued by customers. Any items described in the strategic plan but that cannot be implemented in the 3 to 5 year time frame set for the strategic plan should be removed. For example, it is very difficult to predict the organization's IT needs and management requirements 5 years from now. This should not, however, mean that the strategic plan becomes useless.

Remember, the customers are not in direct contact with strategic planners, and executives but only with operational mangers and their staff. For example,

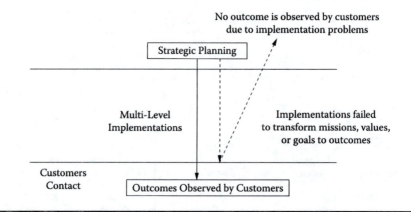

Figure 2.5 A lot can be lost at the implementation layers, even security, mission, and value.

customers will not see the strategic mission or values of the organization, but the outcomes from them.

2.7 IS Security Management Activities

There are many activities that have to be completed before, after, or when performing information security management. These activities are referred to as security management support activities throughout this book. They often relate to performance of IT functions and business processes. Those information security management support activities are not discussed in this book. We are assuming that IT functions and business processes have been designed and are operating in the most optimal way allowed by the organizational business mission. That is, if the computing environment is free of any security disruptions, then all IT functions and business processes will work as owners expect them to. Of course, we do not want, when a problem is due to adoption of an untested technology, to blame poor performance on some security mechanism that is under review. That is, when security management is conducted, we have to assume that the computing environment is functionally sound, and we will be reviewing the effects of any security conditions on the performance of systems and not studying performance conditions attributed to IT functions. IT functions are reviewed and audited by IT staff, not security people, to make sure that they perform as expected and that IT goals are met as planned. Electronic data processing (EDP) auditing is responsible for auditing the functionality of the computing environment, and it consists of inspection activities that verify that IT functions work as planned.

Information security management is a continuous process. There are prerequisites for it to start, phases to be accomplished, and recursive continual improvement processes that restart the information security management cycle.

2.7.1 Prerequisites for Information Security Management

In order to perform the information security management function, many conditions have to be in place before the information security management process can start. You need to have a computing environment with known resources, a corporate security policy, a known business mission, and known strategic goals. All company assets have to identified, classified on information sensitivity, and valued. The inventory of company assets is a live database, so information on assets is continuously revised.

That is, at least the following conditions have to be assumed before starting the information security management process:

1. The organization has to be protected with a known business mission.
2. A strategic plan should be in place.
3. A well-defined computing environment with an inventory of assets is in place.

2.7.2 Core Phases of Information Security Management

There are many security activities that make up the core of the information security management process:

1. Security planning
2. Development and revision of security policy
3. Security risk analysis
4. Security assessment (passive or active)
5. Security auditing
6. Security certification and accreditation
7. Development of an information security management system (ISMS)
8. Intrusion detection

2.7.2.1 Security Planning

An information security plan complements the IT plan to define the security requirements for the organization's computing environment and its components. The security plan produces an inventory of all information resources and their security requirements. The security plan recommends a set of managerial, operational, and technical security controls that the organization will need for the next 3 years.

2.7.2.2 Development and Revision of Security Policy

The corporate security of the organization is determined by the acceptable behavior of its computing environment. The business environment of an organization changes, and also its computing environment. Then the corporate security policy will also change and, hence, the security policies for its information resources. The review of security policies is a serious project.

2.7.2.3 Security Risk Analysis

Security risk analysis is needed before recommending any security controls. In this activity, security risks are identified, assessed, and mitigated based on information about the assets, the threats, and available security controls. ISO/IEC 27005 provides guidelines on how to conduct risk analysis [5].

2.7.2.4 Security Assessment (Passive or Active)

The risk analysis activity discussed earlier is not possible before assessing system vulnerabilities and before testing to what extent the computing environment is exposed to dangers. The security assessment task may be completed in a passive way or in an active way. In a passive security assessment task, the testing is conducted without penetration of the system. In an active security assessment task, however, selected systems are penetrated as real hackers do.

2.7.2.5 Security Auditing

A security audit may be conducted by internal agents. It is usually initiated to review the organization for any security weaknesses, and if found, security controls are recommended. ISO/IEC 27001 defines the specifications for developing an ISMS. The standard also presents steps for how to conduct a security audit.

2.7.2.6 Security Certification and Accreditation

In addition to an internal security audit, the organization may request an external audit to comply with a given security standard. In case of compliance, the organization will be certified against that standard. Sometimes, an organization, often a public agency or an auditing firm, will go a step further to obtain accreditation for some standard. That is, the accredited company can now certify other companies and issue certificates against a given standard.

2.7.2.7 Development of ISMS

An ISMS is developed based on ISO 27001. The ISMS defines a risk-driven security program for the organization. The security controls are taken from an annex of security controls defined by the standard. This activity is performed after defining a scope and a security policy for the scoped system. Risks are then identified, assessed, and mitigated before a risk-driven security program and a statement of applicability are devised.

2.7.2.8 Intrusion Detection

Intrusion detection is a very important step in information security management. Log information about incidents is useful in understanding the changes in the system. Reports about intrusions in the computing environment are needed to estimate the frequency of threats, and their impact. In information security management, it is vital to monitor the computing environment and detect intrusions before attacks occur. Recovery decisions and corrective actions are planned based on reports generated by intrusion detection systems.

2.7.3 Recursive Continual Improvement for Security Management

Information security management produces an ISMS with a statement of applicability, or a risk-driven security program. Neither, however, can guarantee a stable and secure computing environment for the organization. That is, a thorough review of current risks is needed to ensure that risks are still below their accepted levels. The vulnerability of assets may change; the threats may change; company resources may change, including people, activities, data, technology, and networks. Any of those changes may lead to changes in current risks. The recursive continual security improvement task will restart the information security management process.

2.8 Do We Really Need an Independent Information Security Functional Unit?

Every company, small or large, needs an information security unit. Can this security unit be small and come under the IT functional unit, as shown in Figure 2.6, or does it have to be independent, as shown in Figure 2.7, parallel to the IT unit? There is no exact answer to this question. It all depends on the politics of the organization and the size of its computing environment. If the information security is a part of the IT functional unit, then there will be no chief information security officer (CISO) but, instead, an information security management officer (ISMO) or information system security manager (ISSM) who will report to the chief information officer (CIO). That is, in this case, none of these information security management officers will report directly to the CEO of the organization. If, however, you have an independent information security functional unit, then there will be an independent CISO who will report directly to the CEO of the company.

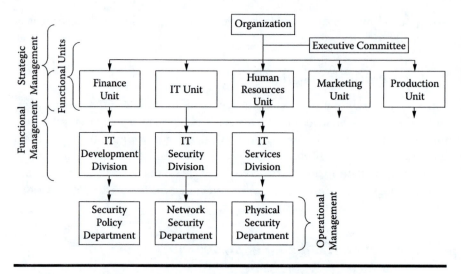

Figure 2.6 Organizational structure without a separate security unit.

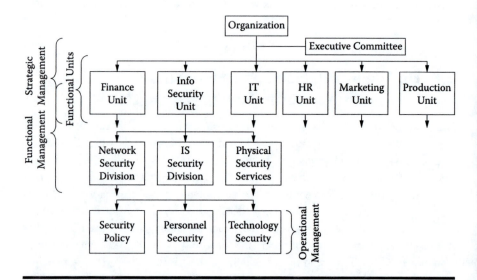

Figure 2.7 Organizational structure with an independent functional security unit.

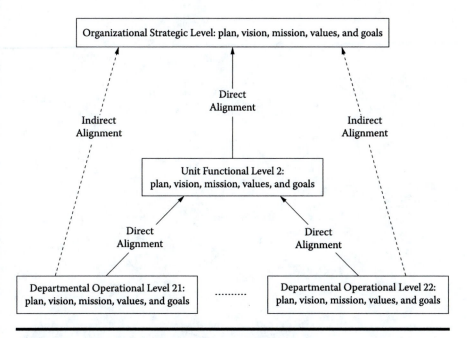

Figure 2.8   Alignment requirement for a functional unit.

Any functional unit or division has to be aligned with the organizational strategic plan. Alignment requirements may be organized into three subsets of managerial requirements:

1. The company's organizational strategic plan, company's strategic vision, strategic mission, strategic values, and strategic goals
2. The company's functional plan, functional vision, functional mission, functional values, and functional goals
3. For each one of its departments, its operational plan, operational vision, operational mission, operational values, and operational goals

The required alignment scheme for any functional unit is depicted in Figure 2.8.

2.9 The Information Security Management Cycle

2.9.1 Information Security Management Cycle and Management Concepts

The same information security controls apply to most computing environments. The main security goals are set to (1) mitigate security risks until they go lower than or equal to their accepted levels as set in the corporate security policy, and (2)

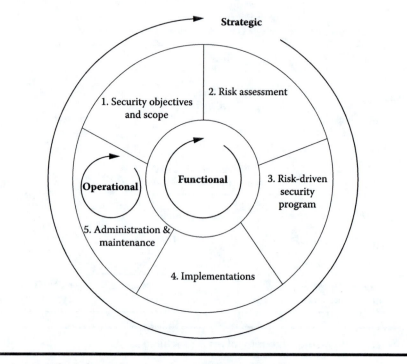

Figure 2.9   The information security management cycle.

maintain a continual security improvement cycle so that when changes occur in the computing environment the current risk-driven security program is reviewed to adjust to any changes that lead to increased security risks.

The information security management cycle involves all levels of information security management: strategic security management, functional security management, and operational security management, as shown in Figure 2.9.

The proposed information security management activities are defining while still preserving the classical management model, which divides managerial activities into three management levels: upper or strategic level, middle or functional level, and lower or operational level. We provide, in Figure 2.10, the same classical management pyramid you may encounter in any management book, but we add the security managerial activities as they apply. Figure 2.11 also provides the same security management pyramid, but we added all information security management titles as they apply.

Irrespective of anything else an information security manager performs and irrespective of the good security he or she is establishing, the manager cannot rest as long as the interactions between assets and the adopted risk-driven program are not under control. Unfortunately, the operational information security manager has to closely manage the interactions between each critical asset and the established security program. So, do not think you are done because you established the best risk-driven security program possible! No, you are certainly not done. You have

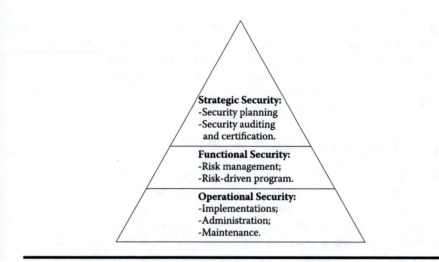

Figure 2.10   The information security management pyramid.

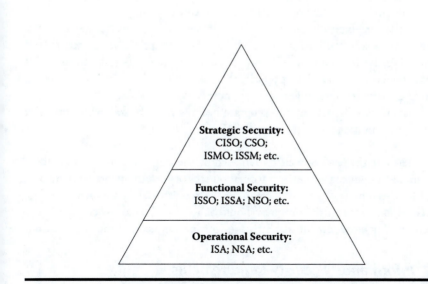

Figure 2.11   The information security management pyramid with security management titles.

to continue managing those interactions between critical assets and the security program. Any change in the computing environment can change its behavior, and security risks of assets may change. The security manager, at the security operational level, has to monitor the interactions between assets and the security program. If the security risk of an asset goes beyond its accepted risk level, then the security controls added to the security program to protect this asset have to be revised.

2.9.2 Information Security Controls

Information security controls are any security activities designed to reduce security risks, including security policies, practices, procedures, or mechanisms.

Information security controls are adopted to maintain security risks at their accepted levels as prescribed in their relevant security policies. As a result, company operations will continue as planned, and business will continue as expected, bearing in mind that the only risks that mitigated were known ones and that unknown risks were not part of the risk-driven security program. Also, this is not to be confused with business continuity, which is discussed in a later chapter. ISO 27001, however, suggests that to ensure their effectiveness, security controls must satisfy the security requirements defined at an earlier stage.

Moreover, after implementing the security controls that match the security requirements on hand, there is no guarantee that security requirements will stay the same, nor are there guarantees that the security risks for which we devised a risk-driven security program will stay the same. The vulnerabilities of assets can change. The threats can change. The business environment, including its operations, its activities, its technologies, its resources, can all change.

Given the foregoing discussion, the risk-driven program we devised earlier is not sufficient to keep the mitigated risks below their accepted levels. There should be something else that effective security management can undertake to solve this problem, perhaps, an iterative approach that can adjust the security controls as needed to cope with any changes that can increase security risks.

That is, any risk-driven security program has to satisfy the following three risk management conditions:

1. Determine the level of security required by the target system. This attribute should be deduced from the information security requirements on hand.
2. All the recommended security controls have to satisfy the security requirements.
3. The risk-driven security program should be able to adjust to any changes in the computing environment that affect the business mission of the organization.

2.9.3 Information Security Requirements

Information security requirements define the states of information resources that business owners accept as sufficient to fulfill the business mission set for the organization.

Those states are written in terms of confidentiality, integrity, and availability requirements recognized as sufficient to fulfill the intended business mission.

The information security requirements may be acquired in different ways, even though we here only present two of them:

1. Company documentation and references
2. Risk analysis

The documentation approach to security requirements bases its security requirement definition on security policies, laws, and regulatory and contractual requirements with customers, suppliers, and partners. Principles and information processing requirements are also possible sources of information security requirements.

In theory, the corporate security policy defines the acceptable behavior of the enterprise. That is, security requirements may be defined based on what the corporate security policy sets as states leading to fulfillment of the business mission. Unfortunately, not all corporate security policies are well written, and basing information security requirements on them may compromise the security of the enterprise. On the same lines, the corporate security policy is the integration of security policies for the information resources constituting the computing environment. That is, the corporate security policy is also the source of any security requirements for any information resources constituting the computing environment.

Alternatively, because everything we do to add security anywhere in the company has to be motivated by risk reduction, it is only sensible to base our information security requirements on risk. In fact, ISO 17799, ISO 27001, and ISO 27002 recommend exactly that. That is, the security requirements may be obtained from risk assessment conducted in the organization's computing environment.

2.10 IS Security Management versus Functional Management

2.10.1 Strategic and Functional Levels: Security Managers

Security managers are responsible for assessment, security planning, and maintenance of effective security requirements within the organization. Security managers therefore hold a senior management rank, and are responsible for getting the organization to develop security management programs. The following activities provide information on the strategic and functional processes that security managers must consider when developing a continual security management program:

Identifying and prioritizing information security
Identifying, valuing, and defining business-driven security rules

Identifying, assessing, and prioritizing security risks

Mitigating and managing identified risks

Reviewing risk-driven security programs to provide for continual improvement

Monitoring, responding, and contingency planning

2.10.2 Operational Management Level: Security Administrators

Security administrators are responsible for the operational management of security within the organization. For example, given a security policy and risk-driven security program, the security administrator performs the following:

Deploys and configures security solutions

Maintains the delivery of security solutions

Monitors the computing environment

Evaluates potential security problems that may occur on a system

Reports on security matters to security managers and information and system owners

2.10.3 Roles, Responsibilities, and Qualifications for an IS Security Manager

Even though an ISO's role varies depending on the size of the organization, its organizational structure, and its internal regulations, the following ISO responsibilities generally apply:

1. Enforce the corporate security policy
2. Advise and participate in defining the corporate security strategy
3. Review the security policy
4. Identify, assess, mitigate, and manage security risks
5. Periodically audit security
6. Plan, test, and manage disaster recovery and business continuity
7. Develop, plan, and evaluate IS security training and awareness programs

Usually, an ISO would have completed at least a BS in computer science, information systems, or a comparable field. An ISO's minimal education would consist of network computing, operating systems, and major security concepts. Certification in network administration or in information security is important. While there are many networking and security certificates an ISO may obtain, it is recommended that he or she obtain at least the CISSP.

CISSP is a certification for information security professionals. It is offered by the International Information Systems Security Certification Consortium ((ISC)²). This organization is internationally recognized for educating and certifying information security professionals. Some of the professional certifications it provides include the following:

CISSP: Certified Information Systems Security Professional
ISSAP: Information Systems Security Architecture Professional
ISSMP: Information Systems Security Management Professional
ISSEP: Information Systems Security Engineering Professional
CAP: Certification and Accreditation Professional
SSCP: Systems Security Certified Practitioner

The CISSP is often taken by individuals who intend to develop and manage information security policies, standards, and procedures. This certification will generate self-confidence and trust, as some employers may require new security staff to have the CISSP before they are hired.

The CISSP exam is concerned with the following 10 security areas:

1. Access Control Systems & Methodology
2. Telecommunications & Network Security
3. Security Management Practices
4. Security Architecture & Models
5. Cryptography
6. Physical Security
7. Operations Security
8. Applications & Systems Development
9. Business Continuity Planning
10. Law, Investigation, and Ethics

Even though it all depends on the organizational structure of the company, the ISO usually heads the information security unit and has information security staff working for him or her, typically with the following titles:

Network administers
Information security analysts
Incident response staff
Forensic staff
Security technicians/operators

In the absence of a security functional unit that is established parallel to the IT functional unit, the ISO will report directly to the CIO.

2.10.4 ISO Personality Traits for Effective IS Security Management

The qualifying conditions for the ISO position are necessary, but not sufficient to deliver effective security management. The following personality traits have to be present in every ISO who intends to deliver effective information security management:

Up to date
Reliable
Collaborator/cooperator
Business-oriented
Flexible
Well connected
Responsible/accountable
Communicator

Up to date: Technology changes very rapidly; in fact, even the concepts behind it are susceptible to change, especially in the relatively new information security field. New malicious tools will emerge as often as new defense tools are developed. The ISO has to adopt a continuous-learning attitude. He or she and the concerned staff should be up to date.

Reliable: Reliability for an ISO's position is a must; he or she must be reliable in performing activities and in his or her interactions with staff. Any small inconsistency or mistrust will easily and quickly spread to the rest of the team. If this continues, the security of the entire computing environment may be compromised.

Collaborator/cooperator: This role has to be evident to all members of the security team, as well as to users and partners. All players have to feel comfortable when interacting with the ISO in planning security, monitoring security, and correcting security. Any weakness in collaboration on the ISO's part will lead to security staff, users, or partners not cooperating in important security matters, as workers are usually reluctant to be involved in investigations linked to undesired events.

Business-oriented: All security incidents have to be studied in terms of their impact on business. If there is no impact on business, there will be no risks associated with those incidents. Security decisions have to be made based on risk, and therefore, on business impact. It is vital that the ISO think in a business-oriented manner. This behavior should be evident to his or her staff so they behave in the same way, and to system owners so they can trust him or her with their business interests.

Well connected: The ISO has to be well connected to the community, as often major support may be needed from law enforcement, major suppliers, independent security experts and consultants, etc. It is important that the ISO belong to professional associations where members can discuss developments in the security management field. It is also important that the ISO attend conferences that address security management topics. This networking will connect the ISO to colleagues who can provide assistance when undesired incidents take place.

Flexible: Technology and security concepts change without prior notice, and the computing environment is also considerably affected by such changes. This will also affect people, their activities, data, and the network of resources. The ISO needs to absorb all these effects by demonstrating flexibility when interacting with users and partners. Often, contracts with partners will need to be rewritten; tremendous support from various suppliers may be needed; extended hours of works may be required from the ISO and his or her staff; temporary security policies may be enforced; etc.

Responsible: The ISO has to be courageous enough to accept all consequences of his or her actions. Accountability is a very honorable attitude. This attitude has to be evident to all staff and users. They will understand that they expect the same from him or her.

Communicator: The ISO has to be a good communicator. Staff, users, and partners have to fully understand what the ISO communicates to them. At times, his or her tone has to be strong to reinforce the message of an oral or written communication to them. If the ISO lacks this quality, he or she can hire an assistant who is a champion in communication. It is really worth it to set some security rules straight to all instead of leaving them at the mercy of misinterpretations or bad judgment.

2.10.5 The Information Security Management Team

We earlier saw common management principles from traditional management schools. We discussed what managers do and how do they organize, direct, and control, and we saw the skills managers need to have in order to perform effective management. Let us see how we can apply what we have learned so far in this chapter to information security management.

As shown in the pyramid in Figure 2.10, effective information security management, as in any theory of management, requires three managerial levels: strategic security managers, functional security managers, and operational security managers:

Strategic security management: This level of security management is concerned with strategic management. The main activities initiated at this level include security planning, and security auditing and certification. A generic name for any responsible at this level is *strategic information security manager*, even though, in the real world, we find titles such as chief security officer, chief information security officer (CISO), information system security manager (ISSM), information security management officer (ISMO), etc.

Functional security management: This level of security management is concerned with functional management in information security. Activities at the functional level include risk management and security design. A generic name for any responsible at this level is *functional information security manager*, even though in the real world we find titles such as information security analyst (ISA), information system security officer (ISSO), network security officer (NSO), etc.

Operational security management: This level of security management is concerned with operational management in information security. Activities at the functional level include security implementation, security administration, and security maintenance. A generic name for any responsible at this level is *operational information security manager*, even though in the real world we find titles such as information security administrator (ISA), network security administrator (NSA), etc.

Figure 2.11 shows a typical hierarchy organizing the information system security management team.

Enterprise security management, as depicted in Figure 2.12, shows active interactions among the assets and the security controls. For example, Asset A is affected by existing threats that can at any time exploit asset vulnerabilities to compromise the security of the asset. The asset controls included in the risk-driven security program to protect Asset A continue to struggle to protect the asset. Hence, there are many interactions between the asset and its security controls to protect the asset.

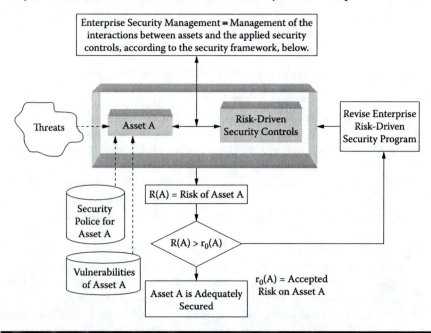

Figure 2.12   A simple framework for operational security management.

When the asset security policy is violated, causing an increase in the asset risk above its accepted risk level, then the risk-driven security program has to be revised to enhance security by implementing new security controls. That is, enterprise security management administers the interactions between the asset in question and its security controls and handles any changes in those interactions to ensure that any change in those interactions does not increase risks above accepted risk levels. Those interactions involve the asset itself and the security controls:

Asset: The asset is classified and valued; its accepted risk level is defined, and it is protected to achieve its business mission

Security controls: Those security controls, part of the risk-driven security program, act on the asset to ensure that its security policy is enforced, and its security requirements are defined, implemented, measured, and controlled.

2.10.6 ISO Self-Assessment to Deliver Effective IS Security Management

The strategic information manager cannot develop a good strategic plan without having good strategic goals. We here propose Ike Krieger's SMART goals [6]. Ike Krieger is a speaker, author and mentor, who coaches people on how to build business success. Those goals are as follows:

S: Specific goals
M: Measurable goals
A: Attainable goals
R: Realistic goals
T: Timely goals

A specific goal has to be written to explicitly list the goals you intend to accomplish in the next 3 to 5 years for a strategic plan, in less than a year for a functional plan, and in less than a month for an operational plan. A measurable goal should include evaluation criteria needed to evaluate the progress of the goals. The more specific the goal, the more measurable it is. The goal must be attainable. If your goal is not measurable, then you will not be able to manage it. If you cannot manage your goal, then you cannot attain it. Are you confident you can achieve your goals using the current resources? For example, achieving a fault-free intrusion detection system is not an attainable goal.

Your goal has to be realistic. Do not set a goal that you cannot achieve. A security risk-free computing environment is not a realistic goal because it is not something doable. The security manager may look at benchmark data or at his or her company security data to make sure that the security goals are, in fact, realistic. It is certainly good to have specific, measurable, attainable, and attainable security goals, but those goals are only useful if they are timely.

In addition to achieve SMART security goals, an effective security manager has to satisfy several conditions to qualify for the strategic security management position. We next provide a set of questions that we propose security managers answer before they qualify for any effective security management position. Each set of questions applies to a specific body of knowledge the security manager needs to have.

Here are the main questions that information security managers have to answer:

1. Do you know the organization?
2. Do you know your strategic thinking?
3. Do you know the corporate security policy?
4. Do you know your security training programs?

These questions provide the main topics discussed in an interview to hire an information security manger. Those questions may be addressed but not directly answered. We present four subsets of secondary questions that the candidate should answer. The consolidation of those intermediary answers will give an idea about how well the candidate knows his or her organization, the company's strategic thinking, the company security policy, and security training programs.

A good security manager should make sure that he or she can answer these questions. A candidate who cannot answer those questions will not be able to provide effective security management.

Subset 1: Do you know the organization?
To what extent do you understand the organization's vision, values, and goals?
To what extent do you understand the business processes?
To what extent do you understand the functional processes?
To what extent do you understand the budget process?
To what extent do you understand the culture of the organization?
To what extent can all that you know about the organization help you in obtaining an adequate budget for security needs?

Subset 2: Do you know your strategic thinking?
To what extent do you plan sufficiently early?
Do you know how to align security with the organization's mission?
Do you have a strategic plan for information security?
Do you know how to relate the security strategic plan to the business mission?
Do you have a strategy to sell your strategic security program?
Do you know how to obtain users' support for your strategic security program?
Do you know how to identify benefits and value to users that are generated by the proposed security programs?
It is an accepted tenet that agents who benefit more from security will provide more support to the security program. So, have you come up with effective ways to persuade users of how they will benefit by adopting better security?

Do you have a plan to manage security?

Demonstrate how you will implement the SMART process to develop your own goals for information security management?

Subset 3: Do you know your security policy?

To what extent do you understand the corporate security policy?

Do you understand why all security policy statements are defined?

Do you understand how security policy statements counter the threats behind their writing?

To what extent do you understand the threats for which a security policy is written?

Do you understand all the risks associated with the written security policy?

To what extent can you support the security policy?

Do you inform your security management agents of all changes with timely briefings?

Subset 4: Do you know your security training programs?

Do you have a sound security education or work experience?

Do you know how to convince upper management to provide support for training programs?

2.11 Summary

The theory of management is well established and accepted in research and also in practice. We attempted to relate information security management concepts to the general foundation and practices of management.

We introduced some useful management concepts, and we showed how to adapt them to information security management. For instance, we redefined Mintzberg managerial roles and extended them to include the information security management roles that apply to effective security management. Information security managers were defined in terms of the traditional organization structure found in both public and private sectors. We defined information security managers' roles and responsibilities based on the same organizational structure.

Effective management is a prerequisite for any organization to achieve success by generating the greatest business value possible in a cost-effective way. Because organizations have understood and appreciated the significance of effective management, many researchers and management practitioners write about and share their applied models and experiences with the rest of the world. After a thorough review of the literature [3,4], we encountered a wide range of principles and guides for effective management, but we could select and reduce those concepts to Fayol's minimal set of managerial functions: (1) Define goals, (2) plan how to achieve those goals, (3) organize resources to define who will do what, (4) direct personnel to define how their tasks are to be done, and (5) control activities by checking that desired results are being achieved.

2.12 Review Questions

1. Briefly compare the management theories of Fayol, Taylor, Weber, and Mintzberg.
2. How do the planning, organizing, directing, and controlling functions apply to IS security management? Give examples.
3. Define computer literacy, information literacy, and security literacy. Give examples demonstrating a general manger's need to know all of them.
4. Redefine in your own way the following Mintzberg managerial roles to add all IS security management roles that are relevant to it: the interpersonal roles. You may add new roles that are needed in IS security management and are relevant to the interpersonal roles.
5. Redefine in your own way the following Mintzberg managerial roles to add all IS security management roles that are relevant to it: the informational roles. You may add new roles that are needed in IS security management and are relevant to the informational roles.
6. Redefine in your own way the following Mintzberg managerial roles to add all IS security management roles that are relevant to it: the decisional roles. You may add new roles that are needed in IS security management and are relevant to the decisional roles.
7. Give an example of an information security management unit's strategic plan.
8. Give an example of strategic goals for an Internet service provider. Use the SMART features when developing your goals.
9. Write a complete fictitious resume/vita for the position of an IS security manager. In order to maximize your chances of getting the job, include all the qualifications that make you the best candidate for the job.
10. Explain how information security management fits in the traditional organizational structure in management theory.
11. How do you develop an ISMS? You may use the Internet to answer this question.
12. Explain the information security management cycle. Give a simple example.
13. How can corporate security be a threat to its organization? Explain how mistaken security requirements may be obtained if the security policy is used to produce security requirements.

2.13 Workshops

Workshop 1

Assume that managerial levels are concerned with information security management in different ways. Assume that managers play roles in managing the security of various computing environments' components: people, activities, data, technology, and network, as explained in Chapter 1. Draw a 3 × 5 matrix showing the managerial levels as columns and the computing environment components as rows. In each cell of the matrix, identify the three main security management roles that the corresponding management level manager plays in managing the computing environment's component in this cell.

Now that you defined the roles in security management that various managerial levels should play, use Chapter 1 and literature from the Internet to define the appropriate security training program for each of the managerial levels. Use the management concepts you learned in this chapter to distinguish between managerial duties at different managerial levels.

Workshop 2

In a small business, most managerial roles and functions overlap. Discuss how this overlap affects information security management. Devise a solution that circumvents any negative effects and defines strategic, functional, and operational plans that are favorable to effective security management in the small business. You may either redefine managerial roles and functions in the small business, or define new information security positions.

References

1. ACRL, The Information Literacy Competency Standards for Higher Education by the Association of College and Research Libraries, http://www.ala.org/acrl/ilstandardlo. html, accessed on November 6, 2008
2. Elwell, F., 1996, Verstehen: Max Weber's HomePage, http://www.faculty.rsu. edu/~felwell/Theorists/Weber/Whome.htm, accessed on November 6, 2008.
3. Galbraith, Jeffery, The Evolution of Management Thought, http://www.ejeff.net/ HistMgt.htm, accessed on November 6, 2008.
4. Halsall, P., 1998, Modern History Sourcebook: Frederick W. Taylor, http://choo.fis. utoronto.ca/fis/courses/lis1230/lis1230sharma/history2.htm, accessed on November 6, 2008.
5. ISO/IEC 27005, Information technology—Security techniques—Information Security Risk Management, ISO/IEC 2008.
6. Krieger, I., Would You Like to Feel More Confident When You Talk About Your Business? http://www.businesssuccessbuilder.com/, accessed on November 6, 2008.
7. Mintzberg, H., *The nature of managerial work*, 2nd edition, by Henry Mintzberg. Englewood Cliffs, NJ: Prentice-Hall, 1980.
8. National Forum on Information Literacy, http://www.infolit.org, accessed on November 6, 2008.
9. Wilson, M., NIST Special Publication 800-16, Information Technology Security Training Requirements: A Role- and Performance-Based Model, http://csrc.nist.gov/ publications/nistpubs/800-16/800-16.pdf, 1998.

Chapter 3

The Information Security Life Cycle

Learning Objectives

After reading this chapter, students are expected to achieve an understanding of:

What a security life cycle is
How a security life cycle is planned
How security is analyzed in the security life cycle
How to conduct an impact analysis
How to compute asset exposures to threats
How to conduct a risk analysis
How to design security in the security life cycle
How to mitigate security risks
How to review security in the security life cycle

3.1 Introduction

The security life cycle describes all the steps necessary to achieve confidentiality, integrity, and availability for a given information asset in an organization. The security objectives are written in accordance with its current security policy. This applies to a single piece of information, an entire information system, or any com-

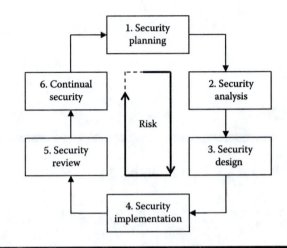

Figure 3.1 Information security life cycle.

ponent of an organization's computing environment. The security life cycle of a target information asset consists of the following steps:

1. Security planning
2. Security analysis
3. Security design
4. Security implementation
5. Security review
6. Continual security

The security life cycle, depicted in Figure 3.1, shows how the security of an information asset is achieved. The security is initially planned in terms of the asset security policy, its scope, its security objectives, a limited preliminary impact analysis, and a limited risk assessment analysis. Once a plan is defined, the security of the information asset is analyzed to define its security requirements. The security requirements are established based on information about the levels of impact the asset has on the business mission of the organization and based on information generated by a thorough assessment of risks that is sufficient for understanding of real security needs of the asset. Security analysis often acquires information on current threats, current security controls, and asset vulnerabilities and their exposure.

Once an initial set of security requirements is obtained, security is designed accordingly. Security design will conduct a more detailed risk assessment to obtain further information on the design of a feasible risk-driven security program. Once the security design is ready, the design of the risk-driven security program is ready for implementation.

Once the security program is in place, it is then designed and implemented. The security review process may then start. It consists of the certification, accreditation, and authorization of the security program. Once the security program is authorized, security audit may take place in a periodic manner.

Continual improvement is the final process in the security life cycle, where the security of the information asset is continuously monitored. If risks change, then corrective actions have to be taken to restore the security of the asset to its accepted state, as prescribed in its security policy. Often, however, the security objectives, security policy, and computing environment all change, which will necessitate a new scope for the security of the asset. In this case, a new security planning phase is started to initiate a new iteration of the security life cycle of the target information asset.

3.2 Security Planning in the SLC

Security planning is the foundation on which the development of a security program rests; it should not, in any case, be skipped. Security planning should be initiated and approved by the organization's upper management, satisfy the corporate security policy, and constantly remain aligned with the organizational strategic plan. We will see, later in this book, that this is not only the responsibility of security administrators and security officers, but also system owners, management, and users. Network administrators and managers cannot proceed with security analysis, security design, or implementation until planning is completed.

This section explains how the security of the information asset is planned. It describes all steps that are involved in the entire project of providing for the security of the information asset in accordance with its security policy. The security policy of the asset contains a detailed description of the acceptable behavior of the asset. Any deviation from such behavior is a violation of the asset security policy. This policy also describes all acceptable interactions between the asset and the rest of the components of the computing environment. The following steps are needed for planning the security of the information asset throughout the entire security life-cycle project:

1. Asset definition
2. Security policy
3. Security objectives
4. Security scope

3.2.1 Asset Definition

The identification and definition of assets is the first step in any security analysis. We need to identify the information asset for which an approved budget is made available for its protection. The corporate security policy identifies the information assets that are to be secured. A special budget is usually divided among the identified information assets based on their criticality scores and in accordance with the corporate security policy and their individual security policies. However, often there are two approaches used in the initial identification of the information assets that are candidates for a security project: problem-based approach and objective-based approach.

In a problem-based approach, an information asset may be identified as a candidate for a security project if this asset has been involved in an undesired incident that has been blamed for compromising one of the security objectives of the organization or one of its information systems: confidentiality, integrity, or availability. The identified information asset has become a candidate for an eventual security project because, if it is not adequately protected, its business mission will be compromised. This situation can then directly or indirectly affect the security of one of the components constituting the information asset, the security of the information system, or the security of the computing environment where it resides, or even the security of the entire organization.

The objective-based approach for asset identification is based on upper management or executive directives. A security project is then initiated for any information asset that is part of an executive directive. The only restrictions are the ones entailed by the asset security policy, its risk position, its prescribed budget, or its feasibility study results.

Of course, in real life, we certainly hope that a security project for any information asset in the organization will be initiated by an objective-based approach. Otherwise, instead of preempting malicious attacks, we would be waiting until an undesired event occurred in order to plan corrective actions, which may be too late for full recovery. Waiting until we see something harmful threatening an information asset before a decision is made to protect it is not the appropriate thing to do. Detecting undesired incidents, planning a response, and recovering from the resulting damage caused by discovered undesired incidents may be considerably more expensive and riskier than initiating a security project to protect the information asset.

After the identification of an asset, we have to know its location in the organization, and its constitution. For example, we need to know all of its components and their placement in the computing environment: people, activities, data, technology, and networks. We obviously cannot protect the asset without protecting its components. There are also many other properties characterizing the information asset, for example, its vulnerabilities, impacts, exposures, that we need to study before we can devise a security program for this asset; these properties will be studied later throughout the security life cycle of the asset. This chapter will discuss those properties in later sections.

What are the critical assets? Suppose that a disgruntled employee, who was fired 2 months earlier, was successful in accessing and obtaining a copy of your company's classified projects. How do you cope with this undesired event? The handling of this security disruption will certainly depend on the gravity of the incident. It is important to estimate the effects of this incident on the business mission of the organization before planning the appropriate responses. Upper management and the relevant system owners will jointly discuss how the asset is critical to the business mission and how much security is needed, in accordance with its security policy. Given its multiple security objectives, then, in addition to confidentiality and integrity, the availability requirements for this information asset have to be studied to determine how much redundancy and availability are required.

Most of the literature identifies assets as information assets, software assets, physical assets, and people. Information assets include data/information, and data stores (files, databases, etc.). Software assets include any versioned computer programs. Physical assets include any tangible assets in the organization. People include employees, users, customers, and partners.

It does not really matter what asset identification taxonomy we adopt, as long as we have sufficient information about the contribution of the identified asset to the business-value-generation capability in the organization. An information asset is always associated with people, activities, data, technology, and networks. For example, an information system consists of people, activities, data, technology, and networks, and without these components, no information will be produced that the organization can use to support its business mission.

Usually, an organization requires an asset inventory, with asset profiles being maintained for each asset. An information asset, however, has users and owners.

Even though the authorization of operations is usually effected by the authorizing official (see Chapter 4), the asset owner will be in charge of asset valuation and all asset operations once this asset has been authorized. The asset valuation will determine the business-value-generation capability of this asset, based on which the security requirements are defined.

The asset owner is the person who knows the business value of the information asset. There may be other agents who interact with the information asset, for example, to revise some of its properties or to explore some of its services, but nothing is permitted on the information asset without the permission of its owner. Even though the owner of a database may be the person who knows and manages its business value, the database administrator of the database may play the role of asset owner because no interactions with the database are permitted without his or her permission. In an inventory database of an inventory management system, no item may be deleted, changed, or added without the authorization of the owner of the database, if one exists, or the owner of the inventory management system. The ownership of an information asset has to be known before we can define any security requirements. These requirements are closely tied to the true business-value-generation capability of the asset, which can only be obtained from its owner.

3.2.2 Security Policy

The security policy of an information asset is its acceptable computing behavior. The security policy should define the acceptable asset interactions with the rest

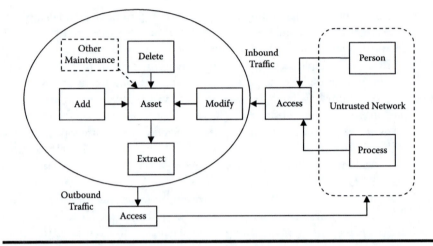

Figure 3.2   Computing behavior of an asset expressed in its security policy.

of the components in the computing environment. For example, it defines which users and processes are authorized to access the information asset, and once granted access, what the operations they are authorized to perform. The computing behavior of the asset is depicted in Figure 3.2.

Any violation of the acceptable computing behavior of an information asset undermines its business-value-generation capability. The security of the information asset can therefore only be achieved with strict enforcement of its security policy. If an unauthorized user succeeds in accessing the information asset, its security will be compromised. The security of the information asset will also be compromised if an authorized user accesses the information asset and performs an unauthorized activity.

Imagine an authorized user who is a technical staff working in an inventory management system. This staff has a userid, a password, and is authorized to update all databases in the inventory management system except the supplier database; this staff member can only extract information about suppliers. The staff member may be tempted to modify supplier information to privilege a particular supplier who is granting him or her the highest commission. The staff member would be violating the information asset security policy if he or she modifies records in the supplier database. The business mission of the information asset would be compromised if an authorized staff member performed an unauthorized operation.

All members of the security planning team have to understand the security policy of the information asset for which a security project is initiated. The security requirements of an information asset cannot be defined by staff members who do not fully understand the working of its security policy. All acceptable interactions between the information asset and other components of the computing environment, including people, activities, technology, data, and networks, should be defined in the existing security policy and recognized by the security staff members. Later in the security project, the existing security policy will be studied and revised according to the new security controls selected for the security of the target information asset.

3.2.3 Security Objectives

The most common security objectives set for the security of an information asset are the security objectives defined in the security star presented in Chapter 1: confidentiality, integrity, availability, authentication, and non-repudiation. These security objectives may be further tailored, as shown in Figure 3.3, to the security policy of the information asset in question. For example, how much availability is sufficient to maintain an acceptable business-value-generation capability for an information asset? Or, how and under what conditions should non-repudiation be verified in order to achieve the business goal set for an information asset?

The security requirements for an information asset also depend on its security objectives. These requirements will obviously change if we drop an old security objective, add a new one, or modify an existing one. It is important that these security objectives be closely linked to the business mission of the information asset and that they be well defined. Any incompleteness or ambiguity in their definition will

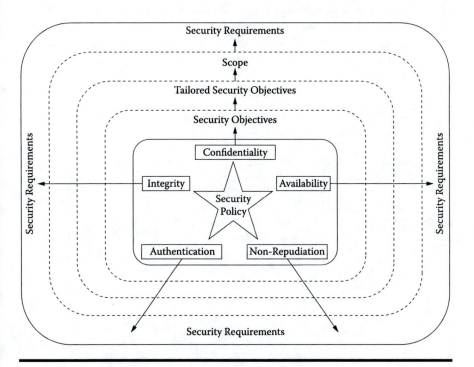

Figure 3.3 Defining the scope for an information asset.

translate into deficient security requirements that will lead to inadequate security for the target information asset.

3.2.4 Security Scope

The scope of the asset security project defines the security depth and breadth of the project. Not all security requirements can be met, but enough should be satisfied to establish the acceptable security risk level established by the asset security policy. The scope defines the depth of the security design and the breath of the security requirements that must be addressed to achieve the security objectives set for the information asset. Figure 3.4 shows how information is processed to define the scope of the security project.

There are also additional constraints that influence the definition of the scope of the security project for an information asset. This project has to respect budget constraints and any feasibility conditions established by the project feasibility study.

A preliminary impact analysis for an information asset defines its criticality in terms of any impact on confidentiality, integrity, availability, authentication, and non-repudiation. For example, unauthorized disclosure of information could be expected to have limited, serious, or severe adverse effects on organizational operations and organizational assets. Unauthorized modification or destruction of information could be expected to have limited, serious, or severe adverse effects on organizational operations and organizational assets. The disruption of access to, or use of, information or an information system could be expected to have limited, serious, or severe adverse effects on organizational operations and organizational assets.

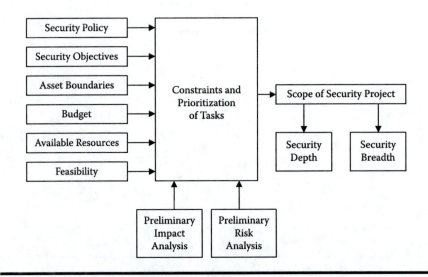

Figure 3.4   Scope in the security life cycle.

The preliminary impact analysis indicates the level of impact the target information asset has on the organization's business mission. In other words, the analysis reveals what the impact of the asset on the organization's capability to generate business value as stated in its business mission would be if the information asset is compromised . If the impact is low, then the asset is of low criticality. If this impact is moderate, then the criticality level of the asset is moderate. If this impact is high, then the asset is highly critical. Sometimes, it may be useful to study the impact from the standpoint of the consequences to the organization in order to understand the intensity of the impact. On the other hand, there may be more significant long-term consequences of the threat, such as the result of violation of privacy, civil lawsuits, loss of proprietary technology, fines, loss of human life, major embarrassment for the organization, loss of trust, etc. Estimating the impact in those cases is not easy because the consequences take a long time to be realized. Independently of how the impact is studied, the level of the impact is, however, needed when conducting a preliminary assessment of asset risks.

In addition to the preliminary impact analysis, preliminary risk assessment may also be needed to further prioritize security tasks constituting the scope of the security project. Preliminary risk assessment only produces a brief initial description of the basic security needs of the information asset, enough to guide the definition of the security scope of the project. A formal and detailed security risk analysis will be conducted later in the analysis phase to determine the security controls capable of feasibly mitigating those risks.

We saw earlier that the need for information security is expressed in terms of the need for confidentiality, integrity, availability, authentication, and non-repudiation. A preliminary risk assessment defines the threat environment in which the target information asset operates. This risk assessment activity will guide the security planning team in defining a scope that is sufficient to provide for the protection of the information asset in its intended operational environment.

3.3 Security Analysis

The objective of security analysis in a security life cycle is to define the security requirements needed to adequately protect the target information asset. The security requirements should reflect the results of risk assessment in terms of risks to the confidentiality, integrity, and availability of the system and its information.

Figure 3.5 explains how the security life cycle works in the security analysis phase to produce the security requirements needed to protect the target information asset. The security analysis of an information asset often basically starts with simple questions such as, why is security needed for this asset? Obviously, the security of the information asset is required to first enforce the corporate security policy as this asset belongs to a larger computing environment adequately protected to support the organizational business mission and, secondly, to enforce the asset security

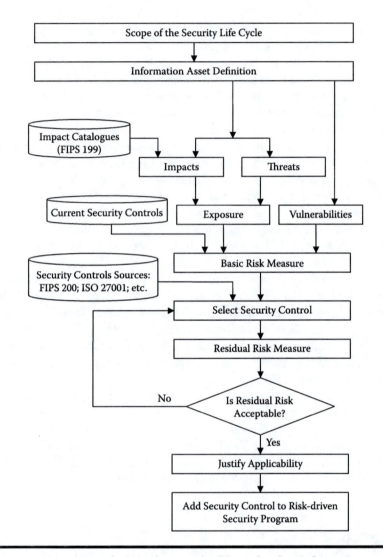

Figure 3.5 Security analysis in the security life cycle of an information asset.

policy to make sure the security of this asset is not compromised in a way that menaces the overall business-value-generation capability of the organization. For example, what are the valuable components of the information asset that require protection? What are the threats to the target information asset? How is this asset vulnerable? What are the risks or threats that can cause harm to the asset, considering the asset vulnerabilities and the resulting impacts of the damage? What are the acceptable risks for the information asset?

Finding answers to these questions might be time consuming, depending on the complexity of the asset, and might be costly or even infeasible. Security analysis is an investment for the organization. It includes assessing the threats and risks, managing the risks, and revising or establishing a security policy for the information asset. There is, however, no doubt that the outcomes of these activities should always be in accordance with the existing organizational security policy, which regulates how the organization manages, protects, and distributes resources to achieve the organization's security objectives (defined earlier). Such a security project permits extension of the organizational security requirements to the information asset. Once the security requirements for this asset are clearly defined, it becomes easier to design a security program that will efficiently satisfy the requirements.

Security analysis identifies existing and potential threats that may affect the information asset and estimates the risk that these threats will compromise the security of the information asset and harm the organization.

Independently of the security analysis methodology the organization may use, the outcome of the security analysis should always be the security requirements of the target information asset, which define the appropriate level of protection required, and the security program, which consists of cost-effective and feasible security controls. Figure 3.6 depicts the information exchange used to produce the risk levels and the security requirements that have to be translated into security design.

Any security analysis methodology adopted by an organization should include at least the following activities:

1. Asset analysis: The asset has to be studied in terms of its acquisition cost, operating cost, maintenance cost, its benefits, and its contribution in generating the business value of the enterprise.
2. Impact analysis: Estimating potential harm that might be inflicted on the asset as well as resulting impacts for the organization.

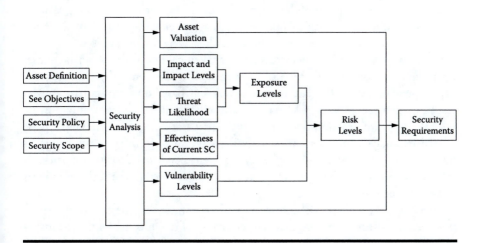

Figure 3.6   Security analysis outputs.

3. Threat analysis: Identifying and defining threats to the target information asset, and estimating their likelihood of occurrence.
4. Exposure analysis: Independently of its vulnerabilities, the asset may be exposed in such a way that if the threat materializes the worst of the possible impact levels may be realized.
5. Vulnerability analysis: Analyzing asset vulnerabilities and estimating asset exposure levels.
6. Analysis of current security controls: Estimating the effectiveness of the current security controls.
7. Risk analysis: Measuring the risks using exposure rating, asset vulnerabilities, and the effectiveness of current security controls.
8. Security requirements: Defining the security requirements to use in designing the security of the information asset.

3.3.1 Asset Analysis

We first need to identify all components constituting the information asset and assign value to them. For example, if the information asset is an information system, its main components are people, activities, data, technology, and network. All parts of the information asset have value, but some components of the asset are obviously more valuable than others. If the information asset is a single element, its value will be the business value it generates for the organization.

If the information asset is a wide-area network, identifying its components and valuing them is not very straightforward, given the large number of connected resources and the varied information they process. Security analysis, in this case, may require initial screening or sometimes even sampling if consideration of all network components and the associated large amounts of information is not feasible. Of course, at this point of the security life cycle, are not we conducting security analysis based on the security scope produced at the planning phase? And are not the tasks we are processing expected to be feasible? Why do we have to worry about the scope again, when I thought this all was taken care of in the planning phase? This is certainly a good point to raise. However, we need to remember that the security scope obtained in the planning phase was only based on a preliminary impact analysis and a preliminary risk analysis. Those preliminary analyses only provide initial support information that serves in the preparation effort for the next phase of security analysis. In the security analysis phase, we perform more detailed tasks that will produce more detailed security requirements. More detailed information is hence sought about the scope of the security project even in the security analysis phase, as needed.

However, the valuation of information assets cannot be done effectively before its criticality is thoroughly studied. The criticality of the information asset consists of two components: sensitivity, and availability. Of course, the criticality of an information asset should be defined in terms of the criticality values of all of its components. If the information asset is made of many components, its criticality will be the highest criticality among the criticality values of all of its components.

The criticality concept is closely related to business value. If an information asset has no business value, its criticality will be nil. Often, the higher the business value, the higher the criticality of the asset. Criticality can, however, be alternatively defined in terms of potential losses that may take place if the security of the information asset is compromised.

That is, the value of the asset can also alternatively be represented in terms of potential losses. These losses may be presented in terms of the replacement value, the immediate impact of the loss, or any other consequences to the organization. An easy way to value the asset may be to represent the losses using linguistic terms or qualitative ranking of low, medium, or high losses. This ranking is very general and can represent not only the replacement cost of the asset, but also any other impacts on the organization's business mission. You may assign numbers that correspond to the linguistic terms or ranks you decide to adopt, for example, 5 = very high, 4 = high, 3 = moderate, 2 = low, and 1 = very low. Assigning linguistic values to the impact may ease not only the valuation of the asset but also the definition of security requirements at a later stage.

For example, FIPS 199, Standards for the Security Categorization of Federal Information and Information Systems, issued in February 2004, requires agencies to categorize their information systems as low-impact, moderate-impact, or high-impact for the security objectives of confidentiality, integrity, and availability. Then, based on this categorization of the asset, the baseline security controls may be extracted from FIPS 200. The use of FIPS 199 and FIPS 200 in defining security requirements will be presented in greater detail in Chapter 4.

3.3.2 Impact Analysis

Once threats are identified for an asset, the security analysis staff then determines the potential immediate impact on the asset if a threat takes place. Given this information, we can estimate the impact level on the information asset and the organization if the threat occurs.

The impact of the target information asset may be estimated by measuring the business value of the organization when all assets work as expected, and then measuring the new business value after the asset fails. Figure 3.7 shows that when all assets A1, A2, and A3 are fully operating, the generated business value is b1 + b2 + b3. Suppose A2 fails, then, as shown in Figure 3.8, because the business value of asset A2 is b2, then the new business value of the enterprise is equal to b1 + b3. The impact of the failure of asset A2 is the loss of the amount b2 corresponding to the business value of asset A2.

The impact of the threat of information leakage, information corruption, and denial of service, which usually points to immediate near-term security problems, potentially results in the following:

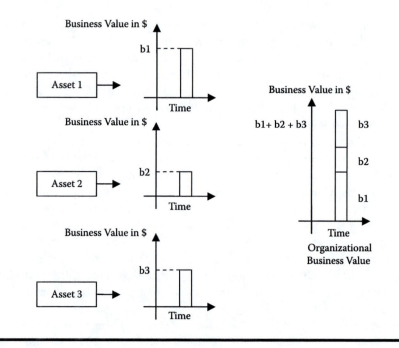

Figure 3.7   Assets generate business value.

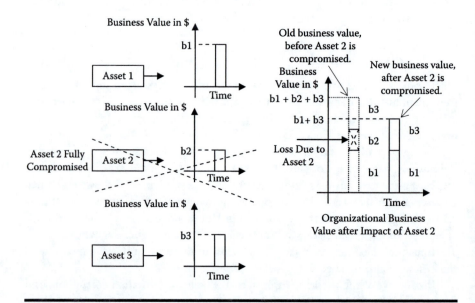

Figure 3.8   Security is the mitigation of risk of loss of business value.

1. Unauthorized access: An unauthorized agent (human or process) gains access to the information asset in an unauthorized manner. Even though this situation does not always cause actual harm to the asset, it may lead to other effects such as the ones list here.
2. Unauthorized disclosure of information: An agent (authorized or not; human or process) divulges information processed at the information asset in an unauthorized manner (intentionally or unintentionally).
3. Unauthorized modification to data: An agent (authorized or not; human or process) modifies data/information processed at the information asset in an unauthorized manner (intentionally or unintentionally).
4. Unavailability: This consists of disruption of asset services and functions. The threat temporarily or permanently disrupts services provided by the information asset so that it is not fully available as configured according to its security policy. The disruption of asset services and functions includes the denial of services provided by the information asset, including unavailability of data or services.
5. Deceptive actions: This occurs when the agent (human or process) that disrupts the security of the information asset cannot be detected, identified, or caught.

The occurrence of a threat can, in fact, produce, through information leakage, information corruption, and denial of service, and multiple impacts (presented earlier) such as unauthorized disclosure of information, unauthorized modification to data, disruption of functions/unavailability, and deceptive actions. Unavailability is a general term to mean that the information sought is not present at the time it is needed; it includes denial of service, destruction of hardware, software, or data, deceptive actions, etc.

Once the impacts are known for the target asset, the impact levels have to be estimated for each impact. Figure 3.9 depicts a worksheet that contains a template that has to be filled out for the information asset. For an information system, for example, one copy of the impact worksheet has to be filled out for every component of the information system. The resulting impact worksheets are then consolidated to form one overall impact worksheet that corresponds to the impact on the entire information system.

In order to assess impacts and their levels on a given information asset, we need to study the asset exposure levels to threats for each of the impacts. For example, consider the information asset to be a fitness center membership database. A disgruntled IT staff member in the fitness center requested to cancel his membership without accepting a contract buyout deal of 40% of the value of his annual membership. This staff member is trusted by his colleagues, who have authorized him to update the customer database and to perform standard maintenance operations. The disgruntled staff member is the assumed threat in this example. This threat, if it occurs, may lead to unauthorized modification of data for the purpose of compromising the integrity of the database, which may lead to potential loss of business

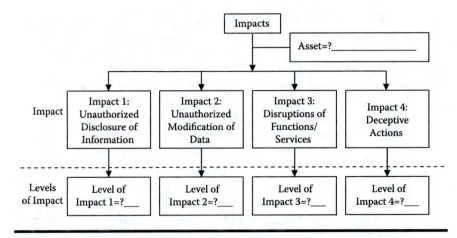

Figure 3.9   Impacts and impact levels for a threat to a given asset.

if customers who discover that their records are corrupted decide to cancel their memberships. The impact here is data corruption. The size of loss of business presents the level of the impact, which is high if a large number of customers leave, or low if only a small number of customers leave.

The disgruntled customer can also delete some support files, causing the operating system or the membership database server to stall, and can hence cause denial of service for the main server of the fitness center. He can, alternatively, misconfigure the server to cause it to stall for a more prolonged period of time. In both cases, the disgruntled employee has caused unavailability. The second impact here is unavailability. Assume that customers who sign up today find out that the server is down and make additional attempts in the next few days when the server is brought back online. If we also assume that only a small number of customers will be lost if the server is fixed quickly, the impact level would be low. The impact worksheet for this situation is depicted in Figure 3.10.

3.3.3 Threat Analysis

While elsewhere in the book we adopt other taxonomies for threats depending on the context of the discussion, threats are usually organized into two main categories: natural and man-made. The latter category of made threats may be accidental or intentional. Natural threats are related to the conditions of the environment in which the information asset is operated. These threats occur in a random way and are fully independent of the purpose, function, and conditions of the information asset. The main consequence of the occurrence of natural threats is probably unavailability of services at the information asset. Accidental threats are associated with mistakes committed by individuals, bugs in processes, etc. They can take place anywhere and any time, but cannot target a preselected resource. The consequences

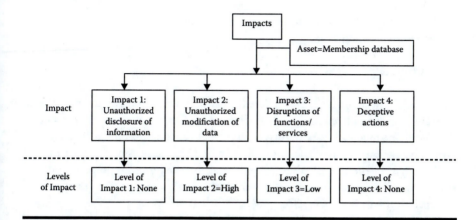

Figure 3.10   Impacts and impact levels for a given asset.

can, however, be unpredictable as we cannot predict what the misconfiguration of the information asset may lead to, and cannot know what bugs may exist in the processes associated with the information asset. These threats can, however, cause unauthorized access, security disruption, and loss of services.

Intentional threats are often man-made attacks that are deliberate and often target a preselected victim. Their consequences are usually calculated in advance by the attackers. They can result in unauthorized access to the information asset, unauthorized disclosure or modification of sensitive data, denial of services, or any other effects programmed by the attackers. The intentional threats are usually motivated by returned gain or other opportunities, or vicious intent to avenge by causing great harm to the targeted victims.

The definition of a threat may embrace several levels because it starts at the source of the threat, called the root threat, and then reaches a first perimeter or environment; then, within this environment, it reaches a first system; then, within this system, it reaches a first subsystem; and then, within this subsystem, it reaches a first component, and so on. After the root threat, also called the first-order threat, the *i*th threat is called the *i*th-order threat. Knowing the distribution of threats originating at the same source is sometimes very useful because the countermeasures and responses are independent. For example, if there is a power outage, you will automatically get a flashlight or a new power supply independently of whether the power outage is caused by a thunderstorm or some other cause. Figure 3.11 depicts a simple taxonomy of threats that is seen in most of the literature.

For example, a thunderstorm may cause a fire, which may cause a power outage. The power outage may cause failure of the freezer. The consequence may be, for example, loss of frozen food, which may, say, amount to a loss of about $400. The thunderstorm, the fire, the power outage, and the failure of the freezer are all threats, but they are ordered as follows:

Root threat = Thunderstorm
Secondary threat = Fire
Third-order threat = Power outage
Fourth-order threat = Freezer failure

Even though those threats may be related to the planning responses and safeguards, they are often considered independent. If there is a fire, the first response to undertake would be to get a fire extinguisher to put out the fire. It is only when planning preventive actions that we attempt to understand the cause and effect path to get to the origin of the undesired event and determine the most appropriate preventive measures we need to undertake. Table 3.1 provides some examples of general threats and their immediate effects on an information asset.

At this point, we know how to identify and estimate the threats to a target information asset, impacts, and impact levels. We then need to obtain a likelihood measure to be associated with each (asset, threat, impact) scenario. That is, for the information asset in question, what is the likelihood that a particular threat occurrence produces an impact on the asset? The organization would usually have its own risk analysis methodology that recommends candidate methods to use to measure likelihood. Except for those natural threats associated with industrial accidents, for which data is often available, estimating likelihood measures for other types of threats is a very subjective process. Depending on the type of information asset, knowledge and expertise regarding technical aspects of the information asset and knowledge of operational aspects of the organization are very valuable in determining likelihood measures of accidental and intentional threats.

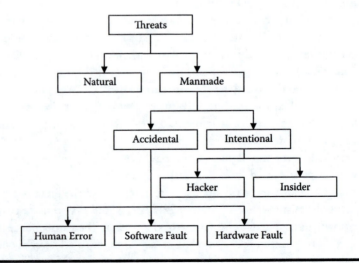

Figure 3.11   Threat taxonomy.

Table 3.1 Example of Threats and Effects

Root Threat Category	Effect of Threat to Asset (Secondary Threat)	Threat Impact and Consequences
Natural Threats		
Earthquake, fires, flooding, thunderstorms	Power outage, fires	Loss or degradation of communications, destruction of equipment
Biological incidents	Diseases, death of security experts	Disruption of functions/ denial of service
Accidental Threats		
User error	File/data deletion, mishandling of equipment, invalid input	Disruption of functions, unauthorized modification to data
Administrator error	Misconfiguration of information asset	Unauthorized access to the information asset, which may lead to unauthorized disclosure of information, modification of data, disruption of asset services, deceptive actions
Hardware/software failure	Failure of servers, loss of Internet connections, failure of communication devices	Disruption of functions/ services, destruction of equipment, unauthorized modification of data
Intentional Threats		
Hackers	Password cracking, eavesdropping, spoofing, trojan horse, virus, masquerading	Unauthorized disclosure of information; and unauthorized access to the information asset, which may lead to unauthorized disclosure of information, modification of data, disruption of asset services, deceptive actions

As seen earlier, if we need to have linguistic terms to measure impact levels, we then may need such terms when measuring the likelihood of threats. A broad scale based on linguistic terms or based on a several-point Likert scale can in fact simplify the likelihood assessment task. We can employ, for example, a five-point Likert scale that consists of the following options:

1. Very rare occurrence
2. Rare occurrence
3. Moderate occurrence
4. Frequent occurrence
5. Very frequent occurrence

We may alternatively adopt a three-point Likert scale that is defined as follows:

1. Low occurrence
2. Moderate occurrence
3. High occurrence

Whether we adopt a three-point, a five-point, or a higher-point scale, all depends on the level of details you want to represent when expressing a score for your decision parameter. More points on the Likert scale will produce more levels, and you can hence represent more scores on it, which will ease the ranking and prioritization processes but make interpretation difficult. Lower-point Likert scales are easier to use, but because the number of levels you can present is small, you will end up having many candidates with identical levels, which will make prioritization a difficult task.

The likelihood of threat occurrence and the resulting impact levels need to be assessed in order to obtain an estimate of the risk associated with each (asset, threat) pair.

3.3.4 Exposure Analysis

Up to this point, we should all know how to estimate impact levels and likelihood of occurrences. We will now see how to measure exposure levels to threats for the information asset. Exposure rating is a measure the organization may use to determine which threat scenario it is most exposed to. It is important to note that because the exposure rate is not related to asset vulnerabilities or current security controls, the exposure rate we describe here is not a risk level. Figure 3.12 shows an example of exposure when the target asset is the cheese and the threat is a mouse. The exposure rate would be the highest when cheese is not stored in a box. If the cheese is stored in an open box, the exposure level would be moderate. If the cheese is stored in a closed box, the exposure level would be low.

The Guide for Threat and Risk Assessment for Information Technology (GTRAIT) [1] suggests calculating the exposure rating using a table similar to

Situation 2: Medium Exposure (Rate = 3):   Situation 1: Very Low Exposure (Rate = 1):
The cheese is in an open box.   The cheese is in a closed box.

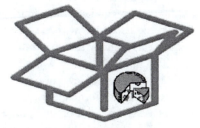 

Situation 3: Very High Exposure (Rate = 5):
The cheese is fully out of the box.

Threat

Figure 3.12   Example of asset exposure.

**Table 3.2   Exposure Rates Given
Likelihood and Impact Levels**

		Impact Levels		
Likelihood	Precedence >	L	M	H
	L	1	2	3
	M	2	3	4
	H	3	4	5

Table 3.2, where impact level takes precedence over likelihood. The precedence rule here assigns higher rates for the impact level when you have two symmetric situations for the pairs (likelihood, impact level). For example, when the pairs (High, Medium) and (Medium, High) are encountered, the pair (High, Medium) gets a score higher than the pair (Medium, High). Usually, the score for (High, Medium) is equal to the score of (Medium, High) augmented by one.

3.3.5 Vulnerability Analysis

In order to estimate the current risk position of the organization, we certainly have to identify system vulnerabilities and the current security controls that are in place. We have to understand the weaknesses of the target information asset and understand why despite all of the existing security controls the asset is still at risk. This means that the current risk of the asset is higher than the accepted risk level defined by its security policy.

The adequate identification of existing vulnerabilities and existing security controls is essential to correctly assess the level of risk associated with each scenario. But now that we know the exposure ratings, we can identify the vulnerabilities of the asset that the identified threats can exploit to harm the asset. We should also identify existing security controls to determine if the current level of protection is appropriate, considering the asset level of exposure and its vulnerabilities.

An information asset vulnerability describes a characteristic of, or weakness in, an asset or one of its component that tends to support the occurrence of a threat. All known vulnerabilities associated with the asset, technical or nontechnical, should be listed.

It is important to note that there are many factors affecting how an information asset interacts with the threats, depending on the computing environment where it resides and its own security policy enforcement trends.

3.3.6 Analysis of Effectiveness of Existing Security Controls

Evaluating the current security controls will help in determining whether or not adequate protection against specific threats is in place. It is easier to verify that managerial and operational security controls are in place, but it is not easy to verify that they work as they should. Most technical controls are, however, not easy to identify but it is easy to verify that they are working as expected.

Existing security controls should also be studied to determine if they are currently providing the prescribed protection. If a control is not providing adequate protection, it can be considered a vulnerability. If the organization of those security controls produces conflicts in the computing environment, then those controls where the conflicts originate are a vulnerability.

Existing security controls should be identified for each (asset, threat, impact) scenario. A security control is retained in the security program if it consists of measures that will prevent or reduce the likelihood of threats that attempt to exploit asset vulnerabilities. Those security controls normally provide functionality in at least one of the following areas: confidentiality, integrity, availability, and physical security.

Once appropriate asset vulnerabilities and security controls are identified, the effectiveness of the existing security controls needs to be assessed in order to get an estimate of the risk level associated with each (asset, threat, impact, exposure, vulnerabilities, existing security controls) scenario.

3.3.7 Risk Analysis

The definition of cost-effective security solutions that are capable of reducing the risk associated with an information asset to an acceptable level specified in the asset security policy is not an activity that can be performed without the adoption of an effective risk analysis methodology. Such a methodology has to be simple to understand, communicate, and use, but it also has to be complete, effective, and efficient in producing the feasible security controls that work. If this methodology is lengthy and difficult to use, or if it requires detailed data inputs that cannot be feasibly acquired, or if it generates results that are not implementable, then it will not be feasible to adopt this methodology. Recommendations are not implementable when security staff members cannot translate them into tasks they can perform and see expected outcomes. Those outcomes should reflect the true risk targeted by the risk-driven security program produced by the adopted security analysis methodology. The recommendations may also be not implementable when the security staff members are not trained to deploy the proposed security controls constituting the security program. The methodology should describe how risk is estimated by estimating the threats, their likelihood in terms of occurrence frequency, the consequences of threat occurrence and resulting impact, asset vulnerabilities, and existing security controls.

The risk can be defined as a measure indicating the likelihood and consequences of threat events or undesired events that could compromise the security of the information asset, considering its vulnerabilities and given the effectiveness of existing security controls. The outcome of this process should indicate to the organization the degree of risk associated with the target information asset. This outcome is important because it is the basis for making security control selection, as needed, and risk mitigation decisions.

We present here a generic approach to estimating risks. The estimation of security risk rests on three parameters: asset exposure levels, vulnerability levels, and the effectiveness of current security controls. To determine each risk level, the exposure levels, vulnerability levels, and effectiveness measures of present security controls are combined.

We earlier presented the exposure rates to be points on a five-point Likert scale. You may come up with your own consistent linguistic terms that correspond to those five points. The following is an example of the exposure linguistic terms:

1. Very low exposure
2 Low exposure
3. Moderate exposure
4. High exposure
5. Very high exposure

The exposure rates represent a measure of the likelihood that a threat will occur and cause potential damage to the asset and the organization should it materialize. The vulnerability levels model the asset weakness that the threats can exploit. The vulnerability levels may be generically rated using any Likert scale of your choice. We may use, for example, a three-point Likert scale as follows:

1. Low vulnerability level
2. Moderate vulnerability level
3. High vulnerability level

For example, suppose that the information asset in question is a network administration LAN and that some staff members are allowed to work from home as needed. The vulnerability of the administration LAN is obviously high because the connection may be intercepted by intruders and confidential information may be compromised. If, however, we protect those connections using a VPN, the connection between the remote endpoint and the private LAN will be protected through end-to-end encryption, and the vulnerability of the LAN would be low.

The effectiveness of the existing relevant security controls should be estimated. The effectiveness of a security control is a measure of the effect that a security control has on the probability of a threat to exploit asset vulnerabilities and on the resulting impacts should the threat materialize.

For example, the implementation of a VPN (encrypted tunnel with a firewall at every end) between a remote access point and a private network at the main office is a security control that is very effective at preventing unauthorized information disclosure or information leakage. On the other hand, applying a single firewall between the remote access point and the main office may provide an effective solution to prevent information leakage, but the rate of effectiveness of this security control would only be moderate. Any security solution relying on logical access control based on just identification, authentication, and authorization would be less effective. The effectiveness of such a logical access control mechanism would be low.

In order to estimate the effectiveness of the security controls, it is important to know the factors that affect their implementation, their configuration, and their applicability. Those factors include asset vulnerabilities, continuous applicability, adequate maintenance, operational feasibility, and interdependence with other security controls. The eventual objective of applying a security control is to mitigate the risk of exposure of the information asset. That is, a high level of effectiveness for a security control is achieved when the probability that asset vulnerabilities would be exploited is considerably reduced when this security control is applied. We can express the effectiveness rates for a security control as follows:

1. Low: Minimal reduction of probability that asset vulnerabilities would be exploited when the security control is implemented.
2. Moderate: Moderate reduction of probability that asset vulnerabilities would be exploited when the security control is implemented.
3. High: High reduction of probability that asset vulnerabilities would be exploited when the security control is implemented.

The security analysis team now has at hand all the information needed to estimate risks. In the real world, your organization will impose the risk methodology that the security analysis team has to adopt. Here, however, we intend to discuss generic risk analysis methods and explain how the risk analysis process really works. The generic methods we discuss may be extended as needed and adapted in any organization where security risks are computed. Security risks are usually estimated using qualitative approaches, quantitative approaches, or both combined. This chapter will, however, only cover the qualitative approach.

Let us (arbitrarily) employ a five-point Likert scale for risks. We will estimate risks using five risk levels that may be expressed as follows:

1. Very low risk
2 Low risk
3. Moderate (or medium) risk
4. High risk
5. Very high risk

Risk levels will be determined based on asset vulnerability levels, asset exposure levels, and security control effectiveness levels. One may obviously choose a lower- or higher-point Likert scale. The lower-point scale presents a disadvantage when risks are prioritized because, due to the small number of risk levels available to represent risk, many components will end up having the same risk levels, which will make ranking/prioritizing them a difficult task. The higher-point scale offers more granularity, which will ease the ranking process but will later make it more difficult to justify any risk mitigation decisions.

As you may see in Tables 3.3, 3.4, and 3.5, there are many entries representing identical risk levels. The duplication of the risk levels is due to the small number of risk levels offered by the five-point Likert scale we adopted. The security analysis team may need to go back and reevaluate the criticality of each of the candidate components when conflicts arise. When the candidate components all have the same risk levels, the ones with the highest criticality scores have to be considered first in the security program.

Table 3.3   Risk Levels When Vulnerability is Low

SC Effectiveness >	Low Vulnerability		
	1	*2*	*3*
Exposure Levels 1	1	1	1
2	2	1	1
3	3	2	1
4	4	3	2
5	5	4	3

Table 3.4   Risk Levels When Vulnerability is Moderate

SC Effectiveness >	Moderate Vulnerability		
	1	2	3
Exposure Levels 1	2	1	1
2	3	2	1
3	4	3	2
4	5	4	3
5	5	5	4

Table 3.5   Risk Levels When Vulnerability is High

SC Effectiveness >	High Vulnerability		
	1	2	3
Exposure Levels 1	3	2	1
2	4	3	2
3	5	4	3
4	5	5	4
5	5	5	5

The risk analysis methodology that you decide to adopt does not really matter as long as you use it consistently for all security projects and as long as it is easy to understand and apply in risk mitigation.

3.3.8 Security Requirements

This section is the last step in the security analysis phase. So far, we have completed the following steps:

1. We defined the target information asset of the security project.
2. We identified existing threats and estimated their likelihood.
3. We estimated impacts and impact levels for the information asset.
4. We estimated asset exposures based on threat likelihood and impact levels.
5. We estimated asset vulnerabilities.
6. We estimated levels of effectiveness for the existing security controls.
7. We estimated risk levels based on threat likelihood, threat vulnerabilities, and asset exposure levels.

Given the foregoing information, we can now define the security requirements for our information asset. To do so, we need to answer the following three questions:

1. How much confidentiality do we need to provide to protect our information asset?
2. How much data integrity do we need to provide to protect our information asset?
3. How much availability do we need to provide to protect the information asset?

Once these answers are answered, the security design team will interpret the outputs provided by the security analysis team and determine which risks should be mitigated.

3.4 Security Design

The security design activity aims at devising security to meet the security objectives defined for the target information asset. We have seen earlier that the security star presents five security objectives: confidentiality, integrity, availability, authentication, and non-repudiation. We then design a risk-driven security program that consists of a variety of security controls that are cost-effective and can collectively provide for the security we just defined. The security design activity will therefore consist of five security design tasks:

1. Security design for confidentiality
2. Security design for integrity
3. Security design for availability
4. Security design for authentication
5. Security design for non-repudiation

The security design activity is performed based on security analysis information obtained in the previous phase of the security life cycle. We now have at hand the following information:

1. Information about the information asset
2. Information about current threats
3. Information about impacts and impact levels
4. Information about asset security exposure levels
5. Information about asset vulnerabilities
6. Information about the effectiveness of existing security controls
7. Information about security risk levels

At this point, we can ask the question: Where do we find security controls that can ensure confidentiality, integrity, availability, authentication, and non-repudiation?

The answer to this question is always linked to security risk mitigation because the bottom line is always to search for cost-effective safeguards to reduce risks below the accepted risk levels specified in the asset security policy. The first phase in security design, as we will see later, is always risk mitigation; refers to the security activity comprising security design and discussion of the security design objectives listed earlier. There are, however, three possible solutions: (1) design our own security controls for each of the five security objective set for the target information asset; (2) hire security experts who can recommend the appropriate security controls that correspond to the security objectives on hand; and (3) select security controls from prescribed security control catalogs.

The first security design solution option requires a great deal of expertise that the organization may not currently have. While training security staff to acquire the security knowledge, we need to define the security controls that correspond to the asset security objectives that need to be met. Even though it is very useful, training may be very costly and time consuming. In this case, waiting too long may increase the security risks we are striving to control and maintain at our accepted levels. The second security design solution option is certainly acceptable and may be quick to implement. This option will, however, often be more expensive than any of the other methods.

The third security design solution option is only feasible if one or more security standards are adopted. Usually, a security standard, such as ISO 17799, ISO 27001, or NIST SP 800-53, comes with security control catalogs from which security controls are selected. The selection of security controls depends on the security risk levels estimated in the security analysis phase.

That is, the security design phase consists of the following steps:

1. Risk mitigation
2. Design of security training programs
3. Design of security planning programs
4. Design of the risk-driven security program

3.4.1 Risk Mitigation

The risk mitigation process aims at reducing the security of the asset to its acceptable risk level as specified in its security policy. Risk mitigation may be then performed by selecting the most appropriate security controls that are capable of reducing the asset security risk as explained earlier.

Before determining the candidate security controls to be selected for risk mitigation, we have to compute the current risk position of the information asset. The basic risk of the asset is the current risk of the asset before any new security controls for risk mitigation have been implemented. A model for computing basic security risks is depicted in Figure 3.13. Residual risk of the asset is its new risk after

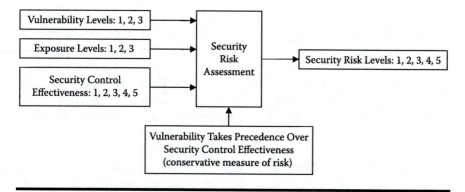

Figure 3.13   Computing basic security risks.

applying the recommended security controls. A model for computing residual security risks is provided in Figure 3.14.

In addition to the effectiveness of the security controls and their cost, the process of selecting security controls takes into account many other factors, such as the corporate security policy, the asset security policy, legislation and regulation, safety and reliability requirements, technical requirements, etc. A security control that reduces the basic risk for the asset to a risk level that is still above the accepted risk level of the asset security policy will be not be selected. Once the security program is devised for the purpose of mitigating the asset risk below the acceptable risk level of the asset, it is still not final unless it gets approved by management, including the appropriate authorizing officials. Usually, however, the security control selection process is iterative and, often, final decisions are not immediately obtained.

When the candidate security controls are sufficiently documented, then security management staff members will have the opportunity to study their contributions to

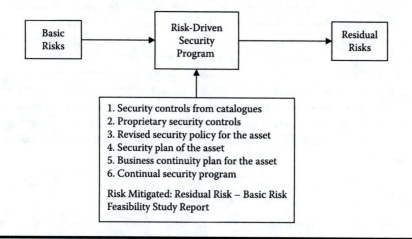

Figure 3.14   Computing residual security risks.

security requirements and determine what new security risk levels can be achieved. On very rare occasions, management may opt for security controls that do not lead immediately to acceptable risk levels, owing to extraordinary circumstances. After all, upper management, accountable as they are, may override any risk mitigation and security selection decisions as they see needed. Under those conditions, the acceptance of those security controls despite their lack of providing the expected acceptable risk levels is related to higher criticality and immediate need, which will make the identification of better security controls very time consuming and infeasible.

On the other hand, there will be many situations where there are sufficient reasons to leave things the way they are without seeking any additional security controls to further mitigate risks:

■ Basic risk is acceptable
■ Candidate security control does not mitigate sufficient risk.
■ Economic feasibility
■ Social feasibility
■ Operational feasibility
■ Ethical and legal feasibility
■ Technical feasibility

When all candidate security controls are examined and the total budget reserved for the target information asset is exhausted, the resulting risk-driven security program is assembled, approved, and implemented. At this point, residual risks should be evaluated to start planning any possible security improvement.

The main security solution for the information asset consists of two main subsets of solutions: cataloged security controls and proprietary security controls.

There are many government-recommended annexes and catalogs or international standards that the security design team can consult in order to extract the security controls applicable to the information asset. Of course, those repositories include a large number of security controls to choose from. There are usually conditions for selection. The subset populated by applicable security controls may be adapted or extended to make them suitable for our security solution. Sometimes, the design team does not find the security controls that can feasibly satisfy all the security requirements. Sometimes also, the security design team decides that none of the cataloged security controls is applicable as is or after minor revisions, and decides that the organization has to design its own security control.

3.4.2 Design of Security Training Programs

The security maintenance team is in charge of the continual security of the information asset target of our security life cycle. Most members of this team have at least professional-level skills in the following areas:

1. Access control systems and methodology
2. Telecommunications and network security
3. Security management practices
4. Security architecture and models
5. Cryptography
6. Physical security
7. Operations security
8. Applications and systems development
9. Business continuity planning
10. Law, investigation, and ethics

The foregoing security areas are, in fact, the CISSP examination areas, which represent the minimal requirements to qualify for working in the information security field. The appropriate security training program should be designed for members of the security maintenance team. The contents of this training program will depend on the definition of the information asset in question and its security policy.

In addition to the specialized security training program reserved for the security maintenance team, there is a need to design a security awareness program for users and other individuals who interact in some way with the information asset. Even the janitor who cleans the computer rooms at night has to be trained in physical security matters related to the operations of the information asset.

3.4.3 Design of Security Planning Programs

Security planning consists of mainly two aspects: the design of a security plan that defines security requirements of information for the next 3 years, and the design of a business continuity plan that defines the actions to be taken to continue business operations when a disaster takes place. This book devotes two separate chapters to the development of security plans and business continuity plans, respectively.

3.4.4 Design of the Risk-Driven Security Program

At this point of the security life cycle of the target information asset, we have all the security controls recommended for the protection of the information asset given its security policy, identified security threats, the effectiveness of current security controls, the asset's vulnerability levels and exposures, and basic risk levels. All steps that lead to the selection of the security controls, that are capable of mitigating basic risk levels below the asset's accepted risk levels specified in the asset security policy, have to be fully documented. The documentation of the risk-driven security program has to include a table similar to Table 3.6, summarizing the retained security controls constituting the security program and their justification. A model for producing a risk-driven security program is provided in Figure 3.15.

Table 3.6 Summary of Retained Security Controls for Risk-Driven Security Program

Security Control	Catalog	Description (Type/Family)	Asset Component	Basic Risk	Residual Risk	Acceptable Risk Level
SC123	FIPS 200	Operational security control	Component 1	5	3	4
SC11	ISO 27001 Annex A1	Operational security control	Component 2	4	3	3
etc.	etc.	etc.	etc.	etc.	etc.	etc.
Whole asset				5	3	3

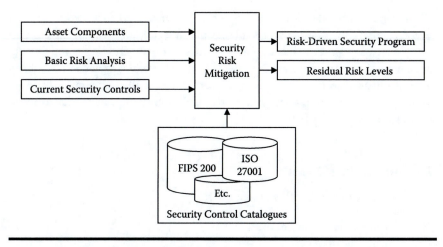

Figure 3.15   Risk-driven security program.

3.5 Security Implementation

This phase consists of the implementation of the risk-driven security program. Remember, the target information asset is only authorized to operate when the designated authorizing official approves it. The authorizing of operation of the target information asset is only determined after its certification and accreditation. The latter two steps are only performed in the review phase.

The implementation step must ensure both usability and sustainability of the security program. This may be substantiated by some design verification activities. Those activities constitute a testing period, during which the security program's usability and sustainability will be inspected. The security implementation staff should develop their own testing procedures, which should simulate real-world intrusion attempts to break or circumvent certain security aspects embedded in the target security design. The security implementation team may elect to discontinue the process if the security-tested mechanism was found incomplete or vulnerable.

Even though security design is the territory of capable security specialists, because users of the final system where those security mechanisms are embedded are not security professionals, there are many social factors that will contribute, as much as security, to the performance of the designed security features. Ignoring social factors when designing and implementing any security mechanisms can only diminish the usability and sustainability of the protected system. Even though it is obviously very difficult to account for social factors in security design, usually such factors may be mitigated by providing for flexible interface design.

The interface design should not be viewed as a layout of nice buttons appealing to users but should incorporate appropriate policies, technologies, and standards that are familiar to users. There may, however, be some balance between usability and security in a protected system, but even if this balance remains unknown it is still common sense that a security design that does not yield a secure system with acceptable usability is not an acceptable design. In fact, both usability and sustainability are two goals to be incorporated in any security design. While the security implementation team will make any possible effort to hide any added complexity due to embedded security controls, it is imperative that all configurations applied on the target information asset yield to adequate security implementation as specified in the asset security policy.

3.6 Security Review

The review phase consists of two main steps:

1. Security review for authorization
2. Security auditing

The purpose of this phase is to ensure that the authorizing official and the asset owner agree on the proposed security program, including the asset's documented security requirements, before the certification agent begins the assessment of the security controls in the information asset. If the information asset in question is small, for example, a simple desktop to register customers at a reception desk, then upper management may allow the authorizing official's designated representative or the system owner to administer the certification and accreditation steps needed before the information asset is authorized to operate.

The security certification phase aims at determining the extent to which the security controls in the information asset are implemented correctly, operating as intended, and producing the desired outcomes. When the certification and accreditation steps are completed, the information asset owner will either have authorization to operate the information asset, a provisional authorization to operate the information asset under specific terms and conditions, or a denial of authorization to operate the information asset.

Upper management assigns the authorizing official, who reviews the information needed from the security certification to determine the risk to asset operations, and the organization; thus, the official will be able to arrive at an appropriate security accreditation decision for the information system.

The accreditation step will determine if the remaining known vulnerabilities in the information asset pose an acceptable level of risk to asset operations, and the organization.

3.7 Continual Security

Continual security consists of continuous monitoring activities intended to ensure that security risks stay at accepted levels and that if the effectiveness of current security controls diminish and cause the accepted risk levels to be violated, corrective actions are planned to bring the risk levels back to their accepted levels. The following steps are usually planned to achieve continual security:

1. Configuration management and control
2. Monitoring of security controls
3. Monitoring of the computing environment for any changes
4. Reporting of changes and documentation

That is, the purpose of the continual security phase is to monitor the security controls in the information asset on a continuous basis and inform the authorizing official and the asset owner when changes occur that may impact the security of the asset and the organization. The activities in this phase are performed continuously throughout the security life cycle of the information asset.

Completing a periodic security audit will lead to the reaccreditation of the information asset to ensure that it is being operated with appropriate management review, that there is ongoing monitoring of security controls, and that reaccreditation occurs periodically in accordance with the corporate security policy and whenever there is a significant change to the system or its operational environment.

The continual security phase may include the following activities:

■ Periodic assessments of risk, including the magnitude of harm that could result from the unauthorized access, use, disclosure, disruption, modification, or destruction of information and information systems that support the operations and assets of the agency
■ Periodic review of policies and procedures that are based on risk assessments, cost-effectively reduce information security risks to an acceptable level, and ensure that information security is addressed throughout the security life cycle of the information asset
■ Security awareness training to inform personnel of the information security risks associated with their activities and their responsibilities in complying with organization's policies and procedures designed to reduce these risks
■ Periodic testing and evaluation of the effectiveness of information security policies, procedures, practices, and security controls to be periodically performed
■ A process for planning, implementing, evaluating, and documenting remedial actions to address any deficiencies in the information security policies, procedures, and practices of the agency
■ Procedures for detecting, reporting, and responding to security incidents

3.8 Summary

This chapter presented the security life cycle of an information asset. The security life cycle consists of six phases: planning the security life cycle, security analysis, security design, security implementation, security review, and continual security. The chapter also discussed all the phases of the security life cycle. In particular, we explained how to estimate impacts and impact levels for a target information asset. We also explained how an asset's security exposures are estimated.

The chapter also discussed how to assess security risks and how to mitigate security risks in the context of a holistic risk-driven security program for the target information asset.

3.9 Review Questions

1. How is the security life cycle of a given information asset planned? Explain the steps.
2. How is security in the security life cycle of a given information asset analyzed? Explain the steps.
3. How is security in the security life cycle of a given information asset reviewed? Explain the steps.
4. Explain how to compute asset security impacts and impact levels. Give an example.
5. Explain how to compute asset security exposure levels for threats. Give an example.
6. Explain how to compute asset security risk levels. Give an example.
7. Explain the pros and cons in selecting lower- or higher-point Likert scales in representing security risk levels. Give examples as needed.
8. How are asset security risks in the security life cycle of a given information asset mitigated? Explain the steps.
9. Explain how the security project scope in a security life cycle of a given information asset is defined. Explain the steps.

3.10 Workshops

Workshop 1

Consider a small business that has established an online presence using its Web site. Assume that the business hosts its own Web site. Follow all the steps of the security life cycle, treating the small business Web site as the target information asset. Also assume that the enterprise has a current security plan and current business continuity plan.

Workshop 2

A computing environment consists of people, activities, data, technology, and network. Apply the information security life cycle to ensure the security of the computing environment. Draw a 5 × 6 matrix with the computing environment components on the columns and the security life cycle phases on the rows. In each cell, show the types of security objectives that are most important among confidentiality, integrity, and availability.

Reference

1. NIST, Special Publication 800-30, Risk Management Guide for Information Technology Systems, http://csrc.nist.gov/publications/nistpubs/800-30/sp800-30.pdf

SECURITY PLAN

II

Chapter 4

Security Plan

Learning Objectives

After reading this chapter, students are expected to achieve an understanding of:

How the security planning process works

How system categorization in security planning is performed based on Federal Information Processing Standard (FIPS)

How risk management is addressed in security planning

What system security plan (SP) responsibilities are

How the system SP is approved

How the certification and accreditation process works in security planning

How to define SP scope and system boundaries

How to conduct SP analysis

How to apply scoping guidance

How to define compensating controls

How to specify common security controls

How to apply common security controls

How to select justifiable security controls

How to maintain ongoing system security

How the proposed SP methodology works

How to distinguish between a security program and a security plan

How to distinguish between a major application and a general support system

How to perform all phases of the SP methodology

How to perform system definition

How to perform SP analysis
How to perform SP design
How to assess system sensitivity
How to assess system availability requirements
How to recognize when restructuring or process reengineering
becomes necessary in security planning

4.1 Introduction

This chapter adapts the work of NIST's great authors, Ron Ross, Stu Katzke, Arnold Johnson, Marianne Swanson, Gary Stoneburner, and George Rogers, who jointly developed the only extant standard for the formulation of a security plan. This chapter attempts to communicate this standard (or guidelines, the team used in some of the literature) to students, researchers, and professionals in both the public (which is already mandatory in the United States) and the private sector, where it is adopted to gain competitive advantage. This chapter translates this standard into a user-friendly methodology based on a older version of the same standard (NIST SP 800-18) published by Marianne Swanson in NIST publications. From time to time, we reproduce some of the definitions that are better communicated the way they are instead of paraphrasing them [3].

There are obviously many international security standards we can study and conform to, but before we seek any compliance with any security requirements those standards propose, we have to look around us and understand all the local, regional, or national security standards and regulations. The organization has to study the benefits and feasibility of any security standards and satisfy the security requirements that affect its business community. In the United States, however, most security standards that apply to security planning are the product of the government and should apply to all public agencies and any other enterprises that have any type of interaction with the government. Usually, any company, small, medium, or large will be members of the same business communities as the government through sharing users, customers, partners, or event services and products. It is very difficult to find a company that will not benefit from the adoption of the security standards that the Government recommends for public agencies in the area of security planning. Many companies in the private sector can, however, gain a great deal of competitive advantage by feasibly complying with selective national security standards.

Federal Information Processing Standard (FIPS) 200, Minimum Security Requirements for Federal Information and Information Systems, specifies the minimum security requirements for federal information and information systems in 17 security-related areas. Even though the original target is federal agencies, this literature applies to any type of organization, whether in the public sector or in the private sector.

While public agencies have to meet the minimum security requirements defined in FIPS 200, there is no doubt that even organizations in the private sector can benefit from them. Public agencies and organizations in general can gain great security by adopting security controls in NIST Special Publication 800-53 [5], called "Recommended Security Controls for federal Information Systems." NIST SP 800-53 contains the managerial, operational, and technical safeguards or countermeasures prescribed for an information system. The controls selected or planned must be documented in a system security plan. Most of the information used in discussing effective security planning is borrowed from selected NIST publications, for example, NIST SP 800-18 [3], NIST FIPS 199 [1], NIST SP 800-37 [4], and NIST 800-53 [5].

4.2 SP Development Guidelines

4.2.1 The Security Planning Process

The purpose of a security plan for an information system is to define its security requirements for the long term. Those security requirements will be specified depending on the criticality of the information system, which is often expressed in terms of the sensitivity of its information and its availability requirements. On the other hand, the criticality of the information may be also expressed in terms of the information system's impact on the business mission of the organization. The government recommends to its public agencies the use of FIPS 199 in conducting impact analysis for their information systems. FIPS 199, *Standards for the Security Categorization of Federal Information and Information Systems*, issued in February 2004, was the first standard that NIST developed to meet FISMA requirements. FIPS 199 may be used by both public agencies and organizations in general to categorize their information systems when an SP project is initiated. Those information systems are categorized as low-impact, moderate-impact, or high-impact systems for the security objectives of confidentiality, integrity, and availability.

Coupled with FIPS 199 is another security standard that is adopted by public agencies to determine which security controls are applicable and effective in providing for the security of their target information systems. FIPS 200, *Minimum Security Requirements for Federal Information and Information Systems*, which was approved on March 9, 2006, is the second standard that was specified by FISMA. After agencies have categorized their systems in accordance with FIPS 199, they are required to determine minimum security requirements for 17 security-related areas and to select an appropriate set of security controls to satisfy the minimum requirements. Security controls, which are specified in NIST SP 800-53 [5], are organized to match the 17 security-related areas identified in FIPS 200 [2]. The application of controls is an essential component of a broad-based, balanced information security program.

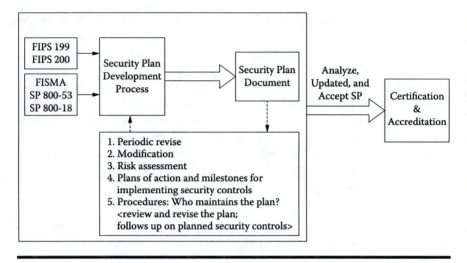

Figure 4.1   The security planning process.

The security planning process, as depicted in Figure 4.1, relies on several federal standards defining minimal security requirements—FIPS 199 and 200, the Federal Information Security Management Act (FISMA), and several NIST special publications, NIST SP 800-53 [5] and NIST SP 800-18 [3]—to study the target system and define its security requirements for the long term, usually, for a period of 3 years. The main output of the security planning process is the SP for the target system.

The SP will consist of the organization's security requirements in terms of managerial, operational, and technical security controls that are capable of providing adequate security for the organization for the next 3 years. The Office of Management and Budget (OMB) Circular A-130 [6], Appendix III, defines adequate security in terms of the levels of security risks and the magnitude of harm resulting from information leakage, information corruption, and denial of service.

The SP is approved by an authorizing official designated by upper management before it is analyzed, updated, and accepted for the purpose of being certified and accredited. The SP will also include a schedule for periodic reviews, modification, and plans of action and milestones for implementing the planned security controls.

NIST SP 800-53 [5] presents the fundamental concepts concerning the selection and specification of security controls. It discusses the structural components of security controls and how the controls are organized into families of controls:

- The baseline, or minimum, controls that can be selected
- The common controls that can be applied in more than one organizational information system
- The controls needed to protect systems in exchanges with external information systems

- Implementation of controls within an information system with assurance that the controls are effective
- NIST's plans for periodic review of the controls and maintenance of a catalog of effective controls

NIST SP 800-53 [5], Revision 1, *Recommended Security Controls for Federal Information Systems*, was written by Ron Ross, Stu Katzke, Arnold Johnson, Marianne Swanson, Gary Stoneburner, and George Rogers, and published by NIST in December 2006. Most of the security planning guidelines and concepts discussed in this chapter are the work of those great authors. We, occasionally, lightly bend some of those concepts to extend their use beyond public agencies to the private sector. While this publication, when used with other standards and guidelines, assists federal agencies in protecting the information systems that support federal government operations and assets, there is no doubt that the same benefits extend to most organizations outside the public sector provided a through feasibility study is performed before full adoption.

The guide describes the recommended comprehensive process that organizations should follow for selecting and specifying security controls for an information system. Topics covered include the steps that an organization should take to manage risks; the requirement for federal agencies to categorize their information systems as low impact, moderate impact, or high impact for the security objectives of confidentiality, integrity, and availability; how to select and tailor an initial set of minimum, or baseline, controls; how to supplement the tailored baseline controls to achieve needed security protections; and how to update controls through regular reviews as part of a risk management process.

NIST, in fact, has not missed any security planning concepts that organizations need to employ effective security management. Further information is provided in the appendices to NIST SP 800-53 [5], which offer extensive support in the selection and specification of security controls. Included are a list of references, a glossary of terms used in the publication, and a list of acronyms. One table lists the catalog of minimum security controls in summarized form and indicates the appropriate control and any applicable control enhancements that would be needed to protect low-impact, moderate-impact, and high-impact information systems.

Another part of the appendix explains the minimum assurance requirements for the security controls listed in the catalog, and provides supplemental guidance concerning how the minimum requirements are to be applied. One large section of the appendix provides a catalog of security controls organized into families with supplemental guidance and with information associated with each control to allow for the enhancement of the control. Mappings of the relationships of security controls to government and voluntary industry standards and to other control sets, mappings of the relationships of security controls to NIST standards and guidelines, and guidance on the application of controls to industrial control systems complete the appendices.

4.2.2 System Categorization in Security Planning

Each system identified in the organization's inventory of assets must be categorized using FIPS 199 (Figure 4.2). NIST Special Publication 800-60, *Guide for Mapping Types of Information and Information Systems to Security Categories,* provides implementation guidance for completing this activity.

Consider the example of the local subway system. It employs an information system that informs the public about the schedule of all available trains, but the same system also advises engineers on train maintenance and rail routing. On one

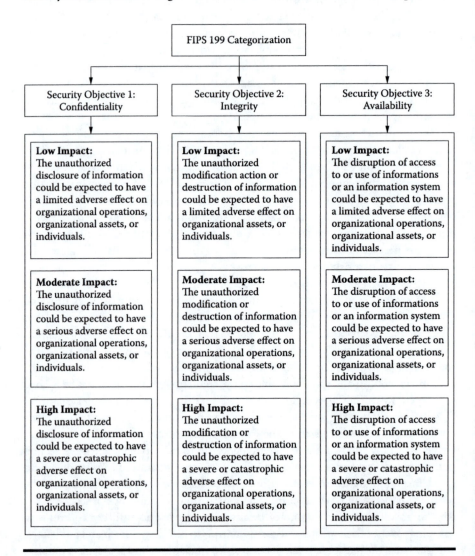

Figure 4.2   FIPS 199 categorization of information systems.

hand, for the part of the system that displays public information, the unauthorized disclosure of information could be expected to have a limited adverse effect on organizational operations, organizational assets, or individuals. On the other hand, for the part of the system dealing with train maintenance and rail routing, any disruption of access to, or use of, information or an information system could be expected to have a severe or catastrophic adverse effect on organizational operations, organizational assets, or individuals. The question is how to classify this system. The first part of the system is classified as "low impact," according to FIPS 199 categorization. The second part of the system is classified as "high impact," according to FIPS 199 categorization. Applying the weak link principle, the entire system should be classified as "high impact."

4.2.3 Risk Management in Security Planning

According to NIST SP 800-53 [5], risk management is essential in developing a security plan. It should provide an effective framework for the selection of appropriate security controls. However, although a risk analysis activity is certainly needed before even thinking of studying the information system security requirements, it is important to understand that this risk activity is only a preliminary risk, assessment step, whose purpose is to gather the limited information support needed to compare security controls based on how they affect the security risk position of the information system. A thorough risk analysis of the kind that is employed in security audit with independent certification is very time consuming and costly and will not be appropriate in security planning. The precision required in a through and detailed security risk analysis activity is not needed in an SP project.

The risk-based approach enables organizations to protect the information systems that store, process, and transmit organizational information, to make well-informed risk management decisions, and to apply system authorization and accreditation processes. NIST SP 800-53 [5] recommends the following steps to manage risks, as part of a security plan:

1. Categorize the information system and its information in accordance with FIPS 199 [1].
2. Select an initial set of baseline, or minimum, controls from NIST SP 800-53 [5], based on the categorization and the minimum security requirements defined in FIPS 200 [2]. Apply the tailoring guidance from NIST SP 800-53 to identify the starting point controls.
3. Supplement the initial set of tailored security controls based on the assessment of risk and the organization's specific requirements.
4. Document the security controls, including refinements and adjustments to the initial set of controls, in the system security plan.
5. Implement the security controls in the information system, and apply security configuration settings.

6. Assess the security controls to determine if they have been implemented correctly, are operating properly, and are meeting security requirements.
7. Authorize information system operation, using security certification and accreditation procedures. Security accreditation is the decision to authorize operation of an information system and to accept the risk to agency operations, agency assets, or individuals based on the implementation of an agreed-upon set of security controls. Security certification is a comprehensive assessment of the system's security controls to determine the extent to which the controls are implemented correctly, operating as intended, and meeting the security requirements of the system.
8. Monitor and assess selected security controls to track changes to the information system on a continuous basis, and reassess the effectiveness of controls.

4.2.4 System SP Responsibilities

Organizations need to have a security policy that guides them through security planning. Security plans are living documents, usually with about a 3 year life cycle, that require periodic review, modification, and plans of action and milestones for implementing security controls. In order to distribute SP development responsibilities, we need to know the process of security planning and all procedures or activities involved in the production of a security plan. Usually, organizations either have a project management division that supervises all project management processes initiated in the organization or have a project management policy that describes the project management methodology that should be employed. The SP project should be treated as any other project for which a project management process is initiated.

Also, there will be a need to define the procedures that have to be in place, describing who reviews the plans, keeps the plan current, and follows up on planned security controls. Moreover, security plans have to be developed and reviewed before proceeding with any eventual security certification and accreditation process for the system.

The work breakdown structure (WBS), as in Figure 4.3, is a simple but powerful tool to define the scope of a project, similar to our SP project. It represents the project in terms of the hierarchy of deliverables it will produce. The role of the WBS is to:

■ Partition the major security project deliverables into smaller components to improve the accuracy of cost estimates
■ Provide a mechanism for collecting and controlling actual costs
■ Provide a mechanism for performance measurement and control

Figure 4.3 describes only an example of the standard activities constituting an SP development process, not the entire SP project that we will be seeing in more detail

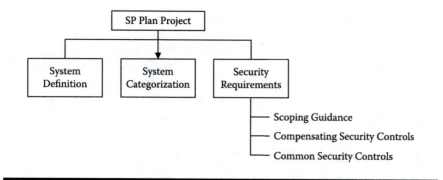

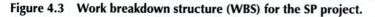

Figure 4.3   Work breakdown structure (WBS) for the SP project.

in Chapter 5. The box at the top of the diagram represents the total system and is referred to as WBS level 1. Lower levels that describe project components in increasing detail are numbered 2, 3, 4, and so on.

The concept of WBS level is important as it allows you to designate the level of detail at which you report cost estimates and project cost performance figures. For example, to effectively manage a large project, a senior manager typically needs summary details of cost variance at level 2. On the other hand, the team leader responsible for developing a level 2 software component needs cost performance reports at level 3. The lowest levels of a WBS represent discrete deliverable items against which costs will be tracked and performance measured.

4.2.5 System SP Approval

The corporate security policy should define who approves any system security plan. This policy should also explicitly define the SP submission process. Prior to the certification and accreditation process, the designated authorizing official approves the plan. The authorizing official should be different from the system owner.

4.2.6 Certification and Accreditation Process

During the security certification and accreditation process, the system SP is analyzed, updated, and accepted. The certification agent verifies that the security controls described in the system SP are consistent with the FIPS 199 security category determined for the information system, and that the threat and vulnerability identification and initial risk determination are identified and documented in the system security plan, risk assessment, or equivalent document.

The results of a security certification may be employed to reassess the risks, develop the plan of action and milestones that are required to track remedial actions, and update the system security plan. The information assembled so far provides all the decision support information an authorizing officer needs to determine whether or not the target information system should be accredited. NIST SP 800-37 provides further information on the certification and accreditation processes. NIST Special Publication 800-37 defines a minor application that requires attention to security due to the risk and magnitude of harm resulting from the loss, misuse, or unauthorized access to, or modification of, the information in the application. Minor applications are typically included in a general support system.

4.2.7 SP Scope and System Boundaries

Before initiating a security plan, FIPS 199 should be used to determine the impact and the category of every candidate information system and its information. Based on this impact analysis, the SP team can determine which systems in the SP scope have to be logically grouped together into major applications or general support systems. The impact levels produced by the FIPS 199 impact analysis are needed to define system boundaries and to select the initial set of security controls, known as the security control baselines defined in NIST SP 800-53 [5].

Preliminary risk assessment will later be needed to tailor those baseline security controls given local conditions, including organization-specific security requirements, specific threat information, cost-benefit analyses, the availability of compensating controls, or special circumstances. The tailoring process will be discussed later in this chapter.

Security planning management defines the boundary of the scope of an SP by assigning information resources to an information system. There should be some flexibility in determining what constitutes a major application or a general support system. If some information resources are added to the SP scope, they should generally be under the same direct management control. In addition to direct management control, all resources in the same SP scope often have to satisfy the following conditions, as required in NIST SP 800-18 [3]:

■ They have the same function or mission objective and essentially the same operating characteristics and security needs.
■ They reside in the same general operating environment (or in the case of a distributed information system, reside in various locations with similar operating environments).

Authorizing officials and senior information security officers should consult with prospective information system owners when establishing information system boundaries. The process of establishing boundaries for the SP scope and the associated security implications should include careful negotiation among all key participants, taking into account the mission/business requirements of the organization, the technical considerations with respect to information security, costs, and available budget.

FIPS 199 defines security categories for information systems based on potential impact on organizations, assets, or individuals should there be a breach of security that produces a loss of confidentiality, integrity, or availability. FIPS 199 security categories can play an important part in defining information system boundaries by partitioning the organization's information systems according to the criticality or sensitivity of the information and information systems and the importance of those systems in accomplishing the organization's mission.

FIPS 199 requires that information resources in the SP scope be secured to the highest impact level when grouping minor applications/subsystems with varying FIPS 199 impact levels into a single general support system or major application unless there is adequate boundary protection that guarantees the right protection level at the right impact level for all resources in the SP scope. Moreover, NIST SP 800-18 requires that there be assurance that the shared resources, that is, networks, communications, and physical access within the whole general support system or major application, are protected adequately for the highest impact level [3].

4.2.7.1 Major Applications

In an organization, all applications have business value and require adequate protection. Certain applications, because of their criticality and the business value they generate, deserve special security management attention. Based on their strict security requirements, some applications are known as major applications. A major application is expected to have a FIPS 199 impact level of moderate or high. Based on OMB Circular A-130 [6], major applications are applications that require special management attention because of their importance to an organization mission; their high development, operating, or maintenance costs; or their significant role in the administration of organizational programs, finances, property, or other resources. NIST SP 800-18 defines major applications as systems that perform clearly defined functions for which there are readily identifiable security considerations and needs [3]. This NIST SP standard requires that if a major application is run on another organization's general support system, the major application owner be responsible for the following activities:

- The major application owner accepts associated risks.
- The major application owner notifies the general support system owner that the application is critical and provides specific security requirements.
- The major application provides a copy of the major application's system SP to the operator of the general support system.
- The major application requests a copy of the system SP of the general support system and ensures that it provides adequate protection for the application and information.
- The major application includes a reference to the general support system SP in the major application system security plan.

4.2.7.2 General Support Systems

NIST SP 800-18 defines a general support system as an interconnected set of information resources under the same direct management control that share common functionality [3]. A general support system often includes people, technology (hardware, software), data/information, communications, and facilities; and it provides support for a variety of users and applications. The following are examples of general support systems: LAN, backbone, communications network, data processing (DP) unit, etc. A general support system may include a major application, but in this case, the general support system plan should reference the major application system security plan.

A general support system may have a FIPS 199 impact level of low, moderate, or high. The security categorization depends on the criticality and sensitivity of included subsystems and major applications. A general support system is considered a major information system when special management attention is required, for example, with high development, operating, or maintenance costs, or when the system/information plays a significant role in the administration of organizational programs. When the general support system is a major information system, the system's FIPS 199 impact level is either moderate or high.

4.2.8 What Is a Security Plan?

FIPS 200 provides 17 minimum security requirements for federal information and information systems. The requirements represent a broad-based, balanced information security program that addresses the managerial, operational, and technical aspects of protecting the confidentiality, integrity, and availability of information and information systems. These requirements are also valid for the private sector. Organizations can gain a great security advantage by planning their security according to NIST SP 800-18 [3].

The security requirements recommended by NIST for security planning are divided into three classes of security controls: managerial security controls, operational security controls, and technical security controls. As shown in Table 4.1, NIST defines four families of managerial security controls; nine families of operational security controls; and four families of technical security controls.

An organization must meet the minimum security requirements in this standard by applying security controls selected in accordance with NIST SP 800-53 and the designated impact levels of the information systems. The organization should have the flexibility to adapt the security control baseline in accordance with the terms and conditions set forth in the standard. Adapted activities include (1) the application of scoping guidance, (2) the specification of compensating controls, and (3) the specification of common security controls, as needed. The system SP should document all adapted activities.

In order to understand how an SP is developed, we need to understand the following three activities:

Table 4.1 Security Control Class, Family, and Identifier

Class	Family	Identifier
Management	Risk Assessment	RA
Management	Planning	PL
Management	System and Services Acquisition	SA
Management	Certification, Accreditation, and Security Assessments	CA
Operational	Personnel Security	PS
Operational	Physical and Environmental Protection	PE
Operational	Contingency Planning	CP
Operational	Configuration Management	CM
Operational	Maintenance	MA
Operational	System and Information Integrity	SI
Operational	Media Protection	MP
Operational	Incident Response	IR
Operational	Awareness and Training	AT
Technical	Identification and Authentication	IA
Technical	Access Control	AC
Technical	Audit and Accountability	AU
Technical	System and Communications Protection	SC

1. The application of scoping guidance
2. The specification of compensating controls
3. The specification of common security controls, as needed

4.2.9 SP Analysis

4.2.9.1 Scoping Guidance

4.2.9.1.1 What is Scoping Guidance?

Let us examine the definition of *scoping guidance,* as provided by NIST in NIST SP 800-18, 2006 [3]:

Provides organizations with specific technology-related, infrastructure-related, public access-related, scalability-related, common security control-related, and risk-related considerations on the applicability and implementation of individual security controls in the control baseline.

Scoping guidance, as shown in Figure 4.4, offers specific terms and conditions that the organization is advised to use to determine the applicability of any security controls taken from NIST SP 800-53. It is very important to understand the conditions of implementation of the selected security controls before recommending them to system owners. Even though strictly satisfying all the conditions and terms provided in the scoping guidance recommended by NIST in the process of selecting security controls is not mandatory, those organization that are seeking the certification of their security plans or the accreditation of their information systems may be better off closely following most of it to facilitate any eventual certification or accreditation processes.

4.2.9.1.2 How Is Scoping Guidance Applied?

Let us also examine what can be done to understand how the baseline security controls can affect the security of the organization. Are there any prerequisites that have to be studied or any considerations that have to be looked at that can maximize the chances that all selected security controls will in fact achieve any of the security requirements that were initially defined? In other words, it is important to find ways to justify any security controls we included in the security plan. The SP should include all justifications employed when the security controls are chosen for inclusion in the security plan. That is, any considerations or specific conditions associated with the security requirements being studied have to be adopted as part of any justifications cited in the security plan.

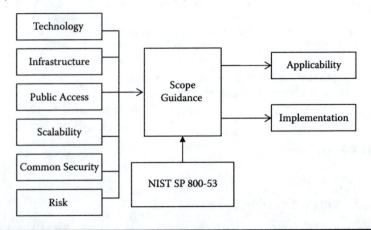

Figure 4.4 Using scope guidance to select security controls for the security plan.

That said, any justification process has to be discussed with owners, who should explicitly approve them before they are added to the security plan. The SP should explicitly identify the security controls that were justified based on the scoping guidance and clearly present any justifications employed. Those scoping-guidance justifications of the security controls have to be evaluated and approved by the authorizing official for the system.

We next explain some of the considerations that have to be addressed when the scoping guidance is followed: (1) technology-related considerations, (2) common security control-related considerations, (3) public access information systems-related considerations, (4) infrastructure-related considerations, (5) scalability-related considerations, and (6) risk-related considerations.

a. Technology-related considerations:

The technology-related concerns that ought to be addressed when security controls are recommended are expressed as simple rules of applicability:

Rule of applicability 1:

Applicability requires that any specific technologies needed by a security control can only be approved if those technologies exist in the computing environment of the information system under study.

Rule of applicability 2:

A security control is only applicable if the target information system components meant by this very security control provide the minimal security power required by the minimal security requirements and no more.

Rule of applicability 3:

Any security control that is supported, implicitly or explicitly, by an existing automated mechanism will not require the development of the mechanism, unless it already exists or is available commercially. If this mechanism is not available or is not technically feasible, then the minimal security requirements have to be satisfied through compensating security controls that are implemented through nonautomated mechanisms. The nonautomated mechanisms still satisfy the prescribed minimum security requirements.

b. Common security control-related considerations:

A common security control is designed, developed, implemented, and evaluated by the organization and also managed by an organizational element other than an information system owner. Figure 4.5 depicts the process of defining common security controls.

That is, every security control defined in NIST SP 800-53 is studied by an organizational official as a common security control or by an information system owner as a security control designated for a specific information system.

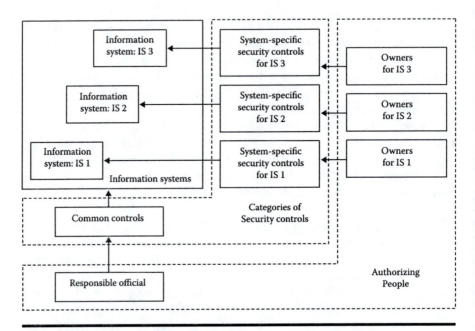

Figure 4.5 Common security controls versus security controls.

It is important to note that the designation of a common security control to target a set of information systems or other components of the computing environment should not discharge the organization from its obligation to define the most appropriate security controls for individual information systems.

c. Public access information systems-related considerations:

The baseline security controls require identification and authentication of organizational personnel who maintain and support information systems that provide public access services. It is important to note that those same controls are not necessarily required for users when they access those systems through public interfaces to obtain publicly available information. Despite the latter assertion, identification and authentication must be required for users accessing information systems through public interfaces to access their private or personal information.

Most security controls associated with public access information systems should be carefully studied and handled with discretion because some of the security controls from the specified security control baselines may not be applicable to users accessing information systems through public interfaces.

d. Infrastructure-related considerations:

Physical security controls for an information system are only concerned with the physical resources that are deployed to protect the information system.

All those security controls that refer to infrastructure, including equipments, facilities, physical controls, etc., will be applicable only to those sections of the facilities that directly provide protection to, support for, or are related to the information system. Examples of physical resources include its information technology assets such as electronic mail or Web servers, server farms, data centers, networking nodes, communication equipments, etc.

e. Scalability-related considerations:

Scalability is concerned with the implementation of a security control, from the breadth and the depth directions of the security control, and the impact level of the information system. That is, a security control is scalable by the size and complexity of the organization. Systems owners should apply discretion as needed in scaling the security controls to a particular environment. This will ensure a cost-effective, risk-based approach to security control implementation.

For example, the security controls for a business continuity project are not defined the same way as for controls in a smaller environment with a low-impact information system.

f. Risk-related considerations:

The selection of security controls from the minimal baselines should be performed based on risks. Those security controls that uniquely support the confidentiality, integrity, or availability security objectives can be downgraded to the corresponding control in a lower baseline if, and only if, the downgrading action (1) is consistent with the FIPS 199 security categorization for the corresponding security objectives of confidentiality, integrity, or availability before moving to the high watermark; (2) is supported by an organization's assessment of risk; and (3) does not affect the security-relevant information within the information system.

Security-relevant information at the system level must be distinguished from user-level information within an information system. An organization must make sure that no downgrading activity affects any security-relevant information within the information system.

4.2.9.2 Compensating Controls

4.2.9.2.1 What Are Compensating Controls?

Compensating controls constitute the managerial, operational, and technical controls employed by an organization in lieu of the recommended controls in the low, moderate, or high baselines described in NIST SP 800-53, that provide equivalent or comparable protection for an information system.

4.2.9.2.2 How to Specify Compensating Controls?

An organization can only adopt compensating security controls for the protection of an information system under the following conditions:

1. The organization selects the compensating controls from the security control catalog in NIST SP 800-53.
2. The organization provides a complete and convincing rationale and justification for how the compensating controls provide an equivalent security capability or level of protection for the information system.
3. The organization assesses and formally accepts the risk associated with employing the compensating controls in the information system.

The use of compensating security controls must be reviewed, documented in the system security plan, and approved by the authorizing official for the information system.

4.2.9.3 Common Security Controls

4.2.9.3.1 What Are Common Security Controls?

A centralized view of an eventual information security program can only ease the identification of common security controls. The common security controls should, by definition, apply to a set of information systems or a wide cross-section of the computing environment of the organization.

A common security control is a security control that can be applied to one or more information systems in the organization, and has the following properties:

1. The development, implementation, and assessment of the control can be assigned to a responsible official or organizational element, other than the information system owner.
2. The results from the assessment of the control can be used to support the security certification and accreditation processes of an agency information system where that control has been applied.

In order to understand the security planning process, it is better to organize security controls into two categories: common security controls and system-specific controls. Partitioning security controls into common security controls and system-specific security controls can result in significant savings to the organization in system development and implementation costs. Security planning based on this partitioning schema may yield a more reliable application of the security controls throughout the entire organization.

Consequently, a more efficient security planning process can only lead to more cost-effective certification and accreditation processes. It is all about the simple process of emphasizing common security controls as needed. There will be no need to assess security controls for each information system alone. We instead assess, as needed, common security controls in every information system. The partitioning of security controls into common security controls and system-specific controls is certainly simple and intuitive, but the application of this principle within an agency requires effective security planning.

4.2.9.3.2 How to Apply Common Security Controls?

A computing environment includes information systems, subsystems, or applications (i.e., common hardware, software, and firmware) deployed at one or multiple operational sites of the same organization. Common security controls are usually the result of close cooperation among the CIO, CISO (if one exist), authorizing officials, information system owners, and information system security officers, etc. As shown earlier when we defined common security controls, it is noteworthy that the development, implementation, and assessment of common security controls cannot be assigned to information system owners but to responsible agency officials or organizational elements, and that often the results of any assessment activities are adopted in any eventual security certification or accreditation processes for selected information systems.

Common management and operational controls include contingency planning controls, incident response controls, security awareness and training controls, personnel security controls, and physical security controls. All these security controls apply to most of the organization, and they are hence called common security controls.

The objective of adopting common security controls is to reduce security costs by centrally managing the development, implementation, and assessment of the common security controls selected by the organization. These security controls will, consequently, share assessment results with the owners of information systems where those common security controls are applied. Security controls not selected as common controls are considered system-specific controls and are hence the responsibility of the information system owner. System security plans should clearly identify which security controls have been designated as common security controls and which as system-specific controls.

However, in order to produce an efficient security plan, common security controls should be documented once and then inserted or imported into each system SP for any target information systems within the organization.

The individual staff member responsible for implementing a given common security control should be recorded in the security plan. The effective adoption of common security controls in security planning depends on the following factors:

1. The organization develops, documents, and communicates its specific guidance on identifying common security controls.
2. The organization assigns the responsibility for coordinating common security control identification and review and obtaining consensus on the common

security control designations to a management official with security program responsibilities such as the CIO or ISO.
3. The organization briefs system owners on the system security planning process, including use of common security controls.
4. Consultation with security experts in the organization associated with the specific area of the common security control in question.

4.2.10 Security Control Selection

In preparation for documenting how the NIST SP 800-53 [5] security controls for the applicable security control baseline (low-, moderate-, or high-impact information systems), as shown in Figure 4.6, are implemented or planned to be implemented, the security controls contained in the baseline should be reviewed and possibly tailored. The scoping guidelines explained in Section 2.5.1 should be used when determining the applicability or tailoring of individual controls. Additionally, the controls that are common among numerous systems or within the whole agency should be identified and then documented in the plan (see Section 2.5.3 for guidance on how the common controls should be determined, documented, and coordinated). The process of selecting the appropriate security controls and applying the scoping guidelines to achieve *adequate security* is a multifaceted, risk-based activity involving management and operational personnel within the agency and should be conducted before the security control portion of the plan is written.

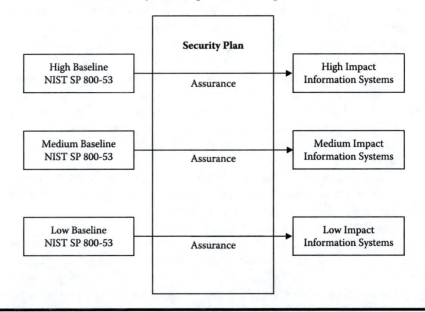

Figure 4.6   Relationship between security baselines of NIST SP 800-53 and security planning.

■ For *low-impact* information systems, an agency must, at a minimum, employ the security controls from the low baseline of security controls defined in NIST SP 800-53 and must ensure that the minimum assurance requirements associated with the low baseline are satisfied.

■ For *moderate-impact* information systems, an agency must, at a minimum, employ the security controls from the moderate baseline of security controls defined in NIST SP 800-53 and must ensure that the minimum assurance requirements associated with the moderate baseline are satisfied.

■ For *high-impact* information systems, an agency must, at a minimum, employ the security controls from the high baseline of security controls defined in NIST SP 800-53 and must ensure that the minimum assurance requirements associated with the high baseline are satisfied.

Now that the security controls have been selected, tailored, and the common controls identified, in a thorough documentation effort, you will need to describe each control. The description should contain the following:

1. The security control title
2. How the security control is being implemented or planned to be implemented
3. Any scoping guidance that has been applied and what type of consideration
4. Indicate if the security control is a common control and who is responsible for its implementation

Security controls in the security control catalog (NIST SP 800-53, Appendix F) have a well-defined organization and structure. The security controls are organized into classes and families for ease of use in the control selection and specification process. There are three general classes of security controls: managerial, operational, and technical. Each family contains security controls related to the security function of the family. A standardized, two-character identifier is assigned to uniquely identify each control family. Table 4.1 summarizes the classes and families in the security control catalog and the associated family identifiers.

Security control class designations (i.e., managerial, operational, and technical) are defined in the following text for clarification in preparation of system security plans.

Managerial controls focus on the management of the information system and the management of risk for a system. They are techniques and concerns that are normally addressed by management.

Operational controls address security methods focusing on the 17 security control families in NIST SP 800-53 [5] are associated with one of three security control classes (i.e., managerial, operational, technical). Families are assigned to their respective classes based on the dominant characteristics of the controls in that family. Many security controls, however, can be logically associated with more than one class. For example, CP-1, the policy and procedures control from the Contingency Planning family, is listed as an operational control but also has characteristics that are consistent with security management as well. Operational security controls concern mechanisms primarily implemented and executed by people (as opposed to systems). These controls are put in place to improve the security of a particular system (or group of systems). They often require technical or specialized expertise and often rely on management activities as well as technical controls.

Technical controls focus on security controls that the computer system executes. These controls can provide automated protection against unauthorized access or misuse, facilitate detection of security violations, and support security requirements for applications and data.

4.2.11 Ongoing System SP Maintenance

Once the information system SP is developed, it is important to periodically assess it, review any change in system status, functionality, design, etc., and ensure that the plan continues to reflect correct information about the system. This documentation and its correctness are critical for system certification activity. All plans should be reviewed and updated, if appropriate, at least annually. Some items to include in the review are:

- Change in information system owner
- Change in information security representative
- Change in system architecture
- Change in system status
- Additions/deletions of system interconnections
- Change in system scope
- Change in authorizing official
- Change in certification and accreditation status

4.3 SP Methodology

We propose a methodology, for the private sector and foreign enterprises, for the writing of a security plan. This SP methodology will satisfy most known requirements defined for the federal agencies.

However, why does a private agency have to obey federal guidelines? Simply, because these are the only ones that exist, and the only ones that have been developed with rigor. Moreover, now or later, any private agency will have to deal with the federal guidelines for certification, accreditation, etc.

Why should a foreign agency follow U.S. federal guidelines? It need not if it is unrelated in any way to any system that has to satisfy ISO 15408. This international standard is the merging of ITSEC and TCSEC, but more likely to agree with the U.S. standard TCSEC, which in one way or another is related to the U.S. federal guidelines.

One of the interesting federal guidelines for automated information systems that is concerned with security planning is Appendix III of OMB A-130 [6]. The purpose of this appendix is to add a minimum set of controls, and assign federal agency responsibilities for the security of automated information. Other countries may find these guidelines useful in defining their national security directives.

While federal agencies are required to implement and maintain a program to ensure that adequate security is provided for all information collected, processed, transmitted, stored, or disseminated in general support systems and major applications, there is no doubt that the private sector and the rest of the world define similar requirements.

4.3.1 Security Program versus Security Plan

An SP is a cost-effective process for identifying and implementing a set of security controls in response to a thorough security risk analysis activity. A security program is associated with a security risk management process, usually for a short time period. You may consider a given organization with a mission M, a budget b, and a set of assets A. Let the current set of threats be denoted T, and the set of available security controls S. The task of a security program is to identify a set of security controls within S that, when implemented, will minimize the organization's security risk given its budget b and its current mission M.

The report that includes all the implementation programs of the selected security controls is called a security program. It is usually set for a short period that does not exceed 1 year. On the other hand, an SP contains detailed technical information about the system, its security requirements, and the controls implemented to provide protection against its risks and vulnerabilities.

An SP should establish a set of rules of behavior concerning the use of the system, its security, and its acceptable level of risk. The rules should be based on the needs of the various users of the system. The security required by the rules should be only as stringent as necessary to provide adequate security for information in the system. Such rules should clearly delineate responsibilities and expected behavior of all individuals with access to the system. They should also include appropriate limits on interconnections to other systems and should define service provision and restoration priorities. Finally, they should be clear about the consequences of behavior not consistent with the rules.

The SP should ensure that all individuals are appropriately trained in how to fulfill their security responsibilities before allowing them access to the system. Such training should ensure that employees are familiar with the rules of the system, comply with guidance issued by NIST and the Office of Personnel Management (OPM), and learn about available assistance and technical security products and techniques. Behavior consistent with the rules of the system and periodic refresher training should be required for continued access to the system.

The SP should explain how to formally screen individuals who are authorized to bypass significant technical and operational security controls of the system. Such screening should occur prior to an individual being authorized to bypass controls and periodically thereafter.

The SP should ensure that there is a capability to provide help to users when a security incident occurs in the system and to share information concerning common vulnerabilities and threats. This capability should include sharing information with other organizations, consistent with NIST coordination, and should assist the agency in pursuing appropriate legal action, consistent with Department of Justice guidance.

The SP should establish and periodically test the capability to continue providing service within a system based on the needs and priorities of the participants of the system.

The SP should ensure that cost-effective security products and techniques are appropriately used within the system.

The SP should have obtained written management authorization, based on the acceptance of risk to the system, prior to connecting with other systems. For federal agencies, where connection is authorized, controls should be established that are consistent with the rules of the system and in accordance with guidance from NIST.

4.3.2 Applications and Systems

Even though we try throughout this book to stick to the meaning that NIST applies to terms, some of the terms encountered may not necessarily conform to the definition given in NIST documentation.

Whenever it is used in this book, the term *adequate security* means security commensurate with the risk and magnitude of the harm resulting from the loss, misuse, or unauthorized access to or modification of information. This includes ensuring that systems and applications used by the enterprise operate effectively and provide appropriate confidentiality, integrity, and availability, through the use of cost-effective management, personnel, operational, and technical controls.

The term "application" means the use of information resources to satisfy a specific set of user requirements.

The term *general support system* or *system* means an interconnected set of information resources under the same direct management control that shares common functionality. A system normally includes hardware, software, information, data, applications, communications, and people. A system can be, for example, a local area network (LAN) including smart terminals that support a branch office, an agency-wide backbone, a communications network, a departmental data processing center including its operating system and utilities, a tactical radio network, or a shared information processing service organization.

The term *major application* means an application that requires special attention to security due to the risk and magnitude of the harm resulting from the loss, misuse, or unauthorized access to or modification of the information in the application. All federal applications require some level of protection. Certain applications, because of the sensitive information in them, however, require special management oversight and should be treated as major applications. Adequate security for other applications should be provided by security of the systems in which they operate.

4.3.3 Main Phases of the SP Methodology

This methodology for the writing of an SP consists of 5 phases:

1. Strategic security definition
2. Strategic security analysis
3. Strategic security design
4. Strategic security choice
5. Strategic security review

4.3.3.1 Strategic Security Definition

The strategic security definition phase is the first phase of developing an organization's security plan. The security plan writer (SPW) defines all security-relevant components constituting the system being studied.

The SPW may need to study the current vision, mission, and security objectives of the organization before starting the SP project. More time should be spent on functional missions and security objectives, especially in the functional unit that contains the system being studied. Usually, in the case of a general support system, the system for which an SP is being developed belongs to more than one functional unit. In this case, all members of the SP team should be fully aware of the organization's operational missions in the concerned functional units.

While an e-business application, for example, seems to be more concerned with the marketing functional unit, its SP cannot be studied if members of the SP team are not familiar with the organization's operational missions in the production/manufacturing, finance, and human resource functional units.

Often, only the SP writer would know all the security-relevant components of a given system, but there are several components, identified by NIST, that should be studied in every security plan.

These security relevant components are identified as follows:

- SP certification and acceptance page
- SP document handling/control
- Date of study
- Responsible organization

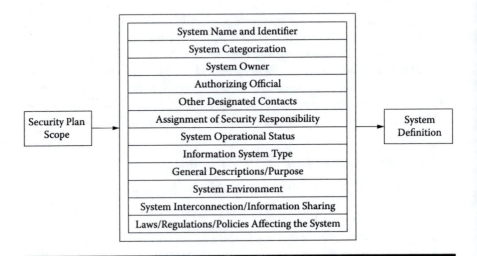

Figure 4.7 Steps for the SP system definition phase.

- System name/title
- System category
- General description and purpose
- System environment and special considerations
- Systems interconnections and information sharing
- Information contacts

The activities constituting the system definition phase are illustrated in a hierarchical structure in Figure 4.7.

4.3.3.1.1 System Definitions

This section provides information about (1) how the security of the SP is to be handled, (2) the date this SP is delivered and accepted by information owners, (3) the organization responsible of developing this security plan, and (4) and contact information.

The date of an SP is the date of the delivery of the SP to the information owners. The SP developer and information owners or their representatives negotiate the SP final product. Information owners accept the security plan, and both parties sign it.

This section contains identity information about the agency responsible for the SP under study. At least the name, address, and phone numbers of the responsible agency should be provided in this section of the security plan.

This section lists the name, title, organization, and telephone number of one (or more persons) designated to be the point(s) of contact for this system. One of the contacts given should be identified as the system owner.

The strategic security definition phase is mainly an information-gathering activity to understand the organization's existing computing and networking environment for which an SP is being developed. This phase should at least collect information that can provide answers to a dozen sets of questions listed in the following subsection. Each set of questions is answered in a separate document. The documents produced may be then automatically merged to generate the SP section concerned with the strategic security definition of the system/application under study.

4.3.3.1.2 System Definition Information Gathering

In the system definition activity, we employ 12 folders to collect information about the system definition following the steps specified in the NIST SP standard. Each folder contains answers to questions used to define the system target of the security plan. The following folders are used to store the information needed to define the system:

SD folder: SDA.1: Application/System Name/Title
SD folder: SDA.2: Application/System Category
SD folder: SDA.3: Responsible Organization
SD folder: SDA.4: Authorizing Official
SD folder: SDA.5: Information Contact(s)
SD folder: SDA.6: Assignment of Security Responsibility
SD folder: SDA.7: Application/System Operational Status
SD folder: SDA.8: Information System Type
SD folder: SDA.9: General Description/Purpose
SD folder: SDA.10: Application/System Environment
SD folder: SDA.11: Application/System Interconnection/Information Sharing
SD folder: SDA.12: Applicable Laws or Regulations Affecting the Application/
System

The detailed list of questions and folders containing their answers are as follows:

SD folder: SDA.1:
Title: Application/System Name/Title
Questionnaire for gathering information:
Size: 1 question
Question A.1: Give a unique identifier and name to the system.
SD folder: SDA.2:
Title: Application/System Category
Questionnaire for gathering information:
Size: 1 question
Question A.2: Identify the appropriate FIPS 199 categorization: Low, Moderate, and High.
SD folder: SDA.3:
Title: Responsible Organization
Questionnaire for gathering information:

Size: 1 question

Question A.3: Give the IS owner's name, title, agency, address, e-mail address, and phone number.

SD folder: SDA.4:

Title: Authorizing Official

Questionnaire for gathering information:

Size: 1 question

Question A.4: Give name, title, agency, address, e-mail address, and phone number of the senior management official designated as the authorizing official.

SD folder: SDA.5:

Title: Information Contact(s)

Questionnaire for gathering information:

Size: 1 question

Question A.5: List other key personnel, as needed; include their titles, addresses, e-mail addresses, and phone numbers.

SD folder: SDA.6:

Title: Assignment of Security Responsibility

Questionnaire for gathering information:

Size: 1 question

Question A.6.1: Persons responsible for security of the application/system and an alternate emergency contact (name, title, address, phone number, fax number, e-mail address).

SD folder: SDA.7:

Title: Application/System Operational Status

Questionnaire for gathering information:

Size: 1 question

Question A.7: Indicate the operational status of the system (or part of the system if more than one status is selected): operational, under development, or major modification.

SD folder: SDA.8:

Title: Information System Type

Questionnaire for gathering information:

Size: 1 question

Question A.8: Indicate if the system is a major application or a general support system. If the system contains minor applications, list them in Section 9, General System Description/Purpose.

SD folder: SDA.9:

Title: General Description/Purpose

Questionnaire for gathering information:

Size: 3 questions

Question A.9.1: Describe the function or purpose of the application/system and the information processed.

Question A.9.2: Describe the processing flow of the application/system from input to output.

Question A.9.3: List user organizations (internal and external) and the type of data and processing provided.

SD folder: SDA.10:

Title: Application/System Environment

Questionnaire for gathering information:

Size: 4 questions

Question A.10.1: Provide a general description of the technical application/system. Include any environmental or technical factors that raise special security concerns (dial-up lines, open network, etc.) Include a diagram of architecture here or in an appendix, if applicable.

Question A.10.2: Describe the primary computing platforms used and a description of the principal application/system components, including hardware, software, and communications resources.

Question A.10.3: Include any security software protecting the application/system and information.

Question A.10.4: List the physical locations of the application/system.

SD folder: SDA.11:

Title: Application/System Interconnection/Information Sharing

Questionnaire for gathering information:

Size: 3 questions

Question A.11.1: List interconnected applications/systems and application/system identifiers (if appropriate).

Question A.11.2: If connected to an external application/system not covered by a security plan, provide a brief discussion of any security concerns that need to be considered for protection.

Question A.11.3: A description of the rules for interconnecting applications/systems and for protecting shared data must be included with this security plan.

SD folder: SDA.12:

Title: Applicable Laws or Regulations Affecting the Application/System

Questionnaire for gathering information:

Size: 1 question

Question A.12: List any laws or regulations that establish specific requirements for confidentiality, integrity, or availability of data/information in the application/system.

4.3.3.2 Strategic Security Analysis

The purpose of the strategic security analysis is to analyze the security of the existing system. The outcome of this analysis will aid in the selection of security con-

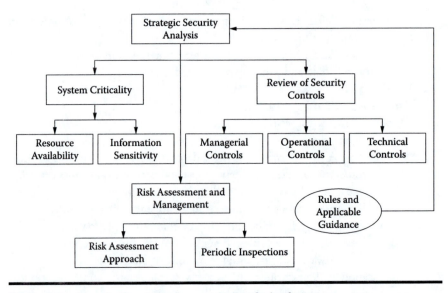

Figure 4.8   Steps in the strategic security analysis phase.

trols that the organization will implement according to an SP schedule/control mechanism defined in the SP that covers an economic life cycle of 3 years.

Eventually, the organization's assets are valued, the threats to these assets are identified, the threats' effects on the assets are evaluated, and the most appropriate security controls are recommended. These steps are, in fact, the same steps followed when designing a security program. However, for an SP where the target system is a major application, or a general support system, the steps are more comprehensive and strategic, and the life cycle is longer.

The steps constituting the security analysis phases are represented in the hierarchical structure of Figure 4.8, and are listed as follows:

- System criticality;
  Information sensitivity
  Information resource availability
- Review of security controls;
  Managerial controls
  Operational controls
  Technical controls
- Risk Assessment and Management;
  Risk Assessment Approach
  Periodic reviews

As in the strategic security definition phase, information gathered concerning the strategic security analysis is also obtained through questions. The SP writer should prepare documented answers to all of the relevant questions.

4.3.3.2.1 System Criticality

This section describes the type of protection needed for the system. Protection is often expressed in terms of confidentiality, integrity, and availability needs. That is, respectively, owners' information requires protection from unauthorized information leakage and information corruption (unauthorized, unanticipated, or unintentional modification); and owners information and services require continuous availability with no disruptions or denial.

The criticality level of an information resource may be simply defined using two components:

1. Sensitivity of the information processed by the information resource
2. Availability of the information resource that processes the information

The sensitivity of the information is the need to protect it from information leakage or corruption. The criticality of the availability of the information is the need to protect the information resource from any service denial.

The information resource manager should measure the security level of the system on both counts, the sensitivity of the information and the availability of the information resource, and then adopt the higher rating to determine the overall security level of the system.

This kind of measurement should support the confidentiality, integrity, and availability security requirements defined by the Office of Management and Budget (OMB):

Confidentiality: The system contains information that requires protection from unauthorized disclosure.

Integrity: The system contains information that must be protected from unauthorized, unanticipated, or unintentional modification, including the detection of such activities.

Availability: The system contains information or provides services that must be available on a timely basis to meet mission requirements or to avoid substantial losses.

Sensitivity levels for information resources are assigned based on the type of information/data processed and the requirements of specific laws governing the protection or disclosure of information; for example, the Privacy Act.

4.3.3.2.1.1 Sensitivity Levels of Information Resources—The sensitivity levels of information adopted in this book are defined as follows:

1. Sensitivity Level 1: Low Sensitivity
   This category identifies information/data that requires minimal protection. Threats to these data are minimal, and only minimal precautions to protect

the information/data need to be taken at the user site. Unintentional alteration or destruction is the primary concern for these types of data.

2. Sensitivity Level 2: Moderate Sensitivity

This category identifies information/data that has some importance to the organization and must be protected against such acts as malicious destruction. However, because these types of information/data are usually collected for analytical purposes, disclosure problems are not usually significant.

3. Sensitivity Level 3: High Sensitivity

This category contains the most sensitive unclassified information/data (other than unclassified data whose loss could adversely affect national security interests). The information/data in this category requires the greatest number and most stringent security safeguards at the user level. This category identifies all information resources that process national security classified information and all those that contain other sensitive, but unclassified information, the loss of which could adversely affect national security interests.

4.3.3.2.1.2 Availability Levels of Information Resources—Availability criticality levels are assigned to information resources based on the relative importance of their processing capabilities to the organization they support. For example, availability Level 1 rating is used for an information resource with the lowest availability requirements of data processing relative to the organization it supports, and availability Level 3 rating is used for an information resource with the highest availability requirements.

1. Availability Level 1: Low Availability

This category identifies information resources with data processing capabilities that require minimal protection. These include information resources that, in the event of alteration or failure, would affect the organization minimally or could be replaced with a minimum of staff time or expense. This category also includes information resources that generate, store, process, transfer, or communicate data which are considered to have low or no sensitivity.

2. Availability Level 2: Moderate Availability

This category identifies information resources with data processing capabilities that are considered important but not critical to the internal management of an organization. This category includes:

a. Information resources whose failure to function for an extended period of time would not have a critical impact on the organization they support

b. Information resources that generate, store, process, transfer, or communicate data which are considered to have moderate availability requirements

3. Availability Level 3: High Availability

This category identifies information resources with data processing capabilities that require high availability. This category includes:

   a. Information resources whose failure to function for even a short period of time could have a severe impact on the organization they support
   b. Information resources that generate, store, process, transfer, or communicate data which are considered to have high availability requirements

Organizations in the private sector are not really required to follow the sensitivity classification we have just presented. They can, in fact, use their own security level measurement as long as they are consistent throughout the information security life cycle.

This section describes, in general terms, the information handled by the system and the need for protective measures in terms of the three basic protection requirements: confidentiality, integrity, and availability.

4.3.3.2.2 Security Analysis Information Gathered on Criticality

In system security analysis, we employ one folder to collect information about the information sensitivity and availability requirements as defined in the NIST SP standard. This folder contains answers to questions used to define information criticality (sensitivity and availability) of the system target of the security plan. The following folder is used to store the criticality information of the system:

SA folder: SAB.1:

Title: Information Sensitivity and Criticality Assessment

Questionnaire for gathering information:

Size: 6 questions

Question B.1.1: Describe, in general terms, the information handled by the application/system and the need for protective measures.

Question B.1.2: List the types of sensitive information the application/system accesses. Examples may include administrative, financial, grant/contract, patent, proprietary, research, Privacy Act.

Question B.1.3: Relate the information processed to each of the three basic protection requirements.

Question B.1.4: For each of the three protection requirements (confidentiality, integrity, and availability), indicate if the sensitivity is classified as high, medium, or low.

Question B.1.5: A more detailed chart may be used if the application/system processes information with different levels of application/system protection requirements.

Question B.1.6: Include a statement of the estimated risk and magnitude of harm resulting from the loss, misuse, or unauthorized access to or modification of information in the application/system.

4.3.3.2.3 Review of Current Security Controls

This section identifies all existing security controls or those being planned. This section should provide information on the performance of these security controls and to what extent they are achieving their objectives.

OMB states that at least every 3 years, an independent management review or audit of the security controls for the system must be performed. This review or audit should be independent of the manager responsible for the major application or general support system. The objective of these reviews is to provide verification that the controls selected or installed are sufficient to provide a level of protection corresponding to an acceptable level of risk for the system.

This section should therefore include information about the last independent audit or review of the system and who conducted the review. It should discuss any findings or recommendations from the review and include information concerning correction of any deficiencies or completion of any recommendations. If an independent audit or review has not taken place, this fact should be placed on record.

The FIPS 200 standard recommends 17 minimum security requirements for the information system target of the security plan. These requirements offer a broad-based, balanced information security program that covers the managerial, operational, and technical security controls for protecting the confidentiality, integrity, and availability of the information system. We have seen earlier in Table 4.1 that NIST defines four families of managerial security controls; nine families of operational security controls; and four families of technical security controls.

An organization must meet the minimum security requirements in this standard by applying security controls selected in accordance with NIST SP 800-53 and the designated impact levels of the information systems. The organization should have the flexibility to adapt the security control baseline in accordance with the terms and conditions set forth in the standard. The security analysis phase of our SP includes activities such as (1) scoping guidance, (2) specification of compensating controls, and (3) specification of common security controls.

The SP writer may formulate and answer the set of questions, stored in the following security analysis (SA) folders, to identify the current security controls that are in place and the ones that are planned or under development.

SA folder: SAM.1:
Title: Risk Assessment and Management
Questionnaire for gathering information:
Size: 3 questions

Question SAM.1.1: Describe the risk assessment methodology used to identify the threats and vulnerabilities of the application/system.

Question SAM.1.2: List the group that conducted the assessment, and the dates on which the review was conducted.

Question SAM.1.3: If there is no application/system risk assessment, include a milestone date (month and year) for completion of the assessment.

SA folder: SAM.2:

Title: Review of Security Controls

Questionnaire for gathering information:

Size: 2 questions

Question SAM.2.1: List any independent security reviews conducted on the application/system in the last 3 years.

Question SAM.2.2: Include information about the type of security evaluation performed, who performed the review, the purpose of the review, the findings, and the actions taken as a result.

SA folder: SAM.3:

Title: Rules of Behavior

Questionnaire for gathering information:

Size: 3 questions

Question SAM.3.1: A set of rules of behavior in writing must be established for each application/system. The rules of behavior should be made available to every user prior to the user receiving access to the application/system, with a signature page to acknowledge receipt.

Question SAM.3.2: The rules of behavior should clearly delineate responsibilities and expected behavior of all individuals with access to the application/system. They should state the consequences of inconsistent behavior or noncompliance. They should also include appropriate limits on interconnections to other application/systems.

Question SAM.3.3: Attach the rules of behavior for the application as an appendix, and reference the appendix number in this section or insert the rules into this section.

SA folder: SAM.4:

Title: Planning for Security in the Life Cycle

Questionnaire for gathering information:

Size: 5 questions

Question SAM.4.1: How is security planned in the initiation phase?

Question SAM.4.2: How is security planned in the Development/Acquisition phase?

Question SAM.4.3: How is security planned in the Implementation phase?

Question SAM.4.4: How is security planned in the Operation/Maintenance phase?

Question SAM.4.5: How is security planned in the Disposal phase?

SA folder: SAM.5:

> Title: Authorization to Process
>
> Questionnaire for gathering information:
>
> > Size: 3 questions
> >
> > Question SAM.5.1: Provide the date of authorization, name, and title of management official authorizing processing in the application/system.
> >
> > Question SAM.5.2: If not authorized, provide the name and title of manager requesting approval to operate and date of request.
> >
> > Question SAM.5.3: Attach Authorization to Process memo.

SA folder: SAO.1:

> Title: Personnel Security
>
> Questionnaire for gathering information:
>
> > Size: 7 questions
> >
> > Question SAO.1.1: Have all positions been reviewed for sensitivity level?
> >
> > Question SAO.1.2: Have individuals received background screenings appropriate for the position to which they are assigned?
> >
> > Question SAO.1.3: Is user access restricted to the minimum necessary to perform the job?
> >
> > Question SAO.1.4: Is there a process for requesting, establishing, issuing, and closing user accounts?
> >
> > Question SAO.1.5: Are critical functions divided among different individuals (separation of duties)?
> >
> > Question SAO.1.6: What mechanisms are in place for holding users responsible for their actions?
> >
> > Question SAO.1.7: What are the friendly and unfriendly termination procedures?

SA folder: SAO.2:

> Title: Physical and Environmental Protection
>
> Questionnaire for gathering information:
>
> > Size: 2 questions
> >
> > Question SAO.2.1: Discuss the physical protection in the area where application/system processing takes place (e.g., locks on terminals, physical barriers around the building and processing area, etc.).
> >
> > Question SAO.2.2: Factors to address include physical access, fire safety, failure of supporting utilities, structural collapse, plumbing leaks, interception of data, and mobile and portable systems.

SA folder: SAO.3:

> Title: Production, Input/Output Controls
>
> Questionnaire for gathering information:
>
> > Size: 12 questions
> >
> > Question SAO.3.1: Is there a help desk or group that offers advice and can respond to security incidents in a timely manner? Are there procedures in place documenting how to recognize, handle, report, and

track incidents and/or problems? Do these procedures outline how to categorize and prioritize incidents?

Question SAO.3.2: Are there procedures to ensure unauthorized individuals cannot read, copy, alter, or steal printed or electronic information?

Question SAO.3.3: Are there procedures for ensuring that only authorized users pick up, receive, or deliver input and output information and media?

Question SAO.3.4: Are there audit trails for receipt of sensitive inputs/outputs?

Question SAO.3.5: Are there procedures for restricting access to output products?

Question SAO.3.6: Is there internal/external labeling for sensitivity (e.g., Privacy Act, Proprietary?)

Question SAO.3.7: Is there external labeling with special handling instructions (e.g., log/inventory identifiers, controlled access, special storage instructions, release or destruction dates)?

Question SAO.3.8: Are there audit trails for inventory management?

Question SAO.3.9: Is there a media storage vault or library containing physical, environmental protection controls/procedures?

Question SAO.3.10: Are there procedures for sanitizing electronic media for reuse?

Question SAO.3.11: Are there procedures for controlled storage, handling, or destruction of spoiled media or media that cannot be effectively sanitized for reuse?

Question SAO.3.12: Are there procedures for shredding or other destructive measures for hardcopy media when no longer required?

SA folder: SAO.4:

Title: Contingency Planning

Questionnaire for gathering information:

Size: 4 questions

Question SAO.4.1: Briefly describe the procedures (contingency plan) that would be followed to ensure the application/system continues to be processed if the supporting IT application/system were unavailable. If a formal contingency plan has been completed, reference the plan. A copy of the contingency plan may be attached as an appendix. Include descriptions for the following: agreements of backup processing; documented backup procedures including frequency (daily, weekly, monthly) and scope (full, incremental, and differential backup); and location of stored backups and generations of backups.

Question SAO.4.2: Are tested contingency/disaster recovery plans in place? How often are they tested?

Question SAO.4.3: Are all employees trained in their roles and responsibilities relative to the emergency, disaster, and contingency plans?

Question SAO.4.4: Coverage of backup procedures, for example, what is being backed up?

SA folder: SAO.5:

Title: Application/System Hardware and Software Maintenance Controls

Questionnaire for gathering information:

Size: 18 questions

Question SAO.5.1: Are there restrictions/controls on those who perform hardware and software maintenance and repair activities?

Question SAO.5.2: Are there special procedures for performance of emergency repair and maintenance?

Question SAO.5.3: Are there procedures used for items serviced through on-site and off-site maintenance (e.g., escort of maintenance personnel, sanitization of devices removed from the site)?

Question SAO.5.4: Are there procedures used for controlling remote maintenance services where diagnostic procedures or maintenance is performed through telecommunications arrangements?

Question SAO.5.5: Are software warranties managed to minimize the cost of upgrades and cost-reimbursement or replacement for deficiencies?

Question SAO.5.6: Was the application/system software developed in-house or under contract?

Question SAO.5.7: Does the government own the software? Was it received from another agency?

Question SAO.5.8: Is the application/system software a copyrighted commercial off-the-shelf product or shareware?

Question SAO.5.9: Has the software been properly licensed, and have enough copies been purchased for the application/system?

Question SAO.5.10: Are there organizational policies against illegal use of copyrighted software and shareware?

Question SAO.5.11: Are periodic audits conducted of users' computers to ensure that only legal licensed copies of software are installed?

Question SAO.5.12: What products and procedures are used to protect against illegal use of software?

Question SAO.5.13: Describe any formal change control process in place.

Is there version control that allows association of application/system components with the appropriate application/system version?

Are all changes to the application/system software or application/system components documented?

Are there impact analyses to determine the effect of proposed changes on existing security control including the required training for both technical and user communities associated with the change in hardware/software?

Are there change identification, approval, and documentation procedures?

Are there procedures for ensuring that contingency plans and other associated documentation are updated to reflect application/system changes?

Question SAO.5.14: Does the change control process require that all changes to the application/system software be tested and approved before being put into production?

Question SAO.5.15: Are there procedures for testing and approving system components (operating system, other system, utility, applications) prior to promotion to production?

Question SAO.5.16: Is test data live data or made-up data?

Question SAO.5.17: Do test plans trace back to the original security requirements?

Question SAO.5.18: Are test results documented?

SA folder: SAO.6:

Title: Data Integrity/Validation Controls

Questionnaire for gathering information:

Size: 9 questions

Question SAO.6.1: Is virus detection and elimination software installed? If so, are there procedures for updating virus signature files, automatic and/or manual virus scans, and virus eradication and reporting?

Question SAO.6.2: Are reconciliation routines used by the application/system, that is, checksums, hash totals, record counts? Include a description of the actions taken to resolve any discrepancies.

Question SAO.6.3: Are integrity verification programs used by the application/system to look for evidence of data tampering, errors, and omissions?

Question SAO.6.4: Is an intrusion detection tool installed to monitor the application/system?

Question SAO.6.5: Are procedures in place to handle and close out security incidents?

Question SAO.6.6: Are other network security software packages used?

Question SAO.6.7: Is application/system performance monitoring used to analyze performance logs in real time to look for availability problems, including active attacks, and application/system and network slowdowns and crashes?

Question SAO.6.8: Is penetration testing performed on the application/system? If so, what procedures are in place to ensure that tests are conducted appropriately?

Question SAO.6.9: Is message authentication used in the application/system to ensure that the sender of a message is known and that the message has not been altered during transmission?

SA folder: SAO.7:

Title: Documentation

Questionnaire for gathering information:

Size: 3 questions

Question SAO.7.1: List the documentation maintained for the application/system. Examples may include vendor documentation of hardware/software, functional requirements, design specifications, source code documents, testing procedures and results, records of verification reviews/site inspections, standard operating procedures, user rules/manuals, emergency procedures, contingency plans, and risk assessments.

Question SAO.7.2: Describe the procedure used to update documentation.

Question SAO.7.3: List the physical location of documentation.

SA folder: SAO.8:

Title: Security Awareness and Training

Questionnaire for gathering information:

Size: 3 questions

Question SAO.8.1: Describe the type and frequency of application/system-specific training provided to employees and contractor personnel (workshops, formal classroom, focus groups, role-based training, and on-the job training).

Question SAO.8.2: Describe the procedures for ensuring that employees and contractor personnel have been provided adequate training.

Question SAO.8.3: Describe the awareness program for the application/system.

SA folder: SAO.9:

Title: Incident Response Capability

Questionnaire for gathering information:

Size: 4 questions

Question SAO.9.1: Are there procedures for reporting incidents handled either by application/system personnel or externally?

Question SAO.9.2: Are there procedures for recognizing and handling incidents, that is, what files and logs should be kept, whom to contact, and when?

Question SAO.9.3: Who receives and responds to alerts/advisories, for example, vendor patches, exploited vulnerabilities?

Question SAO.9.4: What preventative measures are in place, that is, intrusion detection tools, automated audit logs, penetration testing?

SA folder: SAT.1:

Title: Identification and Authentication

Questionnaire for gathering information:

Size: 11 questions

Question SAT.1.1: Describe the application/system's user authentication control mechanisms (password, token, and biometrics).

Question SAT.1.2: Indicate the frequency of password changes, describe how changes are enforced, and identify who changes the passwords (the user, the system administrator, or the application/system).

Question SAT.1.3: Provide the following if an additional password system is used in the application/system:

Password length (minimum, maximum)

Allowable character set

Password aging time frames and enforcement approach

Number of generations of expired passwords disallowed for use

Procedures for password changes (after expiration and forgotten/lost)

Procedures for handling password compromise

Procedures for training users and the materials covered

Question SAT.1.4: Describe the level of enforcement of the access control mechanism (network, operating system, and application/system).

Question SAT.1.5: Describe how the access control mechanism supports individual accountability and audit trails (e.g., passwords associated with a user ID that is assigned to a single person).

Question SAT.1.6: Describe the self-protection techniques for the user authentication mechanism (e.g., passwords encrypted while in transmission, automatically generated, or checked against a dictionary of disallowed passwords).

Question SAT.1.7: State the number of invalid access attempts that may occur for a given user ID or access location (terminal or port), and describe the actions taken when that limit is exceeded.

Question SAT.1.8: Describe the procedures for verifying that all application/system-provided administrative default passwords have been changed.

Question SAT.1.9: Describe the procedures for limiting access scripts with embedded passwords (e.g., scripts with embedded passwords are prohibited, scripts with embedded passwords are only allowed for batch application/systems).

Question SAT.1.10: Describe any policies that provide for bypassing user authentication requirements, single-sign-on technologies (e.g., host-to-host, authentication servers, user-to-host identifiers, and group user identifiers), and any compensating controls.

Question SAT.1.11: Describe any use of digital or electronic signatures and the standards used. Discuss the management procedures for key generation, distribution, storage, and disposal. If digital signatures are used, the technology must conform to FIPS 186, *Digital Signature Standard* and FIPS 180-1, *Secure Hash Standard* issued by NIST [1].

SA folder: SAT.2:

Title: Logical Access Controls

Questionnaire for gathering information:

Size: 7 questions

Question SAT.2.1: How are access rights granted? Are privileges granted based on job function?

Question SAT.2.2: Describe the application/system's capability to establish an ACL or register.

Question SAT.2.3: Describe how users are restricted from accessing the operating system or other application/system resources not required in the performance of their duties.

Question SAT.2.4: Describe controls to detect unauthorized transaction attempts by authorized or unauthorized users. Describe any restrictions to prevent users from accessing the application/system outside of normal work hours or on weekends.

Question SAT.2.5: Indicate after what period of user inactivity the application/system automatically blanks associated display screens and/or disconnects inactive users. After what period of user inactivity does the application/system require the user to enter a unique password before reconnecting?

Question SAT.2.6: Indicate if encryption is used to prevent access to sensitive files as part of the application/system access control procedures.

Question SAT.2.7: Describe the rationale for electing to use or not use warning banners, and provide an example if banners are used.

SA folder: SAT.3:

Title: Public Access Controls

Questionnaire for gathering information:

Size: 1 question

Question SAT.3.1: If the public has access to the application/system, discuss the additional security controls used to protect application/system integrity. What additional controls are used to protect the confidence of the public in the application/system? Such controls include segregating information made directly accessible to the public from official agency records. Others may include:

Some form of identification and authentication

Access controls to limit what the user can read, write, modify, or delete

Controls to prevent public users from modifying information in the application/system

Digital signatures

CD-ROM for online storage of information for distribution

Copies of information for public access available on a separate application/system

Controls to prohibit the public from accessing live databases

Verification that programs and information distributed to the public are virus free

Audit trails and user confidentiality

Application/system and data availability

Legal considerations
SA folder: SAT.4:
  Title: Audit Trails
  Questionnaire for gathering information:
    Size: 6 questions
    Question SAT.4.1: Does the audit trail support accountability by providing a trace of user actions?
    Question SAT.4.2: Are audit trails designed and implemented to record appropriate information that can assist in intrusion detection and remediation? Does the audit trail include sufficient information to establish what events occurred and who (or what) caused them (e.g., type of event, when the event occurred, user ID associated with the event, program or command used to initiate the event)?
    Question SAT.4.3: Is access to online audit logs strictly enforced?
    Question SAT.4.4: Is the confidentiality of audit trail information protected if it records personal user information?
    Question SAT.4.5: Describe how frequently audit trails are reviewed and whether guidelines exist.
    Question SAT.4.6: Does the appropriate application/system level administrator review audit trails following a known application/system software problem, an unexplained application/system or user problem, or a known violation of existing requirements by a user?

The security analysis phase includes a statement of the estimated risk and magnitude of harm resulting from the loss, misuse, or unauthorized access to or modification of information in the system. The impact should be described in terms of cost, inability to carry out mandated functions, timeliness, etc.

This phase also describes all security evaluation methods conducted over the past 3 years. Two categories of security reviews are identified: a formal risk assessment approach and the rest of the periodic security inspections. It also describes the methods used to assess the nature and level of risk to the system. The section has to explain how the risk assessment approach addresses the crucial elements of the security planning process. It indicates the date on which the system risk assessment took place. It also explains how the identified risks relate to the requirements for confidentiality, integrity, and availability determined for the system.

If a risk assessment for your system did not take place, indicate the projected date (month and year) when a risk assessment will be completed. If the risk assessment is more than 3 years old or there have been major changes to the system or its functions, a risk assessment is recommended. Indicate the projected date (month and year) when the recommended risk assessment will take place.

In addition to a formal risk assessment approach, often, other system evaluations approaches are applied periodically. This section has to provide information about who performed the review, when the review was performed, the purpose of the review, the findings, and the actions taken as a result of the review.

4.3.3.2.4 Applicable Guidance

This section should indicate specific standards or other guidance used in the design, implementation, or operation of the protective measures used on the system (e.g., relevant federal or industry standards). In addition to listing any Federal Information Processing Standards (FIPS) issued by NIST that may apply, this section should include all relevant guidance documents.

4.3.3.2.4.1 Flexibility—Flexibility is an important property in writing a security plan. You do not want to establish features that are not easy to modify or guidelines that nobody follows. For example, in the case of an SQL server, assigning permissions to a global group is not very flexible. You may alternatively assign permissions to roles instead of assigning them directly to a global group. This capability lets you add SQL Server-authenticated logins to your SP with little additional effort. Even if you never expect to use SQL Server login accounts, it still recommended that you assign permissions to roles so that you are prepared in case your requirements change in the future [Pascal, 2001].

4.3.3.2.4.2 Simplicity—SQL Server-authenticated logins are simple to implement and easier than NT authenticated logins to code into programs, but they are difficult to manage when the number of users exceeds 25, when you have multiple servers, when each user has access to multiple databases, or when the database has multiple administrators. Even in small installations in which the database administrator has other responsibilities, simple plans alleviate the problems of remembering each user's permissions and how he or she got them. This problem is made more complex because SQL Server does not have a tool that shows users' effective permissions. The best recommendation, therefore, is to use NT-authenticated logins and to manage database access with a carefully selected set of global groups and database roles.

With proper planning, you can handle all maintenance of access rights and permissions on the domain controller so that changes are reflected in all the servers you manage.

4.3.3.2.5 Rules of Behavior

This section includes the "rules of behavior" that have been established for the system. Documents that contain additional rules should be attached in an appendix to the plan.

The rules of behavior shall clearly delineate responsibilities and expected behavior of all individuals with access to the system. They shall also include appropriate

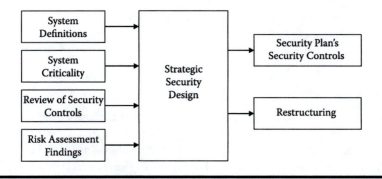

Figure 4.9 **Strategic security design effort.**

limits on interconnections to other systems and define service provision and restoration priorities. The rules must be clear about the consequences of behavior not consistent with the rules. Rules should be in writing and form a basis for computer security awareness activities and training. The rules of behavior should be made available to every user prior to receiving authorization for access to the system.

4.3.3.3 Strategic Security Design

The strategic security design phase is the most important phase in a security plan. It will make use of all the information collected in the previous phases. The SP team members have to be familiar with all available best security practices (BSP) and aware of all possible security controls. Consulting with external security experts and venders is recommended at this stage. The strategic security design effort should output, as shown in Figure 4.8, a new structure that is more favorable to the organization's security policy, and an SP implementable over the next 3 years.

The strategic security design phase defines security control measures for the system or application being studied. It mainly consists of the following steps, also presented in the hierarchical structure of Figure 4.9:

- Restructuring
  Organization
  Process reengineering
- Security control measures
  Management controls
  Operational controls
  Technical controls

The strategic security design phase also includes an additional major activity. This activity scans the existing systems to account for all existing security controls, and applies the rules of minimum security controls, provided in the following subsection, in terms of sensitivity levels. This activity should identify all those minimal security controls that are not currently implemented, and document the reasons.

4.3.3.3.1 Restructuring

In performing the strategic security design, the SP writer should identify all minimal security requirements that are appropriate to the system/application being studied. A list of the minimal security requirements is provided later in this chapter. Every minimal requirement should be present in the existing system. Any minimal security requirement that is not implemented in the existing system should be studied in terms of the following factors:

Is the process constituting the system favorable to the minimal security requirements under study?

Is the current organization of the enterprise favorable to the minimal security requirements?

Usually, the main reasons for which the minimal security requirements are not present in the existing system are either a business process problem or a structural problem.

Following the identification of minimal security requirements that are not satisfied, the SP writer should perform a process reengineering activity whereby all the processes that are relevant to these requirements are identified.

As shown in Figure 4.10, all those processes that are not favorable to one or more minimal security requirements should be redesigned so that these requirements can be feasibly implemented at the presence of these processes.

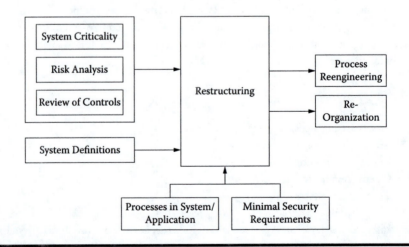

Figure 4.10　Structuring the security design solution.

The structure of a given enterprise may less frequently be too inflexible to host the minimal security requirements needed to protect the system for which an SP is being developed. The enterprise has to be reorganized before implementing the minimal security requirements and before studying any additional security controls.

The higher the security level rating of information resources, the more stringent its security requirements. Information resources with the lowest security level ratings usually require only ordinary security precautions; that is, protection by safeguards that are considered to be good management practice. In all instances, the minimum security requirements of information resources should be equal to or higher than the highest security level rating of any data they process, including data received from other agencies.

Information resource managers must continually evaluate their systems to determine whether they can be circumvented, and must test their security safeguards to ensure that they are functioning as intended. Certification is required at least once every 3 years. Additional reviews are required if the safeguard requirements outlined in the following text change or if an information resource undergoes a significant modification. A waiver must be requested prior to certification if an information resource is not in compliance and cannot be brought into compliance in a relatively short period of time, or if system owners do not approve a particular safeguard requirement.

The minimal security requirements are defined in many different ways depending on the security policy, the mission of the organization, and the size of internal networks and connections. But it is also true that some companies just copy security requirements from similar organizations without examining whether there exists any direct relation to the organization's security policy. Anyway, there is nothing wrong in initially adopting the largest set of minimal security requirements one can have, because the risk analysis, which is a major step in the writing of a security plan, will later only retain and redefine those security requirements that are feasible and clearly go along the organization's security policy.

The following example of a set of minimal security requirements presents these requirements in terms of four security levels of information resources:

1. Level 1 requirements: The controls required to adequately safeguard a Level 1 information resource are those that would normally be considered good management practice. These include, but are not limited to:
   a. An employee AIS security awareness and training program
   b. The assignment of sensitivity ratings to every employee position
   c. Physical access controls
   d. A complete set of AIS documentation
2. Level 2 requirements: The controls required to adequately safeguard a Level 2 information resources include all of the requirements for Level 1, and the following additional requirements:
   a. A detailed risk management program

b. A CSSP (Computer System Security Professional) for systems processing sensitive information
c. Record retention procedures
d. A list of authorized users
e. Security review and certification procedures
f. Required background investigations for all employees
g. Required background investigations for all contractor personnel
h. A detailed fire emergency plan
i. A formal written contingency plan
j. A formal risk analysis
k. An automated audit trail
l. Authorized access and control procedures
m. Secure physical transportation procedures
n. Secure telecommunications
o. An emergency power program

3. Level 3 requirements: The controls required to adequately safeguard a Level 3 information resource include all of the requirements for Levels 1 and 2, and the additional requirement for an inventory of hardware and software.

4. Level 4 requirements: The controls required to adequately safeguard a Level 4 information resource include all of the requirements for Levels 1, 2, and 3, and the additional following requirements:

a. The requirements of National Security Decision Directives, and other federal government directives, for data and systems that are classified
b. The security procedures specified by the source agencies that produce the classified information or systems

4.3.3.3.2 Security Control Measures

The selection of security controls that the organization needs to adopt as part of its security policy is certainly not an exact science, and the SP developer may encounter several security controls that provide overlapping security requirements; moreover, very little information may be available about their feasibility, so it may not be easy to determine the most efficient security controls to be included in the security plan.

Scoping guidance offers, however, specific terms and conditions that the organization is advised to use to determine the applicability of any security controls taken from NIST SP 800-53. It is very important to understand the conditions of implementation of the selected security controls before recommending them to system owners. Even though strictly satisfying all the conditions and terms provided in the scoping guidance recommended by NIST in the process of selecting security controls is not mandatory, organization seeking certification of their security plans or accreditation of their information systems may be better off closely following most of it to facilitate any eventual certification or accreditation processes.

The SP developer has to examine and understand how the baseline security controls can affect the security of the organization. There may be prerequisites that have to be studied, or considerations that have to examined which can maximize the chances that all selected security controls will in fact achieve the security requirements initially defined. The SP developer has to justify all security controls to be included in the security plan.

The justification process has to be discussed with owners, who should explicitly approve them before they are added to the security plan. The SP should explicitly identify the security controls that were justified based on the scoping guidance and clearly present any justifications employed. Those scoping-guidance justifications of the security controls have to be evaluated and approved by the authorizing official for the system.

The SP developer has to take into account the considerations presented in NIST's SP development guidelines, which have to be addressed when the scoping guidance is applied: (1) technology-related considerations, (2) common security control-related considerations, (3) public access information systems-related considerations, (4) infrastructure-related considerations (5) scalability-related considerations, and (6) risk-related considerations.

The SP developer can select compensating controls, which are managerial, operational, and technical controls that may be employed by lieu of the recommended controls in the low, moderate, or high baselines described in NIST SP 800-53, and provide equivalent or comparable protection for an information system.

An organization can only adopt compensating security controls for the protection of an information system under the following conditions:

1. The organization selects compensating controls from the security control catalog in NIST SP 800-53.
2. The organization provides a complete and convincing rationale and justification for how the compensating controls provide an equivalent security capability or level of protection for the information system.
3. The organization assesses and formally accepts the risk associated with employing the compensating controls in the information system.

The use of compensating security controls must be reviewed, documented in the system security plan, and approved by the authorizing official for the information system.

A centralized view of an eventual information security program can also ease the identification of common security controls. The common security controls should, by definition, apply to a set of information systems or a wide cross-section of the computing environment of the organization.

A common security control is a security control that can be applied to one or more information systems in the organization. The SP developer will find it easier to justify the adoption of common security controls because those controls are also needed outside the scope of the SP and should have been justified by the owners of other information systems.

The NIST SP guidelines recommend that the SP developer organize security controls into two categories: common security controls and system-specific controls. Partitioning security controls in this manner can result in significant savings to the organization in system development and implementation costs. Security planning based on this partitioning schema may yield a more reliable application of the security controls throughout the entire organization.

There will be no need to assess security controls for each information system separately. Instead, we assess, as needed, common security controls in every information system. The partitioning of security controls into common security controls and system-specific controls is certainly simple and intuitive, but the application of this principle within an agency requires effective security planning.

The objective of adopting common security controls is to reduce security costs by centrally managing the development, implementation, and assessment of the common security controls selected by the organization. Those security controls will, consequently, share assessment results with the owners of information systems where those common security controls are applied. Security controls not selected as common controls are considered system-specific controls and are hence the responsibility of the information system owner. System security plans should clearly identify which security controls have been designated as common security controls and which controls have been designated as system-specific controls.

However, to produce an efficient security plan, common security controls should be documented once and then inserted or imported into each system SP for any target information systems within the organization.

In preparation for documenting how the NIST SP 800-53 security controls for the applicable security control baseline (low-, moderate-, or high-impact information systems) are implemented or planned to be implemented, the security controls contained in the baseline should be reviewed and, possibly, tailored. Additionally, the controls that are common to numerous systems or within the whole organization should be identified and then documented in the plan. Now that the security controls have been selected, tailored, and the common controls identified, in a thorough documentation effort, you will need to describe each control. The description should contain:

1. The security control title
2. How the security control is being implemented or planned to be implemented
3. Any scoping guidance that has been applied and the type of consideration
4. Indicate if the security control is a common control and who is responsible for its implementation

At this point, the SP writer knows all the risk areas. Before recommending any security controls, he or she should review all published BSPs, minimum security requirements established in similar businesses, and see how they may be applied to the existing system.

If the risk analysis shows lack of compliance with minimal security requirements, then the reasons why the security requirements have not been met must be documented and the document must be made available for inspection.

The following rules identify a minimum set of safeguards, by security level, that should be implemented to protect AISs, AIS facilities, and information services. Justification for nonimplementation of these safeguards should be based on the results of a formal risk analysis (and cost-benefit) study.

IF: Sensitivity level ≥ 1
THEN: Actions are:

A101: Ensure that a complete and current set of documentation exists for all operating systems.

A102: Establish procedures for controlling access to facilities and AISs processing sensitive data.

A103: Furnish locks and other protective measures on doors and windows to prevent unauthorized access to computer and support areas.

A104: Install emergency (panic) hardware on "Emergency Exit Only" doors. Ensure that emergency exits are appropriately marked.

A105: Establish employee security awareness and training programs.

A106: Maintain an accurate inventory of all hardware and software.

A107: Ensure that all personnel positions have been assigned security level ratings.

IF: Sensitivity level ≥ 2
THEN: Actions are:

A201: Require use of current passwords and log-on codes to protect sensitive AIS data from unauthorized access.

A202: Establish procedures to register and protect secrecy of passwords and log-on codes, including the use of a nonprint, nondisplay feature.

A203: Limit the number of unsuccessful attempts to access an AIS or a database.

A204: Develop means whereby the user's authorization can be determined. (This may include answer back capability.)

A205: Establish an automated audit trail capability to record user activity.

A206: Ensure that the operating system contains controls to prevent unauthorized access to the executive or control software system.

A207: Ensure that the operating system contains controls to provide for the logging and the interpretation of logs for the purpose of detecting unauthorized attempts.

A208: Ensure that the operating system contains controls that separate user and master modes of operations.

A209: Install software features that will automatically lock out the terminal if it is not used for a predetermined period of lapsed inactive time, for a specified time after normal closing time, or if a password is not entered correctly after a specified number of times.

A210: Establish controls over the handling of sensitive data, including labeling materials and controlling the availability and flow of data.

A211: Require that all sensitive material be stored in a secure location when not in use.

A212: Dispose of unneeded sensitive hard copy documents and erase sensitive data from storage media in a manner that will prevent unauthorized use.

A213: Prepare and maintain lists of persons authorized to access facilities and AISs processing sensitive data.

A214: Install fire suppression equipment in the computer facility, which may include area sprinkler systems with protected control valves and fire extinguishers.

A215: Provide emergency power shutdown controls to shut down AIS equipment and air-conditioning systems in the event of fire or other emergencies. Include protective covers for emergency controls to prevent accidental activation.

A216: Establish a fire emergency preparedness plan to include training of fire emergency response teams, development and testing of an evacuation plan, and on-site orientation visits for the local fire department.

A217: Secure communication lines.

A218: Establish detailed risk management program.

A219: Establish computer systems security plans for sensitive systems.

A220: Conduct formal risk analyses.

A221: Maintain an accurate inventory of all hardware and software.

A222: Establish a security review and certification program.

A223: Establish a contingency plan.

A224: Establish an emergency power program.

A225: Ensure that all personnel positions have been assigned security level ratings.

A226: Conduct periodic security level rating reviews.

A227: Ensure that all personnel, including contractors, have received appropriate background investigations.

IF: Sensitivity level ≥ 3

THEN: Actions are:

A301: Implement methods, which may include the establishment of encryption, to secure data being transferred between two points.

A302: Record occurrences of nonroutine user or operator activity (such as unauthorized access attempts and operator overrides) and report to the organizational ISSO.

A303: Ensure that the operating system provides methods to protect operational status and subsequent restart integrity during and after shutdown.

A304: Specify fire-rated walls, ceilings, and doors for construction of new computer facilities or modifications of existing facilities.

A305: Install smoke and fire detection systems with alarms in the computer facility. When feasible, connect all alarms to a control alarm panel within the facility and to a manned guard station or fire station.

A306: Provide waterproof covers to protect computers and other electronic equipment from water damage.

A307: Maintain a list of all personnel, including contractors, who have been approved for 6C (High Risk Public Trust), 5C (Moderate Risk Public Trust), 4C (Top Secret, requiring special security considerations), 3C (Top Secret), and 2C (Secret or Confidential) risk level positions.

IF: Sensitivity level ≥ 4

THEN: Actions are:

A401: Ensure that the operating system contains controls to secure the transfer of data between all configuration devices.

A402: Conduct tempest testing of operating system.

A403: Ensure that all requirements of NSDD-145 (National Security Decision Directive) are met.

4.3.3.4 Strategic Security Choice

The SP phases performed so far may produce different versions of a security plan. It is time now for the SP writer to meet with system owners and the security administration to review with them new organizational changes, security policy additions, and security change requests before presenting the prevailing versions of the completed security plan.

The purpose of the strategic security choice is to make sure that all recommendations included in the final version of the SP are the most appropriate possible. System owners have to approve all security controls adopted in the security plan.

It is the responsibility of the writer of the SP to understand system owners' concerns and convince them that the security controls adopted are the only ones that can efficiently reduce the risks defined in the security analysis phase of the security plan.

The final version is then submitted and approved by system owners. It is only now that the SP is delivered. The dated acceptance signature of the SP by system owners is mandatory.

4.3.3.4.1 Implementation of the Security Plan

Before beginning the SP implementation process, the following steps have to be performed:

1. An implementation team has to be constituted.
2. A 3-year schedule has to be defined.

The main members of the SP implementation team are usually the members of the team tasked with writing the security plan. In case the SP development project is outsourced, some of the internal security staff members who participated with the contractors in writing the SP should to be on the SP implementation team.

The implementation of the SP should be continuously supported by security evaluation techniques throughout the life cycle of the security plan. The following evaluation procedures may be periodically performed:

- Audits
- Inspections
- Checklists
- Other evaluation techniques

Usually, the SP is organized in a book, called "Security Plan," that consists of six chapters. The first chapter contains an executive summary that presents to upper management and authorized readers an outline in addition to the big picture of the security plan. The second chapter presents the system definition of the security plan. The third chapter presents the managerial security controls and any relevant security analysis and design information that lead to the production of those controls. The fourth chapter presents the operational security controls and any relevant security analysis and design information that lead to the production of those controls. The fifth chapter presents the technical security controls and any relevant security analysis and design information that lead to the production of those controls. The sixth chapter contains a conclusion and the SP implementation schedule recommended for the next 3 years.

4.3.3.5 Strategic Security Review

4.3.3.5.1 Continual Security

The purpose of the strategic review is to ensure that the system or application behaves according to the design manual containing the security solutions included in the security plan.

The life cycle of an SP is set arbitrarily to 3 years. System owners have to periodically evaluate risks and the validity of the security controls included in the security plan. Any change in the security risks or in the security controls should result in corrective actions being applied.

Security controls become invalid or lose efficiency or effectiveness when an organizational change takes place, when a new technology emerges, when a security policy changes, etc.

Once the information system SP is developed, the NIST standard recommends to periodically assess the plan, review any change in system status, functionality, design, etc., and ensure that the plan continues to reflect correct information about the system. This documentation and its correctness are critical for system certification activity. All plans should be reviewed and updated, if appropriate, at least annually. Some items to include in the review are the following:

- Change in information system owner
- Change in information security representative
- Change in system architecture
- Change in system status
- Additions/deletions of system interconnections
- Change in system scope
- Change in authorizing official
- Change in certification and accreditation status

In order to ensure that the SP is still valid, and in addition to the NIST continual security requirements given earlier, system owners have to be assured that:

1. All estimated risks are still valid.
2. All existing security controls are still efficient.
3. All new threats and their effects on estimated risks and security controls are known with maximum confidence.
4. All new changes have no significant effects on estimated risks and security controls, including:
   New people hired or reappointed
   New activities
   New information resources added
   New networks or components added
   New technologies adopted
   Etc.
5. All changes in security policies have no significant effects on estimated risks and security controls.
6. All new security solutions are known and the reasons that are not adopted documented.

   The security administrator has to explain how a given change can reduce or increase security risks; or otherwise, demonstrate that the security risks are in fact invariant. Any change in security risks will require the revision of the current security plan.

The security team should have its own ways of ensuring that the current SP is still effective. The strategic review should utilize very simple and quick evaluation techniques to monitor how the system or application behaves with respect to the current security plan.

Here is a short list of simple activities that the security team may consider:

1. All members of the security team should understand the security plan.
2. All members of the security team should understand the security policy.
3. Briefly revisit the threats to see if they are still active.
4. Identify possible new threats.
5. Understand and define the effects of the new threats.
6. Redefine risks using quick risk evaluation techniques.
7. Define new security controls to counter the new threats.
8. Make sure the current SP is still valid.

4.3.3.5.2 Quality of a Strategic Review

The quality of a strategic security review depends on many factors, including the performance of members of the security team, management support, security awareness of staff and users, the content and structure of the security plan, understanding of the recommendations presented in the security plan, etc.

The comprehensive quality of the SP certainly depends on the quality of information processed in various phase of writing the security plan, but especially on the strategic security analysis, completeness of the security policy, and management support.

4.4 Summary

This chapter presented NIST SP guidelines under NIST SP 800-18. The development of an SP also rests on other standards such as FIPS 199, FIPS 200, and NIST SP 800-53. We discussed the steps needed to develop an SP according NIST standards.

This chapter provided the definition of an SP and how it is different from a security program. This chapter introduced the various phases constituting a security plan. The detailed definitions of these phases will follow in the succeeding chapters.

This chapter presented the strategic security analysis phase of a security plan. The information gathered throughout this phase is the basis of the strategic security design phase.

The strategic security analysis phase studies the existing system, including, assets, threats, and security solutions. This phase contains three main activities:

the definition of system criticality in terms of information sensitivity and information resource availability; the review of existing security controls that are in place, planned, or under development; and the security risk assessment activity.

4.5 Review Questions

1. Explain how the security planning process works, and give a simple example.
2. Explain how the system categorization in security planning is performed based on FIPS, and give an example.
3. Explain how risk management is addressed in security planning, and give an example.
4. Explain how a system SP is approved.
5. Explain how to define SP scope and system boundaries, and give an example.
6. Explain how to conduct SP analysis.
7. Explain how scoping guidance works, and give an example.
8. Explain how compensating controls are specified, and give an example.
9. Explain how common security controls are specified, and give an example.
10. Explain how to maintain ongoing system security, and give an example.
11. Explain how the proposed SP methodology works.
12. Explain how to distinguish between a major application and a general support system, and give examples.

4.6 Workshops

Workshop 1

Consider a small business, selling small home electronic equipment, hosting their own e-business Web site. Assume that their computing environment includes a server that hosts the Web site, and an independent server that hosts the customer database and the inventory application. These two servers are connected to the only LAN the small business owns. There are seven workstations connected to the LAN used by staff to process customer orders.

The purpose of this workshop is to practice the SP development methodology. Follow the proposed SP methodology to develop an SP for the small business.

Workshop 2

Assume a cybercafé with 20 workstations. Identify the minimal security controls that apply for an SP for the cybercafé. Apply the security analysis process described in NIST SP guidelines.

References

1. Federal Information Processing Standards Publication 199, *Standards for Security Categorization of Federal Information and Information Systems*, December 2003.
2. Federal Information Processing Standards Publication 200, *Security Controls for Federal Information System*, February 2006.
3. National Institute of Standards and Technology Special Publication 800-18, *Guide for Developing Security Plans for Federal Information Systems*, February 2006.
4. National Institute of Standards and Technology Special Publication 800-37, *Guide for the Security Certification and Accreditation of Federal Information Systems*, May 2004.
5. National Institute of Standards and Technology Special Publication 800-53, *Recommended Security Controls for Federal Information Systems*, February 2005.
6. Office of Management and Budget, Circular A-130, Appendix III, Transmittal Memorandum #4, *Management of Federal Information Resources*, November 2000.

Chapter 5

Security Policy

Learning Objectives

After reading this chapter, students are expected to achieve an understanding of:

What a security policy is
What standards are
What guidelines are
How a role-based security policy methodology works
What role-based policy requirements are
How the corporate vital defense strategy (CVDS) works
What CVDS requirements are
How Raggad's IS security taxonomy works
How a security information system works
How a security policy is designed based on CVDS
How security policy flow diagrams (pfd) methodology works
How security policy is designed based on computing environment partition
How a security policy is designed based on computing boundaries
How Benson's security policy methodology works

5.1 Introduction

This chapter starts with a presentation of Raggad's information security taxonomy, which is the basis of policy flow diagrams (pfd) methodology of developing security policy [5]. This taxonomy was published in 2000 at the 23rd National Information Systems Conference of under the title of "Corporate Vital Defense Strategy." Even though it differs from most of the literature we present in this book, it provides a way of managing information security that may be effective for organizations that adopt a problem-based approach. Instead of adopting the information security life cycle as we have consistently done throughout this book, the corporate vital defense strategy discusses information security solutions in terms of attacks, their models, and their consequences.

5.2 Security Policy, Standards, and Guidelines

5.2.1 IT Security Policy

Various definitions of "security policy" follow:

> An IT Security Policy is the most critical element of an IT security program. A security policy identifies the rules and procedures that all persons accessing computer resources must adhere to in order to ensure the confidentiality, integrity, and availability of data and resources. Furthermore, it puts into writing an organization's security posture, describes and assigns functions and responsibilities, grants authority to security professionals, and identifies the incident response processes and procedures.

> **GIAC (http://www.giac.org)**

Raggad defines security policy as follows:

> Security policy of a system is the acceptable behavior of this system, as defined by system owners.

> **Raggad, 2001**

SANS defines policy, standards, and guidelines as follows [6]:

Policy:

A Policy is a formal, brief, and high-level statement or plan that embraces an organization's general beliefs, goals, objectives, and acceptable procedures for a specified subject area. Policy attributes include the following:

Require compliance
Failure to comply results in disciplinary action

Focus on desired results, not on means of implementation
Further defined by standards and guidelines

SANS (www.sans.com)

5.2.2 Standard

A *standard* is a mandatory action or rule designed to support and conform to a
policy. A standard should make a policy more meaningful and effective. A standard must include one or more accepted specifications for hardware, software,
or behavior.

5.2.3 Guideline

A *guideline* is a set of general statements, recommendations, or administrative
instructions designed to achieve the policy's objectives by providing a framework
within which to implement procedures. A guideline can change frequently, depending on the environment, and should be reviewed more frequently than standards
and policies. A guideline is not mandatory, but rather, a suggested best practice.
Hence, "guidelines" and "best practice" are interchangeable.

Although not mandatory, guidelines may be very useful when added to security policy. Guidelines help users better understand the security policy and help
management and owners better understand security best practices. SANS presents guidelines meant to "guide" users to adopt behaviors that increase the security posture of a network; for example, an organization might choose to publish a
guideline on how to secure home networks even though they are not supported by
the corporation [6]. Figure 5.1 depicts the relationship between policy, standard,
and guidelines. Policy is concerned with the "why" aspects of computing behavior.
Standards and guidelines are concerned respectively with the "what" and "how"
aspects of the security policy.

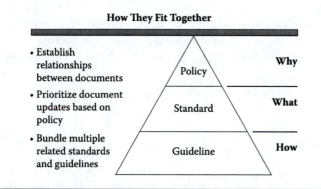

Figure 5.1   Policy versus standard versus guideline.

There are a number of standards and certifications that can be used as the basis for your policy framework [7]:

CoBIT: The Control Objectives for Information and related Technology. This is a set of best practices for IT Management.

ISO27001: Information Security Management—Specification With Guidance for Use; it is the replacement for BS7799-2. It is intended to provide the foundation for third-party audit, and is "harmonized" with other management standards such as ISO 9001 and ISO 14001 (from the ISO27001 Web site).

NIST: National Institute of Standards and Technology.

SSE-CMM: Systems Security Engineer Capability Maturity Model.

CISSP: Certified Information Systems Security Professional (10 domains).

At this point, we have seen that there are many security policy development methodologies we can choose from and many standards we can adopt. So what are the best security methodologies and policy standards we can use? Well, there is not really a best policy methodology or a best standard to adopt, but we have to select what works for the organization. Identifying the most effective security policy methodology an the policy standard to follow can only be known after several trials of selected alternate methodologies and standards. The following factors may influence the selection process: culture, regulations, business mission and organizational values, existing resources, and present and future technology.

SANS requires that a policy should:

State reasons why the policy is needed
Describe what is covered by the policies
Define contacts and responsibilities
Discuss how violations will be handled

Any policy must, however, be implementable and enforceable, concise and easy to understand, and capable of balancing protection with productivity.

SANS presents the key policies every organization needs as follows:

Information Classification Security Policy
Acceptable Use Policy
Minimum Access Policy
Network Access Policy
Remote Access
Acceptable Encryption Policy
Web Server Security Policy
Extranet Policy

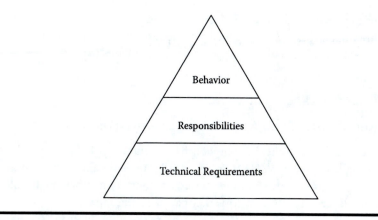

Figure 5.2   Policy: three levels of description.

Application Service Provider Policy
Authentication Credentials Policy

However we develop the security policy and whichever standard we use, the security policy will always be communicated to users as statements expressing computing behavioral requirements they have to respect. Those policy statements target important aspects of computing behavior, and the responsibilities that each user must meet for compliance. More details about the requirements are addressed in the general technical requirements for users or devices to be in compliance with policy. Figure 5.2 shows that policy is expressed at three levels: behavioral level, responsibility level, and technical level.

5.3 Security Policy Methodologies

People develop security policies in their own ways, depending on their business mission, culture, regulations, etc. Policies encountered in the real world vary a great deal, but at least three aspects of definitions can be seen: some policies are very abstract and behavioral, others describe responsibilities assigned to users/employees, and many others provide technical descriptions of resources and staff. The security policy methodologies are also very varied, depending on the ways those policies are defined.

In this chapter, we present several security policy development methodologies as follows:

1. The corporate vital defense security strategy to build a security policy
2. Policy flow diagrams methodology
3. Role-based access control methodology

4. Security policy based on computing boundaries
5. Security policy based on components of the computing environment
6. Iterative security policy building based on Benson templates

5.3.1 Role-Based Security Policy

5.3.1.1 Requirements for Role-Based Security Policy

A *role* is a defined responsibility in terms of behavior, authority, and accountability, given to an employee to complete a function or task. A role should not be confused with an employee's job, title, or position. In fact, an employee may have many roles, and many employees with the same title may have different roles.

RBAC somehow redefines what is meant by roles in the Human Resources department. RBAC defines IT resources and access levels required to fulfill a role's responsibilities [4]. RBAC takes into account roles from both the business process and organizational activities, and the IT application activity requirements. In an attempt to simplify the role definition task, some have taken to differentiating between "IT roles" and "business roles," arguing that the former is at a lower level than the latter. It does not really matter, because the authority and accountability aspects of role definition will always stem from both roles. Both types of roles are useful: the business role describes the functional responsibility of a role, and the IT role describes the resources and assets required to fulfill the role. A top-down role definition may be needed to refine and redefine existing business roles to adapt them for RBAC use.

In a bottom-up approach, current employees' access permissions may be grouped into roles. These roles will correspond to the business-based roles. One may even combine the top-down and bottom-up approaches in order to obtain more precise definition of roles. Current user access permissions may be a good place to start, but these likely include many permissions. The users should be able to identify which function or task each role represents, to describe the role in business terms, and to confirm which individuals currently fill this role.

Users granted membership in a role receive all of the permissions associated with that role. In this way, organizations can grant bundles of permissions to users instead of provisioning the permissions one at a time.

In addition to its cost-effectiveness, as it is assumed to decrease administrative overhead for the IT account administration staff, RBAC is also known for the strategic benefits due to enforcement of security and access policies. The "least-privileges" principle states that each employee should have access to only the IT resources required to do his or her job. Some other advantages include the following:

Once implemented, RBAC simplifies system administration
Strong support for separation of duties

Good auditing support
Considered best practice by many

RBAC also simplifies system administration. When users change positions, their roles are changed to reflect their new positions. Any replacement is assigned his or her old roles, and there is no need to remove a user's old access on each object. If roles are well defined, the system administrator only needs to add a user to their assigned roles. The users will have access to all the resources they require to complete their job.

5.3.1.2 Compliance Controls in RBAC

In a Novell technical white paper entitled "Smart Implementation of Role-based Access Control," Novell proposes automating the provisioning of roles and defines a set of rules that map users to roles based on users' attributes [4]. Required information is taken from the Human Resources Information System (HRIS) or enterprise directories, which describe each identity by attributes such as job code, job title, cost center, and security classification. Based on simple Boolean logic, we can use these attributes to define a set of membership rules for each role. The intention is to attempt to precisely define the set of users that need to be assigned to the role.

Depending on the quality of the role membership rules, administrators may choose from three variations of the provisioning process, each providing varying levels of automation: automated, conditional, and discretional.

If the membership rules are completely accurate, then the provisioning can be fully automated. The RBAC system adds or updates users in the directory, evaluates them according to the membership rules, and if they fall within the membership criteria, it assigns them to the role and provisions the IT resources. If the membership rules are fairly accurate, the system may generate a conditional access-request workflow, but a manager's review and approval will be required before the user can be assigned to the role and the resources provisioned. When the accuracy is low, all provisioning will be performed via a discretionary, manual access-request workflow. In this case, administrators will need to provision these users via a discretionary access-request workflow because the automated rules did not identify them. Figure 5.3, taken from the same Novell white paper, depicts the user provisioning process.

As explained in Novell's white paper, when IT auditors review for compliance with Sarbanes–Oxley, HIPAA, or other standards, they can see appropriate controls for access to IT resources. Sufficient compliance evidence will be available to IT auditors if changes to role definitions are logged, and access to the role management system are secured using RBAC. That is, the auditors can easily verify conformity to the role definitions by querying the target applications and reconciling the application accounts with the rules in the role definitions.

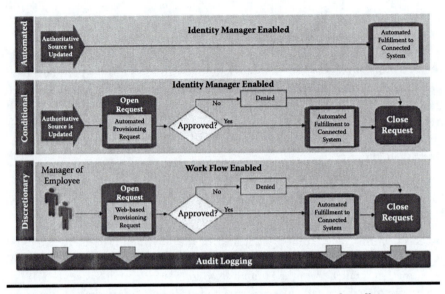

Figure 5.3 Novell's user provisioning scenarios. (From www.hovell.com)

5.3.2 The Corporate Vital Defense Strategy

5.3.2.1 Requirements for the Corporate Vital Defense Strategy

In order to support their operational missions, companies need to guarantee the availability of information, efficient information technologies, and reliable connectivity. Unfortunately, connectivity relies on commercial information resources and networks that are not fully secure. There are, however, IA technology solutions that can provide adequate protection of information. The effectiveness of these solutions should be evaluated based on their impact on operational missions. Full security is not possible, but adequate security can be achieved when IA technology solutions are adopted while balancing risk with cost and performance with operational impact.

The IA technology solutions should be defined with sufficient details to recognize fundamental security services, security technologies, security strategies, interoperability, key management infrastructure, and public key infrastructure. The corporate vital defense strategy should provide a holistic approach in assuming three main roles:

1. Defend enclave
2. Defend the data processing (DP) environment
3. Defend infrastructure support

A company needs to have a framework to support the company's information assurance (IA) needs. The company needs to adopt a clear and deliverable profile of IA strategies. This strategy profile is called vital defense strategy (VDS). The planning, design, and implementation of the VDS should be completed in a well-defined framework called Corporate Information Assurance Technology Framework (CIATF).

The company should always have a clear security mission, and testable policies and regulations. The CIATF contains guidelines on how to acquire, develop, and effectively implant security solutions. The security policy can be satisfied through a balanced implementation between technical security solutions and nontechnical countermeasures. The CIATF provides case studies where trade-offs between cost and risk can yield adequate security. Cases where practical solutions cannot fully satisfy security policies are also explained in the CIATF.

The CIATF identifies a range of risk management methodologies that apply to diverse activities, networks, technologies, conceptual resources, and software systems. The risk management methodologies should be the foundation for additional security assessment models through which the certification and accreditation activities are processed. The CIATF should periodically review and redefine security concepts and diverse roles and functions and new technologies so that current IA technology solutions can be evaluated. Security assessment models should be reviewed and revised as IA security technology changes. New risk assessment models should be developed.

5.3.2.2 *How to Defend the Corporate Enclave through CVDS*

The CIAFT provides structure and sufficient design information on three major areas: the protection of network access originating at the enclave, the protection of remote access by traveling users and remote users, and the protection of interoperability across security levels. The protection of network access should diversify IA technology by considering, for example, firewalls, intrusion detection systems, vulnerability scanners, and virus detection. Defending the enclave also includes defending external connections as required by the CVDS.

5.3.2.2.1 How to Defend DP through CVDS

The defense of the DP environment requires that end-user workstations, servers, applications, and operating systems be protected. CIATF should include explicit details of how security requirements of diverse DP elements are designed. For example, the components of a DP element that should be protected are identified, analyzed before their security solutions are designed, and implemented. End-user applications in the CIATF can include secure e-mailing, secure Web browsing, file protection, and mission-specific applications.

5.3.2.2.2 How to Defend the Infrastructure Support through CVDS

Defending the DP environment, its networks, and its enclave is useless if the infrastructure support itself is not secure. Imagine that agents at the company and its partner's enclaves are all using compromised keys, invalid certificates, or weak cryptographic models. The CIATF cannot help in implementing the company's VDS if the infrastructure support is not adequately secured.

Defending the infrastructure support is obviously an important element of the company's CIATF. At least two major areas should be planned: the KIM/PKI (key management infrastructure/public key infrastructure) and the D&R (detection and respond). The first area concerns the technologies, services, and processes used to manage public key certificates and symmetric cryptography. An information security methodology that agrees with the security life cycle may be needed. This information security methodology (ISM) is a systems approach that produces a user's security needs.

The ISM may be modeled using three main phases, as in Churchman's systems approach (Preparation effort, Solution effort, and Implementation effort), which provide a detailed security analysis of the user's system. This analysis should satisfy all integral requirements defined in the CIATF.

User security should be studied throughout its entire life cycle. The preparation effort is conducted first to understand mission needs, system policies, system regulations, system standards, and threats to owners. The solution effort is concerned with the security design. This phase includes the identification of possible security solutions defined in the CIATF, the definition of choice attributes based on which security solutions are retained, and the selection process. The implementation phase consists of the implantation of security solutions, and their review process.

A good security solution is one that grants the required protection for the security needs stated in the system security policy. Risk assessment is always necessary before the design and after the implementation of a security solution. It is needed in the design process to evaluate how much risk is involved, and after the implementation process to ensure that the adopted security solutions are actually working as desired. The security solutions adopted should only be adequate enough to satisfy a balance between cost to and harm inflicted on system owners.

The certification task is a review process that aims at ensuring that the security solutions are technically feasible. This is, however, a continuous process that persists as long as the system "lives." The certification process continues in order to ensure the system is satisfying operational and security needs and is adequately evaluating relevant threats.

It is very common, however, for the review process to revisit the initial security attributes processed to produce an ISM. Often, the system security policy also needs to be reassessed. When the subsequent revisits generate definitive differences or deviations from findings accepted during the preparation effort, the system security solutions may need to be redesigned.

5.3.2.3 Raggad's IS Security Taxonomy

Attacks are better organized in terms of (1) the identity of the entity carrying out the attack, (2) their effects on system owners, and (3) the models employed in the attacks. The effects of attacks on systems owners are commonly called *security disruptions* [1].

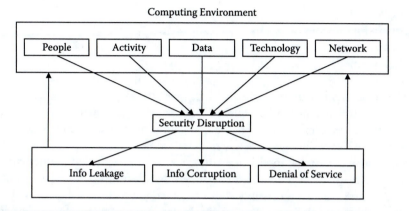

Figure 5.4 Security disruption classes defined by (Effect, Origin) pairs.

There are, however, only five possible acting entities that can have the capability of rooting an attack: (1) an activity, (2) a person, (3) a network, (4) a technology, and (5) a data resource. These entities were introduced first by Whitten, Bentley, and Barlow [9] in systems analysis and design, and used by the author in diverse publications under the term *business computing components*.

These entities consist of people, activities, technology, data, and networks [4]:

People: The role people play in an information system includes who will input data, who will receive output, and so forth.

Activities: The sequence of steps, data flows, security controls and information system environment are defined. The processes and security controls should be defined and documented.

Technology: Technology is studied at any phase in the life cycle of the information system.

Data: Data and information flows are defined at any phase of the system life cycle.

Networks: Network requirements at every location of the business area are studied. Security disruptions are organized, as in Cohen [1], into three main groups: information corruption (C), information leakage (L), and information denial (D).

An attack employs a model to induce an entity to produce one or more security disruptions [1]. Causal links between entities and security disruptions are depicted in Figure 5.4.

5.3.2.3.1 Attack Models

Attacks have models that combine people, data, knowledge, hardware, software, and other resources in order to achieve a specific objective, which is usually to cause harm to system owners. The attack models are organized in four categories:

Probe models
Infrastructure models
Authorized access models
Factory models

Probe attack models are concerned with passive attacks that are designed to identify opportunities that can be explored to cause harm to system owners. A probe model takes the form of any other method conforming to the attack opportunity the attacker is exploring [3].

Infrastructure attack models are concerned with attacks that are designed to induce entities to cause harm to system owners, by affecting an infrastructure attribute. An infrastructure attack model can be generic, such as introducing malicious code, copying traveling data, and attempting to break a security feature; or core, such as attacking a network backbone [3]. An authorized access attack is simply an attack performed by an insider.

Factory attack models are designed to induce an entity to indirectly cause harm to system owners by modifying or substituting of hardware or software at the factory, or during the distribution process. Factory attack models may be designed to embed malicious code through shrink-wrapped software, user swapping media, or path created to import information from an external network. Attacks are usually characterized by the malicious modification of hardware or software between the time the hardware or software is developed and the time it is installed and used. An example would be an entity (a user) with remote access capability who configures his or her computer when the computer is left unattended without any physical protection.

The same attack would take place if the software were shipped through a network or some physical means [3].

5.3.2.4 How to Develop a Security Information System

A security information system is studied in terms of the following three dimensions: (1) attack model (2) security disruption produced, and (3) the entity responsible for the attack. In this manner, the effect of the disruption on the business area in terms of information corruption (C), leakage (L), or denial (D) will be understood. The business information components at the origin of the security disruption, which may be people (P), activities (A), technology (T), data (D), or networks (N), will be known. The models used in future attacks are well defined in terms of their categories: probe models, infrastructure models, authorized access models, and factory models.

In the hierarchy of classes, for each attack model, there are therefore 15 classes defined by the effect and the origin of the security disruption [1]. Because there are four attack models, this hierarchy identifies 4 × 15 = 60 types of security information systems. This article will refer to these systems as Default Functional Security

Information Systems (DFSISs). For a fixed attack model associated with the company's security threats and vulnerabilities, as shown in the company's CVDS, the DFSISs are studied in terms of the following situations:

1. Corrupted People (CP): CP is a security disruption class, where the effect is information corruption and the origin is people at the business area.
2. Corrupted Activity (CA): CA is a security disruption class where the effect is information corruption and the origin is an activity at the business area.
3. Corrupted Technology (CT): CT is a security disruption class where the effect is information corruption and the origin is technology at the business area.
4. Corrupted Data (CD): CD is a security disruption class where the effect is information corruption and the origin is data at the business area.
5. Corrupted Network (CN): CN is a security disruption class where the effect is information corruption and the origin is a network at the business area.
6. Leaking People (LP): LP is a security disruption class where the effect is information leakage and the origin is people at the business area.
7. Leaking Activity (LA): LA is a security disruption class where the effect is information leakage and the origin is an activity at the business area.
8. Leaking Technology (LT): LT is a security disruption class where the effect is information leakage and the origin is technology at the business area.
9. Leaking Data (LD): LD is a security disruption class where the effect is information leakage and the origin is data at the business area.
10. Leaking Network (LN): LN is a security disruption class where the effect is information leakage and the origin is a network at the business area.
11. Denying People (DP): DP is a security disruption class where the effect is information denial and the origin is people at the business area.
12. Denying Activity (DA): DA is a security disruption class where the effect is information denial and the origin is an activity at the business area.
13. Denying Technology (DT): DT is a security disruption class where the effect is information denial and the origin is technology at the business area.
14. Denying Data (DD): DD is a security disruption class where the effect is information denial and the origin is data at the business area.
15. Denying Network (DN): DN is a security disruption class where the effect is information denial and the origin is a network at the business area.

5.3.2.4.1 Default Objectives for the DFSISs

The default objective of a DFSIS is the solution of the security problem or the enforcement of the security directive for which the system is initiated. Unless information system owners approve a new objective, the security information system maintains its default objective.

A security information system is initiated to solve a security problem or to enforce a security directive cited in security policies. The objective of the security information system may be defined as the objective of the class to which the security problem belongs. If it is initiated by a security directive, then the default objective of the security information system will be that of the security directive.

Because a security disruption may reside in different classes, a security problem may also reside in different classes. The security information system may hence have multiple default objectives. Table 5.1 provides default objectives for security information systems associated with the 15 security disruption classes defined earlier. A simple security information system is a system that is initiated by security problems or security directives of members of only one class. The selection of the problem may be done using frequency distribution of security situations. Classes are ranked with respect to the frequency percentage of security situations residing in classes. Classes of corrupted networks, leaking networks, denying networks, corrupted people, and denying activities are ranked 1, 2, 3, 4, and 5, respectively.

Security situations may be ranked according to the number of residences. A situation associated with the highest number of residences is selected first. Every security situation is carefully examined to identify the class where the security disruption resides. Even though the number of classes associated with a situation may indicate that the security information system should be initiated using these classes and their respective default objectives, it is important to think of a threshold beyond which a security situation will be considered as a security problem that will lead to the initiation of the new security information system.

The first simple security information system that is a candidate for initiation will have as an objective the minimization of information corruption originating at networks of the business area.

5.3.2.4.2 Security Information Systems with Multiple Classes

A security information system may be a simple system with one default objective, or a more complex system with multiple default objectives. The complexity of the security information system depends on the number of default objectives involved. Obviously, it is possible for a security disruption to cause any combination of damage, for example, information corruption and information leakage simultaneously. It is also possible for a security disruption to originate at more than one business information component, for example, people and technology both cause the same damage, say, information corruption.

The company DP department either acquires products from vendors identified by their users, or develops systems using vendor products and components made in-house. Functional security information systems, including the 60 types defined earlier, are developed to integrate with these in-house systems and trusted vendor products.

Table 5.1   Default Objectives for Security Information Systems Associated with the 15 Security Disruption Classes

Security Disruption Class	Default Objective
1. Corrupted People (CP):	Minimize information corruption at the business information component: People
2. Corrupted Activity (CA):	Minimize information corruption at the business information component: Activity
3. Corrupted Technology (CT):	Minimize information corruption at the business information component: Technology
4. Corrupted Data (CD):	Minimize information corruption at the business information component: Data
5. Corrupted Network (CN):	Minimize information corruption at the business information component: Network
6. Leaking People (CP):	Minimize information Leakage at the business information component: People
7. Leaking Activity (CA):	Minimize information Leakage at the business information component: Activity
8. Leaking Technology (CT):	Minimize information Leakage at the business information component: Technology
9. Leaking Data (CD):	Minimize information Leakage at the business information component: Data
10. Leaking Network (CN)	Minimize information Leakage at the business information component: Network
11. Leaking People (CP):	Minimize information Leakage at the business information component: People
12. Leaking Activity (CA):	Minimize information Leakage at the business information component: Activity
13. Leaking Technology (CT):	Minimize information Leakage at the business information component: Technology
14. Leaking Data (CD):	Minimize information Leakage at the business information component: Data
15. Leaking Network (CN):	Minimize information Leakage at the business information component: Network

The CVDS requires that all information resources be evaluated, whether they are IT products purchased from vendors or systems developed to satisfy user requirements. For this purpose, a company should maintain a long list of assets that are scheduled for evaluations and reevaluations.

5.3.2.5 How to Build the Security Policy

Raggad's taxonomy introduced 60 default functional security information systems, defined in terms of (1) DoD's attack models (probe, infrastructure, factory, and authorized-access models); (2) Whitten, Withny, and Barlow's entities (data, people, activities, technology, and networks) induced to cause the attack; and (3) Cohen's security disruptions (information leakage, information corruption, and service denial) produced [5].

Automatic information security solutions can be developed. Some automatic security solutions are already provided as a part of the IDS literature. The CVDS should contain a risk and vulnerability assessment that can identify and prioritize the default functional security information systems which should be initiated.

A security policy may be built based on the 60 boxes produced by Raggad's taxonomy. Security specifications are defined for every box of the taxonomy. The specifications provide sufficient description of interactions between the agents, the attack model, and resulting security disruption. The security policy developer can write all the statements that have to be enforced to prevent any interactions between agents, attack models, and security disruptions that can lead to unacceptable behaviors or consequences.

In fact, the writing of the security requirements needed to support the development processes for the default functional information systems proposed earlier are a great source of policy statements. Because of the predefined specifications of these systems, their security requirements and policies are easier to write, and their evaluation processes, which provide for easier enforcement of the security policy, become easier to conduct.

5.3.3 Security Policy Flow Diagrams

This security policy methodology is related to the CVDS and Raggad's taxonomy that we presented earlier. The pfd methodology views the computing environment of an organization as shown in Figure 5.5. The computing environment to protect comprises five interconnected computing components, as assumed throughout this book: people, activities, data, technology, and network. The pfd methodology adopts the security policy definition that views the "security policy of a system as the acceptable behavior of this system, as defined by system owners."

In Figure 5.5, you can see that there are 15 connections, including reflexive connections. These connections represent first- and second-order interactions among

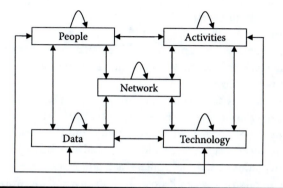

Figure 5.5   Computing environment's connections assumed in pfd.

components of the computing environment. If we consider all possible interactions, including first-, second-, third-, fourth-, and fifth- order connections, we obtain 31 possible interactions among components.

There are, therefore, 31 possible sets of interactions that will be used in developing an information system's security policy. Those interactions are of five types:

First-order policy flow
Second-order policy flow
Third-order policy flow
Fourth-order policy flow
Fifth-order policy flow

In order to provide a structured methodology for developing information system security policy, we need to create 31 security policy flow folders (pff) called pff1 through pff31. They are organized as follows:

First-order policy flow: First-order policy flow describes an interaction between a component and itself. They may be denoted as follows:
pff1: Interactions between People and People
pff2: Interactions between Activity and Activity
pff3: Interactions between Data and Data
pff4: Interactions between Technology and Technology
pff5: Interactions between Network and Network
Second-order policy flow:
pff6: Interactions between People and Activity
pff7: Interactions between People and Data
pff8: Interactions between People and Technology
pff9: Interactions between People and Network
pff10: Interactions between Activity and Data
pff11: Interactions between Activity and Technology

pff12: Interactions between Activity and Network
pff13: Interactions between Data and Technology
pff14: Interactions between Data and Network
pff15: Interactions between Network and Technology
Third-order policy flow:
pff16: Interactions between People, Activity, and Data
pff17: Interactions between People, Activity, and Technology
pff18: Interactions between People, Activity, and Network
pff19: Interactions between People, Data, and Technology
pff20: Interactions between People, Data, and Network
pff21: Interactions between People, Technology, and Network
pff22: Interactions between Activity, Data, and Technology
pff23: Interactions between Activity, Data, and Network
pff24: Interactions between Activity, Technology, and Network
pff25: Interactions between Data, Technology, and Network
Fourth-order policy flow:
pff26: Interactions between People, Activity, Data, and Technology
pff27: Interactions between People, Activity, Data, and Network
pff28: Interactions between People, Activity, Technology, and Network
pff29: Interactions between People, Data, Technology, and Network
pff20: Interactions between Activity, Data, Technology, and Network
Fifth-order policy flow:
pff31: Interactions between People, Activity, Data, Technology, and Network

5.3.3.1 Policy Flow Statement

The pfd methodology describes the flow of policy information defining the interaction between two components of the information system or the computing environment. Each interaction is expressed using a statement <Actor (C), Activity (V), Object (B), Owner (W) , Tool (L)>. A table similar to Table 5.2 may be used to include the structure of pfd statements. Table 5.3 also depicts an example of policy flow diagrams.

An actor may be any component of the computing environment: people, activities, data, technology, or network. An activity may be any activity relevant to the computing environment or any generic activity needed to describe the interaction. An object may be any component of the computing environment. An owner may be any component in the computing environment. A tool may be any tool in technology defined in the computing environment or any generic tool needed to define the interaction in question.

The graphic structure of a security policy interaction is only used to communicate the policy to owners and upper management for approval. Once it is approved, the presentation in Figure 5.6 will be transformed into a statement and added to

Table 5.2 Security Policy Definition in pfd Methodology

1#	Order	Components Involved					Interaction Structure					
		P	A	D	T	N	Actor	Activity	Object	Owner	Tool	Statement

Table 5.3 Example of Security Policy Flow Diagrams

Example of Security Policy Definition in pfd Methodology

pff#	Order	Components Involved					Interaction Structure					Policy Statement
		P	A	D	T	N	C	A	O	W	L	
pff1	1	x					p			p		A parent supervises kids (users).
pff1	1	x					p			p		Ben authorizes access for kids (users).
pff2	1		x				a			a		If view picture, do not print picture.
pff2	1		x				a			a		If view MS Word file, do not save.
pff2	1		x				A			A		If view MS Word file, do not modify.
pff3	1			x			D			D		Password protects data.
pff3	1			x			D			D		Current data replaces old data.
pff4	1				x		T			T		Any new software has to be compatible with Windows.
pff5	1					x	N			N		Do not connect modem to computer after 8:00 pm except during weekends.
pff6	2	x	x				P			A		Ben (admin) defines new activities.
pff6	2	x	x				P			A		Ben (admin) manages activities.
pff7	2	x		x			P			D		Ben owns data files.
pff7	2	x		x			P			D		Ben enters password.

pff8	2	x				x	P	T	Ben (admin) repairs computer.
pff8	2	x				x	P	T	Anybody in the family can connect the moderm.
pff8	2	x				x	P	T	Nobody can unplug the computer.
pff9	2	x			x		P	N	Ben audits connections.
pff9	2	x			x		P	N	Ben replaces cables.
pff10	2		x	x			A	D	Passwords are changed every 3 months.
pff10	2		x	x			A	D	Budget data is revised at the end of the month.
pff11	2		x			x	A	T	Antivirus software is updated once a month.
pff11	2		x			x	A	T	Hard disk cannot be partitioned.
pff12	2		x			x	A	N	Networks is scanned for vulnerabilities periodically.
pff12	2		x			x	A	N	Defective modem is reconfigured immediately.
pff13	2			x		x	D	T	History is erased from Internet Explorer periodically.
pff14	2		x			x	D	N	Configure the system to save log data about Internet access.
pff14	2		x	x			D	N	Use correct information when reconfiguring the modem
pff15	2	x	x			x	T	N	Only use Internet Explorer to connect to the Internet.
pff16	3	x	x	x			P	A	D	Any parent can erase cookies from the computer.

Continued

Table 5.3   Example of Security Policy Flow Diagrams (Continued)

Example of Security Policy Definition in pfd Methodology

pff#	Order	Components Involved					Interaction Structure					Policy Statement
		P	A	D	T	N	C	A	O	W	L	
pff16	3	x	x	x			P	A	D			Only Ben (admin) can change passwords.
												Only parents can create new files.
pff16	3	x	x	x			P	A	D			Any parent can erase cookies from the computer.
pff17	3	x	x		x		P	A				Only Ben can uninstall software.
pff17	3	x	x		x		P	A				A parent can install new software.
pff18	3						P	A				People should not scan the network.
pff18	3	x	x			x	P	A				External people should not access the computer or the printer.
pff18	3	x	x			x	P	A				Ben (admin) changes the passwords.
pff18	3	x	x			x	P	A				Ben (admin) deletes the data files.
pff18	3	x	x			x	P	A				Ben (admin) installs new software.
pff19	3	x		x	x		P		D		T	People only apply existing software to process data.
pff20	3	x		x		x	P		D		N	Ben (admin) owns log data on the Internet connections.

ID												Policy
pff21	3	x		x			P			N	T	Everybody uses Internet Explorer to access the Internet.
pff22	3		x	x		x	A		D	N	T	Existing software should be used to create new data files.
pff23	3		x	x		x	A		D	N		Network logs are archived periodically.
pff24	3	x		x	x	x	A			N	T	No new hardware should be installed on the network.
pff25	3		x	x	x	x	D			N	T	Only use Outlook Express to view your e-mail at the ISP e-mail server.
pff26	4	x		x	X	x	P	A	D		T	Only parents can scan data files for viruses, and the existing antivirus software has to be used.
pff27	4	x			X	x	P	A	D	N		Nobody should download information from the Internet after 10:00 pm.
pff28	4	x		x	x	x	P	A		N	T	Only Ben can download and install software from the Internet.
pff29	4	x		x	x	x	P		D	N	T	Nobody should use remote password crackers to check the strength of passwords.
pff30	4		x	x	x	x	A		D	N	T	Nobody should use remote antivirus software to scan for spyware data.
pff31	5	x		x	x	x	P	A	D	N	T	Ben (admin) is authorized to create personal signature information using MS Word and attach it to e-mails send externally.

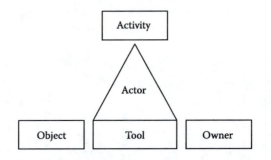

Figure 5.6   Structure of a policy interaction.

the appropriate folder containing the security policy. The graphic presentation of the security policy is also useful when the security policy is studied or audited. The new version of the security policy is presented to management in a graphic format to facilitate communication and approval.

Example

Consider a small family with two kids Mona and Sarah, a husband Ben, and a wife Amy. The family has one computer for the entire family linked to a printer and connected to the Internet via an external modem. The computer includes a keyboard and USB mouse. In addition to Windows XP, the computer includes antivirus software, Microsoft Office 2003, Paint software, and Internet Explorer for the entire family. There are also three games: Solitaire for adults, and FreeCell and Pinball for the kids.

The computing environment contains the following:

1. People: Mona, Sarah, Amy, and Ben
2. Activities:
   Access computer
   Access, Create, Delete, Print files
   View, Print pictures
   Add, Modify, Delete data in files
   Change password, etc.
3. Data:
   House.jpg
   Spring.gif
   Budget.xsl
   Letter to Santa.doc
   Family Plan.doc
   Weekend Rules.doc
4. Technology:
   Hardware: CPU, Monitor, Keyboard, Mouse, Printer, Power supply, and Cable.
   Software: Windows XP, Microsoft Office 2003, Internet Explorer, antivirus software, Paint, Solitaire, FreeCell, Pinball, etc.

5. Network:
   Power supply
   Parallel cable to printer
   Phone cable to modem
   First-order policy flow
   > First-order policy flow describes an interaction between a component and itself. They may be denoted as follows:
   > pff1: Interactions between People and People
   > pff2: Interactions between Activity and Activity
   > pff3: Interactions between Data and Data
   > pff4: Interactions between Technology and Technology
   > pff5: Interactions between Network and Network

pff1: Interactions between People and People:
   A parent supervises kids (users).
   Ben authorizes access for kids (users).

pff2: Interactions between Activity and Activity:
   If view picture, do not print picture.
   If view MS Word file, do not save.
   If view MS Word file, do not modify.

pff3: Interactions between Data and Data:
   Password protects data.
   Current data replaces old data.

pff4: Interactions between Technology and Technology:
   Any new software has to be compatible with Windows.

pff5: Interactions between Network and Network:
   Do not connect modem to computer after 8:00 pm except during weekends.

5.3.4 Security Policy Based on Computing Environment Partition

5.3.4.1 Security Policy for People

Personnel security policy may include any aspects of computing that have to be restricted depending on the security clearance assigned to the staff member and the criticality of the resources involved. We are, however, concerned with at least the following areas:

Hiring policy
Ethics
Password policy
Other computing behaviors

5.3.4.1.1 Hiring Policy

In hiring any staff member, there are obvious steps that Human Resources personnel have to do. They have to explain the job position to potential candidates, conduct a thorough background check, use assessment tools to find honest and trustworthy candidates, and make sure that their assessment tools are fair and non-discriminatory [2].

When hiring security personnel, they have to perform a full background check before making any decision. They have to follow accepted security safeguards to minimize any risks of compromising security due to bad hiring. Personnel security safeguards may be organized into several branches:

1. Qualification assurance: A person is only hired if he or she matches both the specifications of the job and the security clearance for the job. While a candidate's qualification for the job can be easily verified after technical testing and after reviewing his or her work experience, the security clearance task is not an easy process.
2. Screening assurance: Screening and background checks of candidates have to be conducted very thoroughly to make sure that candidates with a history of poor behavior cannot infiltrate into the system. The strength of the security clearance associated with a position depends on the sensitivity/confidentiality of information accessible to this position.
3. Authorizing of process: This consists of granting or taking away any physical or system access privileges at the time of hiring of an employee, his or her transfer elsewhere, or when his or her services are terminated. All privileges of an employee's system access may be granted, modified, or revoked following a formal and auditable process.
4. Security training: Security training programs are made available to employees in accordance with the security requirements of their position.
5. Nondisclosure agreements: All employees who are concerned with any security matters have to sign the appropriate nondisclosure agreements in accordance with their positions. The nondisclosure agreements have to be signed by all individuals who need access to sensitive/confidential information, prior to granting access to that information.

5.3.4.1.2 Ethics

Usually, there are ethical rules that personnel respect, but most of those rules remain undocumented except for some major rules that management wants to enforce. Some organizations document and enforce an ethics code that personnel have to respect. For example, users are not allowed to share accounts or passwords with others. In real life, in many countries, running password checkers on system password files or network sniffers is considered a violation of the ethics code, but in many other countries, those activities are a violation of existing laws, and violators may be prosecuted.

Accepted ethical rules of behavior do not allow a user to do the following:

Break into other accounts
Disrupt services in any way

Abuse system resources
Misuse e-mail
Download pc binaries
Copy unlicensed software, and so on

The following section provides an example of a template for a security policy for ethics, taken from SANS [8].

1. Policy
    1.1. Executive Commitment to Ethics
        1.1.1. Top brass within <Company Name> must set a prime example. In any business practice, honesty and integrity must be top priority for executives.
        1.1.2. Executives must have an open door policy and welcome suggestions and concerns from employees. This will allow employees to feel comfortable discussing any issues and will alert executives to concerns within the work force.
        1.1.3. Executives must disclose any conflict of interest regarding their position within <Company Name>.
    1.2. Employee Commitment to Ethics
        1.2.1. <Company Name> employees will treat everyone fairly, foster mutual respect, promote a team environment, and avoid the intent and appearance of unethical or compromising practices.
        1.2.2. Every employee needs to apply effort and intelligence in upholding ethics.
        1.2.3. Employees must disclose any conflict of interest regard their position within <Company Name>.
        1.2.4. Employees will help <Company Name> to increase customer and vendor satisfaction by providing quality products and timely response to inquiries.
    1.3. Company Awareness
        1.3.1. Promotion of ethical conduct within interpersonal communications of employees will be rewarded.
        1.3.2. <Company Name> will promote a trustworthy and honest atmosphere to reinforce the vision of ethics within the company.

1.4. Maintaining Ethical Practices

    1.4.1. <Company Name> will reinforce the importance of the integrity message, and the tone will start at the top. Every employee, manager, and director needs consistently to maintain an ethical stance and support ethical behavior.

    1.4.2. Employees at <Company Name> should encourage open dialogue, get honest feedback and treat everyone fairly, with honesty and objectivity.

    1.4.3. <Company Name> has established a best practice disclosure committee to make sure the ethical code is delivered to all employees and that concerns regarding the code can be addressed.

1.5. Unethical Behavior

    1.5.1. <Company Name> will avoid the intent and appearance of unethical or compromising practices in relationships, actions and communications.

    1.5.2. <Company Name> will not tolerate harassment or discrimination.

    1.5.3. Unauthorized use of company trade secrets and marketing, operational, personnel, financial, source code, and technical information integral to the success of our company will not be tolerated.

    1.5.4. <Company Name> will not permit impropriety at any time, and we will act ethically and responsibly in accordance with laws.

    1.5.5. <Company Name> employees will not use corporate assets or business relationships for personal use or gain.

2. Enforcement

    2.1. Any infractions of this code of ethics will not be tolerated, and <Company Name> will act quickly in correcting the issue if the ethics code is broken.

    2.2. Any employee found to have violated this policy may be subject to disciplinary action, up to and including termination of employment.

Source: SANS (http://www.sans.org/resources/policies/#template)

5.3.4.1.3 Password Policy

The combination of username and password defines the identity of users on a system. Adopting a good personal password policy is the most important precaution against unauthorized access in current systems. The following is taken from SANS's password policy.

A password should contain a mixture of numbers, capital letters, small letters, and special characters.

A password should be easy to remember and easy to type.

A password should not be written down in any way.

A password should not be communicated in cleartext in any way except for authentication.

Passwords should be stored in encrypted form. The encryption should be strong, resisting brute force decryption for at least weeks on a powerful computer.

Passwords should not be displayed when being entered.

Embedding of cleartext passwords into software should be avoided at all costs. Embedded encrypted passwords are also to be avoided where possible.

A password minimum age, maximum age, minimum length, and history list should be defined in the security policy.

Source: SANS http://www.sans.org/resources/policies/#template)

5.3.4.2 Security Policy for Networks

The network security policy is intended to protect the integrity of internal networks and mitigate the risks and losses associated with security threats to network resources.

Of course, any organization would experience a variety of security incidents associated with a wide range of severity. These incidents range from individual virus infections to network congestion or loss of network connectivity for specific networks or for the entire computing environment.

Attacks and security incidents constitute a risk to the business mission. The loss or corruption of data or unauthorized disclosure of information on company networks could greatly hinder the profitability of current partnerships and may lead to great customer dissatisfaction and, hence, loss of business value.

The network security policy will allow the organization to handle network security effectively. This policy is subject to revision and will be periodically reviewed as the organization gains experience with this policy.

A network security policy is needed to:

Establish comprehensive policies to protect company's networks and computer systems from abuse and inappropriate use.

Establish mechanisms that will aid in the identification and prevention of abuse of company's networks and connected resources.

Provide an effective mechanism for responding to external complaints and queries about real or perceived abuses of university networks and computer systems.

Establish mechanisms that will support the goals of other existing policies.

Network administrators should provide for the following activities as indicated in network security policies:

Monitor in real time, backbone network traffic, as necessary and appropriate, for the detection of unauthorized activity, intrusion attempts, and compromised equipment

Carry out and review the results of automated network-based vulnerability, compromise assessment and guideline compliance scans of the systems and devices on company networks in order to detect known vulnerabilities, compromised hosts, and guideline compliance failures.

Test company wireless network access to ensure compliance with published guidelines.

Prepare summary reports of its network security activities in a periodic manner.

Provide assistance and advice to system administrators to the maximum extent possible with available resources.

Security policy is obviously required, but network administrators will be the first line of defense to answer all questions and plan any responses or corrective actions.

The following section presents a SANS policy template for remote access [8].

SANS' Remote Access Policy Template

This policy is needed to establish an authorized method for controlling mobile computing and storage devices that contain or access information resources. The policy template includes the following outline:

Purpose
Background/History
Persons Affected:
Policy:
Procedures: Minimum Requirements:

Roles and Responsibilities:
  Users
  Enterprise Help Desk
  Information Protection Services Office
  The Information Systems
Definitions

PURPOSE:

The purpose of this policy is to establish an authorized method for controlling mobile computing and storage devices that contain or access information resources at <Company Name>.

POLICY:

It is the policy of <COMPANY NAME> that mobile computing and storage devices containing or accessing the information resources at the <COMPANY NAME> must be approved prior to connecting to the information systems at <COMPANY NAME>. This pertains to all devices connecting to the network at <COMPANY NAME>, regardless of ownership.

Mobile computing and storage devices include, but are not limited to the following: laptop computers, personal digital assistants (PDAs), plug-ins, Universal Serial Bus (USB) port devices, compact discs (CDs), digital versatile discs (DVDs), flash drives, modems, handheld wireless devices, wireless networking cards, and any other existing or future mobile computing or storage device, either personally owned or <Organization Name> owned, that may connect to or access the information systems at <COMPANY NAME>. A risk analysis for each new media type shall be conducted and documented prior to its use or connection to the network at <COMPANY NAME> unless the media type has already been approved by the Desktop Standards Committee. The Desktop Standards Committee will maintain a list of approved mobile computing and storage devices.

Mobile computing and storage devices are easily lost or stolen, presenting a high risk for unauthorized access and introduction of malicious software to the network at <COMPANY NAME>. These risks must be mitigated to acceptable levels.

Portable computing devices and portable electronic storage media that contain confidential, personal, or sensitive <COMPANY NAME> information must use encryption or equally strong measures to protect the data while it is being stored.

Unless written approval has been obtained from the Data Resource Manager and Chief Information Security Officer, databases or portions thereof, which reside on the network at <COMPANY NAME>, shall not be downloaded to mobile computing or storage devices.

Technical personnel and users, which include employees, consultants, vendors, contractors, and students, shall have knowledge of, sign, and adhere to the Computer Use and Information Security Policy Agreement (<COMPANY NAME> 350). Compliance with the Remote Access Standards, the Mobile Media Standards, and other applicable policies, procedures, and standards is mandatory.

PROCEDURES: MINIMUM REQUIREMENTS

■ To report lost or stolen mobile computing and storage devices, call the Enterprise Help Desk at xxx-xxx-xxxx. For further procedures on lost or stolen handheld wireless devices, please see the *PDA Information and Procedures* section.

■ The <COMPANY NAME> Desktop Standards Committee shall approve all new mobile computing and storage devices that may connect to information systems at <COMPANY NAME>.

■ Any nondepartmental owned device that may connect to the <COMPANY NAME> network must first be approved by technical personnel such as those from the <COMPANY NAME> Desktop Support. Refer to the Mobile Media Standards for detailed information.

■ Submit requests for an exception to this policy to the Information Protection Services Office via the Policy Exception Request form (EXEC 205).

ROLES AND RESPONSIBILITIES

Users of mobile computing and storage devices must diligently protect such devices from loss of equipment and disclosure of private information belonging to or maintained by the <COMPANY NAME>. Before connecting a mobile computing or storage device to the network at <COMPANY NAME>, users must ensure it is on the list of approved devices issued by the ISD.

The *Enterprise Help Desk* must be notified immediately upon detection of a security incident, especially when a mobile device may have been lost or stolen.

The *Information Protection Services Office* is responsible for the mobile device policy at <COMPANY NAME> and shall conduct a risk analysis to document safeguards for each media type to be used on the network or on equipment owned by <COMPANY NAME>.

The *Information Systems Division* is responsible for developing procedures for implementing this policy. The Desktop Standards Committee will maintain a list of approved mobile computing and storage devices and will make the list available on the intranet.

Source: SANS (http://www.sans.org/resources/policies/#template)

5.3.4.3 Security Policy for Technology

Let us see how some IT companies, for example, Microsoft, define and develop their security. We next provide an extract of their Windows server security policy. The purpose of this policy is to define standards (even though this is not the way we earlier defined security policy) for the baseline configuration of a client's Windows servers. Before any servers are placed on the production network, standard processes are to be executed to ensure that the servers are installed and maintained in a manner that prevents unauthorized access, unauthorized use, and disruptions in service. For a more detailed description of how Microsoft defines security policy for Windows servers, you may, for example, refer to http://seoutsourcing.com/node/35.

5.3.4.3.1 General Guidelines for Windows Server Security Policy

1. The operating system installation media will come from an approved source.
2. All production servers will be located in a secure facility.
3. Server role configurations are governed by the <Server Role Name> Security Baseline.
4. All servers deployed into production will be registered in the asset management system. The machine name, server role, operating system, IP address, physical location (building/room), and name of contact person will be included.
5. Before any server is put into production, a baseline will be taken in accordance with the Security Technical Implementation Guides (STIGS) WINDOWS 2003/XP/2000 ADDENDUM Version 5, Release 1, Section 2.1. The baseline will be attached to the server's properties in the asset management system.
6. When a server is decommissioned, it must be properly sanitized in compliance with the Media Disposal Policy.

7. Any server identified as compromised will be subject to the practices of the IT Intrusion Response Plan.
8. Logon banners will be displayed before any user signs on to a server as described in Appendix C (of http://seoutsourcing.com/node/35).

5.3.4.3.2 Windows Server Configuration Guidelines

1. The local administrator account will be renamed.
2. Guest accounts will be disabled.
3. All unnecessary Windows services will be disabled.
4. All unnecessary network services will be disabled.
5. Screensaver password will be set.
6. Audit logging will be enabled via Group Policy.
7. Log properties will be configured in accordance with <Company Name>'s Log Configuration Standards.
8. Antivirus software will be installed and updated.

5.3.4.3.3 Patch Update Guidelines for Window Servers

1. All patches will be tested in the lab environment before they are deployed on production systems.
2. High-priority updates will be applied as needed in accordance with <Company Name>'s Change Management Policy.
3. Noncritical fixes will be applied on a quarterly basis in accordance with <Company Name>'s Change Management Policy.

5.3.4.3.4 File System Guidelines for Window Servers

All servers will be configured in accordance with the Security Technical Implementation Guides (STIGS) WINDOWS 2003/XP/2000 ADDENDUM Version 5, Release 1, Section 7.1 and Windows Server 2003 Checklist 5.1.6 Appendix A / A.3 (of http://seoutsourcing.com/node/35).

5.3.4.3.5 Review Guidelines for Window Servers

1. When a new server is deployed, a server deployment checklist will be completed and submitted to InfoSec for approval. The checklist will be entered into the asset management system (Appendix A, of http://seoutsourcing.com/node/35).
2. On a weekly basis, a baseline review will be preformed on all production servers in accordance with the Security Technical Implementation Guides (STIGS) WINDOWS 2003/XP/2000 ADDENDUM Version 5, Release 1, Section 2.1. Any irregularities will be promptly submitted to InfoSec.

Table 5.4   Server Deployment Checklist (after Connecting to the Network)

Action	Notes	Status
Place the server in the applicable production OU.		
Force Group Policy update by executing gpupdate /force.		
Execute gpresult to validate that the server role GPO is applied.		
Once the GPO is applied, execute gpresult > <Server Name>gpresult.txt, and attach the file to the server's properties in the asset management system.		
Confirm that antivirus software is enabled, configured, and updated.		
Run an MBSA scan from the host to audit for compliance.		
Run an Nmap scan against the host to audit for compliance.		

3. On a biannual basis, production server services will be audited, documented, and reviewed by InfoSec (Appendix B, of http://seoutsourcing.com/node/35).

As part of its security policy enforcement program, Microsoft defines configuration baselines that clients follow when installing Windows servers. In addition to those configuration baselines, there are checklists that have to be evaluated after connecting the Windows servers, and server audit criteria to be verified. The server deployment checklist and server service audit criteria are provided in Tables 5.4 and 5.5, respectively.

The following section provides a SANS policy template to protect against viruses.

SANS recommended the following processes to prevent virus problems [8]:

- Always run the corporate standard, supported antivirus software available from the corporate download site. Download and run the current version; download and install antivirus software updates as they become available.

Table 5.5 Server Services Audit

Service	Purpose	Installed	Disabled
Alerter	Alerter: Creates pop-up messages from the system when services fail to start (etc.). Requires Messenger service.		
ClipBook Server	Clipbook Server: Serves up local clipbook pages to other Clipbook Viewers.		
Computer Browser	Computer Browser: Allows for viewing of other computers and resources on the network.		
DHCP Client	DHCP Client: Will automatically contact the DHCP server (Port 67) to acquire the needed network configuration.		
Directory Replicator	Directory Replicator: When configured, will replicate files and directories to other machines.		
Messenger	Messenger: Used to send messages to users or machines and sends messages from the Alerter service.		
Net Logon	Net Logon: Part of the security subsystem, enabling user authentication as well as keeping domain security in sync.		
Network DDE	Network DDE: Transport for Dynamic Data Exchange traffic, used by standard Office applications when sharing data over a network.		
Network DDE DSDM	Network DDE DSDM: DDE Share Database Manager, used by Network DDE service.		

Table 5.5 **Server Services Audit (***Continued***)**

Service	Purpose	Installed	Disabled
Plug and Play	Plug and Play.		
Remote Procedure Call (RPC) Locator	Remote Procedure Call Locator: Used by RPC applications to register availability of resources, and by clients to find compatible RPC server applications.		
Server	Server: Used to provide file and print resources to the network.		
SNMP Trap Service	SNMP Trap Service: Used by network administrators to monitor and to reach remote devices.		
Spooler (unless you need to spool printing)	Spooler: Stores print jobs and queues them to be printed.		
TCP/IP NetBIOS Helper	NetBIOS Helper: Passes normal TCP/IP connection requests to the sockets interface to allow NetBIOS resolution.		
Telephony Service	Telephony Service: Enables a telephony card or phone system to understand commands from an application via the operating system.		
Workstation (Required for Raptor Firewall)	Workstation: Manages connections to network resources such as drive mappings, printer connections, etc.		
Event Log	Event Log: Responsible for creating entries in the Event logs.		

Continued

Table 5.5 Server Services Audit (*Continued*)

Service	Purpose	Installed	Disabled
NT LM Security Support Provider	NT LM Security Support: The LSA handles all authentications before a user is allowed to access a resource.		
Remote Procedure Call (RPC) Service	RPC (RPC) Service: Name service provider that maintains a database with available RPC services on the server, where local RPC services can register themselves. A client can then contact the RPC locator on the server to locate and access the required RPC service.		
Schedule	Schedule: Used to run applications or batch/command files at specific times, using the at command.		
UPS	UPS: Generic uninterruptible power supply service, which shuts the machine down during a power failure.		

■ Never open any files or macros attached to an e-mail from an unknown, suspicious, or untrustworthy source. Delete these attachments immediately, then "double delete" them by emptying your Trash.
■ Delete spam, chain, and other junk e-mail without forwarding, in accordance with <Company Name>'s *Acceptable Use Policy.*
■ Never download files from unknown or suspicious sources.
■ Avoid direct disk sharing with read/write access unless there is absolutely a business requirement to do so.
■ Always scan a floppy diskette from an unknown source for viruses before using it.
■ Back up critical data and system configurations on a regular basis, and store the data in a safe place.
■ If lab testing conflicts with antivirus software, run the antivirus utility to ensure a clean machine, disable the

software, and then run the lab test. After the lab test, enable the antivirus software. When the antivirus software is disabled, do not run any applications that could transfer a virus, for example, e-mail or file sharing.
■ New viruses are discovered almost every day. Periodically check the *Lab Anti-Virus Policy* and this Recommended Processes list for updates

SANS AUDIT VULNERABILITY SCANNING POLICY [8]

This section presents a SANS policy template for vulnerability scanning. This policy defines the requirements and provides the authority for the information security team to conduct audits and risk assessments to ensure integrity of information/resources, to investigate incidents, to ensure conformance to security policies, or to monitor user/system activity where appropriate.

3.0 POLICY

When requested, and for the purpose of performing an audit, consent to access needed will be provided to members of <Internal or External Audit Name>. <Company Name> hereby provides its consent to allow <Internal or External Audit Name> to access its networks and/or firewalls to the extent necessary to allow [Audit organization] to perform the scans authorized in this agreement. <Company Name> shall provide protocols, addressing information, and network connections sufficient for <Internal or External Audit Name> to utilize the software to perform network scanning.

This access may include:

■ User level and/or system level access to any computing or communications device
■ Access to information (electronic, hardcopy, etc.) that may be produced, transmitted or stored on <Company Name> equipment or premises
■ Access to work areas (labs, offices, cubicles, storage areas, etc.)
■ Access to interactively monitor and log traffic on <Company Name> networks

3.1 NETWORK CONTROL

If Client does not control the network and/or Internet service is provided via a second or third party, these parties are required to approve scanning in writing if scanning is to occur outside of <Company Name's> LAN. By signing this agreement, all involved parties acknowledge that they authorize <Internal or External Audit Name> to use their service networks as a gateway for the conduct of these tests during the dates and times specified.

3.2 SERVICE DEGRADATION AND/ OR INTERRUPTION

Network performance and/or availability may be affected by network scanning. <Company Name> releases <Internal or External Audit Name> of any and all liability for damages that may arise from network availability restrictions caused by the network scanning, unless such damages are the result <Internal or External Audit Name>'s gross negligence or intentional misconduct.

3.3 CLIENT POINT OF CONTACT DURING THE SCANNING PERIOD

<Company Name> shall identify in writing a person to be available if the result <Internal or External Audit Name> Scanning Team has questions regarding data discovered or requires assistance.

3.4 SCANNING PERIOD

<Company Name> and <Internal or External Audit Name> Scanning Team shall identify in writing the allowable dates for the scan to take place.

4.0 ENFORCEMENT

Any employee found to have violated this policy may be subject to disciplinary action, up to and including termination of employment.

Source: SANS (http://www.sans.org/resources/policies/#template)

5.3.4.4 Security Policy of Activities

Activities of an information system consist of all procedures, regulations, policies, standards, and protocols governing all interactions between components of the information system, and between these components and the information system and its environment.

Any weakness in any activity of the information system can produce undesired events that can compromise the security of the information system. Any corruption in those activities can damage the information system in unpredictable ways.

A good security policy for activities has to define policy, standards, and guidelines that control the behavior of activities. A wrong policy may compromise the security of any system that has a security policy. This security policy should be revised periodically.

5.3.4.5 Security Policy for Data/Information

Conceptual resources are physically secured to prevent unauthorized disclosure or unauthorized modification of their content as well as destruction of information technology resources. Moreover, equipment used to process conceptual resources and buildings and office space housing information technology resources have to meet organizational physical security requirements. Security safeguards are acquired and maintained to ensure the continued availability and security of each facility's information technology equipment.

Information security is the protection of information resources against unauthorized access. Conceptual resources, such as programs, data, and information, can be secured by applying passwords and digital certificates by authorized users. While passwords prove that a correct code has been entered, we are still unsure that the actual user is, in fact, the one who entered the password. We can obviously employ digital certificates and biometric techniques to authenticate the user and control access to the information resources, but security can still be compromised because there are many other violations such as eavesdropping that can take place.

At the same time, users who have been authenticated and admitted into the system may prove to be dangerous. Such users, once admitted, may initiate unauthorized activities or may even intentionally perform malicious actions that could compromise the security of the system.

A good security policy has to define the behaviors of data and information when stored, when being processed, when transmitted, and when disposed of.

5.3.5 Security Policy Based on Computing Boundaries

In order to define a security policy based on computing boundaries, we obviously have to start with defining local/internal and remote boundaries. For instance, we have to divide the computing environment into internal computing zones and remote/external computing zones. Those computing zones are connected using data flows to each other. External users and personnel/internal users are also connected to various computing zones. Figure 5.7 depicts how a computing environment may be organized to develop a security policy based on computing boundaries.

By examining Figure 5.7, we can see that the security policy for personnel, external users, local computing zones, remote computing zones, and information flows between zones. Resources need to be defined to understand how the computing environment is affected by computing behaviors on various resources

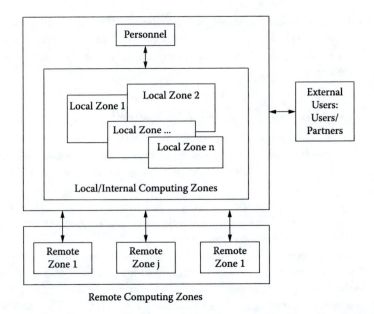

Figure 5.7 The computing environment organized to develop a security policy.

in the computing environments. This will also tell us how to authorize processing on those resources and in various computing zones constituting the computing environments:

Communications Definitions
> The Communications definitions describe the configuration of other systems with which your various zones in the computing environment can communicate. Each CD entry describes an internal computing zone or a remote system.

File Definitions (FD)
> The File Definitions (FD) define data files that are available in various computing zones in the computing environment, including remote computing zones. You can define remote and local files in the FD.

Gateway Definitions (GD)
> The Gateway Definitions (GD) define gateways to other systems with which internal/local and remote zones can communicate.

Monitoring Definitions (MD)
> The Monitoring Definitions (MD) specify the destination and contents of monitoring output from all internal/local and remote computing zones.

Zone Definitions (ZD)
> The Zone Definitions (ZD) define all the parameters that are used by the computing environment. The ZD includes parameters that are used to

define new local or remote computing zones and parameters that are used to configure various information resources in computing zones.

Transient Data Definitions (TDD)

The Transient Data Definitions (TDD) define transient data exchanged between various computing zones. The definition also includes data exchange between local and remote computing zones.

User Definitions (UD)

The User Definitions (UD) define user class information. In order to define security policy for personnel associated with a specific computing zone, we need to know all user access/processing requirements in addition to personnel requirements.

5.3.6 Benson's Security Policy Methodology

5.3.6.1 Methodology for Defining Security Strategies

Benson proposes a methodology for defining a computer security strategy that can be used to implement security policies and controls to minimize possible attacks and threats. The methodology may be used for all types of attacks: malicious, nonmalicious, or natural disasters. This methodology is based on the various types of threats, methods of attack, and vulnerabilities. Figure 5.8 depicts a flowchart outlining the methodology, borrowed from Christopher Benson, Inobits Consulting (Pty) Ltd.

Benson's framework for developing a security strategy is a very powerful tool in developing a security policy too. It starts with predicting attacks and assessing risks; then, based on this information, a proactive security strategy is put in place. If the proactive strategy fails to work as intended, then a reactive strategy is in place to assess damage, determine the cause of damage, repair the damage, and then document and learn and implement a contingency plan as needed. If a simulation is conducted to study the effects of multiple scenarios on the effectiveness of the present security policy, the findings may be used to revise the security policy. The process in Figure 5.8 may be re-iterated when new incidents take place, which will lead to a review of the effectiveness of the existing security policy and its revision. The process in Figure 5.8 can then be used to create and revise the security policy.

5.3.6.2 Proactive Strategy

Proactive strategy defines steps intended to prevent attacks before they occur. The steps are designed to study the effects of potential attacks on the computing environment. The knowledge assembled will be used in implementing security policies that will manage the attacks. These are the three steps of the proactive strategy, as suggested by Benson et al.:

1. Determine the damage that the attack will cause.

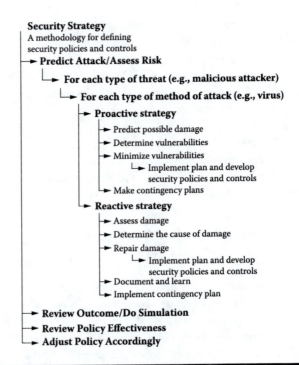

Security Strategy
A methodology for defining
security policies and controls
→ **Predict Attack/Assess Risk**
  ↳→ **For each type of threat (e.g., malicious attacker)**
    ↳→ **For each type of method of attack (e.g., virus)**
      →┌ **Proactive strategy**
       │ → Predict possible damage
       │ → Determine vulnerabilities
       │ → Minimize vulnerabilities
       │   ↳→ Implement plan and develop
       │   security policies and controls
       │ → Make contingency plans
      →└ **Reactive strategy**
         → Assess damage
         → Determine the cause of damage
         → Repair damage
            ↳→ Implement plan and develop
                security policies and controls
         → Document and learn
         → Implement contingency plan
→ **Review Outcome/Do Simulation**
→ **Review Policy Effectiveness**
↳→ **Adjust Policy Accordingly**

Figure 5.8   Flowcharts outlining Benson's methodology.

2. Determine the vulnerabilities and weaknesses that the attack will exploit.
3. Minimize the vulnerabilities and weaknesses that are determined to be weak points in the system for that specific type of attack.

5.3.6.3 Reactive Strategy

A reactive strategy takes over when the proactive strategy fails. The reactive strategy is intended to identify the damage and the vulnerabilities at the origin of the attack, repair the damage, and implement a contingency plan, as needed. Both the reactive and proactive strategies work together to develop security policies. The incident response team will assess the current situation and learn in terms of what has not worked and should be done differently to prevent similar undesired incidents in the future. The knowledge gained will be used to revise the existing security policy.

The reactive strategy consists of the following steps:

Assess the damage
Determine the cause of the damage
Repair the damage
Document and learn
Implement contingency plan

Following the reactive strategy, the present security policy is reviewed and adjusted as follows:

Review outcome/do simulations
Review policy effectiveness
Adjust policy accordingly

5.3.6.4 Assess the Damage

The damage is studied as it occurred in the computing environment. Damage assessment has to be performed in a timely manner. The contingency plan, if one exists, has to be applied in a conservative manner to resume business operations.

5.3.6.5 Determine the Cause of the Damage

In order to determine the cause of the damage, it is necessary to understand the model of the attack and the resources employed. These resources are often dictated by system vulnerabilities. The review of system logs, audit logs, and audit trails may be needed to study all steps of the attack, at its initiation, transition, or execution.

5.3.6.6 Repair the Damage

The damage has to be repaired as quickly as possible to restore normal business operations. Usually, the attacks will not be serious enough to evoke disaster recovery or major business continuity procedures, but recovery procedures should be planned and implemented as needed. The incident response team should be involved in documenting the entire recovery process, and the knowledge gained will be needed to review the effectiveness of the present security policy and adjust it accordingly.

5.3.6.7 Document and Learn

Documentation should cover all steps of managing the attack. This should include information about vulnerabilities, how they were exploited, what the consequences were, what the damage was, and what corrective and recovery actions were needed. The documentation will be needed to modify proactive strategies for preventing future attacks or minimizing damage.

5.3.6.8 Implement Contingency Plan

If a contingency plan already exists, it can be implemented to save time and to keep business operations functioning correctly. If a contingency plan does not exist, it is about time to develop one. The information collected throughout the attack and response process will be needed to develop the contingency plan.

5.3.6.9 Review Outcome/Do Simulations

So far, we have experienced an attack, defended against it, and reviewed the attack's consequences. Reviewing the outcome includes the review of loss in productivity, loss of data, loss of equipment, and corrective actions. The review process has to be fully documented, as it is needed to design the simulation of attack scenarios.

5.3.6.10 Review Policy Effectiveness

Information collected throughout the attack and response process is used to review the current security policy and its revision. If there is no policy in place, then a new one has to developed based on the attack and response information at hand.

5.3.6.11 Adjust Policy Accordingly

If the effectiveness of the security policy is not adequate to handle attacks similar to the one studied using the reactive security strategy steps, the present policy has to be revised. If a security policy does not exist, a new one has to be written. Anyhow, the organization's security policy should respect any standards or guidelines the organization currently follows.

5.4 Summary

This chapter presented several definitions of security policy. It then discussed the Corporate Vital Defense Strategy and Raggad's information security taxonomy. The chapter introduced the policy flow diagram methodology and a generic method based on Raggad's taxonomy. The chapter then showed how to develop a security policy based on a partition of the computing environment and on computing boundaries. A final security policy methodology that you can find at the end of the chapter is Benson's methodology.

5.5 Review Questions

1. Explain how policy, standards, and guidelines relate to each other. How is this relationship relevant in building security policy. Give an example.
2. Explain, in your own way, how role-based security policy works.
3. Give an example of security policy built using the role-based security policy methodology.
4. Develop a security policy for physical security using RBAC.

5. Explain how Raggad's taxonomy works. Explain how is it useful in developing security policy.
6. Explain how Raggad's taxonomy is useful in intrusion detection.
7. Explain how pfd methodology works for developing security policy.
8. How can a security policy based on a computing environment partition be written? Give a simple example.
9. How can a security policy based on computing boundaries be written? Give a simple example.
10. How can a security policy be written using Benson's methodology? Give a simple example.

5.6 Workshops

Workshop 1

Consider a student computer laboratory that has 20 computers connected in a LAN. The LAN is connected to the Internet. A technical assistant is in charge of the lab. Use the pfd methodology to write the lab security policy.

Workshop 2

Consider a student computer laboratory that has 20 computers connected in a LAN. The LAN is connected to the Internet. A technical assistant is in charge of the lab. Use the Benson methodology to write the lab security policy.

Workshop 3

Consider a student computer laboratory that has 20 computers connected in a LAN. The LAN is connected to the Internet. A technical assistant is in charge of the lab. Use RBAC methodology to write the lab security policy.

References

1. Cohen, F. B., *Protection and security on the Information Superhighway*, John Wiley & Sons, New York, 1995.
2. Connolly, J. L., and B. S. Abramowitz, The Trust Technology Assessment Program and the Benefits to U.S. Evaluations, *Proceedings of the 11th Annual Computer Security Applications Conference*, pp. 157–161, New Orleans, LA, December 1995.
3. NSA, Solution Development and Deployment, and Technical Directors, Information Assurance Technical Framework, Release 2.0.2, 1999.
4. Whitten, J. L., L. D. Bentley, and V. M. Barlow, *Systems analysis and design methods*, Irwin, Homewood, IL, 1996.

5. Novell, White Paper: Smart Implementation of Role-based Access Control, http://www.novell.com/consulting/4622046.pdf, visited on November 28, 2008.

6. Raggad, B, Corporate Vital Defense Strategy, http://csrc.nist.gov/nissc/2000/proceedings/papers/029.pdf

7. SANS-1: The SANS Security Policy Project, http://www.sans.org/resources/policies/#template, visited on November 28, 2008.

8. SANS-2: A Short Primer for Developing Security Policies, http://www.sans.org/resources/policies/Policy_Primer.pdf, visited on November 28, 2008.

9. SANS-3: SANS Policy Primer, http://www.sans.org/resources/policies/, visited on November 28, 2008.

Chapter 6

Business Continuity Planning

Learning Objectives

After reading this chapter, students are expected to achieve an understanding of:

- What a business continuity is
- What disaster recovery is
- The difference between business continuity and disaster recovery
- Categories of business disruptions
- How to respond to business disruptions
- Detective actions in business continuity
- Preventive actions in business continuity
- Deterrence actions in business continuity
- Corrective actions in business continuity
- What a business continuity plan is
- What a disaster recovery plan is
- How to develop a business continuity plan
- How to perform business continuity planning
- What a recovery point objective is
- What a recovery time objective is
- What a business continuity strategy is
- What a business continuity scope is
- What a business continuity policy is
- How to conduct a business continuity feasibility study
- How to perform a business continuity analysis

How to perform risk identification
How to perform risk assessment
How to perform business continuity design
How to perform risk mitigation
How to perform risk management
What a business continuity program is
What a business continuity statement of applicability is
How to perform business continuity implementation
How to perform business continuity maintenance
How to perform business impact analysis
How to use SWOT analysis in business impact analysis.

6.1 Introduction

No organization nowadays is immune to business disruptions. These disruptions may be caused by Internet-based attacks, natural disasters, man-made incidents, or technological failures. Financial losses and social consequences may be unbearable. Only those organizations that implement adequate safeguards to deter the agents producing business disruptions, detect them, prevent them, and repair any damage caused have a chance to survive those business disruptions.

AT&T's 2007 study [17] on business continuity and disaster recovery preparedness for U.S. business in the private sector reports that 30% of U.S. businesses are still not prepared for the worst-case scenario associated with both natural and man-made disasters. In the 2007 AT&T Business Continuity Study, companies understand that man-made disasters are a real threat, although many of them have a false sense of security.

The AT&T's Business Continuity Study also surveyed 1000 IT executives at companies with more than $10 million in annual revenue throughout the United States for their views on disaster planning and business continuity trends. In this study [18], New York and Houston business executives indicated that business continuity planning had become a priority in recent years because of natural disasters, security, and terrorist threats.

AT&T has invested, in the last decade, more than half a billion dollars in its Network Disaster Recovery programs. They prepared specially trained managers, engineers, and technicians from across the United States. They additionally committed a variety of resources consisting of more than 150 self-contained equipment trailers, and support vehicles that house the same equipment and components as an AT&T data-routing or voice-switching center [18].

Worms and viruses alone are causing the affected organizations to lose about $2 million in revenues per incident. More than 80% of the organizations surveyed by Aberdeen [2] reported that their business operations were disrupted and disabled by Internet security events during the last 3 years. Although the average rate of disruption of business operations was only one incident per year, about 15% of the surveyed companies said their operations were halted and disabled more than seven times over a period of 3 years [2].

Disruptive agents on the Internet have caused organizations to be concerned about their business continuity. Attacks that can disrupt continuity include worms, viruses, spyware, denial-of-service, and hacker attacks on business resources. Eighty-six percent of the surveyed organizations were worried that their operations may be exposed to Internet-based threats; 80% were also worried about network outages; 80% were worried about compromised IT systems; 85% were worried about threats to data integrity; and 71% were worried about human errors that may lead to Internet business disruptions [2].

Organizations are concerned about several classes of disruptive agents, which we list in descending order of importance, as follows [2]:

1. Internet-based threats
2. Compromises to data integrity
3. Network outages
4. Compromised IT systems
5. Human errors

While many surveys have been conducted recently [3,5,17] to study many aspects of business continuity, disaster recovery, and security, and the effects of disaster recoveries on business assets, we have only reported selected findings from them.

This chapter discusses business continuity concepts and their implementation.

6.2 Business Disruptions

A business can be disrupted in many different ways. Depending on the criticality of the business components that have been hit, the losses can be of any size. While some business components can be fully recovered, others may be only partially recovered or may be lost for good. Also, while some corrective and recovery activities can be easy, quick, and inexpensive, other such activities can be very difficult, slow, and very costly.

We will see later in this chapter that we can use business analysis to study the criticality of business assets and business impact analysis to estimate the effects of business disruption on business. These two activities are very important steps in the business continuity project.

It is difficult to accurately determine business losses following a business disruption. In order to estimate the effects of disruption events on business assets, you have to know a lot more than the specifications of the affected business assets. Business losses are not only financial, but also social, technical, operational, ethical, and legal. You need to be very familiar with the organization's strategic plan, business mission and vision, and strategic objectives and values.

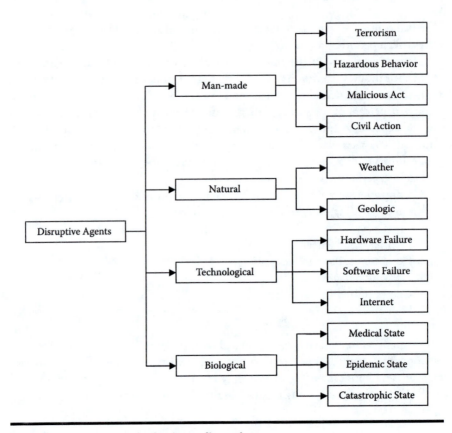

Figure 6.1   Taxonomy for business disruptions.

Many factors can affect the recovery process of a business component, such as the following:

■ Criticality of the business component
■ Cost of the recovery process
■ Type of the disruptive agent
■ Type of the damage inflicted
■ Extent of the damage
■ Time of detection of the disruption

The literature provides many taxonomies [4,6] that organize the disruptive agents into classes in terms of a variety of discrimination parameters. In this chapter, we present, as shown in Figure 6.1, a simple taxonomy of business disruptive agents that divides them into four classes:

1. Natural
2. Technological

3. Man-made
4. Biological

There are many ways to counter business disruptions [7,8], including business continuity, disaster recovery, emergency plans, contingency plans, and so on. However, we will only examine business continuity and disaster recovery plans.

6.3 Business Continuity

Business continuity is the ability of an organization to respond to disaster or business disruption through the timely detection of the disruption event, the accurate measurement of risks and business losses, and the efficient resumption of business operations.

The National Fire Protection Association (NFPA), defined business continuity as follows [9]:

> Business Continuity is an ongoing process supported by senior management and funded to ensure that the necessary steps are taken to identify the impact of potential losses, maintain viable recovery strategies, recovery plans, and continuity of services.
>
> **NFPA**

This definition requires that management fund and support the business continuity effort. Business continuity is an ongoing process that keeps track of all possible losses and their impacts on the organization. It is also responsible for maintaining viable safeguards capable of facilitating an effective and quick recovery and ensuring continuity of business services.

6.4 Disaster Recovery

In addition to business continuity, other activities are concerned with an organization's responsive capabilities to business disruptions. Disaster recovery is an example that is related to business continuity.

Disaster recovery is the activity of resuming computing operations after a disaster, such as floods, severe storms, or geologic incidents, takes place. Restoration of the computing environment is often achieved through the duplication of computing operations. Disaster recovery is also concerned with routine off-site backup, as well as writing and implementing procedures for activating vital information systems in a safer computing environment.

The quality of disaster recovery is given by the organization's ability to recover information systems quickly after a disaster. While a good disaster recovery system allows the organization to have its computing operations running immediately after the occurrence of the disaster, with a poor disaster recovery system, the organization may take several days, or forever, to restore its computing environment.

The scope of the design of a disaster recovery plan depends on many factors, including the type of the incident, data affected, and business losses. The recovery from a disaster attempts to reestablish a computing environment configuration that can produce acceptable business operating conditions.

The World Trade Center in New York was attacked on September 11, 2001. Recovery has been slow and very costly. Some businesses are still recovering, others are yet to recover, and some cannot ever recover. The literature [9] reported that the cost of business interruptions for the World Trade Center attacks reached between $35 billion and $70 billion.

The undesired incidents may be as simple as a faulty connection or as complex as a natural disaster. Incidents can be man-made, such as a fire, or an act of God, such as an earthquake or tornado. In case of a big fire that burns the infrastructure, a local redundancy system may not be effective, and an immediate restoration of business will not be possible. Instead, a disaster recovery plan has to be activated that is capable of rebuilding the necessary components and installing them for the purpose of restoring any acceptable conditions for business operations.

However, management is often in denial, believing that disaster only happens to others, and hence fails to take the necessary precautions to avoid business interruptions due to disruptive events. Business losses due to business disturbances can be prevented if the right business continuity activities have been adequately implemented. Any lengthy business disruptions can be avoided if the necessary disaster recovery actions have been planned.

An organization's computing environment is becoming larger, more complex, and even more integrated. It is very rare that a piece of information, at an information resource, anywhere in the computing environment, can be compromised without affecting other areas of the computing environment. Direct financial losses in one area of the computing environment can rapidly propagate from one functional unit to another functional unit. Indirect financial losses can travel from one unit to another through the losses due to aggrieved customers and their complaints.

That is, any organization of any size will obviously need a proactive business continuity plan to prevent any short business disruptions and a feasible reactive disaster recovery plan to be able to recover from short or long business discontinuities resulting from disasters.

6.5 Responding to Business Disruptions

Business disruptions can happen any time, anywhere in the organization, and without prior notice. The organization, however, should feasibly adopt all available safeguards and defense strategies to minimize the effects of any business disruptions on its business assets. Those safeguards are often divided into four classes:

1. Deterrence safeguards
2. Detective safeguards
3. Preventive safeguards
4. Corrective safeguards

6.5.1 Deterrence Safeguards

The adoption of any deterrence techniques should aim at communicating to disruptive agents that the consequences of committing crimes against the organization surpass the benefits they will obtain from these crimes. The organization should publish previous cases where attackers were caught and punished. Deterrence theory is based on the assumption that when you punish a person for the benefit of society, you will deter others from doing the same [10].

Deterrence can be implemented in several ways:

Sign deterrence
Physical deterrence
Software deterrence
Hardware deterrence

Sign deterrence approaches work by designing appropriate warnings and deterring messages that are communicated in different ways to potential disruptive agents. A domestic example may be the putting of a warning sign saying "watch for the dog," or "private road," or "trespassers will be prosecuted." Most security companies such as ADT and CDT use warning signs stating that the property is protected by the security company at all windows and doors and also around the property.

Many organizations also insert banners containing warning messages, including deterrence for local, state, and federal laws, and stories of previous cases where attackers have been prosecuted and imprisoned, on their Web sites. These deterrence stories do not have to be drawn from cases that happened in the organization, but could be any cases that have been published by other companies in other media but reported here to warn potential attackers of what they expect if they attempt to attack the organization.

The physical deterrence approach employs physical barriers or appliances that scare potential attackers away. Installing barriers at all entry and exit gates to the organization may deter certain types of disruptive agents who employ heavy machinery or vehicles to conduct attacks. A security guard at the door can also scare away potential attackers from attempting to enter with fake IDs.

Software and hardware tools may be useful in deterring potential attackers from conducting harmful attacks against the organization. Installing a firewall at network entry points may scare away those attackers who fear they will be detected and discovered by the firewall.

6.5.2 Detective Safeguards

The earlier you detect a disruptive event, the easier it will be to respond to the disruption and the easier it will be to recover from consequences caused by the disruption. The minute an attack is detected, many activities will be initiated by the organization:

Collect information about the disruptive agent.
Collect information about the attack.
Collect information about the progress of the attack.
Collect information about the impact.
Plan the appropriate incident response.
Initiate recovery procedures.

The feasible adoption of detective mechanisms is a central requirement for the organization. An earlier chapter on intrusion detection systems provides detailed information on how to plan, analyze, design, implement, and maintain these systems.

6.5.3 Preventive Safeguards

Prevention is the recommended way for an organization to protect its computing environment. It can save the organization all the adversity and losses in managing detection and correction activities. Usually, preventive safeguards do not cost the organization more than a fraction of the recovery costs in case a disruptive event takes place.

Preventive controls have to be applied in many areas where risk is not acceptable.

Preventive controls may be applied in human resource management, where hiring procedures have to ensure that only reliable and competent personnel are hired. Candidates for any position in the organization have to go through background checks, drug screening, etc., as stated in the organization's security policy.

The organization's security policy also contains regulations on all types of physical security, such as fire safety, protection from water damage, or other aspects of physical security. Here are examples of preventive actions in the physical security area:

Fire safety:
    Detection systems, tested regularly
    Electrical wiring in good condition

Fire detection in all concealed spaces
Fire-resistant structure
Regular inspection by fire marshall
Insurance:
Claims records maintained safely
Natural disasters covered
Policy up to date
Protection from water damage:
Appropriate dehumidifiers available
No leakage/seepage through walls
No pipe/plumbing leaks
Pipes and plumbing well supported
Water detectors present
Security:
Building exterior well lighted
Intrusion detectors/alarms present and monitored 24 hours
Locks/alarms on all windows and doors

6.5.4 Corrective Safeguards

Unless we have all the information needed about the current attack, the business components that have been attacked, and the damage caused to them, we cannot initiate any corrective actions. As soon as we have this information, the following activities can be initiated:

1. Rank affected business components in terms of their criticality.
2. Rank affected business components in terms of damage extent.
3. Identify alternate corrective actions.
4. Select the most feasible alternate corrective safeguard.
5. Apply the selected corrective actions to the selected business components.

While the foregoing steps should be undertaken whenever a business disruption takes place, there are several business disruptions that have to be managed through more comprehensive corrective approaches, given the extensive damage and losses they can cause to the company. We only examine one comprehensive corrective safeguard: business continuity plan (BCP). A disaster recovery plan (DRP) is simply the part of the business continuity plan that is concerned with the organization's computing environment.

6.5.4.1 What Is a Business Continuity Plan?

Sun Microsystems [11] defines business continuity as follows:

The process of creating, testing, and maintaining an organizationwide plan to recover from any form of disaster is called business continuity planning (BCP). Every BCP strategy includes three fundamental components: risk assessment, contingency planning, and the actual disaster recovery process. BCP should encompass every type of business interruption—from the slightest two-second power outage or spike up to the worst possible natural disaster or terrorist attack.

A business continuity plan (BCP) is a sequence of steps approved by upper management that presents what the organization should do to restore business operations when a disruptive event takes place. This plan concerns the entire organization, including any disaster recovery departments or teams that have been created by the IT unit.

The BCP remains the main source of guidelines defining any activities prescribed for the management of any effort, such as assessing the disruption and its business impact, coordinating the corrective controls needed to restore business operations, and evaluating the business continuity outcomes, intended to restore or enhance business operations when a business disruption occurs.

The BCP aims at providing feasible restoration of all business operations, including information technology, in a prompt manner. The BCP will contain, for each functional unit and its departments, a description of all the requirements necessary for continued operations.

We will see later, when we compare the business continuity effort to a similar effort called the disaster recovery plan, that the duration of business restoration is planned to be as short as possible, when compared to disaster recovery activities. Usually, prompt restoration is possible as business services may be restored using available backup systems. We later present a brief introduction to business backup systems.

Let us examine the BCP definition proposed by The Business Continuity Institute [12]:

> BCP is a holistic management process that identifies potential impacts that threaten an organization and provides a framework for building resilience with the capacity for an effective response that safeguards the interests of key stakeholders, reputation, brand, and value creating activities.

This definition introduces several important requirements for the business continuity process. It emphasizes that the main objective for business continuity is to safeguard the interests of stakeholders, reputation, brand, and value-creating activities. The business continuity process establishes a comprehensive framework for building resilience through scanning the environment for potential business disruption threats, measuring and managing risks, and devising an effective business continuity response system.

6.5.4.2 What Is a Disaster Recovery Plan?

A disaster recovery plan is the sequence of steps approved by management to recover from a disruptive incident so that business may be restored to an acceptable level of operation.

A disruptive incident may be as small as a faulty switch, or as large as the work of terrorism. These undesired incidents may be the work of nature, such as fires, earthquakes, floods, storms, and so on; the work of man, such as man-made attacks, workers' strike, malicious programs, viruses, and so on; or the work of technology, such as network congestion, malfunctioning hardware, or faulty telecommunication devices.

6.5.4.2.1 Why do We Need a Disaster Recovery Plan?

Unfortunately, these days, there is probably nothing easier than justifying the need for a disaster recovery. Terrorism is on the rise. Internet attacks are on the rise. Natural threats and unpredictable weather changes are on the rise. Our dependency on technology is on the rise. Our exposure to unsafe global computing, as well as open connections to the Internet and, consequently, to the rest of the world, are on the rise.

We may need to fight on multiple fronts in order to protect the organization. We need to fight terrorism every single day. Even though the likelihood of this threat seems to be low, its high impact will make it a high priority for the organization. It is better to be safe than sorry. The readiness of the organization to respond to any type of threat is important, despite any risk and feasibility equations that may say otherwise.

Figure 6.2 illustrates the effects of natural, man-made, technological, and biological threats on an organization's computing environment. Disaster recovery is, in fact, IT recovery as business continuity is restored by restoring the computing environment. The restored computing environment may not, however, be good enough to resume the business configuration that was in place when the disaster took place. The latest business configuration that can be reactivated using the restored disaster recovery plan is acceptable.

We obviously need a disaster recovery plan. The following is a list or reasons that can confirm or justify the need for a disaster recovery plan:

Vandalism, riots, and union strikes may affect the computing environment.
Increased likelihood of faulty technology.
Increased likelihood of malicious software and faulty safeguards.
Loss of services if the computing environment is compromised.
Technology dependence on an unstable power supply.
Historical data gives bad news about disaster events.
Significant business impact may be mitigated.

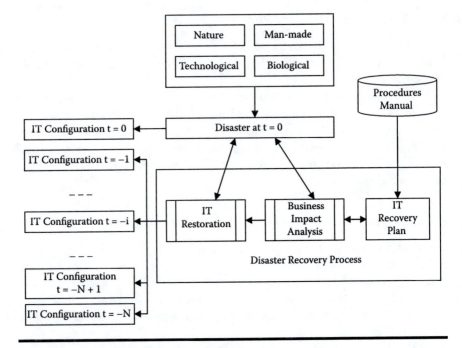

Figure 6.2   A disaster recovery process.

Attractive lower costs of disaster recovery plan compared to business losses when a disaster takes place.

Employees are not ready and do not know what to do if a disaster happens.

A backup of previous configurations becomes available for future restoration when needed.

There is a need to develop a recovery strategy for the recovery effort to succeed.

It is a good idea to make business performance independent of IT failure.

6.5.4.3 Coexistence of BCP and DRP

In real life, most companies that use business continuity plans also use disaster recovery plans. Nevertheless, there is often confusion in the literature in distinguishing between a business continuity plan and a disaster recovery plan. Many people still use the terms interchangeably. People also refer to both plans as contingency plans.

The business continuity plan is actually the result of a comprehensive business process that includes the disaster recovery plan, meant for the IT functional unit. Figure 6.3 shows that the IT unit is in charge of the computing environment for the entire company and that the disaster recovery program documented in the disaster recovery plan is concerned only with the computing environment and not the business system of the organization. The disaster recovery plan is a very important component of the business continuity system.

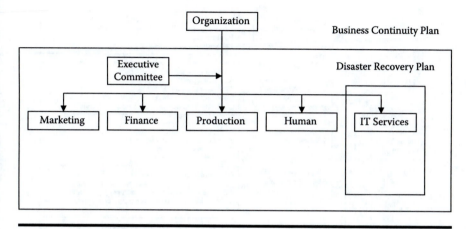

Figure 6.3 Coexisting business continuity and disaster recovery plans.

6.6 Developing a BCP

The development of a business continuity plan, as depicted in Figure 6.4, requires five phases:

1. Business continuity planning
2. Business continuity analysis
3. Business continuity design
4. Business continuity implementation
5. Business continuity maintenance

The business continuity planning phase is intended to generate ideas for creating and organizing the business continuity project. The business continuity analysis phase is needed to analyze business continuity conditions and study business criticality and requirements, risks, and business impact. The business continuity design phase aims at producing a feasible design of the business continuity program that will be documented as a business continuity plan. The last two phases of the business continuity project are concerned with implementing and maintaining the business continuity program and plan. Figure 6.4 illustrates the layout of the business continuity project management process.

6.6.1 Business Continuity Planning

In order to plan the business continuity project, we need to define the scope of the business continuity project, and its objectives. All members of the business continuity project team have to be familiar with the organization's business continuity policy, if one exists. The business continuity policy defines the acceptable behavior of the business continuity program. Before ending the business continuity

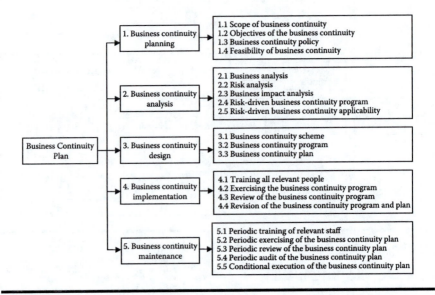

Figure 6.4 Business continuity plan steps.

planning phase, the feasibility study of the project has to be completed and submitted to upper management for approval.

Planning the business continuity project should follow these steps:

1. Scope of business continuity
2. Objectives of business continuity
3. Business continuity policy
4. Feasibility of business continuity

6.6.1.1 Scope of Business Continuity

Business continuity may vary in scope and in budget. While the scope can restrict the BCP to one information resource or one device, it can also be concerned with one location or the totality of the organization. Often, the scope of a BCP is formulated in terms of a set of generic geographic delineations, as follows:

Disruption in computer server
Disruption in computer network
Disruption in one functional unit
Disruption in an office building
Disruption in a remote location
Total disruption

When the scope is fixed, the BCP will serve as a guide that describes how the organization can continue to carry out its business operations as they are initially

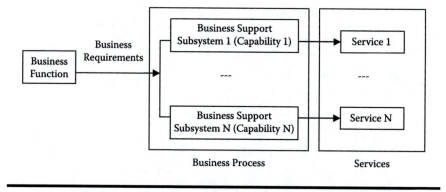

Figure 6.5   Business system structured to make business analysis easier.

defined for this scope. The BCP defines the existing configuration in its working conditions, evaluates any changes effected by the undesired event, and devises the necessary corrective actions needed to restore the business operations back to the initial or to better working conditions.

Figure 6.5 shows how a business process may be managed to produce the business services stated in the organization's business mission. The business support subsystems shown in this diagram are integrated together to produce the business services intended for the business function.

The organization may be viewed as a set of business functions. Each function has very clear business objectives and well-defined business requirements. The business requirements are transformed into business services, using well-defined business processes or capabilities.

A BCP is, in fact, a business function, such as project management, marketing, sales, and so on. It manages a live document describing the proactive process for defining the corrective controls needed to respond to disruptive events for the purpose of bringing the organization's business operations back to normal.

Even though there are many methodologies that may be useful in defining the scope of the business continuity project, they are only used to provide decision support information that upper management may need when it defines the scope of the project.

Usually, however, the scope of the business continuity project should include all critical business functions, business processes and capabilities, and business services, as the budget allows.

Table 6.1 shows a generic example that may serve as a decision aid to help management define the scope of its business continuity project. Given the usual budget constraints, we just cannot include all business components in the scope of the business continuity project. It will not be feasible. A business component is defined in terms of its business function, business process, and business service. For example, the output of a good-quality product or service is a business component

Table 6.1 How to Define Business Continuity Scope

Business Functions	Business Processes	Business Services	Criticality (1–5)	Cost	Rank	Scope
BF1	BP11	BS111	2	280 K	6	E
		BS112	4	120 K	2	I
	BP12	BS121	3	320 K	5	E
		BS122	2	140 K	6	E
BF2	BP21	BS211	1	260 K	15	E
		BS212	3	460 K	5	E
		BS213	5	580 K	1	I
		BS214	2	430 K	6	E
	BP22	BS221	2	340 K	6	E
		BS222	3	160 K	5	E
BF3	BP31	BS311	2	180 K	6	E
		BS312	3	246 K	5	E
	BP32	BS321	4	240 K	2	I
		BS322	4	420 K	2	I
	BP33	BS331	2	250 K	6	E
		BS332	1	240 K	15	E

Note: I—Include in scope; E—Exclude.

associated with the manufacturing/production unit, the total quality management process, and the delivery of service or product, say, the triplet (BF1, BP12, BS122), as shown in Table 6.1.

All business components are assigned a criticality score between 1 and 5 expressed in terms of direct contribution to the organization's business value generation capability, and defined as follows:

1. Noncritical: Negligible contribution to the organization's business value; the organization may incur negligible losses.
2. Little critical: Little contribution to the organization's business value; the organization may incur modest losses.
3. Moderate criticality: Moderate contribution to the organization's business value; the organization may incur moderate losses.

4. Critical: Strong contribution to the organization's business value; without this business component, the organization may incur great losses, but can always be turned around.
5. Very critical: Very strong contribution to the organization's business value; without this business component, the organization will incur major losses and it may not be possible to turn it around.

Once we have criticality scores for all business components (part of the scope study), we need to rank them in descending order. The higher the criticality score of the business component, the lower the business component's rank. Table 6.1 displays the rank for all business components; the first four business components selected to be part of the scope are as follows:

(BF2, BP21, BS213): Rank 1: Cost = $580K
(BF1, BP11, BS112): Rank 2: Cost = $120K
(BF3, BP32, BS321): Rank 2: Cost = $240K
(BF3, BP32, BS322): Rank 2: Cost = $420K

Given a budget of $1500K, and given that the total cost of including the first four critical business components is $1360K, we cannot include more than the afore-mentioned first four critical business components. The first business component that comes after the first four is (BF2, BP22, BS222) with a rank of 5 and a cost of $160K. If we add the fifth critical business component to the scope, we will need a total of $1520K, which exceeds the budget of $1500K. Because the amount needed to include the first five critical business components is greater than the available budget, we decided only to include the first four business components in the scope.

6.6.1.2 Objectives of Business Continuity

Even though the main objective of business continuity is to resume business in case a disruptive event takes place, there are more detailed objectives that are very specific to the type of business services the organization offers. The business continuity team has to discuss with all upper managers whose business functions are candidates for the business continuity project and attempt to elicit their thinking and preferences concerning any business continuity objectives.

Once all candidate business continuity objectives are identified, they are thoroughly studied and negotiated with concerned upper managers to retain only those that can be feasibly achieved. The definition of business continuity objectives is a very important step in any business continuity project as it will considerably affect the feasibility of the project and the effectiveness of the generated business continuity plan.

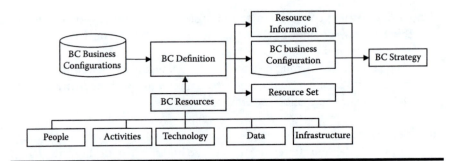

Figure 6.6 Business continuity definition.

6.6.1.3 Business Continuity Policy

The business continuity policy is the acceptable behavior of the organization's business continuity program. Upper managers responsible for all business functions should document their business function policies. These function policies should be fully consistent with all organization's business and security policies.

The business continuity team should thoroughly review the business continuity policy for the purpose of fully understanding it. Managers of the business functions who are members of the initial business continuity team may test the business continuity analysts on their understanding of their respective business continuity policies. It is imperative that all business continuity analysts in the team know the business continuity policy. Any deficiency or lack of understanding of the business continuity policy will be translated into inefficient business operations after resumption, following the business disruption.

As shown in Figure 6.6, the business continuity definition step aims at defining all the resources needed to continue business under any business continuity configuration previously accepted by the organization. All postdisruption business continuity configurations acceptable to the organization are usually specified in the business continuity policy.

6.6.1.4 Feasibility Study

If a business disruption occurs, then the organization will incur great financial and nonfinancial losses. The feasibility of the business continuity project aims at ensuring that the financial and nonfinancial benefits of the project outweigh its financial and nonfinancial costs. Figure 6.7 illustrates feasibility components that have to be studied before determining whether or not the business continuity project is feasible.

The business continuity feasibility has five feasibility components:

Financial feasibility
Social feasibility

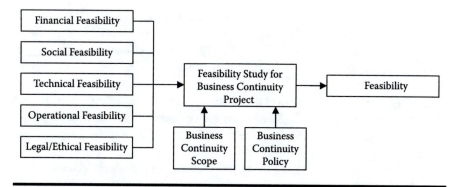

Figure 6.7   Feasibility study for a business continuity project.

Technical feasibility
Operational feasibility
Legal/ethical feasibility

The financial feasibility component is concerned with cost-benefit analyses that ensure that the benefit of the business continuity project is greater than the total costs incurred by the project. Techniques such as the net present value or the internal rate of return may apply.

The social feasibility component aims at ensuring that any social effects caused by the business continuity project inside the organization or in its environment are acceptable. For example, the project should not put any employee's family to hardship when this employee is called to work in the emergency response team; or if a disaster occurs, nobody should be exposed to danger as part of the business continuity plan.

The technical feasibility component is concerned with the availability of the technology or technical solutions needed to implement the business continuity plan and carry out its activity as indicated in the business continuity policy.

The operational feasibility component is needed to ensure that all employees accept the business continuity plan as it is defined in the business continuity policy. Employees cannot boycott or resist the implementation or execution of the business continuity plan.

The legal/ethical feasibility component aims at ensuring that the business continuity project and the produced plan do not violate any organizational policies, local, state, or federal laws, or any adopted ethical codes.

6.6.2 Business Continuity Analysis

The business continuity analysis phase aims at studying the effects of disruptive events on the organization's business-value-generation capability. Business value is produced by business functions, business processes/capabilities, and business services. Obviously, we do not want those business components to be compromised. We have to study the business generated by those business components and prioritize them. We also have to identify the most critical business components, and identify and assess all risks that can potentially diminish their business value.

At the same time, we have to evaluate existing safeguards, determine the impact of the threats on the prioritized business assets, and mitigate and manage risks according to the organization's business continuity policy defined earlier in the business continuity planning phase.

A very important step in the business continuity analysis phase is the business impact analysis step, but before starting it, we need to complete the following activities:

Study the criticality of business components and prioritize them for the business continuity program.
Identify risks, that is, potential threats and disruptive events.
Assess risks.
Study current safeguards and their effectiveness.

All the steps constituting the business continuity analysis phase have to be completed in order. The study of business criticality, risk identification and assessment, and the study of existing safeguards have to be completed before starting business impact analysis. That is, we cannot initiate business impact analysis if we do not know what potential threats exist that can impact business operations. Hence, we need to identify all potential risks and assess them before studying the impact on business. The business analysis phase only deals with the classification of business assets in terms of their criticality and recovery requirements, and can be performed at the beginning of the business continuity analysis phase.

6.6.2.1 Business Analysis

The business analysis step aims at defining the criticality of business components and their recovery requirements, as shown in Figure 6.8. The business continuity analyst has to fully understand how a business function works. He or she has to be familiar with the business system and all business components and how they create business value. It is essential to understand how all business resources work together to produce the organization's business services. In particular, the business continuity analyst must have a good understanding of the roles and responsibilities of people, activities, data resources, technology, and physical resources. It is impossible to determine the criticality of a business function if we do not understand the operation of that function, as well as its business capabilities or processes. Once we understand the operation of the business function, we understand its contribution to the organization's business-value-generation capability.

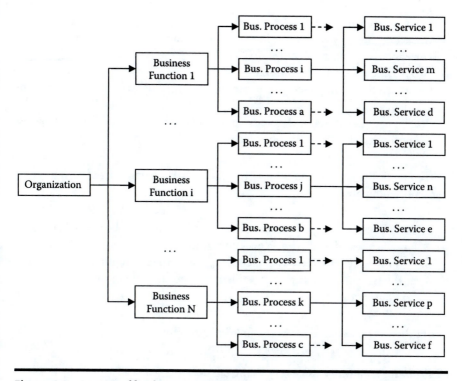

Figure 6.8   Layout of business components.

The organization often stores literature that members of the business continuity team can consult to understand policies, regulations, and procedures relevant to the business continuity project.

Some organizational strategic plans indicate the criticality of functional units and their operational plans. Each unit determines the contributions of people, activities, infrastructure, technology, and data resources integrated to ensure the feasible realization of the unit's business objectives. Each unit establishes the accepted conditions for continuing business in the event undesired events occur. Each functional unit should be able to identify, acquire, and organize the necessary information and tools for the unit to bring business operations back to an acceptable level.

Any information that business continuity management needs to help make business continuity strategic decisions will be valuable to have. Such decisions are usually made based on information obtained from the business analysis step, including information about the recovery point and recovery time objectives. The following information may also be needed in business continuity decisions:

Criticality of business components
Recovery point objectives

Recovery time objectives

Impact of lack of business continuity for some business components

Dependency of business continuity

Geographic information of business components

Duration that components can remain unavailable without affecting the organization

People, activities, data, technology, and infrastructure needed for the business continuity of business components

There are two important questions that cannot be separated from any business continuity program:

1. The system storing your working data is broken after this business disruption, but when was the last time a backup was made of your data?
2. A business component is included in the business continuity scope, but how long can one wait, when a disruption occurs, before this asset resumes functioning?

Let us discuss these questions in the following examples.

Example 1: Infinity Recovery Point Objective and 1-Day Recovery Time Objective

Jamie loves to play Solitaire on her computer. One day, she borrowed a disk that has a game her friend just downloaded from the Internet. It turned out that the disk had a nasty virus in it, and the computer was infected. It is now about 2 weeks, and Jamie cannot use her computer. One day, she met her neighbor Fred, who volunteered to check out the problem.

Fred just figured out that Jamie has no up-to-date antivirus program. She quickly ran to Wal-Mart to get one, but too much damage to her file system had occurred, and Fred has to help her recover her system using the original recovery disk that came with her computer when she bought it. Fred asked Jamie, "I am afraid you will lose most of your data; when was the last time you save a backup copy of it?"

Jamie replied, "I think I have a copy of what I need; Solitaire, that is it." Jamie really did not care much about storing a backup for anything. She just needed the Solitaire game that she could get for free when the computer is restored.

If we attempt to answer the first question (see list before this example) in Jamie's case, then our answer will be "minus infinity." Jamie had no intention of backing up any data. She had never backed up data, which we can represent by $-\infty$. We say that Jamie's recovery point objective equals $-\infty$.

If, however, we pose the second question to Jamie, her answer will be: "Please restore my computer immediately. I cannot stand a day without playing Solitaire or checking the Internet." We say that Jamie's recovery time objective equals 1 day.

Example 2: 1-Day Recovery Point Objective and 1-Day Recovery Time Objective

Hector owns a small business as a local insurance agent. He processes on average about 20 insurance transactions per day. Work completed is mailed the next day to his main insurance company. Every day at 5:00 pm he creates a backup of all the transactions processed on that day.

One day, his computer broke down and he could not fix it on his own. He just could not afford another idle day. He called a local company to see what went wrong. Unfortunately, the computer repair company advised him to wait for 7 days to fix the computer, or rent or buy one.

Two important facts: First, Hector could not lose more than this day. He had a backup that was created the previous day at 5:00 pm. Second, he just could not wait for 7 days until his computer was fixed. The maximum he could wait was one day. He had already lost one day troubleshooting the computer. Hector decided to rent one computer from the computer repair company as he could not afford the stay idle for more than one day, as he feared that his customers would leave him for his competitors. Hector's recovery point objective is 1 day because he creates a backup every day at 5:00 pm when he closes the store. Hector's recovery time objective is also 1 day because he cannot afford to wait for more than 1 day for his computer to be fixed.

WHAT IS RECOVERY POINT OBJECTIVE?

The recovery point objective for a data resource is how long ago its owner backed it up. This backup period is often determined by the purpose of the data and its role in achieving the business mission of the business component.

WHAT IS RECOVERY TIME OBJECTIVE?

The recovery time objective for a business component is how long its owner can afford to wait before it resumes functioning. This time is often determined by the purpose of the business component and its role in achieving the business mission of the organization.

Example 3: Zero, Infinitesimal, or Point of Failure

There are, however, companies that are very sensitive when it comes to recovery point or time objectives. A stock market broker cannot afford to be without a real-time backup system and real-time replacement system in case a disruption occurs. We say that the broker's recovery point objective is zero, infinitesimal, or point of failure. The broker cannot afford any computer failure at all, as his loss can be great. We say that his recovery time objective is zero.

Business functions are the easiest targets in an organization when a business disruption agent strikes. As seen in Figure 6.8, a business function is made of business processes, and each business process is made of business services. After a successful decomposition of business functions, we have now identified all business components. A business component is defined by the triplet <business function, business process, business service>.

Similar to asset classification, business components may be divided into classes of different criticality. This task may be performed jointly by business owners and business continuity analysts.

As discussed earlier when we defined the business continuity scope, all business components are assigned a criticality score between 1 and 5 expressed in terms of direct contribution to the organization's business-value-generation capability, as defined earlier in the business analysis step

After defining the criticality of business components, they should be prioritized for the business continuity program and ranked, as shown in Table 6.2.

In addition to the definition of business criticality of business components and their prioritization for the business continuity program, the following information has to be obtained:

Recovery point objectives
Recovery time objectives
Impact of no business continuity for some business components
Dependency of business continuity
Geographic information of business components
Length of downtime of components without affecting the organization
People, activities, data, technology, and infrastructure needed for the business continuity of business components

6.6.2.2 Risk Analysis

If risks are not identified, they simply cannot be assessed. If the wrong risks are identified, then you will be assessing the wrong risks and will later be mitigating and managing the wrong risks.

If the validity of the risk you assess is not valid, even if the risks have been correctly identified, any mitigation attempt of the identified risks will be ineffective as you may be protecting the wrong business assets. In the same way, if your risk mitigation method is wrong, then your risk management approach will also be ineffective.

Before we move to the business impact analysis step, let us try to understand the kinds of threats that are menacing organizations and assess how serious these threats are. In order to do so, we need to perform two activities: risk identification and risk assessment. Chapter 8, on risk analysis, provides sufficient details of how to identify and assess risks, but we still briefly review these two activities in the next two sections and relate them to business continuity.

6.6.2.2.1 Risk Identification

Organizations learn over time. Their learning may be achieved through two components: internal learning and external learning. Internal learning is achieved through knowledge discovery, data collected and mined, lessons learned, and so on.

**Table 6.2 Generic Example of Prioritization of
Business Components Based on Criticality**

Business Component				
Business Functions	*Business Processes*	*Business Services*	*Criticality (1–5)*	*Rank*
BF1	BP11	BS111	2	6
BF1	BP11	BS112	4	2
BF1	BP12	BS121	3	5
BF1	BP12	BS122	2	6
BF2	BP21	BS211	1	15
BF2	BP21	BS212	3	5
BF2	BP21	BS213	5	1
BF2	BP21	BS214	2	6
BF2	BP22	BS221	2	6
BF2	BP22	BS222	3	5
BF3	BP31	BS311	2	6
BF3	BP31	BS312	3	5
BF3	BP32	BS321	4	2
BF3	BP32	BS322	4	2
BF3	BP33	BS331	2	6
BF3	BP33	BS332	1	15

External learning is concerned with knowledge accumulated from external sources, including lessons learned from others.

With time, the organization should have accumulated an entire inventory of possible threats that can potentially turn into serious business disruption events or even disaster incidents that the organization needs to counter.

At the beginning of the chapter, we discussed disruptive events and organized them into four classes of threats:

1. Natural
2. Technological
3. Man-made
4. Biological

The natural disruptive agent class consists mainly of the following categories:

Weather-related
    Hurricanes
    Tropical storms
    Thunderstorms
    Lightning/hailstorms
    Tornadoes/other wind storms
    Winter storms
    Heat waves
    Fog
    Floods caused by weather conditions
Geologic
    Landslides
    Land subsidence/sinkholes
    Expansive soils
    Earthquakes
    Tsunamis
    Volcano
    Wildfire
    Floods caused by geologic conditions
    Storm surges

The man-made disruptive agent class consists mainly of the following categories:

Terrorism
    Bombing
    Act of violence
    Mass shooting
Hazardous behavior
    Unintentional fire
    Human error
Malicious act
    Vandalism
    Internet-based attacks
    Fire
    Sabotage
Civil unrest
    Strike
    Manifestation
    Riot
    Class action suit

The technological disruptive agent class consists mainly of the following categories:

Software
    Incidents caused by software failure
    Information corruption due to software failure
    Information leakage due to software failure
    Denial of service due to software failure
Hardware
    Incidents caused by hardware failure
    Information corruption due to hardware failure
    Information leakage due to hardware failure
    Denial of service due to hardware failure

The biological disruptive agent class consists mainly of the following categories:

Medical conditions
    Absenteeism
Epidemic conditions
    Contaminated water supplier
    Mass poisoning
    Spread of infectious deceases
    Spread of infestation
Catastrophic conditions
    Nuclear accident
    Chemical disaster

The output of the risk identification step is an inventory of threats and disruptive events. The source corresponding to every threat has to be explained.

It is important to explain how a threat becomes real, how it grows, how it initiates its attack, what types of resources are needed, what are the types of vulnerabilities and weaknesses, and what is the range of those threats.

6.6.2.2.2 Assess Risks

This step considers every threat defined in the inventory of threats produced at the risk identification step, and assess its likelihood of occurring and producing business disruption. Table 6.3 provides an example for a possible output for the risk assessment step.

While the likelihood of a threat of business disruption may be modeled as probabilities that can be calculated based on historical data, organizations usually employ five-point Likert-scales to represent the threat likelihood as follows:

Table 6.3 Example of an Output for Risk Identification and Assessment

Threat Class	Threat	Source	Likelihood
Natural	TN-1	SN-1	4
	—	—	—
	—	—	—
	TN-a	SN-a	3
Technological	TT-1	ST-1	4
	—	—	—
	—	—	—
	TT-b	ST-b	5
Man-made	TM-1	SM-1	3
	—	—	—
	—	—	—
	TM-c	SM-c	2
Biological	TB-1	SB-1	1
	—	—	—
	—	—	—
	TB-d	SB-d	1

1. Very Low; that is, unlikely to occur
2. Low; that is, may occur occasionally
3. Moderate; that is, equally likely to occur or not to occur
4. High; that is, likely to occur
5. Very High; that is, almost certain to occur

6.6.2.3 Business Impact Analysis

6.6.2.3.1 Formal Business Impact Analysis

At this point of the business continuity project, we have already accumulated a great deal of information for use in conducting the business impact analysis step:

A prioritization of business assets
An inventory of threats/disruptive agents

An inventory of current safeguards
RPOs, RTOs, etc.
Likelihood information for identified threats/disruptive agents

The purpose of business impact analysis is twofold:

1. Study the impact of disruptive events on business assets.
2. Assemble decision support information for the creation of a business continuity strategy.

The most important objective of a business impact analysis is to assemble sufficient information to develop a business continuity strategy. Before we proceed further, however, let us first define the term *strategy*.

6.6.2.3.1.1 What Is Strategy? — Strategy is a well-defined set of long-term directions on how to efficiently configure resources toward achieving an organization's business mission. That is, at least according to this definition, a strategy is designed to configure organizational resources, for the long term, for the purpose of a profitable realization of business objectives. We select another definition of strategy that is rather long but complete and simple to understand [1]:

> Corporate strategy is the pattern of decisions in a company that determines and reveals its objectives, purposes, or goals, produces the principal policies and plans for achieving those goals, and defines the range of business the company is to pursue, the kind of economic and human organization it is or intends to be, and the nature of the economic and non-economic contribution it intends to make to its shareholders, employees, customers, and communities.
>
> **Kenneth Andrews (1980)**

A business continuity strategy is the organization's strategy for its business continuity effort. It is intended to efficiently configure all the organization's resources toward achieving business continuity objectives. The business continuity strategy should define a business continuity policy and directions for a sure path to continued business despite business disruptions.

The business impact analysis, depicted in Figure 6.9, provides important strategic information that is needed for the development of a business continuity strategy. User involvement in the business impact analysis and in defining business continuity requirements is indispensable to complete the business impact analysis step.

Once we have identified critical business functions, processes/capabilities, and services, and obtained sufficient information about all these business components, we need to identify all effects of potential business disruptions and determine business

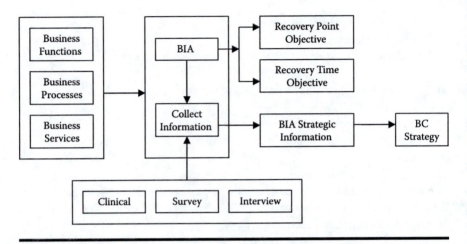

Figure 6.9   Business impact analysis: providing strategic information to define a business continuity strategy.

impacts. These business impacts may be financial or nonfinancial. Figure 6.10 shows what type of information is output by the business impact analysis step.

In a formal business impact analysis, we first need to associate disruptive events with business components. For every association <threat-asset>, we need to evaluate the impact of the threat on the business asset; that is, the impact of the business disruption on the business component.

The business impact information may be presented in a simple matrix, as shown in Table 6.4, where the columns represent the business assets and the rows represent the business disruptions. The table entry where the business disruption intersects the business asset contains a reference r_{ij}, where we store business continuity

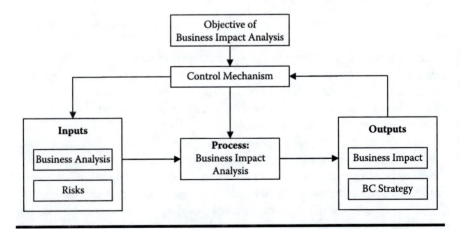

Figure 6.10   Process approach for the business impact analysis.

Table 6.4 Business Impact Analysis Table

Disruption Event/Threat	Business Asset A_1	Business Asset j	Business Asset A_n
D_1	—	—	—
—	—	—	—
—	—	—	—
D_i	—	r_{ij}	—
—	—	—	—
—	—	—	—
D_m	—	—	—

Note: r_{ij} = Reference to access business continuity information for a situation where business disruption *i* hits and affects business asset *j*.

information for the situation when the business disruption *i* occurs and affects business asset *j*.

6.6.2.3.1.2 How to Assess the Impact?—The impact depends on the business value generated by assets, weaknesses and vulnerabilities of assets, and the strength of threats.

Vulnerabilities of business components may be organized into three primary groups:

Technical
Managerial
Operational

While other areas of this testing framework will create tests specifically aimed at extracting these vulnerabilities (particularly technical vulnerabilities), it is useful to explore them during the development of a threat model. Many issues will become obvious before the traditional testing takes place.

Potential vulnerabilities should be identified by looking at the data flow and state transitions of each business component and its operational environment.

Technical vulnerabilities may include issues such as poor authentication mechanisms to control the access of business function systems or one of their components.

Management issues may include poor security policy or lack of compliance with standards for some business components. Operational vulnerabilities may include issues such as having no adequate audit activities to verify the appropriate functionality of critical business functions or of a randomly selected set of business components.

All of the potential vulnerabilities that affect each business component should be identified and studied to determine their effects on the working of the business system.

6.6.2.3.1.3 Explore Potential Threats—Earlier in this chapter, we presented a taxonomy of disruptive agents. We need to conduct a thorough study of each identified disruptive agent, its instigation conditions, and its motives. We can create a matrix showing which disruptive agents affect which business components. It is very important, however, to link the disruptive agent's effects to the vulnerabilities found in business components and the likelihood of the occurrence of those agents.

Here is a sample of preparative questions that need to be answered as part of the business impact analysis:

How is a disruptive agent activated?
What is the likelihood that a disruptive agent will be activated?
How does a disruptive agent attack the victim business components?
How can a disruptive agent be detected?
What damage can a disruptive agent cause to a business component?

The formal business impact analysis method is based on data collection techniques: using questionnaires, interviews, or nominal data acquisition. If questionnaires are used, then the design of the questionnaire is very important. It has to be simple and complete. Assistance (good documentation, online support, live support, and so on) to respondents has to be available to answer their questions. It is better to provide good assistance now than send the incomplete questionnaires back to responders to make corrections.

If interviews are used, then the interview design is very important but administering it is even more important. The interviews should be conducted in a uniform and consistent manner. Follow-up interviews should be rescheduled if initial analysis showed a need to clarify the data previously obtained.

The Nominal method is similar to training for the business continuity analyst, as he or she visits critical business components to study how they work and how they can be restored if a business disruption takes place. For the information collector, the nominal data collection looks like "show and tell," as the staff member shows demos of selected operations. The employee shows how the visited business components work, how they are protected, and how their business is continued if a business disruption occurs.

6.6.2.3.2 Process Approach in Business Continuity Analysis

In order to study the viability of the existing business system, one may follow a process approach, as shown in Figures 6.10 and 6.11. Every business function has very well-defined business requirements. These requirements are processed using business capabilities/processes to produce the organization's business services.

These business services are the output of the organization's business system, which should satisfy all organizational business objectives defined for this business function. If these objectives are not satisfactorily achieved, then corrective actions may be needed to reevaluate the validity of business requirements, the effectiveness of related business processes, and quality of all provided business services.

A business disruption can hit any time and anywhere in the organization, but the only acceptable way to counter it is to ensure that the process' business objectives are satisfied. When a process approach is adopted, any objective's deficiency may be traced back to the process itself if there goes something wrong with it, or the

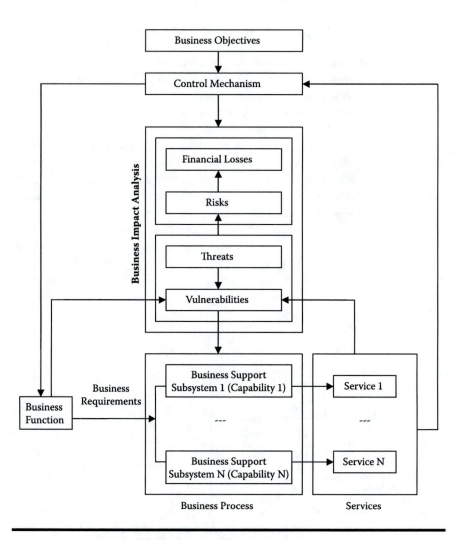

Figure 6.11   Factors affecting business impact analysis.

process inputs if the business requirements are ill defined, or the process' control mechanism, which may be faulty.

6.6.2.3.3 SWOT Analysis in Business Impact Analysis

A SWOT analysis studies the internal and external environments of the organization in terms of internal strengths and weaknesses, and external opportunities and threats that can potentially affect the organization's business performance. The SWOT analysis, as shown in Figure 6.11, may be adopted in estimating business impact and in providing strategic information that may be used in creating a business continuity strategy.

Because a business impact analysis, similar to risk analysis, studies the effects of threats that may exploit weaknesses of business assets and cause business disruptions, the SWOT analysis approach may be very useful in analyzing the impact on business in a victim organization. Figures 6.12 and 6.13 show how a SWOT analysis approach is used in business impact analysis.

The SWOT analysis approach appeared first in the Stanford Research Institute in the 1960s. This approach was originally employed to study business planning failures. That is, the SWOT approach was initially used in understanding a variety of business disruptions, including failure in strategic planning. It seems that early strategic planning studies using SWOT analysis showed that strategic planning may not work effectively unless it is coupled with effective approaches to manage changes and define realistic objectives [13].

The SWOT analysis consists of two components: internal, concerned with strengths and weaknesses; and external, concerned with opportunities and threats. The internal part of SWOT analysis (SW) often plays an important role in the evaluation of strategic effectiveness of an organization. The SW part provides strategic information required for the development of competitive strategic options.

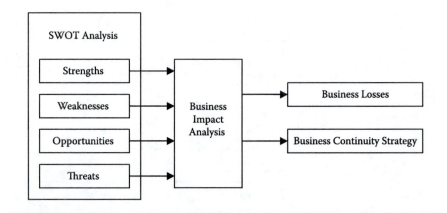

Figure 6.12   Business impact analysis.

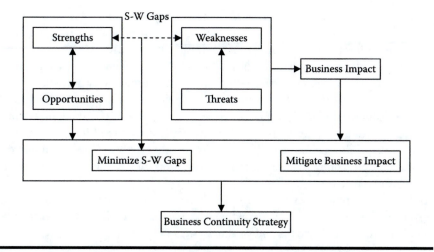

Figure 6.13   Use of SWOT analysis in business continuity strategy.

The organization uses this internal analysis to shape its competitive advantage, by building greater strengths and limiting weaknesses.

The SWOT analysis may be used to revise or reconfigure the key success factors initially defined, to ensure that they are actually achieved.

Once key success factors are defined and adopted for the creation of a competitive advantage, it will be devastating to lose all the gains from competitive advantages if a business disruption or a disaster occurs. While those key success factors are needed to maintain any gained competitive advantages, the organization has to make sure adequate resources and business capabilities remain available.

A business continuity strategy defines the strengths and weaknesses, prioritizes them, enhances organizational strengths, and mitigates risks due to weaknesses and exposures to threats.

The internal analysis part of the SWOT analysis often studies all financial advantages, knowledge management advances, competitive and differentiated services, and diverse advantages. Business continuity should preserve superior quality, superior efficiency, continuous profitable innovation, and loyal and responsive customers.

The SWOT analysis may be a very important tool for the analysis of business impact and also for the development of a business continuity strategy.

The threats and the weaknesses identified in the SWOT analysis are studied to assess the business impact. Often, the threats exploit the existing weaknesses of business functions to cause business disruption, and hence the business impact. The mitigation of the business impact depends on the organization's strengths. The opportunities to the organization, as identified in the SWOT analysis, combined with the organization's strengths, will shape the business continuity strategy, which aims at mitigating business impact. Figure 6.13 depicts how SWOT analysis may be used in business impact analysis and in the development of a business continuity strategy.

Figure 6.10, discussed earlier, shows a more integrated layout of business analysis activities that assess risks, evaluate the business impact, manage risks, and collect strategic information in support of the business continuity strategy.

The organization can also use the SWOT analysis to simulate its strategic business system and suggest effective ways to conduct business continuity activities. To do so, we apply the SWOT analysis for multiple scenarios, compare them, and use the deduced strategic information as decision support in the development of a business continuity strategy. The business system scenarios used in the simulation may consist of alternate strategic business systems that apply to known competitors or just fictitious configurations that the organization thinks work better or provide more business security.

We have defined a set of factors associated with organizational strengths for a strategic business system against which the SWOT analysis simulation may be adopted to evaluate strengths and weaknesses:

Any known advantages
Resources: Activities
Resources: People
Resources: Infrastructure
Resources: Technology
Resources: Data, information, and knowledge
Financial benefits
Social benefits
Technical benefits
Operational benefits
Legal/ethical benefits
Location and geographical
Business processes
IT and telecommunications
Security
Certifications
Main capabilities
Product/service quality
Product/service price

We also have defined a set of factors associated with organizational weaknesses for a strategic business system against which the SWOT analysis simulation may be adopted to evaluate opportunities and threats:

Any known disadvantages
Target weaknesses
Political or legislative effects
Environmental effects

Seasonality, weather effects
Known Internet-based threats
Known compromises to data integrity
Known network outages
Known compromised IT systems
Known human errors
Uncontrollable natural threats
Uncontrollable technological threats
Uncontrollable man-made threats
Uncontrollable biological threats
Technology development and innovation
New markets, vertical, and horizontal
Environmental changes
Partnerships, agencies, and distribution

The information provided in the list of factors affecting a business system and used in the SWOT simulation are integrated and tied to the business impact analysis process and the business continuity strategy, as shown in Figures 6.12 and 6.13.

This simple simulation applies the SWOT analysis to multiple scenarios as follows:

Step 1: Perform SWOT analysis for the organization.
Step 2: Identify multiple scenarios for alternate strategic business systems. They can be scenarios for known competitors or just fictitious configurations that you think work better or provide more business security.
Step 3: Perform SWOT analysis for the identified scenarios.
Step 4: Perform a comparative study for all SWOT analysis outputs.
Step 5: Report information about the business impact and about the business continuity strategy.

Tables 6.5 to 6.6 show templates that may be adopted in conducting the SWOT analysis simulation for three scenarios.

6.6.2.3.4 Need for a Rule Base in a Business Continuity Program

A rule base system for business continuity is a computer program designed to (1) define conditional business continuity rules, (2) make them available to business continuity staff when they need them, and (3) generate a business continuity program or chart specific to the current business disruption that may be added to the existing business continuity plan.

There are many business disruption situations whose signatures we know and for which the organization has formal methods for coping with. Even for those business disruptions that are not known, the organization's business continuity strategy may have formal procedures to tackle them. There are also business continuity best

Table 6.5 Internal SWOT Simulation for Multiple Scenarios

	Organization		Scenario 1		Scenario 2	
	Strengths	Weaknesses	Strengths	Weaknesses	Strengths	Weaknesses
Any known advantages						
Any known disadvantages						
Resources: Activities						
Resources: People						
Resources: Infrastructure						
Resources: Technology						
Resources: Data, information, and knowledge						
Financial benefits						
Social benefits						

Technical benefits				
Operational benefits				
Legal/ethical benefits				
Location and geographical				
Business processes				
IT and telecommunications				
Security				
Certifications				
Primary capabilities				
Product/service quality				
Product/service price				

Table 6.6 External SWOT Simulation for Multiple Scenarios

	Organization		Scenario 1		Scenario 2	
	Opportunities	Threats	Opportunities	Threats	Opportunities	Threats
Target weaknesses						
Political, legal, or ethical effects						
Environmental effects						
Known Internet-based threats						
Known compromises to data integrity						
Known network outages						
Known compromised IT systems						
Known human errors						
Uncontrollable natural threats						
Uncontrollable technological threats						
Uncontrollable man-made threats						
Uncontrollable biological threats						
Technology development and innovation						
New markets						
Partnerships						

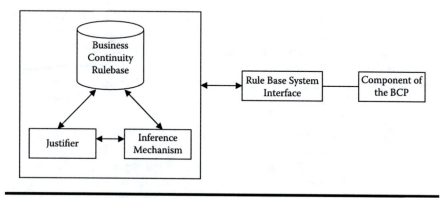

Figure 6.14 A process approach for business impact analysis.

practices that have to be followed in certain types of business disruptions and many redundant tasks that are conditionally structured by nature that apply to all types of business disruption situations. For all the cases just described, a rule base system may be very important. A rule base system is also a very efficient tool to reorganize a business continuity plan. In fact, instead of having a general business continuity plan that works for all situations, the rule base system can just generate the set of rules that apply to the current business continuity situation, once the business disruption event has become known.

The rule base system may also be designed to generate a guide or chart that contains crucial information about handling special situations relative to the current business disruption. For example, while the standard business continuity plan may explain how to conduct business continuity in case of a fire, but does not give specific directions when a custodian strike is taking place at the same time, the rule base can generate instructions on how operational management can cooperate with the business continuity team to handle the additional disturbances generated by the additional unexpected strike.

The rule base system may also be useful in handling business disruption that is not originally included in the business continuity scope. While there is a strategic business continuity plan that defines the business continuity scope and the business continuity strategy adopted by the organization, the organization may experience a variety of business disruptions that are not part of the scope of the current business continuity plan. This does not mean that upper management will just watch the organization go through those devastating conditions only because the affected components are beyond the scope of the business continuity plan. Figure 6.14 shows a rule base system used in business impact analysis.

6.6.2.3.5 Resource Profile Management for Business Continuity

In order to identify the organization's critical priorities, we need to determine all critical needs for all business functions, business processes or capabilities, and business services. Each one of these business components should determine its critical needs in their own way. Survey questionnaires, interviews, or analytical methods may be used to identify the business component's critical needs. For example, business component critical needs may be determined by assessing the critical needs for the people, activities, data, technology, and infrastructure constituting this business component. This assessment of critical needs may include considerations similar to the following:

Identify the primary people involved in the working of this business component.
Identify the primary activities needed to conduct this business component.
Identify the primary data resources needed in the working of this business component.
Identify the primary technology employed by this business component.
Identify any essential infrastructure components that are needed in the working of this business component.
Identify any resources outsourced for the working of this business component.
Identify any known threats, faulty conditions, or vulnerabilities associated with any components of this business component.

Usually, the business continuity strategy will allow for the return to a feasible and acceptable business configuration that is capable of managing any backlogs accumulated throughout the early business disruption period. As soon as the backlogs are satisfied, the organization will be pleased to see any working business configurations, even one that returns a fraction of the original business productivity. Usually, at the start of the business continuity phase, tremendous resources, consisting of people, activities, data, technology, and infrastructure, are needed, and even considerably more resources may be required to handle the accumulated backlog. As soon as the backlog is cleared, only a fraction of the usual resources will be required, keeping in mind that the postdisruption business continuity business configuration may be smaller than any prior original business configuration [14].

For example, business continuity may be carried out after relocating and withdrawing to a safer place, where new resources are assembled and the same business activities are performed under different new conditions. Coping with backlog clearance and change management will require more resources to be made available. Often, a hotline may be installed to answer all types of questions that customers and staff family members may have. Also, there may be a continuous stream of assistance requests for help with technical problems associated with technology and information systems. This may continue for a while even after the clearance of the backlog, as customers may need to inquire about many aspects of the new business conditions, and as the organization may need to engage more resources to improve its reputation and diminish the effects of any damages caused by the business disruption.

Figure 6.15 shows how normal business operations stay almost constant with 60% productivity. Unfortunately, when a business disruption takes place,

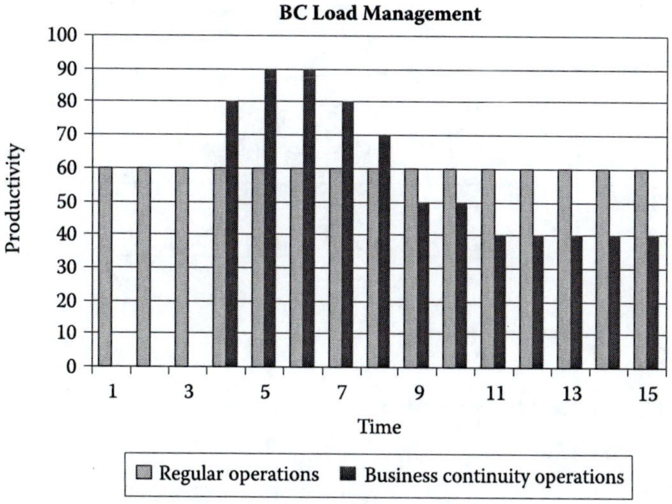

Figure 6.15 Business continuity load management before and after a disruption.

productivity declines and the backlog starts to accumulate until business is resumed. Table 6.7 shows an example of productivity values during the recovery phase. But when business is resumed, all the backlog has to be cleared first, which explains the increase in productivity upon business resumption. When all the backlog has been processed, normal business operations resume, but at lower productivity, for example, 40% productivity.

Figure 6.16 uses the same data represented in Figure 6.15. Figure 6.16 illustrates how productivity increases over time during the recovery period. Of course, this is only possible if the affected business components did not stop working completely and if the recovery process is performed while the business components are operating at lower capacity.

As shown in Figures 6.15 and 6.16, it is important that the business continuity management phase be divided into three stages: normal operations stage before the business disruption; the business continuity stage managing the accumulated backlog; and the continued business continuity stage, where resources are maintained at a lower level as prescribed in the business continuity policy.

Management by exception involves monitoring results of implemented plans and comparing the expected results with the actual results. This feedback allows management to isolate significant variations for further investigation and possible remedial action [15].

Management by exception, when applied to business continuity, relates to those unusual administrative policies that take effect when disruptive events cause the business to deviate from established standards. While, by definition,

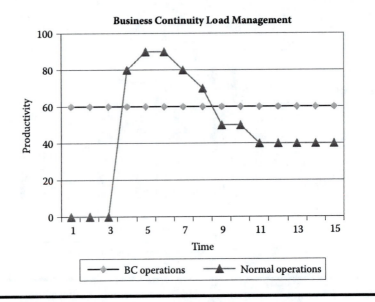

Figure 6.16 Productivity increase before and after a disruption.

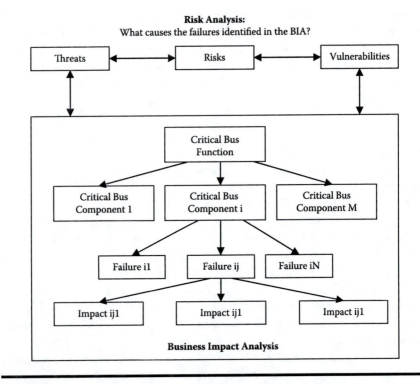

Figure 6.17 An integrated view of business continuity analysis.

Table 6.7 Productivity during Recovery Period

	Business Component 1	*Business Component 2*
Day 1	100,000	180,000
Day 2	160,000	260,000
Day 3	180,000	280,000
Day 4	190,000	290,000
Day 5	195,000	295,000
Day 6	200,000	300,000
Day 8	200,000	320,000
Day 9	200,000	340,000
Day 10	200,000	360,000

management-by-exception practices are established where it has been determined that only those events that deviate from a standard are significant, it is important to understand that every event in business continuity is a critical event throughout the recovery phase.

Management by exception is also very useful in understanding potential business situations and predicting, in addition to new business opportunities, new business disruptions that can be detected, prevented, or corrected prior to their occurrence. Through management by exception, management devotes its time to investigating those situations in which actual results differ significantly from planned results.

The business continuity management team must respect the recovery point and time objectives while performing management by exception for the business continuity phase throughout the implementation of the business continuity plan. Figure 6.16 integrates the business continuity analysis phase. The diagram studies the causes of the failures identified in risk identification and assessment, and for which the business impact analysis steps study their effects.

Earlier, in the business analysis step, we identified all critical business components, as in Figure 6.16, but we also need to identify possible vulnerabilities and potential failures and study their effects on business value.

6.6.2.4 Risk-Driven Business Continuity Program

Before we produce the business continuity plan, we need to define the business continuity program, which contains the sequence of activities and guidelines that will be adopted in case a business disruption takes place.

In order to devise the business continuity program, we first have to identify ways to mitigate risks, then select the best alternative to minimize the business

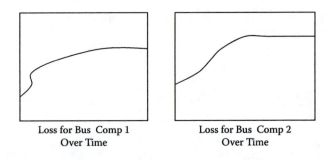

Loss for Bus Comp 1   Loss for Bus Comp 2
Over Time   Over Time

Figure 6.18   Loss of business continuity over time.

impact studied in the business impact analysis step. Once a decision is made on how to mitigate risks to business continuity, we have to come up with an effective program to mange those risks. This program should allow for continual improvement of the organization's ability to respond to all types of business disruption. A final step in the risk-driven business continuity program is the business statement of applicability. The purpose of this step is to ensure that all known business continuity solutions are considered, and the most feasible ones are included in the business continuity program. We will later discuss how to mitigate and manage risks.

6.6.2.4.1 Mitigating Risks

A business continuity strategy should be created after gaining a solid understanding disruptive of the business function's architecture, and creating lists of business processes and services, potential vulnerabilities, and possible disrupting agents threatening the organization. The business continuity strategy should take into consideration the business continuity policy set for the affected business functions and estimate the effects of potential disruption agents prior to determining any course of action to follow in the mitigation of risks.

This business continuity step is intended for the definition of the business continuity solution given business criticality, assessed risks, and their business impact. We need to identify alternative business continuity solutions, define selection criteria, and search for the best business continuity solution based on these criteria. Usually, the business continuity solutions and the selection criteria are extracted from, deduced from, or developed according to business continuity policy and the organization's security policy.

6.6.2.4.2 Risk Management

In order to devise the necessary activities to manage risks in business continuity, we should, at a minimum, discuss the following questions:

What business continuity controls are available to us?
What are the criteria to adopt in selecting the most appropriate business continuity controls?
How much risk can we feasibly mitigate?
What are the business continuity controls that can feasibly mitigate more risks?

A formal way of managing risks is to manage all risks associated with business resources: people, activities, data, technology, and infrastructure. Then, risks for every business function, subsystem, or service should be managed in terms of the risks associated with all business resources, as business impact can usually only happen when those business resources are affected. This formal way of managing risks may be very costly and hence infeasible, and management should prioritize risk management based on business criticality and residual risk. It is, however, often more efficient to manage risks by studying major risk factors and how they impact the prioritized business components. For example, a starting point for managing risks may be the study of the following risks factors and the definition of ways to mange risks associated with them:

Unavailability of business functions
Unavailability of business capabilities/processes
Unavailability of business services
Unavailability of the following business resources: people, activities, technology, infrastructure, and data
Vulnerabilities of any kind
Direct or indirect business losses

Given the identified risks associated with a business function, we can compute the maximum expected business loss for this business function. We can then determine the equivalent maximum expected downtime for this business function and its downtime cost. This way, risk may be managed for a given business function. When risk management information for all business functions is available to business continuity management staff, they can prioritize risks and resolve any existing conflicts, and come up with an integrated risk management program based on which a business continuity program will be produced.

If the downtime lasts T time units, what would be the magnitude of delayed deliveries, the magnitude of buildup of unsatisfied services?

The business continuity team should prioritize the recovery effort by satisfying the backlogged services in an orderly manner. The priority scheme employed in defining those priorities should use criteria expressed in terms of their need for resources: people, activities, data, technology, and infrastructure.

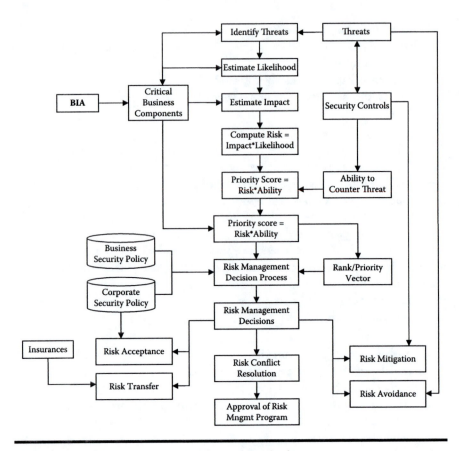

Figure 6.19 Risk management in business continuity management.

6.6.2.4.3 Other Risk Management Methodologies

The literature reports several methods for managing risks in business continuity, and we discussed these in earlier chapters. We have also devoted a chapter to event tree analysis/fault tree analysis, which is often more appropriate in business continuity analysis.

6.6.2.5 *Risk-Driven Business Continuity Management Applicability*

The statement of applicability, in business continuity management, is a very important brief document that assures management that the most appropriate business continuity controls have been adopted and those that are not appropriate have been dropped from the business continuity program. It is important that this document contain information that justifies the adoption of all included controls, and also the rejection of all controls that were left out.

6.6.3 Business Continuity Design

6.6.3.1 Business Continuity Management Requirements

The business continuity scheme is only a framework used to integrate the design of all business components required to devise a business continuity program. The following sections address the design of the business continuity program.

This step is needed to define the business continuity management requirements that will describe the business continuity activities that have to be completed when a business disruption takes place. These activities should be described in sufficient detail in the business continuity plan. The following activities are examples of such activities:

Incident analysis requirements
Requirements for isolating Incidents
Disrupted business assessment requirements
Requirements for protecting facilities
Requirements for withdrawal to safety
Requirements for defining relocations
Business resumption requirements

6.6.3.1.1 Incident Analysis Requirements

This is probably the first step, even though it is the one that may be continue longer than any other step of the business continuity plan. It is not easy to know right away what really happened, unless it is an attack whose signature is known. Usually, if this is a known incident, it is very likely that a response would have been automatically planned and corrective action will be straightforward.

If, however, it is an unknown incident, then we need to investigate to collect more information about the incident. This should take as long as it is needed.

6.6.3.1.2 Requirements for Isolating Incidents

This step is also among the first business continuity plan activities that are begun as soon as the disruptive incident is detected. The isolation of the incident is vital to delimiting the affected resources and areas. If the incident cannot be isolated, it will be very difficult to protect the infrastructure of the organization.

6.6.3.1.3 Disrupted Business Assessment Requirements

Before we initiate any corrective action, we need to know the extent of the damage. We have to identify the affected resources and areas, assess their operations, and provide enough information to management to determine the corrective actions that may mitigate business risks, determine whether or not and how resource withdrawal to safety may be planned, and determine whether or not and how relocations are planned.

Of course, the business assessment step should not wait until the incident analysis step is completed, as this may never happen. Even though any information obtained from the incident analysis step will be very helpful in studying the business impact, business assessment may, in fact, be conducted fully independently of the incident analysis step.

6.6.3.1.4 Requirements for Protecting Facilities

While the other business continuity plan activities, such as disrupted business assessment and incident analysis, continue, corrective actions are performed to save the infrastructure of the organization. Telecommunication networks, buildings, and many other resources have to be protected and restored when feasible. Minimal configurations of business functions may start as soon as the necessary components needed for those functions are restored. The restoration process may be sequential, as business will be recovered sequentially starting from smaller configurations to larger configurations. The business continuity process may bring back the organization to the initial configuration or even to a better one.

6.6.3.1.5 Requirements for Withdrawal to Safety

Once we have obtained enough information from the incident analysis step, disrupted business assessment step, infrastructure protection step, and incident isolation step, we can initiate the step concerned with withdrawal to safety. This step involves identifying the most valuable resources, including people, so that we can evacuate them rapidly. Evacuation maps, for people or other resources, may be needed. This will facilitate the withdrawal of information resources to safer areas and the evacuation of employees.

6.6.3.1.6 Requirements for Defining Relocations

Partial or full relocation of business is sometimes necessary. Many businesses in Manhattan relocated, at least temporarily, when the September 11 disaster occurred. Usually, information about potential new locations of business is available, but the decision to relocate has to be made. The following decisions have to be made:

Full or partial relocation?
Where to relocate?
In case of partial relocation, what parts of business are to be relocated?
Timing of relocations?
What are the new risks, given similar disruptive events?

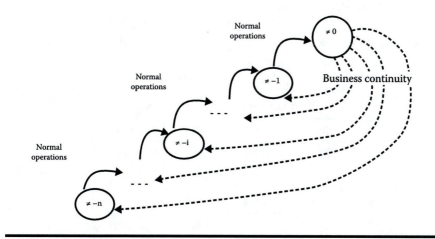

Figure 6.20 Business continuity with migration to past business configurations.

6.6.3.1.7 Business Resumption Requirements

At this point of the business continuity design, we have defined the business disruption incident, and the steps of how to isolate it. We also have defined the steps to follow to assess current business after the business disruption and the steps to protect the rest of the affected business functions, and the other business functions that were not disrupted. We also have defined how to start business withdrawal to safety if needed and how to relocate if necessary.

That is, we have defined all the business continuity requirements that have to be satisfied before starting the resumption of business operations. The step of business continuity resumption is the core step of the business continuity program.

Figure 6.20 shows the transitional states in the business system, which are made up of past business configurations that have been working under certain business conditions that are no longer appropriate. If an unfortunate disaster occurs, the organization will activate its disaster recovery plan. The business continuity plan will, however, fix the current configuration when the impact is minor or bring back the organization to the most feasible previous business configuration available.

Tables 6.8 and 6.9 show current and past business configurations. While all will depend on the type and extent of business disruption, we show here that sometimes organizations prefer to resume business by going back to a previous business configuration that was satisfactorily working in the past if all required resources are available. Table 6.8 shows the current business configuration, called business configuration BC0, which consists of three business functions, BF1, BF2, and BF3, located in Location 1, Location 2, and Location 3, respectively. The business function BF1 consists of two main business processes, BP11 and BP12. The business process BP11 consists of two business services, BS111 and BS112.

The business configuration BC1 consists of the same business configuration BC0, but without the business function BF3. The business configuration BC2

Table 6.8   Current Business Configuration Being Disrupted

Business Function	Business Process	Business Service	Location
Business Configuration BC0			
BF1	BP11	BS111	Location 1
BF1	BP11	BS112	Location 1
BF1	BP12	BS121	Location 1
BF1	BP12	BS122	Location 1
BF2	BP21	BS211	Location 2
BF2	BP21	BS212	Location 2
BF2	BP21	BS213	Location 2
BF2	BP21	BS214	Location 2
BF2	BP22	BS221	Location 2
BF2	BP22	BS222	Location 2
BF3	BP31	BS311	Location 3
BF3	BP31	BS312	Location 3
BF3	BP32	BS321	Location 3
BF3	BP32	BS322	Location 3
BF3	BP33	BS331	Location 3
BF3	BP33	BS332	Location 3

consists of the same business configuration BC0, but without the business function BF2. The business configuration BC3 consists of the same business configuration BC0, but with the business function BF2 only consisting of one business service BP21, which only consists of one business service BS211. The business continuity program may recommend switching back to one of the previous business configurations, BC1, BC2, or BC3, or a combination of them.

6.6.3.2 Business Continuity Program

6.6.3.2.1 Definition of Business Continuity Management Activities

This step takes the business continuity requirements defined in the business continuity requirements specified in the earlier step 6.3.2.7, and translates them into

Table 6.9   Past Business Configurations

Business Function	Business Process	Business Service	Location
Business Configuration BC1			
BF1	BP11	BS111	Location 1
BF1	BP11	BS112	Location 1
BF1	BP12	BS121	Location 1
BF1	BP12	BS122	Location 1
BF2	BP21	BS211	Location 1
BF2	BP21	BS212	Location 1
BF2	BP21	BS213	Location 1
BF2	BP21	BS214	Location 1
BF2	BP22	BS221	Location 1
BF2	BP22	BS222	Location 1
Business Configuration BC2			
BF1	BP11	BS111	Location 1
BF1	BP11	BS112	Location 1
BF1	BP12	BS121	Location 1
BF1	BP12	BS122	Location 1
BF3	BP31	BS311	Location 3
BF3	BP31	BS312	Location 3
BF3	BP32	BS321	Location 3
BF3	BP32	BS322	Location 3
BF3	BP33	BS331	Location 3
BF3	BP33	BS332	Location 3
Business Configuration BC3			
BF1	BP11	BS111	Location 1

Continued

Table 6.9   Past Business Configurations (Continued)

Business Function	Business Process	Business Service	Location
BF1	BP11	BS112	Location 1
BF1	BP12	BS121	Location 1
BF1	BP12	BS122	Location 1
BF2	BP21	BS211	Location 2
BF3	BP31	BS311	Location 3
BF3	BP31	BS312	Location 3
BF3	BP32	BS321	Location 3
BF3	BP32	BS322	Location 3
BF3	BP33	BS331	Location 3
BF3	BP33	BS332	Location 3

structured sequences of deliverable tasks that will be part of the business continuity plan.

6.6.3.2.2 Simulation of Business Continuity Management

BCP analysts need to evaluate assets in relation to potential disruptions. We need to have a clear layout showing the distribution and arrangement of organizational assets, users, and personnel. Simulation can provide a great means of studying possible scenarios for potential disruptive events and alternative ways to prevent them, and to take corrective and recovery actions if a disruptive incident takes place. Nothing can replace a simulation to obtain a good feel of the situation and to gain a good understanding of the actions needed to restore critical business functions.

Usually, simulations may be configured to capture all aspects of the working system while identifying those business processes that contribute the most business value to the organization. Simulation will provide great information support to the BCP analyst, enabling him or her to effectively model disruptions of business operations, effects of disruptions on business operations and their ability to generate business value, and possible corrective and recovery actions. The model is intended to generate decision support information to support various activities of a business continuity plan: incident analysis, disrupted business assessment, infrastructure, protection incident isolation, withdrawal to safety, and relocation definition.

A business continuity program is of no use if it is not successfully tested. The effectiveness of a business continuity plan depends on many factors:

Easy steps.
Complete steps.
All resources required are always in a state of readiness.
Good training program.
Thorough testing activities.
Testing all possible scenarios.
Thorough review process.
Periodic independent audit.
Effective training.
Effective exercising of all possible scenarios.

The simulation process should study all the foregoing factors. The simulation should, for example, test whether or not the steps are easy to exercise and whether or not all relevant staff are well trained to perform all business continuity steps. Also, all resources should be tested for readiness, including business continuity and emergency staff, vendors, and relevant partners, in addition to all data, technology, and physical resources.

The simulation should make sure that the business continuity team can handle special situations that can arise in a business continuity or disaster recovery period. The business continuity team effort may be simulated to ensure that all members know the following:

How to analyze a disruptive incident?
How to isolate a disruptive incident?
How to assess business after the occurrence of a business disruption?
How to protect business components after the detection of a business disruption?
How to withdraw to safety and continue business from a safer place?
How to relocate to a new location and maintain normal business operations?

6.6.3.2.3 Definition of the Business Continuity Program

Up to this point of the business continuity design phase, we have assembled all the business continuity tasks, and simulated them using diversified scenarios. Using the findings produced by the simulation completed in the previous step, we are now in a position to revise the business continuity program. After effecting the necessary revisions, we produce the final design for the business continuity program.

6.6.3.3 Business Continuity Plan

6.6.3.3.1 Testing of the Business Continuity Plan

At this point of the business continuity design phase, we have at hand the business continuity program that was designed earlier. This program should be presented to business continuity staff and tested by them. This testing activity will identify operational faults, which will be reexamined by the business continuity team and corrected. Any inconsistencies or violations of the business continuity policy, security policy, and other organizational regulations and policies should be resolved.

6.6.3.3.2 Documentation of Business Continuity

The business continuity program is now tested and validated. It is then documented and used to generate the business continuity plan. The final business continuity plan is then submitted to management for approval.

The Institute of Professional Business Continuity Managers, also known as the Business Continuity Institute (BCI), defines a business continuity plan as follows [16]:

> A clearly defined and documented plan for use at the time of a Business Continuity Emergency, Event, Incident, and/or Crisis (E/I/C). Typically, a plan will cover all the key personnel, resources, services, and actions required to manage the business continuity management process.

At this point, we have achieved the objective of producing the intended business continuity plan, which is a document presenting, in easy terms, the plan to be followed to restore business if an incident occurs.

6.6.4 Implementation of the Business Continuity Plan

The implementation of the business continuity plan is achieved as follows:

Training all relevant people
Exercising the business continuity program
Review of the business continuity program
Revision of the business continuity program and plan

6.6.4.1 Training All Relevant People

In order to achieve full competency, effective training methods have to be adopted. Diversified training tools have to be used, including videos, lectures, case studies and workshops, and discussion seminars. Training without test measures may not be effective, as we cannot know for sure that the training objectives have been achieved. Diversified testing techniques have to be used, including case studies and workshops.

6.6.4.2 Exercising the Business Continuity Plan

Exercising business continuity is vital. Diversified scenarios for business disruptions have to be selected. The parts of the business continuity plan that concern the selected scenarios have to be acted out as if real business disruption has occured.

Throughout the exercises and at the end of every exercise, all deficiencies of any type have to be documented. The accumulated reports have to be studied, and necessary corrections have to be recommended.

6.6.4.3 Review of the Business Continuity Plan

All findings obtained from earlier testing and exercising activities are used as inputs to the business continuity plan review step. Additionally, many other types of reviews may be performed to make sure the business continuity plan is effective.

It is also recommended that independent internal or external auditors may be called in to audit or review the business continuity plan. The auditors and reviewers submit their reports to the business continuity team. While minor modifications, additions, or deletions may be effected immediately, all major revisions have to approved by upper management.

6.6.5 Maintenance of the Business Continuity Plan

The maintenance of the business continuity plan aims at the continual improvement of the business continuity plan. While the business continuity team may employ any activities or techniques to enhance the effectiveness of the business continuity plan any time they deem necessary, there are circumstances when minor or major revisions are mandatory. Such circumstances include any changes in the business system configuration when new business functions, new business processes, or new business services are added, or when old business components are dropped or reconfigured, or when there are changes in the infrastructure, including new telecommunication networks or buildings, changes in locations, and so on.

Usually, the following steps are included in any maintenance phase of the business continuity plan project:

Periodic training of relevant staff
Periodic exercising of the business continuity plan
Periodic review of the business continuity plan
Periodic audit of the business continuity plan

Finally, in the business continuity plan project, there is always the business continuity execution phase. While one certainly hopes that this phase will never happen, in real life, however, no organization is immune from it.

The business continuity plan should define all conditions, in great detail, regarding the type of the business disruption and the part of the business continuity plan that applies. The business continuity plan will guide the business continuity team in starting the business resumption process. Usually, this business resumption process goes through the steps of analyzing the business disruption incident, isolating the incident, assessing the current business situation, protecting facilities, withdrawing to safer locations, relocating, and resuming business operations.

6.7 Summary

This chapter dealt with business continuity. We defined business continuity and disaster recovery. We discussed business disruption agents and their sources, and organized them in a simple taxonomy. We then discussed deterrence, detective, preventive, and corrective business continuity solutions. We defined business continuity and disaster recovery plans as necessary safeguards.

We also provide a methodology to develop a business continuity plan and used examples to demonstrate the working of various phases and steps constituting the business continuity project. The quizzes, review questions, problems, workshops, and research questions provided at the end of this chapter constitute a learning evaluation mechanism that you need to complete in order to further enhance your knowledge of business continuity.

6.8 Review Questions

1. What is business continuity? Search the literature on the Internet and in your library, and redefine business continuity in your own way.
2. What is disaster recovery? Search the literature on the Internet and in your library, and redefine disaster recovery in your own way.
3. Explain the difference between business continuity and disaster recovery.
4. What are categories of business disruptions? Search the literature on the Internet or in your library, and come up with your own taxonomy for business disruptions.
5. How does one respond to business disruptions? Search the literature on the Internet or in your library, and discuss detective, preventive, deterrence, and corrective actions in business continuity.
6. What is a business continuity plan? Search the literature on the Internet or in your library, and suggest steps to develop such a plan.
7. What is a disaster recovery plan? Search the literature on the Internet or in your library, and suggest steps to develop such a plan.
8. Search the literature on the Internet or in your library, and discuss how to perform business continuity planning.

9. Search the literature on the Internet or in your library, and redefine recovery point objective and recovery time objective. Give an example of each concept.
10. Search the literature on the Internet or in your library, and redefine business continuity strategy. Give a brief example of such a strategy.
11. Search the literature on the Internet or in your library, and redefine business continuity policy. Give a brief example of such a policy.
12. Search the literature on the Internet or in your library, and discuss how to perform business continuity analysis.
13. Search the literature on the Internet or in your library, and discuss how to identify and assess risks in business continuity.
14. Search the literature on the Internet or in your library, and discuss how to perform business continuity design.
15. Search the literature on the Internet or in your library, and discuss how to mitigate and manage risks in business continuity.
16. Search the literature on the Internet or in your library, and discuss how to devise a risk-driven business continuity program.
17. Search the literature on the Internet or in your library, and discuss how to implement business continuity.
18. Search the literature on the Internet or in your library, and discuss how to maintain business continuity.
19. Discuss how to apply SWOT analysis in business impact analysis.
20. Search the literature on the Internet or in your library, and discuss how to perform business impact analysis.

6.9 Workshops

Workshop 1

BCW Inc. started in 1987, on Martine Ave, White Plains, New York, as a furniture store for kids. It operated like that until 1996, when it acquired a new building in the same block and opened a new division called Kids Projects. Kids Projects consisted of two departments that specialized in Kids Toys and Kids Events.

In 2000, BCW Inc. opened a new store in Madison, New Jersey, where two divisions were been created. The first division was called Kids Furniture and consisted of one department specializing in kids furniture. The second division was called General Furniture, and consisted of two departments that specialized, respectively, in office furniture and home furniture.

In 2005, BCW opened a new location in Reading, Pennsylvania where it started three divisions called, respectively, Kids Clothes PA, Kids Projects PA. The Kids Projects division consisted of two departments that specialized in kids toys and kids events. The Kids Clothes division specialized in kids clothes.

Questions

This workshop is intended as a group assignment, where two or three students may sit together, or meet online, for a time period of about 1 hour to study the case. While 1 hour may obviously not be enough to fully complete this workshop, students can jointly understand the case problem, discuss the questions, and define a strategy to answer them. They can then communicate using the Internet, or any available e-learning tool, to jointly complete the workshop. A team leader should be selected to facilitate the workshop project.

1. Given information on BCW Inc., present using the same table structure presented in this textbook chapter, past business configurations of BCW Inc. List all business component triplets for all business configurations.
2. Given information, on BCW Inc. conduct the business analysis step. In addition to business criticality for all business components for the current business configuration of the company, determine a reasonable recovery point and recovery time objectives for BCW Inc.
3. Given the information you obtained in Question 2, prioritize BCW Inc. business components.
4. Given the information provided in Tables 6.11 to 6.13, identify and assess risks. Your identification of risks should be based partially on any literature available to you for the areas of New York, New Jersey, and Pennsylvania, and perhaps the cities where business is located. Risk assessment should be based on Tables 6.11 to 6.13 and any information you know about threats to similar businesses in the areas where BCW Inc. has business.
5. Perform the business impact analysis step using the formal business impact analysis method. In addition to your estimates of financial and non financial losses, what other information did you accumulate that may be needed for the development of the business continuity strategy.
6. Perform the steps of risk mitigation and management. Define a sequence of steps that you recommend should be part of the business continuity program. Write a statement of applicability for all recommended business continuity controls.
7. Transform the business continuity program defined in Question 6 into a business continuity plan.

Table 6.11   Current BCW Inc. Business Configuration

B Function	B Process	B Service	Location
Business Configuration BC0			
BF1: Kids Unit New York	BP11: Kids Projects New York	BS111: Kids Toys New York	Martine Ave, White Plains, New York
		BS112: Kids Events New York	Martine Ave, White Plains, New York
BF2: General Furniture New Jersey	BP21: Kids Furniture	BS211: Kids Furniture New Jersey	Main Street, Madison, New Jersey
	BP22: General Furniture New Jersey	BS221: Office Furniture New Jersey	Main Street, Madison, New Jersey
		BS222: Home Furniture New Jersey	Main Street, Madison, New Jersey
BF3: Kids Unit Pennsylvania	BP32: Kids Projects Pennsylvania	BS321: Kids Toys Pennsylvania	Penn Ave, Reading, Pennsylvania
		BS322: Kids Events Pennsylvania	Penn Ave, Reading, Pennsylvania
	BP32: Kids Clothes Pennsylvania	BS311: Kids Clothes Pennsylvania	Penn Ave, Reading, Pennsylvania

Table 6.12   BCW Inc. Business Value Contributions

B Function	B Process	B Service	Business Value Contribution (%)
Business Configuration BC0			
BF1: Kids Department New York	BP11: Kids Projects New York	BS111: Kids Toys New York	18
		BS112: Kids Events New York	16
BF2: General Furniture New Jersey	BP21: Kids Furniture	BS211: Kids Furniture New Jersey	6
	BP22: General Furniture New Jersey	BS221: Office Furniture New Jersey	12
		BS222: Home Furniture New Jersey	8
BF3: Kids Department Pennsylvania	BP31: Kids Clothes Pennsylvania	BS311: Kids Clothes Pennsylvania	6
	BP32: Kids Projects Pennsylvania	BS321: Kids Toys Pennsylvania	14
		BS322: Kids Events Pennsylvania	16
	BP32: Kids Clothes Pennsylvania	BS311: Kids Clothes Pennsylvania	4
Total of business value contributions			100

Table 6.13 Business Disruption Information for BCW Inc. Locations

		White Plains, NY	Madison, NJ	Reading, PA
Natural	Weather	Floods: Three times a year Thunderstorms/hurricanes: once every 2 years	Floods: Unknown Thunderstorms/hurricanes: Unknown	Floods: once a year Thunderstorms/hurricanes: once a year
	Geologic	Earthquakes: None in recent history	Earthquakes: None in recent history	Earthquakes: Unknown
Technological	Hardware	Uncommon	Very common	Very common
	Software	Very uncommon	Common	Common
	Internet	Very common	Unknown	Uncommon
Man-made	Terrorism	Less common than New York City	Very Uncommon	Very Uncommon
	Hazardous behavior	Uncommon	Common	Uncommon
	Malicious act	Possible	Possible	Possible
	Civil unrest	Unknown	Unknown	Unknown
Biological	Medical conditions	Less common than in New York City	Unknown	Unknown
	Epidemic conditions	Less common than in New York City	Unknown	Unknown
	Catastrophic conditions	Unknown	Unknown	Unknown

Workshop 2

The following is a list or reasons that can confirm or justify the need to have a disaster recovery plan:

Vandalism, riots, and union strikes may affect the computing environment.
Increased likelihood of faulty technology.
Increased likelihood of malicious software and faulty safeguards.
Loss of services if the computing environment is compromised.
Technology dependence on unstable power supply.
Historical data gives bad news about disaster events.
Significant business impact may be mitigated.
Attractive lower costs of disaster recovery plan compared to business losses when a disaster takes place.
Employees are not ready and do not know what to do if a disaster strikes.
A backup of previous configurations for future restoration when needed.
Need to develop a recovery strategy for the recovery effort to succeed.
It is a good idea to make business performance independent of IT failure.

Use a quantitative model that combines risk equations (related to risk identification, assessment, and mitigation), business impact equations, and benefits from security and disaster recovery safeguards to justify the adoption of a business continuity plan. Give a quantitative example that demonstrates the working of your model.

References

1. Andrews, K. (1980), *The concept of corporate strategy*, 2nd edition, Dow-Jones Irwin.
2. AberdeenGroup (2004), The Attack of the $2 million Worm, http://www.news.com/ The-attack-of-the-$2-million-worm/2100-7355_3-5258769.html?tag=cd.top.
3. CERT, CERT Statistics (2007), http://www.cert.org/stats/cert_stats.html.
4. SEI, CMU (2007), SEI CERT° Program and FSTC Introduce Resiliency Engineering Framework to Help Organizations Manage Operational Resiliency; URL: http://www.sei.cmu.edu/about/press/releases/ref.html.
5. CSI (2007), CSI Computer Crime and Security Survey 2007, URL: https://www.cmp-netseminars.com/ars/eventregistration.do?mode=eventreg&F=1000609&K=7AL.
6. CERT (1995), An Analysis of Security Incidents on the Internet URL: http://www. cert.org.
7. Continuity Forum: Creating Continuity (2007), http://www.continuityforum.org.
8. U.K. Home Security, Expecting the Unexpected: Business Continuity in an Uncertain World, http://www.thebci.org/London%20Firsts.pdf.2003.
9. NFPA 1600, entitled "Standard on Disaster/Emergency Management and Business Continuity Programs," the National Fire Protection Association (NFPA).
10. Daniel Whiteneck, Deterring Terrorists: Thoughts on a Framework, http://www.twq. com/05summer/docs/05summer_whiteneck.pdf.

11. Sun Microsystems, (2007) Business Continuity—Disaster Recovery, URL: http://www.sun.com/datacenter/continuity/recovery/.
12. The Business Continuity Institute. http://www.thebci.org, 2009.
13. Businessballs, (2007) SWOT Analysis, URL: http://www.businessballs.com/brainstorming.htm.
14. ASIS International, (2005) Business Continuity: A Practical Approach for Emergency Preparedness, Crisis Management, and Disaster Recovery, URL: http://www.asisonline.org/guidelines/guidelinesbc.pdf.
15. CRF: Credit Research Foundation, Glossary of Terms, www.crfonline.org/orc/glossary/m.html.
16. BCI (2002) Glossary of General Business Continuity Management Terms, URL: http://www.thebci.org/Glossary.pdf.
17. AT&T (2007) Continuity Study 2007 AT&T Business, http://www.att.com/gen/press-room?pid=7922.

SECURITY
ANALYSIS

Chapter 7

Security Risk Management

Learning Objectives

After reading this chapter, students are expected to achieve an understanding of:

What security risk management is
How security risk management works
What strategic, functional, and operational risks are
How security risk is mitigated
How productivity, security compromise, and recovery work together
How ALE works
How the Naval Safety Center risk management process works
Understand how the ABLE risk methodology works
Understand how asset analysis works
Understand how threat analysis works
Understand how security control analysis works
Understand how to compute ABLE values
Understand how to assess effects of threats on productivity
Understand how to compute life-cycle security risks
Understand how to compute annual security risks
Understand how to compute present security risks
Understand how to compute discounted security risks for long risk
    life cycles

7.1 Introduction

This chapter is mainly concerned with security risk management. We will discuss several security analysis methodologies, for example, ABLE and ALE. The ALE methodology and our new ABLE methodology are presented later in this chapter. Before we do so, however, we need to discuss several issues related to security risk, including strategic, functional, and operational risk management. Because operational management deals with day-to-day business matters, we will also present operational risk management. Even though the operational risk management approach adopted by the Naval Safety Center that we present here applies to military personnel, it is also very effective in risk management for any business or service organization.

Every organization may have its own risk management strategy, but such a strategy should consist of a sequence of phases that are often organized in a security management cycle such as the one shown in Figure 7.2. Let us present now some simple definitions of some of the concepts needed to discuss the risk management cycle.

> **Risk:** It is a measure of the potential inability to achieve overall project objectives within defined cost, schedule, and technical constraints. It has two components: (1) the probability/likelihood of failing to achieve a particular outcome, and (2) the consequences/impacts of failing to achieve that outcome [7].
>
> **U.S. Department of Energy [2]**

Events are elements in the computing environment that should be assessed to determine the level of risk, for example, things that could go wrong that affect the business mission of the organization. The events should be defined at a level where we can comprehend the potential impact and its causes. For example, a potential risk event for a production system may be the congestion of one of its resources. The congestion of a given information resource is related to other potential risk events that should be selected, examined, and assessed by subject-matter experts. There are two components of risk: probability and consequence/impact.

7.1.1 Various Layers of Risk

Risk involves many components across assets, threats, vulnerabilities, and controls. Studying risks may be initiated by discussing the following questions, which will translate into specific risk assessment terminology and categories used to prioritize risk:

What asset are you protecting?
How valuable is the asset to the organization?

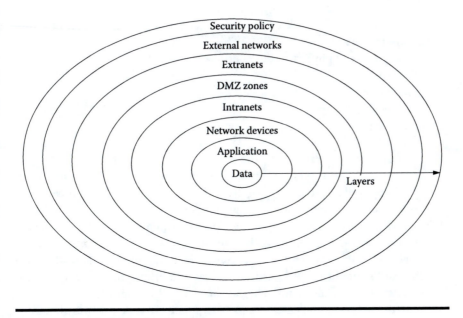

Figure 7.1 Defense-in-depth system.

What are you trying to avoid happening to the asset (both known and potential threats)?

How might loss or exposures occur?

What is the extent of potential exposure to the asset?

What are you doing today to reduce the probability or the extent of damage to the asset?

What are some actions that we can take to reduce the probability in the future?

One may also adopt the defense-in-depth model to study all relevant elements of risk. The defense-in-depth layers may be useful in defining a simple framework for risk management. This is, however, only sufficient to gather preliminary risk information that will be used later to guide the risk management process. A more extensive view of architectural layers will probably include more layers, as shown in Figure 7.1, including starting at the most external peripheral: organizational policy, external networks, extranets, demilitarized zones, intranets, network devices that interface network zones systems, applications, and data. Often, adopted security controls will apply to one or more layers of an organization's technical architecture.

Physical security: This refers to barrier placed around a computing system to deter unauthorized physical access to that computing system. In the event of an attack, there should be a low probability of success and a high probability of the attack being detected either during the attack, or subsequent to penetration.

It describes several physical access control areas:

Physical access

Fire safety

Supporting utilities

Plumbing

Interception of data

Mobile and portable systems, and so on

Physical security strategies concern methods for creating a secure environment, guarding equipment, preventing theft, safeguarding portable resources, regulating power supplies, and protecting production.

Network security: A well-designed and properly implemented network architecture provides highly available, secure, scalable, manageable, and reliable services [1]. When the organization includes multiple networks, then networks should be evaluated individually to ensure that they are appropriately secured and that the high-value networks are protected from unsecured networks. Implementations of internal network defenses should be achieved in terms of network design, wireless network security, and security protocols to ensure that only trusted computers have access to critical network resources [1].

Application security: This is essential to the security model. Applications exist within the context of the overall system, so you should consider the security of the entire environment when evaluating application security. Each application should be thoroughly tested for security compliance before running it in a production environment. The implementation of application defenses includes proper application architecture and ensuring that the application is running with the least amount of privilege with the least exposure possible [1].

Data security: Data is the most valuable organizational resource because it produces organizational information. At the client level, data is often stored locally and may be particularly vulnerable to attack. Data can be protected in different ways even though cryptography and backup remain the most popular methods of protection.

7.2 The Risk Management Life Cycle

Security risk management, as shown in Figure 7.2, consists of a set of recurrent and documented phases: risk planning, risk analysis, risk assessment, risk treatment, and risk monitoring. This is also referred to as the risk management life cycle in some of the literature.

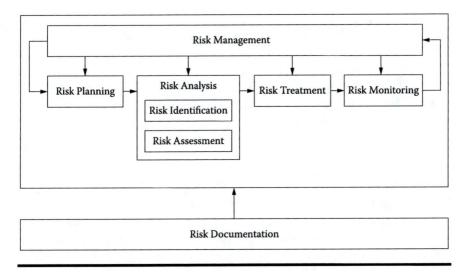

Figure 7.2 **Risk management life cycle.**

Risk management: It is the activity of controlling risk to maintain it within its acceptable range. It includes planning for risk, assessing risk areas, developing risk-treatment options, monitoring risks to determine how risks change, and documenting the overall risk management program [7].

Risk planning: It is the process of developing and documenting an organized, comprehensive, and interactive strategy and methods for identifying and tracking risk areas, developing risk treatment plans, performing continuous risk assessments to determine how risks change, and assigning adequate resources [7].

Risk assessment: It is the determination of the level of risk and the potential impact of identified risk by measuring the likelihood and impact if associated incidents were to take place. Risk assessment is needed to prioritize any risk treatment effort devised to protect the system in question. The amount of risk assessed will be compared against expected benefits before any risk treatment is approved.

Risk analysis: It is the process of examining each identified risk area or process to refine the description of the risk, isolate the causes, and determine the effects. It includes risk rating and prioritization, in which risk events are defined in terms of their probability of occurrence, severity of consequence/impact, and relationship to other risk areas or processes.

Risk treatment: It is the process of defining, selecting, and implementing security controls in order to bring back risks to acceptable levels as defined in the security policy. This includes the terms of what should be done, when it should be accomplished, who is responsible, the schedule, and relevant costs.

Risk monitoring: It is the process of systematically tracking and evaluating the performance of risk treatment actions against established metrics and developing further risk treatment options, as needed. This process revisits the other risk management activities of planning, analysis, and treatment, as shown in Figure 7.2. This represents the cycle in the risk management process.

Risk documentation: It is the recording of information describing various phases of risk management.

7.3 The Preparation Effort for Risk Management

Why risk it (i.e., the asset)? Let us do something about it. Let us take the necessary actions to protect it. The asset is exposed to a chance of "loss," that is, loss of availability, confidentiality, or integrity. If the asset is exposed to a chance of loss of this type, then the owner is exposed to a chance of other types of loss: loss of business and loss of noneconomic benefits (or social benefits).

The loss of confidentiality, integrity, or availability of an asset will translate into loss of business value to the organization. The organization will also lose its reputation, the trust of its partners and customers, in addition to many other undesirable social outcomes. If the loss occurs, because of an undesired event that we failed to prevent, the organization will lose all the revenues generated by the normal operations of the victim asset throughout the asset recovery period, in addition to social benefits. Unless those undesired events are prevented and asset vulnerabilities are mitigated, there is always a chance that losses would take place. This situation is depicted in Figure 7.3.

If you believe that there are threats, internal or external, that menace the normal business-value-generation capability of a given asset, then this asset is at risk. Owners have to be aware of asset exposure conditions that can increase the risk of damage to the asset that can occur as a result of attacks by known threats. Owners need to reduce the risk that the regular business value generated by an asset would decline if certain exposure conditions occur in the computing environment. But what is risk?

7.3.1 What Is Asset Risk?

Asset risk is the potential of an adverse condition occurring on the asset that can cause the asset to not meet its business objectives. As shown in Figure 7.4, the adverse condition is often expressed in terms of two components: a weakness in the asset and a threat capable of exploiting this weakness to cause harm to the asset. Direct harm affects the asset, and it is usually expressed in terms of three security disruptions: loss of confidentiality, loss of integrity, or loss of availability. Indirect harm affects owners, and it is usually expressed in terms of loss of business value and loss of noneconomic benefits.

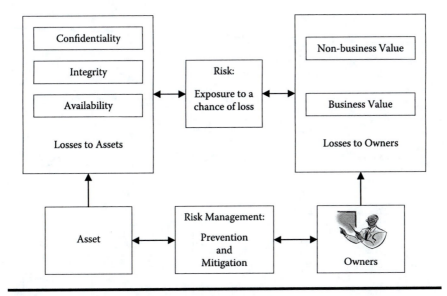

Figure 7.3   Business value versus risk management.

7.3.2 What Is Enterprise Risk?

Organizations should be clear about their security objectives and the risks they are willing to tolerate. Owners should understand the business objective set for their assets. They are responsible for defining the levels of risk they are willing to tolerate for their assets. The asset security policy should state the tolerated risk level of the asset. The organization's security policy should include the tolerated risk levels for all systems and assets belonging to the organization.

Each functional unit, division, and department should have a policy manual with clearly stated objectives and constraints so that employees and users know the type of risks taken by the organization.

Uncertainty about an organization's computing environment, its components, and the achieving of its organizational objectives can often indicate risk, which is the possibility of loss, damage, or any other intolerable consequences. We all seek low risks, hoping to guarantee a steady generation of business value with minimum security disruptions.

Assume that all the assets in a customer service LAN are working as planned, with full capacity. This situation is in complete agreement with the business mission of the enterprise, and it is also in agreement with the predefined security policy of the LAN. Due to overtime work by the security administration staff of the department, some staff members fell sick and could not make it to work the next day. This undesired situation caused the main database server to shut down, as no replacement could have been found to fill in for the absent staff. Can this situation be anticipated? May be not, but this situation should be modeled using the risk

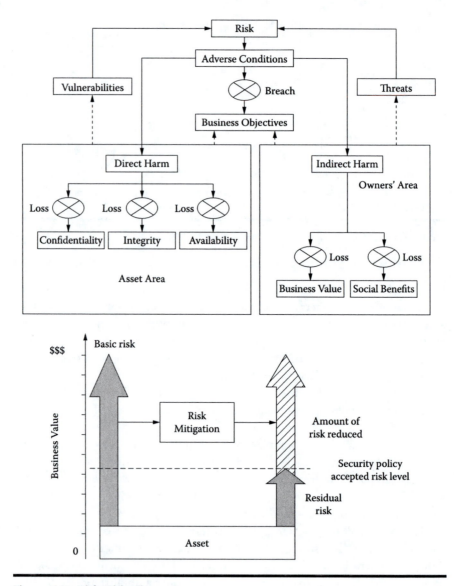

Figure 7.4 Risk mitigation process.

concept we are discussing in this chapter, as the probability of the asset getting hit by an undesired event, such as the absence of its operator.

Once all risks have been identified, a model is needed to measure the risks. Measuring risk means assigning a quantitative value or penalty to the risk, to help you decide whether the risk is worth taking. For example, if there is a 30% chance of getting a computer virus by leaving the computer connected overnight, costing you $100 out of your own pocket to fix the problem in the morning, that might be a risk you are willing to take. But there is a 5% chance of losing all the customers who may request your product overnight, knowing that there is a $10,000 penalty, you might be less willing to take that risk.

Risk may be understood as the probability that a threat would lead to harm. Vulnerabilities and threats are certainly not dangerous if they are related. For example, the vulnerability in leaving a window open in an office building and the threat of the e-mail virus Bubbleboy are not related. On the other hand, the threat of heavy rain will put computers at risk when the office windows are left open.

Fortunately, security management can always apply managerial, administrative, and technical controls to keep risks below a tolerable risk level, often stated in the organization's security policy.

7.4 A Sustainable Security Culture

Effective security management develops a broader view that allows them to study the entire computing environment before planning any security programs. Security management should be aware of the organization's weaknesses and vulnerabilities that increase the organization's exposures to existing threats. A simple security objective, in this context, would be "to ensure that threats do not turn into intolerable consequences."

In addition to implementing plans to prevent intolerable consequences, effective security management should lead to the creation of a new culture of staying secure. This new security culture should promote the attitude of behaving and handling tasks and documents in a secure way, that is, as stated in the organization's security policy. Security awareness, literacy, training, and education are all important components of the new security culture.

In a different domain—but still a good analogy with the security culture—a health-aware culture would require that a person wash his or her hands every time he or she gets back from outside. In another example, cited by Mona Lilly Raggad (my younger daughter, who was 9 years old when she volunteered to contribute), would be to stay at least three feet away from a cougher in order not to get the flu, and not to share drinks or lollypops with friends.

If an organization does not get to the position where a sustainable security culture is in place, this is an indication that the organization still has to go through many steps of training and retraining in behavioral security.

Security management should ensure that undesired events do not occur, by planning the necessary prevention and mitigation actions needed to improve the security position of the organization. Preventive actions attempt to counter the possibility that an event will result in intolerable losses. Mitigation actions, on the other hand, concern processes to reduce vulnerability to known threats. In this manner, security management can manage security risks.

A sustainable security culture consists of good habits of behaving in secure ways to prevent any harm from being caused to yourself or to any component in the organization. Such a culture is made up of security habits, commonsense best practices, and volunteered policies that are not written as part of any security policy. Violations of any implicit behaviors are not considered security breaches and are not subject to any legal or ethical pursuits.

7.4.1 Hazards

Hazards are dangerous conditions associated with people, activities, data, technology, or infrastructure that can result in exposures or vulnerable situations that may be exploited by disruptive agents to produce harm or violate the organization's security policy.

In order to estimate security risks, at least two parameters have to be estimated before computing the security risk value: the probability of occurrence of the exposure and the expected loss generated by the victim asset. The probability of the occurrence of the exposure constitutes the probability that hazardous conditions can be exploited by known threats. The expected loss due to the realization of an attack should be expressed in terms of the amount of business value lost during the entire recovery period. For example, if this asset generates a profit equal to $365,000 annually, then a recovery period of 5 days produces a loss of $5000.

An attacker cannot just penetrate into a system without any preparation. There are several stages that have to be completed before an attacker can penetrate the system and start causing harm. A very important initial step before an attack is initiated is the discovery phase. In this phase, the attacker collects information about the system's vulnerabilities.

This chapter is limited to risk management, but you may read Matthew V. Mahoney and Philip K. Chan's study entitled "An Analysis of the 1999 DARPA/Lincoln Laboratory Evaluation Data for Network Anomaly Detection" [1], found at http://www.cs.fit.edu/~mmahoney/paper7.pdf, or Jelena Mirkovic, and Peter Reiher's paper entitled "A Taxonomy of DDoS Attack and DDoS Defense Mechanisms" [3], found at http://www.cis.udel.edu/~sunshine/publications/ccr.pdf. Both documents provide a full description of DARPA taxonomy that discusses the phases followed by attackers in planning an attack.

Obviously, a system that has no vulnerabilities is not at risk of being attacked. Vulnerability may, for example, consist of an incompatible security policy, an erroneous managerial control, or a technical bug in a computer program. An attacker who knows about the weaknesses of the security policy, the managerial control, or the code bug can plan the appropriate tools with which to exploit those vulnerabilities.

A vulnerability may be easy to exploit by threats if the tools to do so are easy to acquire and simple to use. We say that this asset is highly exposed to those threats, or that the vulnerability generates high exposure, for the asset, to known threats. Sometimes, the vulnerability exists, but the tools are difficult to obtain or use. We say that the vulnerability generates low exposure to known threats.

Usually, however, attackers would first need to identify vulnerabilities associated with high exposures; systems with such vulnerabilities are very easy to attack. The objective of system owners and the security management is to fight back by devising security programs capable of mitigating risks, as shown in Figure 7.4.

7.5 Information Needed to Manage Risks

There are risks anywhere you look in an organization. Every asset in the organization is at risk. Some assets will, however, be associated with risks lower than the risk level tolerated by management, and others will be menaced by risks higher than the accepted risk levels determined by owners for those assets. In the former case, the risk level associated with the asset is accepted by owners, and no additional security will be provided to the asset. In the latter case, the risk level is higher than the tolerated level, and there is an immediate need to invest in securing the asset enough to take it back to an acceptable risk position.

The maximum accepted level of risk is defined for every asset in its security policy. We will refer to this tolerated risk level as the asset security policy accepted risk level (ARL).

In order to manage risks, security management needs to identify risks, assess them, and mitigate them. Figure 7.5 depicts the transition from basic risks to mitigated risks by the application of the appropriate security controls. In addition to those three steps, security management has to devise a risk-driven security program capable of managing those risks by keeping them always lower than the security policy's accepted risk level. Security management has to collect information about assets and their vulnerabilities, threats, the organization's current security policies, and the current security controls. As in developing any information system or IT product, the development of an information security system goes through the phases of planning, analysis, design, and implementation.

The planning phase aims at collecting information about the development of a risk-driven security program for the purpose of managing risks associated with a given asset, as shown in Figure 7.5. We need five types of folders or databases:

1. Inventory of assets
2. Inventory of vulnerabilities

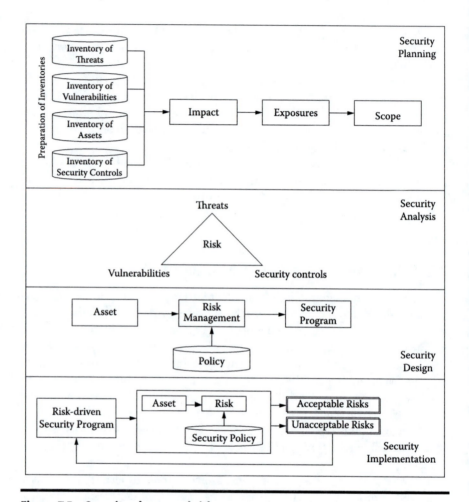

Figure 7.5   Security phases and risk.

3. Inventory of threats
4. Inventory of current security controls
5. Inventory of security policies

7.6 Factors Affecting Security Risk

Sometimes, the asset is not fully out of service, but there is partial loss of productivity from the time of crash until normal operations resume. The security management of the victim asset determines how the recovery process is planned. Corrective actions are performed in two modes: compromised productivity mode, or full unavailability mode. In the compromised productivity mode the security

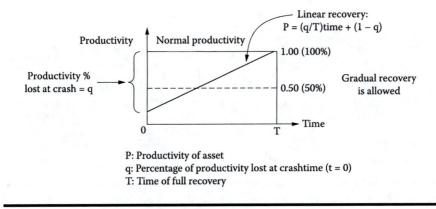

Figure 7.6   **Linear recovery in case of partially compromised productivity.**

team performs the necessary corrective actions while the asset continues to operate at the compromised productivity rate $c(t)$. The function is usually an increasing function because we assume that the corrective actions supervised by the security team can only improve the security of the asset and hence improve its compromised productivity rate. Figures 7.6 and 7.7 show examples of linear compromise and recovery rates.

In real life, this assumption is not necessarily true. If the tools employed in the corrective actions are not adequately secured—for example, if a compromised recovery disk was used—then those corrective actions can in fact produce more harm than the damage created by the compromised productivity rate. In this case, the recovery process will produce a lower productivity rate, and the function $c(t)$ will not be an increasing function.

Sometimes, there is loss of $c(t_0)\%$ at the time of the crash, but the recovery will progressively improve productivity until full recovery is reached, at which point the asset gets back to normal operations.

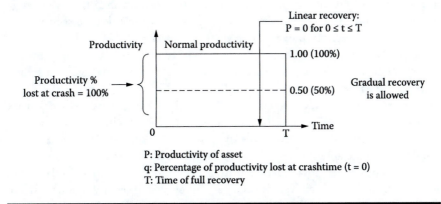

Figure 7.7   **Linear recovery in case of full unavailability.**

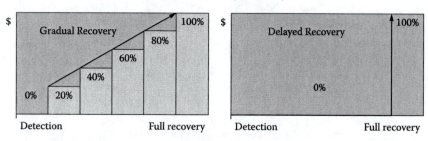

Figure 7.8 Examples of incremental recovery rate functions.

Figure 7.8 shows a situation where the asset was attacked using a denial-of-service attack. The asset may be, for example, a local area network for the printing department of a medium-sized company. The server schedules print jobs depending on the size of the document and the type of paper needed to print it. At the time of detection of the attack, the productivity of the printing department slipped to 20%. The recovery process began by replacing the server by a desktop where jobs were printed manually. On the first day, the productivity continued at 20% as staff members were still initiating the recovery process and productivity remained unchanged. On the second day, the productivity increased to 40% due to installation of a new desktop. On the third day, a second computer system managing a printing station was added, which increased the productivity by another 20%. The productivity was now 60%. The next day, a second printer was added, which increased the productivity back to 80%. On the last day of the recovery, an entirely new computer system is in place, and operations are back to normal.

Independently of the shapes of productivity functions, compromise rates, and recovery rates, any security management program has to be evaluated in terms of its effectiveness in security risk management. System owners and security management should understand that security management is equivalent to security risk management. A security program that does not lower risks below the maximum accepted risk levels as specified in relevant security policies is a failing program. Figure 7.9 depicts how risk mitigation fits in the general risk management framework for the entire organization.

Figure 7.9 also provides a graphical interpretation of an asset security risk. Risk increases when threats increase. As long as the asset risk stays in the area of acceptable risks, the asset is in an acceptable risk position. Risk mitigation is achieved by implementing the appropriate security controls in a feasible manner. The diagram shows that no matter how much security is added to the asset, its risk level will never reach the zero level. This is called asymptotic risk. The asymptotic residual risk level is the lowest risk level that an asset can reach if sufficient security is added for its protection.

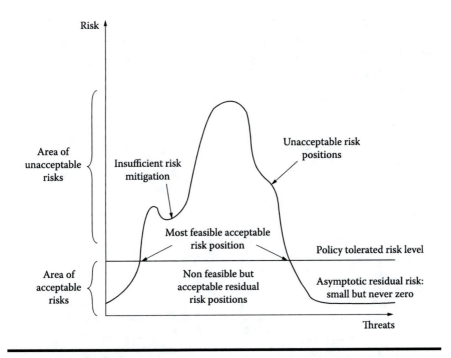

Figure 7.9   Risk treatment effects.

Risk is never zero. It can, however, be below or above the policy-tolerated level. This level is determined by asset owners and is stated the asset security policy. Any risk position equal to or below the policy risk level is acceptable, and any investment in any security controls for the purpose of adding protection to this asset may not be justifiable.

On the other hand, if the current asset risk position is above its policy risk level, then there is an immediate need to move this asset to a risk position equal to or below the policy risk level.

7.6.1 Annual Productivity

Let us assume, at least in theory, that owners know the productivity of their assets for the entire year. Any asset that does not play a role in achieving the organization's business mission has no reason to exist and should be removed. If this asset does, however, play a significant role, then its owner has to be able to plan its productivity for at least the current year. If this asset productivity is not known to its owner, then the owner should be replaced by a new owner who knows this asset productivity, the role it plays in achieving the organization's business mission, and its business-value-generation capability.

Usually, the annual productivity function of an asset is known to its owner. In rare cases, for smaller-sized companies, there are too many factors that can affect

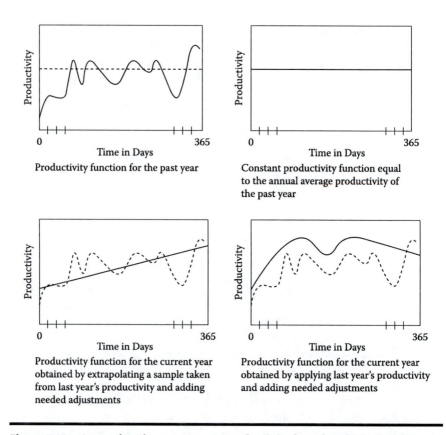

Figure 7.10 **Approximating next year's productivity based on historical data.**

the fluctuations of the annual productivity function; in this case, the owner can either use the past year's annual productivity function as representative for the current year, with or without adjustments, or use the annual average productivity for this purpose, as shown in Figure 7.10.

Let us denote the productivity function by $b(t)$, where t represents the time in a predefined time unit, for example, the day of the year, and where N is the number of time units in a year. If the time unit is the day, then N is 365 days. Table 7.1 provides fictitious productivity data, showing how productivity is compromised and recovered.

The total annual productivity is equal to $\int_0^N b(t)dt$. The annual average productivity of an asset equals $(1/N)\int_0^N b(t)dt$.

7.6.2 Corrective Actions

Once an intrusion is detected, security management has to decide on the following:

Table 7.1 Fictitious Productivity Data, Showing How Productivity Is Compromised and Recovered

		Day t	Productivity during Normal Operations	Compromised Productivity Rate (%)	Productivity during Recovery
		1	2600	100	
		2	2600	100	
		3	2800	100	
		—	—	—	—
		—	—	—	—
		—	—	—	—
Recovery period	t_0	100	2400	40	960
	$t_0 + 1$	101	3000	46	1380
	$t_0 + 2$	102	3200	52	1664
	$t_0 + 3$	103	3400	58	1972
	$t_0 + 4$	104	3600	64	2304
	$t_0 + 5$	105	3600	70	2520
	$t_0 + 6$	106	3800	76	2888
	$t_0 + 7$	107	3800	82	3116
	$t_0 + 8$	108	3400	88	2992
	$t_0 + 8$	109	3600	94	3384
	T	110	3800	100	3800
		111	3800	100	
		112	3800	100	
		113	3600	100	
		114	3600	100	
		115	3400	100	
		116	3200	100	
		117	3200	100	

Continued

Table 7.1 Fictitious Productivity Data, Showing How Productivity Is Compromised and Recovered (*Continued*)

		Day t	Productivity during Normal Operations	Compromised Productivity Rate (%)	Productivity during Recovery
		118	3200	100	
		–	–	–	
		–	–	–	
		–	–	–	
		363	3800	100	
		364	3800	100	
		365	4000	100	

1. What is the current productivity level?
2. How long does it take to fully recover and go back to normal operations?
3. If t_0 is the time at which corrective actions are invoked and T is the time at which the asset goes back to normal operations, what is the productivity level at any time between t_0 and T?

7.6.3 Managing Productivity at Time of Disruption

Let us assume that the security disruption takes place in $[t_0, T]$. We assume that the security disruption starts at $t = t_0$, after which productivity is compromised at the rate $c(t)$ in the time period $[t_0, T]$. The term $c(t)$ is called the compromise rate term. It means that at any point of time in $[t_0, T]$ there is a loss of productivity amount of $c(t)b(t)$. Figure 7.11 depicts the situation where productivity is compromised at a $c(t)$ rate, assuming no recovery in $[t_0, T]$.

You can see in Figure 7.12 that there is a drop of productivity of $c(t) = 60\%$ in the period $[t_0, T]$. The new productivity after being compromised becomes $(1 - c(t))$ * $b(t)$ in the compromise period $[t_0, T]$. If we start the recovery process immediately after the security disruption is detected at $t = t_0$, the compromise rate will be reduced in terms of the recovery rate $\rho(t)$. The new compromise rate becomes $(1 - \rho(t))c(t)$ for the period $[t_0, T]$. Because the recovery rate is applied, the drop in productivity will decrease in terms of the decrease associated with the compromise rate. The resulting productivity during the compromise period $[t_0, T]$ becomes $(1-(1 - \rho(t))c(t)))b(t)$. Figure 7.12 shows the change in the drop of productivity when recovery activities are started at $t = t_0$.

Let us look at all the equations all together:

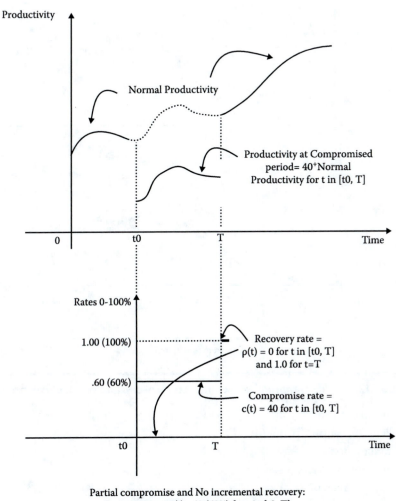

Partial compromise and No incremental recovery:
Compromise =c(t)=.60 (60%) for t in [t0, T]

Figure 7.11 Partial compromise and no incremental recovery with constant compromise.

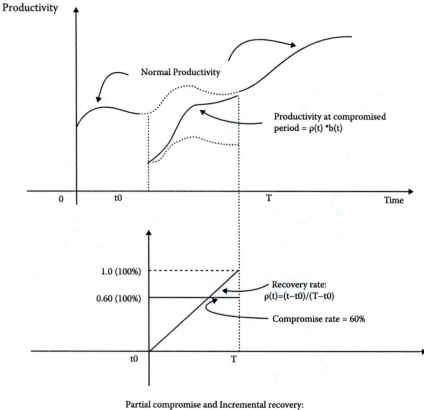

Figure 7.12 Partial compromise, incremental recovery, and constant compromise.

Time parameter: $[0, \infty]$
Compromise time period: $[t_0, T]$
Productivity: $b(t)$
Compromise rate: $c(t)$
Recovery rate: $\rho(t)$.

Given the foregoing parameters, we can write the productivity equation as follows:

$$\text{Productivity } (t) = \begin{cases} b(t) & \text{if } t < t_0 \\ 1 - (1 - \rho(t))c(t))b(t) & \text{if } t \in [t_0, T] \\ b(t) & \text{if } t > T \end{cases}$$

We can obviously make all the assumptions we want about the shapes of the equations of $b(t)$, $c(t)$, and $\rho(t)$, but nothing can be known for sure until the security disruption occurs, and its effects on productivity are measured; and the recovery process begins, and its effectiveness in mitigating the effects of the security compromise is measured. We can, however, define the initial productivity plan expressed using the function $b(t)$, but it is not easy to predict how the security disruption and the recovery process will affect the initial shape of the productivity curve. We are leaving as an exercise the study of several scenarios that may be of interest to security management.

At any point of time in the recovery period $[t_0, T]$, and given the compromised productivity rate $c(t)$, the recovery period productivity is equal to $(1-(1 - \rho(t))c(t))$ $b(t)$, as discussed earlier.

The amount of productivity compromised or lost at any time t between t_0 and T is given by $(1 - \rho(t))c(t))b(t)$. The total productivity lost at any time of recovery t_1 is expressed as follows:

$$\int_{t0}^{t1} (1-(1 - \rho(t))c(t)))b(t)dt$$

The average productivity loss is equal to $1/(T - t_0) \int_{t0}^{T} (1-(1 - \rho(t))c(t)))b(t)dt$.

7.7 The ALE Risk Methodology

The ALE value may be estimated in terms of two parameters: annualized rate of occurrence (ARO) and single loss expectancy (SLE). The ARO represents the frequency of attack occurrence in 1 year. An attack should be here understood as the situation where a system vulnerability is exploited by a threat. We, however, throughout this chapter, assume that every vulnerability included in risk assessment is exploited by an existing threat. Based on this assumption, we will interchangeably use vulnerability occurrence, as in some of the literature, to mean threat occurrence or attack occurrence. The SLE represents the most likely loss from an attack. ALE is computed as follows:

$$ALE = SLE \times ARO$$

Once you've compiled lists of assets and vulnerabilities (and considered likely attackers), the next step is to correlate and quantify them. One simple way to quantify risk is by calculating annualized loss expectancies (ALEs).

We first consider an asset, and then we identify all vulnerabilities associated with it. We then consider a vulnerability and estimate the cost of replacing or restoring the asset; this is the asset's single loss expectancy. We then estimate the vulnerability's expected annual rate of occurrence. You then multiply these to obtain the vulnerability's annualized loss expectancy.

Remember, we need to compute the risk of the entire computing environment, which has many assets and vulnerabilities associated with them. That is, what do we do with the rest of the vulnerabilities and assets?

Assume that we have n assets $\{A_i, i = 1,n\}$. Also let $\{V_{ij}, j = 1,f_i\}$ be the vulnerabilities associated with asset A_i. That is, we can compute ALE_{ij}, which denotes the ALE for asset A_i and V_{ij}, as follows:

$$ALE_{ij} = ARO_{ij} \times SLE_{ij}.$$

The ALE of the entire computing environment may be computed as follows:

$$ALE = \sum_{i\,=\,1,n} \sum_{j=1,ji} ARO_{ij} * SLE_{ij}.$$

Consider the server hosting an e-business Web site. Assume that the server crashes takes 5 hours to replace, and business is lost at the rate of $12,000 per hour. Let us estimate the current SLE. The SLE should include the replacement cost, the business lost, and opportunity costs. Assume that the total replacement cost is $8000. Without assuming any side effects from the unavailability of the server, the SLE is estimated at $8000 + 5 × ($12,000) = $68,000. We also need to estimate the ARO value based on the annual frequency of similar attacks/incidents associated with same vulnerability associated with the e-business server. Let us say that the same incident repeats every 4 years. In this case, the ARO is equal to 0.25.

Based on the foregoing information, the ALE risk value is equal to ARO × SLE = (0.25) × ($68,000) = $17,000. This simply means that if the cost of replacing the server is higher than $17,000 then the optimal decision will be to go ahead and replace the e-business server; otherwise, the risk has to be accepted.

In real life, however, it is very difficult to obtain the information we need to estimate the ARO and SLE parameters, and even if we do get the information, we have to worry about its precision. If the information at hand is not valid, the computed ALE will not be valid. Of course, we always hope that historical data is available and valid values for both the ARO and SLE will be available so that we can produce an acceptable ALE.

7.8 Operational, Functional, and Strategic Risks

Risks can appear at any level of business management: at the strategic, functional, or operational level. Strategic risks are risks associated with strategic planning activities. Functional risks are concerned with functional performance. Operational risks are concerned with operational activities. Managers of operational risks can only see risk effects associated with business operational activities. Even though sometimes risks are assessed at operational activities, they may originate at higher levels, at the functional level, or at the strategic level. Losses caused by any events are felt at the

Table 7.2   ALE for the Computing Environment and Individual ALEs

Assets	Vulnerability	AROs	SLEs	ALEs
A_1	V_{11}	ARO_{11}	SLE_{11}	$ARO11 \times SLE11$
	—	—	—	—
	V_{1j}	ARO_{1j}	SLE_{1j}	$ARO_{1j} \times SLE_{1j}$
	—	—	—	—
	V_{1j1}	ARO_{1j1}	SLE_{1j1}	$ARO_{1j1} \times SLE_{1j1}$
	—	—	—	—
A_i	V_{i1}	ARO_{i1}	SLE_{i1}	$ARO_{i1} \times SLE_{i1}$
	—	—	—	—
	V_{ij}	ARO_{ij}	SLE_{ij}	$ARO_{ij} \times SLE_{ij}$
	—	—	—	—
	V_{iji}	ARO_{ij1}	SLE_{ij1}	$ARO_{ij1} \times SLE_{ij1}$
	—	—	—	—
A_n	V_{n1}	ARO_{nj}	SLE_{nj}	$ARO_{nj} \times SLE_{nj}$
	—	—	—	—
	V_{nj}	ARO_{nj}	SLE_{nj}	$ARO_{nj} \times SLE_{nj}$
	—	—	—	—
	V_{njn}	ARO_{njn}	SLE_{njn}	$ARO_{njn} \times SLE_{njn}$
ALE for the entire computing environment				$\Sigma_{i=1,n}\Sigma_j = 1, ji\, ARO_{ij} \times SLE_{ij}$

operational level but they are caused by a faulty major production system, a functional plan, or the organization's strategic plan. Consider the stalling of a major server resulting from the misconfiguration of the administration network or the poor maintenance of the server. A simple event such as this can lead to denial of service, which can have disastrous effects that can tarnish the image of the company. Figure 7.13 gives an example of strategic risks, functional risks, and operational risks.

The organization has to identify, assess, and mitigate risks at every managerial level. Bear in mind that risks at all managerial levels are interdependent. Operational risks can have significant effects on functional risks and strategic risks. For example, a simple incident at the operational level can disrupt the performance of a functional unit or affect the public image of the organization. On the other hand, a wrong

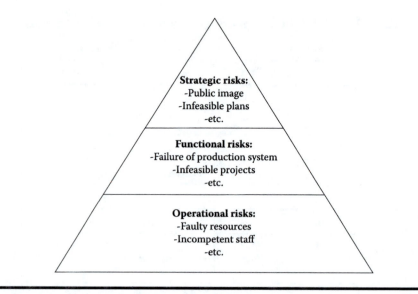

Figure 7.13   Risks at various managerial levels.

strategic decision, for example the initiation of an infeasible project or misconfiguration of a segment of the production system, can disrupt operational activities.

Organizations have to be concerned with all types of risks. This will certainly require a comprehensive strategic approach to enterprise risk management. According to Sippy [6], taking a strategic approach to risk management not only anticipates and diminishes problems, but can also create business opportunities. To be successful, a strategic and mature approach to enterprise risk management must focus on risk avoidance, protecting existing assets, enhancing future growth opportunities, and creating competitive differentiation.

Adopting a reactive approach will limit the organization's ability to adequately assess critical risks and their interdependencies. The adoption of a strategic approach to risk management can achieve great business value and alleviate the effects of any potential undesired events. Organizations have to translate their risk management processes from reactive to proactive, and from tactical to strategic.

Sippy [6] explained that managing risk strategically requires organizations to:

Automatically identify and monitor top enterprise risks
Embed risk management into existing business processes so that lines of business can effectively mitigate risks
Plan for cross-enterprise risk scenarios
Add risk analysis to strategy and decision-making processes

For the organization to sustain a competitive advantage, it has no choice but to maintain an acceptable level of security and a risk position that is competitive enough not to lose profitable partners and good customers. The organization has to maintain a computing environment in which confidentiality and privacy requirements are met and integrity and availability are assured.

The organization has to study which of the following risk management strategies will provide the competitive advantage discussed earlier: risk avoidance, risk transference, risk mitigation, and risk acceptance. Risk acceptance is, however, more of a risk management rule rather than a risk management strategy.

Risk avoidance: This is concerned with applying the security controls that eliminate or reduce the remaining uncontrolled risks for the vulnerability. Risk Avoidance is the risk control strategy that is primarily concerned with any attempts to prevent the exploitation of the vulnerability. Risk avoidance may be implemented by adopting one of the following:
Enforcement of security policy
Providing the necessary information assurance literacy, awareness, and training and education programs
Effective management of present and future threats
Adoption of the most appropriate security controls

Risk transference: This is concerned with shifting the risk to other areas or to outside entities. Risk transference is the control approach that is concerned with any attempts to shift the risk to other assets, processes, or organizations. This type of strategy may be achieved as follows:
Reevaluation of the business functions
Outsourcing to other organizations
Purchasing insurance
Implementing service contracts with providers where risk is transferable

Risk mitigation: This is concerned with reducing the impact after the vulnerability has been exploited. Risk mitigation is the control approach that is concerned with any attempts to reduce, by means of planning and preparation, the damage caused by the exploitation of a vulnerability. This approach requires a disaster recovery plan, an incident response plan, and a business continuity plan. Mitigation capabilities will obviously depend on the ability to detect and timely respond to attacks.

Risk acceptance: This is concerned with understanding the consequences and accepting the risk without putting in place control or mitigation. Risk acceptance is the decision to accept risks when investing in security controls is not feasible. It is probably not a risk management strategy but a rule that imposes the acceptance of risks under infeasibility conditions. The risk acceptance rule only applies when the following are satisfied:
Risks are known with reasonable accuracy.
Vulnerabilities and how they can be exploited are known.
Probabilities of events are known.
Attack's consequences are known.

Table 7.3   RAC Matrix

		Mishap Probability			
		Likely	Probably	May	Unlikely
Hazard Severity	Critical	1	1	2	3
	Serious	1	2	3	4
	Moderate	2	3	4	5
	Minor	3	4	5	5
	Critical	1	1	2	3

A feasibility study has been completed.

A thorough cost-benefit analysis has been performed.

Adopting new security controls is infeasible.

7.9 Operational Risk Management: Case of the Naval Safety Center

The Naval Safety Center adopts four risk principles that are effective in security management [4]. Table 7.3 shows a document summarizing the risk management steps associated with those risk principles. This document is similar to the statement of applicability adopted in the information security management system (ISMS) developed when complying with ISO 27001 (see Chapter 10).

The Naval Safety Center adopts four principles for applying operational risk management (ORM) [4]:

Principle 1: Accept risk when the benefit > risk.

> Risk is inherent in the nature of military action.
>
> Leaders who are in the risk-taking business must be top-quality risk managers.
>
> Risk is usually proportional to gain.
>
> You cannot eliminate all risk.

Principle 2: Accept no unnecessary risk.

> An unnecessary risk is any risk that, if taken, will not contribute meaningfully to mission accomplishment.
>
> Leaders who accept unnecessary risks are gambling with the lives of their staff—for nothing.
>
> The gambler does not know what will happen; the risk-managing leader can reasonably predict what the outcome will be.

Principle 3: Anticipate and manage risks by planning.

> Risks are more easily controlled when identified in planning because more time, assets, and options are available to deal with the risk.

It improves efficiency and saves money if ORM is integrated early in the
planning process. If risk controls are tacked on as an afterthought in
training or in combat, they will probably fail.

Proper prior planning prevents poor performance.

Principle 4: Make risk decisions at the right level.

The leader directly responsible for the operation makes risk decisions.

If risk > benefit or goes beyond the commander's stated intent or help is
needed to implement controls—communicate with a higher authority.

The risk assessment adopted by the Naval Safety Center is based on hazard identification, hazard classification, and the assessment of probabilities of hazard occurrence.

Identification of hazards: There are two types of hazards: inherent and induced
hazards. Inherent hazards are characteristic of and intrinsic to the type of
equipment. Examples are electrical systems, radioactive materials, etc. Induced
hazards arise from oversights or wrong decisions. Examples are design, production, or operations errors.

Classification of hazards: Hazards are grouped into severity of component failure/
environment/malfunction/personnel error/procedural difficulties, etc. An example is Class 1: Catastrophic; Class II: Critical; and Class III: Marginal damage.

Probability: Probability addresses the likelihood that an identified hazard will
cause a mishap. It is estimated as A: Likely to occur; B: Probably will occur;
C: May occur; and D: Unlikely to occur.

To quantify the risks within a hazardous operation, codes were developed using the
severity classes together with the probability estimates: RAC 1—Imminent danger,
initiate abatement procedures immediately; RAC 2—Serious condition exists, priority attention required; RAC 3 to 5: Nonserious condition exists, correct ASAP.
The risk assessment codes are shown in Table 7.3.

The Naval Safety Center employs five steps for performing operational risk
management [5]:

1. Identify hazards
2. Assess hazards
3. Make risk decisions
4. Implement controls
5. Supervise

7.9.1 Step 1: Identify Hazards

This step aims at defining the major steps of the target operation. This requires a
limited operational analysis to define the scope of the risk analysis. The following
tasks are performed by the Naval Safety Center for identifying hazards:

Conduct an operational analysis.
List major steps of the operation.
Conduct a preliminary hazard analysis.
List the hazards associated with each step.
List the possible causes of the hazards.

7.9.2 Step 2: Assess Hazards

The second step of the ORM aims at assessing hazards associated with the target operation. The degree of risk associated with hazards should be expressed in terms of two important measures: severity of the hazard and its probability. The following tasks are performed by the Naval Safety Center:

Determine degree of risk for each hazard in terms of severity and probability.
Use of a matrix is recommended but not required. A matrix provides a consistent framework for evaluation and shows the relative perceived risk between hazards. It also prioritizes which hazards to control first.
Any matrix that supports the specific application may be used.
Risk Assessment Code (RAC) is a scale used to measure the level of the risk:
Critical
Serious
Moderate
Minor
Negligible
The following is a scale used to measure the hazard severity:
Critical: May cause death, loss of facility/asset, or grave damage to national interests.
Serious: May cause severe injury, illness, property damage; or damage to national or service interests.
Moderate: May cause minor injury, illness, property damage; or damage to national, service, or command interests.
Minor: Minimal threat.
The following is a scale for measuring the probability of a mishap:
Likely: Likely to occur immediately or in a short period of time. Expected to occur several times to an individual item or person, or continuously to a group.
Probably: Probably will occur in time. Reasonably expected to occur some time to an individual item or person, or continuously to a group.
May: May occur in time. Reasonably expected to occur some time to an individual item or person, or several times to a group.
Unlikely: Unlikely to occur.

7.9.3 Step 3: Make Risk Decisions

This step is concerned with making risk decisions. What are the feasible security controls that are capable of minimizing risks? The organization cannot feasibly treat every hazard identified in the target operation but can prioritize and select the most serious hazards first. How to make a risk decision? We have to make sure that the controls in place are such that benefits are higher than risks. Risks are accepted if the benefits are higher than risks. Those risks have to be communicated to a higher authority if risks are higher than benefits, if risks exceed the decision maker's (commander in the case of the Naval Safety Center) stated intent, or if help is needed to implement the security controls.

The following tasks are proposed by the Naval Safety Center:
Develop controls for each hazard to eliminate the hazard or reduce the risk until the benefit exceeds the risk.
Determine residual risk.
Make risk decision.

7.9.4 Step 4: Implement Controls

This step is concerned with the implementation of security controls. This step has to involve all relevant managers and concerned staff and operators in order to minimize potential undesired events that may take place in later monitoring activities. The following steps are proposed by the Naval Safety Center:

Incorporate selected controls into relevant activity in the target operation.
Communicate selected controls to the lowest level. Who will do what by when?

7.9.5 Step 5: Supervise

This step is concerned with managing security according to relevant standards and controls. The following tasks are performed by the Naval Safety Center:

Enforce standards and controls.
Remain alert for changes and unexpected developments.
Take corrective action when necessary.

A summary of Operational Risk Management from the Naval Safety Center that we slightly changed is provided in Table 7.4 (http://www.combatleadership.com/documents/00036.rtf).

Table 7.4 Summary of Operational Risk Management from Naval Safety Center (Slightly Changed)

Mission:

Date Worksheet Prepared:

Operation Phases	Step 1: Identify Hazards		Step 2: Assess Hazards	Step 3: Make Risk Decisions		Step 4: Implement Controls	Step 5: Supervise
	Hazards	Causes	Initial RAC	Develop controls	Residual RAC	How to Implement	How to Supervise
—	—	—	—	—	—	—	—

Accept Risks: Yes   No

Communicate with upper management: Yes   No

Lessons Learned:

Source: http://www.combatleadership.com/documents/00036.rtf.

7.10 The ABLE Methodology

7.10.1 Introduction

The ABLE methodology was originally developed to assess annual security risk as in ALE in terms of their time frame. The ABLE methodology accounts for both economic and noneconomic benefits, whereas ALE is limited to economic values. The computations are very different in both methods. This chapter still maintains the same name for ABLE, where the letter "A" indicates the annual benefits accounted for, even though we extend the ABLE methodology to assess risks through any time span of the risk life cycle. We give enough flexibility in defining the time unit used and the length of risk life cycle. We also allow for the discounting of economic benefits when their effects are realized in the future.

This chapter introduces three types of risks based on the risk life cycle length and the category of benefit risked: operational security risk, functional security risk, and strategic security risk. Usually, operational risks are concerned with the direct economic benefits that are generated in the short term. Functional security risks are system performance and semieconomic benefits usually measured in the midterm range. Strategic security risks are concerned with noneconomic benefits that are usually measured for the long term.

A parameter is semieconomic if it may be translated to an economic value but a direct relationship is not known; for example, we know that system performance is related to productivity, but we do not know the direct relationship. Functional risk is associated with the loss of system performance, whereas operational risk is associated with system productivity. Even though we know that better system performance produces higher productivity, we do not know exactly how the two quantities are related.

Strategic security risk is associated with noneconomic benefits, for example, social, technical, operational feasibility, and legal/ethical benefits. The main difference between operational security and strategic security is that once the latter is compromised, this compromise lasts for longer periods, whereas compromise due to operational risk goes away at the end of the recovery period.

The pyramid in Figure 7.14 shows that operational risks are associated with the organization's business-value-generation capability which is studied in terms of economic benefits generated by the organization. Operational risk is concerned with the probability and value of the loss of economic benefits. Functional risk relates to systems performance and is assessed in terms of the probability and the opportunity of improving systems performance (which would indirectly lead to higher productivity). The general idea here is that if an incident occurs once and the appropriate corrective actions are taken, this incident should not occur in the near future or at least, if it occurs, the effects should be a lot milder. If, however, the same incident keeps recurring, there must be deeper security problems that are

Figure 7.14 Risks, benefits, and time frame.

often related to the configuration of the system and security management controls that regulate system performance.

Independently of the type of security risks just defined, those risks all depend on asset exposure, asset vulnerabilities, and the effectiveness of existing security controls. As shown in Figures 7.15, 7.16, and 7.17, asset exposure is defined in terms of the types of known potential threats and their impacts on assets. The impact depends, however, on the types of benefits that are compromised. For operational security risks, those impacts are associated with economic benefits; for functional risks, with system performance, semieconomic benefits, and midterm range; and strategic security risks, with noneconomic benefits and long-term range.

Figure 7.18 explains the relationship between operational, functional, and strategic risks. If an intrusion takes place, there will be immediate compromise of operational and strategic security, but the functional security of the computing environment will not affected directly by the intrusion. Functional security is related to systems performance, which can be compromised, not directly by the intrusion, often by a sequence of operational security incidents; not after a single one, but by the definitions and configurations of various components of the computing environment. The appropriate response will terminate the intrusion by implementing the necessary corrections and the relevant recovery procedures for the purpose of restoring normal business operations. However, when normal operations resume, all economic benefits are recovered, but noneconomic benefits remain compromised for a longer time period. Strategic security stays compromised until the security strategy, security policies, ethics code, regulations, and all relevant noneconomic benefits are reviewed and improved. Their effects will last for longer periods, and some effects even may be permanent when the image of the organization is touched.

In order to enhance functional security, it is important to review systems performance after multiple security incidents and conduct a comparative study to identify new performance opportunities. This can be accomplished in two ways:

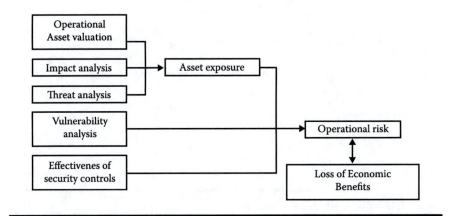

Figure 7.15   Operational risk assessment.

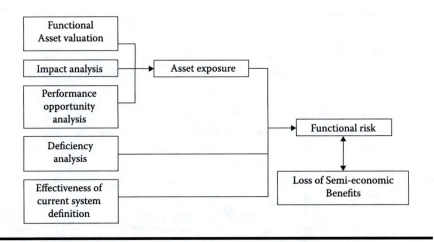

Figure 7.16   Functional risk assessment.

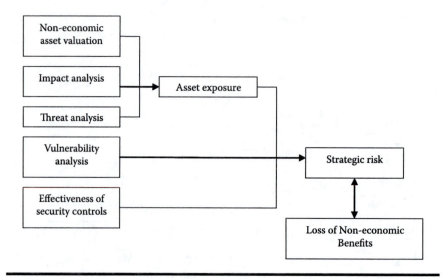

Figure 7.17   Strategic risk assessment.

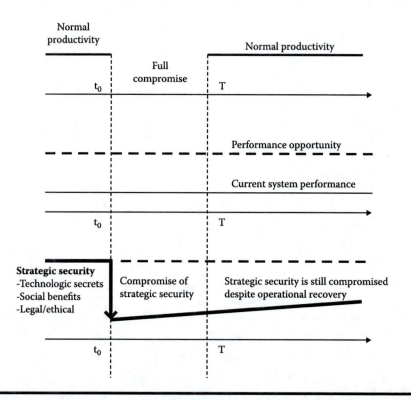

Figure 7.18   Interactions between operational, functional, and strategic risks.

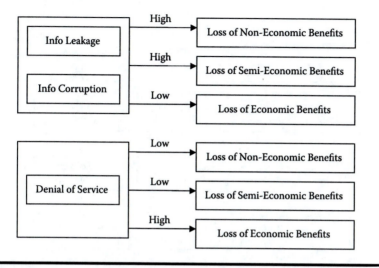

Figure 7.19 Security disruptions and loss of benefits.

based on a simulation study or based on competitive advantage intelligence. The simulation is needed to study to what extent systems performance can be feasibly elevated. The simulation will identify new opportunities to enhance system performance, which will indirectly lead to higher productivity. Alternatively, or in parallel to the simulation approach, we need to collect intelligence about what competitors are doing to generate higher performance. Once we know the definition of competitors' systems, we can study possible results if organizational systems are redefined in a feasible manner.

Figure 7.19 may be summarized simply by saying that denial-of-service attacks produce loss of economic benefits. Information leakage or corruption may produce losses of semieconomic and noneconomic benefits.

7.10.1.1 Measuring Functional Risk

Functional risk is concerned with risks related to system performance. We need to identify any feasible changes we can effect in the computing environment that can produce significant improvements in system performance in the midterm. Because the computing environment consists mainly of people, activities, data, technology, and network, we then need to study what changes can be effected on people, activities, data, technology, or the network that can enhance system performance in the midterm.

We can estimate the total system performance produced if those changes are implemented. While this depends on the information asset in question, simulation may be used to estimate any gain in system performance. The gain, per time unit,

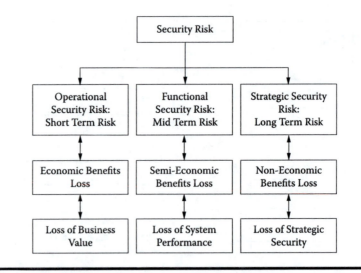

Figure 7.20   Relationship between benefit losses and types of risks.

of performance is assigned to the single functional security benefit loss expectancy of the asset, or single performance loss expectancy.

Alternatively, it is possible to collect information about the quality of people, activities, data, technology, and network adopted by competitors who are known for their higher system performance. Based on this information, and the information assembled following a series of operational security incidents, we can compute the added performance per time unit that is assigned to single loss expectancy.

7.10.1.2 Measuring Strategic Risk

Strategic security risk is concerned with changes in the computing environment that can improve system security in the long run. Usually, those changes are associated with the revision of current strategies, including security risk strategies, initiating new R&D projects for the purpose of enhancing security, acquiring social assistance and involving users in reorganizing social benefits, revising security policy and regulations, identifying new ways to enforce the ethics code and security policy, etc. Strategic security risk measures noneconomic security risks associated with the asset in question.

We can estimate the total loss of noneconomic benefits when information leakage, information corruption, or denial of service takes place. Historical data may be used to estimate the single noneconomic benefit loss expectancy, or single strategic loss expectancy. Figure 7.20 depicts the relationship between benefit losses and operational, functional, and strategic risks.

7.10.2 Risk Analysis Using ABLE

7.10.2.1 The ABLE Risk Methodology

The risk life cycle length and the time unit should both be fixed before using the ABLE risk methodology. The ABLE methodology may be used to compute three categories of risks: Present security risk (PSR), annual security risk (ASR), or life cycle security risk (LSR).

The LSR risk is concerned with all incidents that take place throughout the entire risk life cycle. The LSR methodology is often needed to budget security throughout the enterprise. The PSR risk is concerned with the next potential incident that would take place any time from now. Operational security risk is an example of a present security risk.

The purpose of a risk management program is to determine the level of protection currently provided, the level of protection required, and a cost-effective way of providing needed protection for the organization's computing and networking environment (CNE).

The most fundamental element of risk management is the evaluation of the security position of the CNE. Risk management identifies the impact of events on the security position and determines whether or not the impact is acceptable and, if not acceptable, provides for corrective actions.

However, a risk management program can only be effective if it is based on a sound risk analysis process. Risk analysis, security tests and evaluations, and contingency planning are essential components of any risk management program.

The primary purpose of conducting a risk analysis is to evaluate the risk to the computing environment activities and assets and identify the most cost-effective security controls for reducing the risk of operating those activities and protecting those assets. Based on this analysis, appropriate security controls can be sought, selected, and implemented to prevent or minimize risk. A risk analysis is a procedure within the accreditation process and is conducted prior to a new system design approval, whenever a significant change to a system is made or at least once every 3 years.

A risk analysis involves a detailed examination of the assets and procedures of the CNE. It includes the threats that may exploit the vulnerabilities of the operating environment, resulting in information leakage, information corruption, or denial of system services. Risk analysis activities are planned in terms of the current status and mission of the CNE operations.

System owners determine which risk analysis methodology is to be used. This decision is based on the complexity of the system environment, which is governed by the sensitivity classes of data processed, the availability classes of information resources, security mode of operations, system configurations and locations (stand-alone, networked), and the criticality of the mission.

The ABLE method is a generic security risk analysis method that ranks risk exposure on multiple attributes: economic, noneconomic/social, technical, operational, and legal/ethical. It determines how organizational assets are affected by potential threats and what security controls should be implemented to protect them for each security disruption class or impact category (information corruption, information leakage, and service denial).

7.10.2.2 Roles and Responsibilities

The following people are responsible for the validity and effectiveness of a risk management program:

Systems owners: They are responsible for the overall effectiveness of a risk management program. They ensure that a continual risk analysis process is in effect to minimize the potential for unauthorized disclosure of sensitive information, modification or destruction of assets, or denial of service. Risk analysis is applied throughout the system life cycle.

Security administrators: They are responsible for implementing an effective risk management program. Their duties in this area are to:
1. Ensure that a risk analysis is conducted.
2. Review threats and vulnerabilities in order to properly assess risks and determine appropriate security controls.
3. Select a risk analysis team to conduct the risk analysis and act as the Risk Analysis Team Leader.
4. Provide ongoing risk analysis during the system life cycle; review and evaluate the security impact of system changes.
5. Initiate certification and accreditation of activities under direction from system owners.

7.10.2.3 Risk Analysis Team

The risk analysis team comprises security staff personnel. It is desirable that team members possess some technical qualifications and have training in system security prior to the risk analysis.

The risk analysis team is responsible for:

1. Gathering information for the risk analysis, which consists of in-depth interviews and reviewing documentation.
2. Documenting the findings and completing the forms required for the risk analysis.
3. Compiling the risk analysis information.
4. Developing the risk analysis report.

7.10.2.4 ABLE's Phases

The ABLE methodology consists of the following phases:

1. Planning the security program
2. Asset analysis
3. Threat analysis
4. Security control analysis
5. Design of the security program
6. Final report

7.10.2.4.1 Planning the Security Analysis

The procedures for performing the risk analysis method are as follows:

1. Preparation procedures
    a. It is recommended that the organization performs security surveys of information resources prior to conducting risk analysis to understand the computing environment, threats, and the present defense system. The results of the surveys determine the scope of the risk analysis effort.
    b. Prior to the start of the risk analysis, the team leader schedules a project presentation to upper management to seek its support and provide information so that all company personnel are aware of the risk analysis team's efforts. The briefing provides an overview of the risk analysis process and addresses the following:
        i. The team's goals during the risk analysis process
        ii. The level of participation expected from relevant personnel
        iii. The risk scope, life cycle, and end results of the risk analysis process and its management
    c. The risk analysis team members conduct a kickoff meeting to discuss their approach to the risk analysis process. Areas of consideration for the meeting include division of work, assignment of individual responsibilities, and categories of assets and threats on which to concentrate during risk analysis interviews. The team also reviews documentation such as system security survey, security plan, previous risk analysis findings, etc.

Interviews may be conducted to gather data pertinent to the system operating environment. The data are used to complete the risk analysis documentation. The level of detail depends on the risk analysis method used and the size of the system being analyzed.

7.10.2.4.2 Asset Analysis

This phase aims at valuing the current system. It analyzes the security of the existing system by identifying and analyzing each asset or asset group and comparing its current operating costs to its annual revenues in terms of the relevant economic parameters and noneconomic factors (social, technical, operational, and legal/ethical attributes). It also produces life-cycle benefits of the existing system on all the attributes.

The asset analysis phase consists of the following steps:

1. Identify all assets or asset groups.
2. For each asset or asset group, explain its value added as follows:
   Estimate its current replacement cost.
   Estimate its current life-cycle operating costs.
   Estimate its current revenues throughout the risk life cycle.
   Estimate life-cycle noneconomic benefits in terms of
      Noneconomic/social factors
      Technical factors
      Operational factors
      Legal/ethical factors
3. Percentage of noneconomic benefits with respect to life-cycle net benefits.

7.10.2.4.3 Threat Analysis

This phase aims at estimating the impact of threats on the current system. The threat analysis information needed to compute security risks is provided in Table 7.5. It identifies all possible threats and studies their effects on all assets in the three security disruption areas: information leakage, information corruption, and service denial.

This phase produces estimates for the likelihood of threats, and for each threat and asset, the likelihood that the threat would impact the asset. These latter estimates are actually subjective conditional probabilities. These probabilities will change value when security controls are implemented.

This phase consists of the following steps:

1. Identify all threats.
2. For each threat and for each asset, explain how this threat impacts this asset in each of the security disruption areas, as follows:
   2.1 Information leakage:
      2.1.1 Estimate the threat's impact, in terms of information leakage, on the asset's current net business value generated throughout the defined risk life cycle (a number between 0 and 1).
      2.1.2 Estimate the threat's impact, in terms of information leakage, on the asset's current noneconomic benefits for the economic, non-economic/social, technical, operational, and legal/ethical factors,

Table 7.5 Threat Analysis Worksheet for the Existing System

1. Threat ID:	Official use only:
	– Accept
	– Reject
2. Asset number:	– Redo
3. Given the historical data at hand, what is the likelihood that this threat would take place? (a number between 0 and 1):	
4. How often would this threat take place in the defined risk life cycle?	
Note: Make sure that the information you provide in items (4) and (3) are consistent. The probability estimate you provided in (4) should be equal to the frequency you provided in (3) should be equal to the frequency you provided in (4) divided by the number of opportunities for the incident to take place. The number of opportunities decreases when security increases.	
5. If this threat has taken place, what is the likelihood that it would actually affect this asset (a number between 0 and 1)?:	

identified in the Asset Valuation Worksheet provided in Table 7.6. Give the percentage of the net business value generated that would be lost due the effect of information leakage on those noneconomic factors (a number between 0 and 100).

2.2 Information corruption:

2.2.1 Estimate the threat's impact, in terms of information corruption, on the asset's current net business value generated throughout the defined risk life cycle (a number between 0 and 1).

2.2.2 Estimate the threat's impact, in terms of information corruption, on the asset's current noneconomic benefits in terms of the economic, noneconomic/social, technical, operational, and legal/ethical factors, identified in the asset valuation worksheet. Give the percentage of the net business value generated that would be lost due to the effect of information corruption on those noneconomic factors (a number between 0 and 100).

Table 7.6 Asset Analysis Worksheet

1. Asset name: _____ _____	Official use only: – Accept – Reject
2. Asset number: _____ _____	– Redo – Override
3. Asset replacement cost: _____ _____	

4. Current profitability of the asset:
4.1 Estimate the asset's current annual operating costs in terms of Economic factors: _____
4.2 Estimate its current revenues: _____
4.3 Identify its noneconomic benefits in terms: social, technical, operational, and legal/ethical factors. Use this 5-point Likert scale 1: Very insignificant; 2: Insignificant; 3: Moderate; 4: Significant; and 5: Very significant.   Social factors (Choose 1, 2, 3, 4, or 5): _____   Technical factors (Choose 1, 2, 3, 4, or 5): _____   Operational factors (Choose 1, 2, 3, 4, or 5): _____   Legal/ethical factors (Choose 1, 2,3, 4, or 5): _____
4.4 Total net business value generated by asset = (4.2) – (4.1) =   _____
4.5 If there is an incident where the asset is fully compromised, the entire amount in (4.4) is fully lost for the entire recovery period. But at the end of the recovery period, when business operations resume, the amount of (4.4) will be restored except for a small percentage amount that is associated with noneconomic benefits identified in (4.3), for example, company reputation, technological secrets, etc. What is your assessment of this percentage of business value that is lost for every due to loss of noneconomic benefits?: _____%.
5. Quality of information collected: _____   _____

2.3 Service denial:
  2.3.1 Estimate the threat's impact, in terms of denial of service, on the asset's current net business value generated throughout the defined risk life cycle (a number between 0 and 1).
  2.3.2 Estimate the threat's impact, in terms of denial of service, on the asset's current noneconomic benefits with respect to the economic, noneconomic/social, technical, operational, and legal/ethical factors, identified in the asset valuation worksheet. Give the percentage of the net business value generated that would be lost due to the effect of service denial on those noneconomic factors (a number between 0 and 100).

7.10.2.4.4 Security Control Analysis

This phase aims at identifying possible security controls for the purpose of reducing risks in all security disruption areas. It analyzes each security control in terms of its effects on the threats. Security control information is provided in Table 7.8. For each threat, each security control, and each asset, the effects of the security control on the threat's impact on the asset are studied. A comparative study of the impacts of threats on assets before and after the implementation is conducted.

This phase consists of the following steps:

1. Identify all possible security controls.
2. For each new security control and for each asset identified in the asset analysis phase, explain how risk is reduced in the security disruption areas as follows:
  2.1 Information leakage:
    2.1.1 Estimate the threat's impact, in terms of information leakage, on the asset's current net business value generated throughout the defined risk life cycle (a number between 0 and 1).
    2.1.2 Estimate the threat's impact, in terms of information leakage, on the asset's current noneconomic benefits for the economic, noneconomic/social, technical, operational, and legal/ethical factors, identified in the asset valuation worksheet. Give the percentage of the net business value generated that would be lost due the effect of information leakage on those noneconomic factors (a number between 0 and 100).
  2.2 Information corruption:
    2.2.1 Estimate the threat's impact, in terms of information corruption, on the asset's current net business value generated throughout the defined risk life cycle (a number between 0 and 1).
    2.2.2 Estimate the threat's impact, in terms of information corruption, on the asset's current noneconomic benefits in terms of the economic, noneconomic/social, technical, operational, and legal/ethical factors, identified in the asset valuation worksheet. Give the

Table 7.7 Postimplementation Impact Analysis Worksheet

1. Security control Id: _____	Official use only: – Accept
2. Security objective: _____	– Reject – Redo
3. Threat number: _____	
4. Asset number: _____	
5. If this threat has taken place, what is the likelihood that it would actually affect this asset (a number between 0 and 1)?: _____	
6. Revision of threat impact on the asset after implementing this security control:	
6.1 Information Leakage:	
6.1.1 Estimate the threat's impact, in terms of information leakage, on the asset's current net business value generated throughout the defined risk life cycle (a number between 0 and 1):	
6.1.2 Estimate the threat's impact, in terms of information leakage, on the asset's current noneconomic benefits for the economic, noneconomic/social, technical, operational, and legal/ethical factors identified in the asset valuation worksheet. Give the percentage of the net business value generated that would be lost due to the effect of information leakage on those noneconomic factors (a number between 0 and 100):	
6.2 Information Corruption:	
6.2.1 Estimate the threat's impact, in terms of information corruption, on the asset's current net business value generated throughout the defined risk life cycle (a number between 0 and 1):	
6.2.2 Estimate the threat's impact, in terms of information corruption, on the asset's current noneconomic benefits in terms of the economic, noneconomic/social, technical, operational, and legal/ethical factors identified in the asset valuation worksheet. Give the percentage of the net business value generated that would be lost due to the effect of information corruption on those noneconomic factors (a number between 0 and 100):	

Table 7.7 Postimplementation Impact Analysis Worksheet (*Continued*)

6.3 Service denial:
6.3.1 Estimate the threat's impact, in terms of denial of service, on the asset's current net business value generated throughout the defined risk life cycle (a number between 0.00 and 1.00):
6.3.2 Estimate the threat's impact, in terms of denial of service, on the asset's current noneconomic benefits with respect to social, technical, operational, and legal/ethical factors identified in the asset valuation worksheet. Give the percentage of the net business value generated that would be lost due to the effect of service denial on those noneconomic factors (a number between 0.00 and 1.00):
7. The effect of this threat on the economic benefits of this asset is estimated at: (6.1.1) + (6.2.1) + (6.3.1) = _____
8. The effect of this threat on the noneconomic benefits of this asset is estimated at: (6.1.2) + (6.2.2) + (6.3.2) = _____ Note: Make sure that this estimate is consistent with item 4.5 in the Asset Valuation Worksheet. This item elicits the following information: Item 4.5 of the Asset Valuation Worksheet: If there is an incident in which the asset is fully compromised, the full amount in (4.4) is fully lost for the entire recovery period time. But at the end of the recovery period, business operations resume, and the amount of (4.4) will be restored except for a small percentage amount that is associated with noneconomic benefits identified in (4.3), for example, company reputation, technological secrets, etc. What is your assessment of this percentage of business value that is lost for every due to loss of noneconomic benefits?
9. Quality of information collected: _____

Table 7.8   Security Control Analysis Worksheet

1. Security control name:	Official use only:
	– Accept
	– Reject
2. Security control number:	– Redo
3. Annual total relevant cost:	
4. Quality of Information:	

> percentage of the net business value generated that would be lost due to the effect of information corruption on those noneconomic factors (a number between 0 and 100).
>
> 2.3 Service denial:
>
> 2.3.1 Estimate the threat's impact, in terms of denial of service, on the asset's current net business value generated throughout the defined risk life cycle (a number between 0 and 1).
>
> 2.3.2 Estimate the threat's impact, in terms of denial of service, on the asset's current noneconomic benefits with respect to the economic, noneconomic/social, technical, operational, and legal/ethical factors, identified in the asset valuation worksheet. Give the percentage of the net business value generated that would be lost due the effect of service denial on those noneconomic factors (a number between 0 and 100).

In fact, the foregoing steps are the exact steps we included in threat analysis, and we now revisit them to see whether the new security controls we just implemented produced the desired defense effects. The security control effectiveness information is obtained from the Post Implementation Impact Analysis Worksheet, provided in Table 7.7.

7.10.2.4.5   Design of the Security Program

This phase aims at implementing security controls that minimize risks. Security controls are very expensive. It is very important to select the set of cost-effective security controls that minimizes the total annual benefit loss expectancy of the system.

For every security control, for every threat, and for every asset, analyze the security control's effect on the threat's impact on the asset. If there are N assets, M threats, and K security controls, then the risk analysis team has to fill out $N \times M \times K$ worksheets.

The algorithm for selecting and implementing the security controls follows:

> While there is budget and there are still available security controls,
>   do the following:
> Begin

1. Fill out the Post-implementation Impact Analysis worksheets for all remaining security controls.
2. For every remaining security control, compute the system risk position after the implementation of this security control.
3. Rank remaining security controls in descending order of system risk positions.
4. Implement the security control with the lowest system risk position.

> End;

The postimplementation threat analysis is intended to study the expected behavior of assets after the implementation of security controls. The actual postimplementation period is a part of the risk management process that executes the security program recommended by the ABLE security analysis.

The postimplementation threat analysis also includes the study of the postimplementation profitability of assets. The postimplementation threat analysis worksheet reserves a section on estimating postimplementation annual operating costs, annual revenues, and annual benefits on all the attributes: economic, noneconomic/social, technical, operational, and legal/ethical.

This information is needed to compute the ABLE values (annual benefit loss expectancy).

It is not possible to analyze a security control by only looking at the values of assets and how they are currently protected. Unless the security control counters the threats, there will be no risk reduction due to the implementation of this security control.

It is therefore necessary to study the security control's effect on each threat's impact on assets.

The rest of this chapter presents the computation of security risks: life-cycle risks, annual risks, and present security risks. As seen earlier, we distinguished between three main term security risks: short-term risk, midterm risk, and long-term risk. The short risk is also referred to as operational risk or present risk. The midterm security risk is the annual security risk or the functional risk. The long-term risk is also referred to as life-cycle risk or strategic risk.

Because every type of risk is either directly or indirectly computed in terms of the ABLE values, the time unit is the year and the value of N is expressed as a number of years. This is certainly a computational requirement, but it is easier to interpret risks when the length of the risk life cycle is measured in years. Any risk mitigation budget planning is performed after discounting any future values to their present worth. It is important, however, to make sure that if the risk life cycle is N years, then the time unit has to be the year. If the risk life cycle is less than a year, then the time unit can be any number as long as one year equals N time units.

Let us start by defining some variables that are needed to present the ABLE methodology:

n_j = random variable representing the annual frequency of threat Z_j.

$\check{n}$ = random variable representing the annual frequency of any incident involving any threat.

$p(\check{n})$ = probability distribution of $\check{n}$.

$F = E(\check{n})$ = mean of $\check{n}$.

A_j = asset number j (Assets: $\{A_i\}j = 1,n$).

Z_j = threat number j (Threats: $\{Z_j\}j = 1,m$).

Z = any threat.

A = any asset (Assets: $\{A_i\}j = 1,n$).

i = represents asset A_i (unless it is a mute index).

j = represents threat Z_j (unless it is a mute index).

k = kth time of incident, $k = 1,K$.

K = maximum number of incidents in a year.

t_{jk} = time of occurrence of threat Z_j.

t_k = time of occurrence of any threat (when threats are averaged out to simplify computation).

T_{jk} = end of security compromise period from threat Z_j's occurrence that started at t_{jk}.

T_k = end of security compromise from any threat (when threats are averaged out to simplify computation).

$d_{jk} = T_{jk} - t_{jk}$ = duration of compromise period $[t_{jk}, T_{jk}]$.

$d(.,j) = d_{.j}$ = average duration of compromise period on all assets when threat Z_j is considered.

$d(i,.) = d_{i.}$ = average duration of compromise period on all threats when asset A_i is considered.

d = average of $d_{jk} j = 1,m; k = 1,K$.

$C(i,j) = C_{ij}$ = cost of corrective actions to restore asset A_i's operations affected by threat Z_j.

$C(.,j) = C_j$ = average cost of corrective actions on all assets when threat Z_j is considered.

$C(i,.) = C_{i.}$ = average cost of corrective actions on all threats when asset A_i is considered.

C = average of C_{ij}; $i = 1,n$; $j = 1,m$.

$s(i,j) = s_{ij}$ = Percentage of unitary business value/productivity modeling the lasting noneconomic benefits lost after the recovery of all economic benefits when asset A_i and threat Z_j are considered. This loss is assumed to last until the end of the risk life cycle.

$s(.,j)$ = average $s(i,j)$ for all assets when threat Z_j is considered.

$s(i,.)$ = average $s(i,j)$ for all threats when assets A_i is considered.

s = average of $s(i,j)$ for $i = 1,n$; $j = 1,m$.

$F(Z_j) = F_j$ = frequency of threat Z_j in the risk life cycle.

F = frequency of a threat (when threats are averaged out to simplify computations).

$ABLE(i,j) = ABLE_{ij}$ = annual benefit loss when asset A_i and threat Z_j are considered.

$ABLE(.,j) = ABLE_{.j}$ = annual benefit loss on all assets in the risk scope when threat Z_j is considered.

$ABLE(i,.) = ABLE_{i.}$ = annual benefit loss on all threats when asset A_i is considered.

$ABLE$ = annual benefit loss when all assets and all threats in the risk scope are considered.

$SBLE(i,j) = SBLE_{ij}$ = single benefit loss when asset A_i and threat Z_j are considered.

$SBLE(.,j) = SBLE_{.j}$ = single benefit loss on all assets in the risk scope when threat Z_j is considered.

$SBLE(i,.) = SBLE_{i.}$ = single benefit loss on all threats when asset A_i is considered.

$SBLE$ = single benefit loss when all assets and all threats in the risk scope are considered.

$LBLE(i,j) = LBLE_{ij}$ = life-cycle benefit loss when asset A_i and threat Z_j are considered.

$LBLE(.,j) = LBLE_{.j}$ = life-cycle benefit loss on all assets in the risk scope when threat Z_j is considered.

$LBLE(i,.) = LBLE_{i.}$ = life benefit loss on all threats when asset A_i is considered.

$LBLE$ = life-cycle benefit loss when all assets and all threats in the risk scope are considered.

$PBLE(i,j) = PBLE_{ij}$ = life-cycle benefit loss when asset A_i and threat Z_j are considered.

$PBLE(.,j) = PBLE_{.j}$ = life-cycle benefit loss on all assets in the risk scope when threat Z_j is considered.

$PBLE(i,.) = PBLE_{i.}$ = life benefit loss on all threats when asset A_i is considered.

PBLE = life-cycle benefit loss when all assets and all threats in the risk scope are considered.

h = number of years in the risk life cycle.

N = number of times units in a year.

tu = time unit.

7.10.2.4.6 What Is the ABLE Value?

The ABLE value is the annual benefit loss expectancy, which accounts for both economic and noneconomic benefits. You will encounter $ABLE(\omega)$, which refers to the expected annual value of economic and noneconomic benefits that would be lost for the organization or computing environment ω when all assets in the security scope and all known threats are considered. When the arguments i and j are added, we denote $ABLE(i,j)$ or $ABLE_{ij}$ to mean the expected annual value of economic and noneconomic benefits that would be lost for asset A_i when only threat Z_j is considered.

That is, $ABLE(\omega)$ is equal to $\sum_i\sum_j ABLE_{ij}$. This amount is the total annual security risk for ω, denoted $TASR(\omega)$. Sometimes, it is useful to compute the weighted average annual security risk of assets, which is denoted by $AASR(\omega)$; it is equal to $\sum_i\sum_j w_i \times ABLE_{ij}$, where w_i denotes the weight for asset i.

The ABLE values are all assessed based on the risk analysis worksheets provided in this chapter. Any other values of risks are deduced from the ABLE values. This chapter introduces present security risks and life-cycle security risks, which are all based on the ABLE values estimates, which are in turn based on data collected using the ABLE security analysis worksheets.

In general, except for present security risks, which address the immediate security risks usually assessed to understand the current organization's security risk position, any other security risk has to specify the target length of the risk life cycle. Two important parameters have to be defined: the time unit (tu) adopted throughout the security life cycle and the length, in time units, *N* of the risk life cycle. That is, we need at least the following:

1. Scope of risk: ω
2. Life-cycle length: *N* time units
3. Time unit: tu

The security risk consists of three risk components: loss of economic benefits, loss of noneconomic benefits, and cost of corrective actions. The risk may be therefore written as follows:

$$\text{Life-cycle risk } (\omega, N) = r(\omega, N) + \rho(\omega, N) + c(\omega, N)$$

where

$r(\omega, N)$ = expected economic loss throughout life cycle

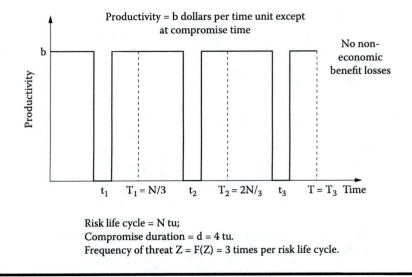

Risk life cycle = N tu;
Compromise duration = d = 4 tu.
Frequency of threat Z = F(Z) = 3 times per risk life cycle.

Figure 7.21   Layout of the threat intervals in the risk life cycle.

$\rho(\omega, N)$ = expected noneconomic loss throughout life cycle
$c(\omega, N)$ = expected cost of corrective actions throughout life cycle

The economic life-cycle length may be short term, midterm, or long term, but it depends on both the value of N and the value of the time unit tu. For example, if N equals 36 months and the time unit is the month, we are dealing with long-term risk. If, however, N equals 180 days and the time unit is the day, then we are dealing with short-term risk.

While the productivity of the organization in question or its computing environment that is considered in the risk scope may be of any form or shape, we are approximating it by a simple constant productivity function equal to the average value throughout its risk life cycle. This is a safe approximation that makes the ABLE risk methodology effective and user-friendly. That is, the productivity is equal to b dollars for any t in the risk life cycle $[0, N]$. We also assume that, if a threat Z occurs $F(Z)$ times in the risk life cycle, its occurs in the equidistant intervals $[t_i, T_i]$, $i = 1, F(Z)$, where $T_i - t_i = d$ for all i's. The amount d is called the security compromise duration. Because the intervals are equally distant, we then have $t_i = i \times (N/(F(Z) + 1))$. Figure 7.21 depicts the layout of the threat intervals in the risk life cycle.

7.10.2.4.7 Effects of Threats on Productivity

Let us see what we have here: The threat Z will occur $F(Z)$ times at $t_1, t_2, ..., t_{F(Z)}$ and will require a recovery period of d time units. This will cause two types of losses: loss of economic benefits that are worth $b(i)d(i,j)$ dollars, and loss of non-economic benefits that are worth $b(i)(1 - s(i,j))$ dollars for the remaining of the risk life cycle. The computation of losses of economic and noneconomic benefits in the $F(Z)$ consecutive intervals of security compromises is provided in Table 7.9, where N is either a fixed number of years when the risk life cycle is one or more years; or a fixed number of time units if the risk life cycle is less than a year. If we replace T_i's by their values, we obtain the results provided in Table 7.10. The sequential single life-cycle benefit loss expectancies are depicted in Figure 7.22.

In general, $[t_k, t_k + d]$, $k = 1,K$ are the intervals of security compromise where productivity is zero for d time units. For any incident $Z(k)$, there are economic losses amounting to $bd(1 - s)^{k-1}$ and noneconomic benefit losses that amount to $b(1 - s)^{k-1}(N - t_k)$. Let us assume that risk term range consists of N time units. That is,

Table 7.9 Summary of Life-Cycle Risk Computations on Both Economic and Noneconomic Components

Time of Incident	Incident Intervals	Economic Benefit Loss	Noneconomic Benefits Loss
t_1	$[0, T_1[$	$db + C$	$sb(N-t_1)$
t_2	$[T_1, T_2[$	$db(1-s) + C$	$sb(1-s)(N-t_2)$
- - -	- - -	- - -	- - -
t_k	$[T_2, T_k[$	$db(1-s)^{k-1} + C$	$sb(1-s)^{k-1}(N-t_k)$
- - -	- - -	- - -	- - -
t_F	$[T_{F-1}, T_F[$	$db(1-s)^{F-1} + C$	$sb(1-s)^{F-1}(N-t_F)$
Totals		$bd\sum_{k=1,F} (1-s)^{k-1}$	$b\sum_{k=1,F} (1-s)^{k-1}(N-t_k)$.

Total life cycle risk = $bd\sum_{k=1,F} (1-s)^{k-1} + b\sum_{k=1,F} (1-s)^{k-1}(N-t_k)$.

Where:

$b(i)$ = unitary business value generated by the system in the defined risk scope (in \$/tu)

$d(i,j)$ = length of security compromise (in tu)

$C(i,j)$ = Average cost of corrective actions per incident

$F(Z)$ = Frequency of occurrences of incidents in the risk life cycle

$s(i,j)$ = percentage of business value lost due to loss of noneconomic benefits per time unit

N = length of the risk life cycle in tu

PS. The arguments i and j are hidden to better see and understand the equations above.

Table 7.10 Summary of Life-Cycle Risk Computations on Both Economic and Noneconomic Components

Time of Incident	End of Security Compromise	Economic Benefit Loss	Noneconomic Benefits Loss
t_1	T_1	$db + C$	$\Delta sb[2(F-1)+1]$
t_2	T_2	$db(1-s) + C$	$\Delta s(1-s)b[2(F-2)+1]$
- - -	- - -	- - -	- - -
t_k	T_k		$\Delta s(1-s)^k b[2(F-k)+1]$
- - -	- - -	- - -	- - -
t_F	T_F	$db(1-s)^{F-1} + C$	$\Delta s(1-s)^{F-1}b$
Total		$db(1-(1-s)^{F(Z)})/s + FC$ if $s>0$ or $(db + C)F$ if $s=0$.	$asbN/(F+1)*[\Sigma_{k=0,F-1}\ (2(F-k-1)+1)(1-s)^k]$

If $s(i,j)>0$ then: $\text{Risk} = d(i,j)b(i)(1-(1-s(i,j))^{F(Z)})/s(i,j) + F(Z)C(i,j) + \Delta sbN/(F+1)*[\Sigma_{k=0,F-1}\ (2(F-k-1)+1)(1-s)^k]$

If $s(i,j)=0$ then: $\text{Risk} = F(Z)b(i)d(i,j)$

Where:

$\Delta = N/2F$

$b(i)$ = unitary business value generated by the system in the defined risk scope (in \$/tu)

$d(i,j)$ = length of security compromise (in tu)

$C(i,j)$ = Average cost of corrective actions per incident

$F(Z)$ = Frequency of occurrences of incidents in the risk life cycle

$s(i,j)$ = percentage of business value lost due to loss of noneconomic benefits per time unit

N = length of the risk life cycle in tu

PS. The arguments i and j are hidden to better see and understand the equations above.

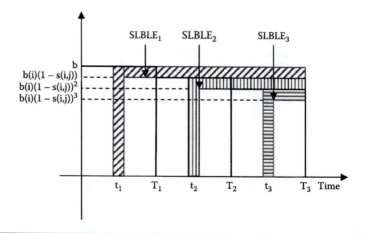

Figure 7.22 Sequential single life-cycle benefit loss expectancies.

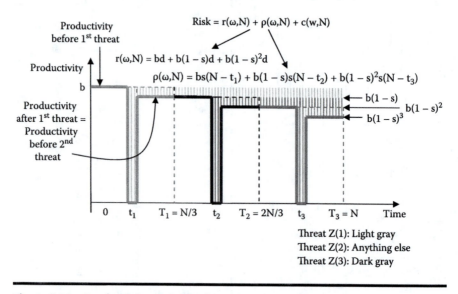

Figure 7.23 Productivity and security compromise effects.

in any risk life cycle of N time units, the total economic losses add up to $bd\sum_{k=1,F} (1-s)^{k-1}$ and $b\sum_{k=1,F} (1-s)^{k-1}(N - t_k)$. The total security risk for the entire risk life cycle amounts to $bd\sum_{k=1,F} (1-s)^{k-1} + b\sum_{k=1,F} (1-s)^{k-1}(N - t_k)$.

The total risk area is depicted in Figure 7.23. The productivity function changes with the sequential effects of the $F(Z)$ occurrences of the threat Z. The productivity function is depicted in the same figure, and it may be written as follows (F represents $F(Z)$):

$$
\text{Productivity} = \begin{cases}
b & \text{if } t \leq t_1 \\
0 & \text{if } t_1 \leq t < t_1 + d \\
bs & \text{if } t_1 + d \leq t < t_2 \\
0 & \text{if } t_2 \leq t < t_2 + d \\
b(1-s) & \text{if } t_2 + d \leq t < t_3 \\
0 & \text{if } t_3 \leq t < t_3 + d \\
b(1-s)^2 & \text{if } t_3 + d \leq t < t_4 \\
\cdots & \\
0 & \text{if } t_F \leq t < t_F + d \\
b(1-s)^{F-1} & \text{if } t_F + d \leq t < t_F = N
\end{cases}
$$

Before we further proceed, let us examine some simple examples:

Example: Three incidents

After averaging all relevant parameters associated with the three threats $Z(1)$, $Z(2)$, and $Z(3)$, we obtain the following information:

Duration of compromise = d = 16 hours
Percentage of noneconomic benefit loss = s = 1%
Unitary productivity = b = $400/hour
Risk life cycle = N time units = 8760 hours
Time unit = tu = hour
Δ = half of any interval $[T_k, T_{k+1}]$ = 8760/5 = 1752 hours

The incidents take place at t_1, t_2, t_3, t_4, and t_5. We have, by definition, $T_k = t_k + \Delta$, for $k = 1,5$.

The first threat hits at $t = t_1$ and causes full security compromise for d time units. That is, productivity is zero from t_1 to $t_1 + d$. At $t = t_1 + d$, all normal operations are resumed and, hence, all economic benefits. The noneconomic benefits are, however, lost for long periods or sometimes even forever. Noneconomic benefit losses due to threat 1 are estimated as $bs(N - t_1)$.

The second threat occurs at $t = t_2$ and lasts until $t_2 + d$. That is, productivity is zero between t_2 and $t_2 + d$. The amount of economic benefits lost when $Z(2)$ occurred is equal to $b(1 - s)d$. At the end of the compromise, for this incident, all economic benefits are restored, but noneconomic benefits are lost forever. The amount of noneconomic benefits lost when $Z(2)$ took place is equal to $sb(1 - s)$ $(N - t_2)$.

The third threat is predicted to occur at $t = t_3$ and to last until $t = t_3 + d$. This incident will generate economic benefit losses of about $db(1 - s)^2$. Then, even though all economic benefits are restored at the end of the compromise period,

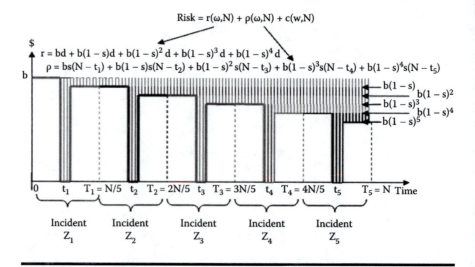

Figure 7.24 Productivity and compromises: case of five incidents.

there will be a loss of noneconomic benefits that amounts to $sb(1 - s)^2(N - t_3)$, and so on. The life cycle risk is computed as follows:

Economic benefit losses:

$$\rho(\omega, N) = bs(N - t_1) + b(1 - s)s(N - t_2) + b(1 - s)^2 s(N - t_3) +$$
$$b(1 - s)^3 s(N - t_4) + b(1 - s)^4 s(N - t_5) = \$86{,}555$$

Noneconomic benefit losses:

$$r(\omega, N) = bd + b(1 - s)d + b(1 - s)^2 d + b(1 - s)^3 d + b(1 - s)^4 d = \$31{,}366$$

$$\text{Life cycle risk} = \$ \ 117{,}922$$

Figure 7.24 provides a layout of risk computations for this example. The detailed computation is provided in Table 7.11.

7.10.2.4.8 Life-Cycle Security Risks

We are mainly interested in four types of life-cycle security risks: (1) Life-cycle security risk of A_i considering Z_j, (2) life-cycle security risk of asset A_i, (3) total life-cycle security risk on ω, and (4) weighted average life-cycle security risk on ω:

1. Life-cycle security risk of A_i considering Z_j:

$$LSR(A_i, Z_j, N) = \text{Life-cycle security risk of } A_i \text{ considering } Z_j \text{ only}$$

$$= \sum_{y=0,\infty} p(n_j = y) \, LBLE_{ijy}(N)$$

Table 7.11 Computations for Life-Cycle Risk: Case of Five Incidents

Security Incident	Time of Incident	Economic Benefit Loss ($)	Noneconomic Benefit Loss ($)
Z_1	t_1	6,400	31,536
Z_2	t_2	6,336	24,282
Z_3	t_3	6,272	17,171
Z_4	t_4	6,209	10,199
Z_5	t_5	6,147	3,365
	Total	$31,366	$86,555
	Life-cycle risk	$117,922	

$$= \Sigma_{y=0,\infty} \, yp(n_j = y) \, SLBLE_{ij}(N)$$

$$= SLBLE_{ij}(N) \times \Sigma_{i=0,\infty} \, yp(n_j = y)$$

$$= F(Z_j) \times SBLE_{ij}(N)$$

2. Life-cycle security risk of asset A_i:

$LSR(A_i,N)$ = Life security risk of asset A_i considering all known threats

$$= \Sigma j=1, m \ F(Z_j) \times SLBLE_{ij}(N)$$

3. Total life-cycle security risk:

$TLSR(\omega,N)$ = Total life-cycle security risk of ω for a life cycle of N time units

$$TLSR(\omega,N) = \Sigma_{i=1,n} \, \Sigma_{j=1,m} \, F(Z_j) \times SLBLE_{ij}(N)$$

4. Weighted average life-cycle security risk:

$$WALSR(\omega,N) =$$
Weighted average life-cycle security risk of ω for a life cycle of N time units

$$= \Sigma_{i=1,n} \, \Sigma_{j=1,m} \, w_i \times F(Z_j) \times SLBLE_{ij}(N)$$

The decision tree depicting the computation of life cycle security risks is provided in Figures 7.25, 7.26, and 7.27.

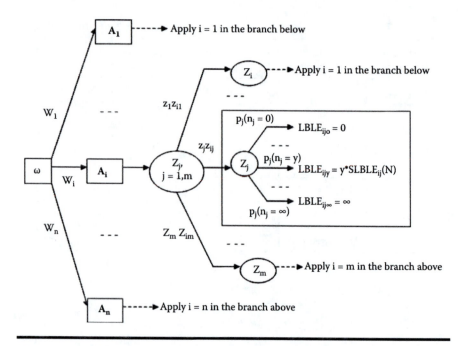

Figure 7.25 Life-cycle security risk computation for asset A_i and threat Z_j.

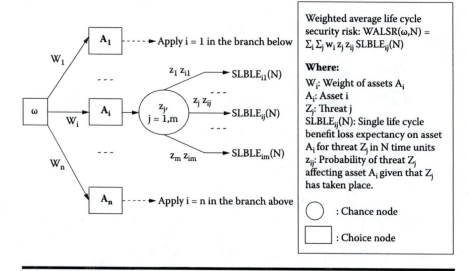

Figure 7.26 Weighted average life-cycle security risk computation on all assets and all threats.

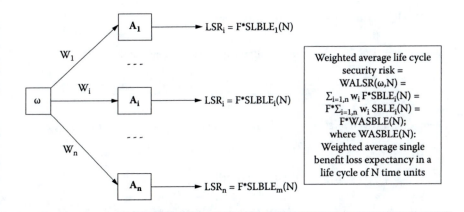

Figure 7.27   Weighted average life-cycle security risk computations summary.

7.10.2.4.9 Annual Security Risks

We are mainly interested in four types of annual security risks: (1) annual security risk of A_i considering Z_j, (2) annual security risk of asset A_i, (3) total annual security risk on ω, and (4) weighted average annual security risk on ω:

1. Annual security risk of A_i considering Z_j:

$$ASR(A_i, Z_j) = \text{Annual security risk of } A_i \text{ considering } Z_j \text{ only}$$

$$= \Sigma_{y=0,\infty}\, p(n_j = y) ABLE_{ijy}$$

$$= \Sigma_{y=0,\infty}\, yp(n_j = y)\, SBLE_{ij}$$

$$= SBLE_{ij} \times \Sigma_{i=0,\infty}\, yp(n_j = y)$$

$$= F(Z_j) \times SBLE_{ij}$$

2. Annual security risk of asset A_i:

$$ASR(A_i) = \text{Annual security risk of asset } A_i \text{ considering all known threats}$$

$$= \Sigma_{j=1,m}\, F(Z_j) \times SBLE_{ij}$$

3. Total annual security risk:

$$TASR(\omega) = \text{Total annual security risk of } \omega$$

$$TASR(\omega) = \Sigma_{i=1,n}\, \Sigma_{j=1,m}\, F(Z_j) \times SBLE_{ij}$$

4. Weighted average annual security risk:

$WAASR(\omega)=$ Weighted average annual security risk of ω

$$= \Sigma_{i=1,n} \ \Sigma_{j=1,m} \ w_i \times F(Z_j) \times SBLE_{ij}$$

The decision tree depicting the computation of life-cycle security risks is provided in Figures 7.28, 7.29, and 7.30.

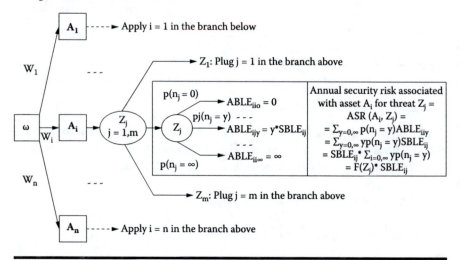

Figure 7.28 Annual security risk computation on asset *i* and threat *j*.

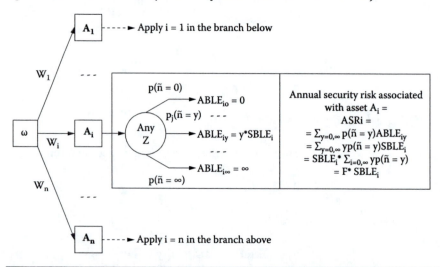

Figure 7.29 Annual security risk computation on any asset A_i.

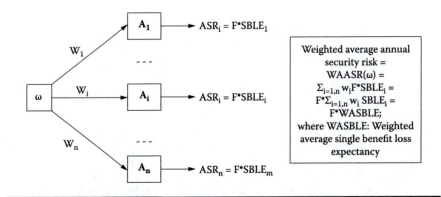

Figure 7.30 Annual security risk computation: Weighted average annual risk.

7.10.2.4.10 Present Security Risks

Present security risks are concerned with events that can potentially take place anytime. Once the incident has occurred, security management will apply corrective actions, following which the economic benefits are recovered and normal operations will resume; but most of the noneconomic benefits will be lost until the end of the risk life cycle.

$$PSR\ (i,j) = d(i,j) \times b(i) + C(i,j) + s(i,j) \times b(j) \times (N - t)$$

where

$b(i)$ = unitary business value generated by the asset in the defined risk scope (in \$/tu)

$d(i,j)$ = length of security compromise (in tu)

$C(i,j)$ = average cost of corrective actions per incident

$F(j)$ = frequency of occurrences of the threat in the risk life cycle

$s(i,j)$ = percentage of business value lost due to loss of noneconomic benefits per time unit

$$PSR(\omega) = \sum_i \sum_j PSR\ (i,j) = \sum_i \sum_j d(i,j) \times b(i) + C(i,j) + s(i,j) \times b(j) \times (N - t)$$

The computations of present security risks are provided in Figures 7.31, 7.32, and 7.33.

7.10.2.4.11 Discounted Security Risks for Long Risk Life Cycles

For long life-cycle risks, the incidents may take place in the last year in the risk life cycle. Security management will budget security controls against some losses that may happen 10 years from now, and those loss amounts should be discounted back to current present when security control budgets are planned.

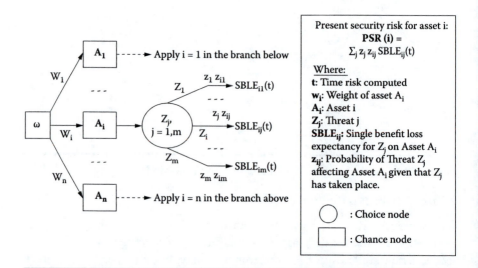

Figure 7.31   Present security risk computation on asset *i*.

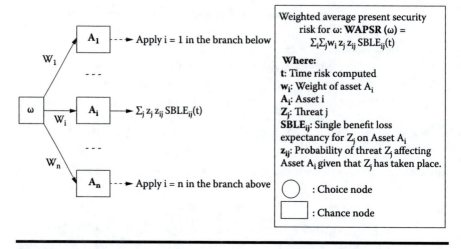

Figure 7.32   Weighted average present security risk computation.

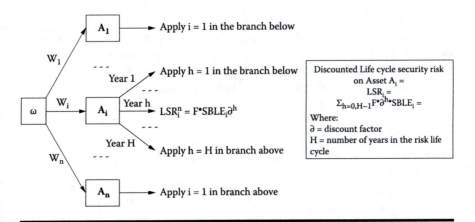

Figure 7.33 Discounted life-cycle security risk computation on asset A_i.

The discounted life-cycle security risk on asset A_i is expressed as follows:

$$DLSR_i = \Sigma_{h=0,H-1} F \times \partial^h \times SBLE_i$$

where
∂ = discount factor
H = number of years in the risk life cycle

The weighted average life-cycle security risk may be expressed as follows:

$$WADLSR(\omega) = \Sigma_{i=1,n} \Sigma_{h=0,H-1} w_i F \times \partial^h \times SBLE_i$$

$$= F \times WASBLE \Sigma_{h=0,H-1} \partial^h$$

$$= F \times WASBLE \times (1 - \partial^H)/(1 - \partial)$$

where
$WASBLE$ = weighted average single benefit loss expectancy
∂ = discount factor
H = number of years in the risk life cycle

The computations of discounted life-cycle security risks are provided in Figures 7.20 and 7.21.

7.10.2.4.12 Minicase Example

Consider an online electronic store called Digicity. The store serves 10 customers per hour with an average business value of $40 per customer. That is, the unitary business-value-generation rate is $b = \$400$ per hour. Our risk scope is limited to the online store Web site server. Assume a risk life cycle of 1 year with the hour as the time unit. The risk life cycle is hence 8760 hours. Two main incidents occur every year: an external agent attack (Z_1) and a hardware failure (Z_2).

On average, these incidents are described as follows:

EA attack incident:
 Compromise duration = 72 hours
 Cost of corrective action = \$6800
 Annual occurrence = once a year; $F(Z_1) = 1$
HF incident:
 Compromise duration = 24 hours
 Cost of corrective actions = \$3800
 Annual occurrence = once a year; that is, $F(Z_2) = 1$

We desire to compute the annual security risk.

We first need to combine the incidents EA and HF to create one incident, say, EAOHF. While EA occurs once a year and HF occurs once a year, the new combined incident occurs twice a year.

The EAOHF incident is described as follows:

Compromise duration = $(72 + 24)/2 = 48$ hours
Cost of corrective actions = $(6800 + 3200)/2 = \$5000$
Annual occurrence = twice a year; that is, F(EAOHF) = 2.

Security management and business management estimated that security incidents similar to EAOHF produce a lasting loss of 1%. That is, after applying the appropriate corrective actions, all the economic benefits are restored when normal business operations resume, but some noneconomic losses (s is the percentage of unitary business value lost after an incident) are gone for ever (until the end of the risk life cycle).

After the occurrence of the first incident, the productivity becomes only $b(1 - s)$ = $0.99 \times b = \$396/$hour until the end of the risk life cycle.

According to Figure 7.34, the single business value loss for asset Z_1 and threat 1 is equal to $db + C + sb(N - t_1)$ = 48 hours × \$400 + 5000 + (1%)(\$400)(8760 − 2190) = \$19,200 +\$10,000 + \$26,280 = \$50,480. You can see from those numbers that noneconomic benefit losses (\$26,280) can be even higher than the one-time economic benefit losses \$19,200.

Repeating the same for threat Z_2, the single business value loss for asset A_1 and threat Z_2: $db(1 - s) + C + sb(1 - s)(N - t_2)$ = 48 hours × \$396 + \$5000 + (1%)(\$396) (8760 − 6570) = \$19,008 + \$5000 + \$8672 = \$32,680.

The ABLE values for threat Z_1 are computed as follows:

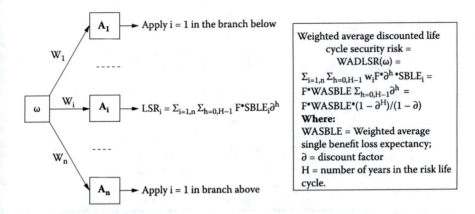

The box on the right reads:

Weighted average discounted life cycle security risk =
$$WADLSR(\omega) =$$
$$\Sigma_{i=1,n} \Sigma_{h=0,H-1} w_i F \cdot \partial^h \cdot SBLE_i =$$
$$F \cdot WASBLE \Sigma_{h=0,H-1} \partial^h =$$
$$F \cdot WASBLE \cdot (1 - \partial^H)/(1 - \partial)$$
Where:
WASBLE = Weighted average single benefit loss expectancy;
∂ = discount factor
H = number of years in the risk life cycle.

Tree labels: A_1 → Apply i = 1 in the branch below; W_1; W_i; A_i → $LSR_i = \Sigma_{i=1,n} \Sigma_{h=0,H-1} F \cdot SBLE_i \partial^h$; W_n; A_n → Apply i = 1 in branch above; ω.

Figure 7.34 Weighted average discounted life-cycle security risk.

$ABLE_{110} = 0$
$ABLE_{111} = \$50,480$
$ABLE_{112} = \$100,960$
$\ldots$
$ABLE_{11\infty} = \infty$

The ABLE values for threat Z_2 are computed as follows:

$ABLE_{110} = 0$
$ABLE_{111} = \$32,680$
$ABLE_{112} = \$65,360$
$\ldots$
$ABLE_{11\infty} = \infty$

The total annual security risk of the Digicity Web site is equal to $ABLE_{111} + ABLE_{121}$ = \$50,480 + \$32,680 = \$83,160. Because we only have one asset, the Web site server, we cannot talk about any weighted average security risk. Because the length of the risk life cycle is 1 year, the annual security risk and the life-cycle risk are identical.

Let us now assume that we have a risk life cycle of 2 years but the threats Z_1 and Z_2 occur on 2 years. It is important to notice that all the information about the two assets is still valid except for the time they occur. The values of t_1, t_2, T_1, and T_2 will be as follows: ($t_1 = 4380$; $t_2 = 13,140$; $T_1 = 8760$; $T_2 = 17,520$).

According to Figure 7.35, the single business value loss for asset Z_1 and threat 1 is equal to $db + C + sb(N - t_1)$ = 48 hours × \$400 + \$5000 + (1%)(\$400)(17,520 − 4380) = \$19,200 + \$5,000 + \$52,560 = \$76,760.

Repeating the same for threat Z_2, we obtain the single business value loss for asset A_1 and threat Z_2: $db(1 - s) + C + sb(1 - s)(N - t_2)$ = 48 hours × \$396 + \$5000 + (1%)(\$396)(17,520 − 13,140) = \$19,008 + \$5000 + \$17,344 = \$41,352.

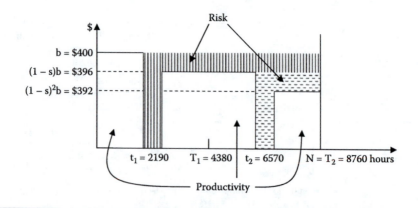

Figure 7.35 Productivity and risks for Digicity: two incidents in 1 year.

The ABLE values for threat Z_1, occurring in year 1, are computed as follows:

$ABLE_{110} = 0$
$ABLE_{111} = \$76,760$
$ABLE_{112} = \$153,520$
...
$ABLE_{11\infty} = \infty$

The ABLE values for threat Z_2, occurring in year 2, are computed as follows:

$ABLE_{110} = 0$
$ABLE_{111} = \$41,352$
$ABLE_{112} = \$82,704$
...
$ABLE_{11\infty} = \infty$

If we use an interest rate of 12% (a discount factor of $1/1.12 = 0.89$), the discounted security risk of the Digicity Web site is equal to $ABLE_{111} + ABLE_{121} \times \partial = \$76,760 + \$41,352 \times .89 = \$113,563$. As we mentioned earlier, because we only have one asset, the Web site server, we cannot talk about any weighted average security risk.

7.10.2.4.13 Problem Areas Still to Be Discussed

Life-cycle security risks may be needed for two reasons:

1. Historical data needed to compute the probability of threat frequency is obtained from h years where $h > 1$; or
2. By security management decision.

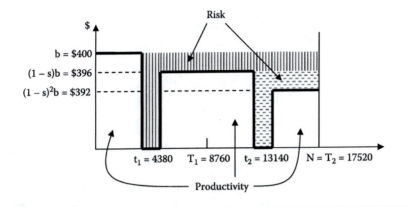

Figure 7.36   Productivity and risks for Digicity: two incidents in 2 years.

Consider two assets: A_1 and A_2. There are also two threats: Z_1, with an annual frequency of 2, which can only affect A_1; and Z_2, with an annual frequency of 1, which can only affect A_2. Assume also that the single benefit loss expectancies for A_1 and A_2 are SBLE1 = \$10,000 and SBLE2 = \$5000. The annual benefit loss expectancies are such that ABLE1 = 1 × 10,000 = \$10,000 and ABLE2 = 2 × 5000 = \$10,000.

The two assets A_1 and A_2 have equal ABLEs. This means that it is feasible to spend \$10,000 to improve the security of A_1 and also to spend the same amount to secure A_2.

Now, if we have only \$10,000 to spend on security, do we secure A_1 or A_2, given that they both have the same ABLEs?

Most people will start by securing A_2 because the annual frequency of threat Z_2 is 2 per year, whereas Z_1 has an annual frequency of 1 per year. It is probably important to think of a ranking mechanism in order to prioritize assets in terms of their security priority pressure. An example of such a mechanism may be the annual frequency weight. In this case, we compute two weights: $w_1(A_1) = 1/(1 + 2) = 1/3$ and $w_2(A_2) = 2/(1 + 2) = 2/3$. You can now see that asset A_2 has a higher priority because $w_2 > w_1$ and, hence, we have to start with A_2.

The latter prioritization mechanism will, however, only work when the assets have identical ABLEs. If the ABLEs are different, we need to think of a new prioritization mechanism that also takes into account the losses or benefits involved. Let us examine the following example, where the annual frequencies are different and the ABLEs are also different.

Consider two assets A_1 and A_2. There are also two threats: Z_1, with an annual frequency $F(1) = 2$, which can only affect A_1; and Z_2, with an annual frequency $F(2) = 1$, which can only affect A_2. Assume also that the single benefit loss expectancies for A_1 and A_2 are SBLE1 = \$10,000 and SBLE2 = \$6000. The annual benefit loss expectancies are such that ABLE1 = 1 × 10,000 = \$10,000 and ABLE2 = 2 × 6000 = \$12,000. What do we do in this case? Do we start with security A_1 or A_2?

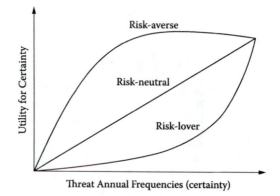

Figure 7.37 Attitude toward risk of security management.

The prioritization mechanism we applied earlier does not work, because the assets do not have the same ABLEs in this example. You may need to distinguish between various types of security management attitudes toward security risk. A risk-neutral security manager will only look at the ABLE values for both assets, and if they are the same, the assets will get the same priority of risk treatment. A risk-averse security manager will give priority of risk treatment to those assets that have higher annual frequency values as long as the ABLEs are not significantly different. A risk-loving security manager will assign higher priority of risk mitigation to those assets that have smaller annual frequency values. Figure 7.37 shows the security management attitude toward security risk when risk treatment priorities are assigned to assets.

7.10.2.4.14 Designing a Security Program

The design of a security program may be completed in three steps, based on (1) the asset analysis information collected using the Asset Analysis Worksheet, (2) the threat analysis information collected using the Threat Analysis Worksheet, and (3) the security control analysis information using the Security Control Analysis Worksheet. The following algorithm is reserved for annual security risks, but it is still valid for life-cycle and present security risks; you just need to replace the annual security risk formulas by any other risk formula that is relevant to your security risk project.

As long as there is a budget and there are still remaining security controls to be considered, do:

Begin
1. Collect the postimplementation threat analysis information using the Postimplementation Impact Analysis Worksheet.

2. Compute the risk position R_k after applying a security control S_k, for all remaining security controls, as follows:

$$R_k = \sum_i \sum_j w_i z_i z_{ijk} \, ABLE_{ij}$$

Note that the subscript k does not show in the term $ABLE_{ij}$, because the security control S_k used to counter the threat Z_j does not change the annual benefit loss expectancy value but the conditional probability that the threat would impact the asset given that the threat has occurred. This conditional probability is used to model system exposures to potential security incidents as defined in the risk scope. This conditional probability is decreased from its initial value t_{ij} to its new value z_{ijk} after applying the Security Control S_k.

3. Select the security controls to be added to the security program.

End.

You may compute the new security risk position as follows:

$$R = \sum_i \sum_j \sum_k w_i z_i z_{ijk} \, ABLE_{ij}$$

The total security risk reduction produced by the proposed security program may be then computed as follows:

$$\sum_i \sum_j \sum_k w_i z_i (z_{ij} - z_{ijk}) \, ABLE_{ij}$$

where

$ABLE_{ij}$: Annual benefit expectancy of A_i after the impact of Threat Z_j

z_{ij}: Probability of Threat Z_j affecting Asset A_i

z_{ijk}: Probability of Threat Z_j affecting Asset A_i after the implementation of the Security Control S_k

z_j: Probability of Threat Z_j occurring

w_i: Weight of risks associated with A_i

The risk reduction attributed to the security control S_k is illustrated in Figure 7.38.

Also, note that because the implementation of one security control can affect the likelihood of impact of many threats, the Postimplementation Impact Analysis Worksheet should be executed every time a security control is added to the security program.

7.10.2.4.15 Final Report of the Security Analysis

This phase generates a final report containing the recommended security program. This security program explains the implementation of the security controls retained for the security management process.

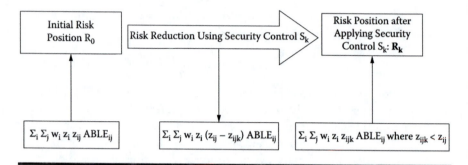

Figure 7.38   Risk attributed to one security control.

The computation of risk weights and the selection and implementation of security controls are beyond the scope of this book.

The chapter is only concerned with the design part of the security program. Many methods may be used to select the feasible security controls: a scoring method, a linear program where the risk reduction quantity is maximized subject to budget constraints, a knowledge-based approach, etc.

A forthcoming book on the writing of security plans will contain the implementation part of the security program.

7.11 Summary

This chapter defined and discussed security risk management. We defined the risk management life cycle. We also presented the risk management process as adopted in the Naval Safety Center. Even though there are several risk analysis methodologies in the literature, we only presented the ALE methodology as it is the simplest and most popular around. The second half of the chapter, however, presented Raggad's ABLE methodology.

This methodology is a generic methodology that can be implemented in many different ways using any numeric processing or knowledge-based approach.

The purpose of the ABLE methodology is to analyze economic benefit and noneconomic benefit losses that can be prevented by implementing the appropriate security controls. Most other security methods do not account for noneconomic benefit losses and do not discount for losses that take place in the far future. The ABLE methodology provides a more comprehensive framework to minimize risks of organizational benefits losses of any type.

7.12 Review Questions

1. Explain how the security risk management life cycle works.

2. Define and give the differences between strategic, functional, and operational risks. Give examples of each type of risk.
3. Explain how security risk is mitigated and give an example.
4. Give an example of linear productivity, constant security compromise, and incremental recovery. Compute total productivity lost in $[t0, T]$.
5. Give an example of constant productivity, constant security compromise, and incremental recovery. Compute total productivity lost in $[t0, T]$.
6. Give an example of linear productivity, linear security compromise, and incremental recovery. Compute total productivity lost in $[t0, T]$.
7. Explain how ALE works and its pros and cons.
8. Search the Internet, and identify five security risk methodologies. Define each one. Compare them in terms of their precision, cost, and ease of use.
9. Explain the relationship between risk treatment and continual security.
10. Give a risk treatment model that incorporates the ALE method and the company's business-value-generation capability.
11. Distinguish between risk analysis and risk management.
12. What is a risk-driven security program?
13. How does the ABLE methodology work?
14. Distinguish between the Threat Analysis and the Postimplementation Impact Analysis Worksheets.
15. Where are the subjective conditional probabilities expressing a threat's impact on assets collected?
16. Where are the expected annual benefits of assets after the implementation of security controls collected?
17. Why are risks computed at every iteration of the security control selection and implementation algorithm?
18. Explain how economic benefit losses are computed in the ABLE methodology. Give an example.
19. Explain how noneconomic benefit losses are modeled. Give an example.
20. Explain how future benefit losses are accounted for. Give an example.
21. Explain the utility of the risk life cycle in security risk analysis. Give an example supporting your argument.
22. Explain the differences between ALE (Chapter 8) and the ABLE risk methodology.

7.13 Workshops

Workshop 1

Consider the computing environment in Figure 7.39. Explain how to use the ALE risk methodology to budget its risk treatment program.

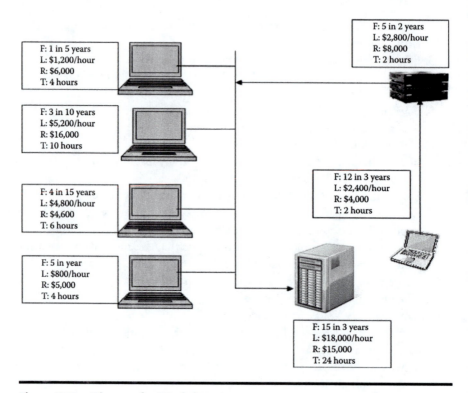

Figure 7.39 Diagram for Workshop 1.

Workshop 2

Consider a small business with self-hosted e-business Web site presence. In addition to the e-business server, the company manages its own independent database and e-mail servers. Assume that the e-business server is located in the DMZ zone. There are also five workstations and a printer linked to the local area network. Give a possible layout for the small business computing environment. Use the Naval Safety Center's operational risk management process, as revised in this chapter, to devise a risk treatment program for the small business. Give a table similar to Table 7.4 summarizing the proposed operational risk treatment program.

Workshop 3

Consider an online electronic store called Digithall. Digithall is concerned about two severs: Asset A_1, consisting of the Web site server; and Asset A_2, consisting of the corporate database server. The store serves 20 customers per hour with an average business value of $40 per customer. The $40 is thought to be shared as follows: the Web site server generates a business value of $25 per hour, and the database server generates a business value of $15 per hour.

Sales cannot be made if the Web site server is out of order. If the database server is out of order, sales are possible but with a rate of 20% of normal operations. Based on this information, the weights for assets A_1 and A_2 are as follows: weight of A_1 = w_1 = 80% and weight of A_2 = w_2 = 20%. Noneconomic losses are estimated at s = 1%.

Three main incidents occur every year: Z_1, Z_2, and Z_3, as follows.

Duration of any incident = d = 18 hours.
Average cost of corrective actions = \$4200.
Scenario 1: Consider a risk scope of 1 year. Compute the security life cycle for A_1, and that for A_2.
Scenario 2: Consider a life cycle of 3 years and an interest rate of 15%. Compute the discounted life cycle risk for A_1, and for A_2. Compute the weighted average discounted security risk for the enterprise.

References

1. Mahoney, M. V., and P. K. Chan, An Analysis of the 1999 DARPA/Lincoln Laboratory Evaluation Data for Network Anomaly Detection, http://www.cs.fit.edu/~mmahoney/paper7.pdf.
2. Microsoft, Chapter 4: Assessing risk, published security risk management guide, Updated: March 15, 2006, http://technet.microsoft.com/en-us/library/cc163154.aspx.
3. Mirkovic, J., and P. Reiher, A Taxonomy of DDoS Attack and DDoS Defense Mechanisms, on http://www.cis.udel.edu/~sunshine/publications/ccr.pdf, visited November 7, 2008.
4. Naval Safety Center 1, 4 Principles of Applying ORM, http://www.safetycenter.navy.mil/orm/generalorm/introduction/4principles.htm
5. Naval Safety Center 2: Operational Risk Management, http://www.safetycenter.navy.mil/ORM/generalorm/downloads/introtoorm.doc, visited on December 6, 2008.
6. Sippy, N., Moving from Reactive to Strategic Risk Management, *GRC Journal*, Managing People, Process, and Technology, http://www.grcjournal.com/?mc=strategic-risk-management&page=gp-viewarticle
7. U.S. Department of Energy, Risk Management, Project Management Practices 4, Rev E, June 2003.

Chapter 8

Continual Security: Integrated Fault-Event Analysis and Response Framework (IFEAR)

Learning Objectives

After reading this chapter, students are expected to achieve an understanding of:

> How FTA works
> How ETA works
> How IFEAR works
> How to compute probabilities in FTA
> How to compute probabilities in ETA
> How to manage risks using FEA-integrated methodology
> How to mitigate risks using simulation

8.1 Introduction

This chapter proposes a layered security assessment and enhancement methodology intended to provide information continual security for an organization. This methodology is not intended to replace the security risk management approach required

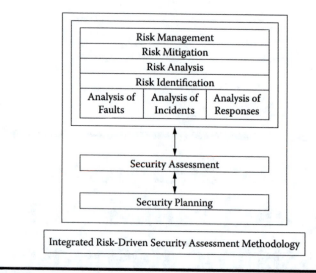

Figure 8.1   IFEAR methodology for continual security and security planning.

by ISO 27001 as a part of the technical audit performed to develop an Information Security Management System (ISMS). This methodology integrates the fault tree analysis (FTA) and the event tree analysis (ETA) [1] approaches to link detection-failure episodes and their effects on harmful consequences caused by events generated by system failures. The integrated approach will be called, throughout this book, the fault event analysis (FEA). The FTA approach generates information about the consequences of undesired incidents caused by system failures [2,4,6]. We apply an incident response approach to plan any corrective actions to alleviate the effects of undesired events. The security assessment and enhancement methodology we are proposing is called Integrated Fault Event Analysis and Response framework (IFEAR). Findings from applying IFEAR are also useful in defining information security requirements produced in security planning.

The IFEAR methodology rests on a low-level security analysis, where components failures, incident consequences, and existing incident responses are analyzed. Those three security analyses constitute the basis of the security assessment methodology needed in continual security and in security planning. This bottom layer serves as a risk identification phase. The upper layers consist of risk analysis, risk mitigation, and risk management. Figure 8.1 depicts the layers constituting the IFEAR security assessment and enhancement methodology.

8.2 IFEAR Methodology

This book presents different methodologies for assessing security risk. The information security management team and system owners can select one methodology

IFEAR Framework			
Preventive Power	Deterrive Power	Detective Power	Corrective Power
Fault Analysis: Deductive model		**Incident Analysis:** Inductive model	
Tool: Fault tree analysis **Output:** Probabilities of undesired events		**Tool:** Event tree analysis **Output:** Probabilities of consequences	
IFEAR Output: Risk-driven security program			

Figure 8.2   Framework for the IFEAR methodology.

or another, depending on the security management project they initiated. The IFEAR method is a probabilistic risk management process that is designed to study system faults, security incidents, and responses for the purpose of devising a risk-driven continual security program. Such a security program is written in terms of applicable preventive, detective, and corrective security controls. As shown in Figure 8.2, this method is based on two information-gathering processes: the first one is a deductive process called FTA; the second one is an inductive process called ETA.

Before we further proceed, let us present and discuss the main security objective of this chapter. So, what do we really want to achieve by developing the IFEAR methodology? A set of questions should probably help in starting this discussion:

Question 1: Why the worries?
Question 2: What can go wrong in the computing environment that can compromise our business mission?
Question 3: If something goes wrong, what can really happen that can produce undesired consequences?
Question 4: If something bad happens, what can we do to respond? How can we mitigate risks?

To start our discussion, we worry simply because we do not want to be put out of business. In order to answer the second question, we need to identify major undesired events that can potentially take place. For each undesired event, we have to study how it can occur. That is, we have to collect sufficient information on all possible conditions that can produce each identified undesired event. Those conditions are defined in terms of a chain of events that, if they occur as specified in those conditions, will bring about the undesired event.

We can then formally write as follows:

$$Z_i = z_i(E_{i1}, \ldots, E_{in})$$

where z_i is a hierarchical scheme that connects all the events, $\{E_i\}_{i=1,n}$, to produce Z_i.

This equation explains our incident search framework. We attempt to uncover any situation that can lead to the realization of an undesired event. Certain conditions can form and cause failures in diverse components of the computing environment. These failures can affect people, activities, networks and infrastructure, data, and technology. Figure 8.2 provides the framework used to design the IFEAR methodology.

The main principle behind the IFEAR methodology is to answer at least two questions among the ones we presented earlier, which may be combined in the following question: How can an undesired event Z occur, and what happens after it occurs?

The FTA method will produce information about the occurrence of the undesired event, Z, and the ETA method will provide information about the production of the undesired consequences that follow. Figure 8.3 depicts the joint effort that both the FTA and the ETA exert together to prepare for the estimation of risks and their mitigation.

There is great power in integrating FTA and ETA; in fact, every undesired event produced by FTA is further studied by ETA to analyze any negative effects and define its consequences. Based on these consequences and their probabilities, the appropriate response will be planned. Figure 8.3 also depicts the link between FTA and ETA in this context.

ETA is an inductive procedure that shows all possible outcomes resulting from an undesired event, taking into account whether installed safeguards are functioning or not.

Effective security management studies mainly four types of security controls or safeguards: preventive, detersive, detective, and corrective actions.

Preventive security controls are adopted to prevent information leakage, information corruption, and denial of service in an organization's computing environment. Some administrative security controls such as security policy, operational security controls such as firewalls, or technical security controls such as authentications techniques are examples of preventive security measures.

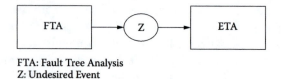

FTA: Fault Tree Analysis
Z: Undesired Event
ETA: Event Tree Analysis

Figure 8.3   FTA and ETA joint effort to analyze undesired events.

Detective security controls are adopted to monitor the computing environment and detect known intrusions. Common examples include log analysis, intrusion detection systems, and fire alarms.

Corrective security controls are adopted to plan responses to intercept and abort intrusions. Reconfiguring affected system resources is an example of corrective security control. Corrective security controls are the result of studying the information collected by detective security controls. Corrective security controls also include all recovery procedures activated to ensure business continuity or to return the system to normal operations.

This chapter reserves the next section for a discussion of FTA. Two other sections are reserved for ETA and incident response analysis (IRA). A later section will present a risk-driven integration of all of the three methods: FTA, ETA, and IRA.

8.3 Fault Tree Analysis

FTA is not new. It has been around since 1962. Bell Labs developed the FTA concept for use in system reliability and safety analysis. Leading users of the FTA approach were the U.S. Air Force and Boeing. The FTA was also called *negative tree analysis* in some of the literature. It is a visual top-down logical diagramming approach that presents the state of the target system in terms of the states of its components. The system represents the undesired or negative event. Its components are the basic events constituting the target system [9,10].

FTA uses a visual model defining the paths that lead to a probable failure or undesirable event. A path from a source event to the event of the fault tree defines a logical combination of events that produces the undesired event [7].

The reader may wonder why we do not emphasize the study of system success instead of looking for negative events. If those negative events remain unknown, we will not know when they can be realized, and they may take us by surprise.

Do not confuse the root cause, which is a leaf of the fault tree, with the top event, which is the root of the tree, specifying the undesired event produced by the FTA tree, and is placed at the foot of the tree as shown in Figure 8.4. Even though a hierarchical structure is expected, there is not really any acceptable or standard layout you have to follow. Most designers will, however, prefer having parallel rows of nodes that provide details as they go deeper down to the leaves of the tree.

If our objective is to secure the success of a target system, why do we have to worry about the faults of the system? It is through studying why our systems fail that we know how we can achieve success. If failures and faults are identified and fixed on a system, then success is easier to obtain. If we are successful in uncovering what is wrong in a target system, then we can achieve system success.

As shown in Figure 8.5, FTA is, however, a joint effort where users, security staff, security management, and system owners all participate. Security staff plan, define, construct, analyze, and report. System owners review, modify, and accept.

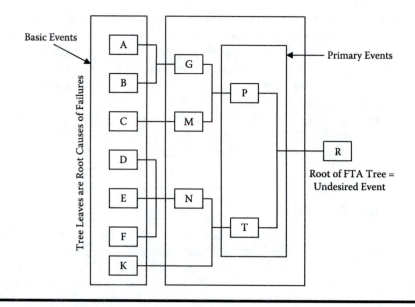

Figure 8.4   General layout of the FTA tree.

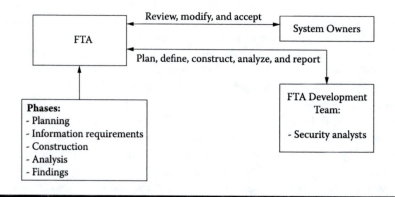

Figure 8.5   FTA environment.

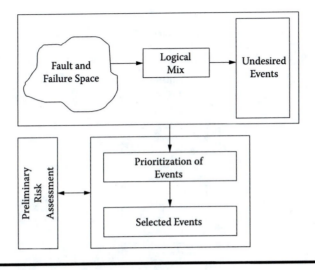

Figure 8.6   Fault search in an FTA.

FTA is a process that searches for undesired events. The output may be prioritized according to preliminary risk assessment based on asset criticality. The search process uses a deductive information-gathering process that builds logical combinations of events representing failures and faults in system components. FTA is hence a fault search process that combines identified failures and faults to produce undesired events. Figure 8.6 depicts the fault search process.

8.3.1 FTA Development

The FTA method, as shown in Figure 8.7 consists of the following steps:

1. Planning of FTA
2. Information requirement for FTA
3. Construction of FTA
4. Analysis of FTA
5. Report of FTA Findings

The planning phase consists of several preparatory steps. The first step aims at defining the objective of the analysis. FTA may be used for many different reasons—for example, in risk analysis of information systems, for the identification of improvements in security management systems, and in other protection functions.

FTA should obviously have its scope where boundaries for the study are delineated, often with respect to feasibility constraints. The scope is defined before the starting the design of the fault tree. Information requirements and the construction of the tree can, however, expand beyond information security analyst control. Some

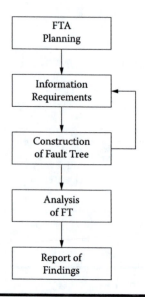

Figure 8.7 Major phases of FTA.

events cannot be studied without expanding local studies on one path to other branches that cannot be overlooked [2,10]. This pattern of expansion sometimes cannot be predicted, which will let the information requirements phase go on for prolonged periods. That is, the scope of a FTA project may not be easy to define in earlier phases and only becomes definitive halfway through the project. Once underway, you cannot just stop the study before examining all events contributing to the production of the undesired event.

As with any other methodology, FTA has its pros and cons. The main advantages of FTA are the following:

It is visual.
It is easy to learn, apply, and communicate.
It provides a simple and logical graphical representation.
It is easy to communicate to users and system owners.
Its clear presentation makes it simple to implement.
It provides a cause-effect analysis.
It can model complex systems.
It can combine people, activities, networks, data, technology.
It provides a probability model.
It is logically acceptable.
It produces significant findings even with incomplete information.

Known disadvantages include the following:

It does not converse well when time is added.

Representing loops is a complex task.

Even though there are some in the market, an excellent FTA software package does not exist.

If you can successfully collect the information requirements needed to construct the fault tree, there is nothing easier than constructing a fault tree. A simple and small number of symbols may be used to show a fault tree representing a simple causal logical scheme. The causal logical scheme defines paths showing how a root failure evokes faults that lead to new faults until the top undesired event is produced. The security management team can now understand the chain of events that lead to an undesired event.

A simple tree is one that uses simple logical gates like AND and OR, or minimizes the use of constraint symbols and the use of transfer connectors.

In the ETA section, most information resources have one or more security controls that are implemented to stop or reduce the consequences of potential accidental events. The probability that an accidental event will lead to unwanted consequences will therefore depend on whether these controls are functioning or not. The consequences may also depend on additional events and factors. Examples include:

Whether or not the security control works
Whether or not the security disruption is detected
Whether or not there has been information leakage
Whether or not there has been information corruption
Whether or not there has been a denial of service
What the criticality of affected resources is

Security controls employed as safeguards to various information resources in the computing environment may be managerial controls, operational controls, or technical controls.

Example: An Authorized Access by a Hostile Agent

The example in Figure 8.8 depicts a fault tree explaining how a security disruption is produced. If there is a hostile agent (B) and a firewall failure (A) occurring at the same time, then an unauthorized access (C) attempt will take place. If the authentication (D) mechanism also fails, then a security disruption (X) will occur. The Inhibit gate is like an AND gate, but the fault only passes if the condition specified in the oval symbol is satisfied. Even though the inhibit gate usually contains a condition or a probability, in this case, it is associated with the condition specified in D. Table 8.1 shows the main gates commonly used in FTA.

Fault trees produce vital planning and auditing data. These data will be needed in the evaluation and enhancement of system security. The meaningfulness of any FTA process rests on the accuracy of the identification of critical undesired

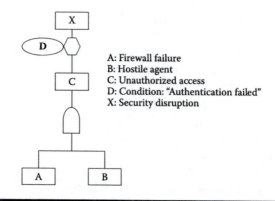

A: Firewall failure
B: Hostile agent
C: Unauthorized access
D: Condition: "Authentication failed"
X: Security disruption

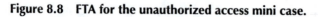

Figure 8.8 FTA for the unauthorized access mini case.

Table 8.1 Limited FTA Symbols

Operator	Symbol	Description
AND gate		The output event will occur only if all of the input events occur simultaneously.
OR gate		The event will occur if at least one of the input events occurs.
Rectangle		It represents a negative event or any intermediary events contributing in the causal analysis. This is the only symbol that will have a logic gate and input events below it.
Circle		It represents a base event in the tree, usually situated on the bottom of the tree and requires no further development or breakdown. No gates or events are found below the base event.
Diamond		It represents an undeveloped terminal event; sometimes due to a lack of information or significance. A fault tree branch can end with a diamond.
Oval		It represents a special situation that can only be seen if certain circumstances occur.
Triangle		This is a an extension connector representing a transfer of a fault tree branch to another location within the tree

events. If we start with the wrong top event, then the FTA will be meaningless. The success of any FTA project depends first on the selection of the appropriate undesired events, and second, on the ability of the information security analyst, who should be effective in identifying all failures and faults capable of producing the top event.

FTA is capable of representing most useful interactions between people, activities, data, technology, and the infrastructure, and modeling any faults, failures, human errors, and any external conditions that can cause undesired incidents in the computing environment. The FTA method is also useful to identify system vulnerabilities, estimate the probabilities of threats, and identify new accidental events produced by the exploitation of system vulnerabilities. The investigation is usually conducted by security analysts familiar with the working of the computing environments who may acquire the support of knowledgeable security experts.

FTA itself is not capable of assessing security risks, because the consequences of the occurrence of undesired events will only be produced by the ETA method; but the preparation of the risk management project may be initiated. FTA is useful in identifying events and threats that can result in undesired events. Frequencies of failures may be assessed by the FTA method. A list of contributing events may be obtained. Preliminary recommendations of ways to mitigate risks may be generated, but a sound risk-driven security program will not be possible without anticipating the consequences of undesired events. The ETA method will be presented in a separate section later in this chapter.

FTA is, however, applicable to most risk assessment applications, but it can be more useful in studying the true causes of specific accidents associated with relatively complex combinations of events.

Example: A Fault Tree Representing a Smurf Attack

A Smurf attack is a well-known attack in which an ICMP echo request is directed to a broadcast network address, which will act as an amplifying agent with a spoofed source address. That is, a stream of ICMP echo replies from that network develops. If the size of the reply is massive enough, then this attack may easily crash the victim's network. Even after early detection, the victim will not be able to plan a timely incident response because the link is simply congested with packets.

The Smurf attacks involve several events:

F: Smurf attack
A: Crash victim network
B: Return address is spoofed
C: Storm of replies from network
D: Misconfigured router forwarding the broadcast request to the subnet
E: Link is overloaded with packets
G: Unencrypted data
H: Storm of ICMP Echo request
I: Connection to a broadcast network acting as an amplifying agent

The top event F representing the undesired event consists of three primary events as follows:

$$F = A + B + C \text{ where}$$

+: union symbol
A: Crash victim network
B: Return address is spoofed
C: Storm of replies from network

Let x.y.z.0–255 be the address range assigned to our company with an amplifier. The attacker uses the destination x.y.z.255 to direct packets. As soon as this packet reaches the amplifier which observes the broadcast address (x.y.z.255), the amplifier forwards the request to all the resources on the network (referred to in the literature as directed broadcast).

The security analyst then studies the fault tree analysis and alerts system owners to similar situations that can produce the Smurf attack. For example, for the Smurf attack event to be realized, the events A, B, and/or C have to occur. In addition to the primary events directly linked to the top event of the fault tree, there are other components that are crucial to the production of the Smurf attack event. These are the basic events that constitute the root causes of failures that have to be prevented, and if prevented, the top event of the fault tree will not occur. The Smurf attack is depicted in Figure 8.9. Figure 8.10, however, depicts the fault tree corresponding to the Smurf attack.

In such an attack, the amplifier also makes itself and its network a victim because the link between the victim machine and the network gets overloaded, and the network gets congested. Usually, victim addresses are obtained from IRC bots, where information is exchanged about the addresses and the mechanisms

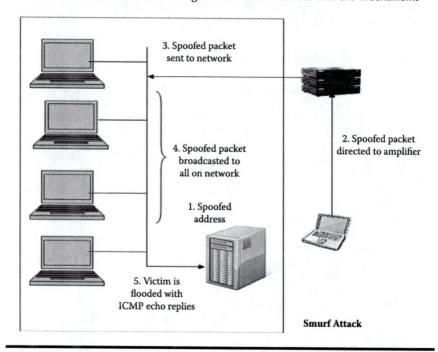

Smurf Attack

Figure 8.9 Framework for the Smurf attack.

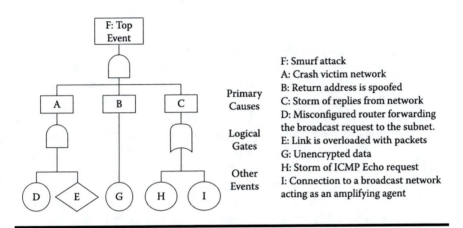

F: Smurf attack
A: Crash victim network
B: Return address is spoofed
C: Storm of replies from network
D: Misconfigured router forwarding
  the broadcast request to the subnet.
E: Link is overloaded with packets
G: Unencrypted data
H: Storm of ICMP Echo request
I: Connection to a broadcast network
  acting as an amplifying agent

Figure 8.10   FTA representing a Smurf attack.

of performing attacks. Hackers often exchange the information about amplifiers with one another so that when a mass attack occurs, nobody will know for sure from where it originates. IRC bots are scripts that connect to Internet Relay Chat as client, and this way the client will appear to other IRC users as another ordinary user. It differs from a regular client in that instead of providing interactive access to IRC for a human user, it performs automated functions.

The FTA method is useful in understanding what is really happening that can produce the Smurf attack. The security analyst can then recommend to system owners how to protect against such an attack. The following are the steps needed to protect against the Smurf attack.

STEP 1: AMPLIFIER CONFIGURATION

You first need to make sure that the router is not configured to forward directed broadcasts onto networks; otherwise, a simple command such as no ip-directed broadcast on Cisco routers should do it. It is, however, a good practice, to disable this type of broadcast on all routers, in addition to external routers. If the internal router does not allow for directed broadcast, then internal users on company networks cannot conduct the Smurf attack.

STEP 2: CONFIGURE THE SERVER'S OPERATING SYSTEMS

Second, you need to make sure that your servers are not configured to respond to a directed broadcast request. Some operating systems, like FreeBSD, are configured by default not to respond to a directed broadcast request, but many systems are not, for which manual configuration should apply.

STEP 3: ISP HAS TO BLOCK ICMP ECHO REPLIES

When a Smurf attack takes place, the link from the victim to the network may be flooded with replies. That is, the victim machine may not be able to do much as the link itself may be congested. The victim's ISP has to block ICMP echo repliers to prevent overloading the victim's link to the ISP and to the network.

8.3.2 Design of a Fault Tree

There are certainly other methods that may be adopted to study system faults and failures. FTA seems to be, however, more straightforward in searching for those negative events that lead to the realization of undesired events. This provides a clear means to communicate root causes to system owners. Information security managers can gain a better understanding of the security of the system being studied. The security management team can use FTA to visualize complex systems and delineate all events capable of producing the undesired event, identify relevant events and conditions producing undesired events, and define the logical conditions combining relevant events to produce the undesired events.

Once we have sufficient information on all known negative events, at least as much as one can feasibly have, it becomes easier to conduct any risk assessment activities. It is simpler to identify system vulnerabilities and estimate the probability of the undesired event. Sufficient information on negative events will produce better risk assessment information as follows:

Identify vulnerable components, and define how they can produce the undesired event.

Identify and define possible conditions capable of exploiting component vulnerabilities that can lead to the undesired event.

Estimate the likelihood of an occurrence of events and that of the undesired event.

Moreover, the identification and study of negative events is useful in understanding the security policy of all components associated with the negative events. It is the violation of a component security policy that produces information about relevant negative events. For any information system, it is important to view the system as comprising people, activities, data, technology, and network and study possible undesired events and how they can be caused. Table 8.2 shows a worksheet where the security analyst can assemble FTA information in an information system. That is, the study of negative events is a good means to assemble information security requirements. The following steps are needed for gathering information security requirements:

Understand how security policy is enforced on all components associated with the undesired event. Identify the components where security policy is not adequately enforced.

Understand the causes of any security deficiencies in relevant components.

Define new security requirements and prioritize them in terms of how they can prevent the occurrence of the undesired system.

FTA is sometimes required by users, customers, and partners, and the company is obligated to show FTAs for major undesired events as part of security planning.

Table 8.2   Worksheet—FTA Target: Undesired Event Information

Undesired event #: _____ of _____

Project: _____

Undesired Events	Information System Components				
	People Affected	Activities Affected	Data Resources Affected	Technology Affected	Infrastructure Affected
Number of IS Components					
Component 1					
Name					
S: 1 to 5					
A: 1 to 5					
C: 1 to 5					
Component 2					
Name					
S: 1 to 5					
A: 1 to 5					
C: 1 to 5					
Component 3					
Name					
S: 1 to 5					
A: 1 to 5					
C: 1 to 5					
Component 4					
Name					
S: 1 to 5					
A: 1 to 5					
C: 1 to 5					

Continued

Table 8.2 Worksheet—FTA Target: Undesired Event Information
(***Continued***)

	Information System Components				
Undesired event #: _____ of _____ Project: _____					
Undesired Events	*People Affected*	*Activities Affected*	*Data Resources Affected*	*Technology Affected*	*Infrastructure Affected*
Component 5					
Name					
S: 1 to 5					
A: 1 to 5					
C: 1 to 5					
Total					
S: 5 to 25					
A: 5 to 25					
C: 5 to 25					
Security analyst: _____ Date: _____ Initials: _____					S: 25 to 125
Comments: _____ _____					A: 25 to 125
					C: 25 to 125

Some certification bodies also request that FTAs be conducted by internal security analysts. These reports are very useful in speeding up security planning and auditing activities and in making them more cost-effective. Many security auditors will appreciate having those reports ready. This will cut time and expenses in audit testing activities as auditors will only need the available findings and perform minor tests to amend or confirm those findings. The changes in findings are by themselves a very important indication of the presence of deficiencies if those changes are negatives or for security enhancement if the changes are positive.

Systems owners also may request that FTAs be prepared when risks become high. The FTA process itself will uncover most potential dangerous incidents and risky anomalies. In a later section, you will see how event trees are used to study the effects of security controls and safeguards when selected undesired incidents take place.

Even though an FTA is usually designed to explain how failures and faults can jointly contribute to produce an undesired event, there are many security assessment activities that are performed as part of the FTA process that can be very useful in many other security assessment projects:

Evaluating unintentional security disruptions attributed to carelessness and unpreparedness.
Estimating the probabilities of major security disruptions.
Identifying rogue users.
Identifying accidental activities that can lead to ugly consequences.
Evaluating system failure of all types.
Evaluating unnecessary deployment of infeasible countermeasures.
Estimating probabilities for major undesired events.
Evaluating the current layout and effectiveness of current intrusion detection systems and their components.

All the activities just listed are needed in security planning, security auditing, vulnerability assessment, etc.

When the fault tree is ready, there may be various ways of analyzing it depending on our security objectives. Usually, independently of our security objective, we have now identified what the undesired events are and how they are realized. We have to prevent the undesired event from taking place. We also have to prevent any event that leads to the undesired event or its production. Preventing all those events from taking place may be something that is not feasible, but it is certainly a necessary security project to plan for. Events leading to the undesired event in a complex or large fault tree may be very costly to achieve.

In order to adopt an efficient way of mitigating security risks associated with the realization of the undesired event of the fault tree, we have to identify the cut sets of the fault tree and manage their risks. Figure 8.14 gives an example showing the need for cut sets. The following definitions may be useful in analyzing a fault tree:

1. Cut set (CS): Set of events that together cause the top event to occur.
2. Minimal CS: CS with a minimum number of events that can still cause the top event to occur.
3. Super set: CS that contains a minimal CS plus additional events to cause the top event to occur.
4. Critical path: The highest probability CS that drives the top event probability.
5. CS order: The number of elements in a CS.
6. CS truncation: Cut sets may be removed from the tree when the FT is evaluated. CSs are truncated when they exceed a specified order or a fixed probability.

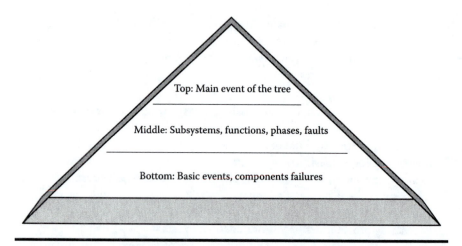

Figure 8.11 Trees are developed in layers, levels, and branches.

When the fault tree is constructed, three thick layers may be designed. The top layer includes information and visual presentation of the main event of the fault tree. The boundaries between the layers are somehow arbitrary, but the middle layer is usually the thickest layer because there are many intermediary events that participate in the production of the undesired event. The basic events make the bottom layer of the fault tree. This is also the most critical layer of the fault tree because risks are mitigated by preventing the basic events from occurring. Risk mitigation will then occur at the bottom layer of the tree. Figure 8.11 displays the three-layer pyramid depicting the layout of the fault tree.

It is important to relate risk management with various layers of a fault tree, as shown in Figure 8.12. Usually, the top event of the tree represents the target system

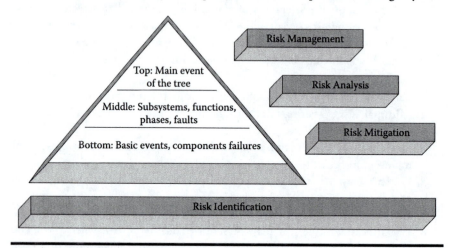

Figure 8.12 Risk layers and fault tree layers.

for which security risk is managed. Risks are analyzed based on the states of intermediary events leading to the main undesired events producing the undesired consequences. However, when security controls are applied to mitigate risks we have to identify those safeguards that can have effects on the basic events of the fault tree. The undesired event at the top of the fault tree may be prevented or controlled by controlling the basic events situated at the bottom of the fault tree.

E-mail bombing is a malicious attack by a hostile agent, a human, or a computer program, where massive numbers of e-mails are intended to target a specific system or a user account of that system. The e-mail bombs will usually fill the assigned space on an e-mail server for the user's e-mail, and can result in crashing the e-mail server, or at least diminishing the performance of the server and rendering it useless when the e-mail client continuously attempts to download the huge amounts of e-mail.

E-mail spam usually concerns unsolicited commercial messages sent in bulk by people who were not authorized to use your e-mail address and were unknown to you. E-mail spam is the traditional junk mail, except that it is sent at a considerably lower cost. The cost of sending junk mail through the post office is very real, and the spammer is paying for it. The cost of sending e-mail spam is, however, very small, and most costs are not paid by the spammer. The cost factor encourages spammers to continue their spamming effort, which can bring with it tremendous destructive power as servers can easily crash and networks can easily get congested. There is no doubt that, because of this low cost of sending unsolicited e-mail and the potential profit entailed, only strict legal enforcement can stop e-mail spamming

Sending spam violates any acceptable use policy. Usually, an acceptable use policy is a set of rules and regulations that system owners enforce to restrict the way systems are expected to behave computationally. Acceptable computing policies are designed in terms of the security policies of systems. New users are asked to accept and sign the security policy of systems before they are granted access to them.

The security policy will be easier to enforce if it is more comprehensive. It will be more effective to enforce the security policy of an organization if the policy lists deterrence methods, including sanctions that should be applied if a user violates the security policy. In the United States, the states enacted their own antispam laws, which have since been preempted by the CAN-SPAM Act of 2003. The CAN-SPAM Act of 2003 (15 U.S.C. 7701, et seq., Public Law No. 108-187, was S.877 of the 108th United States Congress), signed into law by President George W. Bush on December 16, 2003, establishes the United States' first national standards for the sending of commercial e-mail and requires the Federal Trade Commission (FTC) to enforce its provisions [3,5,8].

The CAN-SPAM Act is commonly referred to by antispam activists as the You-Can-Spam Act because the bill does not require e-mailers to get permission before they send marketing messages [5]. It also prevents states from enacting stronger antispam protections, and prohibits individuals who receive spam from suing spammers. The act has been largely unendorsed, despite a letter to the FTC from the Senator Conrad Burns, who noted that "Enforcement is key regarding the CAN-SPAM legislation." In 2004 less than 1% of spam complied with the CAN-SPAM Act of 2003 [8].

Spam is legally permissible according to the CAN-SPAM Act of 2003 provided it follows certain criteria: a truthful subject line; no false information in the technical headers or sender address; "conspicuous" display of the postal address of the sender; and other minor requirements. If the spam fails to comply with any of these requirements, it is illegal. Aggravated or accelerated penalties apply if the spammer harvested the e-mail addresses using methods described earlier.

Several countries have passed laws that specifically target spam, notably Australia and all the countries of the European Union. Article 13 of the European Union Directive on Privacy and Electronic Communications (2002/58/EC) provides that the EU member states shall take appropriate measures to ensure that unsolicited communications for the purposes of direct marketing are not allowed either without the consent of the subscribers concerned or in respect of subscribers who do not wish to receive these communications, and the choice between these options to be determined by national legislation. In Australia, the relevant legislation is the Spam Act 2003, which covers some types of e-mail and phone spam, which took effect on 11 April, 2004.

There are software packages available that you can acquire to support qualitative or quantitative analysis. Qualitative analysis employs computational methods that use cut sets to identify what combinations of events produce the undesired event (that is, the top event of the fault tree). Quantitative analysis uses a variety of exact calculation methods to determine the probability of occurrence of the top event based on maintenance data on the failure or maintenance data entered for leave events of the tree.

For example, Relex is a software that supports several calculation results, including unavailability, unreliability, importance measures, frequency, and number of failures.

Most organizations provide e-mail services to their users. Just because they have a valid e-mail address, your users are vulnerable to e-mail bombing and spamming. E-mail spamming is almost impossible to prevent because a user with a valid e-mail address can spam any other valid e-mail address, newsgroup, or bulletin-board service. How does a denial-of-service attack materialize?

When large amounts of e-mail are directed to or through a single site, the site may suffer a denial of service through loss of network connectivity, system crashes, or failure of a service because of overloading network connections using all available information resources filling the disk as a result of multiple postings and resulting syslog entries.

There are two information resources that are a common target of this type of DoS attacks: consumption of bandwidth and consumption of all types of memory. A hostile agent, a human or a computer program, may be able to consume most of or all the available bandwidth on your network by generating and directing a

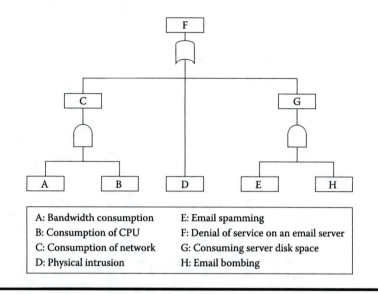

Figure 8.13   FTA for e-mail server example.

large number of packets to a critical network. Even though those packets can be of any type, often these packets are ICMP ECHO packets. A more hostile agent can produce more harm by operating or coordinating several machines on different networks to achieve more destructive power.

In addition to network bandwidth, the hostile agent may be able to consume other information resources that your system cannot function without. For example, the agent may be able to consume data structures, holding process information by writing a simple program or script that repeatedly create copies of itself. Most operating systems have quota facilities to protect against this problem, but many systems are vulnerable to it. Often, however, even if the process table is not yet full, the CPU may be consumed by a large number of processes and the associated time spent switching between processes.

Figure 8.13 presents a fault tree where the undesired event is the failure of the company e-mail server. The security analyst has to thoroughly study the computing environment, potential threats, current system vulnerabilities, and current safeguards. This study will identify security risks associated with the undesired event and explains with sufficient details how the identified undesired event can actually occur.

The failure of the company's e-mail server, in this example, may be produced through a disjunction of three main faults:

Fault: disjunction—denial of service on an e-mail server (Event F)
    Failure: consumption of network (Event C)
    Failure: physical intrusion (Event D)
    Failure: consumption of server disk space (Event G)

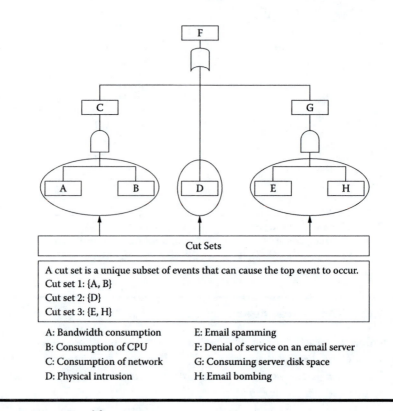

Figure 8.14 FTA with cut sets.

That is, at least one of the events C, D, and G has to occur in order for the e-mail server to fail. This area corresponds to the middle area of the fault tree layout presented earlier. You may note that event D is also a basic event (in addition to being a primary event) that is a leaf connected directly to the top event of the tree, and should be studied as a part of the risk mitigation process. The event D may be at the same time a member of the middle layer or the bottom layer of the fault tree. If event D cannot be prevented then the top (undesired) event, e-mail server failure, will take place.

If we go down a step deeper, we will reach the bottom layer where basic events reside. Because of the AND gate's combining events A and B to produce C, the intermediary event C can only occur if both basic events A and B occur at the same time. In a similar manner, the event G defined by the consumption of the e-mail server disk space can only occur if both basic events F and H occur at the same time. That is, if e-mail bombing and e-mail spamming cannot both be prevented, there will be consumption of e-mail server disk space.

Failure: bandwidth consumption (Event A)
Failure: consumption of CPU (Event B)

Failure: e-mail spamming (Event E)
Failure: e-mail bombing (Event H)

8.4 Event Tree Analysis

Event tree analysis (ETA) is an inductive method that shows all possible outcomes resulting from an accidental event, taking into account all other events and parameters and whether or not installed security controls are functioning [1].

By studying all relevant accidental events, the ETA method can be used to identify all potential accident scenarios and sequences in the computing environment or a target system. System vulnerabilities can be identified, and probabilities of the various outcomes from a security incident can be determined.

Figure 8.15 provides an ETA representing what can go wrong if a buffer overflow takes place. The event tree has a root containing the main event to be analyzed. When you draw an event tree similar to the one in Figure 8.15, you will notice that there are paths going from the root of the event tree to the final consequences that may be caused by the undesired event. Every path represents a specific security disruption scenario that can take place. All those scenarios have to be studied in order to enhance security toward mitigating risks associated with the negative consequences defined in the event tree.

ETA method is often needed to perform two main activities in information security management:
Risk analysis of information resources
Identification of improvements in security controls and security management systems.

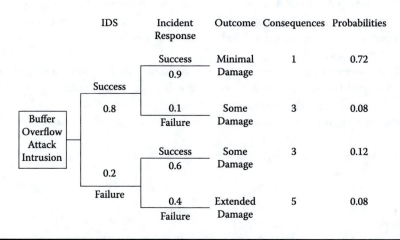

Figure 8.15 An event tree for a buffer overflow example.

8.4.1 ETA Steps

The ETA method is usually conducted using the following steps:

1. Define the incident to study.
2. Identify the safeguards or security controls in place to protect against the root incident and related events.
3. Construct the event tree.
4. Define the resulting incident sequences.
5. Determine the frequency of the accidental event and the conditional probabilities of the branches in the event tree.
6. Calculate the probabilities/frequencies for the identified consequences.
7. Write ETA report.

ETA is always performed within a larger project and not alone. For example, ETA may be one step in security planning, security auditing, risk analysis, or any other security management projects. Most of those projects often require the identifications of threats and undesired events that have to be studied in terms of the existing managerial, operational, and technical security controls.

There may be incidents, and undesired and accidental events that are candidates for an ETA, and it is sometimes difficult to select the ones you need to include in an ETA and use as root or initiating events. The following set of questions may be helpful when an accidental event is selected:

What type of event is more relevant to the security management project in question? For example, information leakage, information corruption, denial of service, fire, and so on.

Where does the event take place? For example, physical security, people, infrastructure, technology, activities, data resources, technology, and so on.

When does the event occur? For example, during normal operation, during maintenance, etc.

Which event is thought to be closer to the source of the problem or potential danger? For example, is it a virus at the origin of information corruption? Is it a physical break at the origin of the denial of service?

Which event presents a more serious violation of the security policy?

An accidental event may be caused by:

People, like rogue users
Human error
System failure
Poor quality or corrupted data
Hardware failure

Accidental events may be previously known or new ones. The new ones, for example, new types of attacks for which we do not know the signature, are not candidates for initiating accidental events, obviously because we do not have sufficient information to expand the event tree. The security analyst has to have sufficient information on expanding the tree, including the effects of existing security controls and possible consequences produced by the root accidental event. The security analyst should know how the root accidental event appears and how it progresses, system dependencies, and intermediary responses. Table 8.3 shows an example of a template that can be followed in defining the consequences of an event tree.

The security analyst should also know how the defense system provided by existing security controls works. The security analyst has to define the sequence of activation of security controls to counter the root accidental events and any other events. For example, the following information may be needed:

Intrusion detection components activated and in order
Sequencing of alarms activated
Sequencing of people informed
Sequencing of corrective actions taken
Sequential risk mitigation as a result of applying incident responses

Existing safeguards that are in the path of the initiating accidental event of the event tree under construction have to be put in the event activation sequence in a chronological manner. To make sense to the event tree analysis in terms of the security objective of the project in question, safeguards my be described using an adverse statement, for example,

"Access server R1 does not function." Assume that our initiating event is "Erroneous user authentication." This means that the access control server does not fulfill its user authentication mechanism as mentioned in its security policy. Additional events may also be described by adverse statements. The path originating at the initiating accidental event and containing the sequence of generated child events tells the story behind the negative consequences produced throughout the chronological sequence of events. Figure 8.16 provides a generic example depicting the general layout of an event tree.

In practice, an easy way to develop an event tree will be to proceed as follows:

1. Identify the root event.
2. Identify the first event resulting from the root event.
3. Events are safeguards defending the system against the root event.
4. After certain safeguards events as many as needed, a final event concludes by generating the final consequences of the event tree.
5. Estimate the probabilities of the consequences.
6. Report findings.

Table 8.3 Consequences in an Event Tree

Path #	Frequency	Outcome	Damaged Components						Economic Loss	Noneconomic Loss
			People	Activities	Technology	Data	Network			
1										
2										
n-1										
n										

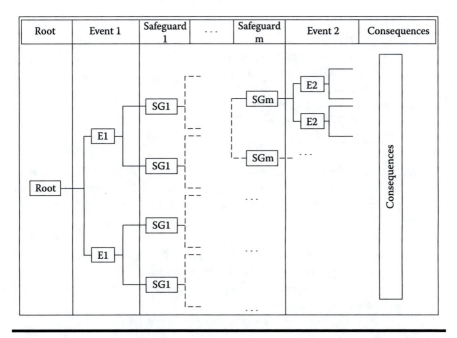

Figure 8.16   General event of an event tree.

The consequences in the event tree are produced by the realization of the undesired event despite the activation all existing safeguards. That is, all that we see as consequences are those residual effects which have not been stopped by the existing security controls that are in place. Those consequences have effects on all components of the computing environment, including people, activities, network and infrastructure, data, and technology. Those consequences may be economical, social, technical, operational, and legal/ethical.

While identifying root events of an event tree seems to be not so complicated after all, as shown earlier, this negative event cannot be studied in isolation from the affected assets. There may be a large number of assets that are affected by the undesired event, which will make the definition of the event tree scope something as easy. It will not be feasible to include all relevant assets in the event tree scope when their number is high. The scope should only include the most critical assets that are affected by the undesired event. An asset criticality has two components: sensitivity, and availability. Asset sensitivity and availability are defined using a five-point scale as follows:

Asset sensitivity:
1. Very low sensitivity
2. Low sensitivity
3. Average sensitivity

4. High sensitivity
5. Very high sensitivity

Asset availability requirements:

1. Very low availability requirements
2. Low availability requirements
3. Average availability requirements
4. High availability requirements
5. Very high availability requirements

The computation of criticality in terms of sensitivity and availability information is provided in Table 8.4, with precedence given to sensitivity. In order to ease the computation of criticality values, we use a 9-point Likert scale to represent them, as follows:

1. Very low criticality (very low sensitivity and very low availability)
2. Little sensitivity and little availability requirements
3. Low criticality (low sensitivity and low availability)
4. Low-to-medium criticality
5. Moderate criticality (moderate sensitivity and moderate availability)
6. Moderate-to-high criticality
7. High criticality (high sensitivity and high availability)
8. High-to-very high criticality
9. Very high criticality (very high sensitivity and very high availability)

The security analyst can now adopt the asset criticality scores to determine the undesired events to use in event trees. To provide a sound method for the selection of the most critical events those are to be used in the event tree analysis. Any sound selection method has to be risk driven. At this point, however, we can only perform a preliminary risk assessment given the negative events candidates for the event tree analysis. Any risk assessment, on the other hand, has to take into account

Table 8.4 Criticality Values with Precedence to Sensitivity

		Sensitivity				
Precedence >		1	2	3	4	5
Availability	1	1	2	3	4	5
	2	2	3	4	5	6
	3	3	4	5	6	7
	4	4	5	6	7	8
	5	5	6	7	8	9

the probability of the undesired event and its criticality. You may note that at this point we do not yet know the consequences of the undesired events to include in any preliminary risk assessment. Remember, the main objective of ETA is the production of the consequences to be caused by the undesired events. We will not have sufficient information about the consequences before we complete the ETA for which we are attempting to select the root event.

Event trees are useful in many areas of industrial engineering and in computing. The results from the event tree analysis may be used to:

Judge the acceptability of the system
Identify improvement opportunities
Make recommendations for improvements
Justify allocation of resources for improvements

8.4.2 How Is an Event Tree Constructed?

Sometimes, in order to assess the security of a target system, an event tree analysis can be of great help to security analysts. An event tree is a diagram of all the events that can occur in a system. It is like presenting a truth table. This is something very useful in sensitivity analysis. Answering what-if questions, like "What if event E happens?" Studying all paths initiated at event E will explain possible consequences which will provide information support for the making of any response planning decisions.

An event tree is started with a root event beginning at the left of the diagram; then new branches are added that represent new events that occur following preceding events. Every branch introduces new events, and so on, until known consequences are attained. The final tree structure will clearly present paths leading to consequences. Every path on the tree may be studied in terms of the probabilities of events on the path to produce estimates of security risks associated with the target system.

Once the security objective is defined, an event tree diagram may be started. Sorting all relevant events chronologically may be a good start. The root event E_0 will produce several states $s_{01}, s_{02}, \ldots, s_{0a}$; The resulting structure is depicted in Figure 8.17.

8.4.2.1 Advantages and Disadvantages of ETA

While it provides great benefits in security monitoring and continual security enhancement, ETA, as with any other computing methodology, has its own advantages and disadvantages:

Advantages:
Visualize event chains following an accidental event.
Visualize barriers and sequence of activation.

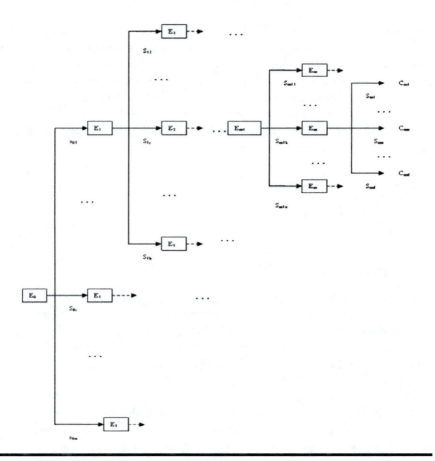

Figure 8.17 General layout of an event tree.

Good basis for evaluating the need for new/improved procedures and safety functions.

Disadvantages:

No standard for the graphical representation of the event tree.

Only one initiating event can be studied in each analysis.

Easy to overlook subtle system dependencies.

Not well suited for handling common cause failures in the quantitative analyses.

The event tree does not show acts of omission.

8.4.3 Computing the Probabilities of Event Tree Paths

This section provides information about ETA and how it relates to information security management. An event tree is a visual representation of events that can occur in a system. As the number of events increases, the picture fans out like the branches of a tree. This tool is useful to analyze systems in which all components are continuously operating. Every event tree has a root event, also called the initiating event, that is considered the initial security disruptor. The event tree displays the sequences of events involving success and/or failure of the system components.

In risk analysis, an event tree is used to identify the various possible outcomes of the system following a given initiating event, which is generally a security disruption event.

The event tree (Figure 8.17) is constructed to analyze the possible outcomes of an intrusion detection and response system. The system has two components designed to handle this event: intrusion detection subsystem and an automated response subsystem. If the intrusion detection system detects the intrusion, then the automatic response system will plan a response. This response can succeed or fail. If the intrusion detection system fails, then the incident response may or may not plan a manual incident response.

The goal of event tree analysis is to determine the probability of a root event, based on the outcome of child events in the chronological sequence of events leading up to it. The analysis of all possible outcomes determines the percentage of outcomes which lead to the probabilities in question. The probabilities of damage due to buffer overflow attacks are computed as follows:

P(minimal damage due to Buffer Overflow Attack) = P(success of ids) × P(success of incident response).

P(some damage due to Buffer Overflow Attack) = P(success of ids) × P(failure of incident response) + P(failure of ids) × P(success of incident response).

P(extended damage due to Buffer Overflow Attack) = P(failure of ids) × P(failure of incident response).

8.4.4 Simulation-Based Event Tree Analysis for an Introduction Detection System

We now know how to perform an ETA, including how to identify undesired events and selecting the most critical ones to serve as root events for the event trees. Recall that the objective of the event tree is to understand how the undesired event produces the undesired consequences at the presence of the existing safeguards. But how do we acquire the information about the paths of events that take place in a sequential manner until the consequences are realized? Usually, security assessment tests are conducted to evaluate what can happen that leads to negative effects. These tests include, for example, vulnerability assessment tests, active security assessment test, and invasive penetration tests.

An example of an active security assessment test is a simulation-based security assessment test. In such a test, a well-defined set of attack scenarios are injected in various entry points of the computing environment to induce the undesired

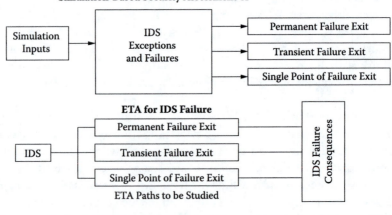

Figure 8.18   Simulation-based ETA for IDS failures.

event. After its induction, the simulation continues to study the sequential effects to record possible types of negative effects, including the behavior of existing security controls. The differences between a simulation-based security assessment test and a penetration test include the following:

A penetration test simulates hackers subject to a well-defined security policy.
A penetration test exploits system vulnerabilities and studies their effects.
A simulation-based security assessment test injects a set of well-defined scenarios and measures their consequences.
A simulation-based records the behavior of a prescribed set of controls implemented to counter known incidents.
A simulation-based security assessment test target a prescribed set of undesired events, whereas a penetration test searches for undesired events to be explored.

In the example depicted in Figure 8.18, the simulation-based security assessment test target an intrusion detection system. A set of attack scenarios are injected in the computing environment, and the IDS is studied for three failure exits:

Permanent failure exit
Transient failure exit
Single point failure exit

8.4.5 Transient Failure Exit

A transient failure is characterized by the detection of the intrusion or correct recognition of the problem that leads to the recovery from a temporary fault. Such a failure is usually caused by external interference, probing, or environmental factors, such as excessive heat, unstable power supply, or humidity, for example.

Faults are usually of the transient type and generally lead to successful recovery. Intrusions of unknown signatures may not be detected easily, and they are not necessarily of the transient type. For intrusions with known signatures, several stages may pass before the real attacks are executed. A good intrusion detection system may be able to have enough time to detect the initiation effort or even more time to detect the transition effort, and can hence detect the intrusion before the execution stage takes place. Corrective actions such as, for example, reconfiguring the system or switching to a safer configuration may be sufficient to prevent system failure.

We then need to reach this exit successfully, for example by:
  Promptly detecting any probe or any errors produced by one of the components
  Promptly detecting any performance deficiencies
  Preempting and stopping an intrusion in a feasible manner

If a problem remains after applying all known and appropriate rollback and reconfiguration attempts, then the security analyst may confirm to system owners that the problem is judged to be produced by a permanent fault. The security control needed will be a permanent fault recovery action. At this time, the faulty component is dropped from the system. It has to be reconfigured without the faulty component. The security assessment activities should continue to uncover faulty subsystems.

The permanent fault recovery process in this case removes the root causes of the problem. The permanent scale-down procedure is adopted against a persisting transient fault or against a permanent fault.

8.4.6 Single Point Failure Exit

Sometimes we are dealing with a single point of failure. A single point of failure causes the entire system to fail. This can happen if the intrusion detection systems are not able to uncover the intrusion at the earlier stages of initiation or transition, and the intrusion is successful in executing its planned attack. Antivirus systems are kept current through the automatic updating of virus signatures. When a virus is detected, the system can be scanned, cleaned, and restored without prolonged delays.

Alternatively, the intrusion may be caused by an error that was not detected by the IDs and was successfully propagated through the system, similar to the effects of a virus, and cause system failure. The propagation of the consequences can also expand if the affected subsystem cannot be isolated. This may lead to prolonged delays if the system cannot be reconfigured or corrected to resume normal operations.

8.4.7 Permanent Failure Exit

Sometimes, some faults are within the risk range, and corrections tend to lack feasibility; system owners accept those risks and define an acceptable configuration of the system at risk. Usually, an older version of the business configuration is available and can be reproduced and implemented to resume business, albeit as a less profitable system. In such a situation, system owners need to determine and accept the permanent nature of the fault, and acknowledge the successful isolation and removal of the faulty component.

A simulation approach will be useful in studying the operations of the system by identifying failures and faults and by measuring their effects on the profitability of system. If a faulty component tends to permanently affect the system, it has to be dropped from the system. This prudent attitude of implementing a permanent coverage model establishes lower but steady operating conditions of the system. This situation applies to people who are judged unfit in the operation of the system because they are not trusted or are determined incompetent to perform required activities.

8.5 FTA-ETA Integration

Security assessment has been always a difficult task to complete. The reasons for this difficulty are many, but two of them stand out and may be expressed in three questions: The first question is "What can go wrong in the system?" The second question is "If something goes wrong, how does it negatively affect the system?" The third question is "When something goes wrong and negatively affects the system, what can be done to correct, recover, and resume normal operations?

We posed three questions that we address in section. We initially propose a solution made up of three parts: the identification of major failures, the study of incidents and their consequences, and the response to incidents. Each part of the solution will only make sense if it is feasible in terms of associated risks. That is, the three parts of the proposed solution should be performed subject to effective security management. This means that the devised security program should be risk driven. A fourth part should be added to the proposed solution: security risk management.

The solution we propose here is a simple probabilistic risk management methodology that we refer to throughout this book as IFEAR. It is designed to study system faults, security incidents, and responses for the purpose of devising a risk-driven security program. Figure 8.19 shows how FTA produces the undesired event, which is then analyzed by ETA, where its consequences are studied given current security controls.

The security assessment solution we are discussing here requires four complementary components: the first component searches for failures that can potentially bring undesired incidents; the second component starts where the previous step ended, by studying the consequences that may be produced by the undesired

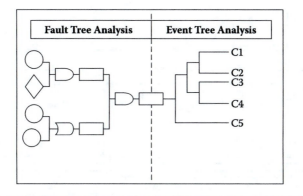

Figure 8.19   Information exchange between FTA and ETA.

Figure 8.20   Four-part security assessment solution in IFEAR.

incidents; the third component aims at planning incident responses to correct, recover, and resume normal operations; the fourth component is intended to review all steps to make sure that risks are identified, assessed, and mitigated in a feasible manner. The four components are integrated in the security assessment project to produce an adequate risk-driven security program. The four-part security assessment project is presented as shown in Figure 8.20.

8.6 Risk Management

At this point we have three sets of findings obtained from FTA, ETA, and response planning analysis. Findings of FTA produced information on how undesired events may be produced. Findings of ETA produced information on the consequences of the occurrence of the undesired events studied in the FTA phase. The response planning phase produced information on the corrective security controls planned to counter all the events resulting from the occurrence of undesired events. Figure 8.21 depicts the informational support acquired through the fault-incident-response process just discussed.

We now know what can happen, how it happens, the produced consequences, and how to plan corrective actions. We also collected sufficient probabilistic information to estimate all risks, but there is still one important step missing: the risk

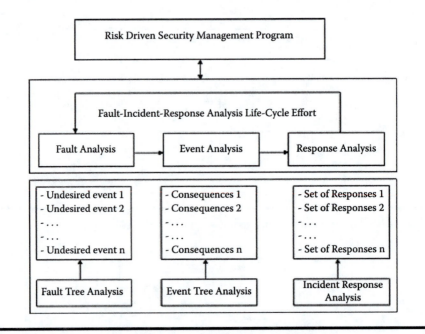

Figure 8.21   Fault-incident-response analysis life-cycle effort.

management step. That is, given all the information we now have, how can we optimally mitigate risk and devise a risk-driven security program that works.

As shown in Figure 8.19, the fault-incident-response analysis concluded was only a one-way analysis. It does not really tell us what can happen if the new corrective actions are taken. How do corrective actions affect the fault analysis information and the event analysis information we have, as well as the consequences produced by the event tree analysis. We need, however, to go back and study the effects of the incident response effort on the conducted fault and event analyses. Figure 8.19 is revisited to give Figures 8.20 and 8.21, which add the incident response life cycle effort to fault-incident-response analysis.

Using the integrated framework, we can now achieve two computational steps: in the first step, we compute the probability of the undesired event; in the second step, we compute the consequences originating at the undesired event. Figure 8.22 shows a simple example without the recursive effect.

8.6.1 Computation of Probabilities in FTA–ETA Integration

We intentionally provide a simple example where the undesired event is the system failure that can only take place if two root events A and B occur. The system fails with a probability $p(F) = p(A)p(B)$.

The undesired event F will generate the consequences L1, L2, and L3 through the existing barriers and safeguards, SG1 and SG2, adopted to counter the undesired

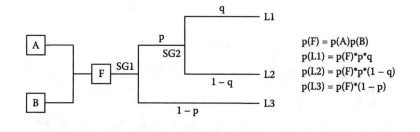

Figure 8.22   Simple example of information exchange between FTA and ETA.

event F. The probabilities of safeguards SG1 and SG2 of functioning properly are given by p and q. We can then compute the probabilities of the various consequences L1, L2, and L3 as follows:

$$p(L1) = p(F) \times p \times q$$

$$p(L2) = p(F) \times p \times (1 - q)$$

$$p(L3) = p(F) \times (1 - p)$$

The utility of the integrated framework is to study the effects on the consequences of any variation in the states of the root events A and B. For example, how much change may be effected consequently to L1, L2, and L3, if we realize a change of 10% in the probability of a root event, due to the application of some risk mitigation strategies?

8.7 Simulation and Sensitivity Analysis

In this section we intend to answer the question "How can we change FTA inputs to produce desired changes in ETA consequences?" If we can feasibly do this, then we can minimize the negative consequences and hence mitigate risks. Of course, this risk mitigation, even though based on FTA and ETA, requires the application of new incent responses order to mitigate risks. Those responses are designed based on information obtained from the FTA–ETA process. Figure 8.23 shows how a simulation process works to control consequences.

8.7.1 Risk Management Chain

Security risks should be understood in terms of threats and system vulnerabilities. Security assessment can, however, identify major undesired events and study them using a deductive approach to understand how they occur. The fault tree

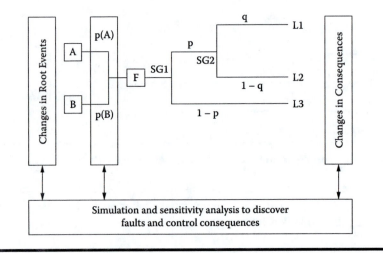

Figure 8.23 Simulation-ready framework for FTA–ETA–IR analysis.

analysis method is very useful in defining all the paths of events that lead to the realization of the undesired event, once we obtained the fault tree describing the production of the undesired event. This latter is then studied in an inductive way to understand what can happen when the undesired event occurs and how the consequences are produced.

The security program shown in Figure 8.24 is a one-way security program in the sense we go only in one direction, source faults to consequences. Figure 8.25 depicts the same system as in Figure 8.24 but with risk management added. We first use a deductive approach to define the deductive paths that lead to the top event of the fault tree, then we obtain the undesired event. In a second step, we apply an inductive approach to identify and define the inductive paths of the event tree that produce the consequences. In a third step, we define two sets of counter-measures: preventive countermeasures to serve as barriers on the deductive paths of the fault tree, and corrective countermeasures to serve as barriers to the inductive paths of the event tree.

In order to devise an effective risk-driven security program, we have to allow for the improvement of preventive countermeasures and the corrective countermea-sures. This requires that we simulate or review all recommended security controls to make sure that they are really mitigating risk up to an acceptable level as it is stated in the relevant security policy. We hence go back to the security management life cycle as shown in the PDCA framework. The security management cycle starts with identifying the top event of the fault tree and applies a deductive approach to identify and define all possible ways to produce the undesired event. In the incident response analysis phase, we will recommend all the feasible preventive security con-trol we need to prevent the undesired event from take place.

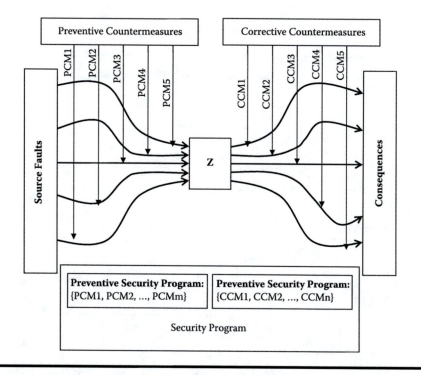

Figure 8.24 Preventive and corrective countermeasures throughout the FTA–ETA process.

If the undesired event takes place, then it may be late to go back and prevent this one but we can do better next time and prevent similar events from happening. We will then use an event tree analysis to identify all possible consequences. The incident response analysis phase will recommend all the corrective countermeasures for the purpose of stopping and intercepting the destructive paths to mitigate expected consequences. Figure 8.26 provides the framework needed for the security design for IFEAR.

8.8 Summary

This chapter presented the FTA methodology and the ETA methodology, and tells how to integrate them. The FTA methodology is a very powerful tool to identify faults that lead to failures. When those faults are fixed in a timely manner, continual security may be achieved. FTA produce possible undesired events that may be caused by existing faults. ETA, on the other hand, identifies possible undesired events and studies their consequences. When those consequences are defined, the security analyst reviews present security controls and studies their effectiveness for

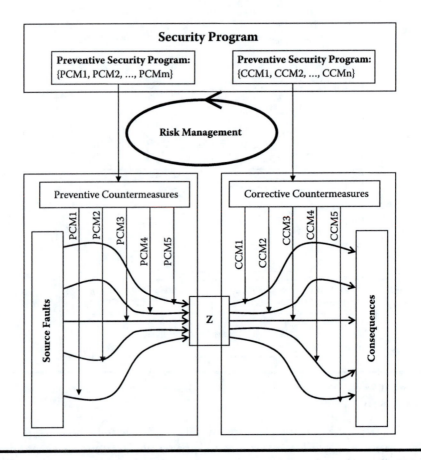

Figure 8.25 Preventive and corrective countermeasures throughout the FTA–ETA process, with risk management added.

the purpose of defining new ways to reduce and/or control the effects of those undesired events on business value.

The FTA and the ETA processes were integrated to produce a fault event analysis (FEA). The FEA methodology adopts the FTA methodology to produce the undesired event, then adopts the ETA methodology to study the consequences caused by the undesired events. The incident response step added to FEA will define the needed responses. The IFEAR goes a step further by evaluating risks and prioritize identified undesired events and devise a risk-driven security program that recommends those incident responses that best mitigate risks.

This chapter presented the IFEAR framework and was not intended to propose a development process. That was intentionally left for readers to develop.

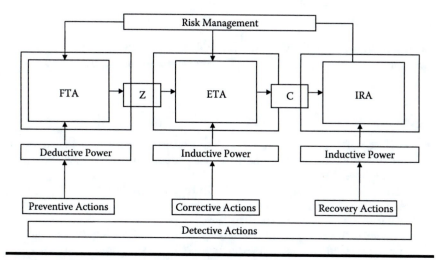

Figure 8.26 Complete framework needed for IFEAR design.

8.9 Review Questions

1. Explain how FTA works. Use a simple example.
2. Explain how ETA works. Use a simple example.
3. Explain how FEA works. Use a simple example.
4. Explain how to plan responses based on FEA. Give a simple example.
5. Explain how risks are managed using FEA. Give a simple example.
6. Explain how IFEAR works.
7. Explain how to apply IFEAR in business continuity.
8. Explain how to apply IFEAR in a security audit.
9. Explain how to apply IFEAR in intrusion detection.
10. Explain how to apply IFEAR in security planning.
11. Review Figure 8.5 of this chapter. Explain how do staff plan define, construct, analyze, and report in FTA? How do system owners review, modify, and accept in FTA?

8.10 Workshops

Workshop 1

Consider the ISO/IEC 27001. Write an IFEAR model based on ISO/IEC 27001. Compare the risk-driven security program produced by this approach to an ISMS-based ISO/IEC 27001.

Workshop 2

Give a case study, on your own, where you replace an intrusion detection system in a small business with an IFEAR model. Explain what is gained or lost by doing so.

References

1. Andrews, J. D., and S. J. Dunnett, Event Tree Analysis Using Binary Decision Diagrams http://www.lboro.ac.uk/departments/ma/research/preprints/papers99/99-25.pdf, visited on November 18, 2008.
2. Breukelen, E. D., Hamann, R. J., and E. G. Overbosch, Qualitative Fault Tree Analysis Applied as a Design Tool in a Low Cost Satellite Design: Method and Lessons Learned, 2006, on www.lr.tudelft.nl, visited on November 18, 2008.
3. Californian Business and Professions Code, Spam Laws, 2004, http://www.spamlaws.com/state/ca.shtml, visited on November 18, 2008.
4. Chelson, P. O., National Aeronautics and Space Administration, Technical Report 32–1542, Reliability Computation Using Fault Tree Analysis, http://ntrs.nasa.gov/archive/nasa/casi.ntrs.nasa.gov/19720005773_1972005773.pdf, 1971.
5. GP-Canada, Personal Information Protection Act, Chapter 63, SBC 2003, http://www.qp.gov.bc.ca/statreg/stat/P/03063_01.htm, visited on November 18, 2008.
6. NASA, The Team Approach to Fault Tree Analysis, Practice No. PD-AP-1312, http://paso.esa.int/5_training_materials/training_14_team%20approach.pdf, visited on November 18, 2008.
7. Sullivan K. J. et al., The Galileo Fault Tree Analysis Tool, http://www.cs.wm.edu/~coppit/wiki/images/a/a8/GalileoFTATool.pdf, visited on November 18, 2008.
8. U.S. Congress, PUBLIC LAW 108–187—DEC. 16, 2003 117 STAT. 2699, http://www.spamlaws.com/f/pdf/pl108-187.pdf, visited on November 18, 2008.
9. Vesely, W. F. et al., NUREG-0492, U.S. Nuclear Regulatory Commission, Fault Tree Handbook, 1981.
10. Xiang, J., Fault Tree Analysis of Software Reliability Allocation, http://www.jaist.ac.jp/~jxiang/publications/FTA%20in%20SRA.pdf, visited on November 18, 2008.

Chapter 9

Active Security Assessment

Learning Objectives

After reading of this chapter, students are expected to achieve an understanding of:

The existing standards for active security assessment
The limits of active security assessment
The vulnerabilities of various components of the computing environment
Ethical hacking
The proposed strategies for active security assessment
How the active security assessment project works
How the reconnaissance effort is conducted
How to conduct passive security assessment
How to conduct the active security assessment effort
How the NSA Triad for security assessment works
How to penetrate the system as hackers do
The cognitive ability of hackers
How some ASA resources work

9.1 Introduction

This book is about effective security management. Major activities in security management include security planning, intrusion detection, risk management, and security auditing. There are not, however, any activities among these that does not require major testing activities that include both passive and active security assessment. This chapter is concerned with active security assessment. There are many types of testing activities presented in the literature with different names, such as vulnerability assessment, penetration testing, ethical hacking, and security assessment, and even these testing activities have single definitions acceptable to all.

Penetration testing activities, for example, mean different things to different people. It all depends on the purpose and the scope of the test. Some people use it in vulnerability assessment, others use it in security planning, and many others use it in security auditing. People not only differ on the name but also on the contents of penetration testing activities. Penetration testing activities are variously defined, depending on the security objectives, test scope, and test security policy.

Anyway, before we propose our own definition of penetration testing, it is important to note that no matter how we define it in this book, how other people define it, and how different those definitions are, everyone agrees on the fact that the penetration test consists of active testing activities where the work of hackers is simulated. This simulation embraces hackers' effort when they discover, identify system vulnerabilities, and exploit them.

Let us propose a working definition of a penetration test that we will adopt throughout most of this book as follows:

> A penetration test is an active security assessment that is performed according to a well defined security objective, a well defined scope, and a well defined penetration security policy. This security assessment activity has to (1) blindly discover access information, (2) identify system vulnerabilities, (3) exploit them for the purpose of studying the system ability to resist adverse actions that can potentially compromise system security, and (4) generate security recommendations and act upon them according to the assigned penetration security policy.

In the literature, however, penetration testing tends to emphasize the invasive property of testing activities, while in this book we additionally emphasize the comprehensiveness of the test. No test can be useful in security management if it does not provide a comprehensive look at all aspects of the target system, including people, activities, data, infrastructure, and technology. To distinguish between our view of penetration testing and other views that take more myopic approaches in penetration testing, we propose using the name of active security assessment (ASA) instead.

Formal penetration testing activities define the scope of the project, its objectives, and adopt a methodology that the penetration test team uses throughout the project. The bottom line of any penetration test project is to identify vulnerabilities, prioritize them, study how to eliminate any conditions that bad guys can exploit to cause damage, and finally generate recommendations. Penetration testing employs the same tools, tricks, and techniques that hackers use but with prior authorization from system owners. We will later propose a set of steps that constitute the active security assessment project.

9.2 Standards for Active Security Assessment

There are many standards and guidelines that apply to various security planning and auditing activities, and security in general. Even though these standards are related to active security assessment and penetration testing in one way or another, they do not directly apply to active security assessment or penetration testing. We bring them up here because they may be useful in guiding your testing activities in several ways.

Security management, owners, and partners may be familiar with those standards, and unless your final report relates to those security requirements your active security assessment effort may not be highly valued. Security standards accepted by partners, competitors, and the security community in general may be referred to, as needed, in the project, or in its final report. Security guidelines and methods accepted by your system owners and confirmed by your security management may be useful in active security assessment.

Moreover, it is the responsibility of testers in their active security assessment to verify that those security controls that your company adopted to protect target systems based on its compliance with those standards or other accepted guidelines are in fact working and are effectively protecting the target systems; otherwise, your report should identify and present security deficiencies that existed despite the company compliance with those standards, and in this case, you have to propose corrective actions to enhance system security.

In fact there are many standards that you can adopt when planning your active security assessment project, but while many of them are relevant but not very practical the few we present in this book are very useful and often required in order to achieve effective security management: ISO 17799, ISO 27001-05, BS 25277, NIST Security Plan Guidelines, and OSSTMM.

9.3 Limits of Active Security Assessment

Do not even think for a minute that we are doing active security assessment to mimic the work of hackers. Testers just simulate hackers' work. In doing so, they

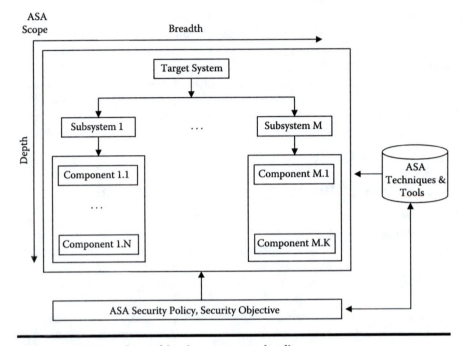

Figure 9.1 ASA project: objective, scope, and policy.

are limited by the ASA objective, its scope, and its security policy, as shown in Figure 9.1. In addition to those definitional limitations of an ASA project, there are limitations associated with our incapacity to compete with hackers. We most likely will not have sufficient resources to invent a new countermeasure against every attack they launch against us. Just read security publications here and there, and daily you will see their newest tools and the destruction they produce. This however should not eliminate the utility of those active security assessment activities based mainly on penetration tests. We may not be able to stop everything hackers do but we can make it difficult for them to harm us, and we certainly can minimize the effects of their malicious work on our systems.

You may be successful in testing an exploit of certain vulnerabilities you identified in your penetration test, and even in correcting them by applying the appropriate corrective security controls. In real life, however, there may be other exploits, even more destructive than the ones you just corrected, that can emerge immediately after you closed your ASA project, and cause greater security disruptions. Does this mean that your penetration test has just failed?

The answer is no. There may be new vulnerabilities that just appeared when you are trying to end your ASA project. There may be also new ways to exploit some of the old vulnerabilities that despite your successful active security assessment can still take place. We should not, however, think to stop this type of testing activity because conditions did not improve immediately after the penetration test ended. It is only through those activities that we can understand the effects of what hackers can do, which will certainly minimize security risks. Those active security assessment activities are very effective in aborting new attacks and in reducing the intensity and the success of many known attacks. Usually, the objective of active security assessment is not to eliminate the occurrence of attacks but to reduce their effects and their probability of success when they take place.

Many people think that active security assessment using penetration testing is a magic stick that eliminates all security problems. This is obviously very wrong. It is wishful thinking to believe that because you just finished a successful ASA project you can now enjoy a peaceful truce period where hackers will leave you alone, even for a short period of time. Do not rest; sneak attacks are always possible.

The completion of a successful ASA project is only one step towards risk mitigation. You are not proving much, other than risk reduction, when showing that new responses can be planned to detect certain system conditions if attempts are made to penetrate some components to exploit certain vulnerabilities. In fact, even the opposite does not prove much—that is new attempts, contrary to your expectations, could not be prevented. This is simply not the purpose of an ASA project or a penetration test to stop new hackers' attempts. A penetration test is not designed to prove any security trends based on single instances of technical tests. A penetration test is used to understand the effects of discovered technical conditions, good or bad (even though we have to do something about it immediately when it is bad), based on which we can proceed to implement baseline security controls that can reduce the probability of success of similar threats when they take place.

There should not be any intention to replace regular vulnerability assessment activities, the implementation of up-to-date vendors' upgrades and patches, security policy enforcement, planning and auditing efforts, etc.

9.4 Can You Hack Your Own System?

This is an active security assessment project that consists of active security testing activities that are often full of penetration tests simulating the real work of hackers. In an ASA project, it is proper that systems owners give testers permission to simulate what hackers do from the early footprinting effort to the final effort of reporting the effects of testers' attempts to exploit the identified systems vulnerabilities.

If you are a penetration tester, you will then act like a real hacker, but your penetration testing activities are limited. That is, a penetration test, also called *ethical hacking*, consists of a sequence of penetration activities authorized by systems owners. Every penetration test has a security objective, a well defined scope, and a well-defined security policy. An active security assessment scope does not only define the target system and its components involved in the penetration test, but it should also define all penetration test activities allowed. The security policy defines the behavior of the active security assessment project. An active security assessment project is intended to:

Explore what real hackers can do without causing damage to the target system
Identify risks
Explain risks to system owners
Generate recommendations to counter any intrusion aspects seen when hacking activities are simulated

This project is intended to experiment with the security disruptions that are the result of the exploiting, by testers, of those system vulnerabilities identified throughout the active security assessment activities. It is vital that you know that even though you are there simulating a hacker's activities, you are not a real hacker, so do not get destructive and follow as thoroughly as possible your ASA security policy. Here are some differences between real hackers and testers:

Testers have a security objective to respect, and a real hacker has a destructive objective to expend as much as possible.
While testers are limited by the scope of penetration testing activities, which limits the techniques and the tools to use, the real hacker who has a destructive objective to achieve is not limited to any techniques or tools.
Testers have a security policy to comply with, but the hacker is not bothered with such restraints.
While testers attempt to record every single step taken to study effects and possible remedies, the real hacker will attempt to hide the traces of all steps to make it difficult for forensic analysts to identify or catch.

The ASA project not only imposes the ASA scope that defines the target system and its components, but also a clear security objective set by system owners, and a security assessment security policy. The ASA scope also defines the testing activities and the methodologies testers are authorized to adopt when conducting their active security assessment activities.

Well, now we have a clear understanding of ASA limitations and testers' expectations. ASA testers simulate hackers for the purpose of identifying, studying by exploiting, and mitigating risks caused by vulnerabilities in the target system. It is, however, important to notice that a target system cannot be found by itself, but it is a important member of a company's information system or its computing environment. As we described in Chapter 1, an information system (of the company's computing environment) is a collection of people, activities, data, infrastructure, and technology. The vulnerabilities you are looking for may hence reside in any of the information system components described in earlier chapters.

9.5 Ethical Hacking of a Computing Environment

Let us discuss how ASA testers simulate their ethical attackers on various components of the information system.

9.5.1 Attacks on People

Testers' simulated hacking effort can target people holding critical positions and manipulate them, through social engineering, to trick them into divulging information that can be of use to them to penetrate protected components in the target system. Social engineering exploits are powerful ways to gain access information from innocent and trusting users for well planned malicious purposes.

9.5.2 Attacks on Infrastructure

The information infrastructure referred to in this book includes all physical resources except the technology part, which is included in another class. The technology components of information systems belong to a different class, as in Raggad's taxonomy [13], adopted throughout this book (see attack on technology below).

For example, an information system infrastructure may include company facilities, equipment, network infrastructure, and so on. That is, infrastructure attacks on information systems may be physical, where testers can break into rooms or facilities containing assets to be stolen or physically damaged. These assets can be laptops, desktops, servers, or any other equipment of great value to hackers. Critical information may also be obtained in dumpsters, trash cans, and recycling or sanitation stations where valuable information is disposed of.

Information system infrastructure attacks can also target network infrastructure available almost anywhere you are in your company. Locally, this can be done physically while a hacker is walking in company facilities. The network infrastructure may also be attacked by a remote hacker when the company's internal network is connected to the Internet and is hence available to all users worldwide. Testers, as simulated hackers, may test how real hackers exploit weaknesses in network protocols TCP/IP, or NetBEUI or how they can plan DoS attacks on company networks.

Common infrastructure attacks, as studied by [17], include the following:

1. *Lower-layer attacks*

   When an attacker has access to a physical link, this often results in downtime for the link. Of course, this is normally something benign but it could be catastrophic when connected systems have high availability requirements. It can however be even uglier when the malicious intent behind the attack is to prolong the unavailability to allow hackers to install eavesdropping or man-in-the-middle devices.

2. *Generic DoS on the router*

This attack is initiated by overloading a router using various techniques, for example, by sending traffic exceeding the router's forwarding capacity, by sending special transit packets that go through slow-path processing, or by sending some packets directed at the router itself.

3. *Cryptographic exhaustion attacks*

The previous attack may manifest in many other ways, some of them more malicious, such as those attacks targeting a protocol that uses cryptographic mechanisms, for example, TCP-MD5 or IPsec. Valid protocol messages are sent with cryptographic signatures or other properties to the router, which is forced to perform cryptographic validation of the message.

4. *Unauthorized neighbor attacks*

Sometimes when authentication is not adequate, unauthorized nodes obtain a routing protocol adjacency, and this may result in many kinds of attacks including traffic redirection.

5. *TCP RST attacks*

TCP sessions can be terminated by attackers who can send a TCP RST packet with guessed spoofed endpoint identifiers and a sufficiently close sequence number.

6. *ICMP attacks*

An ICMP attack may be initiated by sending an ICMP type which indicates a hard-error condition. ICMP errors must be propagated to applications, and most applications detect the errors or by closing a connection or session.

9.5.3 Attacks on Technology

The information system technology component consists of hardware and software. Hacking attacks on computer equipments are very common, and they are even more common on software components. There are mainly two types of software components known to be continuously attacked: Operating systems and computer applications like HTTP, SMTP, PTP, and VoIP. Hacking can easily apply fingerprinting techniques to identify operating systems on remote systems. Once the operating system is known on a computer system, the hacker can exploit known vulnerabilities of the operating system and then conduct the appropriate attacks to cause higher destructive affects.

As soon as the operating system is identified, testers start finding, on the system, vulnerabilities of different levels of gravity. While white-hat hackers report to system owners to warn them of potential dangers and ways to counter them, black hat hackers save no time in exploiting all known vulnerabilities to produce the highest destructive power, given the resources they have to cause extended damage to target systems. Those black hackers can exploit specific configurations of embedded authentication systems, for example, passwords on cryptographic schemes.

Attacks on operating systems exploit bugs in the operating system software. Usually, when these problems are identified, they are promptly fixed by the operating system developer. If one, however, frequently applies the latest security patches, then this will certainly reduce system vulnerabilities. Developers usually provide sites when users can automatically download the latest patches needed.

Hackers also often attack popular computer applications like HTTP, SMTP, FTP, and others. Attackers often do not need much resource to successfully complete their application attacks. Application level attacks target resources limitations within the application and do not require many compromised intermediary systems or large bandwidth. Often, the weakest link is the first point to be targeted in an application attack. For example, if a computer cluster is attacked, then the front- or back-end hosts that balance loads or distribute tasks are first to attack. Moreover, application attacks are not easy to trace, even though the application layer attacks use familiar protocols like HTTP and HTTPS. Proxy servers can therefore be used to hide the true origin of the attacker, and many are available for attackers to redirect their malicious traffic. Many of these proxy servers do not keep logs of connection attempts and could therefore successfully cover the true origin of the attacking host.

9.5.4 Attacks on Data

Data is a very valuable resource in any information system. If corrupted, data can cause extended damage to all output subsystems. Hackers can corrupt data and information residing in all components of the information system. They can also attack the information system using denial of service attacks, and users will not be able to access the data or information they need in a timely manner. Files containing critical information that are not adequately protected may be posted in systems with major vulnerabilities that rogue users and hackers can exploit in malicious ways.

More and more Web applications use databases widely to store data, which is accessed and modified infrequently. Dynamic data is used to manage user sessions. Database operations, however, incur overhead cost in terms of storage space and processor time.

Attackers need access to a large amount of bandwidth should they wish to attempt to flood the victims' Internet connection. Considerably fewer resources may be required if the attack is, instead, directed at a few carefully selected database queries.

9.5.5 Attacks on Activities

Activities in an information system consist of all tasks, procedures, policies, and regulations. Those activities can be easily corrupted by rogue insiders. Imagine that in order to prevent virus contamination of staff desktops, your organization imposes a new policy that prohibits employees from taking their laptops outside the organization. This new policy will cause great loss of business to the organization due to lost productivity. This new policy is wrong and has to be corrected, for example, by imposing an antivirus solution instead.

Telecommunication and computing protocols are considered activities designed by people and executed by processes often to effectively and efficiently manage networks and computing resources. Most of those are, however, vulnerable to all types of attacks: ARP, ICMP, SNMP, TCP, IP, etc. You will notice that most of the examples associated with those protocols also apply to network and infrastructure security. This overlapping is justifiable because networks cannot operate without the use of those protocols. So, the security of activities in a computing environment extends to networks and the infrastructure that use those activities.

SYN attacks exploit vulnerabilities in the TCP/IP connection mechanism. SYN flood attacks are mounted using programs to send a flood of TCP SYN requests to congest pending connection queues on servers. During this time, other users are not allowed to establish new network connections.

Internet Control Message Protocol (ICMP) is a TCP/IP protocol needed to share error and control messages with users—for example, to inform them that the node they are trying to reach is not available. A ping utility sends ICMP echo requests to verify the existence of an IP address. Routers use ICMP to notify users that their destination node is not available.

Denials of Service attacks are based on the simple concept of generating extended amounts of traffic to make resources unavailable to the general user. Those attacks are known to be simple and almost costless to activate. What is it going to cost for the attacker sending a spoofed ICMP echo packet to a broadcast address? DDoS attacks require the participation of thousands of end hosts to generate the traffic necessary to render a host unusable.

Address Resolution Protocol (ARP) spoofing, also known as ARP poisoning or ARP Poison Routing (APR), is a technique used to attack Ethernet networks, which will let attackers sniff data on a local area network, modify the traffic, or even stall the traffic to cause denial of service.

Using ARP spoofing one can capture traffic on all or just parts of the network from a single machine within the network. Of course, we can always opt to monitor all data packets on a LAN by using a network switch, instead of a hub, and track all packets passing through all ports of the switch. When information resources are connected to a switch port, instead of a hub, we will be unable to directly read the data due to the definition of switched networks, but there are attackers who may use other techniques to sniff data on any target network.

9.6 Ethics in Ethical Hacking

The code of ethics that applies to active security assessment or ethical hacking is very lengthy, and it is beyond the topic discussed in this chapter. Ethics of security testing is extensively covered in most of the literature [10]. We, however, provide four important rules that need to be included in any code of ethics written especially for active security assessment. These rules have to be incorporated in one way or another in any ASA security policy.

The first rule of ethics in active security assessment is to stick to the security objective and scope, and to enforce the project security policy. Going beyond any limits set by the scope, the security objective, and the security policy, even to explore new risks, is not allowed.

The second rule of ethics that has to be applied is respect for privacy. All information collected throughout the penetration testing process should be kept confidential. Every penetration testing activity has its own code of ethics. Testers have to respect them.

The third rule of ethics, in active security assessment, is to avoid any destructive effects. Remember that the purpose of conducting those penetration testing activities is to figure out new ways to secure the target system and minimize risks. That is, crashing your system is not an option in a penetration test and any other adverse effects should not be allowed.

The fourth rule of ethics, we would like to present here, would be to report any violation of any code of ethics by a member of the penetration testing team.

9.7 ASA through Penetration Testing

An ASA project should be initiated by system owners. The ASA plan should be approved and supported by management. It is important to apply a "need to know policy" in informing people about the initiation and execution of the ASA project. Users of the target system should not be alerted to the ASA project in order to prevent any change of usage behavior so that users will show normal behavior throughout the ASA project.

An active security assessment project is a special IT project that you plan, analyze, design, implement, and use. The planning effort in active security assessment (ASA) is a very critical phase of the project. In this phase, you need to constitute the ASA team, define project objectives, delineate its scope, and write its security policy.

The ASA project scope should specify that the following tasks be defined:

Target system and its components
Timing of the project
Risks to be accepted throughout the ASA project
Strategy of the project in terms of visibility, place, and direction
Delivery requirements
Response activities and testing limitations throughout the ASA project

9.7.1 Target Systems and Components

The ASA project cannot start if the target system is not well defined. In addition, there may be components of the system that are intentionally left out. It is very important to define all the components of the system that are also targeted in the ASA project. This is, in fact, often more valid when the target system is large, and budget and timing constraints are restrictive. For example, the ASA team may study an entire LAN but not a print server connected to this LAN.

9.7.2 Delivery Requirements

ASA projects may be initiated in a routine manner or for other specific reasons usually expressed in the ASA project objectives. Independent of the motivation behind the initiation of the ASA project, timing is a very important factor in defining the success of the project. Sometimes, delays in identifying major vulnerabilities of a target system or one of its major components can increase security risks associated with the target system, and adequate countermeasures may be extensive and very costly, given the absence of accurate information of system vulnerabilities. Alternatively, system owners may think that no major vulnerabilities exist, because they are not yet known due to delays of the production of ASA findings of the current ASA project.

That is, due to the absence of any information on major vulnerabilities in the target system, system owners do not act to implement the appropriate countermeasures. Imagine the consequences if the danger takes place at the target system. That is, the scope of the ASA project should define the deliverables and their timing throughout the ASA project. Respecting the timing of those deliverables is critical for the success of the ASA project. As explained earlier, delays in identifying major system vulnerabilities may be destructive if those vulnerabilities are exploited by hackers before we discover them.

9.7.3 Timing in the ASA Project

The ASA project scope should define the timing of all major penetration test steps of the ASA project. Some ASA steps should not be initiated when the production system is running so that the production outputs are not affected by those steps. Some testing activities may slow down the performance of some components of the target system, which may compromise the performance of the target system. That is, determining when the ASA tests are conducted is critical in the ASA project.

In many ASA projects, testing activities are performed in weekends, late at night, or early in the morning to eliminate any effects on productivity. Of course, the ASA team cannot make the timing decision alone. When users or workers within the target system are included in the ASA team as observers or in any other capacity, they can help in determining the best timing of ASA activities. Because they are directly related to the target system, they will know how ASA test activities can affect the productivity of the target system. Involving them in your timing decisions will alleviate any risks associated with your ASA testing activities.

Usually, the scope of the ASA project provides enough information about the breadth of testing activities but a lot less on the depth of ASA activities. Sufficient guidelines are usually given to the ASA team on the depth of the ASA project. Testers apply those guidelines to limit their digging in the target system.

In the case of an internal ASA project where testers belong to the target system, the unit containing the system, or the company containing the unit containing the system, testers are relatively more familiar with the target system and can easily decide, given the depth guidelines provided by the ASA scope, how deep they need to go to discover more vulnerabilities in the system. On the other hand, if they are dealing with an external ASA project, then testers are external to the target system, its unit, and its company, and they are not sufficiently familiar with the target system and company security policies. External testers, in this case, will have a hard time knowing how deep they have to go to uncover new vulnerabilities or follow leads to collect further information on major system vulnerabilities.

Hackers' hacking process is usually sequential in nature. At the starting of their hacking project, hackers have sufficient motivation to initiate their project but their planning phase goes through a cold start up where they slowly collect information about domain names, IP addresses, and states of systems before they start testing and retesting the responsive systems to identify sufficient vulnerabilities they can exploit to produce extended destructive power. Blind ASA testing goes through a cold start where testers do not have sufficient information about the domain, IP addresses, and states of systems to be targeted in the ASA project. Visibility, on the other hand, may be added when tester are provided with access information to the target systems.

The scope of the ASA project should provide sufficient information regarding to what extent a ASA project is blind on visible. Defining a framework for the pretesting and testing activities and the information collection process needed to guide the identification of system vulnerabilities will require defining a strategy for the ASA project. ASA strategies are discussed in the next section.

9.7.4 Responses Available to ASA Testers

What do the ASA testers do when immediate danger is discovered? Can they just continue collecting information on more vulnerability until a final report is due to system owners? Assume that while testers are collecting new information on new vulnerabilities, some hackers manage to identify some of the vulnerabilities they earlier associated with immediate danger but did not do anything to counter. Imagine the consequences if those hackers exploit them to produce extended destructive power? How can this ASA project be useful if the identified security holes remain open for hackers to exploit? There should be some limited responses that ASA testers are allowed to take to prevent the exploitation of all identified vulnerabilities instead of waiting until the ASA report gets to security management who will then plan their responses. It is just too much risk. In addition to misleading system owners and users to a false sense of security throughout the ASA project, potential hackers can uncover, on their own, the same vulnerabilities and exploit them before ASA findings are reported to security management.

9.8 Strategies for Active Security Assessment

Our active security assessment strategy has three components: *place, visibility*, and *direction*. The place component expresses the position of the testers defined for the active security assessment project. The visibility component is defined in terms of two variables: v_1, defining whether or not the tester obtains partial access information from systems owners before the starting of testing activities; and v_2, defining whether or not systems users and management are informed of testing activities by system owners before the start of testing activities. The third strategic component, *direction*, takes two values: one way or two ways. The active security assessment project does not usually allow real-time interactions between testers and security management staff. In rare occasions, mainly in military organizations, the two-ways direction is allowed.

9.8.1 Place Strategies for Active Security Assessment

The place component expresses the position of the testers which can be *external* or *internal*. An external tester performs the active security assessment activities outside the organization using the Internet or any other untrusted external network. An internal tester connects to an internal or DMZ network in the company when performing his or her active security assessment activities.

9.8.1.1 External Active Security Assessment Strategy

The external active security assessment strategy, as depicted in Figure 9.2, is characterized by placing testers outside an organization, using a public network to perform their testing activities according to the security objective, security scope, and security policy defined for the active security assessment project. These testing activities usually begin with an external discovery process to study the organization's public information and public access information in order to scan networks and ports, and collect information about relevant systems. The testers then identify vulnerabilities and exploit them as hackers do but with full respect for the organization's security assessment security policy. The external testers study the

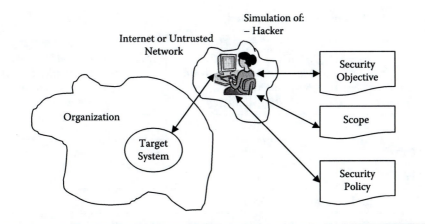

Figure 9.2   External active security assessment strategy.

effects of compromising the security of all systems, including HTTP, SNMP, and DNS servers and other systems and application servers that are externally visible to hackers.

9.8.1.2 Internal Active Security Assessment Strategy

The internal active security assessment strategy, as depicted in Figure 9.3, is characterized by placing testers inside the organization. They use an internal or DMZ network to perform their testing activities according to the security objective,

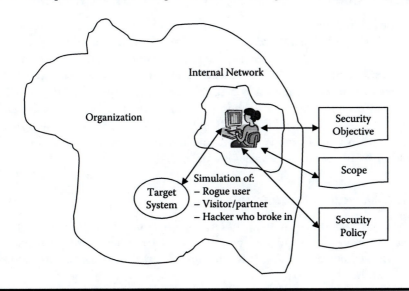

Figure 9.3   Internal active security assessment strategy.

Table 9.1   Visibility Values Defined

Visibility Values	The Tester Obtains Partial Access Information from System Owners before Testing Activities	Systems Users and Management are Informed of Testing Activities by System Owners before Testing Activities
Double visible	Yes	Yes
Visible	Yes	No
Blind	No	Yes
Double blind	No	No

security scope, and security policy defined for the active security assessment project. Testing activities in an internal active security assessment project are similar to those performed in an external active security assessment project, but while the latter simulates a real external hacker, the former simulates a rogue user who may be an internal disgruntled employee or an authorized visitor or partner who possesses standard processing privileges. The internal testers will study the effects of compromising system security by rogue users or those hackers who were successful in breaking in the perimeter of the company and use internal networks to access the company's critical systems.

9.8.2 Visibility Strategies for Active Security Assessment

As depicted in Table 9.1, the visibility component takes four values: *visible, double visible, blind,* and *double blind.* These linguistic values are described in terms of two variables: v_1, defining whether or not the tester obtains partial access information from systems owners before the starting of testing activities; and v_2, defining whether or not systems users and management are informed of testing activities by system owners before the starting of testing activities. The visibility value is "Visible," when v_1 = Yes and v_2 = No; "Double Visible," when v_1 = Yes and v_2 = Yes; "Blind," when v_1 = No and v_2 = Yes; "Double Blind," when v_1 = No and v_2 = No. Table 9.1 recaps the visibility values just defined.

9.8.3 Direction Strategy

This security assessment strategy is concerned with double-active security assessment where warring is allowed between the testers and security management staff. Throughout the book, this is sometimes referred to as *double-active security assessment.*

The warring strategy for active security assessment involves system security management and security assessment staff. The active security assessment policy will set the rules defining interactions between system security staff and active security assessment staff. The warring setting may be synchronous or a synchronous. In synchronous warring, active security assessment members attempt to hit internal systems while security management staff fights back by detecting and planning effective responses against intruder's attacks. In asynchronous warring, active security assessment members attempt to hit internal systems for a fixed time period. In a posterior time period, security management staff is allowed to fight back by detecting and planning effective responses against intruder's attacks in the future.

9.9 Guidelines and Terms between Testers and the Organization

There are two ways to initiate the active security assessment project. The organization chooses an internal or an external active security assessment team. In the former, all members of the team are employees of the client's company. In the latter approach, the members of the team are external and independent testers.

Independently of the type of active security assessment, internal or external testers, a contract should be written, even though for the internal testers, the contract will only serve to contain the security objective, scope, and the security policy written specially for the active security assessment project. This way, the internal tester will have good understanding of the specifications of the job they are assigned to throughout this project.

The contract should clearly state the objective being pursued by the organization, the scope of the project, and the security policy to enforce throughout the project. The most common objectives relevant here are:

Achieve a better risk position through active security assessment.
Find system vulnerabilities.
Study effects of exploiting them as hackers do.
Enhance security according to current assessment

By writing the active security assessment contract, even when the testers are internal, testers avoid unnecessary misunderstandings and risks and ensures that the penetration test is adapted to the client's needs.

The scope of the active security assessment project should include individual techniques used in the penetration tests. The security policy of the project should explain the extent and consequences of dealing with ethical conditions, as in social engineering and its effect on agents involved in it. There are also problematic situations when, for example, testers attempt to physically break in, attempting to simulate an active penetration test where physical resources and facilities are involved.

Usually, the client has to sign for accepting potential consequences associated with damaging measures during testing activities. It is advisable that the contract is signed by a legal representative of the client. A person authorized to represent the client—for example, for your organization, the general manager, or any other authorized person with the appropriate signatory authorization, such as the department head—may commission the performance of all penetration testing activities constituting the active security assessment project. Usually, the tester is not allowed to outsource certain activities of the project to external agents, unless it is explicitly allowed in the project security policy.

The security policy should explain how matters are resolved when unconventional testing procedures such as social engineering or the circumvention of physical security measures have been planned. This will protect both parties by helping them preventing any unnecessary misunderstandings.

9.10 The Active Security Assessment Project

We now know what active security assessment project consists of, and we are ready to launch the project. As shown in Figure 9.4, the following phases are proposed:

1. Planning effort:
   Objective
   Scope
   Policy
2. Reconnaissance effort
3. Passive assessment effort
4. Active assessment effort
5. Corrective effort
6. Reporting effort

9.10.1 Planning Effort

ASA projects are not identical because they have different objectives, different scopes, and different security policies. So the 10 system vulnerability scanners and the 10 Web application vulnerability scanners recommended earlier may not all apply. However, the general phases constituting the ASA project itself are very similar independently of the objective, scope, or security policy. Most ASA projects follow a similar plan, as follows:

1. Find access information as specified in the ASA project scope.
2. Understand the target system.
3. Test the target system for vulnerabilities, as specified on the ASA project scope.

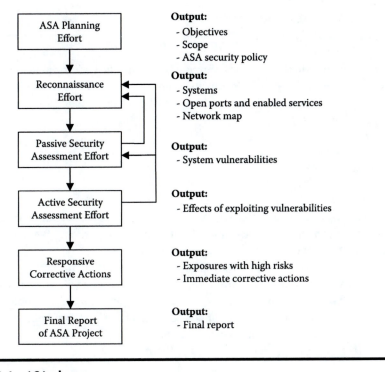

Figure 9.4   ASA phases.

4. Test the target system by exploiting the vulnerabilities identified in step 3, as specified in the ASA project security policy.
5. Report findings and generate recommendations.

The scope of the ASA project is designed to guide ASA testers throughout the various steps of the ASA project. ASA testers obtain minimal ASA information before they start the ASA project. This information is needed to plan the ASA project. While a blind ASA project is evoked with a very cold startup period where ASA testers proceed by collecting sufficient access information for the target system, in a visible ASA project, ASA testers are given minimal access information to start with. In either way, ASA testers still need a great deal of access information that can only be acquired in a sequential manner. Access information will be used by ASA testers to scan the target system and get familiar with it by knowing what ports are open and what services are enabled by the target system.

Sufficient understanding of the system and its components may be needed before ASA testers can start testing the system for its vulnerabilities, as specified in the ASA project scope. ASA testers should simulate hackers in exploiting selected major vulnerabilities and study the effects of their work on system security. ASA testers may recommend immediate corrective actions to mitigate risks to lower levels.

9.10.2 Reconnaissance Effort

9.10.2.1 Search for Preliminary Information

The reconnaissance effort starts on public ground. The easiest public area for collecting information on target companies and their systems is probably the Internet. Hackers use mainly three approaches to gather initial public information about your organization:

Web search
Web crawling
Web navigation

As hackers do, you may search the Web to obtain a great deal of public information about your company. Google.com is the champion source of any Web search effort you need to initiate. You do not need to search further.

You may also use Web crawling tools to download, as hackers do, all public files available on your organization Web site. All those files will be available to you offline so you can thoroughly study any sensitive information that should not have been made public, or any display or configuration flaws that should be corrected to prevent any malicious intent to exploit them.

Web search can produce information about:

Organizational mission, vision, and values
Press releases about organizational services and products
Organizational structure, including functional units and departments and their
    locations
Employee names and contact information including managers
Past and coming events organized by the company
White papers and Webcasts that provide further information about the
    organization

All these tools will allow you to examine all public files available on your company Web site, to study its layout and configuration, to review the HTML code of Web pages, various tags and command fields, and to study to what extent hackers can easily access folders containing files that are visible to them through simple Web crawling tools. Why do you want those hackers to know developers' names and email address or the names and contact information of your IT staff? Even worse, why do you want them to be able effortlessly to pick up your company server names, software versions, and your network internal addressing schemes?

There are also Web sites that provide useful information about companies and their employees including management and security administrators.

Let us present a brief before we proceed to discussing the testers' reconnaissance effort. A review of some of the concepts associated with the World Wide Web and that are relevant to this phase may be helpful in introducing the footprinting steps in the reconnaissance phase, as described in Table 9.2.

The Domain Name Service (DNS) is a distributed Internet directory service intended for determining Web host locations (IP addresses) to the domain names easiest to read and memorize. There are the common Generic Top Level Domains (gTLDs), such as .com, .net, and .org, as well as more specialized and restricted Special Top Level Domains (sTLDs) such as .edu, .gov, and .mil. There are about a hundred two-character Country Code Top Level Domains (ccTLDs) and the hundreds of subdomains from around the world.

The Internet Corporation for Assigned Names and Numbers (ICANN; see www.icann.org) was created to assume responsibility for IP address space allocation and protocol parameter assignment, as well as the Domain Name System (DNS) and root server system management functions. ICANN can develop and authorize new TLDs with various partners, such as the recently added gTLDs .aero, .biz, .coop, .info, .museum, .name, and .pro.

Host countries can also grant agreements to registrars to represent and perhaps manage specific domain extensions and subdomains or country code TLDs. For example, VeriSign Global Registry Services (see www.verisign-grs.com) maintains the definitive directory of some 30 million dot-com and dot-net domain-name Web addresses, and propagates this information from its root server throughout the Internet. It also responds to billions of DNS look-ups daily.

DoS and information corruption attacks are very common on DNS directories worldwide. Protecting those DNS resources is very critical to the entire international community. The ICANN site lists accredited registrars (see www.icann.org/registrars/accredited-list.html), whereas a complete list of ccTLD registrars and contact info reside on the Internet Assigned Numbers Authority (IANA) site (www.iana.org/cctld/cctld-whois.htm).

Real malicious attacks cannot be performed without first identifying the target operating system. Of course, some amateurs and script kiddies do not adopt any methodologies in hacking systems. They just keep searching for open ports and perform a large variety of exploits in a trial-and-error manner, hoping that one of them will work. Unless you are sure about the vulnerabilities that your target system has, you may not know for sure what exploits will actually work on the system. Scrip kiddies have sufficient time and patience, and usually will not give up until some destructive goals are achieved. That is, script kiddies and many novice intruders do not care about identifying operating systems on target systems. This sounds funny, but saving time by knowing the operating system and by aiming better at the target is not an important decision parameter for them. They have enough time to try anything, knowing something will work. They may be good and cost-effective testers in a regular vulnerability assessment project but, unfortunately, they are under age and cannot be legally hired, at least in the United States.

That said, professional security assessment requires the identification of operating systems on target systems as early as possible in the project.

Table 9.2 Reconnaissance Phase of the Active Security Assessment Project

Steps and Their Objectives	Descriptions of Steps	General Activities of Steps	Examples of Applicable Techniques
Footprint-based passive reconnaissance: Objective: Gathering information about company network to create a unique profile of its computing environment.	Gather public information about the company	Manual research of Internet resources to accumulate contact information, locations and branches, partners and press releases, privacy policies, and so on.	Web search Web crawling Web site study
	Gather public information about the company's computing environment	Gather information about company networks and systems to understand how the computing environment works.	Whois SmartWhois NsLookup Sam Spade
Scanning-based active reconnaissance: Objective: Identify open ports and enables services.	Identify active machines	Perform external or internal network scanning, and ping resources.	NMap Ping Traceroute Superscan Netcat NeoTrace Visual Route
	Discover open ports and access points	Port scan individual systems.	

	Fingerprint the operating system	Perform any needed scanning techniques to grab banners to identify operating systems.	
Enumerating the computing environment: Objective — Identify users and groups, network resources and shares, and applications.	Network mapping	Perform any networking mapping activities needed to identify users and groups, network resources and shares, and applications.	Obtain active directory information
			Identify vulnerable user and group accounts
			Use NBTscan to identify NetBIOS name enumeration
			Use snmputil for SNMP enumeration
			Query Windows DNS records
			Use TCP scanning techniques to discover new alive systems

Testers tend to use different techniques and tools to identify operating systems on target systems. Some techniques and tools will work better than others as in any other project. While probing with ICMP packets may work on systems, it will not work as good on systems where firewalls prevent scanning when incoming ICMP packets are blocked.

The literature seems to favor well accepted fingerprinting techniques that employ a variety of TCP/IP scanning techniques. Most scanning techniques used to identify open ports and enabled services on them. Those services tend to reveal information about system operating systems in their login banners, as it does Telnet, FTP, SMTP, and many other Web applications.

That is, testers can easily obtain operation systems information by looking at server banners on open ports. Of course, this assumes that you trust the login information provided by those Web applications. Well, do not be so sure! The prudent application administrators who suspect that hackers may take advantage of login banners and learn information on operating systems (which they may use to speed up their malicious access to owners systems), can actually trick you by displaying the wrong login information. If this is the case, then you still have not identified the accurate operation systems running on your target systems.

Alternatively, testers can grab email headers to learn not only the operating system on the sender's system but also information about remailers, firewalls, and proxies belonging to the email path.

Testers can also use port sweeps which will identify open ports and indirectly information on operating systems in most cases. The most popular way, for good and bad guys, for identifying operating systems remains always the evoking of Nmap. What is making Nmap even more attractive to all of us is its continuous expansion with new fingerprinting techniques [19].

Nmap is an open source tool for network mapping towards vulnerability assessment and security auditing. Even though it is very useful in scanning single hosts, it is originally designed to rapidly scan large networks. You may use Nmap to determine what hosts are available on the network, what services are enabled, what operating systems are running, what firewalls are in use, etc. While Nmap is commonly used for security planning and auditing, system administrators also frequently use it to monitor and manage their networks. Here is an example of using Nmap to scan a target host:

```
nmap -A -T4 myhost.mysite.com
```

This command scans the host myhost.mysite.com. The A and T4 options enable OS and version detection, and set the timing template to "aggressive."

Nmap may be used to collect the initial sequence numbers received from the target to recognize patterns indicative of the way they are incremented. These patterns may be useful in identifying some operating systems; for example, some UNIX systems use a constant increment, while others apply random increments. Other operating systems, as in some Windows platforms use time-based increments.

Of course, the accuracy of your operating system identification is only as good as the information gathered by Nmap. Remember that your information is extracted from the target system where there are no guarantees that it has not been corrupted before its extraction. In addition to this deficiency, it is also possible that NAT (Network Address Translation) firewalls at the borders of those target systems intentionally corrupt or transform those sequence numbers for the purpose of hiding them from operating systems identifying agents.

9.10.2.2 Examples of Tools Applicable to the Reconnaissance Phase

We earlier proposed some tools that testers need to conduct various steps of the reconnaissance phase. We have seen earlier that some tools like Whois, port scan, ping, Nmap apply to most of the steps in the reconnaissance phase. For instance, you can use Nmap in footprinting, scanning, and in enumerating as well. In fact, most of network analyzer tools may be useful in gathering information about company networks and connected resources in most steps of the reconnaissance phase. The following is a list of tools that may be useful in the reconnaissance phase:

DNS lookup
Finger
Name lookup
Ping
Port scan
Throughput
Trace route
Whois

9.10.2.2.1 DNS Lookup

Host names are simple names for IP addresses in your language. Every host name can be translated into an IP address; and every IP address can be translated into a host name. DNS lookup is intended to identify the IP address of a given host name. The DNS lookup tool accepts queries to retrieve any information available in reachable domain name servers on the Internet [7].

9.10.2.2.2 Finger

The finger utility is intended to retrieve information about another Internet user. This utility queries Remote User Information Protocol (RUIP) servers for information about users who are logged on to a given host with a known host name. Various options, available with this utility, allow you to specify the content of your query output. For example, you may opt for the long response format, and your query output will contain more detailed information about the user in question.

9.10.2.2.3 Name Lookup

The name lookup utility is intended to connect a host name to an IP address or an IP address to a host name. This command accepts a host name or a domain name as an argument. A name lookup is performed for each address in a specified range of IP addresses.

9.10.2.2.4 Ping

The ping utility is intended to check whether or not a computer is operating and whether or not the network connections are good. Ping uses the ICMP (Internet Control Message Protocol) echo function. A small packet is sent through the network to a particular IP address. If the sender receives back the echo packet then the connections are good, and the target computer is up. The ping command can also tell the user the number of hops that separate the two computers and the round-trip time, which is the amount of time it takes for a packet to make the complete trip. Extended waiting time is indicative that something may be wrong.

In addition to the ping command, there are ping scans that are intended to discover active nodes on a given network. As in the ping utility, A ping scan uses the ICMP protocol to send echo requests to a range of IP addresses. This query can be executed at different times when new machines are added or removed from the network to provide new information about the state of the network.

9.10.2.2.5 Port Scan

A port scan is intended to query a specified range of ports on a single host to search for available services. Usually, operating systems like most versions of Unix, most versions of Windows, and others open multiple ports by default. The open ports pose great risks for the hosts that are connected to the Internet. Tools like service scanners may be used to test for services being offered on a particular port by any hosts within a specified range of IP addresses.

9.10.2.2.6 Throughput

The throughput utility is intended, on the Internet, to measure the speed of a connection. The throughput of a connection is the number of bytes per second this connection is capable of transferring. This utility measures the rate at which files are downloaded from specified HTTP or FTP servers. This utility can also create a data stream to be analyzed by network diagnostic tools, including EtherPeek.

Etherpeek is a comprehensive network analyzer that helps network managers configure, manage, and troubleshoot Ethernet networks by monitoring and capturing network traffic and simplifying traffic analysis [22]. Just think of two computers sharing data over an Ethernet LAN. One PC broadcasts a data packet labeled with the second PC's network address. All the other network cards on the LAN can see this header, but only the designated PC receives the packet. As any simple packet sniffer, Etherpeek works by making its PC's network card accept every packet, in what is called the *promiscuous mode*.

9.10.2.2.7 Traceroute

The traceroute utility is intended to trace your data from your computer to an Internet server. This utility can also provide time information showing where the slow connection segments constituting the path are. Trace route is a standard part of the Internet Protocol suite. The traceroute utility can also calculate and displays the round-trip time required for each hop. If the routers have DNS entries, their names are also displayed.

9.10.2.2.8 Whois

The whois utility is intended to find information about networks, domains, and hosts. The output usually include data on the organizations and the contacts associated with these networks and domains. There are many implementations of the whois protocol. Whois services operate through a whois server. You can connect to a whois server and send a query. The whois server will then reply back and end the connection. You can run your own whois server. For example an organization can implement its own whois server that provides information about its various departments and staff.

There are many varieties of implementations of the WHOIS protocol.

Another member of the whois family is Active Whois. It is a simple network tool designed to retrieve reconnaissance information such as country, e-mails, and postal addresses for the owners of IP addresses and Internet domains. As with other versions of the whois client, Active Whois does not require special skills to collect the company information. You may use Active Whois to explore DNS aliases and can display the domain and IP address information together. As any other whois client, you can investigate any Web site including international top level domains, and retrieve its ownership details and the location of the servers hosting the site, but some are easier than others, and some provide the information in just one single click.

Even if you are not involved in any security assessment testing activities, the whois client is still very useful. I am sure that, like any other concerned security staff member, you may be, for example, very interested to examine your Web server logs to check who were your visitors last night, and may be also be curious about whether or not mistakes have taken place while you are asleep. Even if you are not a security management staff member, some other system owners may be interested in knowing who your customers are, how much time they spent on your site, and what time of day they visited. No problem. You simply need to examine the IIS logs that include the IP addresses for visitors and obtain their domain names using any reverse DNS tools. You can use the whois utility to obtain the name of your customers. Usually, you obtain the names of the customers' companies or ISPs so that the whois client can only produce the ISP or customer company instead of the name of the real human visitor.

Active Whois can access information located in a large number of whois servers (about 90). This can dynamically determine the correct server based on replies from other whois servers. Active Whois is also useful for investigating hacker scans, spam, suspicious Web sites, or IRC/Instant Message/chat nicknames. As an exercise, you may download an evaluation version of Active Whois, install it, and use it to track some of your spammers.

Active Whois generates a report that includes the following information:

DNS records
Domain owner
IP address
HTTP header

That is, the report shows DNS records where individual host names are connected with their corresponding IP addresses. One computer on the Internet that is configured as a host may sourced to several IP addresses and host names, Active Whois displays all records occurring in the DNS directory with their full domain names and IP address aliases. Additionally, the Active Whois tool is capable of tracing these aliases back to their original DNS results.

This report also displays information about the domain registrant assumed to be the same as the domain holder. Active Whois also provides about top level domain (TLD) with a link to the domain registrar and the name of the country. As with other whois tools, this reports provides information about IP addresses. Often, you will have the IP addresses corresponding to the individual or the organization that you are seeking. In many other occasions, the IP addresses will corresponds to ISP's where the domains are hosted, but even in this case, this information can help you to determine the physical location of the Web site or remote computer. This report may also include HTTP headers. Information about the Web server software, and about the files and their creation may be useful.

9.10.3 Passive Security Assessment

Hackers will use a simple ping utility to scan hosts that are reachable from the Internet. Information is collected by documenting the pinged hosts, using either their specific host names or their IP addresses. In addition to scanning your hosts, you also need to apply war dialing to identify all unsecured modems on your systems, and scan network ports to identify open ports and services enabled on them

War dialing is a popular example of passive security assessment, a common technique to identify one telephone number owned by a target entity and then to dial the entire prefix that number belongs to. For example, if your target is Pace University in upstate New York, you would dial every number starting with (914) 422. If war dialing one telephone number takes half a minute, then in one day, you may be able to dial a prefix of $245 \times 60 \times 2 = 2880$ phone numbers.

Of course, war dialing can be performed manually, but dialing a thousand telephone numbers by hand will take forever, and it would be very boring and embarrassing at times due to repetitions.

As in http://www.tech-faq.com/war-dialing.shtml, ToneLoc was a popular war dialing computer program for MS-DOS written in the early to mid-1990s by two programmers known as Chris Lamprecht and Mucho Maas. The name ToneLoc was short for "tone locator" and was a word play on the name of the rap artist known as Tone Lōc. The utility was created for the purpose of scanning for dial tones or modem carriers in order to find PBXes, long distance carriers, or other modems.

PhoneSweep was introduced in 1998 as the first commercial software that performed war dialing. PhoneSweep aims at establishing connections by calling a range of phone numbers. Repeated calls are made to the same number in order to determine useful features in the called modems.

There are also networks analyzers that allow you to listen to network traffic. A network analyzer is a device that is installed on a network to enhance protection against malicious activities. Network analyzers provide detailed statistics for network activities, test antimalware programs and vulnerabilities, detect unusual levels of network traffic, identify packet sources or destinations, configure alarms for defined threats, and monitor bandwidth utilization over time.

System vulnerability is a weakness that a potential impostor can exploit to harm the system. Harm to the system may be produced through information leakage, information corruption, or denial of service. For example, a misconfiguration error or a logical flaw in a computer program in an information asset may be exploited by somebody to gain unauthorized access to the system.

A system consists of many components, including hardware components, software components, security policy components, and configuration components. Vulnerability assessment (VA) is the process of identifying and profiling vulnerabilities on a system. For each identified vulnerability, the VA process provides the identity of the vulnerability, its name, the component affected, and the scope of the vulnerability.

9.10.3.1 CVE to Standardize Vulnerabilities

Common Vulnerabilities and Exposures (CVE) represents the standard for vulnerability names. CVE provides a dictionary where it standardizes the names of all publicly known vulnerabilities and security exposures. It provides access to other vulnerability databases and security tools. Entries are reviewed by an editorial board constituted by representatives from numerous security-related organizations such as security tool vendors, academic institutions, government agencies, and selected security experts. Members of the board evaluate new entries before they are added to the CVE as vulnerabilities or exposures. The board assigns a name and enters a description for all new vulnerabilities and security exposures.

The MITRE Corporation manages the CVE editorial board and moderates all board discussions, providing guidance throughout the process to ensure that CVE serves the public interest. All board meetings and discussions are archived and made available for review on the CVE Web site.

The MITRE Corporation (www.mitre.org) is a not-for-profit organization chartered to work in the public interest. It manages three federally funded research and development centers (FFRDCs): one for the Department of Defense (known as the DOD Command, Control, Communications and Intelligence FFRDC), one for the Federal Aviation Administration (the Center for Advanced Aviation System Development), and one for the Internal Revenue Service (the Center for Enterprise Modernization). MITRE also has its own independent research and development program that explores new technologies and new uses of technologies to solve our sponsors' problems in the near-term and in the future.

For those standard vulnerabilities, it is sufficient that the VA process identifies vulnerability with its CVE reference and its scope. The CVE dictionary will provide further information about how the standard vulnerability or security exposure affects system risks. For those nonstandard vulnerabilities identified on the system, it is very important that the VA process describes the scope of the vulnerability in great details. Table 9.3 shows an example of a Microsoft component identified on an information asset.

This vulnerability is identified as CVE-2000-0884. It affects a Microsoft component called Microsoft IIS 4.0. The description of the scope of the vulnerability should explain its cause, and indicate ways of exploiting the vulnerability. In this example, an intruder can apply any code of his/her choice to execute on the vulnerable Web server. Even though the harm caused by a specific code is limited by the server configuration, the risk associated with this vulnerability is high, given the ability of any user who logs into the server to install and run code, or perform other actions like adding, changing, deleting files, and Web pages.

After obtaining the VA process report, the system owner is now aware of the risks associated with the vulnerable system. Usually, risk analysis is the right step that comes next, before making any decisions on the security controls to adopt in order to mitigate risks, given the vulnerabilities identified by the VA process. If risks are not too high, the system owner may decide to keep some of the vulnerabilities and take necessary actions to protect the system from all known ways of exploitation. Alternatively, the system owner can proceed by eliminating some of

Table 9.3   Vulnerability Assessment Finding Sheet

Information asset ID (from Asset Inventory)	as3471
Asset class (from Asset Inventory)	Server
CVE Reference	CVE-2000-0884
Name	Web Server Folder Traversal
Affected Component	Microsoft IIS 4.0 and 5.0
Scope	The vulnerability results because it is possible to construct an URL that would cause IIS to navigate to any desired folder on the logical drive that contains the web folder structure, and access files in it. An intruder can apply any code of his/her choice to execute on the vulnerable Web server. Even though the harm caused by a specific code is limited by the server configuration, the risk associated with this vulnerability is high given the ability of any user who logs into the server to install and run code, or perform other actions like adding, changing, deleting files and Web pages.
Prescriptions	Vulnerability assessment process recommendations for system owners: Actions to be taken

the vulnerabilities if at all possible, or apply the necessary patches, if they exist, to reduce risks of exploiting the vulnerabilities.

As explained earlier, VA is needed to identify system vulnerabilities throughout the computing environment of the organization. Usually, the organization maintains an asset inventory defining all information assets constituting its computing environment. Examples of information assets include servers, routers, security appliances, databases, software applications, operating systems, etc.

Ideally, each information asset should be evaluated using VA to discover its vulnerabilities. In real life, however, only those information assets with higher criticality scores and a random sample of the asset inventory will undergo a vulnerability assessment. Information owners will then decide how to control those vulnerabilities.

Of course, the main objective in protecting the affected information asset is to mitigate risks associated with vulnerabilities and security exposures identified on the asset. That is, those security risks have to be evaluated before selecting the security controls to be adopted. The relationship between risk analysis and vulnerability assessment should now be clear. There is no risk analysis without a prior vulnerability assessment, and there is no response to any vulnerabilities and security exposure before performing a risk analysis on the affected asset.

Risk analysis, however, requires other activities in addition to vulnerability assessment. First, a security policy has to be in place. This security policy defines the risk analysis methodology to be used and the risk levels tolerated for various information assets. A risk analysis also requires several inventories, in addition to vulnerabilities, to be maintained: an information asset inventory, a threat inventory, and an inventory of existing security controls. The risk analysis process will study the effect of security threats, given system vulnerabilities and security exposures, on information assets and estimate the organization risk position. If this risk position is higher than the security policy-tolerated risk level, then a security program should be defined. The objective of this risk-driven security program is to implement a cost-effective set of security controls capable of bringing back the current organization risk position to an acceptable risk position as defined in the organization's security policy.

The main objective of a security policy is to define the acceptable behavior of the organization's computing environment. The security policy also defines all security activities and projects needed to protect the organization's computing environment, including a security every 3 years and a security audit once a year.

Most all other known vulnerabilities are documented in cert.org, nist.org, and mitre.org.

Information on less common vulnerabilities should be obtained from vendors. Even though there is an abundance of vulnerability assessment tools, some of them are capable of providing a stateful view of the entire system and explain how those vulnerabilities can jointly be exploited by a hacker to cause extended damage.

9.10.4 Active Security Assessment Effort

9.10.4.1 The NSA Triad for Security Assessment

As seen in Chapter 1, NSA's security assessment Triad is a top-down approach to studying the security posture of an organization. It consists of a sequential process made of three phases: assessment, evaluation, and penetration testing [15].

9.10.4.1.1 Assessment

In the first phase, the agency starts with a high-level review of the organization's critical assets. This is part of security planning where potential security incidents are studied to understand their effects on business in the next 3 years. The security objective is to recommend long-term directions about how improve the overall information security posture of the organization.

9.10.4.1.2 Evaluation

In a second phase, the agency initiates an evaluation activity. This is a detailed review of the organization's information systems in terms of their strengths in enforcing their security policies. The security objective of the evaluation phase is to recommend medium-term directions on how to use technology to support information security. The evaluation activity is conducted internally with the collaboration of all relevant plays, like information owners, users, and customers.

The evaluation report should show where policy cannot be effectively implemented, and where policy was not effectively implemented, and how closely the agency is in achieving its security expectations. In addition to this evaluation phase, the evaluation phase can also result in certification and accreditation of the systems evaluated.

The NSA has developed a methodology for system evaluation, called INFOSEC Assessment Methodology (IAM). The evaluation also provide assurance that the systems are enforcing relevant policy, that configurations in place are working, and that potential undesired events are ranked and prioritized.

9.10.4.1.3 Penetration Testing

The penetration testing activity is a technical activity that goes deeper in the computing environment to identify vulnerabilities that are ready to be exploited by existing threats and harm the organization. It searches for short-term weaknesses that can yield to undesired incidents. This is a noncooperative activity where the testers simulate real hackers to compromise the security of an organization's computing environment.

The assessment phase remains a preliminary study that is characterized by the following properties:

Not technical, often qualitative
Does not involve any testing
Collaborative, often shared by users, managers, and owners

The evaluation phase remains preliminary but involves intensive testing. It satisfies the properties:

Technical but not invasive
Passive testing required for self-study
Collaborative to some extent
Involves diagnostic tools
Involves internal auditors

The penetration testing phase is invasive in nature. The following properties are required:

Noncollaborative
Technical in nature

Invasive in nature
Involves external auditors
Active penetration tests
Designed to avoid risks of compromising the target system
Active assessment expertise

Usually, the NSA security assessment triad is conducted in the context of a certification process and accreditation process. In this process, the certifier evaluates an organization's system against a well-defined set of prescribed security controls defined in terms of the criticality and sensitivity of the system security requirements.

9.10.4.2 How to Penetrate the System as Hackers Do

At this point of the ASA project, we have finished identifying vulnerabilities, and have set aside a set of major vulnerabilities that we will exploit, as hackers do, to reveal the effects of hacking on system security.

Before proceeding to penetration actions, sufficient information about any system to be penetrated and its components has to be available to testers. While penetration activities vary depending on the target systems, their operating systems, the vulnerabilities to be exploited, the ASA scope, and the tools available, a combination of the following activities are often taken:

Prepare an access point through obtaining a remote command prompt.
Disable logging and any adverse security controls.
Capture snap shots for critical states of the system.
Gain elevated or root privileges.
Perform appropriate attacks, for example, DOS, buffer overflow, etc.
Leave a message or a file recording your penetration actions.

9.10.4.3 Active Security Assessment on Network

Performing ASA on a network is reduced to several ASA projects where the target systems are all those systems connected to the network, for example, routers, firewalls, servers, etc. Every ASA project has its own scope, which describes restrictions on systems components to be assessed, timing schedule, tools to be adopted, and so on. Despite the limited ASA scope, there are still thousands of vulnerabilities and thousands of techniques that may be concerned with the ASA project. So, the ASA team should have a consolidated view of the entire network, which if adequately patched, will enhance the overall security of the network.

Often, your best bet is to proceed to patch your network hosts with the last vendor software and firmware patches. This way, you have eliminated all known network-related vulnerabilities and satisfied the minimal security best practice requirements that apply to your network.

Usually, you have to worry a lot more about rogue users (malicious) and internal users (unintentional) who are internal to company networks, and can plan great destructive power for all hosts and other resources connected to your internal networks. Most company hosts are internal, hence not accessible to external users; even if hackers manage to reach those internal hosts the damage will not be as extensive. There are, however, always new vulnerabilities that we need to identify and counter to mitigate any risks associated with them.

Network infrastructure touches all data transmission functions and is the foundation for any information system activities. This means that network infrastructure vulnerabilities affect every process running on your network. That is, you cannot mitigate information system security risks without eliminating all known vulnerabilities on your network infrastructure. We showed earlier in this chapter that minimizing system security risks is only possible after eliminating vulnerabilities found in people, activities, company infrastructure, data, and technology.

Our ASA project aims at identifying vulnerabilities through hackers' simulation of attacks. This should include testing activities from the outside of the computing environment as hackers do, and testing activities from the inside by simulating what rogue users do.

9.10.4.4 What to Look for, as a Hacker Would

Testers are selected based on some hackers' profiles accumulated by security management. Testers should simulate the hackers and follow their approach in looking for vulnerabilities they can exploit. It may be very useful if testers can answer some of the following questions:

What hackers learn when they scan ports?
How do hackers exploit identified vulnerabilities?
Knowing the network layout simplifies the planning of testing activities as testers know how hosts are connected.
Knowing the layered defense system is useful in planning the penetration testing activities.
Knowing the places for all security appliances including routers, firewalls, intrusion detection systems, etc.
Knowing the protocols used is necessary.
Knowing how hosts and security appliances are configured.

Before you perform any testing activities, you have to make sure that your partners have no objection that you test for vulnerabilities on common borders to make sure that their ports are protected and their firewalls are adequately configured.

9.10.4.5 Simulating What Hackers Do

Hackers often first search the Web for information about the company owning the target system. Hackers use a variety of tools available on the Internet for free, even though some of the sources will require that you register or provide some personal information that they have no way of checking as valid.

As an internal ASA tester, you already know sufficient information on your own organization and the target system that can save the delays caused by the cold startup phenomenon characterizing most hackers' reconnaissance effort. Despite this advantage, you still have to go through what real hackers go through when they collect initial access information. This duplicate effort on your own part will show you what a great deal of information about your organization anybody can obtain just by searching the Web and how harmful this information is, as hackers can use it to figure out the access information they need to initiate their hacking activities.

In a second step, hackers will identify the discovery tools they need to perform network scans, port scans, and other vulnerability assessment tools needed to determine in-depth information about company network layouts, and resources connected to them, and open ports and enable services at those ports. Hackers now have very specific information on how to access various resources of the target organization.

You, as a ASA tester, can simulate all of this using your own safe tools, accumulated earlier within your ASA resources as specified in the ASA scope or ASA security policy.

Of course, the real hacker has no restrictions on the tools he/she can use, nor do hackers at any time have constraints to satisfy. One may ask why a ASA tester should be restricted by any of those constraints if he/she is simulating a real hacker. Well, we have to be realistic here. The real hacker can crush your system but you are not allowed to do that. There are always many constraints that an ASA tester must abide by, including limitations on availability of tools, a budget, and timely completion of a project. These constraints are imposed on ASA testers to ensure that the ASA project remains feasible—economically, technically, operationally, socially, and ethically and legally.

9.10.4.6 Port Scanning

A port scan provides information on what is there on the network. Port scanners also produce a layout of the network. Testers can study port scan information to identify unauthorized resources and poor network configurations. Most port scanners produce lengthy information from which testers can detect vulnerabilities. Usually, this information is generated independently of the operating systems found on the network or on hosts connected to the network. Unfortunately, different port scanners may generate different information and testers may produce different systems vulnerabilities. Testers are encouraged to use multiple port scanners and consolidate their results. Probably because some applications do not know how to reply to some UDP scans, UDP scans tend to be not as reliable as TCP scans. Imagine, you have 65,535 TCP ports to scan and 65,535 UDP ports to scan. Tables 9.4 and 9.5 list UDP and TCP ports. So how many hosts you have to scan? Port scanning is really very time consuming and their reports are voluminious, so how much time and how much patience can you really afford?

Table 9.4   Selected UDP Ports

echo	7	Pop2	109	at-nb p	202
discard	9	Pop3	110	at-echo	204
daytime	13	sunrpc	111	at-zis	206
msp	18	ntp	123	Qmtp	209
chargen	19	pwdgen	12	z3950	210
fsp	21	loc-srv	135	ipx	213
ssh	22	netbios-ns	137	imap3	220
time	37	netbios-dgm	138	pawserv	345
rlp	39	netbios-ssn	139	zserv	346
tacacs	49	imap2	143	fatserv	47
re-mail-ck	50	snmp	16	rpc2portmap	369
domain	53	snmp-trap	162	codaauth2	370
tacacs-ds	65	cmip-man	163	clearcase	371
bootps	67	cmip-agent	164	ulistserv	372
bootpc	68	mailq	174	ldap	389
tftp	69	xdmcp	177	imsp	406
gopher	70	nextstep	178	https	443
www	80	bgp	179	snpp	444
kerberos	88	prospero	191	microsoft-ds	445
acr-nema	104	irc	194	saft	487
csnet-ns	105	smux	199	isakmp	500
rtelnet	107	at-rtmp	201		

Table 9.5   Selected TCP Ports

tcpmux	1	gopher	70	irc	194
echo	7	rje	77	smux	199
discard	9	finger	79	at-rtmp	201
systat	11	www	80	at-rbp	202
daytime	13	link	87	at-echo	204
netstat	15	kerberos	88	at-zis	206
qotd	17	supdup	95	qmtp	209
msp	18	hostnames	101	z3950	210
chargen	19	iso-tsap	102	ipx	213
ftp-data	20	acr-nema	104	imap3	220
ftp	21	csnet-ns	105	pawserv	345
ssh	22	rtelnet	107	zserv	346
telnet	23	pop2	109	fatserv	347
smtp	25	pop3	110	rpc2portmap	369
time	37	sunrpc	111	codaauth2	370
nameserver	42	auth	113	clearcase	371
whois	43	sftp	115	ulistserv	372
tacacs	49	uucp-path	117	ldap	389
re-mail-ck	50	nntp	119	imsp	406
domain	53	ntp	123	https	443
mtp	57	nextstep	178	snpp	444
tacacs-ds	65	bgp	179	microsoft-ds	445
bootps	67	prospero	191	saft	487
bootpc	68	irc	194	isakmp	500

Of course, the scope defines all constraints associated with the ASA project. However, despite all of those constraints, you should find ways, as feasible as possible, to scan as many resources on the network. Even though you are encouraged to scan as many resources on the network, as many ports, using as many tools, and as many techniques as you can to ensure that the information produced is consistent, this may not happen in real life due to the constraints explained earlier.

9.10.4.7 How Do Port Scanners Work?

Once a ping is performed to identify all live resources on a network, the tester can use a port scanner to identify vulnerabilities on hosts and the resources on the network. A TCP scan is done by sending TCP SYN requests to a host or a range of hosts. Then the port scanner waits for selected replies from available hosts. The port scanner probes for all hosts of the networks on selected ports, from 0 to 65,535, to detect available hosts.

The information produced by port scanners include information on active hosts that are reachable on the network, their network address, and information on enabled services and applications that are running.

Your ASA project should first find out if any of the known vulnerabilities are present on the target system. The ASA project should then simulate the work of hackers to study the effects of potential hackers on system security. Findings of the ASA project will be used to assess risks and generate recommendations to enhance system security. Vulnerabilities are often listed on cert.org, nitre.org, and nist.org.

9.10.4.8 How to Map Company Networks as Hackers Do

Before you can perform any system scanning or play social engineering tricks to obtain system access information for later use in penetration testing, you need simple network mapping tools to obtain the following information:

General domain registrations
Hosts containing email applications for given domains
How to reach those hosts

In order to obtain the information above, you need to use one of the whois utilities you can download from the Internet. For example, such utilities are available from your ISP, whois.org, or from any domain registration sites, like www.register. com, or www.networksolutions.com. You can use your whois utility to look up the Internet domain name information you need and to identify DNS servers responsible for your domain name.

9.10.4.9 How to Scan Your Systems as Hackers Do

As soon as your whois information is digested, you should start scanning the hosts, modems, and ports to see information the way real hackers see it while those hosts are live. Your network mapping activity provides information about how your systems are connected together and information on IP address, internal and external host names, running protocols, open ports, enabled services, and running applications.

Usually, internal hosts are not visible to hackers, and simulating hackers may not allow you to test those internal hosts hidden by your internal addressing schemes. But internal hosts are often part of your ASA scope, and you may need to simulate as malicious internal users can do to compromise the security of those internal systems. Anyway, you can easily scan further by simply connecting your laptop to the network, loading your tools, and gathering the information you need.

9.10.4.10 Cognitive Ability of Hackers

We said earlier that the ASA project simulates the work of hackers and studies effects on the target system for which we generate security recommendations based on the findings of the ASA project. But what types of hackers should we simulate in the ASA project? Do we also simulate their profiles and motivations? Hackers evolved from being knowledge seekers and explorers who may have compromised systems security without intentionally planning any destructive power, to becoming destructive power seekers who maliciously break into systems to obtain personal gain.

The literature reports that most hackers are internal users who are often malicious employees, unhappy customers, trusted auditors, or partners who abuse company systems by gaining higher computing privileges that allow them to access sensitive information and transmit it to competitors or enemies to harm the company. Usually, those insiders are extremely dangerous because they know the system in greater details and enjoy privileged access information. They can easily, rapidly, and stealthily produce greater destructive power. Of course, there are certainly internal users who have no malicious intent but unintentionally corrupt sensitive information, and delete or communicate critical data to unauthorized recipients. Even though those insiders are not malicious, they can compromise system security unintentionally and create greater destructive power as professional malicious hackers. Usually, those insiders are not knowledgeable users who plan malicious attacks, but their ignorance can lead to the same consequences hackers plan to produce.

So, what types of hackers should we simulate in our ASA effort? The literature reports that 80% of hackers are insiders and the rest are external hackers who are either very savvy hackers with malicious intents and personal gain, or script kiddies who are not knowledgeable users but have patience and time to unintentionally produce harm. Those simple hackers do not plan their attacks but can link to target systems directly using Telnet, for example, without hiding their identities. They often get caught rapidly and easily.

The script kiddies do not necessarily go through prolonged discovery phases, but instead they act without thinking and without any initial accurate information to access systems. Usually, they do not bother to identify the operating system of the victim system or even what services are available to tone their hacking effort. Common sense may suggest to simulate hackers in the same proportions reported in the literature, that is, 80% of the simulated hackers are insiders who are selected from the company, 10% of the simulated hackers are savvy with malicious intent, and 10% are regular users without computer knowledge who are given sufficient time to compromise the security of the system. In real life, however, this common sense may not make sense for our hacking simulation process. This process can be prolonged and costly. Simulation results may not be predicted, while risks of our compromising system security during the ASA project may increase to unacceptable levels. That is, in selecting good ASA testers we need to study current hackers and their work before we make a final selection. Capturing the mind of hackers, understanding the way they think, and capturing their cognitive ability in a formal profile for intruders and hackers may be needed. The profile should identify hackers' personal traits that can be predictive of their malicious behavior.

9.10.5 Resources Available for ASA Testers

9.10.5.1 Active and Passive Security Assessment Tools

Before we proceed, it is important to note that the same vulnerability assessment tools may be used in passive or active ways. Usually, the good guys will use them for good purposes and the bad guys will use with malicious intent. Moreover, ASA tools may be ineffective or inefficient in detecting main vulnerabilities of the target system. Certain tools may also be corrupted, and they can harm the target system or its components. That is, ASA testers should be limited to the tools and ASA resources that system owners provide for them. If ASA testers have special tools they intend to use in any step of the ASA project, these tools have to be tested independently before they are added to ASA resources provided by system owners. Because there is no single tool that will uncover all vulnerabilities on a target system, owners usually provide multiple diversified tools that are made available to ASA testers. In this book, we recommend the top 10 vulnerability scanners suggested by insecure.org:

1. Nessus
2. GFI LANguard
3. Retina
4. Core impact
5. ISS Internet Scanner
6. X-scan
7. SARA
8. Qualys Guard

9. SAINT
10. MBSA

Good tools should come with adequate documentation, generate detailed reports about system vulnerabilities, provide information on how those vulnerabilities are exploited by hackers, and recommend ways to fix those vulnerabilities. Good ASA tools also provide updates and user support. The above 10 tools are mainly appropriate to scan hosts, but insecure.org also suggests another set of top 10 vulnerability scanners when the target system is a Web application. The top 10 Web application vulnerability scanners produced by an insecure.org survey conducted in 2006 are as follows:

1. Nikto
2. Paros Proxy
3. WebScarab
4. WebInspect
5. Whisker/LibWhisker
6. Burpsuite
7. Wikto
8. Acunetix Web Vulnerability Scanner
9. Watchfire AppScan
10. N-Stealth

Insecure.org initiated two surveys on security tools in 2000 and 2003. They lately released a new survey in 2006. In an ASA project, insecure.org seems to be a great source of information on active security assessment and penetration testing activities. In insecure.org's 2006 survey on vulnerability scanners, Fyodor, the creator of Nmap, invited Nmap hackers' mailing list users to participate in the survey by sharing their review of familiar vulnerability assessment tools.

There was no restriction on the source, platform, or type of vulnerability assessment tools to include in the survey. Subjects were permitted to submit reviews on open source or commercial tools on any platform. Because respondents were taken from a Nmap mailing list, Nmap was not included in the study to eliminate any biases or subjectivity. Survey authors also note that there may be slight biases toward hacking or attack attitude may rather than a defensive stance. In the case of ethical hacking where testers are expected to simulate hackers, a survey of types of biases will be more appropriate than any survey where subjects show defensive behavior in their evaluation process.

Criteria employed in the selection process for the 2006 survey are as follows:

It is new with respect to the last survey of 2003.
Even though it generally costs money, a free limited/demo/trial version may be available.

Works natively on Linux.
Works natively on OpenBSD, FreeBSD, Solaris, and/or other UNIX variants.
Works natively on Apple Mac OS X.
Works natively on Microsoft Windows.
Features a command-line interface.
Offers a GUI (point and click) interface.
Source code is available for inspection.

9.10.5.2 General System Vulnerability Tools

The following top 10 vulnerability scanners are provided at http://sectools.org/vuln-scanners.html:

1. **Nessus:** Premier UNIX vulnerability assessment tool
   Nessus is the best free network vulnerability scanner available, and the best to acquire on UNIX at any cost. It is constantly updated, with more than 11,000 plugins for the free feed. Key features include:
   Remote and local authenticated security checks
   A client/server architecture with a graphical interface
   An embedded scripting language for writing your own plug-ins
   Nessus is the most popular utility intended to automate the testing and discovery of known security vulnerabilities [14]. Nessus is a free program released under the GPL. Nessus also has a great community of developers anchored by the primary author, Renaud Deraison. When allowed to fairly compete in reviews against other vulnerability scanners, Nessus has performed better than many other products costing thousands of dollars.
   A very powerful feature of Nessus is its client server technology. Servers can be placed at any optimal points on a network allowing tests to be conducted from various points. Servers may be controlled from a central client or from multiple distributed clients.
   The server portion will run most favors of Unix. It even runs on MAC OS X and IBM/AIX, but its installation and configuration on Unix seem to be simpler. These features provide a great deal of flexibility for testers. Clients are available for both Windows and Unix. The Nessus server may be configured to complete all testing activities while the client provides management, reporting, and interpretations.
2. **GFI LANguard**: A commercial network security scanner for Windows
   GFI LANguard scans IP networks to detect all live hosts. In the next step, it tries to identify the operating system on the host, and enabled services and running applications. This utility can also collect Windows machine's service pack level, missing security patches, wireless access points, USB devices, open shares, open ports, services/applications active

on the computer, key registry entries, weak passwords, users, and groups. Scan results are saved to an HTML report, which can be customized/queried. It also includes a patch manager which detects and installs missing patches.

3. **Retina**: Commercial vulnerability assessment scanner by eEye

This utility is intended to scan all the hosts on a network and report on any vulnerabilities found. It was written by eEye, who are well known for their security research [4].

Some of the features claimed by eEye:

Network security scanner: Retina enables prioritized policy management, patch management, and vulnerability management.

Network vulnerability assessment: Identify network security vulnerabilities, missing application updates, plus zero day threats.

Network discovery and policy assessment: Retina discovers all devices, operating systems, applications, patch levels, plus policy configurations.

Vulnerability management: Enables prioritized policy management, patch management, and vulnerability assessment.

Fast and accurate scans: Accurately scan a Class C network of devices, operating systems, and applications in about minutes.

Policy compliance: Identify and simplify your corporate and regulatory requirements (SOX, HIPAA, GLBA, PCI, and others).

4. **Core Impact**: An automated, comprehensive, penetration testing product

Despite its high cost of tens of thousands, Core Impact is still widely considered to be the most powerful tool available, with invasive testing activities. It maintains an updated database of professional exploits, performs smart exploits on one host, and then establishes an encrypted tunnel through that host to reach and exploit other boxes. Alternatively, you can obtained similar efficiency while saving considerably with Canvas, or the excellent and free Metasploit Framework (go to http://www.metasploit.com/framework/).

5. **ISS Internet Scanner**: Application-level vulnerability assessment

Internet Scanner emerged in the early '90s as a small tiny open source scanner by Christopher Klaus. The company is now a billion-dollar company with a myriad of security products.

6. **X-scan**: A general scanner for scanning network vulnerabilities

This is a multithreaded, plug-in-supported vulnerability scanner. It includes many features, including full NASL support, detecting service types, remote OS type/version detection, weak user/password pairs, and more. You may be able to find newer versions available here if you can deal with most of the page being written in Chinese.

7. **SARA**: Security Auditor's Research Assistant

SARA is a vulnerability assessment tool that was derived from the infamous SATAN scanner [18]. They try to release updates twice a month and leverage other software created by the open source community (such as Nmap and Samba).

8. **QualysGuard**: A Web-based vulnerability scanner

   Delivered as a service over the Web, QualysGuard eliminates the burden of deploying, maintaining, and updating vulnerability management software or implementing ad hoc security applications. Clients securely access QualysGuard through an easy-to-use Web interface [2]. QualysGuard features 5,000+ unique vulnerability checks, an Inference-based scanning engine, and automated daily updates to the QualysGuard vulnerability KnowledgeBase.

9. **SAINT:** Security Administrator's Integrated Network Tool

   SAINT is another commercial vulnerability assessment tool (like Nessus, ISS Internet Scanner, or Retina) [16]. It runs on UNIX and used to be free and open source, but is now a commercial product.

   The SAINT scanning engine is very indispensable for your vulnerability assessment program. SAINT features a graphical user interface that is intuitive and easy to use. SAINT's features include:

   Vulnerability scanner is integrated with SAINTexploit penetration testing tool so you can exploit vulnerabilities found by the scanner

   Scans IPv4 and IPv6 addresses

   PCI compliance reporting

   Correlation of CVE and CVSS scores and vectors

   Allows designing and generating *vulnerability assessment reports* quickly and easily. Present the findings of even the largest network scans in an easy-to-read format with colorful charts.

   PCI compliance reports permit you to see if your network is compliant with PCI security standards.

   Trend analysis report option allows you to quantitatively analyze your remediation program

   Cross reference codes. SAINT includes the following identification numbers, which can be automatically correlated in reports: CVE, IAVA, OSVDB, BID, CVSS 2.0, SANS/FBI Top 20, etc.

   Data localization. SAINT allows you to store the vulnerability data locally or remotely. Other products require that your vulnerability data be sent across the Internet to their location.

   New threats to your networks can emerge in an instant. SAINTexpress provides complete, automatic updates to SAINT whenever a scan is run. Updates are released every two weeks, or sooner for a critical vulnerability announcement.

10. **MBSA:** Microsoft Baseline Security Analyzer

    This utility may be useful to improve your security management process by using simple MBSA techniques to detect common security misconfigurations and missing security updates on your computer systems [8].

Microsoft Baseline Security Analyzer (MBSA) is an easy-to-use tool designed for the IT professional that helps small- and medium-sized businesses determine their security state in accordance with Microsoft security recommendations. It also offers specific remediation guidance.

9.10.5.3 Top 10 Web Application Vulnerability Scanners

The following top 10 Web applications vulnerability scanners suggested in an insecure.org survey may be found at [6]:

1. **Nikto**: It is a more comprehensive Web scanner. Nikto is an open source Web server scanner that performs comprehensive tests against Web servers. Further information may be obtained from insecure.org or http://www.cirt.net/nikto2. According to this review, it scans for the following:

   Multiple malicious items

   More than 3200 potentially dangerous files

   Versions on over 625 servers

   Version-specific problems on over 230 servers.

   It allows for automatic update for new scan items and plugins. Insecure.org rates it as as a great tool, but the value is limited by its infrequent updates. Therefore, the newest and most critical vulnerabilities are often not detected.

2. **Paros proxy**: This is a Web application vulnerability assessment proxy. It uses a Java based Web proxy for assessing Web application vulnerability. It supports editing/viewing HTTP/HTTPS messages on-the-fly to change items such as cookies and form fields. It includes a Web traffic recorder, Web spider, hash calculator, and a scanner for testing common Web application attacks such as SQL injection and cross-site scripting. Further information may be obtained from insecure.org or [11].

3. **WebScarab**: It provides a framework for analyzing applications that communicate using the HTTP and HTTPS protocols. Further information is available on [20].

   In its simplest form, WebScarab records all observed requests and responses conversations and transfers them to the operator to review them. WebScarab is designed to be a tool for anyone who needs to expose the workings of an HTTP(S) based application, whether to allow the developer to debug otherwise difficult problems, or to allow a security specialist to identify vulnerabilities in the way that the application has been designed or implemented.

4. **WebInspect**: This is a powerful Web application scanner intended for security assessment to identify known and unknown vulnerabilities within the Web application layer. This utility is also useful to check that a Web server is configured properly, and to attempt common Web attacks such as parameter

injection, cross-site scripting, directory traversal, and more. Further information may be obtained at http://www.spidynamics.com/products/webinspect/ SPI Dynamics' WebInspect application security assessment tool helps WebInspect can also help.

5. **Whisker/libwhisker**: Rain.Forest.Puppy's CGI vulnerability scanner and library Libwhisker is a Perl module geared geared towards HTTP testing [3]. It provides functions for testing HTTP servers for many known security holes, particularly the presence of dangerous CGIs. Whisker is a scanner that used libwhisker but is now deprecated in favor of Nikto which also uses libwhisker.

6. **Burpsuite**: This is an integrated platform for attacking Web applications. The tester can use this utility to combine manual and automated techniques to enumerate, analyze, attack and exploit Web applications. Burp provides an integrated environment where a variety of tools work together effectively to share information. It allows the consolidation of findings to understand the origin of the attacks. You may further information on the Burp suite on insecure.org or [12].

Key features unique to Burp Suite include:

Ability to "passively" spider an application in a non-intrusive manner, with all requests originating from the user's browser.

One-click transfer of interesting requests between tools, e.g. from the Burp Proxy request history, or the Burp Spider results tree.

Detailed analysis and rendering of requests and responses.

Extensibility via the IBurpExtender interface, which allows third-party code to extend the functionality of Burp Suite. Data processed by one tool can be used in arbitrary ways to affect the behaviour and results of other tools.

Centrally configured settings for downstream proxies, Web and proxy authentication, and logging.

Tools can run in a single tabbed window, or be detached in individual windows.

All tool and suite configuration is optionally persistent across program loads.

Runs in both Linux and Windows.

7. **Wikto**: This is a Web server assessment tool. It is intended to check for flaws in Web servers. You will find the same features as in Nikto but this latter will also provide addeded, for example, a Back-End miner. You may find further information on insecure.org or [21].

8. **Acunetix Web Vulnerability Scanner**: This is a commercial Web vulnerability scanner. This utility is intended to check Web applications for vulnerabilities such as SQL injection, cross site scripting, and weak password strength on authentication pages. Acunetix WVS offers a comfortable GUI

and a capability to generate professional Web site security audit reports. You may find further information on insecure.org or [1].

9. **Watchfire AppScan**: This is a commercial Web vulnerability scanner AppScan is intended to perform security testing throughout the system development lifecycle for the purpose of early discovery of common vulnerabilities, such as cross site scripting, HTTP response splitting, parameter tampering, hidden field manipulation, backdoors/debug options, buffer overflows and more. You may find further information on insecure.org or [5].

10. **N-Stealth**: This is a Web server scanner utility. Because it is a commercial Web server security scanner, it is generally updated more frequently than free Web scanners such as Whisker/libwhisker and Nikto. N-Stalker Web Application Security Scanner 2006 is a Web security assessment solution developed by N-Stalker. It incorporates N-Stealth HTTP Security Scanner and its 35,000 Web Attack Signature database.

Insecure.org evaluates that the claims of "30,000 vulnerabilities and exploits and dozens of vulnerability checks are added every day are highly disputed. Web scanners, as vulnerability assessment tools, are encountered almost everywhere in security assessment, as in Nessus, ISS Internet Scanner, Retina, SAINT, and SARA." You may find further information on insecure.org or [9].

9.10.6 Corrective Effort

The purpose of the corrective effort is to preempt hackers from exploiting the vulnerabilities and deficiencies discovered throughout the ASA project. The security analysts should be able to organize the discovered set of vulnerabilities and deficiencies into two subsets: a subset of highly critical vulnerabilities and deficiencies requiring immediate corrective actions, and a subset of less critical vulnerabilities and deficiencies. The first subset of vulnerabilities and deficiencies requires that security analysts take immediate corrective actions to preempt potential hackers from exploiting those vulnerabilities and deficiencies. Bear in mind that no matter how dangerous the critical vulnerabilities and deficiencies are, none of the corrective actions can take place without the written authorization of upper management. The second subset of vulnerabilities and deficiencies will wait until the final report is approved by the designated authorizing official.

9.10.7 Active Security Assessment Report

At the end of the active security assessment report, security analysts working on the ASA project, should assemble a final report identifying all discovered vulnerabilities and their recommendations to mitigate security risks. For every vulnerability or deficiency, the report describes how risk can be mitigated. Are the identified vulnerabilities patchable? How can we circumvent the security deficiencies? How can we preempt hackers to prevent them from exploiting the discovered vulnerabilities and deficiencies?

The ASA report has to devise a security program capable of circumventing all deficiencies discovered throughout the ASA project. Table 9.6 provides an example for a template summarizing the deficiencies and vulnerabilities discovered and ASA actions documented in the ASA report.

9.11 Summary

As seen in the information security life cycle that good security design depends on a good security analysis. A good security analysis however has to assess security effectiveness to redefine the security requirements assembled based on business impact analysis and risk analysis. Security assessment may be conducted in a passive way, with invasive testing, or in an active way with guided penetration testing. This chapter presented the security assessment process in general and a systematic methodology that, if followed, can lead to effective security assessment. The chapter also recommended several tools for both passive and active assessment testing.

9.12 Review Questions

1. Discuss possible attacks on people in a computing environment. Give examples.
2. Discuss possible attacks on activities in a computing environment. Give examples.
3. Discuss possible attacks on data in a computing environment. Give examples.
4. Discuss possible attacks on technology in a computing environment. Give examples.
5. Discuss possible attacks on networks and infrastructure in a computing environment. Give examples.
6. Discuss the working of the NSA security assessment triad. Give an example.
7. Discuss the timing of an active security assessment project.
8. Discuss the strategies of an active security assessment project. What are the differences among strategies? Use a table summarizing those differences.
9. Discuss the recursive effects between the discovery, passive, and active assessment phases. Give examples as needed.
10. Discuss the usefulness of Web search, Web crawling, and Web navigation in security assessment. Give examples as needed.
11. Discuss the objective of footprint-based passive reconnaissance and how it works. Suggest steps and tools when applicable. Give examples as needed.

Table 9.6 Passive and Active Security Assessment Output

Vulnerability/ Deficiency	System	Source	Patchable	Exploitable	ASA Action	Report Control	ASA Policy	Tester Initials	Date

12. Discuss the objective of scanning-based active reconnaissance and how it works. Suggest steps and tools when applicable. Give examples as needed.
13. Discuss the objective of enumerating the computing environment and how it works. Suggest steps and tools when applicable. Give examples as needed
14. Discuss the cognitive ability of hackers and give examples as needed.
15. Define ethical hacking and discuss its advantages and risks. Give examples as needed.

9.13 Workshops

Workshop 1

The bottom line of any penetration test project is to identify vulnerabilities, prioritize them, study how to eliminate any conditions that bad guys can exploit to cause damage, and finally generate recommendations. Discuss this penetration test objective and give an example how it can be achieved. Suggest a sequence of steps and relate those steps to risk assessment and the design of a risk-driven security program. You may demonstrate your method using a small business case.

Workshop 2

The objective of this workshop is to develop a methodology based on security assessment capable of generating a risk-driven security program. Your methodology has to start with studying the components of the computing environment. You may need to apply security assessment on people, activities, data, technology, and network to identify the security posture of each of those components. Hint: Once you know the vulnerabilities of those components and existing threats, you can then estimate their security exposures.

Apply your methodology to a small business example.

References

1. Acunetix, White Paper: Audit Your Website Security with Acunetix Web Security Scanner, http://www.acunetix.com/, accessed on November 7, 2008.
2. CSI, White Paper: QualysGuard Intranet Scanner, http://www.csisoft.com/Security/Qualys/qualysguardintranetscanner.php, November 7, 2008.
3. Desai, N., White Paper: Using Libwhisker, http://www.securityfocus.com/infocus/1798, August 2004.
4. eEye, White Paper: eEye Digital Security, http://www.visus-it.com/eeye.php, accessed on November 7, 2008.
5. IBM, White Paper: Rational AppScan, http://www-01.ibm.com/software/awdtools/appscan/, November 7, 2008.

6. Insecure.org, White Paper: Top 10 Web Vulnerability Scanners, http://sectools.org/web-scanners.html, November 7, 2008.
7. Jung, J., E. Sit, H. Balakrishnan, and R. Morris, DNS Performance and the Effectiveness of Caching, http://nms.lcs.mit.edu/papers/dns-ton2002.pdf, accessed on November 7, 2008.
8. MSDN, White Paper: How To: Use the Microsoft Baseline Security Analyzer, http://msdn.microsoft.com/en-us/library/aa302360.aspx, November 7, 2008.
9. N-Stalker, White Paper: N-Stalker Web Application Security Scanner, 2006, http://www.nstalker.com/products/, accessed on November 7, 2008.
10. Palmer, C. C., Ethical hacking, *IBM Systems Journal*, Vol. 40, No. 3, 2001.
11. Paros, White Paper: Paros—for Web Application Security Assessment, http://www.parosproxy.org/index.shtml, November 7, 2008.
12. Portswigger.net, Burp Suite: Web Application Security, http://portswigger.net/suite/, August 2004.
13. Raggad, B., Corporate Vital Defense Strategy: A Framework for Information Assurance, *23rd National Information Systems Security Conference*, NIST/NSA, Baltimore, 2000.
14. Renaud Deraison, R., Nessus Network Auditing, Syngress, September 2004.
15. Rogers, R. et al., Security Assessment: Case Studies for Implementing the NSA IAM, Syngress, USA, 2004.
16. Saint, White Paper: Vulnerability Scanning, http://www.saintcorporation.com/products/vulnerability_scan/saint/saint_scanner.html, November 7, 2008.
17. Savola, P., Backbone Infrastructure Attacks and Protections, March 2006, http://tools.ietf.org/html/draft-savola-rtgwg-backbone-attacks-00, accessed on November 7, 2008.
18. Security Forest, White Paper: Category: Vulnerability Scanning, http://www.securityforest.com/wiki/index.php/Category:Vulnerability_Scanning, accessed on November 7, 2008.
19. Spangler, R., Analysis of Remote Active Operating System Fingerprinting Tools, May 2003, http://www.packetwatch.net/documents/papers/osdetection.pdf, accessed on November 7, 2008.
20. WebScarab, White Paper: Category:OWASP WebScarab Project, http://www.owasp.org/index.php/Category:OWASP_WebScarab_Project, November 7, 2008.
21. Wikto, White Paper, Wikto: Web Server Assessment Tool, http://www.sensepost.com/research/wikto/, accessed on November 7, 2008.
22. WildPackets, EtherPeek NX Real-Time Expert Protocol analysis, http://www.netcomp.monash.edu.au/fit3030/resource/WildPackets/EPNX_10CoolThings.pdf, accessed on November 7, 2008.

Chapter 10

System Availability

Learning Objectives

After reading this chapter, students are expected to achieve an understanding of:

Why computer clustering is needed

What are the main cluster types

Distinguish between high-availability/failover, high-performance, load-balancing, and grid computing clusters

How Web site availability is achieved

How Web scalability and affinity are achieved

The MS Application Center

When to migrate away from the MS Application Center

What Microsoft offers as a replacement for the Application Center

How to compute availability in high-availability clusters

The difference in design and in computations in both serial and parallel architectures

The definitions of concepts closely related to availability

The Cisco approach of obtaining higher availability

Common configurations for clusters

Self-healing versus availability

10.1 Introduction

This chapter discusses the availability concept of company resources. We review its architecture and its computations, and present examples sufficient to explain differences availability and other related concepts. Availability computations will depend on the architecture of the system and the availability of its components.

10.2 Computer Clustering

The concept of cluster computing has been around for about half a century. The literature, however, does not agree on who actually introduced this engineering concept, and not even on when the concept was invented. It may be DEC or IBM or others who developed this concept, and the invention could date back to the 1960s or even earlier. What, however, could be even more valid, as noted in www.wikipedia.org, is the probability that it was customers who invented clusters, because they could not fit all their work on one computer or needed a backup.

Leaving any conflicting information on the authentic inventor or the date of the invention, computer clustering is a means of achieving high availability through parallel computing. IBM has consistently claimed that one of its staff, Gene Amdahl, introduced parallel processing in 1967 [1]. Amdahl's work consisted of a seminal paper on parallel processing where he showed mathematically that parallel architecture can add speed compared to serial configurations.

This concept should have triggered major innovations taking place about the same time that initiated distributed computing and computer networks. Whether or not the concepts relate to each other, computer clustering and networking cannot be technically separated, as the former can only be realized by connecting computers together, may be with improving availability instead of aiming just to share computing resources or to spread them geographically. There is no doubt, however, that both fields of networking and computer clustering continued to develop in parallel at least at their early stages.

Even though the first commercial clustering product seem to have been developed by Datapoint, in 1977, the first success story in computer clustering only came with DEC's introduction of VAXcluster in 1984 [9]. Both systems, however, combined both the computer clustering concept and storage sharing. IBM also introduced a similar system several years later with different configurations. The virtual super computer technology used TCP/IP communications to provide high-availability computing. The parallel virtual machine architecture started to develop both in the public and the private sectors.

Computer clustering software is now available for both Unix and Windows. The GNU/Linux world supports various cluster software for application clustering. Examples include Linux Virtual Server, Linux-HA, and others that provide clusters allowing incoming requests for services to be distributed across multiple cluster nodes.

Microsoft Windows Compute Cluster Server 2003 based on the Windows Server platform provides software for high-performance computing like the Job Scheduler, MSMPI (MS Message Passing Interface) library, and management tools [7].

10.3 Review of Cluster Concepts

A computer cluster is a group of computers that are closely connected to achieve higher availability and/or enhance system performance. They are known to be much more cost effective than single computers with comparable speed or availability. Clusters may be organized into several categories: High-availability/failover clusters, load-balancing clusters, high-performance clusters, and grid clusters. Figure 10.1 depicts the architecture for a generic cluster.

A generic framework would receive users' requests and process them at the front-end layer. The workload brought by users' requests is distributed to the servers at the back-end layer.

Load-balancing clusters are implemented by distributing a workload evenly over multiple back end nodes. Typically, the cluster will be configured with multiple redundant load-balancing front ends, as shown in Figure 10.1.

Of course, even though a cluster is a group of independent computers that are physically connected together to run a common set of applications, clients still see them as a single system. The computers are logically connected by cluster software.

Network load balancing (NLB) uses a distributed algorithm to distribute traffic across a number of hosts, helping to enhance the scalability and availability of mission critical, IP-based services, such as Web, Virtual Private Networking, Streaming

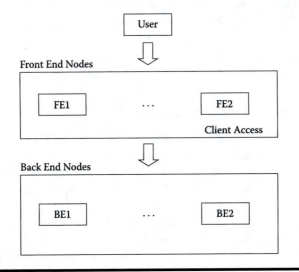

Figure 10.1   Generic cluster architecture.

Media, Terminal Services, etc. It also provides high availability by detecting host failures and automatically redistributing traffic to operational hosts.

These connections allow computers to use problem-solving features such as failover in server clusters and load balancing in application clusters. The next sections further discuss cluster implementations and their architecture scheme.

In Windows, Network Load Balancing (NBL) is used to expand IIS-based Web servers and other stateless applications by adding additional servers when client load increases. This way, clients will only see acceptable performance. This will also hide the failure of any NLB members from users who will not get affected by any extended downtime periods. Because NLB if often a standard addition in Window servers, there will be no need for any special hardware to members in the NLB cluster.

10.4 Types of Clusters

Even though a simple review of the literature can reveal a great deal of information on the types of clusters adopted in both the public and the private sectors, we in fact cannot classify all those types into more than four categories: high-availability/failover cluster; high-performance clusters; low balancing clusters; and grid clusters.

10.4.1 High-Availability/Failover Clusters

Failover clusters are adopted to improve the availability of services. They are implemented using redundant nodes, which take over when the system fails. The purpose of a high-availability cluster is, then, to prevent single points of failure. This is a common cluster category with many commercial packages around. Free software packages may be obtained, for example, from the Linux-HA project for Linux.

10.4.2 High-Performance Computing Clusters

Although the failover clusters aim at high availability, a higher-performance computing cluster is designed to provide higher performance, often adopted in scientific computing. These clusters are implemented by distributing computing tasks across many different nodes on the cluster. Because one computing task is performed on different servers, then those servers have to communicate their results to produce the intended output. An example of this type of cluster is called the Beowulf cluster, which runs on Linux and other free software [8]. For a commercial alternative, Microsoft offers Windows Compute Cluster Server as a high-performance computing platform.

10.4.3 Load-Balancing Clusters

Earlier, we saw two clusters: one intended to enhance availability and the other to enhance performance. Load-balancing clusters are implemented using a front-end row that receives inbound workload and distributes it to a second back-end row of servers. This type of clusters aims both at improving system performance and enhancing availability. Platform LSF HPC, Sun Grid Engine, Moab Cluster Suite, and Microsoft Application Center are examples of commercially available systems that implement load balancing [3]. The Linux Virtual Server project offers free software for Linux.

10.4.4 Grid Computing

Grid clusters are not really computer clusters per se, but they still connect computers for the purpose of optimizing performance. Grid computing manages the distribution of load while optimizing the computation process throughout the grid cluster. Several differences, however, exist between grid computing and other clusters. Grids connect computers that are not configured to trust each other and are often adopted to support more heterogeneous groups than are commonly supported in clusters. The servers of the grid are geographically distributed instead of closely connected.

Grid computing offers an clustered environment where network resources are virtualized to provide a utility framework of computing [2]. This type of cluster is configured to deliver high service availability with a high degree of transparency to users.

As an example, the Open Science Grid (OSG) is a national production-quality grid computing infrastructure for large scale science, built and operated by a consortium of U.S. universities and national laboratories [14]. The OSG Consortium was formed in 2004 to enable diverse communities of scientists to access a common grid infrastructure and shared resources. Groups that choose to join this consortium contribute with great effort and resources to the common infrastructure.

Another example is the Variable Energy Cyclotron Centre (VECC), an R&D unit of the Indian Department of Atomic Energy that performs research in basic and applied nuclear sciences [18]. GARUDA is another Indian Grid Computing initiative connecting 17 cities across the country [5]. The 45 participating institutes in this Indian nationwide project include all the IITs (Indian Institute of Technology) and C-DACs (Centre for Development of Advanced Computing centers) and other major institutes in India.

10.5 Web Site Availability

A computer cluster is a group of computers that are closely connected together. In order to take advantage of available technology, Web applications can benefit from

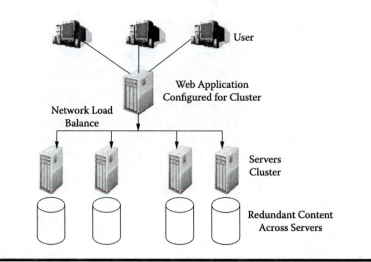

Figure 10.2   An example of a Web site cluster.

the cluster technology, as shown in Figure 10.2, to achieve the most wanted feature any Web site would like to have:

Scalability
Availability

The performance of the Web site can deteriorate when the number of users increases. The failure rate of a Web site will certainly increase. Maybe, a cluster architecture, as shown in Figure 10.3, will enhance the two features above.

10.5.1 Web Scalability

Scalability has two components: Web site scalability and cluster scalability. There is, first, the scalability of the Web site and it means how we can expand the Web site when the population of users expands. If we do not have Web site scalability, when the number of users reaches a high threshold we will then need to drop the current Web site and create a new one that is capable of handling the new large population. If, however, we have sufficient scalability, then we will be able to expand the current version of the Web site without destroying old utilities.

There is, on the other hand, the scalability of the architecture. The lack of this type of scalability may generate high maintenance costs. When the cluster performance slows down, probably due to an increase in the size of user population, we have to redesign the cluster to allow for a new configuration capable of ensuring a higher performance under the new growth conditions. If cluster scalability is present, then when the number of users increases we will be able to, in a linear way,

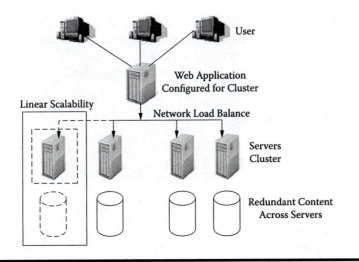

Figure 10.3   Linear scalability in a server cluster.

simply add as many redundant servers as needed. Figure 10.3 depicts how linear scalability is performed.

The Microsoft Application Center is part of the Microsoft .NET Enterprise Servers offering that comprise the Microsoft .NET initiative. To read about other .NET Enterprise Servers you may refer to [10] and [11]. The Application Center can provide content deployment and management facilities for Web sites built on the Microsoft Windows 2000 operating system and Microsoft Internet Information Services 5.0 (IIS). The purpose of this framework is to make scalable, manageable, and secure Web sites.

In Windows, an Application Center will include all the tools needed to manage the Web site. For example, the cluster communicates back with all Web site clients.

The Application center distributes connections across servers and manages the components in a single logical unit which makes the deployment and subsequent management of a site much easier, including deployment across additional servers in the cluster.

State information exchange including servers' logs in a cluster is automatically made available in a single view of a cluster, making the process of cluster wide administration even easier.

10.5.2 Web Availability

Taking advantage of the design scalability by expanding the cluster architecture, in a linear way, provides a very feasible approach to enhance the performance of the cluster in place. Providing for the scalability of a Web site and its cluster architecture is something good to have to add system performance, but it is not enough, on its own, for the system to be available. What then can be done to provide sufficient availability? Of course, the answer is to adopt server cluster for the Web site. This will first prevent any point of failure. Failover will continue to be available to cluster members. Availability should be secured throughout the cluster.

10.5.3 The Web Cluster

We saw earlier that a cluster is simply a group of redundant servers connected together to prevent single point of failure.

By bringing a number of servers together to work as a single unit we have seen that single point of failures can be avoided. This cluster of servers is not a particularly new, on its own, but its application in a Web-based product from Microsoft is. Previously clusters were mainly used in database products such as Microsoft SQL Server or mail servers such as Exchange. Application Center clusters are designed to serve HTTP based clients and target an application based business logic.

The Application Center Server architecture is divided, as shown earlier in the generic cluster architecture of Figure 10.1, into at least two tiers: Web tier and Application tier. This Application Center server is depicted in Figure 10.4.

Even though in the real world we now have a large variety of systems that all provide different implementations for the server clustering and network load balancing approaches, it is still very useful to review the concepts behind all the systems we have available in the market. Most of the examples we provide turn around the Microsoft Application Center model introduced in 2000. Of course, the MS Application Center model is no longer available as an independent system, but the

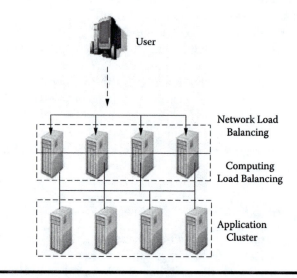

Figure 10.4   The example of the Application Center.

concept is still visible as components of new concepts or their implementations. The major new systems that replaced the Application Center include the Systems Management Server (SMS) 2003, Microsoft Operations Manager (MOM) 2005, and Service Oriented Architecture (SOA) application standards.

The Web tier cluster is the standard cluster that most people know. As shown in Figure 10.4, it provides servers to manage a client requests and may include database, e-mail, and Web servers. The application tier cluster manages any method call constituting a business function. These calls are distributed across cluster members to improve system throughput. This layout is referred to as COM+ application cluster, and it deals exclusively with component load balancing, not the upper network load balancing, which deals with the parent task [16].

We can see scalability is also improved as other servers can be added to the cluster to take on work load which in turn will deliver the intended performance.

Non-NLB balanced clusters can still be adopted but would need another load balancing tool, which can be developed by the company or acquired from other vendors.

10.5.4 Cluster Affinity

Building a cluster is quite simple. The original server, which may be considered a one-node cluster on its own, is connected to redundant servers as needed. The original server has the original up-to-date Web contents and cluster configurations. Often, the cluster members are added on the same network and connecting new servers to the cluster is very simple.

An application server cluster may be configured for the purpose of maximizing Web site performance subject to prescribed Web site scalability and availability. This configuration should also satisfy another important property: affinity.

Usually, the interactions among all members of the cluster are configured using a network load balancing protocol that defines how work load is distributed among the servers. Those inbound client requests for TCP and UDP protocols such as HTTP are distributed across available cluster members using a protocol-based algorithm. All members in the cluster receive the work load coming into the cluster, but a protocol determines which server actually processes the request while the rest of the servers ignored it.

Cluster members exchange messages with the load balancing adapters to manage the load distribution process, but only those servers who responded are involved in the NBL process; the rest of the servers failed to respond and are hence directly dropped from the cluster.

It may be useful to briefly talk about Windows Server 2003, as many people are familiar it. There may be two types of clustering systems on Windows 2003:

Microsoft Server Cluster Services (MSCS)
Network Load Balancing (NLB)

Installing the NLB software component on each node is simple. Often the implementation requires the configuration of a common IP address for the cluster to use, and then the configuration of the IP ports on which the new cluster will receive and respond to network traffic. Network behavior is not the same for both NLB and MSCS clusters. The interested reader needs to check, on his/her own, the differences in implementation and in managing the configuration.

Affinity is how the traffic is directed within the cluster. After a client session is initiated, all communication associated with this session, to and from this client, has to stay on the same node. If this communication is suddenly continued on another node, the connection will fail because the second node has no information on the previous connection.

Single affinity creates an affinity between a single client IP address and an NLB node, determined by an NLB server. When a session is initiated, the first client request is processed by the node assigned thereafter by the NLB; any communication associated with this session is always directed to the same node.

Class C affinity is similar to single affinity but it maps the cluster node with the class C address range from which the traffic comes [11]. Any traffic coming from the client subnet is directed to the same node. Even though replies are directed back to the same subnet, client traffic may come from different sources on the client subnet. The subnet configuration may negatively affect the performance of the cluster; when affinity is broken, it may be due to proxies hiding the source addresses and other security appliances.

Of course, you may say that all of those problems arise because session state information is lost when a session is continued on different nodes and, yes, you are right. You may also easily find ways to go around this by simple maintaining a text file that records all session information and let all nodes share the information as needed. Indeed, cookies may be useful in keeping track of client's session information; in fact, that is what client/server applications do to stay informed on client sessions.

To recap, the NLB provides a way to ensure high availability of company resources in the computing environment using a cluster connection. The cluster network is configured using a load balancing protocol to distribute work to all available nodes on the cluster to maintain acceptable performance. The configuration has to be correct and efficient in order to maximize network performance and prevent extended disruptions.

Microsoft Application Center 2000 started as a deployment and management tool for high availability Web applications built on the Microsoft Windows 2000 operating system. Using the MS Application Center Application Center 2000 rendered managing groups of servers as simple as managing a single computer.

Due to its quick acceptance and its great scalability, the MS Application Center architecture was widely adopted for the purpose of ensuring mission-critical availability through software scaling. Application Center also provided for the cost-effective and easy management of servers' clusters.

10.6 Application Centers No Longer the Only Sound Implementation

While this new Application Center technology started gaining ground, Windows' users found it simple and very useful. Microsoft continued developing new systems that provided, in addition to interoperability, any tools they needed to provide for the mission-critical availability. The MS Application Center 2000 technology was still useful but the release of the .NET platform and Web Services (SOAP) has just introduced the next generation of Web applications [17]. With this new platform, we can have applications that can communicate and exchange data with diverse platforms inside the organization or with external partners.

Scalability and interoperability have become even stronger with the adoption of Service Oriented Architecture (SOA) application standards. This new generation of Web applications brought the new requirements that applications define and manage as a service.

Microsoft just built the next generation for management tools to meet the challenge of managing applications as a service. Microsoft listed the following benefits of migrating from Application Center 2000:

10.6.1 Increased Security

There is reduction of the attack domain of the Web server; this will lead to increased security. There is even more security when Active Directory Group Policy in the context of a larger of security best practices for managing perimeter network servers. To read more about the security of .NET Web Application, you may refer to a white paper on www.microsoft.com entitled "Managing .NET Web Applications with System Center: How to Migrate from Application Center 2000." [12]

The System Center provides integration of applications and security updates using Systems Management Server (SMS) 2003. It provides a comprehensive solution for change and configuration management for the Microsoft platform, enabling organizations to provide relevant software and updates to users quickly and cost effectively. This application deployment allows a single change and configuration management interface to manage both applications and OS security updates.

10.6.2 Application Rollback

Windows Installer comes with built-in application installation rollback. When the installation fails, all system and application changes are made during installation are undone, leaving the system unchanged. The Windows Installer also provides for rollback of database changes during deployment if an installation fails. That is, we have transaction level change control to Web application deployment.

10.6.3 Integration with Centralized Monitoring

With Microsoft Operations Manager (MOM) 2005, administrators and operators can quickly respond to problems or configure the system to automatically respond to events. The MOM 2005 Operator Console uses a remotely accessible Web page to provide a subset of the Operator Console's functionality, in addition to new reporting tools that can automatically receive new reports.

Availability Reporting provides data that may be viewed and customized based on organizational IT goals. Those reports provide tables and graphs describing the availability and reliability of servers.

Availability Reports include detailed information on availability and reliability for supported MS applications, but only basic availability and reliability statistics at the operating system level for the rest of the applications.

10.6.4 Web Application and Enterprise Monitoring

MOM 2005 provides for leading .NET Web application monitoring with simultaneous monitoring capabilities that allow for integration with available enterprise management systems. It is also possible to design, deploy, and monitor .NET Web services to achieve end-to-end availability.

MOM 2005 Availability Reporting Management Pack collects and analyzes data from the event logs of servers, and generates reports that you can study to improve server availability and reliability. This is useful to identify the causes for planned and unplanned downtime and take preemptive actions to decrease downtime in the future.

There are certainly some limitations associated with all those solutions that replaced the Application Center. For example, while real-time application synchronization, with SMS, can ensure near real-time updates and repairs for Web applications, it does not provide change notification using automatic synchronization that can allow for prompt updating when a server is added or dropped from a given group, even though relatively short update delays may be achieved. There are other limitations related to content management that are left for the interested reader to investigate. You may refer to a white paper entitled "What's New with Content Management Server 2002" on http://www.microsoft.com/cmserver/evaluation/overview/whatsnew.mspx. [13].

10.7 Computation of Availability in High-Availability Cluster

Failover clusters are computer clusters that are implemented primarily for the purpose of improving the availability of services using the computer clustering concept. Computer redundancy is the duplication of critical components of a system in order to

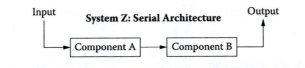

Figure 10.5 A serial architecture for availability.

enhance reliability of the system. This is usually needed to provide backup systems and to absorb failure effects. Failures may be absorbed using fail-safe features that prevent dangers to the computing environment to minimize any negative effects on people.

Computer clustering provides redundant computers that are configured to cooperate in providing service when their system components fail. The availability concept is provided by configuring the computer cluster to provide the failover feature. In order to allow for the failover feature, when a server with a bad application crashes, the application will not be available until this bad component gets fixed so that services of the crashed server can be resumed. Computer clustering solves this problem by detecting the fault, and immediately restarting the application on another system without requiring administrative intervention.

High-availability clustering is costly because of its duplication of resources. It is often employed in file sharing on networks, e-commerce applications, and critical databases. A thorough feasibility study is always needed before determining whether or not high availability is needed and, if so, what clustering architecture will work best for the system in question.

10.7.1 Simple Clustering Architecture

Users only care about end-to-end availability that is directly related to the business processes they need when they attempt to acquire business. That is, system availability should be calculated in terms of all components constituting the system. This may be obtained by modeling the system as an interconnection of parts, often organized in series and parallel. How do we connect system components to achieve higher availability? The following rules are adopted to determine how system components are connected:

Rule 1: If in series, any component that fails results in system failure.
Rule 2: If in parallel, any component that fails results in the other component.

As shown in Figure 10.5, using Rule 1, the two parts A and B are in series, and hence, the failure of either one results in failure of the system.

10.7.2 Serial Availability

The availability of system Z is computed as the product of A's availability and B's availability, as follows:

Table 10.1 Simple Availability Rates for a Serial Architecture

A's Availability	B's Availability	System Availability as a Percentage	System Availability as a Probability
99.00000	99.00000	98.01	0.9801
99.90000	99.90000	99.8001	0.998001
99.99000	99.99000	99.980001	0.99980001
99.99900	99.99900	99.99800001	0.9999800001
99.99990	99.99990	99.9998000001	0.999998000001
99.99999	99.99999	99.999980000001	0.99999980000001

$$a(Z) = a(A) \times a(B).$$

Because availability is always less than or equal to 1, the availability of the system a(Z) is always smaller than or equal to the least availability of the components A and B. That is, $a(Z) \le$ Min (a(A), a(B)).

Table 10.1 provides availability rates for social architecture where two components, A and B, have 2, 3, 4, 5, 6, and 7 availability "nine's."

Table 10.2 provides the downtime in days, hours, minutes, and seconds corresponding to the availability values of the series system Z presented in Table 10.1.

The equation $a(Z) \le$ Min (a(A), a(B)) expresses the weakest link property. That means that even when one of the components, like A in this example, has 7 nine availability, the system's availability will be equal to or smaller than the weakest availability, which is that of B in this example. That is, a chain is as strong as its weakest link. The availability and downtime rates for the serial system, in this case, are provided in Table 10.3, but for different values of A and B.

10.7.3 Parallel Availability

When components operate in parallel, like A and B in Figure 10.6, the system combining them only fails when both fail. That is, the system S is unavailable when both parts A and B are unavailable. We can then write the following:

$$a(S) = 1 - (1 - a(A)(1 - a(B)).$$

You may note that whenever the component A is available, then the system S is available—that is, $P(S) \ge P(A)$. Also, whenever the component B is available, the system S is also available—that is, $P(S) \ge P(B)$. Because S(A) is greater than or equal to P(A) and P(B), we also have S(A) is greater than or equal to the maximum

Table 10.2 Availability and Downtime Rates for a Serial Architecture

Availability Percentage	Availability in Hours	Availability in Days	Downtime in Days	Downtime in Hours	Downtime in Minutes	Downtime in Seconds
98.01	8585.676	357.7365	7.2635	174.324	10459.44	627566.4
99.8001	8742.489	364.2704	0.729635	17.51124	1050.674	63040.46
99.980001	8758.248	364.927	0.072996	1.751912	105.1147	6306.885
99.99800001	8759.825	364.9927	0.0073	0.175199	10.51195	630.7168
99.9998000001	8759.982	364.9993	0.00073	0.01752	1.051199	63.07197
99.999980000001	8759.998	364.9999	7.3E-05	0.001752	0.10512	6.3072

Table 10.3   Availability and Downtime Rates for a Serial Architecture

Comp. A	Comp. B	Availability Percentage	Availability in Hours	Availability in Days	Downtime in Days	Downtime in Hours	Downtime in Minutes	Downtime in Seconds
.9999999	0.99	0.9899999	8672.399	361.35	3.650036	87.60087	5256.052	315363.1
.9999999	0.999	0.9989999	8751.239	364.635	0.365036	8.760875	525.6525	31539.15
.9999999	0.9999	0.9998999	8759.123	364.9635	0.036536	0.876876	52.61255	3156.753
.9999999	0.99999	0.9999899	8759.912	364.9963	0.003686	0.088476	5.308559	318.5136
.9999999	0.999999	0.9999989	8759.99	364.9996	0.000401	0.009636	0.57816	34.6896
.9999999	0.9999999	0.9999998	8759.998	364.9999	7.3E-05	0.001752	0.10512	6.3072

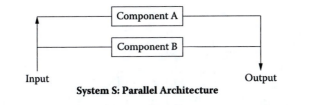

Input   Output

System S: Parallel Architecture

Figure 10.6   A parallel architecture for availability.

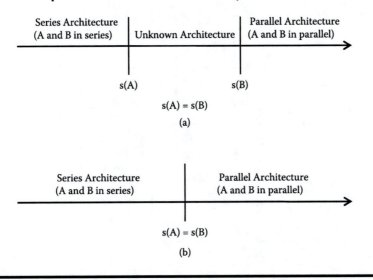

Figure 10.7   A comparison of serial and parallel architecture for availability.

of P(A) and P(B). We can then draw a nice diagram, as shown in Figure 10.7, that explains how availability, is written in terms of the architecture of the system and the availability values of its components.

If A and B have identical availability values, like in Figure 10.7(b), then the space of availability may be divided into two areas: (1) an availability area defined by availability values higher than or equal to a(A) = a(B); (2) an availability area defined by availability values smaller than or equal to a(A)=a(B).

The parallel architecture corresponds to high-availability areas while the serial architecture to a lower availability domain. Table 10.4 gives availability and downtime values in a parallel architecture.

If we examine the diagram in Figure 10.7(a), we see that the only difference between the diagrams in (a) and (b) is that the high availability area and the low availability area are separated by an availability zone [s(A), s(B)] that does not correspond to the high availability area; nor does it correspond to the low availability area. It is somewhere in between; it does not correspond to any one of availability architectures studied, but may be a combination.

Table 10.4 Availability and Downtime Rates for a Parallel Architecture

0.99	0.9999	8759.124	364.9635	0.03650	0.87600	52.56000	3153.60000
0.999	0.999999	8759.991	364.9996	0.00037	0.00876	0.52560	31.53600
0.9999	0.99999999	8760	365	0.00000	0.00009	0.00526	0.31536
0.99999	1	8760	365	0.00000	0.00000	0.00005	0.00315
0.999999	1	8760	365	0.00000	0.00000	0.00000	0.00003
0.9999999	1	8760	365	0.00000	0.00000	0.00000	0.00000

As seen earlier in the availability tables for the parallel and serial architectures, we can now confirm that even though a very low availability for one of the components is used, the overall availability of the system is always much higher for parallel architecture. Thus, parallel architecture offers a very powerful mechanism for making a highly available system from low availability. That is, all mission-critical systems should be configured with redundant parallel components.

10.7.4 Availability Computation

Before providing a formula for computing system downtime, let us agree on some definitions. The length of a year is probably more accurately 365.25 days. Most people, however, use 365 when the year length is included in their computations.

Because most people account for 365 days in a year, we will use this assumption throughout this book. That is, for us, a year is only 365 days. Also, a year is 8760 hours, 525,600 minutes, or 31,536,000 seconds.

The annual uptime of a system is computed as the product of system availability and time length of the year. The annual downtime of a system is equal to the time length of a year minus system annual uptime. We will then have the following:

Period uptime = availability × period time length
Annual uptime = availability × year time length
Annual downtime = year time length – annual uptime
Annual downtime = year time length × (1-availability)

For example, if we consider a system with an availability of 99.98%, then the annual uptime is equal to .9998 × 365 = 364.927 days or 364 days, 22 hours, 14 minutes, and 52.8 seconds. The annual downtime is equal to 0.073 days, 1.752 hours, or 1 hour 45 minutes and 7.2 seconds.

System availability expresses users' perception about systems while system reliability expresses real component failures. While availability distress affects business and may directly affect users, the reliability will directly impact maintenance costs but does not directly impact availability unless business processes are affected.

10.8 Related Availability Definitions

Availability is the probability that a system would operate at a particular point in time. It answers the question: "How likely is it that my system is operating at a specific time?" Availability differs from reliability because it factors repairs into the measurement. To determine availability, the time to perform a repair must be known. Because availability is expressed as a probability, it is a value between 0 and 1. We next present several other definitions that are closely related to availability.

10.8.1 Concepts Closely Related to Availability

10.8.1.1 Downtime or Unavailability

Downtime or unavailability is the compliment of availability. It is a probability value, or a number between 0 and 1, that indicates the likelihood that a system would not be operational at a specified point in time.

10.8.1.2 Reliability

Reliability is the probability that the system would perform as expected without failure for a fixed time period. Reliability takes time into account. The measure of reliability answers the question "How likely is it that my system will remain operational over a period of time?" Because reliability is expressed as a probability, it is always a value between 0 and 1.

10.8.1.3 Fallibility or Unreliability

Fallibility or unreliability is the compliment of reliability. If your reliability is 0.9, the unreliability is equal to $1.0 - 0.9 = 0.1$. It is a probability value, or a number between 0 and 1, that indicates the likelihood that a system would not continuously operate up to a specified point in time.

10.8.1.4 Failure Rate

It is the average number of failures per time unit. For example, if your wireless connection is lost 8 times per month, then your failures rate is $8/(30 \times 24 \times 60) = 1.851$ $e^{-4} = 0.0002$ or 2 per 10,000 minutes. That is, on average, in a period of 10,000 minutes your wireless connection is lost twice.

10.8.1.5 Mean Time between Failures

Mean time between failures (MTBF) is the average number of time units that elapsed between two consecutive failures. If, on average, you can stay connected through your wireless router 1000 minutes without any disconnection, then your MTBF is equal to 1000 minutes. This means that, on average, you can stay connected for 1000 minutes without losing your wireless connection. If we assume a constant failure rate, then the MTBF may be computed as the inverse of the failure rate. For example, if the failure rate is 2 failures per 10,000 minutes, then your MBTF will be equal to $10,000/2 = 5000$ minutes. That is, you can stay connected through your wireless router for about 5000 minutes.

10.8.1.6 Mean Time to Repair

The mean time to repair (MTTR) is the average time to return the failed system to an operable state. This measure is normally expressed in time units and indicates how long it takes to repair a system that is down due to a failure. Although some people do not include logistics time in the MTTR, it is recommended that any elapsed time between failure and the state of operation of the system is accounted for in the MTTR.

System availability may be computed in many ways. We will present the following three methods:

Availability as a percentage
Availability as defect per million
Availability in terms of mean time of failures

10.8.2 Availability versus Defects per Million

Defects per million opportunities (DPMO) is a measurement used to estimate average number of defects in a production phase. It is computed as the ratio of the average number of defects observed to the number of opportunities for a defect to occur during that phase. The ratio is then normalized to the million.

This measurement is useful in any process-based activity. The DPMO will then indicate the number of defects in a process, measured in the number of millions of opportunities. In order to obtain the DPMO we must first calculate the number of defects per opportunity. Once you have the DPO, you multiply by 1,000,000, to get DPMO.

$$DPMO = DPO \times 10^6$$

Process improvement is a very important activity in information security management, as the ISO/IEC 27001 gives specifications for an ISMS that provides continual improvement based on changes in risks and in the performance of security controls. In similar efforts, defects per million opportunities or DPMO is a measure of process performance. In information security management, this concept may be called differently, depending on its use. The DPMO, for example, may be used as the nonconformities per million opportunities (NPMO)), or the violation per million opportunities (VPMO) in information security management when intrusion detection processes are inspected.

In this case:

DPMO = 10^{6*} number of defects/number of units* number of opportunities
NPMO = 10^{6*} number of nonconformities/number of units* number of opportunities
VPMO = 10^{6*} number of violations/number of units* number of opportunities

A defect is defined as a nonconformance of a quality characteristic (e.g., strength, width, response time) to its specification, or a security violation (e.g., unexpected change in indicators, unauthorized attempts by processes, etc). In industrial engineering, the DPMO is stated in opportunities per million units for convenience. Often, only those processes that experience a small number of defects per million units produced are acceptable.

The DPMO concept is indeed a very simple concept, but it should not be confused with the number of defective parts per million (DPPM) because this latter concept does not account for all the defects that cause the part to be defective. In fact there may be many root defects behind this major defect that affected the performance of the defective part. The opportunity for defects is not something easy to capture. A great deal of expertise is needed to account for all defects in a process. The following requirements may be necessary for the valid use of the DPMO concept:

Knowledge of the process under study
Knowledge of Industry standards
Ability to weight defects in a process if multiple types exist
The time, effort, and budget to count and categorize defects

Assume we have a process that makes remote controls that are made from the following parts:

1. Vishay TSOP1138 IR receiver
2. 50v 4.7uF capacitor
3. Two types of bipolar junction transistors: 1N4148 diodes and 4.7K resistors;
4. 7805 voltage regulator

We had a defect detection process capable of identifying 120 opportunities of defection. We also had an inspection station that rejects every unit that has one or more defects.

Assume in a given run, we manufactured 1000 remote controls. In this run alone, we had 100 defects that have been detected by our monitoring process. We however only had 42 units that failed our inspection process and were rejected. The defects were ventilated as follows: 25 defective 1N4148 diodes, 10 missing parts, 25 defective c4.7K resistors, 20 damaged 50v 4.7uF capacitors, 5 missing 7805 voltage regulators, 15 defective Vishay TSOP1138 IR receivers.

Let us sort the breakdown of those defects to identify the parts that contributed most to the number of defective units:

1N4148 diodes: 25
Defective c4.7K resistors: 25
Damaged 50v 4.7uF capacitors: 20
Damaged Vishay TSOP1138 IR receivers: 15

Table 10.5 Equivalence between Availability and DPMO

Availability	DPM
99%	10000
99.9%	1000
99.99%	100
99.999%	10
99.9999%	1

Missing parts: 10
Damaged 7805 voltage regulator: 5

We can easily compute the DPMO and the PDM as follows:

$$DPMO = (10^6 \times 100)/(1000 \times 120) = 833$$

$$DPM = 42/1000 = 42,000$$

In order to relate the DPMO concept to the availability concept, we should view the 99.9999% availability as 999,999 of opportunities free of defects; that is, this availability corresponds to a downtime of 0.000001% which is equivalent to one defect per million of opportunities. Table 10.5 gives the equivalence between 2 to 5 availability 9's and their corresponding DPMO.

10.8.3 Availability versus MTBF and MTTR

MTTR is nothing but an estimate of how long it takes you to restore service in case of failure. Say that your single Web server failed; the MTTR would be the time it takes to call the vendor, order a replacement, rebuild the server, and put it back to work. If the shipment takes 5 days, and all the rest accounts for 3 hours then the total is 5 × 24 = 3 hours. That is, the MTTR is 123 hours. This MTTR could have been reduced if instead of ordering a replacement, you drove to a local store where you acquired your replacement in, say 5 hours. In this case, the MTTR is 5 + 3 = 8 hours.

If we are however dealing with a clustered architecture then the MTTR is the actual time it takes for the high availability software to detect the failure, drop the failing components, and resume operations on a redundant copy of the server. The entire process may take 1 to 3 minutes.

If we have a serial system then the availability of the system is obtained by multiplying the availability of each component together to obtain the overall system availability.

In a clustered system, we have a parallel architecture where all components are required for the system to operate. The components are redundant, and if each of the redundant components is fully functional alone, then the availability of the system is $1 - (1 - A)^n$.

Obviously in the case of redundant components, the system is only failed when both redundant components fail at the same time. That tends to be rare, so redundant systems can have much better availability.

It is also important to understand the relationship between availability, MTBF, and MTTR. This relationship may be simple to comprehend when availability is expressed as the percentage of time the system is though available. The system may be in three states: working, in failure, or being repaired. If we assume that the repair activity starts immediately when failure is detected, the then two states of "in failure," or "being repaired" will be overlapping. That is, the system can only be in one of two states: "working" or "in failure, "or "being repaired." The system availability may be computed as follows:

$$\text{Availability} = \text{MTBF} / (\text{MTBF} + \text{MTTR})$$

Example: Electric Security Gate

A small business owns three facilities built on less than one acre. The property is surrounded by a 5 foot high fence and one strong manual gate. In the last two decades, owners confirmed a fixed failure rate of the gate at twice in 20 years. Every time the gate is broken, it took them on average about 10 hours to fix it.

Given the above information we then have the following:

MTBF = 10 years, 3650 days, or 87600 hours
MTTR = 10 hours

The availability of the gate may be computed as follows:

$$\text{Availability} = 87600 / (87600 + 10)$$

$$= 87600 / 87610 = 99.98858\%.$$

Assume that we remodeled the fence and the gate to add electric power. We now have power supply equipment, an automatic gate, and an electric fence. Figure 10.8 depicts the layout of the physical security at the gate of the small business. Assume the following availability rates:

Electric security gate: 99.98858%.
Power supply: 99.99720%
Perimeter Fence: 99.99860%

The overall availability of the gate is computed as shown in Figure 10.9.

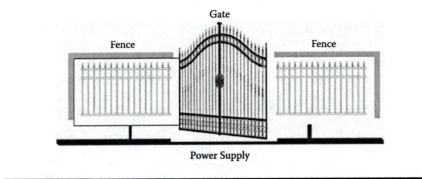

Figure 10.8   Physical security in serial.

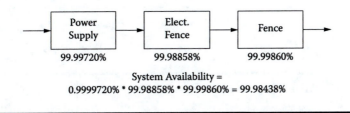

System Availability =
0.9999720% * 99.98858% * 99.99860% = 99.98438%

Figure 10.9   Availability serial architecture for the gate problem.

10.8.4 Computing Availability for Mixed Architecture

We next provide two examples, in Figures 10.10 and 10.11, with mixed architectures. These are two generic layouts that do not require further discussion. We show the layout and the computing for intermediary availability values and the overall availability.

10.9 How to Obtain Higher Availability: The Cisco Process

The case study presented a sequence of steps that lead Cisco to achieve 99.999%. Cisco's global backbone network connects more than 40,000 employees and contractors. They have nodes at 15 locations on four continents. They started with an initial design with backup routers and circuits that nearly eliminated hardware failure and which brought availability to 99.975%.

Cisco had the goal of achieving 99.999% network availability, with 6 seconds of downtime per week.

Based on the steps that Cisco followed to achieve 99.999% availability, other companies with similar conditions may achieve a similar availability. Proposing the same steps to other enterprises will make more sense if they use the same technology.

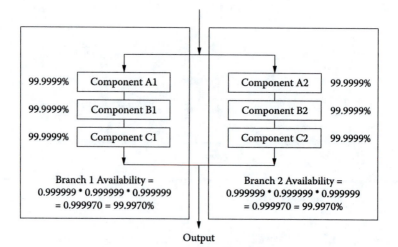

Output

System Availability = $1-(1- a(\text{Branch 1}) (1- a(\text{Branch 2}) = 99.9999\%$

Figure 10.10 Mixed architecture for availability.

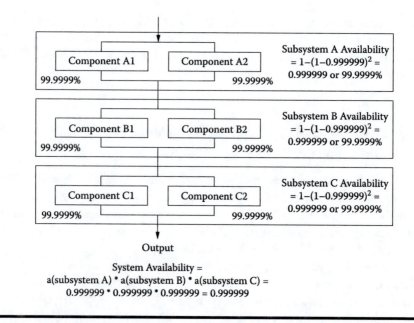

Output

System Availability =
a(subsystem A) * a(subsystem B) * a(subsystem C) =
0.999999 * 0.999999 * 0.999999 = 0.999999

Figure 10.11 A second example of mixed architecture for availability.

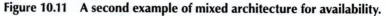

Let us propose Cisco steps as a model for any enterprise that is seeking to achieve high availability. Achieving the five nines of availability may be your goal, but even though your enterprise may not be in the same conditions, as soon as it is feasible, your enterprise has nothing to lose, and can only benefit considerably from following the same Cisco steps.

10.9.1 Feasibility Requirement for Higher Availability

Any enterprise that is interested in following the same steps may have to embed feasibility in every step. Feasibility has to be studied on all of its components: economical, social, operational, technical, and legal/ethical.

10.9.1.1 Economical Feasibility of Availability

Availability should be always be tied to the relevant business processes. Availability for those processes will ensure that end-to-end availability is maintained, and customers will not be lost because a weak link was faulty. The capability of the steady generation of business value through highly available business processes is needed.

10.9.1.2 Social Feasibility of Availability

Some social benefits may be associated with certain features that come with the system availability deployed to provide valuable business functions or processes. For example, the high availability of biometric devices, as iris scanners or fingerprints, deployed 24 hours a day in major entries to the company for the purpose of authenticating employees at every gate may not be socially feasible. Some employees are not willing to enroll in iris scanner databases and similar programs, fearing that their iris scan or fingerprints may be easily corrupted or transferred to imposters.

10.9.1.3 Operational Feasibility of Availability

The most common hurdle in operational feasibility is associated with employees' resistance to using the new technology. As employees may not be willing to stand in front of a digital camera for an iris scan to authenticate their identity. Operational feasibility will affect the availability requirements related to the deployment of those iris scanners. Any security technology has to be confirmed in terms of its operational feasibility for availability.

10.9.1.4 Technical Feasibility for Availability

As we discussed earlier, availability has to be tied to the business processes identified as part of the end-to-end availability requirements. The solution for providing for the availability of relevant systems has to be technically feasible. If the solution cannot be technically available, then the solution will not be delivering the availability requirements set for end-to-end availability. For example, the iris scanner discussed earlier may not be technically feasible if the technology prescribed is not available in the market.

Another example may be a cryptographic mechanism that is part of the solution some system owners want to adopt in Iran to provide for the required availability. If the cryptographic mechanism employs a 256-bit-long key that can only be obtained from the United States and if this chip is not exportable, then the cryptographic solution would not be technically feasible for availability in Iran.

10.9.1.5 Legal/Ethical Feasibility of Availability

The availability of systems should not be provided for if there are laws being broken or any code of ethics being violated.

10.9.2 How to Conduct Cisco Phases

Cisco proposes a three-phase process to achieve higher availability [4]:

Phase 1: Establish reliable availability measurements.
Phase 2: Identify key design and procedural gaps and move to four nines availability (99.99%).
Phase 3: Execute process to upgrade programs and move to five nines availability (99.999%).

10.9.2.1 Phase 1: Measure Availability

The availability measurement is probably the most important phase of Cisco phases. Obviously, if we cannot measure availability, then we cannot improve it. If we were to follow the steps Cisco proposed, we then have to proceed as follows:

Adopt an in-house enterprise management system with sound availability measurement. If those measurements are accessible, then it makes sense to use them. This should save time and cost. Also, do not forget the prior acceptance by management of the availability solution, which will also generate better support by management in any efforts directed towards securing higher availability that is clearly linked to business processes.
Build composite host availability metrics with more meaning for all. The effort of writing availability metrics for all the identified end-to-end availability resources has to be translated into new metrics that apply to the internal network.
Use overall availability measures instead of the availability of individual components. The concept of end-to-end availability requires that we apply a wider

view that includes all components together instead of focusing on individual components. That said, if the effort of translating the host availability metrics defined in the former step into network metrics is successful, then the aggregation of the metrics will be easy to achieve. The fact that the similar and consistent metrics are applied for the hosts and the active network means that we can then guarantee that availability data conflicts will be at a minimum.

10.9.2.2 Phase 2: The Four Nines' Availability

We have seen that the first phase of achieving higher availability was concerned with measurements that start with hosts, translate to the entire network, and then get aggregated to provide for measuring the end-to-end availability scope. This phase will be more concerned with the stability of available systems, which may be achieved with the adoption with accepted configurations and applicable standards. The following steps are needed:

Implement an IP addressing plan that allows route summarization, which simplifies the routing design and reduces instability: Some IP addressing plans produce results that may not be easily interpreted to detect traffic irregularities that are indicative of potential failures. The IP addressing plan that allows route summarization provides a better visualization of patterns that can be easily recognized as triggers for faults and undesired events.

Deploy standard hardware and up-to-date Cisco IOS software releases to simplify network growth, operations, and support: If your enterprise is using Cisco equipment, then standard hardware and Cisco software can add efficiency to your system availability management efforts.

Enforce standard configurations on network devices to reduce problems created by variances and errors: Tested configurations on network devices will obviously add stability, but are there better configurations that have not yet been confirmed but that are worthwhile to experiment with to provide better results? The answer is yes, but if the five nines' are achieved at this stage using the standard configurations on hand, then testing what the untested configurations can give is unnecessary. The third phase will be dealing with several components that have to be thoroughly studied in order add more availability. However, can any of the untested configurations for some of the network devices lead to availability higher than 99.99 or even a five nines' availability?

10.9.2.3 Phase 3: Five Nines' Availability

This phase is concerned with refining operational and support procedures. In fact, this phase contains almost what everybody else does to achieve better availability. Most people, however, have not given importance to measurements and remained attached to standard configuration as success factors for achieving higher network availability.

The three-phase process to achieve higher availability proposed by Cisco is a very powerful means to gain greater availability, but the numbers claimed remain to be tested. Even if achieved at the levels claimed, those numbers may change when network conditions change. This, however, does not diminish anything from the effectiveness of the methodology. In fact, a different enterprise with a smaller computing environment that applies the same proposed phases may achieve even better results than those claimed by Cisco. The method is different from what is seen elsewhere in the literature; imposing measurements and the adoption of standard configurations for telecommunication devices are prerequisite for the success of achieving higher availability through the deployment of the procedures listed in the third phase. For smaller enterprises, higher availability and improved operations may be achieved through the adoption of easier steps than the ones proposed by Cisco.

Cisco reported the achievement of the following results:

Increased network availability to 99.998%
Reduced support staff to a single engineer
Freed other support engineers to work on new programs
Improved network design, standard equipment and configurations, and processes for management and support

Independent of the urgency for applying any phases and steps provided earlier, it is important to accept that the following are outcomes that any availability enhancement effort should seek:

Network design: Facility and circuit planning; resilient technologies for redundancy and fault tolerance
Network management: Host definitions and out-of-band management paths to simplify problem resolution
Network operations: Best practices for Cisco IOS Software upgrades and network changes to reduce disruptions
Fault management and network support: Monitors, alerts, and event procedures to quickly identify problems and minimize impact

10.10 Common Configurations for Clusters

If one node in the cluster fails, then the active cluster will *failover* to another node which will become active. If the failed node is back online, a *failback* can be manually initiated or automatically configured in the cluster group properties.

Every cluster node must have two network interfaces: one network interface for the cluster communication called the private LAN, and one network interface called the public LAN. You can link a cluster with two nodes with a simple cross link cable. If more than two nodes exist in the cluster you have to use a dedicated switch.

The private network interface card is used for the cluster communication. This cluster communication, which is often called the "heartbeat," is much like a ping which can be used to test if the other cluster node is still available. If the heartbeat fails, the failover process occurs.

We next provide several configurations that one finds in cluster implementations: active/active, active/passive, N + 1, N + M, N-to-1, and N-to-N.

10.10.1 Common Cluster Configurations

Let us present some useful cluster configurations. A brief definition is provided, but students are encouraged to obtain further information from the Internet literature [15].

Active/active: In this configuration, the traffic intended for the failed node is either passed onto an existing node or load balanced across the remaining nodes. The latter option requires a homogeneous software configuration.

Active/passive: This configuration provides a fully redundant instance of each node. A node is only brought online when its associated primary node fails. This configuration typically requires the most extra hardware.

N + 1: The N+1 configuration has one node responsible for several active nodes. This one node must be capable of assuming any of the roles the active nodes are responsible for. This configuration provides a single extra node that is brought online to take over the role of the node that has failed. In the case of heterogeneous software configuration on each primary node, the extra node must be universally capable of assuming any of the roles of the primary nodes it is responsible for. This normally refers to clusters that have multiple services running simultaneously. In the case of a single service, this situation is reduces active/passive configuration.

N + M: The N-to-N configuration is a combination of active/active and N + M configurations. In this configuration, each node is active but is capable of reconfiguring themselves to take on any of the responsibilities of the other nodes. This configuration will eliminate the need for back-up nodes but will require additional space on each active node. Whichever configuration is used, a well engineered high availability cluster, along with strong protection against malicious activity, can give your business users a network with consistent availability. The N + M configuration is very similar to the N + 1 configuration but is more useful for large networks where one back-up node is not sufficient to provide high availability. In the N + M configuration, there are several (M) back-up nodes, each able to assume the role of any of the active nodes. This configuration requires that M standby servers are included and available. This is required when a single cluster is managing many services, having only one dedicated failover node. This, however, may not offer sufficient redundancy. The number of standby servers is determined by balancing cost and reliability requirements.

N-to-1: This configuration allows the failover standby node to become the active one temporarily, until the original node can be restored or brought back online, at which point the services or instances must be failed-back to it in order to restore high availability.

N-to-N: This is a combination of active/active, N + M clusters, and N-to-N clusters that can redistribute the services or instances from the failed node among the remaining active nodes. This will eliminate (as with active/active) the need for a standby node, but will require the need for extra capacity on all active nodes.

Related to any high-availability cluster, two terms are usually used to mean the same thing: logical host and cluster logical host. They both describe the network address used to access services provided by the cluster. This logical host is not linked to a single cluster node. It is, instead, a network address/hostname that is linked with the service(s) provided by the cluster. If a cluster node with a running resource goes down, the information resource will be restarted on another cluster node, and the network address that the users use to access the resource will be brought up on the new node as well so that users can access the database again.

10.10.2 Minimal Cluster Design Requirements

Before determining whether or not cluster computing is needed for some business functions, it is important to complete a feasibility study to define the cluster configuration that should be in place. Any cluster computing decision has to be made early at the software analysis and design phases. In order to provide for a high-availability cluster environment, an application must provide at least for the following technical requirements:

The cluster software should include a mechanism that can easily start, stop, and check the status of the application. The application may probably need to have a command line interface or scripts to control the application.

The application should use shared storage.

The application should store as much as possible of its state on nonvolatile shared storage. The application should be able to restart on another node at the last state before failure after obtaining the saved state from the shared storage.

The application should not corrupt data when it crashes or restarts from the saved state. The last two properties are critical to provide for a reliable functionality in a cluster, and are the most difficult to fully satisfy.

10.10.3 Redundancy Reliability

High-availability clusters should be feasibly designed in terms of available approaches. The following approaches are some examples:

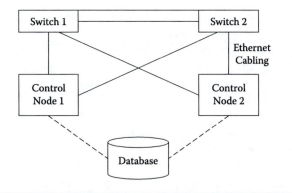

Figure 10.12   Network redundancy.

Disk mirroring: This will prevent the failure of internal disks resulting in a system crash. Disk mirroring, also known as RAID, is the replication of logical disk volumes onto separate physical hard disks in real time to ensure continuous availability. A mirrored volume is a complete logical representation of separate volume copies. RAID 1 creates a mirror, or an identical copy, of a file system on two or more disks. This is effective only when read performance or reliability are more important than data storage capacity. A classic RAID 1 mirrored pair contains two disks, which increases reliability geometrically over a single disk. In a RAID 1 system, if we assume two similar models with a monthly probability of .005, then this means that among 1000 disk units installed about five of them will fail in one month. The probability that RAID 1 would fail is equal to the probability that two disk units simultaneously fail. This probability is equal to .005 × .005 = .000025 or .0025%.

Redundant network: As shown in Figure 10.12, a redundant network provides connections so that single cable, switch, or network interfaces failures do not result in network outages.

High-availability clustering: May be implemented in different ways, but they mostly implement redundancy into a computer cluster in order to eliminate single points of failure. If one network crashes, you may want to have a second one capable of picking up the data traffic and allowing you to use the same resources that you attempted to connect to on the crashing network. The network switches may be made redundant so that if one network fails, another takes over. In the event of a total network failure, in which network cables are disconnected and all the heartbeat network connections between the dual-control nodes fail, both nodes should promptly detect the problem. However, they also detect that the SCSI (Small Computer System Interface, a standard parallel interface between computers and peripheral devices) disk connections to the shared partition are still active. Therefore, services continue to run and are not interrupted. High-availability clusters often use a heartbeat private network connection, which is needed to monitor the health and status of each node in the cluster. Problems, including information corruption that may take place if both networks go down while the nodes remain operating; as a given node, my request resources are ready and active on other nodes. Duplicate instances of services may cause information corruption on the shared resources.

Some redundancy systems may be seen, nowadays implemented in most companies with large computing environments. We provide the following examples:

Redundant storage area network (SAN): SAN data connections are needed so that single cable, switch, or interface failures do not lead to loss of connectivity to the storage. A storage area network, as shown in Figure 10.13, is an architecture needed to attach remote computer storage devices, like disk units or any other storage, to servers where the operating system will treat the device as locally mounted. Due to their high costs, the SAN technology tends to be found more in larger organizations.

Network-attached storage (NAS): An alternative to SAN, NAS employs file-based protocols such as NFS when the storage looks remote, and computers request a portion of an abstract file instead of a disk block.

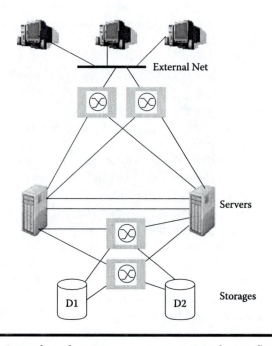

Figure 10.13 Example of a storage area network configured for high availability.

Redundant electrical power: Electrical power inputs on different circuits, usually both or all protected by uninterruptible power supply (UPS) units, and redundant power supply units, so that single power feed, cable, UPS, or power supply failures do not lead to loss of power to the system.

Uninterruptible power supply (UPS): An uninterruptible power supply, also known as an *uninterruptible power source, uninterruptible power system, continuous power supply* (CPS), or a *battery backup,* constitutes a unit that maintains a continuous supply of electric power to connected equipment by supplying power from a separate source when the utility power goes down. A UPS is typically used to protect computers, telecommunication equipment, or other electrical equipment where an unexpected power disruption could cause injuries, fatalities, serious business disruption, or data loss. There are three distinct types of UPS: *offline, line-interactive,* and *double conversion* (also called *online*).

An offline UPS remains idle until a power failure occurs. It then switches from utility power to its own power source, almost instantaneously.

An online UPS continuously powers the protected load from its reserves (usually lead-acid batteries or stored kinetic energy), while simultaneously replenishing the reserves from the AC power. On-line UPS provides protection against complete failure of the utility supply. It also provides protection against all common power problems. It is also known as a *power conditioner* and *line conditioner.*

10.11 Self-Healing and Availability

Every user has dreamed of having a computer that could one day either start by avoiding a recognized component failure, stop the failures, plan a response, and recover from it. Imagine having Unix handling the error messages for you and taking corrective actions in your place [6]. Of course, even though Unix has syslog services that provide error logging, the creators of Unix were not concerned about fault management issues, and they have not embedded features capable of handling complex errors and diagnosing and correcting the system.

Lately, we have started seeing, although still outside the operating system itself, policies and advanced features capable of conducting fault diagnosis, incident response, and system management added to system configurations. Those features are found as hardware, firmware, or patches provided by vendors. That is, the system administrator still has to dig in the log files and manually diagnose, recognize, and respond as appropriate.

An example of vendors who added those capabilities to Unix is Sun, which has designed a new flexible architecture capable of building and deploying self-healing technology, and has implemented this architecture in the Solaris 10. The new software architecture and management tools offer a new model for how to build a self-healing system.

The self-healing architecture will permit rapid conversion of other hardware and software components, as well as adaptation of the technology to other parts of Sun's product line. Sun has identified the following advantages associated with its predictive self-healing feature:

1. Simplifies the task of composing, configuring, and deploying high-availability solutions and continuously measuring their availability;
2. Maximizes the availability of the system and services once deployed by automatically diagnosing, isolating, and recovering from faults and being predictive and proactive wherever possible;
3. Guides system administrators through any tasks that require human intervention, including repairs, and explain problems detected or predicted in the system using clear, concise language and links to continuously updated repair procedures and documentation;
4. Enhances the data-driven feedback loop between the organization (Sun, in this case, but other companies can benefit from the same) and customers to ensure continuous improvement in product quality for both deployed and future products.

10.12 Summary

This chapter defined several concepts related to system availability. We emphasized the importance of higher availability in the generation of business value. Web site availability was related to Web site scalability and Web cluster affinity. We presented a cluster computing taxonomy where four categories are introduced: higher-availability, high-performance, load-balancing, and grid computing clusters.

The chapter also showed how to compute availability for systems with serial, parallel, and mixed architectures. We also presented Cisco's approach to higher availability. This is a simple methodology that companies of different sizes can adopt to obtain the levels of availability the need.

10.13 Review Questions

1. Explain how a generic cluster framework works.
2. Load-balancing clusters are implemented by distributing a workload evenly over multiple back end nodes. Search the Internet and find out how this process works.

3. List, define, and give examples for cluster types defined in this chapter.
4. Explain Web availability. Give an example of how availability of a Web site is useful in maintaining a profitable e-business.
5. Explain Web scalability. Give an example of how scalability of a Web site is useful in maintaining a profitable e-business.
6. Explain Web affinity. Give an example of how affinity is useful in providing for Web site availability.
7. The MS Application Center concept is a very important design needed to provide for availability. Explain what happened in Microsoft that led them to discontinue the Application Center.
8. What does Microsoft now offer to provide for Web site availability?
9. What is SOA? Why is it so useful? Also search the Internet to know more about the evolution of SOA. Explain your findings.
10. Give an example of a serial system with three components. Show how to compute the availability of the system.
11. Give an example of a parallel system with three components. Show how to compute the availability of the system.
12. Give an example of a system with a mixed architecture (serial + parallel) that has five components. Show how to compute the availability of the system.
13. Explain how to compute the availability of a system using information on the MTBF and MTTR on its components. Give an example.
14. Explain how to use the DPMO to estimate the availability of a system. Give an example.
15. Explain how the Cisco approach to higher availability works.
16. Can we apply the Cisco approach for higher availability to a small business? What will happen if we do?
17. Explain the feasibility of availability for a small business. Do all small business need to invest in higher availability?
18. Explain the minimal availability design requirements for a simple cluster.
19. List and define alternate solutions to provide for redundancy.
20. Explain self-healing and how it relates to availability.
21. List possible cluster configurations provided in this chapter and explain the differences in terms of how failover is processed.

10.14 Workshops

Workshop 1

A small business desires to host its own Web site. This business will provide an affordable service to parents in the northeastern United States. It is expected that this business will attract about 10,000 customers.

1. Explain the feasibility of higher availability for this small business.
2. Give a cluster design that is appropriate to this business.
3. Show how scalability can be guaranteed.
4. Does it matter in terms of feasibility if a Microsoft platform or Unix is assumed?
5. Does it matter in terms of better availability if a Microsoft platform or Unix is assumed? Explain.

References

1. Amdahl, G., Validity of the Single Processor Approach to Achieving Large-Scale Computing Capabilities, *AFIPS Conference Proceedings* (30), pp. 483–485, 1967.
2. Buyya, R., and S. Venugopal, A Gentle Introduction to Grid Computing and Technologies, Computer Society of India, http://www.buyya.com/papers/GridIntro-CSI2005.pdf, accessed on November 6, 2008.
3. Choi, D. J., P. Tooby, and N. Wilkins-Diehr, Supercomputing on Demand: SDSC Supports Event-Driven Science, CT *Watch Quarterly*, Volume 4 Number 1 March 2008.
4. Cisco IT Best Practices: How Capnet achieved high availability, http://www.cisco.com/Web/about/ciscoitatwork/downloads/ciscoitatwork/pdf/how_cisco_it_achieved_a_highly_available_wide_area_network.pdf.
5. Garuda: The National Grid Computing Initiative, The Department of Information Technology (DIT), Government of India, http://www.garudaindia.in, accessed on November 6, 2008.
6. Herder, J. N., Bos, H., Gras, B., Homburg, P., and A. S., Tanenbaum, The Design and Implementation of a Fully-Modular, Self-Healing, UNIX-Like Operating System Technical Report IR-CS-020, February 2006, http://www.cs.vu.nl/~jnherder/ir-cs-020.pdf, accessed on November 6, 2008.
7. Iqbal, S., R. Gupta, and Y. C. Fang, Planning Considerations for Job Scheduling in HPC Clusters http://www.dell.com/downloads/global/power/ps1q05-20040135-Fang.pdf, accessed on November 6, 2008.
8. Kopper, K., *The Linux Enterprise Cluster: Build a highly available cluster with commodity hardware and free software*, No Starch Press.
9. Kronenberg, N. P., H. M. Levy, W. D. Strecker, and R. J. Merewood, The VAXcluster Concept: An Overview of a Distributed System, Digital Technical Journal No. 5 September 1987, http://maben.homeip.net:8217/static/S100/DEC/magazine/dtj_v01-05_sep1987.pdf
10. Microsoft .NET, What is .NET Microsoft Framework? http://www.microsoft.com/net/ accessed on November 6, 2008.
11. Microsoft Technet, Network Load Balancing parameters 2005, http://technet.microsoft.com/en-us/library/bb687542.aspx, accessed on November 6, 2008.
12. MS White Paper 1: Managing .NET Web Applications with System Center: How to Migrate from Application Center 2000, http://download.microsoft.com/download/b/8/e/b8e15f0d-9cde-49b9-9081-f1728168d06b/Managing_NET_Web_Applications_with_System_Center_Whitepaper.doc, accessed on November 6, 2008.

13. MS White Paper 2: What's new with Content Management Server 2002 on http://www.microsoft.com/cmserver/evaluation/overview/whatsnew.mspx, accessed on November 6, 2008.
14. OSG: Distributed Computing Grid for data-intensive research, Open Science Grid, http://www.opensciencegrid.org, accessed on November 6, 2008.
15. Pfister, G., *In search of clusters, 2nd edition,* Prentice Hall PTR, 1997.
16. Reynolds, J., and A. Kaur, Content Management, Microsoft Enterprise Services White Paper, April 2000, http://www.microsoft.com/technet/archive/itsolutions/ecommerce/maintain/operate/contmgt.mspx?mfr=true, accessed on November 6, 2008.
17. Seely, S., and K. Sharkey, *SOAP: Cross platform Web services development using XML,* Pearson Education, 2001.
18. VECC: Variable Energy Cyclotron Centre, Department of Atomic Energy, Government of India, http://www.veccal.ernet.in/ accessed on November 6, 2008.

SECURITY DESIGN IV

Chapter 11

Nominal Security Enhancement Design Based on ISO/IEC 27002

Learning Objectives

After reading this chapter, students are expected to achieve an understanding of:

The ISO/IEC 27002
The history of ISO/IEC 27002
How to use the ISO/IEC to enhance security
How to measure the current security posture of an organization
How to implement the ISO/IEC 27002
How to check an organization's compliance with the ISO/IEC 27002
Using the ISO/IEC as a rule-based system
Performing a sensitivity analysis to tone up the security posture
Enhancing security posture using ISO/IEC 27002
Strategies to enhance security posture
The differences between the strategies to enhance security posture

11.1 Introduction

This chapter discusses the international standard ISO/IEC 27002. We present its structure, its 12 security objectives, 39 security practices, and its 135 security controls. We discuss how an organization can use the ISO/IEC 27002 for simple compliance or to enhance its security posture. We present five security enhancement strategies that are based on cost reduction, impact level reduction, threat likelihood reduction, vulnerability reduction, and security control effectiveness enhancement. We also provide generic computing support to most of the methods presented.

The British Standard Institute (BSI) defines an information security management system (ISMS) to be a systematic approach to managing sensitive company information so that it remains secure. It encompasses people, processes, and IT systems. Two international standards, originally developed in the BSI provide guidance and requirements towards achieving the ISMS: ISO/IEC 27001 and ISO/IEC 27002. The ISO/IEC 27002 is the new name for the ISO/IEC 17799.

The ISO/IEC 2702 is an introduction to the practice of information security and describes the key controls necessary to ensure an effective security implementation. On the other hand, the ISO/IEC 27001 specifies the requirements for establishing, implementing, and documenting an information security management system (ISMS) and forms the basis for an assessment of the ISMS. The standard requires a risk assessment and the identification of the most appropriate control objectives. A set of detailed controls are then described which can be used to achieve the control objectives as applicable.

11.2 History of the ISO/IEC 27002

ISO is the International Organization for Standardization. It was founded in Geneva, Switzerland, in 1947. Its purpose is to develop standards that support and facilitate international trade. Also in Geneva, Switzerland, is IEC, the International Electrotechnical Commission. It was founded as early as in 1906. Its purpose is to develop standards for all types of electronic technologies.

BS7799 was introduced by the British Standard Institute, in 1995, as a national security standard. This standard emerged as a result of developing an earlier set of regulations initiated by the British Department of Trade and Industry, in 1992, under the title Code of Practice for Information Security Management.

Some initial opposition slowed down its acceptance in the community, but the standard was then rapidly developed and gained more supporters. A new version of the standard that included accreditation and certification requirements was published in 1999. Despite the great enhancement of the standard the international community did not initially look favorably at the standard. The big six, including the United States, United Kingdom, Canada, France, Germany, and the

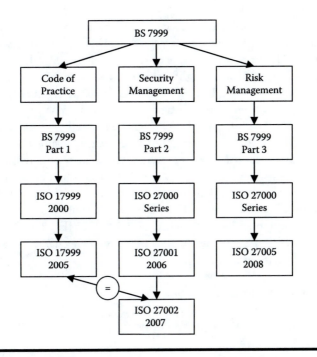

Figure 11.1   History of BS 7799.

Netherlands were still busy working out their differences toward finalizing the ISO 15408, also known as the Common Criteria.

In December 2000, the first part of BS7799 became the ISO 17799. The British Standard Institute has now more acceptance worldwide and was encouraged to publish the second part of the BS7799 in 2002. This part is concerned with the information security management system (ISMS).

The 2000 version of the ISO 17799 describes 127 security controls organized into 10 major sections. Each section specializes in one security area. The security areas are not necessarily independent but they represent each a set of countermeasures that are concerned with a very well-defined security objective. The standard emphasizes the role of security risk management in determining the security controls that have to be implemented. Only considered are those security controls that are relevant to your business process and that can feasibly contribute in mitigating risks. Figure 11.1 presents the history of BS 7799 in terms of the sequential emergence of those international security standards that originated from the BS 7799 standard.

11.3 ISO/IEC 27002

The ISO/IEC 27002 Code of Practice for Information Security Management establishes guidelines and general principles for organizations to initiate, implement, maintain, and improve information security management. This standard provides general guidance on the commonly accepted goals of information security management. Table 11.1 provides the table of contents of the ISO/IEC 27002, which should give you a good idea about the structure of the standard.

As you may see in Table 11.1, the ISO/IEC 27002 is organized into sections. There are 12 sections, from Section 4 on page 5 to Section 15 on page 100. Every section, in the standard, as introduced above, will be referred to as a security objective throughout this book. Each security objective consists of a subset of security practices that have to be adopted in order to achieve the security objective. Each security practice consists of several security controls that have to be implemented in order to adopt the security practices in question. Figure 11.2 depicts the structure linking the security objectives, security practices, and security controls recommended in the code of practice proposed by the ISO/IEC 17799 or ISO/IEC 27002 standards.

The ISO/IEC 27002 standard consists of the following 12 sections:

The content sections are:

C1. Risk assessment and treatment
C2. Security policy
C3. Organization of information security
C4. Asset management
C5. Human resources security
C6. Physical and environmental security
C7. Communications and ops management
C8. Access control
C9. Information systems acquisition, development, maintenance
C10. Information security incident management
C11. Business continuity
C12. Compliance

Every section in the ISO/IEC 27002 is organized into three parts: (1) the title of the section representing the name for the security objective sought in this security section; (2) one or more first-order subtitles representing the security practices; and (3) one ore more second-order subtitles representing the security controls recommended by the standard.

A simple scheme to study the code of practice provided by the ISO/IEC 27002 is to probably adopt a knowledge-based approach that is needed just for restructuring the layout of the standard. The knowledge-based approach suggests that the standard may be interpreted in terms of the structure or scheme shown in Figure 11.3. The security controls, security practices, and security objectives are called the "a," "b, " and "c" concepts, respectively. That is, we have 12 "c" concepts, 39 "b" concepts, and 135 "a" concepts. A "c" concept can only be valid if the corresponding "b" concepts are valid which, in their turn, can only be valid if the corresponding "a" concepts are valid.

Table 11.1   Table of Contents of ISO/IEC 27002

Continued

Table 11.1   Table of Contents of ISO/IEC 27002 (*Continued*)

Table 11.1   Table of Contents of ISO/IEC 27002 (*Continued*)

Continued

Table 11.1   Table of Contents of ISO/IEC 27002 (*Continued*)

We now have restructured the ISO/IEC 27002 for the purpose of easing the interpretation of the code of practice. We still need to determine the approach we will adopt in studying the effects of the implemented security controls on the security objectives defined by the security goals constituting the code of practice. We propose a simulation approach to study the effect of the ISO/IEC 27002 on enhancing the security posture of the organization. This simulation is knowledge-based in terms of the rule base structure of the ISO/IEC 27002 presented earlier.

The standard recommends a set of 10 security objectives to be feasibly achieved. For each security objective, the standard defines a subset of security practices that have to be adopted in order to achieve the security objective. For each security prac-tice, the standard defines a subset of security controls that have to be implemented in order to adopt the security practice. The structure of dependence between secu-rity objectives, security practices, and security controls may be depicted as follows.

11.4 How to Use the ISO/IEC 27002 to Enhance Security

The ISO/IEC 27002 standard expresses the recommended code of practice in terms of

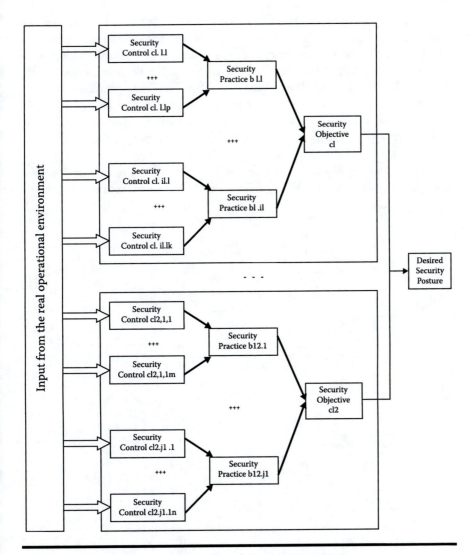

Figure 11.2   The rule-based structure of the ISO/IEC 27002.

12 security objectives
39 security practices
135 security controls

The structure presented in Figure 11.4 shows how the process approach can be used to tone up the security objectives toward the desired levels of security posture, usually set in the corporate security policy. The toning up of security objectives is achieved by adjusting the values of the inputs to the 135 security controls of the ISO/IEC 27002 standard. These values are taken from the operational environment by measuring the appropriate computing parameters that owners and auditors think have effects on the security controls. The outputs from the 135 security controls are input to the 39 security practices and the outputs of the security practices serve as inputs to the 12 security objectives.

After examining Figure 11.5, we can see that the standard recommends a security objective called "Security Policy." This security objective requires two security

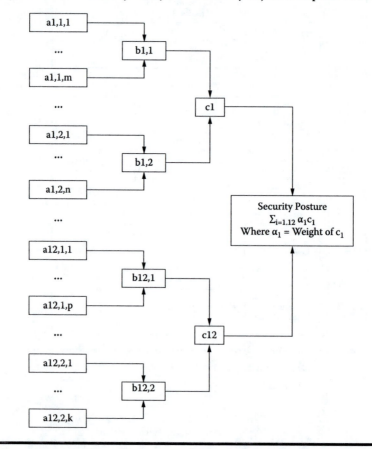

Figure 11.3 Knowledge-based approach to evaluate security in ISO/IEC 27002.

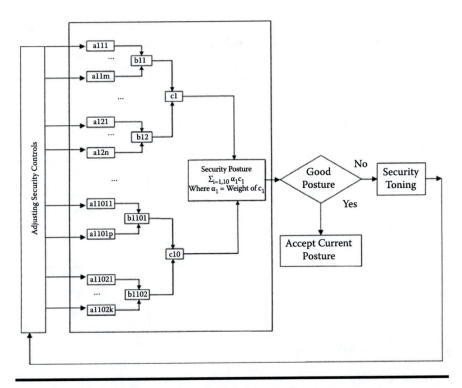

Figure 11.4   Simulation process in toning the security posture.

Figure 11.5   Section 5 of the ISO 27002.

practices called "Information security policy document" and "Review of the information security policy. " The first security practice requires eight security controls, and the second security practice requires three security controls.

The notation we employ in presenting the knowledge-based approach of the standard is "c" for security objectives, "b" for security practices, and "a" for security controls. Table 11.2 provides an example that has the notation employed to represent the knowledge contained in the fifth section of the standard in pages 7 through 8.

The ISO/IEC 27002 does not provide requirements but a code of practice. The code of practice is a knowledge base defining 12 security areas or security objectives $\{c1, ..., c12\}$. Each security objective c_i, $i = 1,12$, is written in terms of several practices b_{ij}, $i = 1,12$, and $j = 1, j_i$ where j_i is the number of practices that have to be adopted in order to achieve the security objective c_i.

Table 11.2 Knowledge-Based Structure for Security Objective c2: Organization of Information Security

Security Objective	Security Practice	Security Control
c2	b2.1	a2.1.1
		a2.1.2
		a2.1.3
		a2.1.4
		a2.1.5
		a2.1.6
		a2.1.7
		A2.1.8
	b2.2	a2.2.1
		a2.2.2
		A2.2.3

Rule Base Structure:

IF: a2.1.1-a1.1.8 THEN: b2.1;

IF: a2.2.1 -a2.2.3 THEN: b2.2.

That is, in order to achieve the security objective c_i, the organization has to adopt the security practices b_{ij}, $j = 1, j_i$. This may be represented as decision rule as shown in Figure 11.6.

The structure above defines a decision rule expressing how the security objective c_i can be achieved by adopting the security practices b_{ij}, $j = 1, i_i$ as recommended in ISO/IEC 20072.

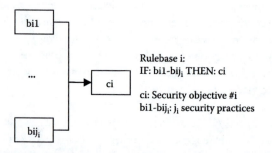

Figure 11.6 Security objective ci achieved by adopting the security practices bij, j = 1,iⱼ as recommended in ISO/IEC 20072.

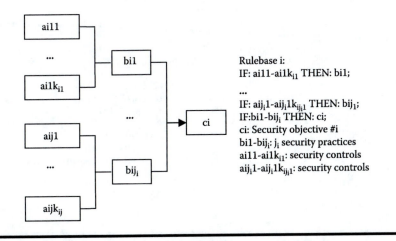

Figure 11.7   Full rule for a security objective in ISO/IEC 27002.

This structure can help the organization in determining the security practices b_{ij}, $j = 1, j_i$ to be adopted and the levels of adoption needed to produce the level of satisfaction of the security objective ci. Every selected security practice will incur some costs depending on the level of adoption. The structure allows for a sensitivity analysis that helps the organization determine, for each security practice, its target level of adoption.

Moreover, each security practice requires a set of security controls that have to be carried out if this practice is adopted. If we consider the security practice b_{ij}, for example, the security controls a_{ijk}, $k = 1, k_{ij}$ have to be carried out. The structure representing this type of knowledge is depicted in the rule base shown in Figure 11.7.

The knowledge management method adopted in studying the ISO/IEC 20072 standard allows for what-if simulations where the organization can get to the desired risk position by trying different security practices and security controls. If computed risk position is still high there is then still need to go back a try more security and controls. Let us illustrate this dynamic knowledge-based process using a simple generic example as shown in Figure 11.8.

Assume without any loss of generalities that security objectives, security practices, and security controls may be adopted at three different levels: Low (L), Medium (M), and High (H). Also assume that security objectives, practices, and controls are related according to the scheme defined in Table 11.3.

If we input L to b_1 and L or M to b_2, or L to b_2 and L or M to b_1 then the output will be L to c. But an input of L to b_1 is caused by an input of L to a_{11} and L or M to a_{12}, or L to a_{12} and L or M to a_{11}. Also an input of L to b_2 is caused by an input L to a_{21} and L or M to a_{22}, or L to a_{22} and L or M to a_{21}. The decision table depicted in Table 11.3 will guide you on how to plan the security practices and controls you need to attain a prescribed level of achievement on the security objective.

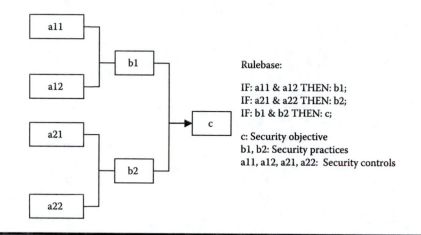

Figure 11.8 Example of a generic rule base representing one security objective, two security practices, and four security controls.

Table 11.3 gives a very simple decision procedure whereby we can fix a target level of satisfaction for security objective, say High. If we desire to achieve this much on the security objective then how do we determine how much should we achieve on each of the security practices b_1 and b_2? After examining Table 11.3 we can see that the only inputs that give H on the security objective c are an input H to b_1 and an input H to b_2. The next question would be how much to achieve on all relevant security controls so we can obtain 'H' on b_1 and 'H' on b_2. Table 11.3 shows that the only inputs that guarantee H on both b_1 and b_2 are H on a_{11} and a_{12}.

11.4.1 c2. Security Policy

A security policy is a document that states in writing how a company plans to protect its computing environment. This latter includes the company's physical and information technology assets. A security policy is a live document that is continuously revised as the computing environment changes. The security policy should define the acceptable behavior of the company's computing environment. The policy also describes how the company plans to educate its users and employees about protecting the company's assets, and how security measurements will be carried out and enforced.

The ISO/IEC 27002 limits the security policy section to one control point; that is, one security practice as follows:

b2.1: information security policy

ISO/IEC 27002 recommends that management documents and maintains an information security policy that defines a feasible information security strategy derived

Table 11.3 Generic Example: Values Taken by the Security Objective (c) Given the Values Taken by Security Practices and Controls

→ or ↓: Input			Values for security objective (c)								
Control a11	**Control a12**	**Practices b1**	Control a11 →	H	H	H	M	M	M	L	L	L
			Control a12 →	H	M	L	H	M	L	H	M	L
			b2 & →	H	M	M	M	M	L	M	L	L
↑ L	L	L		M	L	L	L	L	L	L	L	L
↑ L↓	M	L		M	L	L	L	L	L	L	L	L
↑ L	H	M		M	M	M	M	M	M	M	M	L
↑ M	L	L		M	L	L	L	L	L	L	L	L
↑ M	M	M		M	M	M	M	M	L	M	L	L
↑ M	H	M		M	M	M	M	M	L	M	L	L
↑ H	L	M		M	M	M	M	M	L	M	L	L
↑ H	M	M		M	M	M	M	M	L	M	L	L
↑ H	H	H		H	M	M	M	M	M	M	M	M

Values for security objective c

from management support and participation. A good documentation of the security policy and its enforcement will lead to an effective ISMS. Two security controls are listed as needed to satisfy the information security policy requirements:

a2.1.1: Information security policy document
a2.1.2: Review and evaluation of the security policy

The first requirement, a2.1.1, may be achieved by allowing for the following controls:

The information security policy includes a statement defining the meaning of information security.
It includes a description of the organization's security strategy.
The information security policy includes a statement delineating major ISMS implementation activities.
The information security policy includes a statement defining management support to the security strategy.
The information security policy includes a statement defining established criteria where compliance is important, including any regulations and standards.

The first requirement a2.1.2 may be achieved by allowing for the following controls:

The information security policy includes a description of policy review and maintenance procedures and their frequencies.
The information security policy includes a description for policy enforcement activities.

11.4.2 c3. Organization of Information Security

This control point emphasizes the need for a security management structure to protect the infrastructure, secure outsourcing activities and adequately plan the security of third-party's connections. Possible activities to allow for the controls covered in this section include defining security roles and assigning them; the formation of discussion groups in major security areas; and defining a structure for the computing environment based on the variation in information security requirements.

The ISO/IEC 27002 arranges organizational security into two controls:

b3.1 Internal organization
b3.2 External parties

The security practice b3.1 proposes eight security controls as follows:

a3.1.1 Management commitment to information security
a3.1.2 Information security coordination

a3.1.3 Allocation of information security responsibilities
a3.1.4 Authorization process for information processing facilities
a3.1.5 Confidentiality agreements
a3.1.6 Contact with authorities
a3.1.7 Contact with special interest groups
a3.1.8 Independent review of information security

The security practice b2.2 proposes three security controls as follows:

a3.2.1 Identification of risks related to external from third party access
a3.2.2 Addressing security when dealing with customers
a3.2.3 Addressing security in third-party agreements

11.4.3 c4. Asset Management

This security objective advises that information assets have different sensitivity and availability requirements, and they hence require different safeguards. It is very important that the organization creates an asset inventory where we store information on the sensitivity class, the availability class, the value of the asset, etc.

This control point is organized into two controls:

b4.1 Responsibility for assets
b4.2 Information classification

The first control b4.1 requires one major activity described as follows:

a4.1.1 Inventory of assets
a4.1.2 Ownership of assets
a4.1.3 Acceptable use of assets

The second security practice b4.2 requires two security control items as follows:

a4.2.1 Classification guidelines
a4.2.2 Information labeling and handling

In order to assess the conformity with these control items we need to create a set of questions designed to collect evidence about the information classification scheme. For example, does the organization have a classification scheme? Is there a database where information about all assets is stored? Does this database contain information on all assets? Does the classification envisage both criticality components: sensitivity and availability?

11.4.4 c5. Human Resources Security

This control point aims at minimizing security risks attributed to human resources. Incidents include, for example, human errors, fraud, abuse, misuse, etc. The best practice known for personnel security may be training for all users and staff.

The control point is organized into two major requirements:

b5.1 Human resources security prior to employment
b5.2 Human resources security during employment
b5.3 Termination or change of employment

The security in job definition and resourcing, defined in b5.1, may be achieved by the following security control items as follows:

a.5.1.1 Management responsibilities
a.5.1.2 Information security awareness, education, and training
a.5.1.3 Disciplinary process

The user training requirements, defined in b5.2, may be accomplished by following the security control items as follows:

a.5.2.1 Management responsibilities
a.5.2.2 Information security awareness, education, and training
a.5.2.3 Disciplinary process

The last requirement for achieving personnel security is to respond to security incidents and malfunctions, defined in b5.3. In order to satisfy this requirement, the standard proposes four control measures, denoted as follows:

a.5.3.1 Termination responsibilities
a.5.3.2 Return of assets
8.5.3.3 Removal of access rights

11.4.5 c6. Physical and Environmental Security

Physical security is the protection of personnel, hardware, programs, networks, and data from physical circumstances and events that could cause serious losses or damage to an enterprise, agency, or institution. This includes protection from fire, natural disasters, burglary, theft, vandalism, and terrorism.

Usually, people pay attention when we talk about technical or popular issues such as hacking, viruses, worms, spyware, and so on, whereas nobody takes physical security seriously. This latter is in fact as dangerous, because it can be performed with little or no technical knowledge from the intruder.

Common safeguards include barriers, surveillance. Barriers, fences, and obstacles are installed at entry points to protect against potential attackers and natural disasters. Surveillance and warning systems, including heat sensors, intrusion detectors, and cameras, may be used.

The physical and environmental security objective proposes two security practices:

b.6.1 Secure areas
b.6.2 Equipment security

The first security practice is concerned with physical and environment security areas. It consists of the following security controls:

a.6.1.1 Physical security perimeter
a.6.1.2 Physical entry controls
a.6.1.3 Securing offices, rooms, and facilities
a.6.1.4 Protecting against external and environmental threats
a.6.1.5 Working in secure areas
a.6.1.6 Public access, delivery, and loading areas

The second security practice is dealing with security equipments. This security practice consists of the following seven security controls:

a.6.2.1 Equipment siting and protection
a.6.2.2 Supporting utilities
a.6.2.3 Cabling security
a.6.2.4 Equipment maintenance
a.6.2.5 Security of equipment off-premises
a.6.2.6 Secure disposal or reuse of equipment
a.6.2.7 Removal of property

11.4.6 c7. Communications and Operations Management

This is a security area of great importance. The standard recommends a set of controls for ensuring the security of communications and operations. These recommendations are divided into 10 security practices as follows:

b7.1 Operational procedures and responsibilities
b7.2 Third-party service delivery management
b7.3 System planning and acceptance
b7.4 Protection against malicious and mobile code
b7.5 Backup
b7.6 Network security management
b7.7 Media handling

b7.8 Exchange of information
b7.9 Electronic commerce services
b7.10 Monitoring

For each of the security practices, the standard requires a subset of security control items that have to be adopted in order to satisfy the security practices. These requirements are described in Table 11.4.

11.4.7 c8. Access Control

Access control is the process of limiting access to the resources in the computing environment only to authorized users, programs, processes, or other systems. Access control is any mechanism by which a system grants or revokes the right to access some data, or perform some action. It is important to have in place a system-specific policy to organize the access authorization process. A user must first login to a system, using some authentication system.

This policy describes the management of permissions and restrictions for logging onto a computer or network. Systems typically employ individual profiles that specify which network-attached resources are available to which users.

This section is reserved to the protection of the access to any component in the computing environment, including information systems, technology, data resources, network services, etc. The security requirements are defined in Table 11.5 using the rule-based structure.

The standard reorganizes access control into eight control points, denoted as follows:

b.8.1 Business requirement for access control
b.8.2 User access management
b.8.3 User responsibilities
b.8.4 Network access control
b.8.5 Operating system access control
b.8.6 Application and information access control
b.8.7 Mobile computing and teleworking

11.4.8 c9. Systems Development and Maintenance

Security should be infused in the system development life cycle. This section is also concerned with the security of application and system components including people, inputs, outputs, processes, interfaces, and databases. Safeguards that reduce risks of information, information corruption, and denial of service should be adopted. The security requirement for those security objectives are provided in Table 11.6 as a rule-based system. The standard divides this security area into five control points denoted as follows:

Table 11.4 ISO 27002 Rule Base for c7. Communications and Operations Management

Rule Base:

IF: a.7.1.1–a7.1.4 THEN: b7.1;

IF: a.7.2.1–a7.2.3 THEN: b7.2;

IF: a.7.3.1–a.7.3.2 THEN: b7.3;

IF: a.7.4.1–a7.4.2 THEN: b7.4;

IF: a.7.5.1 THEN: b7.5;

IF: a.7.6.1–a7.6.2 THEN: b7.6;

IF: a.7.7.1–a7.7.4 THEN: b7.7;

IF: a.7.8.1–a7.8.5 THEN: b7.8;

IF: a.7.9.1–a7.9.3 THEN: b7.9;

IF: a.7.10.1–a7.10.6 THEN: b.7.10;

c Concepts: Security Objective	b Concepts: Security Practices	a Concepts: Security Controls
	b.7.1: Operational procedures and responsibilities	a.7.1.1 Documented operating procedures
		a.7.1.2 Change management
		a.7.1.3 Segregation of duties
		a.7.1.4 Separation of development, test, and operational facilities

Continued

Table 11.4   ISO 27002 Rule Base for c7. Communications and Operations Management (*Continued*)

c Concepts: Security Objective	b Concepts: Security Practices	a Concepts: Security Controls
	b.7.2: Third-party service delivery management	a.7.2.1 Service delivery a.7.2.2 Monitoring and review of third-party services a.7.2.3 Managing changes to third-party services
	b.7.3: System planning and acceptance	a.7.3.1 Capacity management a.7.3.2 System acceptance
	b.7.4: Protection against malicious and mobile code	a.7.4.1 Controls against malicious code a.7.4.2 Controls against mobile code
	b.7.5: Back-up	a.7.5.1 Information back-up
	b.7.6: Network security management	a.7.6.1 Network controls a.7.6.2 Security of network services
	b.7.7: Media handling	a.7.7.1 Management of removable media a.7.7.2 Disposal of media a.7.7.3 Information handling procedures a.7.7.4 Security of system documentation

b.7.8: Exchange of information	a.7.8.1 Information exchange policies and procedures a.7.8.2 Exchange agreements a.7.8.3 Physical media in transit a.7.8.4 Electronic messaging a.7.8.5 Business information systems	
b.7.9: Electronic commerce services	a.7.9.1 Electronic commerce a.7.9.2 On-Line Transactions a.7.9.3 Publicly available information	
b.7.10: Monitoring	a.7.10.1 Audit logging a.7.10.2 Monitoring system use a.7.10.3 Protection of log information a.7.10.4 Administrator and operator logs a.7.10.5 Fault logging a.7.10.6 Clock synchronization	

Table 11.5 ISO 27002 Rule Base for c8 Access Control

Rule Base:

IF: a.8.1.1 THEN: b.8.1;

IF: a.8.2.1–a.8.2.4 THEN: b.8.2;

IF: a.8.3.1 & a.8.3.3 THEN: b.8.3;

IF: a.8.4.1–a.8.4.7 THEN: b.8.4;

IF: a.8.5.1–a.8.5.6 THEN: b.8.5;

IF: a.8.6.1–a.8.6.2 THEN: b.8.6;

IF: a.8.7.1–a.8.7.2 THEN: b.8.7;

IF: b.8.1–b.8.7 THEN: c8;

c Concept: Security Objective	b Concepts: Security Practices	a Concepts: Security Controls
Security objective c8	b.8.1 Business requirement for access control	a.8.1.1 Access control policy
	b.8.2 User access management	a.8.2.1 User registration a.8.2.2 Privilege management a.8.2.3 User password management a.8.2.4 Review of user access rights
	b.8.3 User responsibilities	a.8.3.1 Password use a.8.3.2 Unattended user equipment a.8.3.3 Clear desk and clear screen policy

b.8.4 Network access control	a.8.4.1 Policy on use of network services
	a.8.4.2 User authentication for external connections
	a.8.4.3 Equipment identification in networks
	a.8.4.4 Remote diagnostic and configuration port protection
	a.8.4.5 Segregation in networks
	a.8.4.6 Network connection control
	a.8.4.7 Network routing control
b.8.5 Operating system access control	a.8.5.1 Secure log-on procedures
	a.8.5.2 User identification and authentication
	a.8.5.3 Password management system
	a.8.5.4 Use of system utilities
	a.8.5.5 Session time-out
	a.8.5.6 Limitation of connection time
b.8.6 Application and information access control	a.8.6.1 Information access restriction
	a.8.6.2 Sensitive system isolation
b.8.7 Mobile computing and teleworking	a.8.7.1 Mobile computing and communications
	a.8.7.2 Teleworking

Table 11.6   ISO 27002 Rule Base for c9 Information Systems Acquisition, Development and Maintenance

Rule Base:

IF: a.9.1.1 THEN: b.9.1;

IF: a.9.2.1-a.9.2.4 THEN: b.9.2;

IF: a.9.3.1 -a.9.3.2 THEN: b.9.3;

IF: a.9.4.1-a.9.4.3 THEN: b.9.4;

IF: a.9.5.1-a.9.5.5 THEN: b.9.5;

IF: a.9.6.1 THEN: b.9.6;

IF: b.9.1-b.9.6 THEN: c9;

c Concept: Security Objective	b Concepts: Security Practices	a Concepts: Security Controls
Security objective c9: Information systems acquisition, development and maintenance	b.9.1 Security requirements of information systems	a.9.1.1 Security requirements analysis and specification
	b.9.2 Correct processing in applications	a.9.2.1 Input data validation
		a.9.2.2 Control of internal processing
		a.9.2.3Message integrity
		a.9.2.4 Output data validation

b.9.3 Cryptographic controls	a.9.3.1 Policy on the use of cryptographic controls
	a.9.3.2 Key management
b.9.4 Security of system files	a.9.4.1 Control of operational software
	a.9.4.2 Protection of system test data
	a.9.4.3 Access control to program source code
b.9.5 Security in development and support processes	a.9.5.1 Change control procedures
	a.9.5.2 Technical review of applications after operating system changes
	a.9.5.3 Restrictions on changes to software packages
	a.9.5.4 Information leakage
	a.9.5.5 Outsourced software development
b.9.6 Technical vulnerability management	a.9.6.1 Control of technical vulnerabilities

b8.1 Security requirements of systems
b8.2 Security in application systems
b8.3 Cryptographic control
b8.4 Security of system files
b8.5 Security in development and support processes

11.4.9 c10. Information Security Incident Management

This section is concerned with information security incident management. An organization has to satisfy two main security practices:

b.10.1 Reporting information security events and weaknesses
b.10.2 Management of information security incidents and improvements

Table 11.7 provides the rule-based system that links the security objective of information security incident management to two security practices concerned with the reporting of information security events and weaknesses and the management and improvement of information security incident management. This knowledge-based system tells us how much should be invested in the latter security practices in order to achieve the security objective we have in place. There are four security controls that have to be implemented in order to realize the levels of security prescribed for the target information system. The rule-based system provides for continual improvement in the information security incident management area through sufficient sensitivity analysis and toning that produce the security level desired in this area.

11.4.10 c11. Business Continuity Management

This section is concerned with business continuity. The standard recommends a business continuance plan that describes the processes and procedures an organization needs to implement to ensure that essential functions can continue during and after an incident. This is a requirement to prevent any interruptions of mission-critical services, and to reestablish full functioning promptly and as smoothly as possible. This plan should be implemented, tested, and maintained.

The main aspects of the management of a business continuity plan, denoted here as b.11.1, are identified by the standards as the following security controls:

a.11.1.1 Including information security in the business continuity management process
a.11.1.2 Business continuity and risk assessment
a.11.1.3 Developing and implementing continuity plans including information security

Table 11.7 ISO 27002 Rule Base for c10 Information Security Incident Management

Rule Base:

IF: a.10.1.1–a.10.1.2 THEN: b.9.1;

IF: a.10.2.1–a.10.2.2 THEN: b.9.2;

IF: b.10.1–b.10.2 THEN: c10;

c Concept: Security Objective	b Concepts: Security Practices	a Concepts: Security Controls
Security objective c10 Information security incident management	b.10.1 Reporting information security events and weaknesses	a.10.1.1 Reporting information security events a.10.1.2 Reporting security weaknesses
	b.10.2 Management of information security incidents and improvements	a.10.2.1 Responsibilities and procedures a.10.2.2 Learning from information security incidents

a.11.1.4 Business continuity planning framework

a.11.1.5 Testing, maintaining and reassessing business continuity plans

The rule base associated with the ninth security area is given in Table 11.8.

11.4.11 c12. Compliance

There should be established criteria, like regional regulations, laws, polices, and standards, that the organization has to comply with. Periodic audits are needed verify compliance with all established criteria and standards, as required by the security policy. The security requirements translating the compliance security objectives into security practices and security controls are provided in Table 11.9 in a rule-base form.

This section is organized into three security practices, denoted as follows:

b.12.1 Compliance with legal requirements

b.12.2 Compliance with security policies and standards, and technical compliance

b.12.3 Information systems audit considerations

11.5 Measurement and Implementations

Up to this point in this chapter, we have been focusing on the fact that ISO/IEC 27002 is more useful as a rule-based system than a simple checklist for self-assessment and compliance. Using the standard as a rule-based system will allow the internal auditor or the security analyst to estimate the current security posture of the organization, and if the latter is not acceptable, a sensitivity analysis may be performed to determine what new values for the 135 security controls, 39 security practices, and 12 security objectives can produce the desired security posture.

Any of the 135 security controls can be adopted or not adopted, and if adopted it can have any strength between very low and very high. The changes in the set of security controls will change the set of security practices and also the set of security objectives. Those changes will produce the desired security posture. That is, instead of using the ISO/IEC 27002 for simple compliance which will produce two possible outputs, namely, "Found compliant with ISO/IEC 27002," or "Found not compliant with ISO/IEC 27002," we used it to improve the current security posture by adjusting the inputs to the standards as needed. The inputs of the standards are the 135 security controls, and the outputs are the 12 security objectives that are combined to produce the ISO/IEC 27002-based security posture of the organization. The security analyst should undertake the necessary toning up.

Table 11.8 ISO 27002 Rulebase for c11 Business Continuity Management

Rule Base:

IF: a.11.1.1–a.11.1.5 THEN: b.11.1;

IF: b.11.1 THEN: c11;

c Concept: Security Objective	b Concepts: Security Practices	a Concepts: Security Controls
Security objective c11:		
Business continuity management	b.11.1 Information security aspects of business continuity management	a.11.1.1 Including information security in the business continuity management process
		a.11.1.2 Business continuity and risk assessment
		a.11.1.3 Developing and implementing continuity plans including information security
		a.11.1.4 Business continuity planning framework
		a.11.1.5 Testing, maintaining and re-assessing business continuity plans

Table 11.9 ISO 27002 Rule Base for c12 Compliance

Rule Base:

IF: a.12.1.1–a.12.1.6 THEN: b.12.1;
IF: a.12.2.1–a.12.2.2 THEN: b.12.2;
IF: a.12.3.1 THEN: b.12.3;
IF: b.12.1–b.12.3 THEN: c12;

c Concept: Security Objective	b Concepts: security Practices	a Concepts: security Controls
Security objective c12 Compliance	b.12.1 Compliance with legal requirements	a.12.1.1 Identification of applicable legislation a.12.1.2 Intellectual property rights (IPR) a.12.1.33 Protection of organizational records a.12.1.4 Data protection and privacy of personal information a.12.1.5 Prevention of misuse of information processing facilities a.12.1.6 Regulation of cryptographic controls
	b.12.2 Compliance with security policies and standards, and technical compliance	a.12.2.1 Compliance with security policies and standards a.12.2.2 Technical compliance checking
	b.12.3 Information systems audit considerations	a.12.3.1 Information systems audit controls

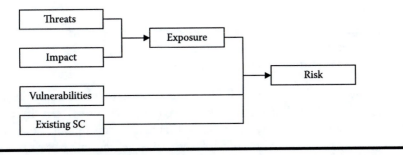

Figure 11.9 Factors affecting security risks.

11.5.1 How Does This Toning Up Work?

It all starts when system owners, upper management, or assigned internal auditors declare (1) that "the current security posture is unacceptable," or (2) that "the organization does not comply with ISO/IEC 27002." We, therefore, can do one of two things: in the first situation (1), we have to proceed to improve the current security posture and determine what security controls are needed to bring back the security posture above its previous level that was declared unacceptable by security analysts; or in the second case (2), we just see where the organization is not in compliance with the ISO/IEC 27002 and make the necessary corrections.

Based on the conclusions obtained from system owners, upper management, or assigned internal auditors, we can either decide to enhance the current security posture or to makes corrections for the purpose of compliance with ISO/IEC 27002. In the first case, we certainly acted to enhance the current security posture; this is the most appropriate action to undertake. In the second case, we acted to make the necessary corrections to produce compliance with the ISO/IEC 27002. This latter action may be inadequate because of the following reasons:

1. The corrective actions will bring back compliance with the standard, but can those corrective actions produce higher security posture?
2. Is it better to have compliance or higher security posture?
3. Does compliance with the standard necessarily imply feasibility?
4. Is it ok to invest in infeasible compliance with ISO/IEC 27002?
5. Where does risk play a role in the compliance decision?

The security analyst may need to discuss the above questions with system owners and upper management to make sure that they prefer compliance to a higher security posture or vice versa. Obviously, however, and independently of whether we are checking for compliance or enhancing the security posture, any decisions to be made in both processes have to be made based on risks. Figure 11.9, however, shows that we can only adjust the organization's risk levels by adjusting one or more of the following four inputs:

1. Threats
2. Impact
3. Vulnerabilities
4. Security controls

Because we are discussing the ISO/IEC 27002 standard, we will skip the threats, impacts, and vulnerabilities, and we will play on the current security controls. Studying the current security controls will reveal two conclusions: either the current security controls are not sufficient, or that the effectiveness levels of some of the current security controls are low. In the first case, we have to go back to the 135 security controls and study them to see which ones have to be added. In the second case, the current security controls are appropriate but lack sufficient effectiveness, and we hence have to enhance their effectiveness levels. In any case, the security analyst has to make sure that all required risk levels for all components of the computing environment have to be respected.

For example, can we talk about compliance while one of the components in the computing environment still has its risk level higher than the acceptable risk level specified in its security policy? The answer is obvious: before investing in any compliance effort, we have to make sure that all components of the computing environment maintain risk levels below the maximum accepted risk levels as stated in their risk policies.

11.6 Strategies to Enhance the ISO/IEC 27002-Based Security Posture

In general, when a strategy is selected for adoption, it is associated with one or more important decision parameters that are studied and optimized as objective functions. Because the ISO/IEC 27002 includes 135 security controls to choose from, we can do this by, for example, minimizing cost. What does this mean?

Let us explain. The main objective of this activity is to enhance the ISO/IEC 27002-based security posture for the organization or a simple target information asset. How do we choose among 135 security controls? In a cost-based strategy, we select the cheapest security controls first, we compute the security posture, and then if this latter is below a certain security level defined by the security policy, we consider a new security control.

Because the primary factors that directly affect risk levels are the input factors for the risk process presented in Figure 11.9, the first strategies that come to mind, in addition to the cost parameter, should focus on threats, impact, vulnerabilities, and security controls.

That is, we propose the following security posture enhancement strategies:

Those strategies are summarized in Table 11.10. The table explains how the security analyst should proceed when searching for the security controls to use

Table 11.10   ISO/IEC 27002-Based Security Posture Enhancement Strategy

Security Posture Enhancement Strategies	*Prioritizing Security Controls*
Threat-based ISO/IEC 27002-based security posture enhancement strategy	Start with the security control that minimizes threat likelihood the most
Impact-based ISO/IEC 27002-based security posture enhancement strategy	Start with the security control that minimizes impact levels the most
Vulnerability-based ISO/IEC 27002-based security posture enhancement strategy	Start with the security control that minimizes vulnerability levels the most
Security control-based ISO/IEC 27002-based security posture enhancement strategy	Start with the security control that maximizes security control effectiveness the most
Cost-based ISO/IEC 27002-based security posture enhancement strategy	Start with the security control that has the least cost

for the purpose of enhancing the ISO/IEC 27002-based security posture of the organization.

11.6.1 Threat-Based ISO/IEC 27002-Based Security Posture Enhancement Strategy

A threat-based strategy should first study the existing threats and see what can be done to reduce their likelihood. The main objective of this activity is still how we can understand the security controls offered by the ISO/IEC 27007 and how we can feasibly adopt them to diminish any negative effects associated with the capabilities of the threats. Let us consider the information asset described in Figure 11.10. We used threats, impact, vulnerabilities, and present security controls to produce its estimated risks.

The computation of asset exposure, given its impact level and the likelihood of threats, is based on Table 2.2 from Chapter 2, called "The Security Life Cycle." The computation of risk, given asset exposure, vulnerability level, and present security control effectiveness, is based on Table 2.3 from the same book chapter. In a threat-based strategy, our immediate objective is to diminish the strength of present threats. Because the only variable we can control, in a threat, is its likelihood, the question becomes "What can be done to reduce the likelihood of present threat?" Remember, because we are in the context of enhancing security using the ISO/IEC 27002, then the range of actions will be limited to the standard's security

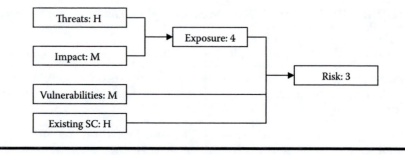

Figure 11.10 Factors affecting security risks.

objectives, security practices, and security controls. Then, because the immediate inputs we can adjust for the purpose of improving the asset security posture are a set of 135 security controls, we have to determine which ones will effectively lower the likelihood of present threats, the subject of the example in question. We therefore need a subset of security controls from the ISO/IEC 27002 that can lower the likelihood of threats so that asset exposure is sufficiently reduced and, consequently, the resulting asset risk level. Suppose, for example, that we selected the security control "a5.3.1: Termination responsibilities" from the security practice "b5.3: Termination or change of employment" from the security objective "c5: Human resources security," and we were able to reduce the present threats from high to low. What would be the gain in risk in this case? Reading Table 2.3, from Chapter 2, called "The Security Life Cycle," when we plug in the new value for threat likelihood, which is now low, we obtain a risk equal to 2. That is, by using a treat-based strategy to enhance the ISO/IEC 27002-based security posture, we succeeded in reducing the asset risk level from 4 to 2. If this risk is acceptable to the asset security policy then we stop here; otherwise, we continue selecting new security controls, as explained in Figure 11.11.

11.6.2 Impact-Based ISO/IEC 27002-Based Security Posture Enhancement Strategy

An impact-based strategy should first study the assets and identify possible impacts when undesired events take place. Undesired events are primarily related to information leakage, information corruption, and denial of service. The impacts that those undesired events can have on the asset have to be studied.

The main objective of this activity is still how we can understand the security controls offered by the ISO/IEC 27007 and how we can feasibly adopt them to diminish any negative effects associated with the impact on the target asset. It is important, however, according to most of the literature, that we assume impacts are independent of security controls, because we express the internal properties of the asset and define the level of impact when the consequences of information leakage, information corruption, or denial of service take place. So it is assumed that even if

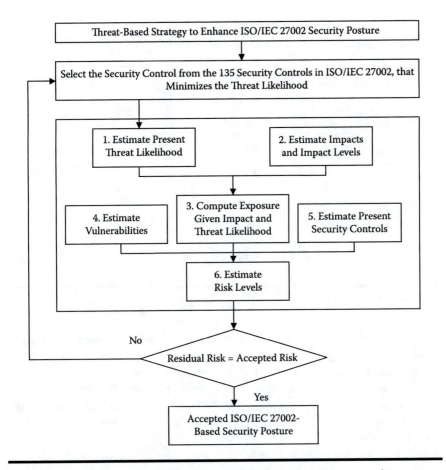

Figure 11.11 Threat-based strategy to enhance ISO/IEC 27002 security posture.

there are no security controls, when those undesired events materialize, there may be no effects when the impact levels are low. This independence assumption is often valid but there are security controls that are defined in a way to reduce the impacts when undesired events take place. That is, those special security controls are, by definition, constructed to reduce the impacts of information leakage, information corruption, and denial of service on assets. For example, if we define a new security control, called "high-availability cluster," then if it is adopted, then the layout and configuration of the computing environment will be redesigned, by definition, for the purpose of ensuring high availability. In this case, the high-availability cluster solution will, by definition, reduce the availability component of the asset's impact to lower levels. This example asserts that there are special security controls that are not independent from asset impact levels. It is then worthwhile to search the 135 security controls of the ISO/IEC 27002 to see whether or not there are security controls that can be used to reduce the asset's impact levels.

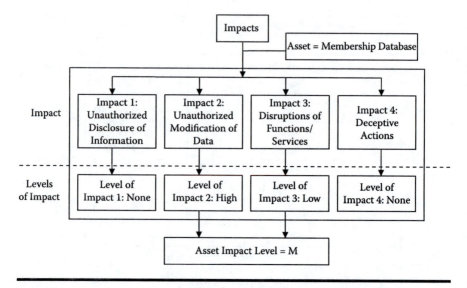

Figure 11.12   Impact level for a target asset to enhance security posture.

Another example would be the special lines or VPNs as security controls. If we consider a larger network where remote users connect to the main office using those special lines or VPN connections, the network impact levels for unauthorized access to or modification of data, will be reduced. In fact, if we enhance the cryptographic level of the VPN we can considerably reduce the network impact level. This explains the dependence of asset's impact levels on certain security controls.

Let us consider the information asset described in Figure 11.12. We used threats, impact, vulnerabilities, and present security controls to produce its estimated risks. The computation of asset exposure, given its impact level and the likelihood of threats, is explained earlier. Remember, because we are in the context of enhancing the ISO/IEC 27002, then the range of actions will be limited to the standard's security objectives, security practices, and security controls.

Let us also study the reasons behind the value taken by impact levels used in computing the basic risk. We can see, from Figure 11.12, that the level of impact originates at those undesired events: "Unauthorized modification of data" and "Disruptions of functions/services." Now, we can examine the set of 135 security controls proposed by the ISO/IEC 27002 and determine which ones can actually reduce the impact levels of "Unauthorized modification of data," and "Disruptions of functions/services." Of course, sometimes instead of immediately searching in the large set 135 security controls, it is probably easier to search for security solutions in the set of 39 security practices, or even easier if the search takes place in the reduced subset of three security objectives. Bear in mind that even if you start at the reduced subset of security objectives or at the subset of reduced set of security practices, you will always later go back to the real inputs of the ISO/IEC 27002, which are the 135 security controls.

We are leaving it for students to search for security controls among the ISO/IEC 27002's 135 security controls, to identify those controls that reduce asset's impact levels with respect to information leakage, information corruption, and denial of service. After the identification of those security controls, we can use Figure 11.9 and Tables 3.2 and 3.3 from Chapter 3 to estimate the residual risk levels.

You can see that by using an impact-based strategy to enhance the ISO/IEC 27002-based security posture, you will succeed in reducing asset risk levels. If this risk is acceptable to the asset security policy, then you stop here; otherwise, you need to continue selecting new security controls, as explained in Figure 11.13.

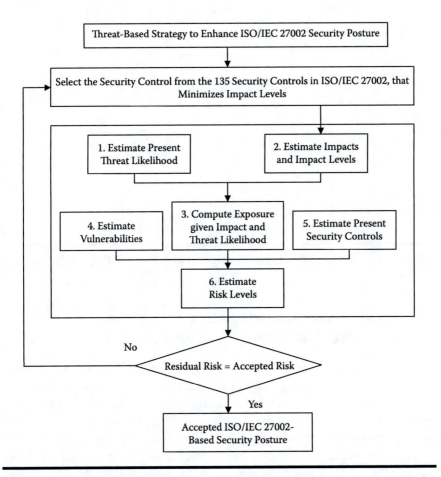

Figure 11.13 Impact-based strategy to enhance ISO/IEC 27002 security posture.

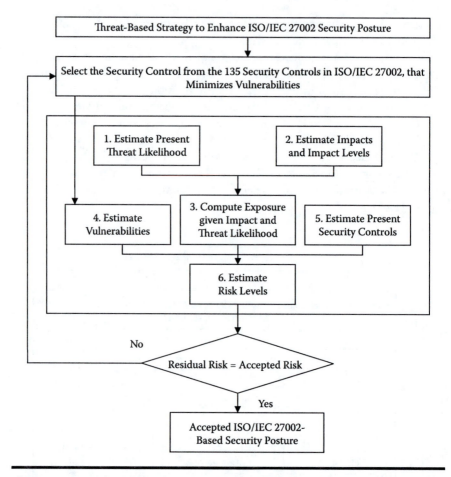

Figure 11.14 Vulnerability-based strategy to enhance ISO/IEC 27002 security posture.

11.6.3 Vulnerability-Based Strategy to Enhance ISO/IEC 27002-Based Security Posture

The vulnerability-based strategy may be used to enhance ISO/IEC 27002-based security posture by adjusting asset vulnerabilities. Figure 11.9 shows that when vulnerabilities are reduced, risk levels are also reduced. This strategy only focuses on vulnerability reduction and is not concerned with threats and impacts. The security analyst needs to identify any security controls in the ISO/IEC 27002 that are related to asset vulnerabilities and adopt them for the purpose of enhancing ISO/IEC 27002-based security posture. The reduction of vulnerabilities will result in risk mitigation and improvement of the security posture.

11.6.4 Security Control-Based ISO/IEC 27002-Based Security Posture Enhancement Strategy

The security control-based strategy is not directly concerned with adjusting impacts, managing threats, or manipulation vulnerabilities. It focuses on studying the effectiveness of present security controls and revising them by enhancing their strength or by adding new security controls to secure a better ISO/IEC 27002-based security posture. Of course, while this strategy is not directly linked to impact, threats, and vulnerabilities, it still can deal with them indirectly through the evoking of one or more of the ISO/IEC 27002's security controls. The security analyst should select the best subset of security controls that can produce the best ISO/IEC 27002-based security posture. Figure 11.15 explains the steps needed to produce the desired security posture using the security control-based strategy.

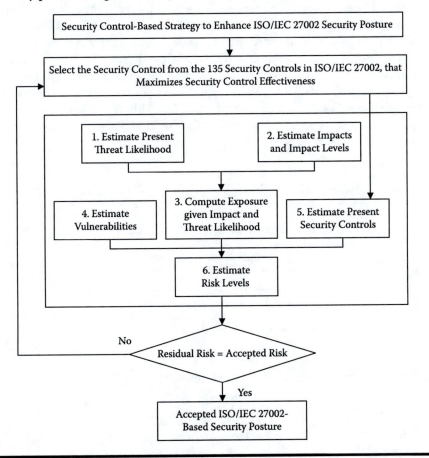

Figure 11.15   Security control-based strategy to enhance ISO/IEC 27002 security posture.

11.6.5 Cost-Based ISO/IEC 27002-Based Security Posture Enhancement Strategy

In a cost-based ISO/IEC 27002-based security posture enhancement strategy, we have to search for those security controls among the 135 proposed by the ISO/IEC 27002 standard that provide the highest reduction in security enhancement cost. As long as there is security posture enhancement budget available and as long as we have not yet reached the target security posture, as specified in the relevant security policy, and as long as we have not yet exhausted all available security controls, we have to consider the next security control with the highest cost reduction.

Of course, and as is always the case in information security, security controls added have to contribute in mitigating risk levels as needed. Any security activity, including the addition of a new security control, is not feasible if current basic risks are with the acceptable range specified in the security policy. You, however, may notice we have not related risk to cost in all of the earlier ISO/IEC 27002-based security posture enhancement strategies. We have always expressed risk levels in terms of asset exposures (indirectly, impact levels and threat likelihood), vulnerability levels, and effectiveness of present security controls. This means that we can only implement this ISO/IEC 27002-based security posture enhancement strategy if we adopt cost-based risk assessment method, like ALE, ABLE, etc. Figure 11.16 depicts the working of the cost-based ISO/IEC 27002-based security posture enhancement strategy.

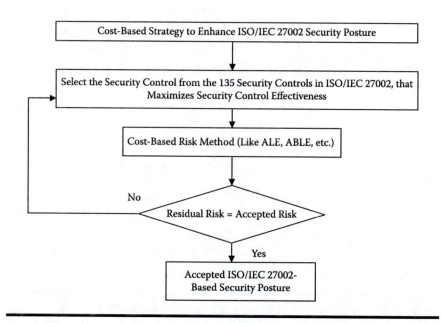

Figure 11.16 Cost-based strategy to enhance ISO/IEC 27002 security posture.

Table 11.11 Additive Effects of Security Posture Enhancement Caused by Security Controls

Original Security Control Level + Enhancement Level	Values of Security Control Effectiveness before Applying New Security Controls				
	1	2	3	4	5
0	1	2	3	4	5
1	2	3	4	5	5
2	3	4	5	5	5
3	4	5	5	5	5
4	5	5	5	5	5
5	5	5	5	5	5

Change produced by applying security controls when enhancing security posture (label for the leftmost column of the table)

11.7 Comparing the ISO/IEC 27002-Based Security Posture Enhancement Strategies

Let us present a generic approach on how to enhance ISO/IEC 27002-based security posture enhancement using the five strategies that we defined earlier. Before we proceed further, we need to apply the same simple Likert scale for all the decision parameters: impact levels, vulnerability levels, threat likelihood, and security control effectiveness. We assume that they all take the following values: (1) very low, (2) low, (3) moderately low, (4) high, and (5) very high. We also assume that the security analyst is very familiar with all the security controls and that he/she has historical data where he/she can estimate the security controls' capabilities to enhance, either by reducing the negative effect decision parameters (such as cost levels, impact levels, threat likelihood, and vulnerability levels) or by increasing the positive-effect decision parameters (e.g, for security control effectiveness). We assume the security control capability to reduce negative effects or to increase positive effects is also measured on the same five-point Likert scale presented earlier. Tables 11.11 and 11.12 provide the computation of the new values of decision parameters after the selected security controls are applied. For example, if the current impact level is 3, and the security control reduction amount is 1, then the new impact level is 3 − 1 = 2. On the other hand, if the security control reduction amount is 4 instead of 1, then the new impact level is 3 − 4 = 1 (and not −1). Along the same line, if the current security effectiveness is 4 and the new security control increase amount is 3, then new security effectiveness is 4 + 3 = 5 (and not 7).

As shown in Table 11.13, in a threat-based ISO/IEC 27002-based security posture enhancement strategy, we have to start with the security control that minimizes threat likelihood the most. In Table 11.13, we had five security controls (s1, s2, s3, s4, and s5) that are capable of producing threat likelihood reduction

Table 11.12 Reduction Effects of Security Posture Enhancement Caused by Security Controls

Original Impact, Likelihood, Vulnerability Level— Enhancement Level		Value of Impact, Likelihood, or Vulnerability Levels before Security Controls				
		1	*2*	*3*	*4*	*5*
Change produced by applying security controls when enhancing security posture	0	1	2	3	4	5
	1	1	1	2	3	4
	2	1	1	1	2	3
	3	1	1	1	1	2
	4	1	1	1	1	1
	5	1	1	1	1	1

amounts of 2, 1, 2, 1, and 2, respectively. In enhancing the ISO/IEC 27002-based security posture, the security controls are considered in this order: s1, s5, s3, s2, and s4. Of course, we have to stop considering security controls when the target security posture is reached.

On the other hand, with the impact-based ISO/IEC 27002-based security posture enhancement strategy, we have to start with the security control that minimizes impact levels the most.

In Table 11.13, we had five security controls—s1, s2, s3, s4, and s5—that were capable of producing impact-reduction amounts of 1, 2, 3, 1, and 0, respectively. In enhancing the ISO/IEC 27002-based security posture, the security controls are considered in this order: s3, s2, s1, s4, and s5.

In the vulnerability-based ISO/IEC 27002-based security posture enhancement strategy, we have to start with the security control that minimizes vulnerability levels the most.

In Table 11.13, we had five security controls—s1, s2, s3, s4, and s5—that are capable of producing vulnerability reduction amounts of 0, 2, 2, 2, and 1, respectively. In enhancing the ISO/IEC 27002-based security posture, the security controls are considered in this order: s1, s2, s3, s5, and s1.

In the same manner, in the security control-based ISO/IEC 27002-based security posture enhancement strategy, we have to start with the security control that maximizes security control effectiveness levels the most. In Table 11.13, we had five security controls—s1, s2, s3, s4, and s5—that are capable of producing security effectiveness enhancement amounts of 2, 1, 1, 2, and 2, respectively. In enhancing the ISO/IEC 27002-based security posture, the security controls are considered in this order: s1, s4, s5, s2, and s3.

Finally, in the cost-based ISO/IEC 27002-based security posture enhancement strategy, we have to start with the security control that maximizes cost reduction

Table 11.13   Priority in Selecting Security Controls in Various ISO/IEC 27002-Based Security Posture Enhancement Strategies

	Impact Level	Threat Likelihood	Vulnerability Level	Security Control Effectiveness	Cost
s1	1	2	0	2	2
s2	2	1	2	1	0
s3	3	2	2	1	2
s4	1	1	2	2	1
s5	0	2	1	2	2
SCBS strategy	Priority: s1, s4, s5, s2, s3				
VBS strategy	Priority: s1, s2, s3, s5, s1				
IBS strategy	Priority: s3, s2, s1, s4, s5				
TBS strategy	Priority: s1, s5, s3, s2, s4				
CBS strategy	Priority: s1, s5, s3, s4, s2				

ISO/IEC 27002-Based Security Posture Enhancement Strategies:

SCBS: Security control-based ISO/IEC 27002-based security posture enhancement strategy;

VBS: Vulnerability-based ISO/IEC 27002-based security posture enhancement strategy;

IBS: Impact-based ISO/IEC 27002-based security posture enhancement strategy;

TBS: Threat-based ISO/IEC 27002-based security posture enhancement strategy;

CBS: Cost-based ISO/IEC 27002-based security posture enhancement strategy the most. In Table 11.13, we had five security controls s1, s2, s3, s4, and s5 that are capable of producing cost reduction amounts of 2, 0, 2, 1, and 2, respectively. In enhancing the ISO/IEC 27002-based security posture, the security controls are considered in this order: s1, s5, s3, s4, and s2.

11.8 Summary

This chapter presented the international standard ISO/IEC 27002. We presented the structure of the standard, its 12 security objectives, 39 security practices, and its 135 security controls. We discussed how an organization may use the ISO/IEC 27002 for simple compliance or to enhance its security posture. We presented five security enhancement strategies that are based on cost reduction, impact level reduction, threat likelihood reduction, vulnerability reduction, and security control effectiveness enhancement. We provide generic computing support to most of the methods we presented.

11.9 Review Questions

1. Explain the history of ISO/IEC 27002.
2. How many security objectives, security practices, and security controls constitute the ISO/IEC 27002?
3. Explain the rule-based structure of the ISO/IEC 27002. Why is it useful?
4. Give an example of how to enhance physical and environmental security, using the ISO/IEC 27002.
5. Give an example of how to enhance access control, using the ISO/IEC 27002.
6. Give an example of how to enhance human resources security, using the ISO/IEC 27002.
7. Give an example of how to enhance asset management, using the ISO/IEC 27002.
8. Give an example of how to enhance security compliance, using the ISO/IEC 27002.
9. Give an example of how to enhance the ISO/IEC 27002-based security posture using the threat-based ISO/IEC 27002-based security posture enhancement strategy.
10. Give an example of how to enhance the ISO/IEC 27002-based security posture using the Impact-based ISO/IEC 27002-based security posture enhancement strategy.
11. Give an example of how to enhance the ISO/IEC 27002-based security posture using the security control-based ISO/IEC 27002-based security posture enhancement strategy.

12. Give an example of how to enhance the ISO/IEC 27002-based security posture using the vulnerability-based ISO/IEC 27002-based security posture enhancement strategy.
13. Give an example of how to enhance the ISO/IEC 27002-based security posture using the cost-based ISO/IEC 27002-based security posture enhancement strategy.
14. Is it possible to combine all or some of the ISO/IEC 27002-based security posture enhancement strategies discussed in this chapter? Explain how.
15. Explain how risk is incorporated in each of the ISO/IEC 27002-based security posture enhancement strategies presented in this chapter.

11.10 Workshops

Workshop 1

ABC Inc. is a small business consisting of 12 staff members and 200 customers. Business is only possible online. The company consists of people, activities (policies, regulations, processes, etc.), data, technology (software and hardware), and network. Apply the ISO/IEC 27002 to estimate the security posture of the company. Using a 5-point Likert scale for the security posture, assume that the security posture assessment gave a score of 3 (say, moderate security posture), which is lower than the minimum accepted level of 4 (say, high security posture). Apply the ISO/IEC 27002 to bring up the security posture of the company to 4. Explain and discuss all the steps.

Workshop 2

Consider ABC, Inc. presented in Workshop 1. Apply the cost-based ISO/IEC 27002 security posture enhancement strategy to bring up the security posture of the company to a higher level. Use the ALE risk methodology and explain and discuss all steps.

References

1. Angelov, P. P. *Evolving rule-based models*. Kindle Edition, 2002.
2. ISO/IEC 27002:2005 (ISO/IEC 17799:2005)—Information Technology Security Techniques—Code of Practice for Information Security Management. International Standards Organization, June 2005. (Source: http://www.iso.org.)

Chapter 12

Technical Security Enhancement Based on ISO/IEC 27001

Learning Objectives

After reading this chapter, students are expected to achieve an understanding of:

Organizations interact with the standards
The general ISMS framework works
ISMS scope is defined
Risks are identified and assessed
Risks are mitigated
The continual improvement process works
Security controls are selected for the risk treatment program
Statement of applicability is designed
How an ISMS is designed
How a system is assessed for compliance with ISO/IEC 27001

12.1 Introduction

As seen earlier, on different occasions, information in an organization is without any doubt the most valuable available organizational resource. It holds the only sure path to a continual generation of business value throughout the organization. Any threat to information resources is a direct threat to the organization's business value generation capabilities. The need to effectively manage security risks the organization faces is urgent. This chapter is concerned with the development of information security management systems.

An information security management system (ISMS) is an information assurance framework adopted to manage information security based on a systematic business risk approach, to establish, implement, operate, monitor, review, maintain, and improve information security. It is an organizational approach to information security. ISO/IEC 27001 is an international standard for information security that focuses on an organization's ISMS. Any information security activity should be planned, implemented, and maintained within this ISMS framework. The ISMS will ensure that the right controls are developed to provide adequate information security and will satisfy all specifications required by users, customers, and partners.

The ISO/IEC 27001 aims to ensure that adequate controls, addressing confidentiality, integrity and availability of information are in place to safeguard organizational information. An ISMS that is conform to ISO/IEC 27001 can help you demonstrate to trading partners and customers alike that you adequately protect the company's information as well as their information. The ISMS design, as shown in Figure 12.1, is actually extracted from Annex A provided at the end of the document containing the ISO/IEC 27001. The obtaining of certification to ISO/IEC 27001 is a strong demonstration of an organization's commitment to effective information security management.

ISO/IEC 27001: 2005 was officially published on October 15, 2005. This standard cancels and replaces the old BS 7799-2 standard (published in 2002 by BSI). The old BS 7799-2 information security standard is no longer valid, and it has been officially dropped.

This chapter provides some practical guidance and advice for those who seek to obtain a certification for their organizations against the ISMS as defined in ISO/IEC 27001. Implementing an information security management system provides assurance that security concerns are being addressed in accordance with currently accepted best practices.

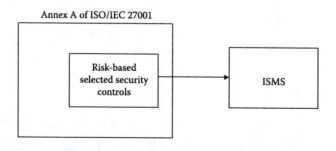

Figure 12.1 Source of ISMS design.

As in any other IS project, the success of your security program is only achievable if you can develop a feasible ISMS plan, measure its effectiveness against this plan, and then take necessary steps to improve your risk position when unexpected incidents take place. The ISMS plan should recognize that the continual improvement of the organization's security posture requires incessant monitoring, management review, and maintenance. This improvement effort requires the availability of adequate resources throughout the organization as needed. This includes the implementation of rigorous training and awareness programs, a careful management of ISMS operations and resources, and the implementation of procedures and other controls capable of enabling prompt detection of security events and response to security incidents.

An ISMS is adopted to systematically operate an organization's information security management system by defining the risk-driven security program the organization needs to correct anomalies and prevent undesired security incidents. The key concept here is that the organization feasibly ensures and improves the confidentiality, integrity, and availability of its information assets.

In ISMS requirements, an organization is required to establish, implement, and continually maintain its documented ISMS, taking into consideration its overall business activities and risks. In this framework, the organization establishes the scope of the ISMS, defines an information security policy, identifies a systematic risk assessment methodology based on prior security policy, identifies the risks associated with the scope defined earlier, manages the risks delineated earlier, devises a risk-driven security program, prepares a plan to treat risk, and prepares a statement of applicability. These steps are discussed in greater detail in the next section.

12.2 How Organizations Interact with the Standards

Most of this book deals with those information security standards the international community has put together to help organizations protect their computing environments. It is important however to know how should organizations interact with those standards.

An organization can interact with the ISO/IEC 27002 (ISO/IEC 17799) and ISO 27001 in different ways, even though there are only three popular approaches organizations can use to take advantage of those standards: compliance, certification, and accreditation.

Compliance is a self-study that the organization voluntarily conducts to verify whether its information security management system complies with one of the standards.

Certification is, on the other hand, awarded by an accredited certification body when an organization successfully completes an independent audit that certifies that the organization's information security management system meets the requirements of a specific standard, for example ISO 27001.

We have seen in an earlier chapter that while the ISO/IEC 17799 or ISO/IEC 27002 provides a code of practice, the ISO/IEC 27001 presents the requirement to develop and maintain an ISMS. That is, an organization can apply for the certification against ISO/IEC 27001 but can only comply with the ISO/IEC 17799 or ISO/IEC 27002.

Accreditation is the effort by which an authorized accreditation body officially grants the authority to a certification body to evaluate, certify and register an organization's ISMS with regard to published standards.

12.3 General ISMS Framework

The ISMS is initiated by establishing the information security policy followed by the definition of the ISMS scope. Given the scope of this ISMS, there is risk assessment where basic risks are estimated, and risk management where possible security controls are evaluated to determine the risk-driven program capable of feasibly mitigating risks below the maximum tolerated risk level. The proposed risk-driven security program ensures continual improvement of the security risk position of the company. That is, the implementation of the ISMS program will set residual risks at an acceptable level. However, new threats and new vulnerabilities keep appearing which will have effects on the current risk position of the company. This situation will lead to a review of the current security policy and a new definition of the scope of the ISMS. The same risk management steps will then follow, as shown in Figure 12.2, which will show the ISMS life cycle.

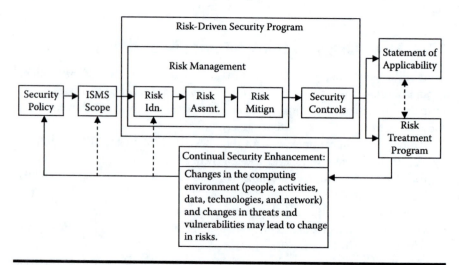

Figure 12.2   ISMS development life cycle.

The ISO/IEC 27001 is self-sufficient in terms of providing all information needed for the ISMS development project. This standard also contains all the specifications needed to produce the ISMS product.

The ISO/IEC 27001 defines steps towards the implementation of ISO/IEC 17799, and describes the process of building an ISMS. The ISO/IEC 27001 proposes six steps for building an ISMS:

1. The scope of the ISMS
2. ISMS security policy
3. Identification of a systematic risk assessment methodology
4. Risk assessment based on the ISMS scope
5. Risk management
6. Preparation of a statement of applicability

12.3.1 Scope of the ISMS

Only considered in the security program are those assets that are highly critical; that is, high availability and/or sensitivity requirements with a risk position above the maximum tolerated risk level. There are many ways to define the ISMS scope. We reserve a special section on ISMS scoping using a risk-based scoping method. The following are approaches for defining the scope for the ISMS:

Business-driven
Policy-driven
Risk-drive
Any combination of the above approaches

Defining the scope may follow a business-driven approach where assets are studied in terms of various features defined for each business process or activity. An alternative approach would follow the structure of the security policy and prioritize areas where the need for security policy enforcement is high. The two approaches may be used together, as shown in Figure 12.3.

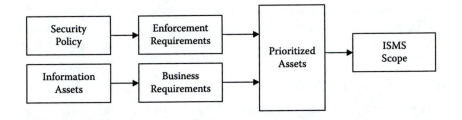

Figure 12.3 ISMS scope based directly on security policy and business requirements.

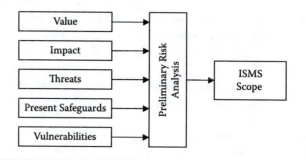

Figure 12.4 ISMS scope based on preliminary risk assessment (and indirectly on policy and business requirements).

Another approach, as depicted in Figure 12.4, would be risk driven. Usually, the risk analysis methodology adopted in the enterprise will determine the approach to be used in defining the scope of the information security project. A good idea would be to construct an inventory of assets if one does not exist. The inventory should define for each asset its value, its sensitivity class, and its availability class, and its owner. The value of an asset may be defined in different ways. The definition should however express the asset value in terms of its operating costs, and its revenues while taking into account economical, social, operational, technical, legal and ethical factors.

12.3.2 How to Define the Scope of the ISMS

The scope of an ISMS can be defined in terms of the organization as a whole, or parts of the organization, covering the relevant data resources, services, technology, and networks. It should clearly define the boundaries. The ISMS could include the entire organization, a computing environment, or one or more of its information systems. An organization may need to define different ISMSs for different parts or aspects of its business.

It is really up to owners to decide what components of the computing environment are to be included in the ISMS study. Owners have to identify those components of the computing environment to be included in the ISMS project. They may decide to select to include the whole computing environment, a limited set of departments, a limited set of applications, or just a limited set of processes.

The main factors that affect the scope decisions include time constraints, budget constraints, local or national laws and regulations, and/or contractual obligations.

12.3.3 Security Policy

In an earlier chapter, we defined security policy as the acceptable behavior of your computing environment. Your computing environment includes people, activities, data, technology, and network [5]. Your policy should provide a criticality classification scheme needed to identify for each asset its sensitivity class and its availability class requirements. The security policy should also specify the maximum accepted security risk level for each of the assets.

12.3.4 Risk Assessment

If the asset inventory is constructed as described earlier, then you are all set for this step. You still need to estimate, for each asset in the scope, its basic risk. If the basic risk is higher than the asset maximum tolerated risk level as defined in the security policy, then we have a problem. The problem may be simply stated as we have a situation where the current security controls implemented to protect the asset are not providing adequate security.

In assessing security risks, you have to take into account all threats that can potentially have effects of the business value generated by any process associated with the asset in question. Of course, those effects depend on asset vulnerabilities; that is, you should be prepared to assess the vulnerabilities on assets and relate them to possible threats so you can estimate the basic risk for this asset.

In defining the ISMS scope, we advised that the organization needs to maintain an inventory of assets. It will be very helpful if the company maintains an inventory of threats, an inventory of vulnerabilities, an inventory of present safeguards, etc. All those inventories are needed in risk assessment. Inventories for vulnerabilities, their effects, and their patches and solutions are available in Carnegie Mellon University's Computer Emergency Response Team. (http://www.cert.org), the National Vulnerability Database (http://nvd.nist.gov/), the Open Source Vulnerability Database and others (http://osvdb.org), the Center for Education and Research in Information Assurance and Security (http://www.cerias.purdue.edu/), and so on.

12.3.5 Risk Management

We now know the basic risks of assets and also the basic risk position for the company. The business-value-generation capability of the company is at risk, and we have to do something about it. There will be obviously many constraints that will restrict your approach of managing risks, example, time, money, regulations, etc. Your way out may be to prioritize your assets based on their basic risk to know which ones should be protected first. Your security policy and security strategy may be of great use in defining the right approach to manage security risks.

Remember that there are always going to be security risks in the organization. You then have to develop business continuity and contingency plans in case something happens. Business continuity was discussed earlier in Chapter 6.

12.3.6 Choose Your Safeguards

After defining the right approach to manage risk at the previous step, you are now well prepared to devise a risk-driven security program capable of continually managing risk.

You should identify the security controls that can bring back the basic risks of assets below the maximum tolerated risk levels as set in the corporate security policy. You need then to devise a risk-driven security program that will consist of feasible managerial, operational, and technical security controls. ISO/IEC 27001 provides a list of security controls that you can choose from [1,2]. The ISO/IEC 27001 requires that security controls should be selected from Annex A provided at the end of the document containing the standard. If, however, compliance and certification against the ISO/IEC 27001 are not sought, then the security controls that work for you may be obtained from NIST SP 800-53 standards, FIPS 200, or other standards which provide alternative safeguards that may be useful [3,4].

12.3.7 Statement of Applicability

The statement of applicability is the justification of the risk-driven security program. For every security control included in the security program, the statement of applicability should show that (1) it is supported by the security policy; (2) it is feasible; (3) it produces mitigation of risk; and (4) it ensures there is continual improvement of the company's risk position. The statement of applicability should also justify the set of security controls considered in the selection process, but not taken from the list of safeguards published by the ISO/IEC 27001.

12.4 The ISMS Model

Seeking a superior competitive advantage based on your ISMS requires a lot more than having an ISMS. Compliance with the ISO/IEC 17799 or ISO/IEC 27002 and certification against the ISO/IEC 27001 are necessary steps. This section and the ones that follow discuss the conformity effort to the ISO/IEC 27001 starting with a detailed description of the ISMS model.

The use of "shall" in the ISO/IEC 27001 is of imperative nature if conformity to the standard is sought. Any organization seeking conformity to ISO/IEC 27001 has no choice but to establish, implement, operate, monitor, review, maintain, improve, and document its ISMS as it is feasible to do so, given the specificity of its business activities and associated risks. This set of requirements is clear in Clause 4.1 of the ISO 27001:2005 standard, called General Requirements.

The standard provides four sections going from Section 4, starting at page 3, to Section 8, terminating on page 12. The early pages and the pages with roman numbers, provide some overhead information, an introduction to the standard and the process-approach employed in interpreting the standard, the scope, and some terms and definitions. The rest of the pages at the end of the standard's document going from page 13 to page 40 present three annexes: Annex A, Annex B, and Annex C. Annex A, from page 13 to page 29, presents a list of security objectives and security controls. This list is the foundation of your risk-driven security program devised as

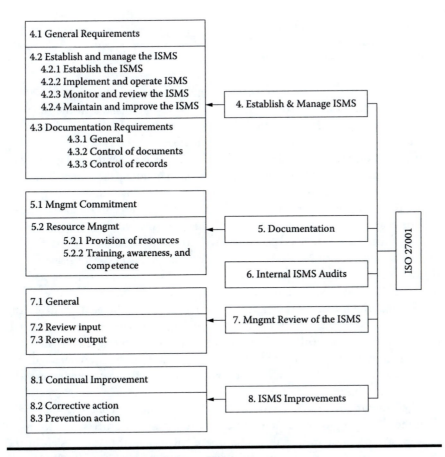

Figure 12.5   Structure for ISO/IEC 27001.

part of writing the organization's statement of applicability (SOA). Every security control listed in Annex A has to be discussed in the SOA. If it is selected by the risk-driven security program, the selection decision has to be justified. If it is rejected, then the rejection decision has to be justified.

Annex B, on page 30, presents OECD (Organization for Economic Co-operation and Development) principles and how they relate to ISO/IEC 27001. Annex C, from page 31 to page 33, is concerned with the correspondence between the standards ISO 9001:2000, ISO 14001:2004, and ISO 27001:2005. Page 34 contains the bibliography used in developing this international standard.

The vital set of requirements defined by the standard for an effective ISMS is provided in Sections 4 to 8. These sections, as shown in Figure 6, present detailed requirements to achieve an effective ISMS:

ISMS: Section 4
Management Responsibility: Section 5

Internal ISMS Audits: Section 6
Management review of the ISMS: Section 7
ISMS Improvements: Section 8

The easiest way to obtain an effective ISMS that is conform to the ISO/IEC 27001 is to thoroughly adopt the specifications and approaches defined in the standard when you plan the development and management of the ISMS. We will discuss the requirements and present ways to implement them.

The ISMS model presented in the ISO/IEC 27001 is presented in Figure 12.6. Several input subsystems feed information needed to build the ISMS model. We list some of them: main organizational objectives, business activities, security requirements, computing environment, size of the company, and organizational structure.

The main organizational objectives of the company will certainly guide the design of the ISMS model as these objectives are the foundation of the definition of risks and any business value generation capability. Security controls that do not significantly and feasibly reduce risks cannot be added to the risk-driven security program. The ISMS will filter out any security controls that are not feasible.

When business activities change, their management requirements change. Any change in people, their activities, data, technology, software, or equipment will require a reevaluation of the ISMS model. New security controls may be added or existing controls may be dropped. Also, the implementation requirements of the current security controls may change to satisfy any new requirements imposed by the changes in business activities.

The structure and size of the company also affect the design of the ISMS model. Securing more people, more data resources, more business processes, more technology, or more equipment will require more enhancement of the design of the ISMS. The size of the company will certainly affect the design of the ISMS and the resulting risk-driven security program. The logical distribution of the company, the infrastructure of the company, and its management structure will also have an effect on the design of the ISMS.

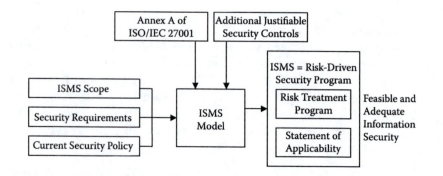

Figure 12.6   ISMS model compliant with ISO/IEC 27001.

Another element that is of great importance in the design of the ISMS is obviously the computing environment. The ISMS itself is part of the computing environment. Any change in the computing environment, whether it is in human or data resources, software, hardware, or activities should be immediately studied to identify any effects for which the risk-driven security program will be reevaluated. Any change in security strategy, security policy, regulations, and contractual obligations should be studied to reconfirm the validity of the ISMS design or its revision.

12.5 The Process Approach Ensures the Continual Improvement of the ISMS

The ISO/IEC 27001 standard adopts a process approach for establishing, implementing, operating, operating, monitoring, reviewing, maintaining, and improving an organization's ISMS. An organization has to manage many activities in order to achieve its strategic objectives. Organization activities may be modeled as processes that transform inputs into outputs.

Similarly, the ISMS may be considered as the integration of many interacting processes sharing the same objective of providing effective information security throughout the organization. A process will then transform inputs made of owners' requirements expectations into security outcomes needed for the effective management of the ISMS.

The ISO/IEC 27001 applies a system of processes within the organization, together with the identification and interactions of these processes, and their management.

The process approach for information security management presented in the ISO/IEC 27001 standard encourages its users to emphasize the need to:

1. Understand an organization's information security requirements and how to establish policy and objectives for feasible information security.
2. Implement and operate controls to manage an organization's information security risks in the context of the organization's overall business risks.
3. Monitor and review the performance and effectiveness of the ISMS.
4. Secure the continual improvement of the ISMS based on objective measurement.

Figure 12.7 illustrates how an ISMS process may be depicted. Each ISMS process gets two types of inputs: information security requirements, and owners' expectations. The process transforms the inputs into information security outcomes. These outcomes are compared to owners' expectations. If a significant gap is detected between the process output and owners' expectations, then it is necessary to review the ISMS process. There could be anomalies in the transformation process that should be resolved. It is possible, however, that owners cannot identify a method

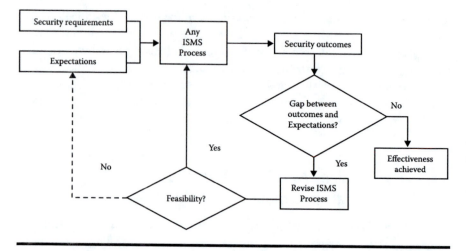

Figure 12.7   Iterative approach to manage an ISMS process.

of transformation that can reduce the gaps detected between the security outcomes and owners' expectations. In this case, owners have to review their security requirements and define new expectations. The same analysis may be iterated until gaps between the process security outcomes and owners' expectations are reduced to a lower level accepted by owners.

A process is simply an activity defined by a clear objective, a set of performance criteria, and a control mechanism, that is designed to transform a set of inputs into a set of outputs using a group of components taken from the organization's computing environment including people, activities, data, technology, and network.

The definition of a process should include the following:

Process objective
Process owner
All components of the computing environment playing a role in the process
Process control mechanism
Process transformation mechanism
Process inputs
Process outputs
Process performance criteria

Every section, from Section 3 to Section 12, is interpreted as a process. The security area treated in one of the sections is interpreted as the security objective set of this security area. For example, Section 3 is concerned with security policy. The security objective defined for this section is the adequacy of the organization security policy. There are practices that have to be adopted in order to comply with this section of the standard, and there are security controls that have to be implemented in order to satisfy the requirements for adopting the security practice.

12.6 Development of the Information Security Management System

ISO/IEC 27001 specifies, as is cited in the standard itself, the requirements for establishing, implementing, operating, monitoring, reviewing, maintaining, and improving a documented ISMS within the context of the organization's overall business risks. We saw earlier that ISO 17799 provides a framework to adopt best practices for information security management. The specifications presented in ISO/IEC 27001 define the requirements for the development and maintenance of an ISMS based on the controls described in the ISO 17799. ISO/IEC 27001 also requires the adoption of the Plan-Do-Check-Act model in the development and maintenance of the ISMS.

The ISMS is developed using four phases, as shown in Figure 12.8:

1. *Plan* phase
2. *Do* phase
3. *Check* phase
4. *Act* phase

The *plan* phase is where the ISMS is established. The *do* phase is where the ISMS is implemented and operated. The *check* phase is where the ISMS monitored and reviewed. The *act* phase is where the ISMS is maintained and improved.

ISO/IEC 27001 describes the following steps in planning the ISMS project:

1. Define the scope of the ISMS.
2. Define a security policy.
3. Undertake a risk assessment/analysis.
4. Manage the risk.
5. Select control objectives and the actual controls to be implemented/applied.
6. Prepare a Statement of Applicability.

The objective of the Corporate Information Security Policy is to provide management direction and support for information security. Therefore, management should set a clear policy direction and demonstrate support for, and commitment to, information security across the entire organization.

The policy document should be approved by senior management, and published and communicated, as appropriate, to all employees. It should state management commitment and set out the organization's approach to managing information security.

a. Define the scope and boundaries of the ISMS;
b. Define an ISMS policy;
c. Define the risk assessment approach of the organization;
d. Identify the risks;
e. Analyze and evaluate the risks;
f. Identify and evaluate options for the treatment of risks;
g. Select control objectives and controls for risk treatment
h. Obtain management approval of the proposed residual risks;
i. Obtain management authorization to implement and operate the ISMS;
j. Prepare a statement of applicability.

a. Implement the identified improvements in the ISMS
b. Take appropriate corrective and preventive actions in accordance with 8.2 and 8.3
c. Communicate the actions and improvements to all interested parties
d. Ensure that the improvements achieve their intended objectives.

Establish the ISMS (4.2.1):

Maintain and Improve the ISMS (4.2.4):

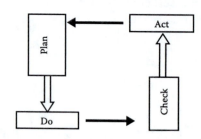

Implement and operate the ISMS (4.2.2):

Monitor and review the ISMS (4.2.3):

a. Formulate a risk treatment plan;
b. Implement the risk treatment plan;
c. Implement controls selected in 4.2.1.g of ISO/IEC 27001;
d. Define how to measure the effectiveness of the selected controls;
e. Implement training and awareness programs as in 5.2.2 of ISO/IEC 27001;
f. Manage operation of the ISMS;
g. Manage resources for the ISMS as in 5.2 of ISO/IEC 27001;
h. Implement procedures and controls for prompt detection of security events and response to security incidents as in 4.2.3a of ISO/IEC 27001.

a) Execute monitoring and reviewing procedures
b) Undertake regular reviews of the effectiveness of the ISMS
c) Measure the effectiveness of controls to verify that security requirements have been met.
d) Review risk assessments at planned intervals and review the residual risks and the identified acceptable levels of risks
e) Conduct internal ISMS audits at planned intervals.
f) Undertake a management review of the ISMS on a regular basis to ensure that the scope remains adequate and improvements in the ISMS process are identified.
g) Update securely plans to take into account the findings of monitoring and reviewing activities.
h) Record actions and events that could have an impact on the effectiveness or performance of the ISMS

Figure 12.8   PDCA model for the development of the ISMS.

The next section illustrates how the PDCA is applied in the ISMS.

12.7 Design of the ISMS

The design of the ISMS is based on information produced by risk assessment and the applicability of Annex A of the ISO/IEC 27001 to solving security problems identified within the ISMS scope. The ISMS design also provides for the continual improvement based on the effectiveness of adopted security controls and any change in the computing environment. Let us create a structured set of security controls A obtained from Annex A. Let us denote A as $\{c_i\}$, $i = 1,n$ where every control in Annex A there exists j such that c_j belongs to A; and vice versa, for any i, $i = 1,n$, if c_i is in A then c_i is also defined in Annex A.

Because Annex A is not intended to be exhaustive, let us also identify all applicable security controls that are not in Annex A but are candidates for adoption in the organization's risk-driven security program. This new set of security controls is called A+. Figure 12.9 depicts the ISMS design process. The following steps have to be followed in the ISMS design:

1. Identify any useful security control that does not violate your security policy but it is not in Annex A; call this new set A+.
2. Compute basic risks for each asset *a*.

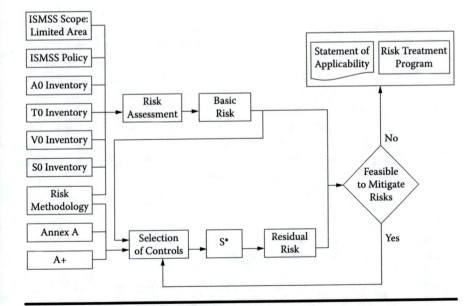

Figure 12.9   Design of ISMS subsystem (ISMSS).

3. For each control c in Annex AUA+, for each asset *a*.
   Compute residual risk of a given *c*.
   Compute its average annual total relevant costs.
   Study feasibility of control for *a* in these aspects:
   > Economical
   > Social
   > Technical
   > Operational
   > Legal/ethical
4. Rank assets in descending order of residual risk.
5. While there is still budget:
   Select the security control *c*.
   Add a record to the statement of applicability (SOA).
   Add a detailed explanation that justifies your adoption of this security control.
6. For any security control in Annex A that was not selected, add a detailed explanation that justifies your rejection of the control. You do not have to justify the rejection of those security controls accumulated in A+. An example of a statement of applicability is provided in Table 12.1.

12.8 Security Inventory Needs

If there are no threats menacing the computing environment, then there will be no security risks despite any existing system vulnerabilities because there are no threats to exploit those vulnerabilities. If there are no vulnerabilities, then even if there are nasty threats out there they still can cause no harm to the computing environment; there are, hence, no security risks. So in order to assess risks we need to have information about current threats, system vulnerabilities, and the effectiveness of present security controls. In addition, in order to study the asset exposures we then need information about information assets, their criticality, and their impact levels, given existing threats. Figure 12.10 shows how risk is computed. Based on the information above, then, in order to be prepared for any risk assessment activities, we need to maintain at least four types of inventories:

A0: inventory of assets
T0: inventory of threats
V0: inventory of vulnerabilities
S0: inventory of present security controls

As shown in Figure 12.11, the computation of risk is directly dependent on vulnerability levels and the effectiveness of security controls, but it is only indirectly linked to asset impact levels and threat likelihood through asset security exposure levels.

Table 12.1 Generic Statement of Applicability

Security Control	A or A+	Decision: A or R	Feasibility: E,S,O,T,L	Basic Risk on All Relevant Assets	Residual Risk on All Relevant Assets	Ref. in Security Policy	Ref. in Regulations/ Contractual Obligations

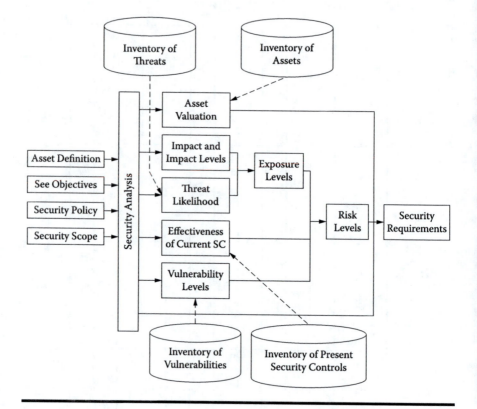

Figure 12.10   Main security inventories needed to manage risks.

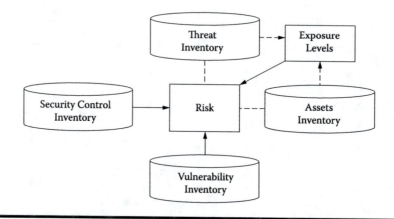

Figure 12.11   Main security inventories maintained for risk assessment.

Asset exposure levels are determined in terms of asset business impact levels and the likelihood of current threats. Basic risk levels can only be assessed if we have information about the assets, their exposure levels, their vulnerabilities, and the effectiveness of present security controls.

In order to follow the process approach in the design of an ISMS as suggested by the ISO/IEC 27001, we need to start by defining the inputs, the outputs, the transformations, the performance criteria, and the control mechanism. But before we further proceed, let us first define the framework for the entire organization's ISMS.

A simple way to do so is to just layout the steps the ISO/IEC 27001 standard requires for establishing the organization's ISMS. They are listed in section 4.2.1 of the standard as follows:

a. Define the scope and boundaries of the ISMS
b. Define an ISMS policy
c. Define the risk assessment approach of the organization
d. Identify the risks
e. Analyze and evaluate the risks
f. Identify and evaluate options for the treatment of risks
g. Select control objectives and controls for risk treatment
h. Obtain management approval of the proposed residual risks
i. Obtain management authorization to implement and operate the ISMS
j. Prepare a statement of applicability

The first step in the process of establishing the ISMS is to define the scope of the ISMS. The organization may be divided into areas with well-defined owners. An area, for example, may be the IT department, or the digital library application. NIST SP 800-18 defines general support systems and major applications [3].

Even though we try throughout this book to stick to the same meaning of terms as used by NIST, some of the terms encountered may not necessarily hold the definition meant in NIST documentation.

The term "general support system" or "system" means an interconnected set of information resources under the same direct management control that shares common functionality. A system normally includes hardware, software, information, data, applications, communications, and people. A system can be, for example, a local area network (LAN) including smart terminals that supports a branch office, an agency-wide backbone, a communications network, a departmental data processing center including its operating system and utilities, a tactical radio network, or a shared information processing service organization.

The term *major application* means an application that requires special attention to security due to the risk and magnitude of the harm resulting from the loss, misuse, or unauthorized access to, or modification of, the information in the application. All federal applications require some level of protection. Certain applications, because of the information in them, however, require special management oversight and should be treated as major. Adequate security for other applications should be provided by the security of the systems in which they operate. Whenever it is used in this book, the term *adequate security* means security commensurate with the risk and magnitude of the harm resulting from the loss, misuse, or unauthorized access to, or modification of, information. This includes assuring that systems and applications used by the enterprise operate effectively and provide appropriate confidentiality, integrity, and availability, through the use of cost-effective management, personnel, operational, and technical controls.

Let us denote the selected areas defined in the ISMS scope as ISMS subsystem areas. This indicates that even though the ISMS subsystem areas overlap, we will still consider that every ISMS subsystem area requires its own ISMS, called ISMS subsystem or ISMSS.

That is, as shown in Figure 12.12, the organization ISMS is the integration of a set of ISMS subsystems delineated by the definition of the ISMS scope and its security policy. The term *integration* is essential to the ISMS as it ensures that there are no information conflicts among outputs produced by various ISMS subsystems constituting the ISMS. A very well written statement of applicability will by construction enforce the integrity property gluing the ISMS subsystems together.

The second step will further emphasize the interactions among all processes of the ISMS including the ISMS subsystems. That is, in addition to the policy associated with the organization of the ISMS, there are separate subsets of policies concerned with the individual ISMS subsystems.

In the third step in designing the ISMS, the organization is required to define the risk assessment methodology to be adopted throughout the ISMS. Usually, the same risk methodology should be adopted throughout the enterprise.

At this point of the design process, we have (1) a well defined scope made of a finite set of ISMS subsystems areas: ISMSS area 1, ISMSS area 2, and so on; (2) a well defined policy for the overall ISMS and a finite set of ISMS subsystem policy chunks; and (3) a well-defined risk assessment methodology.

The next step to complete is to assess risks. This will certainly depend on the security risk methodology selected earlier. However, any good security risk assessment should prepare at least four types of inventories: the inventory of assets A0, the inventory of threats T0, the inventory of vulnerabilities V0, and the inventory of security controls S0.

The inventories represent what owners know they have. For the A0-inventory, owners declare the assets they manage. For the T0-inventory, owners describe the threats menacing them. Remember, an asset owner may not know all the threats that can potentially harm the asset. The zero in T0 means that this inventory only lists the threats the asset owner believe they exist and may harm the asset. If an auditor studies the computing environment and determines that there are additional

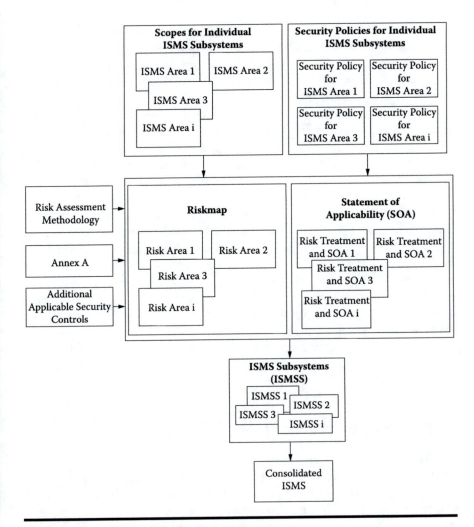

Figure 12.12 ISMS subsystems consolidated.

threats that are not originally declared by the owner, the additional threats should not be listed in the T0 inventory.

In the same line, the owner of an asset declares all know asset vulnerabilities to be listed in the V0 inventory. If an auditor uses vulnerability assessment software to identify additional vulnerabilities on the asset, they should not be added to the V0 inventory.

As a simple rule, any inventory used in computing the basic risks is a level-0 inventory. If additional assets, additional threats, additional vulnerabilities, or additional security controls are involved in computing risks we will then talk about residual risks, and we will use level-1 to denote the inventories of assets, threats, vulnerabilities, and security controls.

Figure 12.13 illustrates the cyclic process approach used in establishing an ISMS subsystem. The inputs are well defined as ISMSS scope limited area, ISMSS policy, A-0 inventory, T0-inventory, V0-inventory, S0-inventory, risk methodology, Annex A of the ISO/IEC 27001 standard, and the set of additional security controls A+ not defined in Annex A.

This process transforms the inputs to produce three important outputs at three consecutive stages. In the first stage, the ISMSS process produces basic risks. In any situation where the basic risk of an asset is above the maximum tolerated level, then a set of security controls have to be selected from Annex A of the ISO/IEC 27001 standard if the controls are listed in Annex A, or from the additional set A+ of security controls proposed to owners.

Residual risks on assets are then recalculated based on the new security controls. While there is still budget available for the ISMSS, and as long as it is feasible, the difference between residual risks and the tolerated risk level is to be minimized. The final set of security controls taken from Annex A and A+ have to be documented and justified in a report called *statement of applicability*. Any security control from Annex A that is not adopted has to be justified. Any security control from Annex A that is adopted has to be justified. Any security control from A+ that is adopted has to be justified.

The set of security controls included in the statement of applicability of the ISMSS is called a *risk-driven security program* or a *risk treatment plan* for the ISMSS.

12.9 The Integration of ISMS Subsystems

The first step in establishing the organization's ISMS gives freedom to owners for defining the scope of the ISMS. This freedom may be something acceptable if the organization decides to seek compliance with the ISO/IEC 17799 or certification against the ISO/IEC 27001 for a special area of the organization or its computing environment. Sometimes, this is also acceptable to please some partners or to satisfy some contractual obligations.

However, this freedom may be misleading, given the fact that owners selection decisions may leave out very critical domains or applications in the organization. If those areas are at risk then the entire organization may be at risk. Normally, the justification of a risk-driven security program is very difficult to support.

At least in theory, the only security solution for the entire organization is to go to an integrated ISMS. ISMS subsystems may be designed independently, but a risk-driven security program will be incomplete without a consolidated statement of applicability where all adopted security controls are justified and all rejected controls are justified. The Conformity decision scheme for an ISMS subsystem against ISO/IEC 27001 is depicted in Figure 12.13.

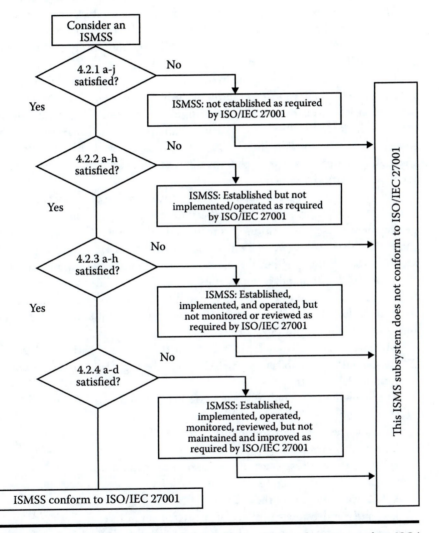

Figure 12.13 Conformity decision scheme for an ISMS subsystem against ISO/IEC 27001.

12.10 Self-Assessment for Compliance

Self-assessment should be done in terms of the PDCA security management cycle to make sure that the developed ISMS is up for compliance with the ISO/IEC 27001. If there are problems that may prevent this compliance, then necessary corrections may be planned to eliminate any deficiencies that can blemish the organization chances of compliance with ISO/IEC 27001. Table 12.2 summarizes compliance assessment information for establishing the ISMS. The conformity decision scheme to the ISO/IEC 27001 is provided in Figure 12.13.

Let us continue using the same five-point scale to measure to what extent ISO/IEC 27001 clauses are satisfied, and arbitrarily fix the score 2 as the minimum satisfaction level to be accepted in assessing compliance to ISO/IEC 27001. Any clause in the ISO/IEC 27001 that is assessed and gets a score higher than 2 is considered complying with the ISO/IEC 27001 on that clause. If all the clauses in all the PDCA phases get a score higher than 2, we then declare that the target system is compliant with the ISO/IEC 27001.

Before we move on to the implementation and operation phase, or the Do phase in the PDCA cycle, let us perform a self-assessment test to make sure that the ISMS development phase was performed as required in the ISO/IEC 27001 standard. If there is any ISMS subsystem for which one of the 10 steps 4.2.1, a through j, has its score less than 2, then the ISMS subsystem does not satisfy the requirements set by the ISO/IEC 27001 standard for establishing an ISMS. If all scores for all steps a to j on 4.2.1 are greater or equal than 2, and if the ISMS subsystem average score is less than 3, then this ISMS subsystem does not satisfy the ISO/IEC 27001 requirements for establishing an ISMS.

Moreover, if there is an ISMS subsystem that does not satisfy the ISO/IEC 27001 standard for establishing an ISMS, then the organization's ISMS does not conform to the standard.

The following steps constitute the ISMS planning process:

a. Define the scope and boundaries of the ISMS.
b. Define an ISMS policy.
c. Define the risk assessment approach of the organization.
d. Identify the risks.
e. Analyze and evaluate the risks.
f. Identify and evaluate options for the treatment of risks.
g. Select control objectives and controls for risk treatment.
h. Obtain management approval of the proposed residual risks.
i. Obtain management authorization to implement and operate the ISMS.
j. Prepare a statement of applicability.

Before we move on to the monitoring and review phase, or the Check phase in the PDCA cycle, let us perform a self-assessment test to make sure that the ISMS

Table 12.2   Self-Assessment for Establishing an ISMS or an ISMS Subsystem as Required by ISO/IEC 27001

Required Steps	Yes or No	If Yes, Show Ref. and Page No.	Show Evidence: Where?	If No, (1) Explain Why and (2) When, If Planned	Enter Satisfaction Score 1: ≤20% 2: >20% & ≤40% 3: >40% & ≤60% 4: >60% & ≤80% 5: >80%
a. Define the scope and boundaries of the ISMS.					
b. Define an ISMS policy.					
c. Define the risk assessment approach of the organization.					
d. Identify the risks.					
e. Analyze and evaluate the risks.					
f. Identify and evaluate options for the treatment of risks.					

Continued

Table 12.2 Self-Assessment for Establishing an ISMS or an ISMS Subsystem as Required by ISO/IEC 27001 (*Continued*)

Required Steps	Yes or No	If Yes, Show Ref. and Page No.	Show Evidence: Where?	If No, (1) Explain Why and (2) When, If Planned	Enter Satisfaction Score 1: ≤20% 2: >20% & ≤40% 3: >40% & ≤60% 4: >60% & ≤80% 5: >80%
g. Select control objectives and controls for risk treatment.					
h. Obtain management approval of the proposed residual risks.					
i. Obtain management authorization to implement and operate the ISMS.					
j. Prepare a statement of applicability.					
Do you think your organization has adequately established an ISMS or an ISMS subsystem?					
Minimum score:					
Average score:					

implementation and operation phase was performed as required in the ISO/IEC 27001 standard. If there is any ISMS subsystem for which one of the eight steps 4.2.2, "a" through "h" has a score less than 2, the ISMS subsystem does not satisfy the requirements set by the ISO/IEC 27001 standard for implementing and operating an ISMS. If all scores for all steps "a" to "h" on 4.2.2 are greater or equal than 2, and if the ISMS subsystem average score is less than 3, then this ISMS subsystem does not satisfy the ISO/IEC 27001 requirements for implementing and operating an ISMS.

Table 12.3 summarizes compliance assessment information for implementing the ISMS.

Moreover, if there is an ISMS subsystem that does not satisfactorily satisfy the ISO/IEC 27001 standard for implementing and operating an ISMS, then the organization's ISMS does not conform to the standard.

Before we move on to the maintenance and improvement phase, or the Act phase in the PDCA cycle, let us perform a self-assessment test to make sure that the ISMS monitoring and review phase was performed as required in the ISO/IEC 27001 standard. If there is any ISMS subsystem for which one of the eight steps 4.2.3, "a" through "h" that has its score less than 2, then the ISMS subsystem does not satisfy the requirements set by the ISO/IEC 27001 standard for monitoring and reviewing an ISMS. If all scores for all steps "a" to "h" on section 4.2.3 are greater or equal than 2, and if the ISMS subsystem average score is less than 3, then this ISMS subsystem does not satisfy the ISO/IEC 27001 requirements for monitoring and reviewing an ISMS. Table 12.4 summarizes compliance assessment information for monitoring and reviewing the ISMS.

Moreover, if there is an ISMS subsystem that does not satisfy the ISO/IEC 27001 standard for monitoring and reviewing an ISMS, then the organization's ISMS does not conform to the standard.

Before we can make a final decision concerning the conformity of the ISMS subsystem, let us conduct a self-assessment test to make sure that the ISMSS conforms to ISO/IEC 27001 standard. If there is any ISMS subsystem for which one of the 4 steps 4.2.4, "a" through "d" has its score less than 2, the ISMS subsystem does not satisfy the requirements set by the ISO/IEC 27001 standard for the conformity of the ISMS. If all scores for all steps "a" to "d" on 4.2.4 are greater or equal than 2, then if the ISMS subsystem average score is less than 3, this ISMS subsystem does not satisfy the ISO/IEC 27001 requirements for conformity. Table 12.5 summarizes compliance assessment information for maintaining the ISMS.

Moreover, if there is an ISMS subsystem that does not satisfy the ISO/IEC 27001 standard, then the organization's ISMS does not conform to the standard.

Any ISMS subsystem for which one the following steps gets a score lower than 3 does not comply with the ISO/IEC 27001:

1. The 10 steps "a" through "j" in section 4.2.1 of ISO/IEC 27001 for establishing the ISMS;

Table 12.3 Self-Assessment for Implementing and Operating an ISMS or an ISMS Subsystem as Required by ISO/IEC 27001

Required Steps	Yes or No	If Yes, Show Ref. and Page No.	Show Evidence: Where?	If No, (1) Explain Why, (2) When, if Planned	Enter Satisfaction Score 1: ≤20% 2: >20% & ≤40% 3: >40% & ≤60% 4: >60% & ≤80% 5: >80%
a. Formulate a risk treatment plan.					
b. Implement the risk treatment plan.					
c. Implement controls selected in 4.2.1.g of ISO/IEC 27001.					
d. Define how to measure the effectiveness of the selected controls.					

e. Implement training and awareness programs as in 5.2.2 of ISO/IEC 27001.				
f. Manage operation of the ISMS.				
g. Manage resources for the ISMS as in 5.2 of ISO/IEC 27001.				
h. Implement procedures & controls for prompt detection of security events and response to security incidents as in 4.2.3.a of ISO/IEC 27001.				

Do you think your organization has adequately established an ISMS or an ISMS subsystem?

Minimum score:

Average score:

Table 12.4 Self-Assessment for Monitoring and Reviewing an ISMS or an ISMS Subsystem as Required by ISO/IEC 27001

Required Steps	Yes or No	If Yes, Show Ref. and Page No.	Show Evidence: Where?	If No, (1) Explain Why, (2) When, if Planned	Enter Satisfaction Score 1: ≤20% 2: >20% & ≤40% 3: >40% & ≤60% 4: >60% & ≤80% 5: >80%
a. Execute monitoring and reviewing procedures.					
b. Undertake regular reviews of the effectiveness of the ISMS.					
c. Measure the effectiveness of controls to verify that security requirements have been met.					
d. Review risk assessments at planned intervals and review the residual risks and the identified acceptable levels of risks.					

e. Conduct internal ISMS audits at planned intervals.				
f. Undertake a management review of the ISMS on a regular basis to ensure that the scope remains adequate and improvements in the ISMS process are identified.				
g. Update securely plans to take into account the findings of monitoring and reviewing activities.				
h. Record actions and events that could have an impact on the effectiveness or performance of the ISMS.				
Do you think your organization has adequately established an ISMS or an ISMS subsystem? Minimum score: Average score:				

Table 12.5 Self-Assessment for Maintaining and Improving an ISMS or an ISMS Subsystem as Required by ISO/IEC 27001

Required Steps	Yes or No	If Yes, Show Ref. and Page No.	Show Evidence: Where?	If No, (1) Explain Why, (2) When, if Planned	Enter Satisfaction Score 1: ≤20% 2: >20% & ≤40% 3: >40% & ≤60% 4: >60% & ≤80% 5: >80%
a. Implement the identified improvements in the ISMS.					
b. Take appropriate corrective and preventive actions in accordance with 8.2 and 8.3.					
c. Communicate the actions and improvements to all interested parties.					
d. Ensure that the improvements achieve their intended objectives.					
Do you think your organization has adequately established an ISMS or an ISMS subsystem?					
Minimum score:					
Average score:					

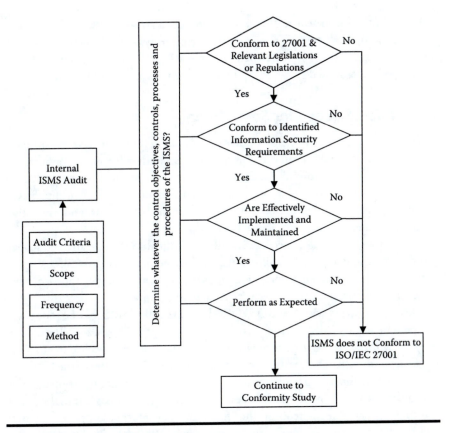

Figure 12.14   Internal ISMS audit.

2. The 8 steps "a" through "h" in section 4.2.2 of ISO/IEC 27001 for implementing the ISMS;
3. The 8 steps "a" through h in section 4.2.3 of ISO/IEC 27001 for monitoring the ISMS; and
4. The 4 steps "a" to "d" in section 4.2.4 of ISO/IEC 27001 for maintaining the ISMS.

Moreover, as shown in Figure 12.14, if there is an individual ISMS subsystem that does not satisfy the ISO/IEC 27001 standard, then the overall organization's ISMS does not conform to the standard.

12.11 Revisiting ISMS Scoping

12.11.1 ISMS Scoping

ISMS scoping is a very important step in developing an ISMS. It is therefore important to prioritize assets and subsystems of the computing environment for their inclusion in the ISMS scope. This section proposes a two-tier risk-based approach (T2-SRI/C) to be adopted for the prioritization of subsystems for their inclusion in the ISMS scope. A small but detailed example was illustrated to demonstrate the working of the proposed two-tier risk-based prioritization approach.

12.11.2 ISMS Scope for Small Enterprises

Small enterprises have limited information infrastructure and have no business objectives that depend on information requiring strict data integrity, confidentiality, and/or availability conditions. Because these subsystems face no major threats, the risks are only minor and a formal ISMS is not required. For these enterprises, risk management through periodic risk identification, assessment, and mitigation is very adequate.

If, however, an ISMS is needed, it will be a limited ISMS that may be scoped using a bottom-up approach. This is usually a fast and precise approach for scoping because in such a small environment, owners know the assets to be protected, their basic risks, the threats, and the security controls that work.

Before complying with the ISO 27001, the scope of the ISMS may be thought of as a preliminary risk identification, assessment, and mitigation process. The conformity to the ISO 27001 will go through all the analyses and steps needed to establish, implement, operate, monitor, review, and improve the effectiveness of the ISMS.

Security threats to information resources and to the availability of operational systems are of minor impact on business operations for small businesses, but these threats may have direct effects on the effectiveness of information systems, which will impact the business value of larger enterprises. While smaller businesses may not require continuity of operations and refined information systems for which a formal ISMS is needed, larger organizations have to invest considerably in establishing, managing, and improving a certified ISMS.

Scoping the ISMS however require many preparation activities. All members of the ISMS development team have to be familiar with the network topology, operating procedures, user practices, and the current policies in use. Even though gathering intelligence about the existing threats, systems vulnerabilities, possible consequences, and how is the organization currently protecting itself, still conducting simulations, vulnerability assessment, and penetration tests to assess major weaknesses may not be needed when the ISMS is being scoped.

For a small organization it may be appropriate to conduct a simple simulation by considering the creation of a set of attack scenarios and acting them out to simulate potential attackers. For this, an attack taxonomy may be useful in defining the attack scenarios and playing them; for example, the tester may perform different sequences of social engineering and determine how users react to these attacks. Scoping the ISMS should not in any way require conducting thorough risk analyses as the objective of ISMS scoping is to identify driver components of the computing environment and select those subsystems that should be included in the ISMS scope.

We do not need to conduct a detailed and precise risk analysis, but we need a simpler, less expensive, and approximate approach that ranks the candidate subsystems the same way the detailed risk analysis does. That is, the candidate subsystems recommended to be included in the ISMS scope, by the detailed risk analysis or by the approximate risk-based approach, should be the same.

This section proposes a risk-based prioritization approach called the *two-tier security risk-based prioritization approach* or the *two-tier security risk index and classification approach* (T2-SRI/C).

12.11.3 Enterprise Modeling for ISMS Scoping

In order to ease the scoping process, it is important to think of a modeling process that reorganizes the organization's computing environment into subsystems as defined earlier.

One way to do this is to envisage a hierarchic structure where the organization's computing environment is arranged into limited support systems, general support systems, and major applications.

Before we advance further, let us all agree on what is meant by a subsystem that is a candidate for inclusion in the ISMS scope. It is very important to realize that we cannot just select assets independently from each other and include them in the ISMS scope, for at least two main reasons: first, there are too many assets to be selected from, and we may end up selecting the wrong one which is known for its low risks; second, assets have to be connected together according to their common objectives, their common management structure, or their common layout. Subsystems of any computing environment may be divided into subsystems that share common objectives, have the same management, and connected in a common layout. These subsystems are of three types: limited support systems, general support systems, and major applications.

12.11.3.1 Major Applications

Most organizations, public or private, medium or large, have applications with significant business value that require a certain level of protection. However, some applications, because of the criticality of their information—stored, processed, or transmitted—require special and stringent management control. These applications are major ones.

Owners are in a position where they can judge and determine whether or not they have major applications. Major applications are systems that perform well-defined functions for which there are clear security objectives and a management group has been identified that is held responsible.

A major application might comprise many individual programs and hardware, software, and telecommunications components. These components can be a single software application or a combination of hardware/software focused on supporting a specific mission-related function. A major application may also consist of multiple individual applications if all are related to a single mission function (e.g., payroll or personnel).

12.11.3.2 General Support Systems and Limited Support Systems

A general support system is defined by NIST as interconnected information resources under the same direct management control which shares common functionality. A general support system normally includes hardware, software, information, data, applications, communications, facilities, and people and provides support for a variety of users and/or applications. Examples of a general support system may be a LAN including smart terminals that support a branch office, a network backbone, a communications network, a departmental data processing center including its operating system and utilities, or any shared information processing service organization.

A limited support system is a set of computing or networking assets that are included in a subsystem where the assets do not share a common functional objective but share a limited security objective for which they are put together—for example, a DMZ group of assets, a VLAN, a set of minor applications that are not part of a general support system, etc.

Usually, owners and managers can easily recognize their major applications and general subsystems. Limited support systems may, however, be constructed as managers if it is appropriate or according to some security policy, as is the case in defining VLANs. It is also possible that some minor applications and secondary information assets are joined together to constitute a limited support system, as in the case, for a DMZ area. Figure 12.15 illustrates a generic enterprise modeling

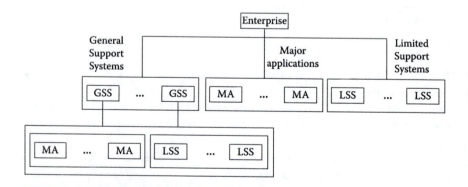

Figure 12.15   Enterprise model for ISMS scoping.

process where the organization is hierarchically arranged into major applications, limited support systems, and general support systems. A general support system may contain major applications and limited support systems.

12.11.4 Preparation for the Two-Tier Risk-Based Prioritization Approach

Assume we have a company with a given budget to start an ISMS. The layout of the organization's computing environment is known, and it consists of a set of subsystems made of general subsystems, limited support systems, and major applications. Every subsystem is made of assets for which we know the criticality, the vulnerability to known threats, the likelihood of known threats, and their impact on the asset. The diagram in Figure 12.16 explains the steps to be taken for the production of two-tier security risk-based priority classes.

In a first phase, for every subsystem that is candidate to be included in the scope of the ISMS project, let us study the two-tier risk-based priority of this subsystem. The criticality of the subsystem is the highest criticality among all assets constituting the subsystem. The vulnerability of the subsystem is the highest vulnerability among all assets constituting the subsystem. The likelihood of subsystem threats is the highest likelihood of threats among all assets constituting the subsystem. The impact of the subsystem is the highest impact among all assets constituting

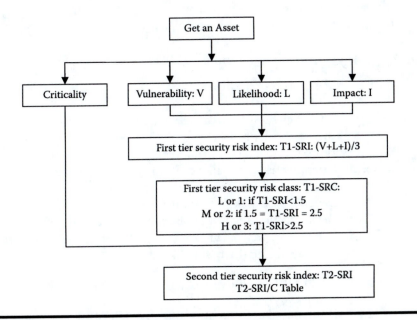

Figure 12.16 Two-tier risk-based prioritization in ISMS.

Table 12.6   Scheme for the T1-SRI Index and T1-SRC Classes

L,V,I = 1,2,3,4, or 5	(L + V + I)/3 < 1.5	1.5 ≤ (L + V + I)/3 ≤ 2.5	(L + V + I)/3 > 3.5
T1-SRC	1 or L	2 or M	3 or H

Table 12.7   T2-SRI

		Criticality		
	Precedence >	L	M	H
T1-SRC	L	1	2	3
	M	2	3	4
	H	3	4	5

the subsystem. The T1-SRI index of the subsystem is the average of subsystem's vulnerability, likelihood, and impact.

Using the T1-SRI/C scheme provided in Table 12.6, we can determine the T1-SRC class of the subsystem. Reiterating the same steps, we just described, we can produce the T1-SRC classes for all candidate subsystems.

In a second phase, as is shown in Figure 12.15, we have to add information about the criticality of subsystems to the T1-SRI/C scheme provided in Table 12.7, and fuse them to produce the T2-SRC classes. The T2-SRI/C approach may be described in more details using the following algorithm:

12.11.4.1 Algorithm for Scoping an ISMS

The TTRP approach consists of the following steps:

1. Identify and define all subsystems candidates for inclusion in the ISMS scope.
2. For every subsystem, s, do the following.
   - 2.1 For every asset, a, in s, do the following:
     - 2.1.1   Determine asset criticality c.
     - 2.1.2   Identify all relevant threats $t(a)$.
     - 2.1.3   Determine likelihood of threats $L(t(a))$.
     - 2.1.4   Determine the asset's vulnerability to the threats $V(t(a))$.
     - 2.1.5   Determine aggregated impact $i(a,t(a))$ of relevant threats on asset a.
     - 2.1.6   Compute the tier-1 security risk index.

$$T1\text{-}SRI(a) = (V(t(a)) + L(t(a)) + I(a,t(a)))/3$$

   - 2.1.7   Determine the T1 security risk class (T1-SRC) of a using the T1-SRC scheme defined in Table 12.6.

2.2 Define the T1-SRC of *s* as the maximum of T1-SRC of *a*, for all *a*'s in subsystem *s*.

2.3 Define the criticality of the subsystem *s* as the highest criticality of all a's in s.

2.3 Define the T2-SRC of s using the T2-SRC scheme provided in Table 12.6.

3. Define the priority vector of subsystems ranked in descending order of priority to be included in the ISMS scope.

12.11.4.2 T1-SRI/C Scheme

The business value of information and business processes should be evaluated before studying risks associated with the current computing environment and scoping any ISMS.

Owners should have prior knowledge about the organization and its computing environment. The ISMS team should be familiar with the structure of the computing environment and its policies. For example, all those assets retained in the ISMS scope have to have a clear and comprehensive security policy to be adopted on establishing the ISMS. All members of the ISMS team and users involved have to fully comprehend the security policy.

Usually, the layout of the computing environment is organized into major applications, general support systems, and limited support systems. If this is not obvious, then the ISMS team has to distribute the assets identified as candidates in the ISMS scope into one or more limited or general support systems and major applications as defined in NIST [3,4]. ISMS scoping will result in selecting one or more general support systems, limited support systems, or major applications to be included in the scope of the ISMS. Some general support systems may include limited support systems and major applications.

Scoping the ISMS for an enterprise with a larger computing environment may be slower and with a higher initial cost. The T2-SRI/C approach is a top-down, methodical, and more formal approach for prioritizing the organization's subsystems for inclusion in the ISMS scope. Remember, the accuracy and precision are not major concerns in the scoping process, even though our objective is to produce without a precise risk analysis method an asset priority vector that lists the same subsystems any other detailed approach produces.

We would like to determine where security is needed to be imperatively improved. This approach aims, through the ISMS, to have a long-term, comprehensive, and well-defined security policy and a security strategy that are supported by owners and management and are well understood and accepted by users.

The T2-SRI/C approach is a systematic scoping approach that involves all the steps any risk-driven security program adopts but to a lesser degree and sometimes even indirectly or in an implicit manner. Before defining the ISMS scope, we need to conduct all of the following, but in a broad manner:

1. Review of security policy and legal requirements
2. Asset preliminary analysis
3. Threat preliminary analysis
4. Vulnerability preliminary analysis
5. Impact preliminary analysis
6. Review of basic security
7. Preliminary risk assessment
8. Scope definition

The objective of risk-based screening is to produce a list of subsystems prioritized in the same order as would be obtained by performing detailed risk analyses but quickly and easily.

We view the company or its computing environment as a set of subsystems. These subsystems may be major applications, general support systems, or limited support systems. Our objective is to scope the ISMS by selecting the subsystems to be included in the scope of the ISMS, given all known constraints, including resources, time, and budget.

We propose a risk-based prioritization approach that owners can use to prioritize the organization's subsystems for inclusion in the scope of the ISMS. We propose using for this a two-tier risk-based prioritization approach (TTRP).

Subsystems are often constituted of multiple assets. The highest T1-SRI for an asset in this subsystem is used as the overall T1-SRI for the subsystem. The T1-SRI is then needed to determine the T1-SRC class of the subsystem.

12.11.4.3 Computing the T1-SRI Index and the T1-SRC Classes

We assume that an asset is defined by four parameters: its criticality, C, which may be high (H), moderate (M), or low (L); the vulnerability to existing relevant threats, V, which may be least vulnerable (1), a little vulnerable (2), moderately vulnerable (3), vulnerable (4), or most vulnerable (5); its likelihood of having existing relevant threats which may be unimportant (1), small (2), moderate (3), high (4), or imminent (5); and the impact of those threats on it which may have least impact (1), a little impact (2), moderate impact (3), great impact (4), or greatest impact (5).

We use the vulnerability, likelihood, and impact parameters to determine the first-tier security risk index denoted as T1-SRI. The minimum value of the T1-SRI index is 3 and the maximum is 15. This is depicted in Table 12.6.

In order to determine the T1-SRC class of a given asset, we first need to compute the T1-SRI value for the asset and then use the T1-SRI/SRC table above to determine its T1-SRC class. For example, if the vulnerability, likelihood, and impact parameters take the values 2, 3, and 4, then their average is the T1-SRI value 3. We can now use the T1-SRI/SRC table to obtain the T1-SRC class is 2.

Before we define the new T2-SRI index, let us explain the need to do so. This can be shown simply by demonstrating that the T1-SRI/SRC scheme is not sufficient alone to prioritize the subsystems that are candidates for inclusion in the scope of the ISMS. Let us consider a simple example, as follows:

1. Let A be an asset with a criticality equal to H and the values $V = 2$, $L = 3$, and $I = 3$. That is, A has a T1-SRI value of 2.66, and it is hence classified in the T1-SRC class 2, according to Table 12.6.
2. Let B be an asset with a criticality equal to L and a the values $V = 5$, $L = 5$, and $I = 5$. That is, A has a T1-SRI value of 5, and it is hence classified in the T1-SRC class 3.

According to the T1-SRI/SRC scheme, B will have a higher priority of 3 and A, a lower priority of 2 despite its higher criticality. That is, the asset B of least critical-ity was given higher priority than asset A which has a high criticality. Therefore, the T1-SRI/SRC scheme is not sufficient to prioritize the organization's subsys-tems without adding the criticality parameter. This justifies the introduction of the T2-SRI/SRC scheme, which adds the criticality parameter to the T1-SRI/SRC scheme.

Let us give an example to demonstrate the transformation of the T1-SRC classes into T2-SRC classes when asset criticality is added. We will revisit the same asset A introduced earlier. A has a criticality equal to H and the values $V = 2$, $L = 3$, and $I = 3$. Initially, A has a T1-SRI value of 2.66, and a T1-SRC class 2. According to Table 12.6, the T2-SRI index of asset A will be 4. On the other hand, B which had a T1-SRI value of 5 and a T1-SRC class of 3, now has a T2-SRI index of 3. That is, asset A gained priority for its inclusion in the ISMS scope, and asset B lost priority when criticality is considered.

The revision of T1-SRI/C approach by adding information about the criticality of the subsystems is represented by the scheme provided in Table 12.7. The com-putation of T2-SRI values are based on the assumption that precedence is given to criticality. The computation method is identical to that of computing asset security exposures (see Chapter 3) based on business impact levels and threat likelihood levels. The use of this method may be simply justified by the fact that the threat and vulnerabilities are all considered threats to the asset.

12.11.5 Example

We are considering, as an example, a fictitious company for which we depict the computing environment in Figure 12.17. A visual examination of the layout of this computing environment identifies the following subsystems:

S1: Major application: A7, A8, A9
S2: Limited support system: A12, A13, A11
S3: General support system: A7, A1, A12, A8, A2, A9, A13, A3, A10, A14, A15, A16, A17, A18, A11

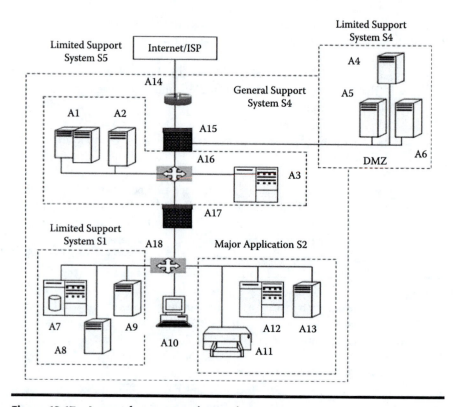

Figure 12.17 Layout for a computing environment.

The enterprise modeling process proposed earlier will produce the enterprise model shown in Figure 12.18 which consists of a major application S2, a limited support system S1, and a limited support system S4, and a general support system S3 containing also the major application S2, and the limited support system S1.

In order to perform the necessary computations for the two-tier risk-based prioritization approach, we need to collect information about the company assets

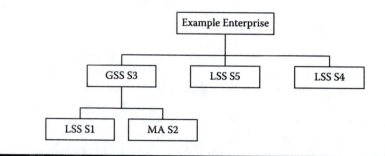

Figure 12.18 Enterprise model for an example enterprise.

constituting the subsystems presented in the enterprise model, their criticality, the threats menacing these assets, and the likelihood of these threats. These steps are presented in the algorithm provided earlier in this chapter.

The information provided in Table 12.8 shows the assets, their criticality, their membership in subsystems of the computing environment, and information about the threat and their likelihood. The notation used in Table 12.8 is as follows:

A: Asset
C: Criticality
S1, S2, S3, S4, and S5: subsystems making the computing environment
L: Likelihood of threats menacing an asset
V: Vulnerability to threats
I: Impact of threats on an asset
T1-SRI index = (L+I+V)/3

The value of the T1-SRI index is obtained by averaging the values of likelihood (L), impact (I), and vulnerability (V). The determination of classes is provided in Table 12.9.

A subsystem consists of multiple assets with varied criticality values. The computation of the first tier security risk index and class (T1-SRI/C) values and the second tier security risk index (T2-SRI) values takes into account of all assets, but when the overall second tier security risk index values for a subsystem are computed, we take the highest values among all second tier security risk index values for all assets in the subsystem. For example, because subsystem S3 consists of assets A1, A2, and A3, which have their respective T2-SRI values equal to 4, 5, and 2, the T2-SRI for subsystem S3 is equal to 5, the highest T2-SRI values given of all assets in S3.

The results of computing the T2-SRI values for all subsystems are provided in Table 12.9.

The T2-SRI/C priority vector is as follows:

S3:5
S5:5
S1:4
S2:3
S4:3

In case there are more than one subsystem in one T2-SRC class, the subsystem with the larger size will have priority to be included in the ISMS scope. In this example, the subsystem S3 is a general support system that includes the subsystem S1 and S2. S3 should hence be selected first to be included in the scope of the ISMS.

Table 12.8 Subsystems, Their Constitution, and Risk Information

A	A7	A1	A12	A8	A2	A9	A13	A3	A10	A14	A15	A16	A17	A18	A11	A6	A5	A4
C	H	H	M	H	H	M	M	M	M	L	L	M	M	M	L	L	L	L
S1	1	0	0	1	0	1	0	0	0	0	0	0	0	0	0	0	0	0
S2	0	0	1	0	0	0	1	0	0	0	0	0	0	0	1	0	0	0
S3	1	1	1	1	1	1	1	1	1	1	1	1	1	1	1	1	0	0
S4	0	0	0	0	0	0	0	0	0	1	1	0	0	0	0	0	1	1
S5	0	1	0	0	1	0	0	1	0	0	0	0	0	0	0	0	0	0
L	5	4	4	3	4	3	3	3	3	2	2	2	2	2	1	4	2	4
I	2	2	3	2	4	3	3	2	3	2	2	2	2	3	3	4	4	3
V	1	3	3	2	4	3	2	2	3	3	2	2	3	3	2	3	4	4
T1-SRI	2.66	3	3.33	2.33	4	3	2.66	2.33	3	2.33	2	2	2.33	2.66	2	3.66	3.33	3.66
T1-SRC	2	2	2	1	3	2	2	1	2	1	1	1	1	2	1	3	2	3
T2-SRI	4	4	3	3	5	3	3	2	3	1	1	2	2	3	1	3	2	2

Note: A, asset; C, criticality; L, likelihood; I, impact; V, vulnerability.

Table 12.9   Obtaining T2-SRC from T1-SRC Give Criticality

Subsystems	T1-SRI	T1-SRC	C	T2-SRI
S1	3	2	H	4
S2	3.33	2	M	3
S3	4	3	H	5
S4	3.66	3	L	3
S5	4	3	H	5

12.12 Conclusion

Electronic information and internet applications are essential to practically all major production systems. Private and public agencies, alike, are experiencing an explosion in the use of electronic data and networked computing. They have rapidly become enormously dependent on these systems and data to support their operations. They certainly realize that if they cannot protect the availability, integrity, and the confidentiality of their information, their ability to carry out their missions will be severely impaired. However, despite the dependence on electronic information and systems, an effective information security management system can deliver a risk-driven security program where preventive and corrective actions are implemented to ensure information security and assurance throughout the organization.

An organization's activities in both the public and the private sector are now considerably dependent on the consistent performance of its business processes. Interconnecting public and private networks, sharing information resources, and investing in networked computing are all indispensable but are also contributing to exposing these business processes to major security threats that could only serve to hamper performance and put the organization information resources at greater risks. Adequately investing in information security is urgent if the organization is to continue allowing for information sharing and collaborative working.

The ISO/IEC 27001 provides the specifications needed to establish an information security management system. This chapter discussed how an organization can plan. Analyze, design, implement, and maintain its information security management system. The chapter showed and demonstrated a complete methodology to develop an information security management system. All steps involved in developing such a system have been discussed very thoroughly based on the technical security audit steps specified in the ISO/IEC 27001.

12.13 Review Questions

1. Explain how the risk methodology adopted by the organization affects the way the ISMS scope is defined.
2. Throughout this book we defined security policy as the acceptable behavior of the computing environment. Find other definitions of security policy on the Internet and compare them with this book's definition.
3. Define system criticality. Explain where is criticality used in the ISO/IEC 27001.
4. Explain how basic risk is estimated. What types of inventories are needed in assessing risks?
5. Explain how a risk-driven program may be obtained.
6. Explain how continual improvement is achieved in the ISMS.
7. Explain how a statement of applicability is designed. Give an example.
8. Explain the utility of the ISO/IEC 27001. How is security enhanced?
9. Explain the differences between nominal security enhancement and technical security enhancement.
10. Give a simple example demonstrating how risks are managed in the ISMS.
11. Give an example where you conduct ISMS development self-assessment towards compliance with ISO/IEC 27001.
12. Give an example where you conduct ISMS implementation self-assessment towards compliance with ISO/IEC 27001.
13. Give an example where you conduct ISMS monitoring and review self-assessment towards compliance with ISO/IEC 27001.
14. Give an example where you conduct ISMS maintenance and improvement self assessment towards compliance with ISO/IEC 27001.

12.14 Workshops

Workshop 1

Murphy's Graphics is a small business in the northeastern United States providing printing services for newsletters, magazines, and black-and-white paperback books. All orders are received online and processed according to several service templates from which customers select their choices online. Murphy's Graphics hosts its own Web site and high availability/backup servers. Murphy's Graphics found the ISO/IEC 27001 a good standard to comply with.

1. Does Murphy's Graphics really need compliance with the ISO/IEC 27001?
2. Assuming that Murphy's Graphics needs to comply with the ISO/IEC 27001, explain all the steps required to do so. How is an ISMS developed

for Murphy's Graphics? Assume real information assets when answering the questions.

Workshop 2

First Direct was launched in 1989 (http://www.thetimes100.co.uk/company_list. php). It offered a new type of banking service. Customers could access all banking services by telephone. The bank was open 24 hours a day, seven days a week, 365 days a year (a 24/7/365 service), with real people always on the end of the phone. This contrasted with the services then offered by the major high street banks. These were available only during traditional banking hours, usually 9 am to 4 pm. The banks closed for most of the weekend. Most transactions had to be made face-to-face. It was difficult to contact the bank unless customers visited a branch.

First Direct's service became highly popular with its customers. The bank won many awards for its service model. By offering additional services such as Internet banking and mobile (on the move) banking, customers could access their accounts and manage their money whenever and wherever they liked. However, convenience was not the only issue, but also that the people at First Direct were courteous, friendly, professional, and adult-to-adult in attitude, not patronizing.

Explain and assess First Direct for compliance with the ISO/IEC 27001. Make up any information on the information assets as needed to demonstrate the working of the ISMS.

References

1. ISO/IEC 27001:2005, Information technology—Security techniques—Information security management systems—Requirements, International Standards Organization, October 2005. (Source: http://www.iso.org.)
2. ISO/IEC 27002:2005 (ISO/IEC 17799:2005)–Information Technology Security Techniques - Code of Practice for Information Security Management. International Standards Organization, June 2005. (Source: http://www.iso.org.)
3. NIST: Guide for Developing Security Plans for Federal Information Systems, NIST Special Publication 800-18, National Institute of Standards and Technology, 2006.
4. NIST: Recommended Security Controls for Federal Information Systems, NIST Special Publication 800-53, Revision 2, 2007.
5. Raggad, B. Corporate Vital Defense Strategy: A Framework for Information Assurance, 23rd National Information Systems Security Conference, NIST/NSA, Baltimore, 2000.

SECURITY IMPLEMENTATION

Chapter 13

Security Solutions

Learning Objectives

After reading this chapter, students are expected to achieve an understanding of:

How the security solution taxonomy works
What security management solutions are
What cryptographic security solutions are
What access control security solutions are
What data traffic security solutions are
What security analysis solutions are
What physical security solutions are
How symmetric cryptography works
How block and stream ciphers work
How public-key cryptography works
How digital signatures work
How VPNs work
How access control works
How biometrics works
How data traffic control works
How network layer firewalls work
How application layer firewalls work
How stateful inspection firewalls work
How security testing is performed
How vulnerability assessment is conducted
How penetration tests work
How forensic analysis is conducted

13.1 Introduction

Users need to connect their computers to other computing resources. They may connect to the Internet or just to their local networks. However they connect, these users subject themselves to the risks of information leakage, information corruption, and service denial. Data sent on the Internet or even on a LAN is placed in data packets with the address of both the recipient and the sender. On a LAN, all machines get all the packets but usually read only the ones intended for them. On the Internet, a packet is routed from one Internet site to another until the final destination is reached. Obviously, someone along the way can examine the contents of the data packet and corrupt it. The sender has no way to know whether or not the intended recipient received the packet. Even if received, the user will have no way to know the received data is actually the same data that was sent to the recipient. Someone on the way could have intercepted the user's message, read it, and modified it. Moreover, to scare even more, logging programs are not restricted to just the programs you are running at the time. There might be a hacker's program out there that intercepts the communication stream and logs all incoming and outgoing messages. Maybe the entire communication is written to a hidden file as it is being sent to the next network interface. That is, there should be many worries for the underprivileged single user and even more worries for those users who enjoy higher privileges. All of those worries will appear very small next to organizations with a large number of users and a complex mix of computing and networking resources. The security distress for organizations can only grow higher with the creepy security reports the literature spreads around from time to time.

After so many years, there is probably no need to still be so pessimistic about this security distress. I am sure there are, by now, all types of security controls that can protect our information assets, computers, and networks from all hackers' transgressions. However, we continue to have problems while improvements for our operating systems are continuously delivered through new versions, new patches, new best practices, and in many other different secure ways.

Just what could go wrong with those new advances in technology? Not so long ago, keyboard logging used to be fairly easy, especially on multitasking operating systems like Windows. The task bar shows us what programs are running, while a program can hide that icon so we cannot be sure which programs are running at any time. I know that with Windows 95 (W95), every time you move or click the mouse, press or release a key, get a packet of data from the modem or network, or use a file, the OD records that event. The event is then placed in a queue and sent to the running programs. Just as W95 is watching the events, so could a hacker program. There might be a program running in the background that monitors keystrokes and places them in a hidden file. All the hacker has to do is get access to this file and read everything you typed.

Anyway, whether you are hooked to an intranet or an external network, you should understand that there is no real information security. This assertion should be accepted by everybody in information security as a security axiom. We redefine information security to enforce a business value. The business value provides added value to information protection, as:

> Information protection is not a goal in itself but rather the reduction of owners' harm resulting from it.

This definition emphasizes owners' benefits from information protection in terms of damage risk minimization. Information security is the protection of the information owner from any harm that can result from effecting information through leakage, corruption, or denial of service. The security solution taxonomy we propose in this chapter is designed with these factors in mind.

Figures of losses due to information security violations are very scary. Some time ago, with a limited internetwork, the American Bar Association, known for its continuous interest in the area of security, reported that hackers caused losses as high as $10 million. This was a decade ago. In more recent studies, losses reached as high as $50 million. The FBI reports that businesses lose $7.5 billion a year to attacks.

In the past, Boeing Computer Systems Inc. lost $75,000 when Charles Anderson and Costa Katsaniotis broke into the computer files of the U.S. District Court in Seattle. Lately, a hacker in Italy penetrated 500 Unix machines at one of the nation's largest telecommunication carriers. In an other example, in a test run by the U.S. Department of Defense's (DoD) Information Services made of about 9000 servers and mainframes, about 8000 stations were been penetrated in a sequence of covert investigations. This is the DoD of the greatest country in the world. In a developing country with minimum security controls, this sort of attempt may not even be detected or known to owners.

In fact, nowadays, anyone with minor technical skills who is willing to gain access to computers can corrupt information, leak information, and disrupt valuable information resources. The technology that provides partial information security is available to everybody, including hackers.

Most information security hardware or software devices that you can acquire is also available to hackers and potential attackers. Usually, the device you adopted has been already explored and analyzed by rivals and hackers before you even think of acquiring it. Even the machines you acquired for your computing needs have to be examined for holes and default accounts, at a minimum.

13.2 Security Solutions

We here define the security solutions and discuss them in terms of their contributions in solving the information security problems.

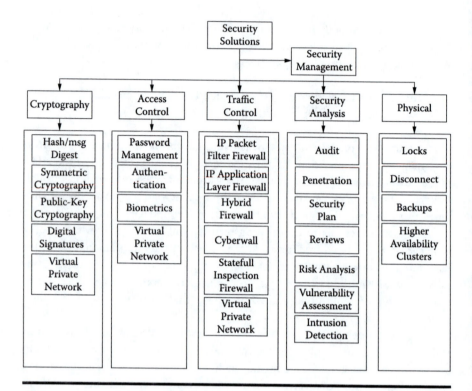

Figure 13.1   Organization of security solutions.

We organize information security solutions into six classes: security management, cryptography, access control, data traffic control, security analysis, and physical solutions. Figure 13.1 shows a visual illustration of our information security solutions organization model.

13.2.1 Security Management

13.2.1.1 Information Security Management System

This is probably the most important class of security solutions. This class of security solutions relate to the organizational security of the company. Is the company doing all it can to effectively secure its computing environment? There are two main components in organizational security: (1) effectiveness in securing the system and (2) information security management system. While the first component of organizational security concerns the 12 security points enforced by ISO 27002 [4], the second component translates all security requirements of ISO/IEC 27001 [3].

Many companies in the United States are, however, still not willing to carefully evaluate the strength of these standards in achieving organizational security and to abide by them. The minimal, simple requirements remain: security policy, best practices, and adequate network management.

An information security management system (ISMS) is an information assurance framework adopted to manage information security based on a systematic business risk approach, to establish, implement, operate, monitor, review, maintain, and improve information security. It is an organizational approach to information security. ISO/IEC 27001 is an international standard for information security that focuses on an organization's ISMS [1]. Any information security activity should be planned, implemented, and maintained within this ISMS framework. The ISMS will ensure that the right controls are developed to provide adequate information security and will satisfy all specifications required by users, customers, and partners.

The ISO/IEC 27001 aims to ensure that adequate controls, addressing confidentiality, integrity, and availability of information, are in place to safeguard organizational information [3]. An ISMS that conforms to ISO/IEC 27001 can help you demonstrate to trading partners and customers alike that you adequately protect the company's information as well as their information. The ISMS design, as shown in Figure 13.1, is actually extracted from Annex A provided at the end of the document containing the ISO/IEC 27001. The obtaining of certification to ISO/IEC 27001 is a strong demonstration of an organization's commitment to effective information security management.

13.2.1.2 Simple Network Management

Major components used in networking are routers, switches, firewalls, and access servers. These components are cabled together to form network topologies. Most configurations run over twisted-pair copper feeding into fiber-optic backbones that move data at speeds from 100 Mbps up to 2.5 Gbps. While these communication components vary in type and size, they usually look like PCs or servers in that they have memories, CPUs, and interface cards. They are diskless and seldom have monitors. They use their interfaces to connect to networks instead of peripherals.

The router is probably the most sophisticated internetworking technology, using a routing protocol that gives networks self-awareness and self adaptation without which configurations would be unpractical. Routers draw a hierarchy of LANs and autonomous systems to find optimal paths to information resources worldwide.

While routers may be able to manage most minute-to-minute issues, there is still need for effective network management according to network security policies defined by system owners. Without persistent review and interventions from network administrators, these communication devices that self-operate will be overwhelmed by a progressive deterioration of operating conditions. All of this explains why this class of security management solutions is very vital to the security of the company.

In addition to the possible deteriorations in network operating conditions, there are all types of security disruptions that communication devices alone cannot deal with. Security administrators have to continuously monitor the behavior of networks to determine risks and detect and respond to security disruptions.

Without a well-defined security management process, even a perfectly configured internetwork will degrade under the strain of added users, increased loads, shifting traffic, new hardware and software versions, and new technology. Network administrators, who are often also security administrators, should monitor, reconfigure, and troubleshoot continuously. There is no single communication device that provides full security, but these devices can make effective internetwork management feasible and ease security administration's tasks.

Historically, computer management tools have evolved from opposite poles of the computing sector: systems and networks. The goal is to bring all computing assets under the management control of a single unit, and the prevalence of placing host systems on networks is driving existing system and network management tools inseparable.

Sophisticated computing management systems, called *system consoles*, have been around for decades. These units were generally hooked up to mainframes sitting in a data center and used to schedule jobs, perform backups, and fix problems. Over time, they developed improved capabilities for managing remote computers.

The most popular product in the data center paradigm is Unicenter made by Computer Associates. Unicenter evolved from a sophisticated console for managing IBM mainframes to an integrated management solution with support for most of the important hardware and software platforms. The objective of Unicenter is the ability to handle the various computer architectures that organizations are likely to put into a configuration.

More recently, a second breed of management tools emerged in the form of network management systems. These tools focus on network infrastructure instead of the data center. They use a console called network management system (NMS). This console takes the networks being managed as the platform for monitoring events.

The leading NMS is OpenView form Hewlett-Packard (HP). HP had committed to Unix as its strategic operating system in 1980s. OpenView became very popular immediately after. While the success of OpenView may be related to its ability to work with devices from various manufacturers, the major contribution HP gave to the world was its built-in design of the IP network management standard Simple Network Management Protocol (SNMP). OpenView was the first major management product that implemented SNMP.

The main difference between system and network consoles is the level at which they operate. While system management tools focus on operating systems, transactions, data files, and databases as they exist across servers, storage controllers, and disks, network management tools focus on packets and connections as they exist over network devices, network interfaces, and transmission links.

System and network consoles are now converging into a single class some call enterprise system management (ESM) tools. The emergence of this hybrid technology

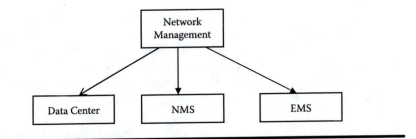

Figure 13.2   System and network management.

is inevitable given the fuzziness in the area separating networks and computers and the development of the client–server technology that moved resources from the data center to internetwork topologies.

The slow pace of integrated management has not impeded the explosive growth in size and use of networks. To remedy for this problem, management teams use several products to track different of their networks. Most large enterprises have an ESM, in addition to dedicated tools to manage critical parts of their networks. Figure 13.2 summarizes the approaches adopted for system and network management.

The Internet Engineering Task Force (IETF) is responsible for the SNMP protocol. Almost all modern internetwork management suites are built on top the SNMP. SNMP is a TCP/IP protocol purpose-built to serve as a communications channel for network management operating at the application layer of the IP stack. SNMP may be directly operated through the command line. But it is often operated through a management application that uses the SNMP communications channel to monitor and control networks.

SNMP has two major components: a network management station and agents. Agents are small code components that reside on managed devices. They can be configured to collect specific pieces of information on device operations. Information collected includes for example, total bytes, total packets, total errors, etc. Agents may be deployed on routers, switches, access servers, hubs, servers, workstations, printers, and UPS power backup systems.

Security administrators should have an agent-deployment strategy based on network security policy. For example, agents may be placed on all network devices and manage the system according to status information sent back.

13.2.2 *Cryptographic Solutions*

13.2.2.1 *Cryptography*

Cryptography remains the most effective method of enforcing data confidentiality. The plaintext message is transformed using a set of mathematical algorithms into a new message in a ciphertext form that reveals no meaningful information to a viewer who does not know how to decrypt it.

Cryptography is the science and art of writing in secret code. In history, it started as ancient art; the first documented use of cryptography in writing dates back to circa 1900 B.C. when Egyptians used nonstandard hieroglyphs in their inscriptions [5]. Cryptography has been around all along even though people only saw forms it more regularly with the widespread development of computer communications. New security requirements related to telecommunication included authentication, confidentiality, integrity, and non-repudiation.

In 1963, Kahn published a popular book that discussed all aspects of the history of cryptography. Cryptography was employed as a weapon tool to protect national secrets and strategies. The wide spread of networking technologies and systems starting in the early 1960s lead to the proliferation of cryptographic solutions both in business and government. Later in the 1970s, Horst Feistel of IBM enhanced existing cryptographic techniques, which lead to their adoption as a U.S. Federal Information Processing Standard for encrypting unclassified information, DES [5]. This data encryption standard is the most well-known cryptographic mechanism in history. It remains the standard means for securing electronic commerce in many financial institutions around the world.

The most outstanding development in the history of cryptography that followed DES happened in 1976 when Diffie and Hellman published their article "New Directions in Cryptography." This paper introduced the revolutionary concept of public-key cryptography and also provided a new and ingenious method for key exchange management [5].

The authors, however, had not presented any implementation methodology for the public-key encryption scheme until 1978 when Rivest, Shamir, and Adleman discovered the first practical public-key encryption and signature scheme, now referred to as RSA [5]. The literature reported more advances in 1980s in this area of cryptography without affecting the security or DES or RSA.

This class of solutions contains mainly five groups of security tools: hash functions, symmetric cryptography, public-key cryptography, digital signatures, and virtual private networks.

13.2.2.2 Main Cryptographic Mechanisms

Cryptography is the use of mathematical techniques to enhance information security such as confidentiality, data integrity, authentication, and nonrepudiation. Two cryptographic methods are very popular: private-key (symmetric cryptography) and public-key (asymmetric cryptography) methods. These two methods may be activated at the application layer of the OSI model when data is traveling.

Private-key algorithms utilize a single key when encrypting or decrypting information. The sender encrypts the message and sends its ciphertext form to the receiver, who should know the secret key and the encryption algorithm in order to be able to decrypt it.

A public-key encryption uses a pair of keys to encrypt and decrypt messages exchanged between senders and receivers. Both keys are independent in terms of that one cannot be feasibly computed from the other. The pair of keys consists of (1) a public key that should be published and is useful to encrypt the message and (2) a private key that remains private to the receiver and that is used to decrypt the message.

Each user needs to keep private his/her own private key. This is very different from the case of symmetric cryptography where the sender and the receiver share the same secret key used for both encryption and decryption. The total number of secret keys required, in this case of symmetric cryptography, for a group of n correspondents, is (n)(n − 1)/2, much larger than the n keys required by the public-key cryptography.

This encyption is so simple. All senders who desire to send a message to a given receiver—say, R—can consult a published directory of public keys and extract R's public key. The senders have to encrypt their messages traveling to R using R's public key. R will then receive the messages and decrypt them using R's private key. Nobody else can read R's messages on their way to R.

On the other hand, R can reply to the senders and digitally sign the messages by encrypting them using R's private key. All users will be able to read R's message after decrypting R's signature using R's public key. This is a good procedure to authenticate R's identity. R, however, has to reply to senders by encrypting their messages using their individual public keys.

Public key cryptography is certainly better in terms of key management than the private-key cryptography because the method has to process an extremely smaller number of keys, especially when the number of communicating users is high. In order to be more efficient, the network using the public key cryptography has to make easier the retrieval of users' public keys.

13.2.2.3 Block and Stream Ciphers in Symmetric Cryptography

Block cipher is an encryption scheme that breaks up the plaintext messages to be transmitted into strings, called *blocks*, of a fixed length over a given alphabet, and encrypts one block at a time. Most well-known symmetric-key encryption techniques are block ciphers. Two important classes of block ciphers are substitution ciphers and transposition ciphers. Substitution ciphers are block ciphers that replace symbols, or groups of symbols, by other symbols or groups of symbols. Transposition ciphers are another class of symmetric-key ciphers that simply permutes the symbols in a block.

A substitution is known to add confusion to the encryption process whereas a transposition is known to add diffusion. Confusion is intended to make the relationship between the key and ciphertext as complex as possible. Diffusion refers to rearranging or spreading out the bits in the message so that any redundancy in the plaintext is spread out over the ciphertext. When combined, substitution and transposition are known add both confusion and diffusion to the encryption. Most modern block cipher systems combine both forms of encryption in succession to encrypt plaintext. That is, simple substitution and transposition ciphers individually do not provide a very high level of security. However, by combining these transformations it is possible to obtain strong ciphers. When substitution and transposition ciphers are combined the result is called product cipher.

Stream ciphers, which are simply block ciphers having block length equal to one, form an important class of symmetric-key encryption schemes. They are very useful in confusing the intruder because the encryption transformation can change for each symbol of plaintext being encrypted. In situations where transmission errors are highly probable, stream ciphers have a great advantage on block cipher because they have no error propagation. They can also be used when data must be processed one symbol at a time—for example, when the device in use has no memory or buffering capability.

A stream cipher employs simple encryption transformations according to the keystream in use. The keystream is often generated at random, or using an algorithm which generates the keystream from an initial seed, or from a seed and previous ciphertext symbols.

The size of the key space is the number of encryption/decryption key pairs possible in a cipher system. A key is a compressed way to specify the encryption transformation, from the set of all possible encryption transformations. For example, a transposition cipher of block length n has factorial n encryption functions to select from. Each selection is described by a permutation, referred to as the *key*.

The security of the encryption scheme seems to depend on the size of the key space. A necessary, but often insufficient, and very important condition for an encryption scheme to be secure is that the key space be large enough to prevent exhaustive searches.

13.2.2.4 Digital Signatures

It is often necessary to prove that a message was generated by the claimed sender. This may be accomplished using a digital signature procedure. Analogous to the U.S. Postal Services practice of processing certified mail, digital certification is also possible. This procedure is referred to as *e-mail non-repudiation* or *non-repudiation of delivery service*. Even though not very common on the network, this new practice is gaining acceptance over time.

A digital signature is an authentication method that aims at providing undisputed evidence that the email sender is the digital signer. A digital signature method uses the public key cryptography. The receiver has to know the signer's public key and a copy of the digital signature software in order to verify the sender's authenticity. The most popular software for email security is called Pretty Good Privacy (PGP).

After generating your own unique private and public key pair, using any careful method of your choice, you may use PGP to generate a digital signature, appended at the end of the traveling message. PGP also provides an encryption function that you may optionally use to ensure privacy.

Digital signatures used in performing authentication tasks and in certifying electronic documents are needed to secure communications on the network and are certainly necessary for the growth of the electronic commerce on the global network.

RSA and almost all other public-key cryptosystems rely for their security largely on the supposed difficulty of factoring an integer into primes or, in some cases, of solving discrete logarithms.

Is it possible that a security device or a system that contains the private key of an RSA key pair may be compromised while performing such functions as obtaining digital signatures, executing authentication tasks, and deciphering encrypted messages? All these functions are important to secure communications, but as electronic commerce applications progress, the need to protect digital signatures from unauthorized use will become essential to the credibility of an electronically based economic structure.

The security of RSA and other digital signature algorithms cannot provide full authentication. In fact, the security of some implementations may be at risk as a result of fault-based cryptanalysis. They may, however, be well protected through simple modifications to the cryptographic processes being performed.

13.2.2.5 Virtual Private Network

A virtual private network (VPN) allows business partners to exchange secure communications between their intranets over the Internet. Such a security solution may be obtained by creating a private secure channel between intranets while the exchanged data is traveling over the public Internet. Firms that afford it used to lease expensive lines between them to send data over a secure link. This security solution will allow partners to link their branch offices in a secure manner (nobody outside the VPN can read the traveling data) without the need to lease private communication lines.

Virtual private network (VPN) is intended to allow remote users to access their network using the Internet without any fear of security. Data is first preprocessed and sent through the Internet to ensure privacy. VPN provides a cost-effective approach to use the company's network to send encrypted data to distributes company branches.

Users can work from home using the same resources available to them when they are in their offices in a very secure manner. The VPN provides reasonable secure transmission with little fear of interception by intruders due to the cryptographic capability applied to all data exchanged on the VPN.

Virtual private network technology is based on the idea of tunneling. VPN tunneling establishes and maintains a logical network connection packets are created in a specific VPN protocol format, which are encapsulated in other secure carrier protocol. These packets are then sent from the client to the server where they are finally deencapsulated and decrypted by the receiver. This private path, which is implemented on public networks, is called a *tunnel*. Firewalls and cryptographic solutions are installed at the ends of tunnels and as needed in the virtual network produced by the VPN.

In addition to efficiency and cost-effectiveness, VPNs offer enhanced speed, flexibility, privacy, financial viability, and customization. Benefits resulting from those advantages may include the following:

Enhanced productivity
Enhanced security
Enhanced profitability due to cost-effectiveness
Simplified network topology
Enhanced scalability

Even though we present in the text to come some technical properties from a behavioral point of view, VPNs may be organized into three main classes: Intranet VPN, Remote Access VPN, and Extranet VPN as follows:

Intranet VPN: This type of VPN is "client transparent." It is often implemented for networks within a common network infrastructure but across various physical locations. Those VPNs are usually implemented by connecting several company buildings to a data center where common mainframe applications are accessed through private lines. Those VPN configurations have to acquire strong encryption methods to satisfy both performance and security requirements, and have to be configured for higher scalability to allow for easy maintenance and upgrading.

Remote Access VPN: This is designed to allow remote users connect to their corporate LAN from remote locations. For example, company representative who travel for work may use their laptops to connect to company information resources through this type of VPNs. The main advantages are flexibility and security. Performance and bandwidth are not crucial as users travel, and they only connect to complete very specific tasks that are not directly related to productivity.

Extranet VPN: This VPN is designed to use the Internet as the main backbone as company branches are assumed to be geographically distributed. It usually includes a wider range of users and locations, enabling customers, suppliers, and branch offices to access corporate resources across various networks. Usually, those VPNs employ VPN standards such as IPSec, presented as follows, to allow for adequate compatibility and adequate security.

There are several types of VPNs that display different technical properties from which we present PPTP, PPP, L2F or L2TP, and IPsec implementations:

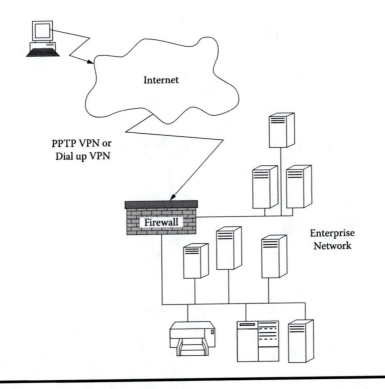

Figure 13.3 PPTP VPN implementation.

13.2.2.5.1 Dial-Up VPN (PPTP VPN)

The simplest VPN that one can install is the PPTP depicted in Figure 13.3. It is a software-based VPN system that uses your existing Internet connection. A secure tunnel is created between two points, allowing a remote user to connect to a remote network. Minimal cost is required to setup this type of VPN, and you can often use your existing equipment and software.

People relate PPTP with Microsoft simply because nearly all flavors of Windows include built-in client support for this protocol. Even though the initial releases of PPTP for Windows by Microsoft contained security features that may be weak, people are still using them. The protocol was developed by a vendor consortium formed by Microsoft, Ascend Communications (today part of Alcatel-Lucent), 3COM, and others.

PPTP technology extends the Point to Point Protocol (PPP) standard, presented in the following text, for traditional dial-up networking. PPTP operates at Layer 2 of the OSI model. As a network protocol, PPTP is best suited for the remote access applications of VPNs, but it also supports LAN internetworking.

PTP VPN, as shown in Figure 13.4, is two or more networks connected using a dedicated line from an ISP. The advantage of using a leased line is to provide for

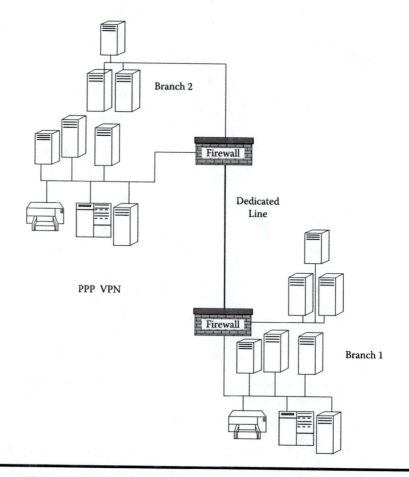

Figure 13.4   PPP VPN implementation.

a circuit-based point-to-point connection that avoids public networks that will prevent any degradation of performance due to unpredicted routing problems, latency, and external congestion.

Similar to PPP VPNs, is the site-to-site VPN with one difference, as the dedicated line is not required and public lines may be used instead, providing that the two firewalls at both ends assure the encryption requirements needed to provide adequate security.

13.2.2.5.2 Layer Two Tunneling Protocol (L2TP)

The main rival to PPTP for VPN tunneling was Cisco's L2F. There was an attempt to improve on L2F by combining its best features with PPTP to create a new standard called L2TP. Like PPTP, L2TP exists at the data link layer, Layer Two in the OSI model.

13.2.2.5.3 Internet Protocol Security (IPsec)

IPsec is actually a collection of multiple related protocols. It can be used as a complete VPN protocol solution, or it can used simply as the encryption scheme within L2TP or PPTP. IPsec exists at the network layer, Layer Three of the OSI model. VPN encrypts IP packets such as SSL with the capability of encrypting UDP traffic one layer deeper in the network model.

13.2.3 Access Control

13.2.3.1 What Is Access Control?

Access control is the mechanism that systems use to identify users and grant them their assigned privileges to access information, systems, or resources.

The protection of private and confidential information from unauthorized users cannot be achieved without the appropriate access control process to systems in place. Most access control methodologies are based on the same fundamental principle of least privilege. This concept applies to access control for any products, systems, or technologies.

Access control devices properly identify people and verify their identity through identification and authentication processes so they can stop any attempts of unauthorized access, catch intruders, and hold them accountable for their actions. Most access control systems record and timestamp all access attempts, communications, and transactions so that access to systems can be audited as needed.

Sound access control systems often provide authentication, authorization, and administration. Authentication is the process by which users are challenged for identity credentials so that it is possible to verify that they are who they say they are. Once a user has been allowed in the system following a successful authentication, authorization determines what resources the user is allowed to access. A user can be authenticated to a network domain, but only be authorized to access one system on that domain. Administration refers to the ability to manage user accounts by adding, deleting, and modifying user accounts and/or user account privileges.

The primary objective of access control is to preserve and protect the confidentiality, integrity, and availability of information resources. Confidentiality refers to the assurance that only authorized individuals are able to view and access data and systems while data integrity refers to protecting the data from unauthorized modification. While information resources need to be secure, they also need to be accessible and available when requested by users in a timely manner.

There are mainly three types of access control systems: discretionary access systems, mandatory access systems, and role-based access systems.

Discretionary access control systems allow the owner of the information to decide who can read, write, and execute files or services. Users can only create or modify files if they are authorized to do so. Owners are granted discretionary access control over the files they own. On end-user laptops and desktops, discretionary access control systems are common.

Mandatory access control systems do not allow the creator of the information to govern who can access it or modify data. Administrators and overseeing authorities prescribe who can access and modify data, systems, and resources. Mandatory access control systems are commonly used in military agencies, and financial institutions.

Role-based access control systems allow users to access systems and information based on their role within the organization. Role-based access allows end-users access to information and resources based on their role within the organization. Role-based access can be applied to groups of people or individual users. Rule-based access control systems allow users to access systems and information based on prescribed and configured rules. Rules can be established to allow access to all end-users coming from a particular domain, host, network, or IP addresses. A very important advantage and property of role-based access systems is that when an employee changes his/her role within the organization, the existing authentication credentials remain in effect and do not have to be reconfigured. The use of rules in conjunction with roles offers greater flexibility because rules can be applied to both people and devices.

13.2.3.2 Access Control Technologies

The most common types of access control technologies often employed to implement enterprise access control solutions are tokens, smart cards, encrypted keys, and passwords.

Biometric devices authenticate users to access control systems based on unique personal physical properties of users, like fingerprint, voiceprint, iris scan, retina scan, facial scan, hand geometry, or signature dynamics. In biometrics, end users do not lose or misplace their personal identifying access features. However, biometrics have not evolved with the same pace we are used to in other technologies because of the high rates of false positives and false negatives that are seen in using biometric technologies.

Smart cards are plastic cards that embed integrated circuits capable of executing transactions as permanently configured in the circuits. These cards may be used to authenticate users to domains, systems, and networks. In addition to smart card, the two-factor authentication feature may be configured on the system by adding a personal identification number.

A token is a handheld device that has a built-in challenge response scheme that authenticates with an enterprise server. Usually, tokens use time-based challenge and response algorithms that constantly change and expire after a prescribed length of time. As in smart cards, tokens may use two-factor authentication when a second challenge request is added. However, unlike smart cards, the two-factor authentication is constantly changing based on timed intervals and when a password is entered, it cannot be reused.

Encrypted keys are mathematical algorithms that are employed to secure confidential information and verify the authenticity of the people sending and receiving the information. Standards such as X.509 for encrypted keys have been created to make sure that security requirements are taken into account, and to allow technologies made by different vendors to work together.

Passwords are used for access control more than any other type of solution because they are easy to implement and are extremely flexible. Passwords can be used to write-protect documents, files, and directories, and to allow access to systems and resources. Unfortunately, passwords are among the weakest of the access control solutions that can be implemented. There are plenty of password-cracking utilities that can be downloaded free from the Internet. If a hacker obtains an encrypted password file he/she can run the password file or document through a password-cracking utility, obtain the password, and then access the system using a legitimate user's account or even modify the existing password by a new one not known to the victim, thus preventing the victim user from accessing his/her account for a prolonged period. Alternatively, by using a protocol analyzer, hackers can easily obtain the network traffic on the wire and obtain passwords in plaintext rather easily. However, despite all those risks, password are here to stay, and there are security policies that have to be enforced to minimize those risks. Some operating systems offer password-cracker programs that users can use to assess the strength of their password. Some organizations also routinely run password crackers on their user accounts to check if users are using easy to guess passwords, or more secure password choices.

13.2.3.3 Authentication

How often have you written a check at a local store for something you bought? Usually, the store required that you present a photo ID or your driver's license. This proof of authenticity also takes place when you access a computer system or a network. It is called *authentication*.

There are many easy ways of mail forgery on the Internet where the intruder impersonates the sender or the sender's station. Hence, e-mail is not so safe, because you cannot be absolutely sure of the sender's identity. If electronic communication weren't possible, the sender's signature would have been a sure method that undeniably identifies the sender. A digital signature may hence be implemented to identify the sender with full certainty.

Encryption can be used not only to hide data from prying eyes, but also to authenticate the sender and the receiver. Encrypted data, if intercepted when going across networks, will look like meaningless garbage, which will defeat any packet snuffers. Attempts to change contents or forge messages, however, will be detected when the messages are decoded by the receiving party.

There are certainly many other cryptographic methods that we do not cover. Our intention is to simply demonstrate the cryptographic class of security solutions. For example, a cryptographic method that we do not emphasize is Tripwire. Tripwire builds a database of cryptographic checksums for selected files. Attempts to modify, add, or delete protected files will be detected by Tripwire. Besides its value in detecting intrusions, Tripwire will shorten the downtime following an attack by helping the system administrator locate compromised files.

13.2.3.4 Biometrics

Biometrics is the automated methods of authenticating or verifying an individual based upon a physical or behavioral characteristic [2].

Users are accustomed to being identified using photo IDs or secret words. Unfortunately, these identification items may be transferred from one user to another, and users may be impersonated when these items are lost or transferred for any reasons. The term *biometrics* was originally used in biology to refer to the development of statistical and mathematical methods applicable to data analysis.

Biometrics therefore refers to technologies for measuring and analyzing a person's physiological or behavioral characteristics, such as fingerprints, irises, voice patterns, facial patterns, and hand measurements, and for identification and verification purposes. Biometrics may be employed to identify or verify a user.

User Identification determines who a person is. It involves taking the measured characteristic and trying to find a match in a database containing records of people and that characteristic. This method can be very costly for it requires a large amount of processing power, especially if the database is large. In law enforcement, it is useful in determining the identity of a suspect from crime scene information.

User verification determines if people are who they say they are. It involves taking the measured characteristic and comparing it to the previously recorded data for that person. This person should have initially enrolled in the verification system. User verification requires less processing power and time, and is often used for accessing places or information.

Biometrics requires the use of (1) code or a device, like a reader, or a scanner that converts the gathered information into digital form, and (2) a database that stores the biometric data for comparison with previous records. The software converts the biometric input into data from which a data pattern is extracted. The match data pattern is then processed using an algorithm into a value that can be compared with biometric data in the database.

There are two types of biometrics: behavioral and physical. Behavioral biometrics is generally used for verification, whereas physical biometrics works for both the identification and the verification.

Examples of physical biometrics include:

Fingerprints—analyzing fingertip patterns
Facial recognition—measuring facial characteristics

Hand geometry—measuring the shape of the hand
Iris scan—analyzing features of colored ring of the eye
Retinal scan—analyzing blood vessels in the eye
Vascular patterns—analyzing vein patterns
DNA—analyzing genetic makeup

Examples of behavioral biometrics include:

Speaker recognition—analyzing vocal behavior
Signature—analyzing signature dynamics
Keystroke—measuring the time spacing of typed words

13.2.4 Data Traffic Control

Before implementing a firewall, we need a clear understanding of the networking requirements in a computing environment. This new data traffic element in the computing environment is likely to have direct impact on every resource residing in any network segment attached to the firewall. Remember that firewalls are needed to implement network security policy, and the design of such a system cannot be defined without first clearly understanding all relevant security rules. The security policy that is relevant to the implementation of a firewall requires at least the following three concepts:

Trust inside. Of course, if we determine that the danger is coming from the outside and we decided to block inbound traffic, then this means that we have to trust the inside. In this case, we are assuming that the most significant threats will come from outside the internal network, and the objective of the security policy should be how to keep outsiders outside. This security policy is often enforced by implementing firewall rules that permit all outbound connections, originating from the inside, and block connections initiated from the outside.

Least privilege. Another important concept is known as "least privilege." This concept assumes that all network connections are blocked in both directions as a starting point, and the policy is incrementally opened to define precisely what needs to be allowed. Most personal firewalls use the least privilege concept and hence deny everything until the user confirms allowing the connection or denying it. New rules are often automatically added to the personal firewall when the user allows or blocks incoming connections.

Selective blocking. A riskier approach is called "selective blocking" and starts with allowing everything, and then rules are added to the firewall to block any connections that are not desired. The security policy for this type of firewall is developed by explicitly denying only selected connections that are thought to be potentially dangerous. This is clearly the most vulnerable approach in building the rule base of a firewall, but such a system may be useful when employed as a first line of defense, like on border routers. One example is the blocking of selected incoming ports using packet filtering on a border router.

For users, a firewall should be viewed simply as a device or a program designed to prevent unauthorized access to or from an internal network. Firewalls are then needed to prevent unauthorized external users from accessing company networks connected to the Internet. Any data that enters or leaves company networks has to pass through the firewall. The firewall examines each packet and blocks any packets that do not meet prescribed security criteria stored in the firewall.

Security management needs to configure firewalls to protect against unauthenticated interactive sessions from the outside world. This way you can prevent intruders from logging into critical machines on your network. While blocking inbound traffic, firewalls should be able to permit users on the inside to communicate with the outside as needed.

Firewalls also play an important role in security auditing because auditors can obtain detailed information about the types of traffic processed through firewall interfaces. It is like having a security guard at a selected entry point in the company, checking on the identity of every person who goes in and every person who comes out.

Firewalls are often organized into three types: packet filters, application-layer firewalls, and stateful inspection firewalls. They are different mainly because of what mechanisms they use to pass traffic from one security zone to another.

Network firewalls generally make their decisions based on the source address, destination address and ports in individual IP packets. A simple router is a network layer firewall, because it is cannot make any decisions related to the packet purpose. Modern network layer firewalls are becoming increasingly more intelligent because they added the capability of maintaining internal information about the state of connections passing through them at any time. The network layer firewalls continue to be very efficient, fast and transparent in routing traffic based on valid IP addresses.

Application layer firewalls are simply hosts running proxy servers that permit no traffic directly between networks, and which have the capability of performing detailed logging and assessment of traffic passing through them. Application layer firewalls are also be used as network address translators. Application layer firewalls tend to provide more detailed audit reports and tend to impose more prudent security assessment than network layer firewalls.

Stateful inspection firewalls intercept packets at the network layer, as in network-layer firewalls, but access, derive, and analyze data from all communication layers for the purpose of understanding the purpose of passing packets and minimize any security risks that can potentially come from allowing the examined packets.

Stateful inspection firewalls use dynamic tables that store state information about other components in the network to provide decision support for allowing or denying the passing packets. This introduces a higher level of security by incorporating context information obtained from communication and application information stored and updated dynamically. Stateful inspection firewalls have become very common and often provide new features like high availability and session failover.

13.2.5 Security Analysis

13.2.5.1 Need for Security Analysis

This class of security solutions is concerned with any security solution where the security of the system is investigated. Some examples we use to demonstrate this security class include the following solutions: security auditing; security planning; risk assessment; security review; vulnerability assessment; and penetration testing.

While we reserve different sessions on these types of security analysis solutions, we briefly describe these examples to demonstrate this class of security solution.

Information resources are always vulnerable one way or another to compromise, spoofing, or denial, no matter how they are configured, no matter where they are located on the network, and despite all traffic control security solutions adopted. With the current increase in connectivity these security disruptions will become more and more likely. Security analysis, including all the security testing activities listed earlier, has hence become very critical, especially for those information resources with highly sensitive information and high availability requirements. Systems owners who fully trust the firewalls, alone, are in great danger and may be seeking disaster.

In the real world, management has been usually against investing in or budgeting for security analysis. Unless a disaster occurs, management will be very reluctant to spend money on testing or acquiring testing security products. Isn't it better to be safe that sorry? Reviewing the entire system and its security controls is a vital requirement. It is needed to evaluate security risks, to enforce security policies, and to ensure that the system behaves as expected. In fact, by investing in security testing, the organization minimizes expected losses, and hence generates higher business value.

When management support is obtained, information system security officers (ISSOs) have to make decisions concerning what types of security analysis activities are needed and when they are needed. Often, security testing activities are different in objectives, scope, and depth. They all, however, aim at enforcing network security policies through identifying trouble spots for which they recommend security controls.

13.2.5.2 Security Testing

Penetration tests perform security reviews from an attacker's point of view, which makes these security tests extremely valuable in protecting highly sensitive information resources.

A penetration test is a legitimate attempt to compromise the current security controls of the system. This type of testing should at least use contemporary hacking tools and techniques to confirm the strength of security controls. Findings will tell whether or not the current security configurations can be exploited in a way that can harm system owners by compromising the system.

The penetration tester does not have to abide by the restrictions imposed on the system, or its security policies, unless there is a special security policy that is explicitly written for how the penetration testing activities should be performed. But a penetration tester has to be familiar with the purpose and security level of all system components in order to tune the tests towards identifying those vulnerabilities that can increase components' security risks. For example, why should a security officer worry about confidentiality protection when an information resource does not include any sensitive information? The officer should instead be concerned about the server availability. The penetration tester should hence test for possible service denial conditions.

Even though there are many ways of performing a penetration test, we only focus on the three most common ones: external source penetration tests, internal source penetration tests, and target system penetration tests. Independently of which one you adopt, a penetration test simply remains a limited process to discover vulnerabilities, without the intention to exhaustively test for all existing security anomalies. Remember, however, that there is certainly no limit on what types of threats can potentially harm the system even after fixing all the vulnerabilities discovered by a rigorous and expensive penetration test.

The term "tiger team" has been employed by the U.S. military to mean a team whose purpose is to penetrate security and thus measure the strength of security controls. Members of a tiger team are paid professionals who are familiar with hacking tools and strategies, and who are hired to induce remote attacks for the purpose of measuring the strength of security controls.

Members of a tiger team are also penetration testers who are allowed to intervene in wider security domains, including the inducing of physical attacks. They are allowed to search anytime and anywhere in the system and may play any role they feel needed for the purpose of discovering vulnerabilities. They can impersonate any entity they think may work better towards identifying the security threats being investigated.

Unlike penetration testers, the tiger team has very specific objectives to be achieved, for example, to compromise a specific physical resource or to seek specific secret information, etc. A tiger team can also intervene to test security policies or the behavior of specific systems.

13.2.5.3 Vulnerability Assessment

A vulnerability assessment test is an extended system security test with specific scope and objectives. This usually does not include penetration testing activities. The purpose of such a test is to provide a fast and low cost analysis, to identify weaknesses, and determine their potential effects. That is, in vulnerability assessment, the tester analyzes threats where potential forces subject to causing compromise, spoofing, or denial of service are thoroughly investigated. The tester identifies system strengths and weaknesses and evaluates system risks before recommending countermeasures.

The intention of the vulnerability assessment test is, however, not to eliminate all vulnerabilities (there will be always some) but to minimize risks. Such a test should not be limited to technical interventions but also include staff posts, their specifications, and how the actual behavior of all users and staff affects the security of the system.

13.2.5.4 Security Review

A security review is a formal analysis of the security controls within a given environment. Unlike penetration and vulnerability assessment tests, a security review is only concerned with the big picture. It primarily identifies all factors that can potentially affect the enforcement of security policies. Usually, security reviewers involve immediate management in the process without the need to communicate findings to upper authorities and system owners.

A security review process can combine and analyze findings obtained from penetration, tiger team, and vulnerability assessment tests but can also call for anyone of these tests to examine a targeted subnet or information resource. Table 13.1 provides a short checklist for vulnerability assessment (www.miora.com).

13.2.5.6 Forensic Investigation

A forensic test is usually initiated after a crime has taken place or following a serious security disruption. Such a test is very limited in scope but has a very well defined structure. This test is not limited to normal data recovery techniques but the investigation should employ very precise procedures and protocols in order to evaluate the state of the system before the incident and its state after the incident. The findings of a forensic investigation should be prepared bearing in mind that they may be later used in possible legal proceedings. This is an extremely laborious and time consuming process. It requires very specialized skills and tools in addition to experience and familiarity with forensic investigations.

Table 13.2 provides a set of standards, borrowed from home.earthlink.net, that forensic investigations should satisfy.

13.2.5.7 Security Audit

A security audit is an independent review and examination of systems records and activities in order to test for the adequacy of security controls. This is to ensure compliance with established security policy and operational procedures, to detect

Table 13.1   Security Review Checklist (www.miora.com; Part 1)

Systems, network and topology evaluation	Mainframe and LAN security implementations
	Network diagram (servers, routers, gateways, multiplexes, workstations, switches)
	Network architectures (token rings, twisted pair, Ethernet, star, etc.)
	Administration responsibility
	W/S configurations (ESP modems and other communications)
	Removable storage media
Administration checklist	Procedures for adding/deleting users
	Procedures for adding/deleting w/s and network addresses network address naming conventions
	LAN administration records
	Documentation and maintenance of server software version levels
	Documentation and maintenance of w/s software version levels
	CM/Records of server hardware
	CM/Records of w/s hardware
	T&E environment isolation
	Application file areas isolation/controlled
	Software licensing/Inventory control
	Software licensing/compliance reviews
	Security/Ops Utilities access restrictions (Syscon, Fconsole, etc.)
File servers & Workstations	File access control mechanisms
	Shared file update authority restrictions
	Login script controls
	Autoexec.bat/config.sys controls
	Compartmentation of user communities sharing file servers
Individual accountability	Guest/anonymous accounts
	Account name policies
	Password policies

Table 13.1   Security Review Checklist (www.miora.com; Part 1) (*Continued*)

	User file areas isolated/controlled
	Determination of access rights
	Assignment of access rights
	Work groups
	Data classification (internal, confidential, public, etc.)
	Access to remote users
Disaster recovery protection	Documentation
	BIA & cost consequences analyses
	Updates
	Testing
	Pre-backup virus scans
	Backup procedures
	Off-site data storage
	Off-site storage of software licenses
	Preventive maintenance
	Fault tolerance
	UPS
	Mirroring
	Electronic vaulting/journaling
	Outage tracking
Connectivity	1. LAN connectivity
	2. Dedicated connections
	Restrictions
	Security devices
	Dial-up tracking
	Dial-up phone number maintenance liaison with carrier
	3. External/Internet connections
	Gateways and firewalls
	Other sites
	Tracking
	International law compliance

Continued

Table 13.1   Security Review Checklist (www.miora.com; Part 1) (*Continued*)

E-mail controls	E-mail system evaluation
	Regulatory requirements for retention/destruction
	Public versus private mail system
Policy review	Change in the computing environment
	New ways to enforce policy
	Historical data on undesired incidents
Logical security	Software security
	Software change control
	Data security
	Communications security
Managerial security	Administrative security
	Personnel security
	Organizational security
Physical security	Physical access security
	Computer location and facility construction

breaches in security, and to recommend any indicated changes in control, policy, and procedures. An audit process is very similar to a security review but the handling of findings and the reporting process is more formal. Also, while a security review does not usually call for penetration testing activities, the technical security audit should require some penetration tests.

The audit process should follow strict standards and protocols. Such a process is very costly and time consuming. Unless cooperation from relevant entities and support from internal resources are obtained, the audit process cannot be successful. The audit process should at least look for security loopholes and compile, for example, activity logs to determine if wrongdoing is taking place.

There are usually three main types of audits: internal audits, external audits, and target audit. The internal audit is performed by internal auditors. The external audit is performed by external auditors. Target audit is conducted for special applications or activities. Table 13.3 provides a list of items that are often included in a security audit. Detailed security audit requirements will be provided in later chapters.

13.2.6 Physical Security

Physical security is the protection of the computing environment, namely people, activities, technology, data, and networks, from physical conditions and incidents

Table 13.2   Some Standards for Forensic Analysis

Use of sterile media	Ensures that all examinations use properly prepared and verified, forensically sterile media. This ensures that there is no contamination by viruses, by previously examined data fro another or the same case, or by other data that could be used on the media.
Hardware documentation	Examines, describes, and properly documents the hardware that is subject of the examination.
Original data	Ensures that the original media and data are maintained in their original unaltered state during the examination. This will prevent loss of data and will be used to authenticate the validity of the data recovered. It will also be a sound defense to lawsuits claiming alteration or corruption of the data or operating system.
Write protected media	Ensures that no unauthorized writes are made to the media by viruses, by "booby trap" defense schemes, by the operating system, by applications that write back to the media to cache data, or by other inadvertent means.
Deleted, hidden, and recovered files	Recovers, unlocks, and accesses deleted files, hidden files or data, password protected files, and encrypted files. Any means of concealing the data is documented for possible use as evidence later.
File revision documentation	Lists all the files in the directory hierarchy, including recovered files. The name, size, starting cluster, time, and date of creation or last modification of each file is documented.
Data manipulation	Examines data in unallocated space (space that is not currently in use by files but which may contain data) for relevancy to the investigation or inquiry at hand. Potentially relevant data is recovered, printed, and the location where found is documented.
	Examines data in file slack (the area within the cluster of a file that is not being occupied by the file) for relevancy to the investigation or inquiry at hand. Potentially relevant data is recovered, printed, and the location where found documented.
	Examines all normal data files individually. Relevant files are printed and the location where found documented.

Continued

Table 13.2   Some Standards for Forensic Analysis (*Continued*)

Files' origination	If requested, examinations are conducted to determine the author and creation or modification date of particular documents or files, to determine who created particular directories, to determine which computer in an office or location created diskettes, and similar comparisons relating to document and file creation, etc.
Potential evidence	All media, exhibits, and other items of potential evidence are properly secured and tightly controlled to maintain their integrity and chain of custody.
Report generation	A report is prepared indicating the physical description of the computer and media, the configuration of the equipment, what was found, any attempt to hide data, and other comments that may be relative to the inquiry at hand. A printout of the directories and files and the potentially relevant data found on the computer is provided. Read-only CD-ROM disks can also be made of relevant data.

that could cause serious losses or damage to an organization. For example, physical security includes protection from theft, vandalism, fire, and natural disasters.

Most of the literature talks about sophisticated technical security solutions intended to protect enterprise assets and money is being invested in acquiring those solutions and in implementing and maintaining them. However, when it comes to physical security, upper management suddenly becomes too thrifty to invest in prevention. Imagine what a small fire can do to your enterprise or what humidity can do to your communication assets; great losses can occur because the easiest physical security solutions needed were neglected.

Many breaches of physical security can be carried out with little or no technical knowledge on cybersecurity, and accidents and natural disasters can happen anytime without prior notice.

The main physical solutions include isolated data backup centers, barriers, locks, surveillance, natural disaster sensors and preventive measures. Isolated data backup centers are useful when something like 9/11 incident takes place. The data back center will contain the latest configuration of business operations and operations may be resumed given the last version of business conditions entered in the backup center. This is certainly a very expensive physical security solution but it may be feasible for some types of organizations. Examples where backup centers may be feasible include pharmaceutical companies, security agencies, etc.

Barriers and obstacles can be placed in entry points to prevent potential attackers from conducting physical attacks. Measures may also include multiple locks, fencing, walls, fireproof safes, and water sprinklers, as all those are physical solutions

Table 13.3   Items That Should be Included in a Security Audit (InfoWorld 1999)

1. Planning the audit	Before starting:
	• Get management support
	• Perform risk analysis
	• Set expectations and goals
	• Revise or draft security policy
	Preparation:
	• Determine the following:
	    – Type of audit
	    – Severity
	    – External/internal/target
	    – Scope/scale
	    – Goals

2. Auditing	Nominal: • Interview personnel • Review documentation • Inventory • Topology • Emergency • Procedures • Logs Technical: • Use currently available tools • Plan for outages, and schedule audits for off-peak hours
3. Report and post-mortem	Safeguard report and distribution Prepare for data overload and set aside time to read and investigate Be aware that the report may raise more questions than it answers Leverage results for a stronger security posture
4. Action	Prioritize action items, set time line, implement Feed findings back into risk analysis, policy Start thinking intrusion/detection and revisit risk acceptance Remember that security is a continuous process, not a static one

that can prevent a variety of physical attacks. Surveillance and alarm systems can be implemented, such as power surge, heat sensors, smoke detectors, intrusion detectors, alarms, and cameras.

13.3 The NIST Security Solution Taxonomy

NIST proposes seventeen security control families, in NIST Special Publication 800-53, that are strongly aligned with the 17 security-related areas in FIPS 200, specifying the minimum security requirements for protecting federal information and information systems [1]. Families are associated with their respective classes based on the dominant characteristics of the controls in that family. As in any taxonomy, many security controls, however, can be logically associated with more than one class. For instance, the policy and procedures control from the Contingency Planning family, denoted CP-1, is designated as an operational control but also has properties that are also consistent with security management.

This standard presents the fundamental concepts associated with security control selection and specification. Security controls in the security control catalog (Appendix F of the standard) have a well-defined organization and structure. The security controls are organized into *classes* and *families* for ease of use in the control selection and specification process. There are three general classes of security controls (i.e., management, operational, and technical) and 17 security control families. Each family contains security controls related to the security functionality of the family. A two-character identifier is assigned to uniquely identify each control family. Table 13.4 summarizes the classes and families in the security control catalog and the associated family identifiers.

Management controls focus on the management of the information system and the management of risk for a system. They are techniques and concerns that are normally addressed by management.

Operational controls address security methods focusing on 17 security control families in NIST SP 800-53 [5], and are associated with one of three security control classes (i.e., management, operational, technical). Families are assigned to their respective classes based on the dominant characteristics of the controls in that family. Many security controls, however, can be logically associated with more than one class. For example, CP-1, the policy and procedures control from the contingency planning family, is listed as an operational control but also has characteristics that are consistent with security management as well. Operational security controls concern mechanisms primarily implemented and executed by people (as opposed to systems). These controls are put in place to improve the security of a particular system (or group of systems). They often require technical or specialized expertise and often rely upon management activities as well as technical controls.

Technical controls focus on security controls that the computer system executes. The controls can provide automated protection for unauthorized access or

Table 13.4 Security Control Classes, Families, and Identifiers

Identifier	Family	Class
AC	Access Control	Technical
AT	Awareness and Training	Operational
AU	Audit and Accountability	Technical
CA	Certification, Accreditation, and Security Assessments	Management
CM	Configuration Management	Operational
CP	Contingency Planning	Operational
IA	Identification and Authentication	Technical
IR	Incident Response	Operational
MA	Maintenance	Operational
MP	Media Protection	Operational
PE	Physical and Environmental Protection	Operational
PL	Planning	Management
PS	Personnel Security	Operational
RA	Risk Assessment	Management
SA	System and Services Acquisition	Management
SC	System and Communications Protection	Technical
SI	System and Information Integrity	Operational

misuse, facilitate detection of security violations, and support security requirements for applications and data.

13.4 The ISO Security Solution Taxonomy

The ISO/IEC 27002 Code of Practice for Information Security Management establishes guidelines and general principles for organizations to initiate, implement, maintain, and improve information security management [4]. This standard provides general guidance on the commonly accepted goals of information security management.

Every section in the standard, as introduced below, will be referred to as a security objective throughout this book. Each security objective consists of a subset of security practices that have to be adopted in order to achieve the security objective.

Each security practice consists of several security controls that have to be implemented in order to adopt the security practices in question.

The ISO/IEC 27002 standard consists of the following 12 sections [4]:

c1. Risk Assessment and Treatment
c2. Security Policy
c3. Organization of Information Security
c4. Asset Management
c5. Human Resources Security
c6. Physical and Environmental Security
c7. Communications and Ops Management
c8. Access Control
c9. Information Systems Acquisition, Development, Maintenance
c10. Information Security Incident Management
c11. Business Continuity
c12. Compliance

Every section in the ISO/IEC 27002 is organized into three parts: (1) the title of the section representing the name for the security objective sought in this security section, (2) one or more first-order subtitles representing the security practices, and (3) one or more second-order subtitles representing the security controls recommended by the standard.

13.5 Summary

This chapter presented taxonomy for information security solutions as discussed in this book. This taxonomy included six classes: security management solutions, access control solutions, cryptographic solutions, data traffic solutions, security analysis solutions, and physical solutions.

For each class of security solutions we provided several examples that we defined and discussed their implementations.

We also presented two other security control taxonomies proposed by NIST and the ISO 27002.

13.6 Review Questions

1. Define and use examples to explain this class of security solutions: security management solutions.
2. Define and use examples to explain this class of security solutions: cryptographic solutions.

3. Define and use examples to explain this class of security solutions: access control solutions.
4. Define and use examples to explain this class of security solutions: data traffic control solutions.
5. Define and use examples to explain this class of security solutions: security analysis solutions.
6. Define and use examples to explain this class of security solutions: physical solutions.

13.7 Workshops

Workshop 1

Consider a midsize business that has three local area networks, a Web site, and several other applications of two types: open to the public, or restricted to internal staff use.

Revisit the taxonomy of security solutions presented in this chapter, and recommend a set of selected security solutions that is appropriate to this business.

If a small business is considered, how is the set of security solutions you just recommended different?

Workshop 2

Discuss the following two definitions of IS security audit. Say which one seems to be more efficient and effective in reducing a company's security risks?

1. "An IS security audit is the identification of violations of corporate security policy and the recommendation of those managerial, operational, and technical security controls that reenforce the corporate security policy."
2. "An IS security audit is an independent review and examination of systems records and activities in order to test for the adequacy of security controls. This is to ensure compliance with established security policy and operational procedures, to detect breaches in security, and to recommend any indicated changes in control, policy, and procedures."

Workshop 3

We represent the class of data traffic control security solutions into several types of firewalls: IP packet filter firewalls, IP application layer firewalls, and stateful inspection firewalls. Search the Internet and define all these firewalls. Using a table, summarize the differences between these data traffic control solutions in terms of cost, performance, and effectiveness in enforcing security policy.

Workshop 4

Explain password management as an access control tool. Give an example of a password management security policy and explain its effectiveness in providing extra security by controlling the access to the system.

References

1. Federal Information Processing Standards Publication 200, *Security Controls for Federal Information System*, February 2006.
2. INFOSEC, ATIS Telecom Glossary 2007, http://www.atis.org/glossary/annex.aspx, visited January 27, 2009.
3. ISO/IEC 27001:2005, Information technology—Security techniques—Information security management systems—Requirements, International Standards Organization, October 2005. (Source: http://www.iso.org.)
4. ISO/IEC 27002:2005 (ISO/IEC 17799:2005)—Information Technology Security Techniques—Code of Practice for Information Security Management. International Standards Organization, June 2005. (Source: http://www.iso.org.)
5. Menezes, A., P. V. Oorschot, and S. Vanstone, *Handbook of applied cryptography*, Boca Raton, FL: CRC Press, 1996.
6. National Institute of Standards and Technology Special Publication 800–53, *Recommended Security Controls for Federal Information Systems*, February 2005.
7. NIST: Recommended Security Controls for Federal Information Systems, NIST Special Publication 800-53, Revision 2, 2007.
8. TechRepublic Pro, Administrator's Guide to VPN and Remote Access, Second Edition—PDF, http://downloads.techrepublic.com.com/abstract.aspx?docid=177620, visited on January 27, 2009.

Chapter 14

The Common Criteria

Learning Objectives

After reading this chapter, students are expected to achieve an understanding of:

  Know who are the main consumers of the Common Criteria (CC)
  Understand how users use the CC
  Understand how vendors use the CC
  Understand how developers use the CC
  Understand how the CC works
  Understand the Evaluation Assurance Levels as used by the CC
  Know what an information resource evaluation methodology is
  Know the common principles of evaluations
  Understand the evaluation process
  Understand different roles of players in the evaluation process.

14.1 The Birth of the Common Criteria

The governments of the North American and European nations, including France, Germany, the Netherlands, the United Kingdom, Canada, and the United States, began in the spring of 1993 to develop the Common Information Technology Security Criteria. This was later referred to as Common Criteria (CC).

There are seven CC international organizations that participated in the development of the CC:

- Communications Security Establishment, Canada
- Service Central de la Securite des Systemes d'Information (SCSSI), France
- Bundesamt für Sicherheit in der Informationstechnik (BSI) or German Information Security Agency (GISA), Germany
- Netherlands National Communications Security Agency, The Netherlands
- Communications-Electronics Security Group, United Kingdom
- NIST: National Institute of Standards and Technology, U.S.
- NSA: The National Security Agency, U.S.

These international organizations were responsible for all North American and European security criteria. In a joint activity, referred to as the Common Criteria Project, they attempted to resolve the conceptual and technical differences among the source criteria, and to combine their separate criteria into a single set of widely useful international IT security criteria.

The CC Project sponsoring organizations formed the CC Editorial Board (CCEB) to develop the CC. They established a formal cooperative liaison with ISO (International Organization of Standardization) and their experts, and contributed several early versions of the CC to ISO. These versions have been adopted by ISO since 1994 as successive working drafts of the ISO criteria.

The resulting Common Criteria experienced extensive international review and testing, beginning in 1996. They were tried out in evaluations of real products prior to being fully accepted for use within Europe and North America. They have been later submitted to ISO as a contribution towards an international standard.

The CCEB had two main tasks: (1) to obtain a clear understanding of the similarities and differences between the source criteria and (2) to develop a CC that can be used by the participating government bodies to replace their existing criteria. The CCEB used the ISO material and the criteria previously developed by the sponsoring organizations as the primary material from which to develop the CC. The CC has to represent a synthesis of the best concepts and components contained in the original material. The CCEB was initially advised to avoid inventing new criteria, although that approach was found to be impractical in the process of achieving a correct and useful synthesis.

They have been many versions produced and reviewed before version 1.0 of the CC was completed in January 1996 and distributed by ISO in April 1996 as a Committee Draft (CD). The CC Project used this version to perform a number of trial evaluations. A widespread public review of the document was also conducted.

The CC Implementation Board (CCIB) extensively revised the CC based on the results of trial use, public review, and interaction with ISO. Version 2.0 was completed in April 1998 following close cooperation between ISO, and the CCIB. In October 1998, ISO slightly revised the document and approved it as final draft International Standard 15408. The document should have become, by now, IS 15408 without further major change.

The ISO has accepted the continued use of the term "Common Criteria" (CC) within the document, while recognizing that the official ISO name for the new IS 15408 is Evaluation Criteria for Information Technology Security.

The seven CC international organizations mentioned earlier are the only organizations that contributed directly in the entire CC project. These organizations are also "evaluation authorities," managing product security evaluation programs for their respective national governments.

Because of the heavy and continuous participation of the international organizations, we all hope that these countries and the rest of the world replace their respective experimental evaluation criteria with the new international standard IS 15408. A mutual recognition among the six countries and the rest of the world of each other's security product evaluation results will produce a wider global market for good IT security products.

The Common Criteria (CC) for Information Technology Security Evaluation becomes the new standard for specifying and evaluating the security features of information resources: IT products or IT systems. The CC is intended to replace previous security criteria adopted by the international community. The CC is the new international standard IS 15408.

The CC is the product of an international project that lasted more than 5 years of full cooperation with the International Organization of Standardization (ISO). Both the NSA and the NIST represented the United States in the CC project. Canada, France, Germany, the Netherlands, and the United Kingdom also participated in the CC project .

The new international standard CC constitutes the foundation for the National Information Assurance Partnership (NIAP), a joint activity of NIST and NSA to establish an IT product security evaluation program supported by a number of accredited, independent testing laboratories. The mission of the NIAP is to establish cost-effective evaluation of security-capable IT products and to promote the wide availability of tested products to federal agencies and others. This will play a central role in helping to protect U.S. information infrastructure.

The CC will be used as the basis for evaluation of the security properties of information resources. The CC provides a common set of requirements for the security functions of information resources and the assurance measures applied to them during a security evaluation.

The evaluation process establishes a level of confidence that the security functions of an information resource and its assurance measures should meet. Users can use the evaluation results to establish whether or not the information resource is sufficiently secure.

The TOE is an IT product or system to be evaluated, the security characteristics of which are described in specific terms by a corresponding ST, or in more general terms by a PP.

It is important that a product or system be evaluated against the specific set of criteria expressed in the ST. This evaluation consists of rigorous analysis and testing performed by an accredited, independent laboratory. The scope of a TOE evaluation is set by the evaluation assurance level and other requirements specified in the ST. Part of this process is an evaluation of the ST itself to ensure that it is correct, complete, internally consistent, and can be used as the baseline for the TOE evaluation.

The CC supports the development of standardized sets of well understood IT product security requirements, in the form of Protection Profiles (PPs) that users can use in procurements and advice to manufacturers.

The TOE security environment is associated with assumptions about the security aspects of the product's expected usage and operating environment, such as value of assets and limitations of use. Assumptions also describe the environment's physical, personnel, and connectivity aspects. The TOE security environment is also associated with threats against which the product or its supporting environment must specifically provide protection, and organizational security policies or rules with which the product must comply. These can be any explicit statements of IT security needs that the product must meet.

Under the Common Criteria, each level of trust rating from the TCSEC can be specified as a Protection Profile (PP). A Protection Profile looks very similar to a level of trust rating but has two fundamental differences. First, where the TCSEC binds sets of features and assurances together, the Common Criteria allows Protection Profiles to combine features and assurances together in any combination. Also, the TCSEC specifies a fixed set of ratings (profiles), but the Common Criteria allows for consumers to write a customized set of requirements in a standard format.

The NCSC is currently developing Protection Profiles that map to the C2 rating referred to in the TCSEC.

The TPEP will continue to conduct evaluations against the Common Criteria at the EAL5 level and above. It will conduct evaluations against the TCSEC at the B2 level and above. All other levels will be evaluated at a TTAP lab.

14.1.1 TCSEC, ITSEC, and CC

The international community has realized the need to produce a common approach to develop IT security criteria. The joint effort of developing the common evaluation criteria benefited from the international initiatives, taking the best features of what had already been done and putting them in a consistent and structured perspective. The criteria have been extended to cover information security areas omitted in various countries participating in the joint effort.

The common evaluation criteria efforts should produce internationally harmonized criteria and provide a compatible basis for certification by the national certification bodies within the participating countries, in addition to allow for international mutual recognition of evaluation results.

The Trusted Computer System Evaluation Criteria (TCSEC), presented earlier, is a widely known and accepted basis for the security evaluation of operating systems. It is used by the U.S. Department of Defense in the U.S. product evaluation scheme operated by the National Computer Security Center (NCSC). The TCSEC criteria are intended to match the security policy of the U.S. Department of Defense. This policy is primarily concerned with maintaining the confidentiality of nationally classified information.

The TCSEC defines seven sets of evaluation criteria called classes (D, C1, C2, B1, B2, B3, and A1), grouped into four divisions (D, C, B, and A). Each criteria class covers four aspects of evaluation: security policy, accountability, assurance, and documentation. The criteria for these four areas become more detailed from class to class, and form a hierarchy whereby D is the lowest and A1 the highest. Each class covers both functionality and confidence requirements.

On the other hand, the criteria designed in the ITSEC permit selection of arbitrary security functions, and define seven evaluation levels representing increasing confidence in the ability of a TOE to meet its security target. Thus, these criteria can be applied to cover a wider range of possible systems and products than the TCSEC. In general, for identical functionality at an equivalent level of confidence, a TOE has more architectural freedom to meet the ITSEC criteria than to meet the TCSEC, but is more constrained in its permissible development practices.

A number of functionality classes have been defined to correspond closely to the functionality requirements of the TCSEC classes C1 to A1. They are included as F-C1 to F-B3. It is not possible, however, to relate the evaluation levels directly to the confidentiality requirements of the TCSEC classes, as the ITSEC levels have been developed by harmonization of various European IT security criteria schemes that contain a number of requirements which do not appear in the TCSEC explicitly.

The intended correspondence between these criteria and the TCSEC classes is as follows (reference):

ITSEC	TCSEC Class
E0	D
F-C1, E1	C1
F-C2, E2	C2
F-B1, E3	B1
F-B2, E4	B2
F-B3, E5	B3
F-B3, E6	A1

There is no functionality class F-A1 as the functionality requirements of TCSEC class A1 are the same as for class B3. A product that has been designed with the objective of successful evaluation against both the ITSEC and TCSEC, and which has been shown to meet one of the classes or combinations in Table 3.1, should pass evaluation against the other criteria at the equivalent class or combination. However, at C1 the TCSEC requires evidence to be provided of system developer testing. Thus, an [F-C1, E1] evaluation would only be equivalent to C1 evaluation if the sponsor decides to satisfy the optional E1 requirement to provide test documentation as evidence of adequate testing against the security target prior to evaluation.

TOEs in a TCSEC evaluation generate additional confidence in higher classes in divisions A and B. Additional confidence result from increasingly rigorous architectural and design requirements placed on the TCB by the TCSEC criteria. TCSEC classes B2 and higher require that access control is implemented by a reference validation mechanism. This reference validation mechanism must be tamper proof, always invoked, and small enough to be subject to analysis and tests, the completeness of which can be assured.

This mechanism should be implemented so that compatibility can be achieved between TCSEC and the ITSEC example functionality classes F-B2 and F-B3. On the other hand, at higher evaluation levels, the ITSEC places architectural and design constraints on the implementation of all the security enforcing functions. Combined with the ITSEC effectiveness requirements that security functionality is suitable and mutually supportive, a TOE meeting the higher ITSEC evaluation levels, and providing functionality matching these TCSEC-equivalent functionality classes, should necessarily satisfy the TCSEC requirements for a TCB and use of the reference monitor concept.

This chapter presented the three main information security criteria developed by various nations: TCSEC, ITSCE, and CC. The chapter also discussed how the criteria approached the evaluations of trusted information resources. The chapter also addressed briefly how one can travel from one set of criteria to another. The concepts retained are the ones adopted by the Common Criteria.

The Common Criteria for Information Technology Security Evaluation (CC) and the companion Common Methodology for Information Technology Security Evaluation (CEM) are the technical basis for an international agreement, the Common Criteria Recognition Agreement (CCRA), which ensures that [1,2]:

Products can be evaluated by competent and independent licensed laboratories so as to determine the fulfillment of particular security properties, to a certain extent or assurance;

Supporting documents are used within the Common Criteria certification process to define how the criteria and evaluation methods are applied when certifying specific technologies;

The certification of the security properties of an evaluated product can be issued by a number of Certificate Authorizing Schemes, with this certification being based on the result of their evaluation;

These certificates are recognized by all the signatories of the CCRA (Common Criteria Recognition Arrangement).

The CC is the driving force for the widest available mutual recognition of secure IT products. This Web portal is available to support the information on the status of the CCRA, the CC and the certification schemes, licensed laboratories, certified products and related information, news, and events [1,2].

14.2 Common Uses of the CC

Even though the successful use of the CC depends on an ability to define the required security capabilities, any CC implementation should be give priority to the business mission, the assets requiring protection, and the purpose of the system under evaluation (the TOE). The CC is continuously evolving, and we see more and more protection profiles (PP) have been developed by the National Security Agency (NSA) and with the cooperation of the National Institute of Standards and Technology (NIST). A working group, called the Protection Profile Review Board (PPRB), is in place to review all proposed Protection Profiles and to work with the authors toward achieving a goal of consistency across PPs [3,5].

The CC is used in two general ways: (1) as a standardized way to describe security requirements, e.g., PPs and STs for IT products and systems, and (2) as a sound technical basis for evaluating the security features of these products and systems.

Users, as shown in Figure 14.1, may use the Common Criteria to (1) find requirements for security features that match their own risk assessment, (2) shop for products that have ratings with those features, or (3) publish their security requirements so that vendors can design products that meet them.

Developers, as shown in Figure 14.2, may use the Common Criteria (1) to select security requirements that they wish to include in their products, (2) to design

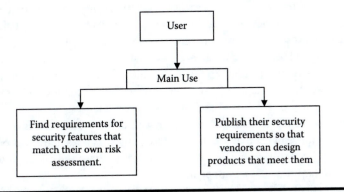

Figure 14.1   Users' common use of CC.

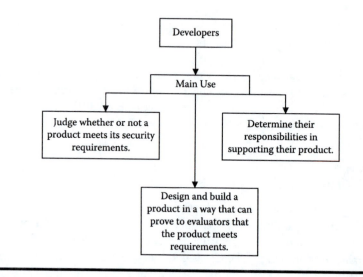

Figure 14.2 Developer' common use of CC.

and build a product in a way that can prove to evaluators that the product meets requirements, or (3) to determine their responsibilities in supporting and evaluating their product.

Evaluators, as shown in Figure 14.3 may use the Common Criteria (1) to judge whether or not a product meets its security requirements, (2) to provide a yardstick against which evaluations can be performed, or (3) to provide input when forming specific evaluation methods.

14.3 The CC Document

The CC consists of three parts: (1) Introduction and General Model, (2) Security Functional Requirements, and (3) Security Assurance Requirements.

The first part of the CC introduces the CC, defines general concepts and principles of IT security evaluations, and presents a general model of evaluation. It also defines constructs for expressing IT security objectives for selecting and defining IT security requirements, and for writing high-level specifications for products and systems.

These constructs are called Protection Profiles (PPs), Security Targets (ST), and packages (briefly defined later). In addition, this part describes the usefulness of each part of the CC in terms of each of the target audiences.

The second part contains a catalog of well-defined and understood security functional requirements that are intended to be used as a standard way of expressing the security requirements for IT products and systems. The catalog is organized into classes, families, and components.

Classes are high-level groupings of families of requirements, all sharing a common security focus (e.g., identification and authentication).

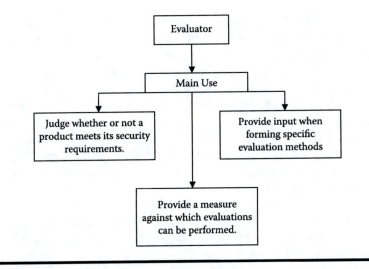

Figure 14.3   Evaluator' common use of CC.

Families are lower-level groupings of requirement components, all sharing specific security objectives but differing in rigor or emphasis (e.g., user authentication).

Components are the lowest selectable requirements that may be included in PPs, STs, or packages (e.g., unforgeable user authentication).

The diagram shown in Figure 14.4 illustrates the hierarchy used in organizing CC operational components.

The second part also includes an extensive annex of application notes for applying the material that it contains. While it is possible to explicitly state functional requirements not included in the second part catalog in building CC-based

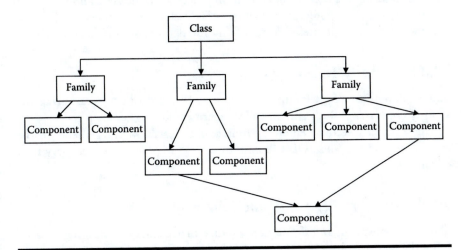

Figure 14.4   Hierarchy used in organizing CC operational components.

constructs (PPs, STs, and packages), this is not recommend unless it is clearly not practical to use Part 2 components. Using functional requirements not part of the catalog could jeopardize widespread acceptance of the result.

The third part contains a catalog that establishes a set of assurance components that can be used as a standard way of expressing the assurance requirements for information resources. The third part catalog is organized into the same class–family–component structure as in the second part.

The third part also defines evaluation criteria for PPs and STs. The third part presents the seven Evaluation Assurance Levels (EALs), which are predefined packages of assurance components that make up the CC scale for rating confidence in the security of information resources.

Both PPs and STs need to go through a formal evaluation. An evaluation of a PP simply ensures that the PP meets various documentation rules and sanity checks. An ST evaluation involves evaluating an actual system (TOE) in addition to examining the ST document.

The ST evaluation is intended to ensure that, to the level of the assurance requirements specified by the ST, the TOE meets the ST's security functional requirements. Customers can determine if the products meet their requirements by comparing STs and PPs.

The creation of PPs or STs uses a process of identifying the security environment consisting of present threats and relevant organizational security policies. After fixing the security scope, you define the security objectives for the product, and select the security requirements that meet the objectives. There are two kinds of security requirements: functional requirements, defining what a product can provide, and assurance requirements defining what measures to inspire confidence that the objectives have been met. The actual creation of PP or ST is not as simple but we need to make sure that the final result show a clear relationship and no critical point are omitted. The process of identifying the security environment, objectives, and requirements is still useful in identifying and defining security requirements.

14.4.1 Security Enforcing Functions

Those components of an information resource that contribute to satisfying the security objectives of the TOE, are called security enforcing components.

The necessary security enforcing functions are established together with the evaluation level that the TOE will have to achieve to provide the necessary level of confidence.

14.4.2 Security Relevant Functions

Those components of an information resource that are not contributing to satisfying the security objectives of the TOE but have to function correctly so they do not disrupt the functions of the security enforcing components, are called *security relevant components.* The security relevant components are hence not security enforcing but must nonetheless operate correctly in order for the TOE to enforce security.

14.4.3 Trusted Computing Base (TCB)

The combination of both the security enforcing components and the security relevant components of a TOE is often referred to as a Trusted Computing Base (TCB).

In the rest of this chapter we define the three main constructs based on which the Common Criteria are defined.

14.4.4 The Protection Profile (PP)

The Protection Profile (PP) is an implementation-independent statement of security needs for a set of IT security products that could be built. A PP is intended to be a reusable definition of product security requirements that are known to be useful and effective. The PP contains a set of security requirements, usually taken from the catalogs in the second and third parts of the Common Criteria, and an evaluation assurance level.

A PP could be developed by user communities, IT product developers, or other parties interested in defining such a common set of requirements. A PP gives consumers a means of referring to a specific set of security needs and communicating them to manufacturers. The PP also helps future product evaluation against those needs.

The PP should, as shown in Figure 14.5, contain the following items:

1. PP introduction: Identifies and describes information that users can use to recognize PPs useful to them.
2. Target of evaluation (TOE) description: Describes the IT product and its purpose, not necessarily from a security perspective. Should address how to counter the threats identified.
3. TOE security environment: Describes the security aspects of the environment in which the product is intended to be used.
4. Security objectives: Addresses what the product intends to accomplish in covering the threats, policies, and assumptions, addressing both the functional and the assurance requirements for compliant TOEs.
5. IT security requirements: This section should include a detailed statement of IT security functional and assurance requirements that the product and its operating environment must satisfy to meet the objectives.
6. Application notes: Additional supporting information that may be useful for the construction, valuation, or use of the product.
7. Rationale: Provides the evidence describing how the PP is complete and cohesive, and how a product built against it would be effective in meeting the objectives.

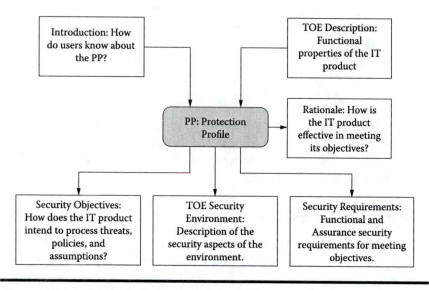

Figure 14.5   A description of a protection profile.

14.4.5 The Security Target (ST)

A Security Target (ST) is a statement of security claims for a particular IT security product or system. Even though it is similar to the PP, the ST has additional elements that include product-specific detailed information. The ST contains a set of security requirements for the product or system, which may be made by reference to a PP. The relationship between the PP and ST constructs is depicted in Figure 14.6.

An ST is the basis for agreement among all parties as to what security the product or system offers, and therefore the basis for its security evaluation. The ST contains a summary specification, which defines the specific measures taken in order for the product or system to meet the security requirements.

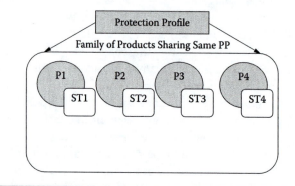

Figure 14.6   Relationship between PPs and STs.

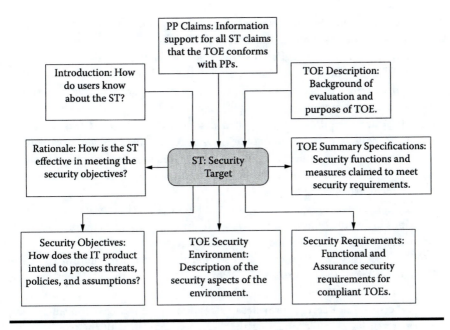

Figure 14.7 A description of a security target.

Opposite to the user's PP, there is the manufacturer's ST that contains a similar set of criteria-based requirements which describe the security capabilities of an IT product. The ST may be used as the basis for security evaluations of a manufacturer's IT product.

Security evaluations are formalized testing and analytic processes that use the criteria to determine whether IT products have been correctly developed. Correct development requires that the product satisfies all product specifications and that the product is effective in countering the security problems as claimed. Users can integrate evaluated IT products into a desired system with increased confidence that their claimed security features will perform as intended.

The ST defines the agreement between the TOE developers, consumers, evaluators, and evaluation authorities as to what security the TOE offers, and on the scope of the evaluation.

The ST, as shown in Figure 14.7, consists of the following sections:

1. An introduction: The introduction provides information concerning the ST identification, the associated TOE, an ST overview for users, and any criteria conformance claim. The ST overview should be suitable to include in an evaluated product list. The conformance claim may include any claim of criteria conformance of the TOE that can be evaluated. This claim may include PPs or a specific level of assurance. A minimum rating strength should be included where appropriate.

2. Security objectives: This section defines security objectives of the TOE and its supporting environment. These security objectives should address the threats and satisfy any organizational security policies and assumptions.

3. TOE description: This section explains the background for the evaluation and describes the type of the TOE, its intended usage, and its general IT features. assumptions, and the application context is provided.

4. IT security requirements: This step describes the functional and the assurance requirements for compliant TOEs. A statement of security requirements should be added where appropriate. Requirements associated with a PP need not be repeated in the ST. Minimum rating strength claims should be included where appropriate.

5. TOE summary specifications: This section briefly defines the security functions claimed to meet the functional requirements, and the assurance measures planned to satisfy the assurance requirements.

6. TOE security environments: This section should describe the threats of the environment, the organizational security policies that the TOE must satisfy, and related assumptions.

7. PP claims: This section provides explanations, justifications, and supporting material for all ST claims that the TOE conforms to with the requirements of one or more PPs.

8. Rationale: This section should demonstrate that the ST contains an effective and suitable set of countermeasures that is complete and cohesive.

In order to evaluate a PP, the evaluator requires an ST describing the security functions of the TOE, which defines the conformance claimed to a specific PP category.

14.4.6 The Package

The package is an intermediate combination of components that expresses a set of requirements that meet an identifiable subset of security objectives. A package is a reusable object that defines requirements that are known to be useful and effective in meeting the identified objectives. A package may be a part of another package, a PP, or a ST.

14.5 The CC Security Approach

14.5.1 A Simple CC Framework

Confidence associated with information resource security can be obtained through the control of its development, evaluation, and operation. The evaluation of an information resource, whether it is an IT system or an IT product, is defined in the CC in terms of three main constructs, defined earlier: (1) the Protection Profile

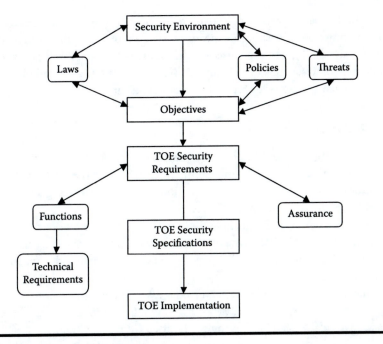

Figure 14.8 Security framework.

(PP), (2) the Security Target, and (3) the Target Of Evaluation (TOE). A possible security framework is presented in Figure 14.8. A Target of Evaluation (TOE) is that part of the information resource that is subject to evaluation [5,7].

A PP contains a set of security requirements that should include an Evaluation Assurance Level. The PP permits the implementation-independent expression of security requirements for a set of Targets of Evaluation (TOEs) that will comply fully with a set of security objectives. A PP is intended to be reusable and to define TOE requirements that are known to be useful and effective in meeting the identified objectives, both for functions and assurance. A PP also contains the rationale for security objectives and security requirements.

A PP could be developed by user communities, IT product developers, or other parties interested in defining such a common set of requirements. A PP gives consumers a means of referring to a specific set of security needs and facilitates future evaluation against those needs.

A ST contains a set of security requirements that may be made by reference to a PP, using the CC functional or assurance components. A ST permits the expression of security requirements for a specific Target of Evaluation (TOE) that are shown, by evaluation, to be useful and effective in meeting the identified objectives.

A ST contains the TOE summary specification, together with the security requirements and objectives, and the rationale for each. A ST is the basis for agreement between all parties as to what security the TOE offers.

The TOE security threats, objectives, requirements, and summary specification of security functions and assurance measures together form the primary inputs to the Security Target (ST), which are used by the evaluators as the basis for evaluation.

Information resource requirements are defined in the CC and used in establishing security requirements for future information resources.

14.5.2 Evaluation

The Common Evaluation Methodology (CEM) is developed as an agreed basis for conducting evaluations against the Common Criteria [7]. The CEM will support the mutual recognition of security evaluations in the United Kingdom, Canada, France, Germany, and the United States.

The inputs for evaluation include the Security Target, the set of evidence about the TOE, and the TOE itself. The result of the evaluation process is a confirmation that the ST is satisfied for the TOE, with one or more reports documenting the evaluations results.

Vulnerabilities and inaccuracies in initial assumptions appear when the information resource is in operations. Reports may require the revision of the TOE. If a revision takes place the TOE has to be submitted for reevaluation.

14.5.3 CC Evaluation Assurance Levels

The CC uses the same evaluation assurance levels defined in the TCSEC. The TCSEC Standard specifies degrees of trust with well-defined assurance levels. These assurance levels express trust ratings in terms of the amount of confidence gained when adding better security features and providing higher assurance to users that these features provide the service for which they are designed. The CC adopted the same EAL initially defined in TCSEC.

Assurance levels define a scale for measuring the criteria for the evaluation of PPs and STs. Evaluation Assurance Levels (EALs) are constructed from the assurance components contained in the third part of the Common Criteria for Information Technology Security Evaluation (CCITSE or CC). These evaluation assurance levels (EALs) define a scale for measuring the criteria for the evaluation of information resources. EALs provide a uniformly increasing scale which balances the level of assurance obtained with the cost and feasibility of acquiring that degree of assurance. There are seven hierarchically ordered EALs. The higher the EAL, the greater the degree of assurance.

14.5.3.1 EAL1: Functionally Tested

EAL1 is applicable where some confidence in correct operation is required, but the threats to security are not viewed as serious. It will be of value where independent assurance is required to support the contention that due care has been exercised with respect to the protection of personal or similar information.

EAL1 provides an evaluation of the information resource as made available to the customer, including independent testing against a specification, and an examination of the guidance documentation provided. It is intended that an EAL1 evaluation could be successfully conducted without assistance from the developer of the information resource, and for minimal cost. An evaluation at this level should provide evidence that the information resource functions in a manner consistent with its documentation, and that it provides useful protection against identified threats.

14.5.3.2 EAL2: Structurally Tested

EAL2 requires the cooperation of the developer in terms of the delivery of design information and test results, but should not demand more effort on the part of the developer than is consistent with good commercial practice. As such it should not require a substantially increased investment of cost or time.

EAL2 is therefore applicable in those circumstances where developers or users require a low to moderate level of independently assured security in the absence of ready availability of the complete development record. Such a situation may arise when securing legacy systems, or where access to the developer may be limited.

14.5.3.3 EAL3: Methodically Tested and Checked

EAL3 permits a conscientious developer to gain maximum assurance from positive security engineering at the design stage without substantial alteration of existing sound development practices.

EAL3 is applicable in those circumstances where developers or users require a moderate level of independently assured security, and require a thorough investigation of the information resource and its development without substantial reengineering.

14.5.3.4 EAL4: Methodically Designed, Tested, and Reviewed

EAL4 permits a developer to gain maximum assurance from positive security engineering based on good commercial development practices which, though rigorous, do not require substantial specialist knowledge, skills, and other resources. EAL4 is the highest level at which it is likely to be economically feasible to retrofit to an existing product line.

EAL4 is therefore applicable in those circumstances where developers or users require a moderate to high level of independently assured security in conventional commodity information resources and are prepared to incur additional security-specific engineering costs.

14.5.3.5 EAL5: Semiformally Designed and Tested

EAL5 permits a developer to gain maximum assurance from security engineering based upon rigorous commercial development practices supported by moderate application of specialist security engineering techniques. Such an information resource will probably be designed and developed with the intent of achieving EAL5 assurance.

It is likely that the additional costs attributable to the EAL5 requirements, relative to rigorous development without the application of specialized techniques, will not be large.

EAL5 is therefore applicable in those circumstances where developers or users require a high level of independently assured security in a planned development and require a rigorous development approach without incurring unreasonable costs attributable to specialist security engineering techniques.

14.5.3.6 EAL6: Semiformally Verified Design and Tested

EAL6 permits developers to gain high assurance from application of security engineering techniques to a rigorous development environment in order to produce a premium information resource for protecting high value assets against significant risks.

EAL6 is therefore applicable to the development of security information resources for application in high risk situations where the value of the protected assets justifies the additional costs.

14.5.3.7 EAL7: Formally Verified Design and Tested

EAL7 is applicable to the development of security information resources for applications in extremely high risk situations and/or where the high value of the assets justifies the higher costs. Practical application of EAL7 is currently limited to information resources with tightly focused security functionality that is amenable to extensive formal analysis.

14.6 Information Resource Evaluation Methodology

14.6.1 Common Principles of Evaluations

While global advances in technology have enabled organizations to share information via computer networks, through the same technology hackers have become even more capable of inflicting more and more destructions around the world.

The ability of the average hacker has increased to a point where they could easily compromise the environment. A solid security plan would provide the direction to secure your information resources. A security plan will document security requirements, review your security policies, and define fundamental causes of security exposures.

A thorough risk analysis will evaluate current security controls and identify gaps where new security solutions need to be implemented.

In order to establish trust among partners and in the business community the enterprise has to initiate the evaluation of its information resources and publish findings to all members of the business community.

Independent of any security evaluation criteria a country decides to adopt, there are common principles of evaluations that have to be satisfied by the evaluators and the evaluation methodology. These principles include (1) impartiality, (2) objectivity, (3) validity, and (4) finality.

1. **Impartiality**

   This principle requires that the evaluation contains no bias. Members of the evaluation team perform their tasks without any influence. Usually, the NEP oversight board should define all unacceptable conflicts of interest and make sure they do not take place.

   In CC evaluations, members shall not have bias against any Protection Profile (PP) being evaluated or any Target of Evaluation (TOE).

2. **Objectivity**

   This principle requires that the evaluation contains a minimum of subjective judgment by members of the evaluation team. Can evaluators be totally free of subjective judgments? Obviously not; but the NEP oversight board should make sure that only a minimum subjectivity be present.

3. **Validity**

   This principle requires that the results of the evaluation are complete and technically sound. The conclusions of the evaluation should show truthful review of the information resource. The NEP oversight board should define all elements of the evaluation process and enforce them.

   In a CC evaluation, there should be evidence that there is good judgment and an accurate technical assessment of the TOE or the PP being evaluated.

4. **Finality**

   This principle requires that the level of assurance that the evaluation process aims for is known to all members of the evaluation team. All members of the team should perform their tasks consistently with the level of assurance sought.

14.6.2 Methodology

The main players in an information resource evaluation methodology are (1) the government, (2) the developer, (3) the evaluator, and (4) the sponsor.

14.6.2.1 Government

A government can indirectly through the NISA control all activities of the evaluation methodology. The NISA and the National Scheme defines all the tasks and responsibilities of the NEP oversight board. In particular, the NEP oversight board should:

Monitor all NEP evaluations
Assure that evaluations satisfy all common principles for evaluations
Provide information support for evaluations
Resolve all conflicts that take place in evaluations

14.6.2.2 The Developer

The developer should provide all product information needed throughout the evaluation process. The developer should develop and maintain evaluation evidence for the purpose of information support.

14.6.2.3 The Evaluator

The evaluator is obviously the main player in an evaluation process. Among his/her main responsibilities, the evaluator:

Receives the evaluation evidence
Performs the evaluation tasks
Satisfies all oversight requirements throughout the evaluation process
Documents and justifies all actions taken
Satisfies common evaluation principles
Obtains information and training support needed from other players

14.6.2.4 The Sponsor

The sponsor prepares for the evaluation by arranging all agreements needed to initiate an evaluation and provides all evidence, training, and support needed throughout the evaluation process.

14.6.2.5 Evaluation Process

An information resource evaluation process consists of three main phases: (1) preparation effort, (2) evaluation effort, and (3) deliberation effort.

The preparation effort is concerned with the first interaction between the sponsor and the evaluator to initiate, together with the rest of the players, an evaluation process. The evaluation effort consists of all evaluation steps. The results of the evaluation process are delivered in the deliberation phase.

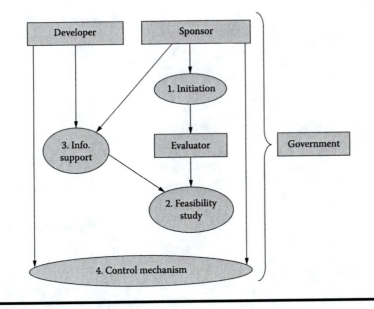

Figure 14.9   Preparation effort.

14.6.2.5.1 Preparation Effort

The preparation effort, as illustrated in Figure 14.9, is started when a sponsor initiates the evaluation process by submitting the target information resource to an evaluator. The evaluator requests support information for an initial feasibility study to estimate the likelihood of success of a possible evaluation process. The sponsor then propose a control mechanism or schedule of the events constituting the evaluation process.

The feasibility study produces a tentative schedule and a set of deliverables that can be useful to all players to jointly monitor and control the evaluation process. An agreement to map out the framework of the evaluation process has to be signed by the sponsor and the evaluator. This agreement should satisfy all laws, rules, and regulations found in NEP documents.

14.6.2.5.2 Evaluation Effort

The evaluation effort, as illustrated in Figure 14.10, is obviously the main effort in the evaluation process. This effort has to be planned according to the control mechanism and deliverables specified by the sponsor. The details of evaluator's activities are set by the NISA and the National Scheme.

The evaluator reviews every item in the evaluation effort according to the assurance criteria defined by the NEP. Often, the evaluator records all information collected through review observations or evidence solicited from the developer, the sponsor, or the NEP oversight board.

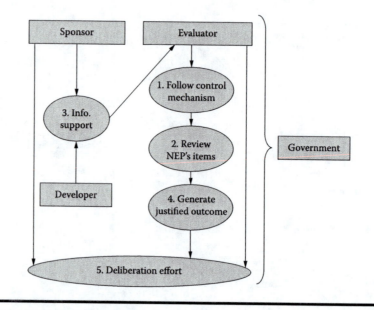

Figure 14.10   Evaluation effort.

In addition to applying the criteria, the evaluator identifies possible vulnerabilities or deficiencies associated to the information resource being evaluated. The NEP oversight board monitors and controls the entire evaluation effort. The evaluator finally generates an Evaluation Technical Report (ETR) which contains justified deliberations.

14.6.2.5.3 Deliberation Effort

The final phase of an evaluation process is the deliberation effort, illustrated in Figure 14.11. In this phase, the evaluator submits the evaluation technical report to the NEP oversight board. This report may contain sensitive data and should be handled accordingly.

The NEP oversight review board reviews the ETR to verify its conformance to NEP's criteria and methodology requirements. The oversight board either confirms the evaluation ruling or rejects it, and transforms the ETR into an evaluation summary report.

The oversight board delivers the summary evaluation report to the evaluation group.

14.7 CC Security Evaluation Programs

Vendors that supply security or security-enabled products to the government have to go through formal security evaluations, as mandated in the

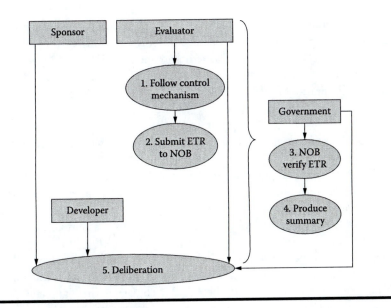

Figure 14.11   Deliberation effort.

U.S. Government's National Information Assurance Acquisition Policy. The Common Criteria (CC) is the first international standard for IT security evaluation and certification. Vendors undertake CC evaluation to differentiate their products from the competition, and to demonstrate to consumers that their security functionality performs as claimed. There are Common Criteria laboratories that vendors may select from to prove that their products meet the requirements of the CC and the U.S. Common Criteria Evaluation and Validation Scheme (CCEVS).

The U.S. government often requires deployment of security products and solutions that have been evaluated and found compliant with well-established criteria. Users of products that protect our national security systems must have a means to validate that these products provide the claimed security functionality. The CC (ISO/IEC 15408) represents the only international standard that is intended to provide for criteria for evaluation of IT security internationally. The National Information Assurance Partnership (NIAP), a joint program sponsored by the National Security Agency (NSA) and the National Institute of Standards and Technology (NIST), is the leading U.S. agency involved in the development of the standard. The "Orange Book" and several other international standards have been at the origin of the CC standard.

The Orange Book, known also as Trusted Computer Security Evaluation Criteria (TCSEC) was released in 1983 but was not published by the DoD until 1985 [12]. There are now specialized organizations that independently assess and determine the level of security adequacy in which commercial transactions are carried out, based on the Orange Book. This report is considered an important cornerstone for defining and designing a set of evaluations or tools for testing the implementation of a sound security certification & accreditation process [11].

The purpose, function and role are specified very well on the Trusted Program Evaluation Program's (TPEP) overview which defines the TCSEC as a standard serving three purposes [13]:

1. Provides product manufacturers with a standard of security features to build into their products
2. Provides DoD components with a metric to evaluate how much trust can be placed in an automated information system for secure processing of classified or other sensitive data
3. Provides a basis for specifying security requirements in acquisition specifications

The publication of the "Rainbow Books" series followed the publication by the DoD of the TCSEC under the name "Orange Book." The following list was compiled by [4] from the information found in the TPEP Web page of the National Computer Security Center (NCSC) Web (Rainbow Series Library, 2000 [8,9,10]):

Orange Book
> Code: 5200.28-STD
> Purpose: DoD Trusted Computer System Evaluation Criteria, 26 December 1985 (supersedes CSC-STD-001-83, dated 15 Aug 83).

Green Book
> Code: CSC-STD-002-85
> Purpose: DoD Password Management Guideline, 12 April 1985.

Light Yellow Book
> Code: CSC-STD-003-85
> Purpose: Computer Security Requirements—Guidance for Applying the DoD TCSEC in Specific Environments, 25 June 1985.

Yellow Book
> Code: CSC-STD-004-85
> Purpose: Technical Rational Behind CSC-STD-003-85: Computer Security Requirements—Guidance for Applying the DoD TCSEC in Specific Environments, 25 June 1985.

Tan Book
> Code: NCSC-TG-001, Ver. 2
> Purpose: A Guide To Understanding Audit In Trusted Systems 1 June 1988, Version 2.

Bright Blue Book
> Code: NCSC-TG-002
> Purpose: Trusted Product Evaluations—A Guide for Vendors, 22 June 1990.

Neon Orange Book
Code: NCSC-TG-003
Purpose: A Guide to Understanding Discretionary Access Control in Trusted Systems, 30 September 1987.
Teal Green Book
Code: NCSC-TG-004
Purpose: Glossary of Computer Security Terms, 21 October 1988. (NCSC-WA-001-85 is obsolete)
Red Book
Code: NCSC-TG-005
Purpose: Trusted Network Interpretation of the TCSEC (TNI), 31 July 1987.
Amber Book
Code: NCSC-TG-006
Purpose: A Guide to Understanding Configuration Management in Trusted Systems, 28 March 1988.
Burgundy Book
Code: NCSC-TG-007
Purpose: A Guide to Understanding Design Documentation in Trusted Systems, 6 October 1988.
Dark Lavender Book
Code: NCSC-TG-008
Purpose: A Guide to Understanding Trusted Distribution in Trusted Systems, 15 December 1988.
Venice Blue Book
Code: NCSC-TG-009
Purpose: Computer Security Subsystem Interpretation of the TCSEC 16 September 1988.
Aqua Book
Code: NCSC-TG-010
Purpose: A Guide to Understanding Security Modeling in Trusted Systems, October 1992.
Red Book
Code: NCSC-TG-011
Purpose: Trusted Network Interpretation Environments Guideline - Guidance for Applying the TNI, 1 August 1990.
Pink Book
Code: NCSC-TG-013 Ver.2
Purpose: RAMP Program Document, 1 March 1995, Version 2.
Purple Book
Code: NCSC-TG-014
Purpose: Guidelines for Formal Verification Systems, 1 April 1989.

Brown Book
   Code: NCSC-TG-015
   Purpose: A Guide to Understanding Trusted Facility Management, 18 October 1989.
Yellow-Green Book
   Code: NCSC-TG-016
   Purpose: Guidelines for Writing Trusted Facility Manuals, October 1992.
Light Blue Book
   Code: NCSC-TG-017
   Purpose: A Guide to Understanding Identification and Authentication in Trusted Systems, September 1991.
Light Blue Book
   Code: NCSC-TG-018
   Purpose: A Guide to Understanding Object Reuse in Trusted Systems, July 1992.
Blue Book
   Code: NCSC-TG-019 Ver. 2
   Purpose: Trusted Product Evaluation Questionnaire, 2 May 1992, Version 2.
Silver Book
   Code: NCSC-TG-020-A
   Purpose: Trusted UNIX Working Group (TRUSIX) Rationale for Selecting Access Control List Features for the UNIX* System, 7 July 1989.
Purple Book
   Code: NCSC-TG-021
   Purpose: Trusted Database Management System Interpretation of the TCSEC (TDI), April 1991.
Yellow Book
   Code: NCSC-TG-022
   Purpose: A Guide to Understanding Trusted Recovery in Trusted Systems, 30 December 1991.
Bright Orange Book
   Code: NCSC-TG-023
   Purpose: A Guide to Understanding Security Testing and Test Documentation in Trusted Systems.
Purple Book
   Code: NCSC-TG-024 Vols. 1/4
   Purpose: A Guide to Procurement of Trusted Systems: An Introduction to Procurement Initiators on Computer Security Requirements, December 1992.
Purple Book
   Code: NCSC-TG-024 Vol. 2/4
   Purpose: A Guide to Procurement of Trusted Systems: Language for RFP

Specifications and Statements of Work—An Aid to Procurement Initiators, 30 June 1993.

Purple Book

Code: NCSC-TG-024 Vols. 3/4

Purpose: A Guide to Procurement of Trusted Systems: Computer Security Contract Data Requirements List and Data Item Description Tutorial, 28 February 1994.

Purple Book

Code: NCSC-TG-024 Vol. 4/4

Purpose: A Guide to Procurement of Trusted Systems: How to Evaluate a Bidder's Proposal Document—An Aid to Procurement Initiators and Contractors.

Forest Green Book

Code: NCSC-TG-025 Ver. 2

Purpose: A Guide to Understanding Data Remanence in Automated Information Systems, September 1991, Version 2, (supersedes CSC-STD-005-85).

Hot Peach Book

Code: NCSC-TG-026

Purpose: A Guide to Writing the Security Features User's Guide for Trusted Systems, September 1991.

Turquoise Book

Code: NCSC-TG-027

Purpose: A Guide to Understanding Information System Security Officer Responsibilities for Automated Information Systems, May 1992.

Violet Book

Code: NCSC-TG-028

Purpose: Assessing Controlled Access Protection, 25 May 1992.

Blue Book

Code: NCSC-TG-029

Purpose: Introduction to Certification and Accreditation Concepts, January 1994.

Light Pink Book

Code: NCSC-TG-030

Purpose: A Guide to Understanding Covert Channel Analysis of Trusted Systems, November 1993.

14.8 The American Model of CC Evaluation Programs

Numerous organizations throughout the world are now implementing the CC, including all of the CC project partners, as well as other European Union nations,

Australia, New Zealand, Japan, Korea, and parts of the former Soviet Union. It is expected that this number will grow significantly as soon as the CC is formally published as International Standard 15408.

The American model for developing an information resource evaluation program included the joint effort of both the NSA and the NIST that produced the NIAP which took the direct responsibility of establishing commercial IT product testing laboratories and accreditation programs. NIAP is dedicated to demonstrating the value of independent testing and validation as a measure of security and trust in IT products. Through its efforts, NIAP fosters the establishment and accreditation of commercial IT product security testing laboratories in the United States [1].

The United States introduced mainly two major stand-alone information resource evaluation programs: (1) the Trusted Product Evaluation Program (TPEP) and (2) the Trust Technology Assessment Program (TTAP) [7].

If a product has been evaluated by the Trusted Product Evaluation Program (TPEP) or Trust Technology Assessment Program (TTAP) to comply with the requirements of a rated class, then it means that an independent assessment showed the product to have the features and assurances of that class. It does not mean that the product is impenetrable.

It is even possible that the independent assessment may overlook some failure to meet the criteria. A vendor claiming to be compliant without an evaluation often doesn't mean very much because the vendor's interpretation of the requirements may not be identical to that of an independent assessor.

14.8.1 The Trusted Product Evaluation Program (TPEP)

In order to encourage the general availability of trusted information resources to information owners and users who wish to protect their valuable information, the TPEP intends to:

- Ensure the availability of useful trusted products that meet the end user's operational needs.
- Provide trusted information resources to be used when developing a trusted system.
- Provide information support with the utility of trusted products.
- Provide information support on the interoperability of the security features and the level of assurance associated with specific features for individually evaluated information resources.
- Establish a continuous and cooperative business relationship with the computer and telecommunications industries.

The Trusted Product Evaluation Program (TPEP) employs security criteria to evaluate computer systems. The TPEP may be used by other organizational units within the NSA to perform computer security evaluations for, and on behalf of, the NCSC. The NSA, however, remains the main agency responsible for the information system security mission with respect to classified and sensitive data [9,13].

The Technical Review Board (TRB) plays the role of a technical advisory panel to the chief of the Trusted Product and Network Security Evaluations Division. The purpose of the TRB is to support the NSA in assuring quality, uniformity, and consistency across evaluations from both a technical and procedural point of view.

The duties of TRB members include the assurance that evaluation team members understand the product they are evaluating. Their duties also include making sure that the documentation satisfies the criteria, in addition to assuring the integrity of the evaluation through quality control and consistency checks during their meeting to review the evaluation. The TRB should gather evidence about TTAP evaluation facility (TEF) processes, for example, by ensuring that [7]:

- The team has performed sufficient analysis of the product design to determine that the design supports the candidate rating.
- The team is prepared to perform thorough product testing.
- Product implementation analysis has been adequately performed.
- The team has performed sufficient analysis and testing to support assignment of the recommended rating and placement of the product on the Evaluated Products List (EPL) [9].

14.8.2 The Trust Technology Assessment Program (TTAP)

The Trust Technology Assessment Program (TTAP) is an evaluation program jointly developed and launched by the National Security Agency (NSA) and the National Institute of Standards and Technology (NIST). The TTAP establishes, approves, and oversees commercial evaluation facilities to perform trusted product evaluations [7,8].

This program is initially intended to target only C2 or lower trust levels of the TCSEC. Higher trust level evaluations may be targeted when this program gains accepted assurance from users and information owners.

TTAP testing services include conformance testing of trusted products, currently including operating systems, database management systems, and network components intended to satisfy the TCSEC C2 class of requirements [7].

14.9 A National Model

The proposed national model for information resource evaluation programs is inspired indirectly from the American model and adapted to the architecture of the government structure configured in a given nation.

The government may establish a National Information Security Agency (NISA; the term *information* is only added to distinguish, in this book, the American NSA from another country's NSA or NISA) that will be in charge of national security, and a National Scheme, in charge of interpreting international information security standards towards the interest of the nation. These security standards are useful in evaluating the nation's capabilities in staying secure, militarily and commercially.

The NISA works jointly with all government departments associated with information security—for example, the Department of Commerce, Department of Telecommunications, and Department of Defense—to organize all information security activities in the country.

The NISA establishes information resource evaluation programs in terms of national information security requirements, in both defense and commerce.

14.9.1 Planning a National Evaluation Program

A country's national information resource evaluation program is simply called, throughout this book, a national evaluation program (NEP). The United States had initially established two NEPs, the TPEP and the TTAP, described earlier in this chapter. These two are now merged in a new program called CC Labs.

The principal participants in NEP are the NEP Oversight Board (NOB), the NEP Evaluation Facility (NEF), and the vendor whose product is being evaluated. A brief description of each of the participants and their roles and responsibilities is provided below.

Vendors have to make a decision concerning which information assurance level they are seeking. The National Scheme has to define the national information assurance system NEFs will use in evaluating IT products. The National Scheme may decide to adopt one of the existing information assurance systems.

The ISO 15408 is obviously the information security standard that all countries need to adopt. Failing to do so may be very costly to a country in terms of national security and commercial trade with IT and telecommunication products. The EAL information assurance levels, defined in Section 8.3.3, are the metrics to apply when evaluating IT products.

The NEP Oversight Board is composed of individuals from NISA and the National Scheme. The Oversight Board has three primary responsibilities: establishing policies for NEP, managing NEP, and representing NEP interests in international evaluation activities.

The NEP Oversight Board is responsible for developing policies and guidance for NEP as a whole. This includes setting the direction of NEP and detailing rules for the operation of the NEP Oversight Board.

The Oversight Board is also responsible for developing the policies for authorization of evaluation facilities (NEF). These policies address areas such as conflict-of-interest requirements, personnel requirements, reporting rules, and training program requirements. As part of its mission, the NEP Oversight Board establishes policies dealing with the use of evaluation criteria and the evaluation methodology and provides support for their development and maintenance.

14.10 Some Other CC Evaluation Requirements

14.10.1 Vendors

The vendor may treat the sought-after NEF evaluation as in seeking any other service. Hence, the vendor can solicit any NEF to perform an evaluation of the vendor's product, including request for proposals from multiple NEFs. It is also possible that the vendor submits a different product to a different NEF for evaluation.

The vendor provides the product's technical and user documentation, reasonable access to appropriate product designers and developers, and access to the product for hands-on testing.

Several items that the vendor should agree to include the following:

- The vendor informs the NEF of any changes to the product during the course of the evaluation.
- The vendor releases proprietary information not only to the NEF, but also to the NEP Oversight Board.
- The vendor must consent to the possible addition of a government participant to the evaluation.
- The vendor agrees that the recommendation to award a rating to a product rests with the NEP Oversight Board.
- The vendor also submits a letter of release for the final evaluation report to the Oversight Board before the evaluated product is placed on the EPL [9].
- The vendor does not make any statements in press releases or other promotional material that might misrepresent the conclusions of the evaluation and trust rating.
- The vendor markets a product as rated only after it has been awarded a rating certificate.
- The vendor does not make any claims about the outcome of the evaluation until a rating certificate is issued. The vendor can, however, make statements that its product is undergoing an evaluation once the product has entered into the evaluation process.

The contract between the vendor and the NEF should specify all the conditions just presented as items the vendor has agreed to satisfy.

14.10.2 NEP Evaluation Providers

The interested evaluating agency should obtain accreditation as a NEP Evaluation Facility (NEF) prior to starting conducting evaluations for the NEP [11]. The candidate agency submits a proposal to the NEP Oversight Board to obtain a provisional status. The successful agency will be granted a trial evaluation authorization as a provisional NEF. The name of the provisional NEFs are added to the provisional NEF list. In the trial period, the provisional NEF will be assigned to work on the evaluation of a trusted product of a specific vendor. If this evaluation is successful, the provisional status of the NEF will be lifted before this latter can start conducting evaluations under the NEP.

To assure fair and consistent evaluations of information resources, the NEP Oversight Board should continue to monitor the work of all practicing NEFs. All NEFs will be available to vendors who are interested in evaluating their information technology products under the NEP. The evaluated products will be published in the NISA's Evaluated Products List.

14.10.3 Authorization of Evaluation Facility

In addition to satisfying the requirements specified in the NEP Technical and Organizational Requirements for Accreditation, authorized NEP facilities must meet the requirements contained in NISA documentation (in the United States this information is provided in Section 285.33, Criteria for Accreditation, in NIST Handbook 150, National Voluntary Laboratory Accreditation Program (NVLAP) Procedures and General Requirements) [11].

The NEP Oversight Board conducts on-site assessments and administers proficiency exams to assess a new agency's ability to conduct evaluations in accordance with the stated requirements. Experts in the field of trusted product evaluations are used to judge an agency's strength in conducting evaluations. Personnel representing the NEP Oversight Board may visit the facility and perform an on-site inspection.

If the NEF successfully completes the trial evaluation, in addition to complying with all the requirements, then the NEP Oversight Board team can grant authorization for one year. This authorization will allow the NEF to:

- Call itself a NEP Evaluation Facility (NEF)
- Perform evaluations against specified evaluation criteria at a particular level of trust (e.g., TCSEC-C2 (Controlled Access Protection))
- Advertise that it is authorized to perform said evaluations

In assessing a facility, the NEP Oversight Board team examines several important factors, namely, (1) impartiality, (2) personnel, (3) reporting and communication capabilities, and (4) equipment.

14.10.3.1 Impartiality

The NEF should be clearly independent of any commercial or social influences and fully independent of the product vendor and developers. Impartiality expresses the independence of the NEF of any influences. The NEF should be able to work as a fully independent unit. If this facility is related to an influencing partnership, the partnership policies and structure should explicitly defined to clearly show that the partnership does not influence the impartiality of the evaluation.

The policies of the procedures of the partnership should also make sure that:

- An evaluation facility member cannot be involved in the development and the evaluation of the same product.
- An evaluator may not provide consulting services to the sponsor or the developer that would compromise the integrity and independence of the evaluation.

In fact, NEP requires that neither the evaluation facility nor any member of the staff concerned with an evaluation can have a vested interest in that evaluation.

14.10.3.2 Personnel

The evaluation facility must demonstrate that its technical staff members playing roles in the evaluation process have the required educational and work experience in the areas of computer science and engineering and information systems security. In addition, evaluators must successfully complete an evaluation training curriculum or demonstrate an equivalent competency.

14.10.3.3 Reporting and Communication Capabilities

There are minimal document generation and storage capability requirements needed to support effective communications with the NEP Oversight Board. For example, an electronic mail capability is required to support communications and document exchange with the NEP Oversight Board, because the NEP Oversight Board requires that all reports be submitted in electronic form.

The facility should also satisfy, as summarized in Table 10.4, the following communication requirements:

- The lab will report changes in personnel to the NEP Oversight Board within 30 days of a change.
- The lab must provide quarterly reports to the NEP Oversight Board listing current staff and evaluations.
- The lab must report any changes in its ownership within, for example, 30 days of the change.

■ The lab will report any new consulting, development, arrangements, or partnerships by the lab or its staff with vendors whose products are currently in evaluation by the lab within 30 days of the establishment of such arrangements/partnerships.

Failure to comply with the NEP authorization requirements may trigger suspension or revocation of authorization.

14.10.3.4 Monitoring

Authorizations are reviewed annually. On-site assessments are not required for each reauthorization. On-site assessments will take place at least once every two years. Additional announced or unannounced monitoring visits may occur as the NEP Oversight Board deems necessary.

14.11 Minicase

InstCorp, a foreign firm, consists of its main technical staff and a number of productivity agents. InstCorp is in the process of planning a NEP Evaluation facility (NEF).

What are the main steps needed in order for InstCorp to become a successful NEF? There are numerous examples on the Internet simulating what security management officers do in real life when they encounter similar problems. There is a wealth of information available on national security evaluation programs that this book's time and space limitations restrict us from presenting, and discussions on relevant information assurance concepts will be found in the literature.

InstCorp mini-case may be studied in terms of a set of sequential phases: planning of the NEF, NEF authorization, NEF operations, and NEF maintenance.

14.11.1 Planning the TEF

InstCorp has to fulfill NEP requirements. In particular, InstCorp should include a facility director, Authorized Representative, Approved Signatories, and key technical people. InstCorp should identify a staff member as quality supervisor who has overall responsibility for the quality assurance and maintenance of the Quality Manual.

It is often better that the facility director and the quality supervisor positions are independently staffed.

Information about InstCorp should be made available in the official personnel folders for NEP assessors to review.

Technical members of InstCorp who are allowed to perform NEP evaluations should have completed at least a Bachelor of Science in computer science, computer engineering, or related technical discipline with demonstrated coursework and/or experience in operating systems, data structures, design/analysis of algorithms, systems architectures, and networking. Exceptions to these conditions should be initially approved by the NEP Oversight Board.

The application package to obtain a NEF authorization includes a description of the facility, a detailed organizational chart, the identification of key facility personnel, and their up-to-date resumes.

The description of the facility should include the legal company name and address, type of ownership of the company, company purpose, and staff size.

The detailed organizational chart of the facility should show the name and position title for all key personnel.

Key NEF staff should include:

1. Authorized Representative of the facility, a person who has facility management authority and responsibility, and will be the primary facility point of contact for NEP
2. Approved Signatory of the facility, the person designated to sign NEP Evaluation Facility test reports
3. Key technical personnel, facility staff with the authority and responsibility to make important technical evaluation decisions.

In the United States, NIST Handbook 150 identifies the types of items that should be specified in a quality manual.

14.11.2 TEF Authorization

It is important that one knows what is meant by NEF authorization; what is meant by authorization to proceed; and how long the period of authorization is. These issues are addressed below, respectively.

NEF authorization is a formal recognition that a facility has met the NEP authorization requirements. Facility authorization identifies the facility as competent and capable to perform trusted product evaluations in accordance with NEP.

The NEP Oversight Board makes grants to prospective NEP evaluation facilities, based on their submitted application package. One may refer to the NEP Scheme (see Chapter 11) for more information.

This initial authorization enables prospective NEP evaluation facilities to conduct a trial evaluation under NEP. The facility will be extended full NEP authorization after the successful completion of the trial evaluation.

The authorization period is indefinite, but facility status is reviewed annually by the NEP Oversight Board to ensure continued compliance.

14.11.3 TEF Operations

In developing this section we first identify several issues that have to be addressed as a part of studying InstCorp operations:

3.1 NEF relationship with vendors
3.2 NEF relationship with the NEP Oversight Board
3.3 NEF support

14.11.3.1 TEF Relationship with Vendors

The relationship between a NEF and a vendor is defined in a mutual agreement. The NEF-Vendor agreement should address (1) the purpose of the agreement, (2) proprietary information, (3) responsibilities, and (4) mutual agreements.

The purpose of the agreement is to delineate the responsibilities and obligations of the parties with respect to the evaluation and maintenance of a rating under the NEP evaluation scheme.

Proprietary Information is the information provided by the vendor, including computer software, that embodies trade secrets or that is privileged or confidential commercial or financial information, or that was developed by the vendor and is not available to the government or to the public without restriction from another source.

The vendor shall:

1. Agree, as a condition to the evaluation, to make the product commercially available.
2. Enter, on a voluntary basis, and at its own risk and expense, into this agreement with the intent of enabling the NEF to determine if the product security features conform to the requirements for the level of trust set forth in the criteria.
3. Provide the NEF with all documentation the NEF requires for its evaluation.
4. Provide the NEF with sufficient quantities of documentation or permit duplication of such documents as required to perform the evaluation.
5. Clearly identify and properly mark all trade secrets and confidential commercial information that are provided to the NEF on a privileged or confidential basis so that such information can be protected to the full extent authorized by law.
6. Not to claim or imply or use language that could reasonably be interpreted to otherwise claim or imply:
   a. Government endorsement, approval, or certification of the product has occurred.
   b. That the results of a favorable NEF evaluation are applicable to this product, until the NEP Oversight Board places this product on the EPL, to any other product, or to other versions of the product.
   c. That the product has been evaluated at any level of trust other than that set forth in the EPL.

7. Agree to the release of all proprietary and privileged information provided by the vendor to the NEF to the NEP Oversight Board or its representatives, including the TRB members.
8. Agree to the inclusion on the evaluation team of a NEP resource or representative assigned by the NEP Oversight Board.
9. Agree to make any and all corrections and enhancements to the product called for by the TRB and/or Oversight Board as a condition of being awarded the certificate.
10. Agree that the final decision on the awarding of a certificate rests with the NEP Oversight Board.
11. Identify a representative of the vendor organization to act as an official point of contact with the NEF and its appointed evaluation team.
12. Provide instructions to team members on the use of the product being evaluated as required for purposes of the evaluation, including product documentation, and vendor-provided classes, and hands-on access time.
13. Make an honest and forthright presentation of the product and its capabilities and deficiencies to the NEF.

The NEF shall:

1. Prepare in conjunction with the NEP Oversight Board, a product bulletin, a summary description of the product and its security features, and candidate level of trust.
2. Evaluate the product and vendor-provided data to determine if the product meets the requirements for the level of trust as set forth in the criteria.
3. Hold in strict confidence the vendor-provided privileged, proprietary, and company confidential information, only disclose the information to the NEP Oversight Board or its representatives (e.g., TRB), and only use vendor information for the purposes of assessing the products compliance with criteria requirements.
4. Perform an honest and forthright evaluation of the product and make an honest and forthright presentation of the product and its capabilities, deficiencies, and compliance with the criteria requirements to the TRB.
5. Assign an appropriately trained team to evaluate the vendor's product.
6. Provide a NEF Technical point of contact and a business point of contact to coordinate activities with the vendor.
7. Make known to the vendor prior to the evaluation any and all information regarding the ownership of the NEF or its subsidiaries, as may be relevant to the vendor.
8. Agree that if, for whatever reason, they cease to be a NEF, then any and all vendor provided proprietary, privileged, and company confidential information they hold, including samples of the product provided by the vendor, shall be returned to the vendor or handled in a manner stipulated by the vendor.

9. Upon successful completion of its evaluation, prepare in a timely manner, a publicly available Final Evaluation Report (FER) delineating that the product has met or maintained the requirements for the level of trust against which it was evaluated. This FER will be submitted to the NEP Oversight Board and to the vendor.

Mutual agreements include the following items:

1. It is mutually understood and agreed that regardless of the best efforts of the vendor and the NEF, the final determination of awarding or not awarding a certificate rests with the NEP Oversight Board. Further, nothing in this agreement imposes an obligation by the NEP Oversight Board to issue an affirmative certification of the product.
2. It is mutually understood and agreed upon that if the vendor can no longer make an evaluated product commercially available, the vendor shall notify the NEF, by letter, at the earliest possible opportunity, and the NEF shall pass this information on to the NEP Oversight Board.
3. It is mutually understood and agreed that the evaluation of the product shall be conducted by evaluators for the NEF. These evaluators may include representatives of the NEP Oversight Board and/or parties under contract with the NEF.
4. It is mutually understood and agreed that the execution of this agreement or the inclusion of the product on the EPL, resulting from the evaluation, shall not be construed as an endorsement of any product of the vendor or a commitment to the vendor by the NEF, NEP Oversight Board, or Government for the procurement of products.
5. It is mutually understood and agreed that no certificate will be awarded prior to the meeting of a TRB and subsequent actions of the NEP Oversight Board. Further, the scheduling of a time for a meeting of the TRB to review and assess the findings of the NEF evaluation team is controlled fully by the NEP Oversight Board.
6. It is mutually understood and agreed that any financial arrangements or conditions laid out in the agreement are strictly agreements between the vendor and the NEF and impose no obligations upon the NEP Oversight Board, the government, or its representatives.
7. It is mutually understood and agreed that the NEP Oversight Board will issue the product bulletin for public dissemination at the onset of the evaluation.
8. It is mutually understood and agreed that upon successful completion of its evaluation, the NEP Oversight Board will recommend an EPL entry be issued that announces the product's rating. However, the product will not be entered into the EPL until the NEP Oversight Board receives the vendor's written concurrence regarding the findings of the FER.
9. It is mutually understood and agreed that entering the product into evaluation imposes no restrictions or guarantees by either party regarding the evaluation of other products.

14.11.3.2 TEF Relationship with the NEP Oversight Board

The NEP Oversight Board is composed of individuals from NISA and the National Scheme. The Oversight Board has three primary responsibilities: establishing policies for NEP, managing NEP, and representing NEP interests in international evaluation activities.

Oversight Board is also responsible for developing the policies for authorization of evaluation facilities. These policies address areas such as conflict-of-interest requirements, personnel requirements, reporting rules, and training program requirements. As part of its mission, the NEP Oversight Board establishes policies dealing with the use of evaluation criteria and evaluation methodology and provides support for their development and maintenance.

The NEP Oversight Board (NOB) supervises all activities of the NEP. The NOB grants and authorizes prospective NEFs and maintains the list of provisional NEFs. The NOB should, for example, monitor their performance and compliance with the terms of NEP.

The NOB grants authorization to proceed with a trial evaluation to prospective NEFs, maintains a list of provisional NEFs, supervising the authorization of evaluation facilities, oversees NEFs, monitors their performance and compliance with the terms of the NEP Scheme, develops and maintains NEP-specific documentation related to evaluation criteria and methodology, ensuring consistency and quality across evaluations, and issues evaluation rating certificate recommendations.

14.11.3.3 NEF Support

The training program may be useful in the success of a NEF evaluator. The training class provides information about the evaluation process and the technical and analytical skills used to evaluate security products. This class is targeted towards facility evaluators who do not have evaluation experience.

14.11.4 NEF Maintenance

In developing this section we first identify several issues that have to be addressed as a part of studying InstCorp operations:

4.1   NEF proficiency test
4.2   NEF on-site assessment

14.11.4.1 NEF Proficiency Test

Proficiency testing will require that InstCorp demonstrates that it can successfully perform conformance testing. NEP evaluations facilities have to undergo proficiency testing and achieve satisfactory results according to the appropriate test methods.

InstCorp should have eventually performed a trial evaluation and obtained the NEP Oversight Board's authorization to proceed. The trial evaluation will provide for InstCorp the initial, necessary evidence that it now has the capability and competence to perform NEP evaluations.

InstCorp may, however, be subject to additional proficiency testing as part of reauthorization. If InstCorp has conducted an evaluation within the 2 years preceding an on-site assessment, a proficiency test will not be required at that time. Otherwise, assessors may administer proficiency testing to test InstCorp evaluator's general knowledge of the evaluation criteria during the on-site assessment.

14.11.4.2 TEF On-Site Assessment

The on-site assessment for NEP facilities will be performed by two or more NEP assessors during a 2-day period. The assessment will take place at the facility site. All observations made by the assessors during the assessment will be held in strict confidence.

The facility shall be prepared to conduct test demonstrations and be ready for examination according to the requirements identified in NISA documents and the facility's quality manual. Efforts will be made to minimize disruption to the normal working routines during the assessment. The assessors will need time and work space to complete assessment documentation during the time at the facility site.

The assessors will use the General Operations Checklist and the NEP Specific Operations Checklist. The checklists, based on Handbook 150 and the technical specifics contained in this document, ensure that the assessment is complete and that all assessors cover the same items at each facility. The checklists have been developed to cover a wide range of possibilities; therefore, not all questions apply in all circumstances. On the other hand, the assessors may go beyond the checklist in order to delve more deeply into a technical issue.

The NEF also needs to pass a proficiency test. It is required that a NEF demonstrates that it can successfully perform conformance testing. Under NEP, facilities will be required to conduct an evaluation, known as a trial evaluation, that will serve as the evidence that a facility has the capability and competence to perform NEP evaluations. Trial evaluations are performed after receiving authorization to proceed from the NEP Oversight Board.

14.12 Summary

This chapter presented the Common Criteria in more details. The evaluation assurance levels adopted by the CC were introduced.

The ISO 15408 is a very complex set of standards. It contains a great amount of notations that can only be understood in the context of evaluations against these criteria. As soon as you change context these terms may have different meanings. Over time, these standards will be more accepted by the international community.

It is only then that the concepts and terminology that emerged with these standards become more and more common knowledge.

This chapter presented basic concepts of an information resource methodology. It provided the main principles of an evaluation process, the main players, and their roles in various steps of the evaluation process.

The chapter also identified the main steps of an information resource evaluation process in the context of the CC.

14.13 Review Questions

1. The EALs have been developed with the goal of preserving the concepts of assurance drawn from the source criteria (TCSEC, ITSEC, and CTCPEC) so that results of previous evaluations remain relevant. Can you explain how EAL1 should be interpreted?

2. The EALs have been developed with the goal of preserving the concepts of assurance drawn from the source criteria (TCSEC, ITSEC, and CTCPEC) so that results of previous evaluations remain relevant. Can you explain how EAL2 should be interpreted?

3. The EALs have been developed with the goal of preserving the concepts of assurance drawn from the source criteria (TCSEC, ITSEC, and CTCPEC) so that results of previous evaluations remain relevant. Can you explain how EAL3 should be interpreted?

4. The EALs have been developed with the goal of preserving the concepts of assurance drawn from the source criteria (TCSEC, ITSEC, and CTCPEC) so that results of previous evaluations remain relevant. Can you explain how EAL4 should be interpreted?

5. The EALs have been developed with the goal of preserving the concepts of assurance drawn from the source criteria (TCSEC, ITSEC, and CTCPEC) so that results of previous evaluations remain relevant. Can you explain how EAL5 should be interpreted?

6. The EALs have been developed with the goal of preserving the concepts of assurance drawn from the source criteria (TCSEC, ITSEC, and CTCPEC) so that results of previous evaluations remain relevant. Can you explain how EAL6 should be interpreted?

7. The EALs have been developed with the goal of preserving the concepts of assurance drawn from the source criteria (TCSEC, ITSEC, and CTCPEC) so that results of previous evaluations remain relevant. Can you explain how EAL7 should be interpreted?

8. The objective of an evaluation process is to enable the evaluator to prepare an impartial report stating whether or not a system or a product satisfies its security target at the level of confidence indicated by the stated evaluation level. How does a security evaluation process in CC work?

9. Explain the security framework presented in Figure 14.8.
10. Who needs to know the criteria?
11. The CC is intended for users, information owners, government agencies, developers, vendors, and evaluators. They all use the CC in their different ways. Why, then, do users need the CC?
12. The CC is intended for users, information owners, government agencies, developers, vendors, and evaluators. They all use the CC in their different ways. Why, then, do developers need the CC?
13. The CC is intended for users, information owners, government agencies, developers, vendors, and evaluators. They all use the CC in their different ways. Why, then, do then evaluators need the CC?
14. The second part of the CC document contains a catalog of well-defined and understood security functional requirements that are intended to be used as a standard way of expressing the security requirements for IT products and systems. This catalog is organized into classes, families, and components. Define and explain the need of the class construct.
15. The second part of the CC document contains a catalog of well-defined and understood security functional requirements that are intended to be used as a standard way of expressing the security requirements for IT products and systems. This catalog is organized into classes, families, and components. Define and explain the need of the family construct.
16. The second part of the CC document contains a catalog of well-defined and understood security functional requirements that are intended to be used as a standard way of expressing the security requirements for IT products and systems. This catalog is organized into classes, families, and components. Define and explain the need of the component construct.

14.14 Workshops

Workshop 1

Assume you are the chairman of the local U.S. Post Office of a midsize town with 20 branches. All branches are connected to the main office where your office is located. We know how the ISO 27001 and ISO 27002 are useful to enhance overall security of your agency but we are confused about the usefulness of the ISO 15408 to the security of your agency. We would like that you explain to us the need for the ISO 15408 for your agency and your national and international partners (a lot of mail comes from overseas). Explain and give detailed steps of how to apply the ISO 15408 to enhance and assure security. Be simple and complete as the steps you recommend will be made available to similar agencies to adopt.

Workshop 2

A public agency in the industrial sector in a developing country is enjoying an outsourcing relationship with organizations in the United States. The developing country cannot afford imposing any security certification against any security standards including the ISO 15408. Recommend security planning steps based on the ISO 15408 that can minimize any security risks that can potentially harm the outsourcing the relationship between entities in these two countries. Explain the relationship between security planning and the ISO 15408.

References

1. Common Criteria, The Common Criteria Portal, http://www.commoncriteriaportal. org/, visited on January, 29, 2009.
2. Common Criteria Evaluation and Validation Scheme for Information Technology Security-Organization, Management and Concept of Operations, Scheme Publication #1, Version 2.0, dated May 1999.
3. Connolly, J. L., and B. S. Abramowitz, The Trust Technology Assessment Program and the Benefits to U.S. Evaluations, *Proceedings of the 11th Annual Computer Security Applications Conference*, New Orleans, LA, December 1995.
4. Arado, E. L., Matrix based on the Rainbow Books Library, http://lacomunidad.elpais. com/el-arado/2008/11/20/matrix-based-on-the-rainbow-books-library, visited on January 30, 2009.
5. Flahavin, E. E., and P. R. Toth, Concept Paper: An Overview of the Proposed Trust Technology Assessment Program, *Proceedings of the 15th National Computer Security Conference*, Vol. I, pp. 84–92, Baltimore, MD, October 1992.
6. Oracle White Paper, 2001. Computer Security Criteria: Security Evaluations and Assessment, http://otndnld.oracle.co.jp/deploy/security/pdf/en/seceval_wp.pdf, visited on January 30, 2009.
7. National Computer Security Center (NCSC), Draft Trust Technology Assessment Program (TTAP) Evaluation Process for C2 Products, Fort Meade, MD, January 1997.
8. National Computer Security Center (NCSC), Ratings Maintenance Phase Program Document, Version 2, Fort Meade, MD, March 1995.
9. National Computer Security Center (NCSC), Evaluated Products List (EPL), INFOSEC Product and Services Catalog, Fort Meade, MD, updated quarterly, March 1996.
10. National Computer Security Center (NCSC), Derived Verification Requirements for TCSEC Class C2: Controlled Access Protection, Fort Meade, MD, January 1997.
11. National Institute of Standards and Technology, National Voluntary Laboratory Accreditation Program, Technical and Organizational Requirements for Accreditation, Gaithersburg, MD, January 1997.
12. Pfleeger C. P., and S. L. Pfleeger, *Security in computing*, Prentice Hall Professional Technical Reference, 2002.
13. TPEP, http://www.radium.ncsc.mil/tpep/process/overview.html, Last updated August 13, 1998.

SECURITY REVIEW VI

Chapter 15

Security Review through Security Audit

Learning Objectives

After reading this chapter, students are expected to achieve an understanding of:

Security audits
Main features of a security audit
Types of security audit
How to manage security risks
Need for a risk-driven security program
Main standards relevant to security audit

15.1 Introduction

A security audit is sometimes very unpleasant, especially for system owners. It is, however, indispensable to maintaining a continual defense system. It is also probably what executives fear the most. Nobody wants to see external agents digging into company records, inspecting every single item in the computing environment; God knows what they can come up with. Just thinking that auditors may find you at fault or lacking adequate security is very worrisome.

In a security audit, an auditor will review your records and activities, and examine the security strategy and mechanisms used to protect your organization. The security audit identifies, assesses, and mitigates risks. The ultimate goal of a security

669

audit is to propose a risk-driven security program that prescribes corrective and preventive actions necessary to bring current risks back to an acceptable level.

The more security deficiencies discovered by auditors, the more disappointments to management and owners. Along with this feeling, there should be some sense of relief now that owners know their systems deficiencies and risks, and they also have learned what corrective and preventive actions they need to take to save the situation.

Despite everybody's discontent, security audit remain a necessary activity that is periodically conducted to determine the risk position of a company. This is a very feasible alternative compared to taking risks from security incidents that would bring great losses to the company, and damage its reputation.

This chapter is intended to discuss issues involved in defining and evaluating security audit. It should provide guidance to organizations on how to design and incorporate an effective audit mechanism into their system, and to present steps for implementers on how to make effective use of the audit capabilities provided by trusted systems. We discuss the information requirements, and security audit processes need to have, in order to produce an effective and efficient risk-driven security program.

Before we further proceed in discussing what is needed to plan a security audit project, we first have to present our own definition of security audit.

15.2 Security Audit Means Different Things to Different People

The more you read on security audits, the more new definitions you will see. Most definitions are valid one way or another and should apply to some tasks in a security audit project. We will see later in this chapter that, usually, none of the definitions is wrong but each of the definitions represents some of the facets in security audit.

We here discuss a representative sample of security definitions from the literature. We look at four security audit definitions: from the NSA and listed in the NSTISSI 4009 standard; from the American National Standard (ANS) listed in T1.523-2001, Telecom Glossary 2000; from WhatIs.com; and from wikipedia.com where many users search for their definitions.

15.2.1 How Does NSA Define Security Audit?

The National Security Telecommunications and Information Systems Security Instruction (NSTISSI) standard No. 4009 provides standard definitions for various specialized terms relating to the disciplines of communications security and automated information systems security. The definitions contained in this glossary are prescriptive for all elements of the U.S. government and for its contractors with respect to national security systems. This document replaces NCSC-9, National Communications Security (COMSEC) Glossary, published in 1982.

Later, in April of 1998, the NSA completed a glossary of terms used in computer security and intrusion detection. Greg Stocksdale of the NSA Information Systems Security Organization was the first who initiated such a comprehensive glossary project. The SANS Institute begun a community-wide program to expand and update the glossary on a continuing basis.

This glossary defines audit as follows:

> Audit is the independent examination of records and activities to ensure compliance with established controls, policy, and operational procedures, and to recommend any indicated changes in controls, policy, or procedures.
>
> **NSA Information Systems Security Organization**

15.2.2 How Does WhatIs.com Define Security Audit?

WhatIs.com is a knowledge exploration and self-education tool about information technology [5]. It is increasingly becoming a place where the IT professional can quickly learn and master new concepts, technologies, skills, and products. In a Glossary published by WhatIs.com, security audit is defined as follows:

> A security audit is a systematic evaluation of the security of a company's information system by measuring how well it conforms to a set of established criteria. A thorough audit typically assesses the security of the system's physical configuration and environment, software, information handling processes, and user practices. Security audits are often used to determine regulatory compliance, in the wake of legislation (such as HIPAA, the Sarbanes–Oxley Act, and the California Security Breach Information Act) that specifies how organizations must deal with information.
>
> **WhatIs.com**

Some of the legislations meant in this definition include HIPAA, the Sarbanes–Oxley Act, and other regional or international standards. Let us briefly talk about what these legislations are. Some other standards are defined later in this chapter but discussed in more details in later chapters.

HIPAA seeks to establish standardized mechanisms for electronic data interchange, security, and confidentiality of all healthcare-related data [6]. President Clinton on August 21, 1996, signed the HIPAA into law, with the intention to enhance the overall efficiency and effectiveness of the healthcare system. The law sets for healthcare the necessary conditions to redefine the management of health information and the assurance of the privacy and security of health information.

This final HIPAA security rule, published in the Federal Register in February of 2003, adopts standards for the security of electronic protected health information to be implemented by health plans, health care clearinghouses, and certain health care providers. The use of the security standards will improve the Medicare and Medicaid programs, and other federal health programs and private health programs, and the effectiveness and efficiency of the health care industry in general by establishing a level of protection for certain electronic health information.

A white paper published in 2005 in Apani Networks Compliance Series provides a simple but thorough presentation of the HIPAA requirements and steps to achieve conformity. This paper gives technical safeguards, policies, and procedures that protect and monitor information access and prevent unauthorized access to data transmitted over a network.

The second legislation mentioned in WhatIs.com's definition is the Sarbenes–Oxley legislation [7]. The Sarbanes–Oxley Act of 2002 is legislation passed as a response to the Enron and WorldCom financial scandals to protect shareholders and the general public from accounting errors and fraudulent practices in the enterprise. The act is maintained by the Securities and Exchange Commission (SEC), which sets deadlines for compliance and publishes rules on requirements.

Sarbanes–Oxley is not a set of business practices and does not specify how a business should store records; rather, it defines which records are to be stored and for how long. The legislation not only affects the financial side of corporations, but also affects the IT departments whose job it is to store a corporation's electronic records. The Sarbanes–Oxley Act states that all business records, including electronic records and electronic messages, must be saved for "not less than five years." The consequences for noncompliance are fines, imprisonment, or both. IT departments are increasingly faced with the challenge of creating and maintaining a corporate records archive in a cost-effective fashion that satisfies the requirements put forth by the legislation.

The third legislation mentioned in WhatIs.com's definition is the California Security Breach Information Act. The California Security Breach Information Act (SB-1386) is a law requiring organizations in California that maintain personal information about individuals to inform them if the security of their information is compromised. For example, if a database containing personal data is compromised, the individual whose information is at risk should be alerted. The act, which went into effect July 1, 2003, was created to help stop the increasing incidence of identity theft.

15.2.3 How Does the ATIS Define Security Audit?

The Alliance for Telecommunications Industry Solutions (ATIS) is a U.S.-based body that is committed to rapidly developing and promoting technical and operations standards for the communications and related information technologies industry worldwide using a pragmatic, flexible, and open approach [2]. ATIS develops standards and solutions addressing a wide range of industry issues in a manner that allocates and coordinates industry resources and produces the greatest return for communications companies. ATIS is accredited by the American National Standards Institute (ANSI).

The American National Standard (ANS) T1.523-2001, Telecom Glossary 2007 proposes an alternative definition of security audit [1]:

> A security audit, when applied to data processing operations, is an independent review and examination of system records and activities to (a) determine the adequacy of system controls, (b) ensure compliance with established security policy and operational procedures, (c) detect breaches in security, and (d) recommend any indicated changes in any of the foregoing.
>
> **Alliance for Telecommunications Industry Solutions**

15.2.4 How Does Wikipedia Define Security Audit?

Wikipedia is an open content online encyclopedia created through the collaborative effort of a community of users known as Wikipedeans. This project started in January of 2001, and it is still growing very rapidly. The Wikipedia Web site encourages readers to contribute to the project's development, for example by submitting needed articles or editing existing content. The Wikipedia also oversees several other open-content projects: Wiktionary, a dictionary and thesaurus; Wikibooks, a collection of free texts and other books; Wikiquote, a collection of quotations; Wikisource, a collection of free source documents; and Meta-Wiki, which coordinates all the other projects.

Many wiki communities now exist privately to support diverse research and development programs. Wikipedia, as the "mother," is designed to support all groups by providing technical support as needed and by validating content with the purpose of sharing information worldwide. Today, the English-language Wikipedia is, by far, the world's largest wiki; the German-language Wikipedia is the second-largest.

Given the growth of Wikipedia and its successful globalization effort, it is certainly a good source of applied definitions, such as for the term *security audit*, as it presents the way users worldwide see things. For example, we can select Wikipedia's definition of security audit [8].

> A computer security audit is a process that can verify that certain standards have been met, and identify areas in need of remediation or improvement. Decades ago, identifying problem areas had to be done by a team of human auditors, but now software can analyze what's on a computer, and present a story that you do not need to be an expert

to comprehend. It is important to use software that stays current with rapidly evolving security threats. Software cannot resolve the whole problem. Computer users need to evaluate the reports, make changes to correct the problems, then rerun the reports. When success is achieved in resolving all the identified problems, we can raise the bar on the standards we are trying to achieve.

Wikipedia

15.3 Some Security Audit Activities

We showed earlier that there are many definitions for security audit. However, they certainly share many properties and testing activities. It is very important to define very clear security objectives for the security audit project and plan it well. Defining the security objective your organization needs is even more crucial now that we know there is a multitude of security audit approaches.

We next present six security audit processes that one may encounter in the real world: (1) vulnerability assessment, (2) penetration test, (3) security checklist, (4) security policy review, (5) physical security audit, and 6) event-driven security audit. Even though the literature reports these security audit processes as different types of security audits, they are in fact not necessarily different security audit methods but simply optional security audit activities from which the auditor makes a selection. For example, the auditor may determine that security policy review and vulnerability assessment are needed but not necessarily a penetration test. That is, we are here dealing with one security audit project where two security audit procedures are needed and not two different security audit projects. This project employs security policy review and vulnerability assessment but does not require a penetration test.

1. **Vulnerability assessment:** This type of security testing is a technical (versus nominal) security audit, that is routinely activated and generally passive in nature, to systematically test for risks from specific system vulnerabilities. For example, there is vulnerability in sendmail that can be exploited to cause a denial-of-service condition and could allow a remote attacker to execute arbitrary code with the privileges of the sendmail daemon, typically root. If you fail to upgrade or apply a patch as specified by your vendor, then you will be at risk. Vulnerability scans may be performed by in-house or out-of-house staff and should be conducted at least once a month and immediately after potentially dangerous vulnerabilities are discovered.

2. **Penetration testing:** While a vulnerability assessment is generally passive in nature, a penetration test is a technical (versus to nominal) security audit that is initiated to actively compromise system, physical, or procedural security.

It's a confident way to assess security posture, practices, and procedures. You cannot have a complete security audit without penetration testing, especially if you have severe security requirements. For smaller organizations, this is an optional form of security audit that may or may not be used during annual security audits or as part of general security reviews.

3. **Security checklist review:** A security checklist review is a semitechnical security testing activity that is periodically conducted to ensure that all systems are operating with the conditions set for them. This test applies current published or publicly available checklists for diverse types of platforms, applications, or services.

4. **Security policy review:** A security policy review is usually a nominal security activity that examines an organization's security policy. These types of testing activities may be conducted by internal staff or by an external security auditor. In the former case, the internal auditor ensures that users, partners, and customers are familiar with the parts of this policy that relate to their interactions with the organization. The internal auditor should also ensure that the current version of the security policy is being enforced throughout the organization. On the other hand, an external auditor, in addition to all the internal auditor activities described earlier, should look into the validity of the current security policy. The external auditor should verify that the existing policy covers all security staff requirements, and all requirements defined for processes, procedures, training, and software and hardware configurations and their operations.

5. **Physical security audit:** A physical security is usually a nominal testing activity where the auditor examines physical access controls and emergency procedures for an organization's sites, buildings, server and equipment rooms, and any areas where proprietary assets are stored or used. This type of test is needed when physical restructuring, mergers, or acquisition take place. In this case, these testing activities are performed by internal staff. Even though external auditors are called for the same physical testing activities, they are more often called for to test for physical access to information systems and related resources.

6. **Event-driven security audit:** The security policy will identify those events for which specialized testing activities are scheduled. The type of testing activities required are prescribed in terms of the possible changes this event can effect in the computing environment. All the security testing activities described may apply in an event-driven audit.

15.4 Our Definition of Security Audit

The following is our definition of security audit:

> A security audit is a systematic, independent evaluation of a company's records and activities to (1) measure its compliance with accepted standards and established controls, policy, and operational procedures; (2) measure its security risk position; (3) attest to the adequacy of its defense system; and (4) recommend a risk-driven security program that includes corrective and preventive actions needed for a continual improvement of the company's security risk position.

This definition of security audit is as close as we can get to the requirements of security standards ISO/IEC 17799, ISO/IEC 27002 (same as ISO/IEC 17799) and ISO 27001 [3,4]). We reserve a special chapter on the Information Security Management System (ISMS), and we will then revisit this definition and discuss it in more detail.

A security audit should assess the validity of owners' assertions regarding the security of their organization. Misstatements may be at the level of the compliance with established criteria, adequacy of its defense system, or security policy and its enforcements. The security mechanisms or appliances installed to implement the security policy may be misconfigured. For example, misstatements may be seen in owners' assertions that the security controls implemented are adequately protecting the organization or that the risk position of the organization is maintained below the maximum permissible level.

The auditor provides reasonable assurance that the security evaluation statements are free of material misstatements. For example, the BS 7799.2 and the ISO 27001 require that the risk-driven security evaluation statements be included in the statement of applicability.

An auditor should be concerned with the organization's security defense system but not with the financial situation, budget constraints, or the wisdom of management's decisions, no matter how great they look in adding business competitive advantage.

15.5 Main Features in Security Audit

As in any other IT project, there is need to gather information on candidates with the skills, experience, and other qualifications required participating in the security audit project. These preparation steps are obviously needed in the case of internal audit. External audits will also go through similar steps in selecting the members who can best serve in the security audit project.

A security audit project should start with a formal opening meeting with the senior management overseeing the security audit project to discuss the planning of the project and any possible concerns. The auditors have to present the methodology and the working steps of the security audit project. Scheduling periodic meetings with senior management to involve them in reviewing the effects of some controls and procedures on business operations—and, as in any IT project, management support and involvement—will obviously alleviate all the difficulties auditors may encounter throughout the audit project.

Auditors usually communicate to senior management their recommendations, which include their attestation to the current security posture of the company and the proposed corrective actions in a formal meeting using a visual presentation. This meeting will provide an opportunity to owners and management to ask implementation questions and present their viewpoints. Owners' and management views are discussed in the final report, and those ideas that are relevant to and in agreement with the implementation of the recommended risk-driven security program should be taken into account in the postaudit evaluation visit.

Our definition requires that a security audit satisfy a dozen features or properties. A checklist table representing a security audit profile, based on those features, is depicted in Table 15.1. The security audit features are as follows:

1. Is a systematic process
2. Requires an independent auditor
3. Applies established criteria or standards
4. Collects evidence of (a) compliance with controls, policy, and procedures or (b) adequacy of an organization's security defense system
5. Detects breaches
6. Applies selective testing
7. Measures the degree of fairness of owners' assertions in representing the state of complying with the criteria or standard, or criteria established, given the samples taken
8. Attests to the current security position of the audited organization
9. Measures the basic and residual risk positions of the audited company
10. Recommends corrective and preventive actions in a risk-driven security program that ensures a continual improvement of the security position
11. Communicates findings to owners
12. A security audit allows for postaudit

These features are easy to follow. We provide a checklist in Table 15.1 Security Audit Profile that provides a description of the features that should be present in any security audit. The security auditor has to consult with this checklist from time to time throughout the security audit project to make sure that there is nothing omitted.

15.5.1 Feature 1: A Security Audit Is a Systematic Process

The security audit has to be conducted in a methodical manner. An acceptable security audit methodology has to be adopted and approved by information owners. References containing a user guide and useful literature have to available not only throughout the security audit project but also as long as the audit report is

Table 15.1 Security Audit Profile

Features	Document of Methodology	Terms of Reference	Management Acceptance	Auditors Acceptance
1. A security audit is a systematic process: List of steps are documented. Templates exist. Automated process for audit.				
2. A security audit requires as an independent auditor. The auditor is internal and independent of target of audit. The auditor is external and independent of target of audit.				
3. A security audit applies established criteria or standards: Internal criteria Security-related standard				
4. A security audit collects evidence of: Compliance evidence Certification evidence				
5. A security audit detects breaches: Corporate policy exists against which violations are identified.				
6. A security audit applies selective testing: Nominal testing applies. Technical testing applies.				

7. A security audit measures the degree of fairness of owners' assertions in representing the state of complying with the criteria or standard, or criteria established, given the samples taken: Owners' assertions exist.					
8. A security audit attests to the current security position of the audited organization: Auditors' attestation is sought.					
9. A security audit measures the basic and residual risk positions of the target of audit. Risk positions are measured.					
10. A security audit recommends corrective and preventive actions in a risk-driven security program that ensures a continual improvement of the security position: Audit-based security program is sought.					
11. A security audit communicates findings to owners: Findings are reported to owners.					
12. A security audit allows for postaudit: Postaudit visits are planned.					

relevant to the security of the audited system. For example, if the security audit project you just initiated lasts 6 months and the generated report is set to expire in 18 months, then the security audit methodology references in questions have to be available at least for the next 2 years.

15.5.2 Feature 2: A Security Audit Requires as an Independent Auditor

The ultimate objective of a security audit is to assess the current security defense system of the organization and owners' assertions about it, in addition to attesting to the current security risk position of the company and recommending a risk-driven security program that ensures a continual improvement in the organization's risk position. Unless the auditor is truthful and unbiased, the security objective just mentioned cannot not be achieved. So, definitely, the auditor has to be an independent agent.

15.5.3 Feature 3: A Security Audit Applies Established Criteria or Standards

Information owners have to present established criteria based on which security audit is to be conducted. Usually, information owners are very sure of the security objectives set for the security audit, but not as sure when it comes to defining the criteria needed in the security audit. These criteria are usually explicitly specified in the corporate security policy. The auditors should discuss with owners the link between the corporate security policy and the objectives of the security audit. There are cases where the security policy is not well written or contains misleading directions. In this case, the corporate security policy is a threat itself, and auditors have to come to an agreement with information owners on the criteria to be adopted in conducting the security audit before such a project is started.

The security audit criteria should obviously include the corporate security policy and internal regulations as a starting groundwork. The main criteria are, however, those established regional, federal, and international security standards that the organization has to conform to in order to attract partners and customers, and satisfy government and international requirements. Examples include the Federal Information Systems Controls Audit Manual (FISCAM), Sarbanes–Oxley Act (SOX), ISO/IEC TR 18044:2004, HIPAA, ISO 27002, ISO 27001, and ISO 15408.

15.5.4 Feature 4: A Security Audit Collects Evidence of Compliance with Controls, Policy, and Procedures, or Adequacy of Its Security Defense System

Let us have a closer look at the security audit project. We are presented with a target system to be audited. Information owners claim that the target system is

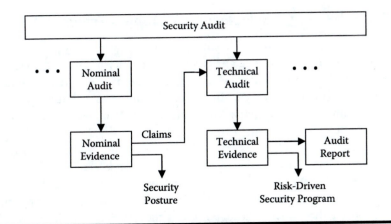

Figure 15.1   Feature 5: A security audit detects breaches.

conformant to the ISO17799 and the corporate security policy, and that systems security risks are adequate. We need then to collect evidence to support those assertions and attest to it.

Where do auditors obtain their evidence? There are at least two sources of evidence where auditors can obtain facts to support, not owners' assertions, but the attestation to owners assertions which will be discussed in the final audit report before it is communicated to owners. In this order, auditors first conduct nominal audit and produce nominal evidence, then uses the nominal audit evidence to conduct technical audit and verify all claims expressed in the nominal evidence. The evidence produced at this level is called technical evidence. Figure 15.1 depicts the relationship between the nominal and technical audit phases in a security audit shown in terms of the nature of evidence exchanged in the audit process.

The security audit is an evidence-based process where auditors first collect facts to verify owners assertions about the security posture of the audited system and then sufficient evidence to support auditors' attestation concerning the current security posture of the system. In addition to the recommendation of a risk-driven security program, auditors' attestation also contains auditors' judgments with an adverse opinion stating that owners' assertions do not fairly present the security posture of the system, or a favorable opinion supporting owners' assertions.

15.5.5 Feature 5: Detects Breaches

At least in theory, any violation of the corporate security policy is a security breach. Some breaches, however, affect high sensitivity and high availability asset classes, and they are hence very dangerous. A security audit should point to problem areas where immediate attention is needed. The testing activities in the technical audit phase where penetration tests are needed will detect a variety of security breaches. This is true in operational security audits but less common in compliance security audits.

15.5.6 Feature 6: A Selective Audit Applies Selective Testing

Nominal evidence is obtained by asking questions about security procedures and processes. The auditors collect claims about the security of assets to accumulate evidence sufficient to estimate the security posture of the system making the assets included in the security audit project. In the technical audit phase, the auditors perform testing activities to verify all the claims gathered during the nominal phase.

Of course, the number of assets is very large. The number of procedures and processes on a given asset is even larger. It is obviously not feasible to test all assets or processes and procedures on a given asset. The auditors only need to perform enough testing activities to obtain enough evidence to form a trustworthy attestation concerning the current security posture of the system and devise a risk-driven security program.

Auditors have to adopt a random selective procedure to determine which assets and which processes and procedures are to be included in the testing activities. Usually, those assets belonging to high criticality classes are associated with higher selection probabilities.

15.5.7 Feature 7: It Measures the Degree of Fairness of Owners' Assertions in Representing the State of Complying with the Criteria or Standard, or Criteria Established, Given the Samples Taken

The evidence collected has to be sufficient to determine whether or not owners' assertions present a fair evaluation of the security posture of the system being audited. The auditors have to develop an acceptable level of belief, throughout the security audit process, that expresses the degree of validity of owners' assertions and also a degree of belief associated with auditors' opinion about the current risk position of the enterprise.

Auditors are never absolutely certain that the security evaluation statements and the estimate of the risk position of the target company are fully accurate. They always have to compute a level expressing the degree of belief associated with the validity of auditors' evaluations of the security posture and the degree of belief associated with how much the recommended risk-driven security program can actually mitigate risks.

15.5.8 Feature 8: A Security Audit Attests to the Adequacy of the Current Security Defense System

The auditors have to attest to the validity of the owners' assertions and attest to the risk-driven security program recommended to enhance the security posture of the enterprise by enhancing the security of the system being audited.

As in financial audits where auditors attest to the truthfulness of owners assertions regarding the financial statements of the company, security auditors should attest to owners' assertions regarding the adequacy of the organization's security defense system.

The attestation should be clear in the audit report. This attestation should express the degree of belief associated with auditors' assessments based on the sampled evidence gathered throughout the security audit project.

15.5.9 Feature 9: A Security Audit Measures the Basic and Residual Risk Positions of the Audited Company

There is no way an auditor can attest to the current security defense system and validate owners' assertions without computing the company's basic risk position. At the same time, a security audit should propose a risk-driven program that recommends corrective and preventive actions needed to mitigate and manage risks. This security program is of no value to owners if auditors fail to show that the recommended actions will actually lead the company to a better security risk position. Auditors have to estimate residual risks, explain how the actions proposed are feasible, and respect the corporate security policy.

15.5.10 Feature 10: A Security Audit Recommends Corrective and Preventive Actions in a Risk-Driven Security Program That Ensures a Continual Improvement of the Security Position

At this point of the security audit project, the auditor should have completed the security policy, performed vulnerability assessment, conducted penetration tests, and carried out enough testing to be able to compute the basic risk position of the company. The auditor can then identify those security policy-compliant controls that can feasibly mitigate risks, and conduct a sensitivity analysis to select the best security controls that can achieve an acceptable residual risk position. The risk-driven security program consists of the set of security controls proposed by the auditor.

15.5.11 Feature 11: A Security Audit Communicates Findings to Owners

The final report of the security audit has to first include all outputs required by the criteria adopted in conducted the very security audit. Additionally, this report should include an explanation of diverse steps followed throughout the security audit process. The report should also contain auditors' attestation concerning the validity of owners' assertions and auditors' recommendations on a risk-driven security program.

Even though the objective of auditor is to add credibility to owners' assertions in evaluating the security of the organization, usually, this objective remains just wishful thinking. As soon as you start the security testing activities to gather facts in support of owners' assertions, the gaps between those assertions and the reality of the security posture of the organization start widening. Auditors, however, need to form their opinion on the overall fairness of owners' assertions, in conformity with the standards adopted in the security audit project, on the basis of selective testing.

15.5.12 Feature 12: A Security Audit Allows for Post-Audit

The security audit project does not have to end with the communication of findings to owners. There is still a lot to do for auditors, not immediately, but after allowing some time for the company to review and implement the proposed security program. Auditors should be available for assistance as needed. Auditors should also plan to visit the company to validate and ensure the company's implementation of the proposed security program. Certain types of security audit will end by issuing an audit certificate showing auditors' attestation and the company's conformity with specific standards.

15.6 Application Audit

In an IT audit, it is possible that an auditor is assigned to carry out a security audit for one application, a major application, or smaller. This application audit will be the audit of a smaller computing environment that includes a set of predetermined servers, databases, operating systems, applications, users, etc. The auditor should seek that the application provides an adequate level of information assurance throughout its domain. In addition to attesting to the adequacy of the application defense conditions, a risk-driven security program should be recommended. Such an application audit should look into the information assurance levels in the application inputs, outputs, processes, interfaces, user support, access control, evolution, continuity, and management.

15.7 How Does Security Audit Relate to the Corporate Security Policy?

We may answer this question in many different ways, but before we do so, it is important that we first agree on an acceptable definition of security policy.

Let us define a security policy of an organization as the acceptable computing behavior of the organization's computing environment. That is, if the organization has no security policy, then there will be no need to conduct a security audit as auditors will be looking for violations of a security policy that does not exist. This

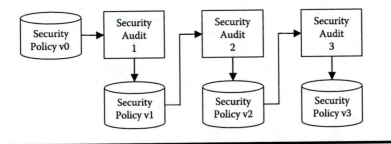

Figure 15.2 **Security policy revision by sequential auditing.**

means that the organization does not prohibit any computing behavior observed in the computing environment. On the other hand, if a poorly written security policy exists; that is, for example, the policy allows incorrect behaviors and rejects acceptable behaviors, and then a security audit will be misleading.

An organization has to have a well-written security policy that evolves with the changing computing needs of the organization in terms of security and business. The security policy should be periodically revised to take into account the new threats and new vulnerabilities that come around and also to implement the new security controls to counter them.

A good security policy should define the requirements a security audit, and the regulations and security auditing standards that have to be adopted in the security audit. The auditors have to have criteria against which a security audit is conducted. Figure 15.2 explains how a sequential security audit produces a sequence of security policies. That is, a security policy is the basis of a security audit, but a security audit is an effective tool for the revision of security policy.

15.8 Structure of a Security Audit

A security audit has two main delivery objectives: compliance and operational. A compliance security audit evaluates the compliance of the target organization with a given standard and recommends a security program to achieve conformity to the standard. An operational security audit evaluates the security posture of the organization before recommending a risk-driven security program.

Moreover, independently of its delivery objective, a security audit consists of two main components: nominal and technical. For example, in a compliance security audit, the nominal phase of the security audit produces nominal evidence on the conformity of the target system to the security audit standard. The technical audit phase produces technical evidence in support of the target system compliance with the security audit standard. On the other hand, in an operational security audit, the nominal audit phase generates nominal evidence on the security posture of the target company. The technical audit phase gathers technical audit on the

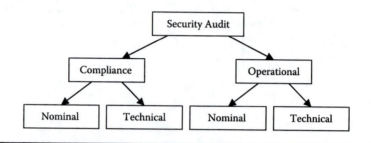

Figure 15.3　Working scheme in a security audit.

security posture of the audited organization. Figure 15.3 illustrates the working scheme followed by a security audit project.

15.9　Security Audit versus IT Auditing

An IT audit, also referred to as electronic data processing audit (EDP audit), is a review of the controls within a computing environment. This type of audit aims at collecting and evaluating evidence of an organization's information systems, practices, and operations. This evidence is needed to make sure that the organization's information systems safeguard assets, maintains data integrity, and is operating effectively and efficiently to achieve the organization's goals or objectives. That is, an IT audit is intended to verify that programs are working as intended, and the data is reliable, and to also verify that none of the data is being tampered with, or can be tampered with.

A computer security audit, while assuming that the work of the IT audit is satisfactorily completed, goes an additional step to ensure that information is adequately secured. The computer security audit collects evidence that the computing environment is adequately protected against information corruption, information leakage, and denial of service. There are certainly some activities that are common between an IT audit and computer security audit, but while the former is limited to functionality and system performance, the latter emphasizes information security, as shown in Figure 15.4.

Some people argue that information security audit is part of an IT audit. This point is still debated in the literature and in the real world. We should also notice that the IT audit continues to expand many system parameters that are traditionally part of an IT audit, like system performance and system integrity, which are now more and more dependent on security configurations and embedded security mechanisms. Those joint system parameters obviously belong to both the IT audit and information security audit. We now know that they overlap, but can we know which one may in fact comprise the other?

Information security has become a very important system performance parameter. The IT audit should therefore be concerned with system security. For, at least

Sound Computing Environment

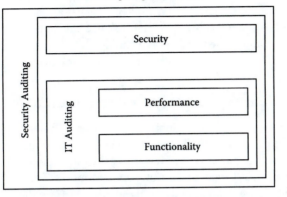

Figure 15.4   IT audit versus security audit.

in theory, information security is a part of an IT audit. In the real world, however, the IT audit and information security audit are still apart. This separation is primarily due to the absence of IT audit methodologies that incorporate information security features needed to evaluate the system for potential information leakage, information corruption, or denial of service. In the future, however, information security should be a part of the IT audit.

Waiting for an integrated IT audit methodology that incorporates both IT audit and information security audit, the IT audit should at least embrace the following activities:

1. **Physical and environmental review.** This includes physical security, power supply, air conditioning, humidity control, and other environmental factors.
2. **System administration review.** This includes security review of the operating systems, database management systems, all system administration procedures, and compliance.
3. **Application software review.** The business application could be payroll, invoicing, a Web-based customer order processing system, or an enterprise resource planning system that actually runs the business. Review of such application software includes access control and authorizations, validations, error and exception handling, business process flows within the application software, and complementary manual controls and procedures. Additionally, a review of the system development lifecycle should be completed.
4. **Network security review.** Review of internal and external connections to the system, perimeter security, firewall review, router access control lists, port scanning, and intrusion detection are some typical areas of coverage.
5. **Business continuity review.** This includes existence and maintenance of fault-tolerant and redundant hardware, backup procedures and storage, and documented and tested disaster recovery/business continuity plan.

6. Data integrity review. The purpose of this is scrutiny of live data to verify adequacy of controls and impact of weaknesses, as noticed from any of the above reviews. Such substantive testing can be done using generalized audit software (computer-assisted audit techniques).

15.10 Applicable Security-Related Standards

There are many national and regional standards organizations. The best known are based in Geneva. They are the International Telecommunication Union (ITU) (since 1865); the International Electro-technical Commission (IEC) (since 1906); and the International Organization for Standardization (ISO; since 1947). They have established tens of thousands of standards covering almost every relevant theme. Many of these are then adopted worldwide, replacing various incompatible regional standards.

In addition to these professional standard organizations, there exist literally thousands of standards organizations that set standards within some more limited context, such as IETF, W3C, or IEEE.

Professional standards organizations are bodies, organizations, and institutions that are formed at the regional level, national level, or international level that produce useful standards. The most popular international standards that are relevant to security audit are the British Standards Institution, the International Organization for Standardization, and the International Telecommunication Union.

Some standards groups are government agencies (like NIST). Some are private research institutes that act like government agencies (like ANSI). There are also private volunteer associations (like IETF) and private industry consortia (like W3C).

International organizations differ in function, membership, and membership criteria. Membership of some organizations is open to all the nations of the world. This category includes the United Nations and its specialized agencies, and the World Trade Organization. Other organizations are only open to members from a particular region or continent of the world, like European Union, African Union, etc.

ISO/IEC TR 18044:2004 provides advice and guidance on information security incident management for information security managers and for information system managers. This standard is intended to provide (1) information on the benefits to be obtained from and the key issues associated with a good information security incident management approach, (2) information on examples of information security incidents, and an insight into their possible causes, (3) a description of the planning and documentation required to introduce a good structured information security incident management approach, and (4) a description of the information security incident management process.

Among the most popular standards relevant to a security audit are the ISO/IEC 17799, the ISO/IEC 27001-27005, and the ISO 15408. The first two standards originated from the British standard BS 7799. This standard consisted originally of two parts: BS 7799-Part 1, and BS 7799-Part 2. BS 7799-Part 3 is in the making at this time. The first part constitutes the standard code of practice and can be regarded as a comprehensive guide to best security practices. The second part is a standard specification for an Information Security Management Systems (ISMS). An ISMS is the means by which senior management monitors and controls security, minimizing the residual business risk and ensuring that security continues to satisfy corporate, customer, and legal requirements.

The ISO 15408, which is also called the Common Criteria standard, is a technical standard. It is intended to support the specification and technical evaluation of IT security features in products. Normally, the products are evaluated as part of the development/production cycle. The Common Criteria standard also has a major usage as a structure, syntax, and catalog of information technology specifications that can be used to describe user technical requirements for security in products.

To see how the Common Criteria can help organizations face their security challenges, please refer to NIST Special Publication 800-23, Guide to Federal Organizations on Security Assurance and Acquisition/Use of Tested/Evaluated Products, which can be downloaded at http://csrc.nist.gov/publications/nistpubs/index.html.

15.11 Security Audit Grades

Security audit, as discussed earlier, may be initiated for different reasons. Based on usual security requirements of an organization, it is useful to organize security audit into four types: Grade 1 audit, Grade 2 audit, Grade 3 audit, and Grade 4 audit. The relationships among those types of audit are depicted in Figure 15.5. The proposed four types of security audits are the following:

Grade 1: Internal audit for self compliance
Grade 2: External audit for independent compliance
Grade 3: Certification by a certifier
Grade 4: Accreditation by an accreditor

15.11.1 Grade 1: Internal Audit for Self Compliance

The enterprise selects a qualified staff member to conduct the internal security audit. The same security audit process may apply to both Grades 1 and 2, but while the internal audit is performed by an internal auditor, the external audit is performed by an independent auditor.

A self study of security weaknesses and security controls to counter these weaknesses will enhance an enterprise security posture. This will achieve management involvement and staff awareness in terms of the enterprise readiness to handle potential security disruptions.

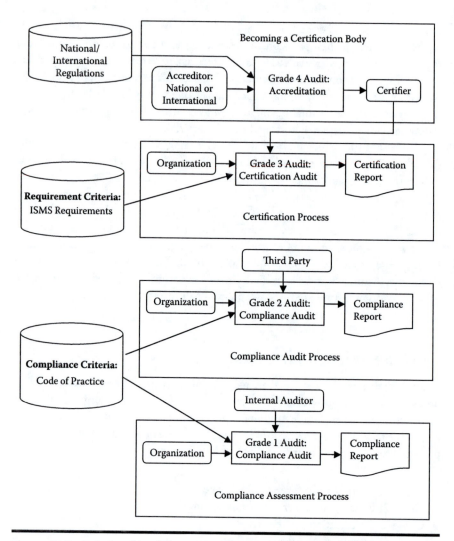

Figure 15.5   Relationships between various grades of security audit.

15.11.2 Grade 2: External Audit for Independent Compliance

An external security audit agency is hired to conduct the external audit to obtain an independent assessment of its security posture, or an independent assessment of its compliance to preselected criteria.

15.11.3 Grade 3: Certification by a Certifier

The certifier is a certification body accredited by an accreditation body to perform a security audit in a candidate enterprise seeking a certification of its security management system. In a Grade 2 grade security audit, the candidate enterprise only seeks an independent evaluation of its security management system against preselected criteria. No certification is issued. Even when the candidate enterprise seeks a certification of its security management system, the certifier cannot be the external security auditor.

While the certification may be needed for client assurance and partners' confidence in terms of the security of shared information at both sides, it is sometimes necessary as an element of a competitive advantage strategy.

If there is a public law requiring the certification, then any enterprise meant by this public law is obligated to obtain the certification. Critical organizations, like health agencies or utility companies, are often required to obtain the certification by a certifier.

15.11.4 Grade 4: Accreditation of a Certifier

A national or international body is designated, respectively, by a nation or the international community to accredit a certification body as a certifier.

15.11.4.1 How to Initiate a Security Audit

Before we start discussing the security audit decisions facing an organization, it is important to note that management and owners should be familiar with the 12 security audit features presented in an earlier chapter. For example, any security audit requires a set of audit criteria. There are three types of criteria: accreditation criteria, certification criteria, and compliance criteria. Accreditation criteria are comprehensive criteria containing national regulations, and national and international accreditation requirements. Certification criteria include any security standards that describe detailed requirements for developing and managing information security management systems, as in the ISO/IEC 27001. The compliance criteria include any established code of practice, like in the ISO/IEC 27002. Figure 15.6 depicts the relationship between security audit types and security standards.

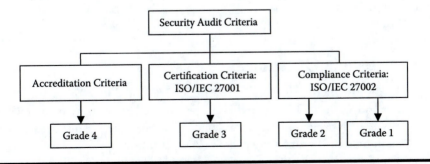

Figure 15.6 How security audit types relate to security standards.

The organization may choose among four types of security audits, from the grades 1 to 4 presented earlier, depending on their needs. The Grade 4 audit is only needed if the organization intends to obtain accreditation for the purpose of accrediting certification bodies. Usually, this type of audit only applies to those agencies involved in writing national standards or which are delivering training, certification, or education curricula developed by the government.

If the organization intends to achieve a better position in the market by, for example, satisfying some customers or partners' requirements, or by meeting some contractual obligations, then it will be appropriate for the organization to seek the certification of its information security management system against some security management requirements criteria, like the ISO/IEC 27001. This type of security audit will serve as assurance to partners and customers.

Organizations may, however, experiment with Grades 1 and 2 of security audits by letting an internal auditor or an external auditor assess the compliance of their information security management systems with established compliance criteria like the code of practice defined in the ISO/IEC 27002 (old ISO/IEC 17799).

The only body who can carry out this certification is a certifier that has been accredited by an accreditation body recognized by the national accreditation agency or by accepted international organisms.

15.12 Conclusion

Students who completed reading this chapter should be able to compare the definitions of security audit presented in the chapter, and come up with their own definition. Any security audit definition should allow, even implicitly, for the 12 features presented in the author's definition. The chapter introduced some of the standards that are relevant to a compliance security audit. The student should comprehend the importance of risk identification, assessment, mitigation, and management in security audit. Any recommendation that is not part of the risk-driven security program should not be included in the final report of the security audit.

15.13 Review Questions

1. Briefly explain the difference between ISO 27002 and ISO 27001.
2. Are both of the ISO 27002 and ISO 27001 needed in a security audit project? If yes, then explain how are the standards applied throughout the security audit project. If your answer is no, then explain why.
3. Explain how a risk-driven security program is devised?
4. Explain the migration from a basic risk position to a residual risk position.

5. Explain how auditors review the validity of owners' assertions on their security defense system.
6. Explain how auditors attest to the current adequacy of the security defense system.
7. Explain the differences between a compliance security audit and an operational security audit.
8. Explain how auditors ensure the continual improvement of their company's risk position.
9. Do security audits detect breaches? Explain the need to do so in operational security audits, and how auditors detect breaches.
10. Explain how evidence is processed throughout the security audit project. How do security audit processes exchange evidence throughout the audit project?
11. Explain the need for a postaudit period. Discuss what the audited company does in this period. What do auditors do when they visit the audited company at the end of the post-audit period?
12. A security audit measures the degree of fairness of owners' assertions in representing the state of complying with the criteria or standard, or criteria established. Explain how auditors do so.
13. Discuss why selective testing is needed. Explain how this works.
14. What happens if a selective testing approach leaves out a high sensitivity or high availability class asset in a security audit project? What do we do about this?
15. How does a penetration test work? Is there a danger of compromising the audited systems when they are being tested? What do auditors do to prevent this from happening?
16. Explain how a vulnerability assessment works. Why is it needed?
17. How does an event-driven audit work? Who needs it?
18. Explain how a security policy review works. Who needs it and when?
19. How does a physical security work? How often is this needed?

15.14 Workshops

Workshop 1

The Web site asos.com is the United Kingdom's leading online fashion store for women and men (http://www.thetimes100.co.uk/company_list.php). Launched in 2000, the online retailer targets fashion-conscious 16–34 year olds. On asos.com there are 9000 products available at any one time, with 450 new fashion items added every week. These include women's fashion, menswear, accessories, jewelry and beauty products. Every month, asos.com attracts 3.3 million unique shoppers and has 1.8 million registered users.

An online service of this scale requires a substantial background operation to fulfill orders and to provide customer service. Five years ago, asos.com had just

550 square meters of warehouse space. Today, to meet growing demand, asos.com now has 32,500 square meters of warehouse space— equivalent in area to nearly five football pitches. In April 2005, asos.com employed 47 permanent staff. By February 2008, it had 250 employees.

Explain the security audit types that apply, the security standards that apply. Use Table 15.1 to define the security audit profile you think is most appropriate for asos.com.

Workshop 2

First Direct was launched in 1989 (http://www.thetimes100.co.uk/company_list. php). It offered a new type of banking service. Customers could access all banking services by telephone. The bank was open 24 hours a day, 7 days a week, 365 days a year (a 24/7/365 service), with real people always on the end of the phone. This contrasted with the services then offered by the major high street banks. These were available only in traditional banking hours, usually 9 am to 4 pm. The banks closed for most of the weekend. Most transactions had to be made face-to-face. It was difficult to contact the bank unless customers visited a branch.

First Direct's service became highly popular with its customers. The bank won many awards for its service model. By offering additional services such as Internet banking and mobile (on the move) banking, customers could access their accounts and manage their money whenever and wherever they liked. However, it was not just about the fact that it was convenient, but also that the people at First Direct were courteous, friendly, professional, and adult-to-adult rather than patronizing.

Explain the security audit types that apply, the security standards that apply. Note that availability requirements are a priority. Use Table 15.1 to define the security audit profile you think is most appropriate for FirstDirect.

References

1. ATIS, ATIS Telecom Glossary 2007. http://www.atis.org/glossary, accessed on November 8, 2008.
2. ATIS, Homepage: The Alliance for Telecommunications Industry Solutions (ATIS). http://www.atis.org, accessed on November 8, 2008.
3. ISO/IEC 27001:2005, Information Technology—Security Techniques—Information Security Management Systems—Requirements, International Standards Organization, October 2005. (Source: http://www.iso.org.)
4. ISO/IEC 27002:2005 (ISO/IEC 17799:2005)—Information Technology Security Techniques—Code of Practice for Information Security Management. International Standards Organization, June 2005. (Source: http://www.iso.org.)
5. Whatis.com, Definition of Security Audit, http://searchcio.techtarget.com/ sDefinition/0,,sid182_gci955099,00.html, accessed on November 8, 2008.

6. Whatis.com, Definition of HIPAA, http://searchdatamanagement.techtarget.com/sDefinition/0,,sid91_gci862786,00.html, accessed on November 8, 2008.
7. Whatis.com, Definition of Sarbanes and Oxley's Legislation, http://searchcio.techtarget.com/sDefinition/0,,sid182_gci920030,00.html, accessed on November 8, 2008.
8. Wikipedia, Definition of security audit, http://en.wikipedia.org/wiki/Computer_security_audit, accessed on November 8, 2008.

Chapter 16

Privacy Rights, Information Technology, and HIPAA

Learning Objectives

After reading this chapter, students are expected to achieve an understanding of:

The problem of privacy
The meaning of privacy
HIPAA
The Privacy Rule
HIPAA Security Rule
Administrative safeguards to comply with the Security Rule
The NIST view of HIPAA standards
How to conduct effective risk analysis

16.1 The Problem of Privacy

Unless residing in a desert or some other isolated environment, no person can escape the onslaught of technological development that has occurred in seemingly geometric progression, particularly in computer technology. The advances, like other major changes in society, bring with them both benefits and detriments.

The former provides a given solution to a societal need while the latter raises problems that a society may have to address. Computers have enabled the expansion of knowledge globally so as to render vast libraries of information accessible to the global community. Although one marvels at the ability to instantaneously acquire knowledge on almost any topic and to communicate with other persons globally within a wisp of the passage of time, nevertheless, the possibility of enormous abuses have proven to be a fruitful area for wrongdoers. Criminal wrongdoing such as the programming of viruses and potentially harmful exposure of private data has led to demands of governments to protect both individual privacy and governmental security.

Historically, few people have had concerns regarding their so-called privacy rights inasmuch as they were rarely threatened with adverse consequences by possible wrongful acquisition and use of personal data. One's personal data was either made available in limited form such as automobile driver's records or was kept confidential by the government. Gradually, credit agencies and other organizations began accumulating data concerning our credit and purchasing habits so that financial companies and marketers could make use of the data. Today, the proliferation of personal data has exacerbated the possible threats to exposure of information we may prefer to remain private.

16.2 The Meaning of Privacy

There are many definitions of privacy but they appear to agree on certain basic fundamental premises. In essence, it is the right to be left alone, free from prying eyes of others including governments, institutions, and other persons. We all possess secrets and other confidential data which we would not want anyone, including those persons closest to us, to learn, inasmuch as it could diminish us in their eyes or have other adverse consequences. We certainly would not want confidential data given to persons who seek to harm our interests.

There are a variety of forms in which the invasion of privacy may take place, depending on the context upon the issue may arise:

■ *Governmental intrusion*: The unwarranted search and seizure of one's body or property. This form may be more onerous and potentially more dangerous than other forms of privacy invasion. Thus, such intrusion tends to be more carefully scrutinized that private conduct. In the United States, the "unreasonable" search and seizure of one's person and residence would run afoul of the U.S. Constitution. Other forms of governmental intrusion include governmental surveillance and even secret courts and trials.

■ *Employer intrusion*. Examples include the requirement of drug testing, uses of lie detector examinations for sensitive and even nonsensitive positions, and searches of personal lockers or e-mails that employees thought were private in nature.

- *Information privacy.* The accumulation and use of personal data such as credit, medical, and driving record reports.
- *Communications intrusion.* Examples are the unwarranted listening-in on telephone conversations, reading of e-mails and facsimiles, and other such modes of communication.

16.3 HIPAA

The United States *Health Insurance Portability and Accountability Act of 1996* (HIPPA) was designed to remedy a serious breach of confidentiality caused in part by revelations that there were numerous incidents of wrongful disclosure of confidential personal medical information, either inadvertently or deliberately, generally to companies seeking to promote products addressing particular medical conditions or anxieties [3]. Examples of such disclosures include Kaiser Permanente, a health maintenance organization (HMO), which allegedly carelessly sent 858 e-mail messages containing personal medical information to unauthorized persons, and by CVS pharmacy that sold such information to drug and other related companies. In addition, there are vulnerabilities such as that of medical charts that are no longer confined to an office, thereby reducing control over their contents; the numerous access points whereby data is transmitted across the country and globally; and the problem of addressing transactions standards involving some 400 formats at the time the legislation was enacted [5].

16.3.1 Purposes of HIPAA

Some key purposes of the act are:

- Improve portability and continuity of health insurance coverage in the group and individual markets
- Combat waste, fraud, and abuse in health insurance and health care delivery
- Promote the use of medical savings accounts
- Improve access to long-term care services and coverage
- Simplify the administration of health insurance

According to the act, Congress was to enact legislation within three years from August 21, 1996, to protect medical privacy or, if not enacted, the Secretary of Health and Human Services would be empowered to promote regulations governing this area of personal privacy. Inasmuch as Congress did fail to enact appropriate legislation, the Secretary, Donna Shalala, caused the publication of Standards for Privacy of Individually

Identifiable Health Information in the Federal Register on November 3, 1999, and the final Privacy Rule on December 28, 2000 and modified on August 14, 2002 [5].

The Act and Regulation provided for its enforcement by the Office for Civil Rights (OCR), which was mandated to assure the balance between privacy of health information with the flow thereof to assure public health.

16.3.2 The Major Vulnerability Addressed by HIPAA

The most important concern that was addressed by the act was the greatly increased risk of invasion of one's privacy in the very important area of health care that arose by the shift of medical records from a paper format to an electronic format. By so doing, it was now possible for records to be transmitted globally instantaneously. The positive aspect of this ability is that a person who is seeking treatment anywhere in the world can have his or her physician or medical care facility access the records at one's home base. The problem is that if the records are carelessly handled, a person's privacy could be greatly jeopardized. An additional benefit of the act is to create a national standard for electronic health-care transactions in place of numerous and often conflicting local standards.

16.3.3 Health Information

Protection is given to health information and individually identifiable health information. "Health information" is defined as follows [5]:

Any information, whether oral or recorded in any form or medium, that:

(1) Is created or received by a health care provider, health plan, public health authority, employer, life insurer, school or university, or health care clearinghouse; and

(2) Relates to the past, present, or future physical or mental health or condition of an individual; the provision of health care to an individual; or the past, present or future payment for the provision of health care to an individual.

"Individually identifiable health information" is defined as a:

Subset of health information, including demographic information collected from an individual, and:

(1) Is created or received by a health care provider, health plan, employer, or health care clearinghouse; and

(2) Relates to the past, present, or future physical or mental health or condition of an individual; the provision of health care to an individual; or the past, present or future payment for the provision of health care to an individual; and

(i) That identifies the individual; or

(ii) With respect to which there is a reasonable basis to believe the information can be used to identify the individual.

It excludes employment records and education and other records, and "de-identifies health information" such as information by a qualified statistician or by the removal of specified identifiers including the individual's relatives, household members, and other such data.

16.4 Regulatory Standards: The Privacy Rule

The Privacy Rule was created to protect the privacy of individuals who may be offended or harmed when its transmission would enable those in possession of it to be able to identify the particular individual about whom the data concerns [5]. The entities who are affected by the rule and the type of information protected are discussed further. Clearly, there are health care providers who need to have the data to better treat particular ailments of the patient, and thus a balance between privacy and the need to have and use the information has to be effected.

Covered entities. The Privacy Rule was enacted to promulgate minimum federal standards for the protection of the privacy of individually identifiable health information. The entities required to take affirmative steps to afford such protection are known as "covered entities." They include persons involved in the electronic billing and payment for services, which may include communication with insurance companies. Researchers conducting clinical studies of participants are also included within the coverage of the act if they are within the covered entities. Unless they are any of the entities mentioned, the rule does not affect other persons or institutions that may also collect the said information, although there may be other federal and state laws and regulations that may also afford protection to the individual. The "covered entities" are defined as including [3]:

- Health plans
- Health care clearinghouses
- Health care providers who transmit any health information in electronic form with respect to a HIPAA transaction

Health plans: They include health, dental, vision, and prescription drug insurers, HMO, Medicare, Medicaid, Medicare+Choice, and Medicare supplement insurers, and long-term insurers. They also cover employer-sponsored group health plans, government and church-sponsored health plans, and multiemployer health plans.

Exceptions to health plans: (1) Nursing home fixed-indemnity policies; (2) group health plans with less than 50 participants administered solely by the employer that establishes and maintains the plan; (3) government-funded programs

(a) whose principal purpose is not to provide or pay for the cost of health care (e.g., food stamp program), and (b) whose principal activity is directly providing health care (e.g., community health centers or making grants to so provide); and (4) insurance entities such as workmen's compensation, auto insurance, and property and casualty insurance.

Health care clearinghouses: They are defined as entities that process nonstandard information received from another entity into a standard format or data content. They include billing services, repricing companies, community health management information systems, and value-added networks and switches performing clearinghouse functions.

Health care providers: They are defined as covered entities including all health care providers, irrespective of size, who electronically transmit health information concerning claims, benefit eligibility inquiries, referral authorization requests, or other transactions under HIPAA Transactions Rule. The rule covers health care providers transmitting directly or by use of a billing service or other third party; and includes all providers or service including hospitals and noninstitutional providers of medical or health services (physicians, dentists, etc.) or person or organization that furnishes bills or is paid for health care.

The Privacy Rule may be avoided through the use of a "hybrid" designation, which concerns an entity that performs business activities that may include both covered functions and those outside of the Privacy Rule. The rule will only affect that part of the entity that has a health care component. So long as the health-related entity does not share the protected data with the noncovered functions of the entity, there will be no violation of the Privacy Rule. For example, a university conducting health-related studies and possess personally identifiable health information of particular information must take steps to protect the privacy of the data collected, but the remaining units of the university are not affected by the Rule, provided it is not in receipt of the protected information.

16.4.1 Permitted Disclosures

The following information disclosures are allowed:

- To the individual, inasmuch as the Privacy Rule protects against other unauthorized persons.
- Treatment, payment, and health care operations of the covered entity. It may share the information with other covered entities with which the individual has had treatment.
- Opportunity to agree or object. Informal consent is permitted such as, for example, the patient giving contact information in the event of an emergency to such persons as a pharmacist, etc.
- Incident to an otherwise permitted use and disclosure.

16.4.2 Authorization

A valid Privacy Rule Authorization is a written and signed consent in plain language for a covered entity to use or disclose an individual's protected health information for the purposes indicated in the authorization. It is required for nontreatment, payment, or as otherwise permitted by the Privacy Rule. Almost all persons who have visited a health care facility will be familiar with forms that state the rights of patients under HIPAA, the permitted uses or disclosures of protected health information, permitted disclosures without an authorization, the rights of patients, and to whom complaints may be made. Treatment of the patient cannot be conditional upon the patient granting such authorization. Use or disclosure of psychotherapy notes require a patient's authorization except for the covered entity's own training, to prevent an imminent threat to public health or safety, to the Department of Health and Human Services for purposes of investigation, or for use in self-defense in a court proceeding.

No authorization from the patient is required under the following circumstances [5]:

A public health authority that is authorized by law to collect or receive such information for the purpose of preventing or controlling disease, injury, or disability

A public health authority or other appropriate government authority authorized by law to receive reports of child abuse or neglect

Food and Drug Administration (FDA) with respect to an FDA-regulated product or activity for which that person has responsibility

A person who may have been exposed to a communicable disease or may otherwise be at risk of contracting or spreading a disease

An employer, regarding an individual who is a member of the workforce of the employer, to determine if the illness was related to workplace activities

Disclosures about victims of abuse, neglect or domestic violence to a government authority, including a social service or protective services agency, authorized by law to receive reports of such abuse, neglect, or domestic violence

Uses and disclosures for health oversight activities; (e) Standard: Disclosures for judicial and administrative proceedings

Disclosures for law enforcement purposes

Uses and disclosures about decedents to coroners and medical examiners

Uses for cadaveric organ, eye, or tissue donation purposes

Uses and disclosures

Uses and disclosures to avert a serious threat to health or safety

Uses and disclosures for specialized government such as for military and veterans activities, and national security

Correctional institutions and other law enforcement agencies

To comply with laws relating to workers' compensation or other similar programs established by law

16.4.3 Minimum Necessary

The Privacy Rule requires that only the minimum quantum of protected health information be disclosed. Exceptions to the Rule include the data authorized by the patient, information to be given to the patient, compliant to the act, to the Department of Health and Human Services, and other uses required by law.

16.4.4 Electronic Data Interchange

A major goal of the act and regulation is the resolution of the need to simplify and improve the administration of the health care system including the Medicare and Medicaid programs and to develop a framework for electronic transactions. Electronic data interchange (EDI), defined as "the electronic transfer of information in a standard format between trading partners," was designed to substantially lessen and lower administrative and operating costs, and improve overall data quality, particularly with respect to the receiving, processing, and storage of documents. As depicted in Figures 16.1 and 16.2, accordingly, a major aspect of Title II of HIPAA was the adoption of Administrative Simplification. Its main purpose was to make more efficient and effective the government's Medicare and Medicaid programs, and was further made applicable to health plans, health care clearinghouses, and health care providers who transmit health care information in electronic form [3].

The Administrative Simplification provisions of the Health Insurance Portability and Accountability Act of 1996 (HIPAA, Title II) were established to deal with the possible compromise of confidentiality and security with respect to information transmitted electronically [3]. It required the Department of Health and Human Services to establish national standards for electronic health care transactions and national identifiers for providers, health plans, and employers. It also addressed concerns of security and privacy of health data.

16.5 The HIPAA Security Rule

We are familiar with security and privacy concepts. The Security Rule of the federal HIPAA or Health Insurance Portability and Accountability Act of 1996 added a very important security component, constituting new policies and procedures.

The HIPAA, as depicted in Figure 16.1, consists of three sections: insurance portability, fraud enforcement, and administrative simplification.

The need for accountability and administrative simplification was imposed by the increasing use of the Internet, involving the distributed manipulation of information, including the storing and transferring of electronic information. It is very crucial to understand who would have access to what information, and how it would be used generated concern [1].

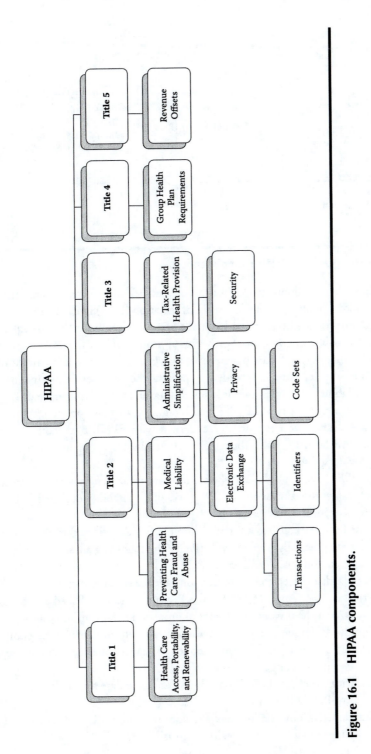

Figure 16.1 HIPAA components.

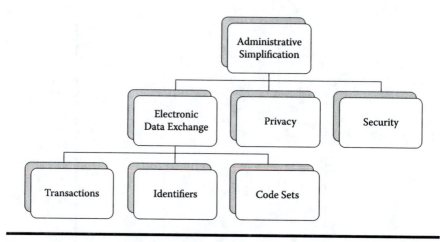

Figure 16.2 Administrative Simplification.

What: The rule applies to electronic protected health information (EPHI), which is individually identifiable health information (IIHI) in electronic form. IIHI is concerned with (1) an individual's past, present, or future physical or mental health or condition, (2) provision of health care for the individual, and (3) past, present, or future payment for provision of health care to an individual. The Security Rule is intended to protect the confidentiality, integrity, and availability of EPHI when it is stored, maintained, or transmitted [1].

Who: Covered entities (CE) like health plans, health care providers, and healthcare clearing houses who are concerned with EPHI, must comply with the HIPAA Security Rule. These CEs include HMOs, group health plans, health providers, and so on [1].

How: CEs have to implement the appropriate security measures that are needed to protect the confidentiality, integrity, and availability of their EPHI against any reasonably anticipated risks [1].

When: HHS established a series of compliance deadlines that allow a covered entity to gradually implement HIPAA. The following are some of the HIPAA major compliance deadlines [1]:

Standards for Electronic Transactions and Code Sets: October 16, 2002.

Privacy Rule: April 14, 2003 (the Privacy Rule established standards that govern the use and disclosure of protected health information).

Standard Unique Identifier for Employers: July 30, 2004. The compliance date for small health plans (defined as health plans with $5 million or less in annual receipts) was August 1, 2005.

Security Rule: April 20, 2005. The compliance date for small health plans is April 20, 2006.

Standard Unique Health Care Provider Identifier: May 23, 2007. The compliance date for small health plans is May 23, 2008.

16.5.1 *What Is the Security Rule?*

The Security Rule presents four requirements for covered entities [3]:

1. Must ensure the confidentiality, integrity, and availability of all EPHI that it creates or receives.
2. Must protect against any reasonably anticipated threats or hazards to the security of EPHI;
3. Must protect against any reasonably anticipated uses or disclosures of EPHI in violation of HIPAA; and
4. Must ensure compliance with the Security Rule by its workforce.

The Security Rule consists of three classes of security controls: administrative, physical, and technical safeguards. Each safeguard includes general standards with which a covered entity must comply. The standards are comprised of "implementation specifications" that are either "required" or "addressable." If an implementation specification is required, then the covered entity must implement those policies and/or procedures. If it is addressable, then the covered entity must assess whether it is a reasonable and appropriate safeguard in the entity's environment.

If a covered entity determines that it is not to implementing an addressable specification required by the standards, it must justify its rejection of the addressable specification and its adoption of any alternative safeguards.

Even though the covered entity has some discretion when implementing the Security Rule, it still has to explain its decisions, for example, as they may be reached, based on factors like size and complexity, the technical infrastructure, the technological capabilities, the cost of implementing the security controls, and so on. That is, the covered entity may adopt security controls that allow it to reasonably and appropriately implement the standards and implementation specifications of the Security Rule.

16.6 Administrative Safeguards

16.6.1 *Security Management Process*

Every covered entity must implement a Security Management Process (SMP) to "prevent, detect, contain, and correct" security violations. This SMP consists of four required implementation specifications [5]:

1. Risk analysis
2. Risk management
3. Sanction policy
4. Information system activity review

The covered entity must conduct risk analysis. This first step is intended to initiate a thorough assessment of potential risks based on vulnerabilities of the covered entity's EPHI. The risk analysis obviously should be performed before any decision is made to implement any specifications.

In a second step, any risk management activity undertaken by the covered entity should result in a significant reduction of risks and vulnerabilities. These security controls adopted to mitigate risks must remain current and should be periodically reviewed to provide continual security as specified in the standards.

The third step requires a sanction policy for the purpose of appropriately sanctioning staff members who fail to comply with the security policies and procedures of the covered entity.

In the final step, the covered entity must have an information system activity review. This may be accomplished by implementing audit activities to regularly review records of information system activity, such as audit logs, access reports, and security incident tracking reports.

16.6.2 Appoint a Security Officer

The covered entity must designate a member of its staff as the HIPAA security officer. This officer will be responsible for implementing the Security Rule's policies and procedures for the covered entity. A corresponding position, as a privacy officer, is also required by HIPAA's Privacy Rule. There is nothing in the standard that says that the security officer cannot be the same person as the privacy officer.

16.6.3 Company Training

The Security Rule requires that a covered entity train its workforce to provide for security awareness. All staff members in an organization, including management and executives, should participate in this training. A continuous record should be maintained to verify the employees who have completed the training.

16.6.4 Amend Business Associate Agreements

HIPAA's Privacy Rule requires each covered entity to have contracts with business associates who have access to the covered entity's PHI. These contracts are called Business Associate Agreements (BAA). If the business associate receives or maintains EPHI on behalf of the covered entity, then the BAA will be amended to include the standards of the Security Rule. These amendments must provide that the business associate will:

a. Implement administrative, physical, and technical safeguards that reasonably protect the confidentiality, integrity, and availability of the EPHI

b. Ensure that any agent to whom it provides EPHI agrees to implement reasonable and appropriate safeguards to protect the EPHI
c. Report to the covered entity any identified security incident
d. Permit the covered entity to terminate the BAA if it determines that the business associate has violated a material term of the contract

16.6.5 Contingency Plan

Each covered entity must establish policies and procedures for responding to an emergency (i.e., fire, system failure, natural disaster, and so on) that damages the systems that maintain EPHI. This contingency plan includes three mandatory implementation specifications:

a. Data backup plan. A covered entity must develop procedures to maintain retrievable, exact copies of its EPHI.
b. Disaster recovery plan. Procedures must be established to restore any loss of data.
c. Emergency mode operation plan. A covered entity must establish procedures to protect the security of EPHI while operating in an emergency mode.

16.6.6 Physical and Technical Safeguards

Physical safeguards are the activities needed to protect physical systems like electronic systems, equipment, and data resources from threats, corruption, and unauthorized disclosure. This may be achieved in part by controlling access to EPHI, setting and isolating off-site computer backups, system security, and data backup and storage.

Technical safeguards consist of the automated processes needed to protect and control access to EPHI. This may include authentication to control access to EPHI, encryption and decryption of EPHI when information is stored, processed, or transmitted, and security controls to prevent information leakage and information corruption.

16.7 NIST on HIPAA

The sections below present how NIST views HIPAA and how it suggests ways to implement it. Accordingly, the National Institute of Standards and Technology (NIST) was called upon to develop standards and guidelines for providing adequate security for agency operations and assets including the HIPAA Security Rule for the safeguarding of electronic protected health information (EPHI). The information that follows is taken from NIST Resource Guide for the Implementation of HIPAA. It applies to all covered healthcare providers, health plans, healthcare clearinghouses, and Medicare prescription drug card sponsors.

16.7.1 Security Goals and Objectives

The security goals and objectives of the HIPAA Security Rule include:

■ The ensuring of the confidentiality (non disclosure to unauthorized persons), integrity (data or information has not been altered or destroyed unless authorized) and availability (data is accessible and usable by aphorized persons) of EPHI that is created, received, maintained or transmitted
■ The protection against reasonably anticipated threats and hazards to the security of EPHI
■ The protection against reasonably anticipated uses of information not allowed under the Privacy Rule

16.7.2 NIST Risk Management Framework

The NIST Risk Management Framework (RMF) consists of six steps for the effective management of risk in the operation and use of information systems by management [4]:

■ *Categorize Information Systems*—Concerns the identification of assets and information systems that create, receive, transmit, or maintain EPHI. The Framework determines the critical nature and sensitivity of the information system and the information being processed. The security controls are to be commensurate with the potential impact on the organizational operations and assets.
■ *Select Security Controls*—Concerns the selection of standards and implementation specifications as the initial security control set. The selection process is threefold: (1) selection of baseline security controls for each information system, (2) application of security control for information systems to allow organizations to adjust their security control baselines in accordance with their missions and business processes, and (3) the supplementation of tailored baseline security controls based on assessment of risk and local conditions.
■ *Implement Security Controls*—Concerns the implementation of security controls that were determined to be reasonable and appropriate to the particular organization. RMF accomplishes the step by employing enterprise architecture and other NIST guidelines for the implementation of security controls in organizational information systems.
■ *Access Security Controls*—Concerns the evaluation of the implementation specifications using assessment methods and procedures to determine the extent to which the controls are implanted and are operating as intended. RMF uses its own standard for the valuation of information security controls for their effectiveness.

- *Authorize Information Systems*—Concerns the acceptance of identified risks that are acceptable to the organization. RMF accomplishes this step by determining the risk to organizations operations and, assets, individuals, and other organizations.
- *Monitor Security State*—Concerns the need for a covered entity to periodically review and update its security measures and documentations as it relates to environmental and operational changes that affect the security of its EPHI. RMF assesses and evaluates the security controls on a continuous basis by providing oversight and monitoring of the security controls to ensure they operate effectively, and includes the documentation of changes to the system, the conducting of security impact analyses of the changes, and the reporting of system security status to appropriate organizational officials on a regular basis.

16.7.3 Security Management Process

According to HIPAA, the covered entities are to implement policies and procedures to prevent, detect, contain, and correct security violations. NIST administrative safeguards to accomplish this goal are as follows:

- *Identify relevant information systems* by identifying all information systems that house EPHI, including its hardware and software, and by analyzing business functions to verify ownership and control of information systems.
- *Conduct risk assessment* by conducting an accurate and thorough assessment of the potential risks and vulnerabilities of the systems used by the covered entity.
- *Implement a risk management program* by enacting security measures sufficient to reduce risks and vulnerabilities.
- *Acquire IT systems and services* even though HIPAA does not require the purchase of particular technologies that are necessary to adequately protect information.
- *Create and deploy policies and procedures* by implementing decisions concerning management operational and technical controls to mitigate risks, create policies that establish roles and responsibilities of persons responsible for the implementation of each control, and create procedures to be followed to accomplish security-related tasks.
- *Develop and implement a sanction policy* by implementing procedures and policies, and applying appropriate sanctions against personnel who fail to comply with security procedures.

16.7.4 Assigned Security Responsibilities

HIPAA requires that a security official be identified for the development and implementation of the required policies and procedures. This may be accomplished by:

- *Selection of a security official who is assigned the responsibility for HIPAA security.* This may be accomplished by the selection of an individual who has final responsibility for the assessment and implementation of the firm's security policy.
- *Assignment and documentation of the assigned individual's responsibility.*

16.7.5 Workforce Security

HIPAA requires the implementation of policies and procedures to ensure that all workforce members have appropriate access to electronic protected health information and to prevent unauthorized workforce members from having access to said information [3]. NIST addresses the issue by suggesting the following:

- *Implement procedures for authorization and/or supervision* of workforce members who work with EPHI.
- *Establish clear job descriptions and responsibilities* by defining roles and responsibilities for all job junctions and identifying all persons who are to be granted permission to access and store EPHI.
- *Establish criteria and procedures for hiring and assigning tasks* by ensuring that the staff members who have EPHI responsibilities have the knowledge, skills, and abilities to fulfill their roles.
- *Establish a workforce clearance procedure* by implementing procedures to determine who are to have access to EPHI.
- *Establish termination procedures* to EPHI when the employment of a workforce member terminates.

16.7.6 Information Access Management

HIPAA requires the implementation of policies and procedures for authorizing access to EPHI. NIST suggests the following be implemented [4]:

- *Isolate healthcare clearinghouse functions* from other functions to ensure that there be no unauthorized access by the other entities of the larger organization.
- *Implement policies and procedures for authorizing access* to EPHI and preventing unauthorized access by selecting appropriate control methods.
- *Implement policies and procedures for access establishment and modification* by establishing standards for granting of access and provide formal authorization to those persons who are granted access.
- *Evaluate existing security measures related to access controls* to determine if the security features involve alignment with other existing management, operational, and technical controls.

16.7.7 Security Awareness and Training

HIPAA requires that there be an implementation of a security awareness and training program for all members of the covered entity's workforce. NIST suggests the following program [4]:

- *Conduct a training needs assessment* by determining the needs of the organization and by interviewing and involving key personnel in its assessment.
- *Develop and approve a training strategy and a plan* by addressing specific HIPAA policies that require security awareness, and have a security awareness and training program.
- *Protection from malicious software; log-in monitoring, and password management* by training employees to guard against and monitor log-in attempts, and by creating changing and safeguarding measures.
- *Develop appropriate awareness and training content, materials, and methods* by using a variety of methodologies and new information in their training materials.
- *Implement the training* by a variety of methods such as e-mails, videotapes, teleconferencing, etc.
- *Implement security reminders* with periodic security updates.
- *Monitor and evaluate a training plan.*

16.7.8 Security Incident Procedures

HIPAA requires the implementation of policies and procedures to address security concerns. NIST suggests the following [4]:

- *Determine goals of incident response* by understanding, determining, and reporting security incidents.
- *Develop and deploy an incident response team or other reasonable and appropriate response mechanism.*
- *Develop and implement procedures to respond to and report security incidents.*
- *Incorporate postincident analysis into updates and revisions.*

16.7.9 Contingency Plan

HIPAA requires the covered entity establish and implement policies and procedures to respond to an emergency or other occurrence that damages systems containing EPHI. NIST suggests the following policies and procedures [4]:

- *Develop contingency planning policy.*
- *Conduct an applications and data criticality analysis* by assessing and relative criticality of specific applications and data.

- *Identify preventive measures* for particular scenarios that could result in the loss of critical service operations involving EPHI.
- *Develop recovery strategy* by having a set of contingency procedures to be implemented for particular emergencies.
- *Data backup plan and disaster recovery plan.*
- *Develop and implement an emergency mode operation plan, and testing and revision procedure.*

16.7.10 Evaluation

HIPAA requires a periodic technical and nontechnical evaluation to respond to environmental or operational changes affecting EPHI. NIST suggests the following policies and procedures [4]:

- *Determine whether internal or external evaluation is most appropriate.*
- *Develop standards and measurements for reviewing all standards and implantation specifications of the security role.*
- *Conduct evaluation.*
- *Document results.*
- *Repeat evaluation periodically.*

16.7.11 Business Associate Contracts and Other Arrangements

HIPAA recognized that a covered entity may permit a business associate to create, receive, maintain, or transmit EPHI on the covered entity's behalf only if the covered entity obtains satisfactory assurances that the business associate will appropriately safeguard the information. NIST suggests that this may be accomplished by the following policies and procedures [4]:

- *Identify entities that are business associates under the HIPAA Security Rule,* such as organizations providing a service or function, including that of claims processing or billing, data analysis, quality assurance, benefit and/or practice management, and hardware maintenance.
- *Obtain a written contract or other arrangement* by documenting the satisfactory assurances required by HIPAA.
- *Establish procedures for measuring contract and terminating the contract if security requirements are not being met.*
- *Implement an arrangement other than a business associate contract if reasonable and appropriate.*

16.7.12 Facility Access Controls

HIPAA requires that the covered entity implement policies and procedures to limit physical access to its EPHI and to the facilities in which they are housed while assuring proper access to them. NIST suggests that the firm [4]:

- *Conduct an analysis of existing physical security vulnerabilities* including data centers, equipment locations, IT staff offices, and workplace locations.
- *Identify corrective measures* by identifying and assigning responsibly to persons necessary to correct deficiencies, and developing policies and procedures to ensure that repairs, upgrades, and other modifications are made.
- *Develop a facility security plan.*
- *Develop access control and validation procedures.*
- *Establish contingency operations procedures.*
- *Maintain maintenance records.*

16.7.13 Workstation Use and Security

HIPAA requires the implantation of policies and procedures to specify the proper function to be performed, the manners they are to be performed, and physical safeguards for all workstations that access EPHI. NIST suggests the following:

- Identify workstation types and functions or uses.
- Identify expected performance of each type of workstation.
- Analyze physical surroundings for physical attributes.
- Identify all methods of physical access to workstations.
- Analyze the risk associated with each type of access; identify and implement physical safeguards for workstations.

16.7.14 Controls

16.7.14.1 Access Controls

HIPAA requires the implementation of policies and procedures for electronic information systems that maintain EPHI to allow access only to persons granted access rights. NIST suggests that the following be implemented:

- Analyze workloads and operations to identify the access needs of all users.
- Identify technical access control capabilities.
- Ensure that all systems users have been assigned a unique identifier; develop access control policy.
- Implement access control procedures using selected hardware and software.
- Review and update user access.

- Establish an emergency access procedure.
- Have an automatic logoff and encryption and decryption.
- Terminate access if it is no longer required.

In addition there should be device and media controls and audit controls.

16.7.15 Person or Entity Authentication

Transmission Security. HIPAA requires that covered entities implement technical security measures to guard against unauthorized access to EPHI that is being transmitted over an electronic communications network. NIST suggests that this can be accomplished by the following:

- Identify any possible unauthorized sources that may be able to intercept and/ or modify the information.
- Develop and implement transmission security policy and procedures.
- Implement integrity controls.
- Implement a mechanism to encrypt EPHI whenever it is deemed appropriate.

16.8 Conducting Effective Risk Analysis

Any implementation of HIPAA final Security Rule without applying an effective risk analysis activity remains incomplete and inadequate. The Security Rule requires covered entities to "conduct an accurate and thorough assessment of the potential risks and vulnerabilities to the confidentiality, integrity, and availability of electronic protected health information held by the covered entity." Additionally, the rule states that "the required risk analysis is also a tool to allow flexibility for entities in meeting the requirements of this final rule ... ." An article published by vgm.com presents a high-level overview of the required risk analysis process [2].

Risk is defined by vgm.com as the likelihood that a specific threat will exploit a certain vulnerability, and the resulting impact of that event [2]. Risk analysis, according to them, is the starting point in an overall risk management process, a systematic and analytical approach that identifies and assesses risks and provides recommendations to reduce risk to a reasonable and appropriate level. This process will enable senior management to understand their organization's risks to electronic protected health information (EPHI), and to allocate appropriate resources to reduce and correct potential losses.

There is no doubt that a thorough risk analysis process is essential for complying with the HIPAA final Security Rule. CEs are advised to adopt a similar risk analysis process to evaluate their risks and determine appropriate and reasonable security controls for protecting their EPHI [2].

16.8.1 *vgm.com Risk Methodology*

The Web site vgm.com proposes eight steps for performing risk analysis that CEs should carry out to support their compliance with the HIPAA final Security Rule [2]:

1. EPHI boundary definition
2. Threat identification
3. Vulnerability identification
4. Security control analysis
5. Risk likelihood determination
6. Impact analysis
7. Risk determination
8. Security control recommendations

16.8.1.1 *Step 1: EPHI Boundary Definition*

The CE initiates its risk analysis process by conducting a detailed inventory of their EPHI and information systems that contain EPHI [2]. The CR needs to employ data collection tools, like questionnaires, on-site interviews and inspections, document review, and automated scanning tools, to gather the following information about its inventory:

- Information system hardware and software details
- Internal and external interfaces of information systems
- Identification of the primary users of the information systems and EPHI
- Basic function and purpose of the EPHI and information system
- Technical controls (e.g., hardware or software access control mechanisms, encryption) and nontechnical controls (e.g., security policies, employee training) being used to protect EPHI and information systems

16.8.1.2 *Step 2: Threat Identification*

The CE should next identify all potential threats to its EPHI and related information systems. A threat is defined by vgm.com as "something or someone that can intentionally or accidentally exploit a vulnerability." The following three types of threats to EPHI are identified:

- **Natural:** Floods, earthquakes, tornados, etc.
- **Human:** Unintentional (incorrect data entry or accidental deletion of data) and intentional (denial of service attack, installing malicious software)
- **Environmental:** Power failures, hazardous material spill, etc.

The Web site bgm.com recommends the following sources to obtain detailed information about threats:

- Hazard identification and vulnerability assessment studies conducted by local and state governments
- Security organizations such as SANS, CERT, and NIPC
- Security Web pages such as www.securityfocus.com and www.searchsecurity.com

16.8.1.3 Step 3: Vulnerability Identification

CEs should then identify the vulnerabilities of their EPHI and related information systems. The site vgm.com defines a vulnerability a flaw or weakness in system security procedures, design, implementation, or internal controls that can be exploited by a threat and result in misuse or abuse of EPHI [2]. The vulnerability identification process identifies system vulnerabilities by reviewing vulnerability sources that publish to the public all known system vulnerabilities and/or by performing security assessments using available tools.

Vulnerability sources include system and data owner questionnaires, on-site review of information systems, audit reports, and information system test and evaluation reports. Vulnerability lists such as the NIST vulnerability database (http://icat.nist.gov), CERT, and Bugtraq, as well as advisories from security vendors and security organizations are all useful tools.

Security assessments use a variety of software tools and resting techniques to check specific data and information systems for possible vulnerabilities.

16.8.1.4 Step 4: Security Control Analysis

CEs should next analyze the security controls that have been implemented or will be implemented to protect EPHI; this includes preventive, detective, deterring, and corrective controls. Preventive security controls are designed to prevent or restrict the exploitation of vulnerabilities. Detective controls detect and report when violations occur. Deterring controls are implemented to deter attackers and scare them away. Corrective controls are needed to respond to known attacks when detected. The analysis should clearly define what security controls are being used to protect specific EPHI. It is only after assessing risks that we can determine what new security controls will be adopted to mitigate risks.

16.8.1.5 Step 5: Risk Likelihood Determination

This step is needed to assign scores to specific risks that indicate the probability that a vulnerability will be exploited by a particular threat. The site vgm.com proposes three factors to be considered: (1) threat motivation and capability, (2) type of vulnerability, and (3) existence and effectiveness of security controls. The three risk likelihood levels that CEs might use are defined as follows [2]:

Likelihood = high: Threat is highly capable, motivated, or likely, and current security controls are ineffective

Likelihood = medium: Threat is capable, motivated or likely, but there are security controls in place that may prevent exploitation of specific vulnerabilities

Likelihood = low: Threat is not capable, motivated or likely, or current security controls will likely prevent exploitation of specific vulnerabilities

16.8.1.6 Step 6: Impact Analysis

In this step, CEs determine the impact that would result if a threat were to successfully exploit a vulnerability. Information system and EPHI owners should be interviewed to determine the impact in the following areas [2]:

Confidentiality: EPHI is disclosed or accessed in an unauthorized manner.
Integrity: EPHI is improperly modified.
Availability: EPHI is unavailable to authorized users.

16.8.1.7 Step 7: Risk Determination

In determining risks, CEs use the information obtained in the above steps to identify the level of risk to specific EPHI and related information systems. For each vulnerability and associated possible threat, CEs should make a risk determination based on [2]:

■ The likelihood a certain threat will attempt to exploit a specific vulnerability
■ The level of impact should the threat successfully exploit the vulnerability
■ The adequacy of planned or existing security controls

The three levels of risk that CEs might use are defined as follows [2]:

Risk level = high: Security controls should be implemented or improved as quickly as possible

Risk level = medium: Security controls should be implemented or improved in a reasonable amount of time

Risk level = low: Existing security controls are likely adequate or the risk is acceptable

16.8.1.8 Step 8: Security Control Recommendations

At this point, we should have all the information we need to determine the security controls that are most appropriate to mitigate EPHI risks. CEs can now conclude the risk analysis process by proposing security controls that can mitigate or eliminate the identified unacceptable risks to EPHI. These controls should reduce the level of risk to EPHI and related information systems to an acceptable level.

16.9 Summary

This chapter discussed the federal HIPAA or Health Insurance Portability and Accountability Act of 1996's Security Rule and its compliance requirements. We covered the problem and meaning of privacy in organizations. We also presented the need for accountability and administrative simplification which was imposed by the increasing use of the Internet, involving the distributed manipulation of information, including the storing and transferring of electronic information.

The chapter also presented how NIST views the HIPAA standards and what ways NIST is suggesting how organizations may comply with HIPAA. The chapter also provided details on how to adopt the needed administrative safeguards to comply with the HIPAA Security Rule.

16.10 Review Questions

1. Explain what the problem of privacy is and give an example.
2. Explain the meaning of privacy in the organization and give an example.
3. Explain the need for HIPAA and complying with it.
4. Explain the Privacy Rule and explain an example of its use.
5. Explain what the HIPAA Security Rule is and explain its usefulness.
6. Explain what administrative safeguards are needed to comply with the Security Rule.
7. Explain how NIST views HIPAA standards. Do you think the steps they recommend are useful or do you feel that you can come up with your own way to comply with HIPAA?
8. Explain how the proposed risk methodology is used to comply with HIPAA.
9. Explain how a covered entity may permit a business associate to create, receive, maintain, or transmit EPHI on its behalf when the covered entity obtains satisfactory assurances that the business associate will appropriately safeguard the information. Does this affect the covered entity's chance for easy compliance with HIPAA? Why the additional risk?
10. Protection is given to health information and individually identifiable health information. Define health information. Suggest minimal requirements to protect health information.

16.11 Workshops

Workshop 1

Consider a small public K1-9 school that includes fewer than 100 students and fewer than 30 instructors and staff members. According to HIPAA, the covered entities are to implement policies and procedures to prevent, detect, contain, and correct security violations. Explain how you can devise administrative safeguards to accomplish this goal. Before you do so, attempt to write a simple security policy that you need to enforce using the administrative safeguards that leads to compliance with HIPAA in a cost-effective way.

Workshop 2

Apply the risk methodology to assess risks in the small public K1-9 school introduced in Workshop 1. Show and orient your risk assessment task toward easy compliance with HIPAA. You may apply the security policy developed in answering Workshop 1.

References

1. Barry, M., A Guide to the administrative safeguards of HIPAA's security rule, by Michael P. Barry, *Utah Bar Journal*, 2006, htttp://webster.utahbar.org/barjournal/2006/04/a_guide_to_the_administrative.html.
2. HIPAA Security Rule: What It Is and How DMEPOS Providers Can Comply with It, http://www.vgm.com/MembersOnly/Presentations/Files/HIPAA_Security_Rule.doc.
3. The HIPAA Security Rule ([US] Department of Health and Human Services, Office of the Secretary, 45 CFR Parts 160, 162, and 164, Health Insurance Reform: Security Standards; Final Rule): http://www.cms.hhs.gov/SecurityStandard/Downloads/securityfinalrule.pdf.
4. U.S. Department of Commerce, National Institute of Standards and Technology, An Introductory Resource Guide for Implementing the Health Insurance Portability and Accountability Act (HIPAA) Security Rule, http://scrc.nisi.gov/publications/nistpubs/800-66-Rev1/SP-800-66Revision1/pdf.
5. U.S. Department of Health and Human Services, Centers for Medicare and Medicaid Services (CMS): http://www.cms.hhs.gov/EducationMaterials/04_SecurityMaterials.asp and http://www.cms.hhs.gov/SecurityStandard/.

CONTINUAL SECURITY

Chapter 17

The Sarbanes–Oxley Act and IT Compliance

Learning Objectives

After reading this chapter, students are expected to achieve an understanding of:

Legal methods of doing business
The Sarbanes–Oxley Act of 2002
Major provisions of SOX
Management Assessment of Internal Controls and IT Compliance
How IT compliance works
How international responses to SOX are planned
What are the advantages to SOX compliance
How foreign whistleblowers appear in the context of SOX
How to reconcile SOX and European conflicting standards
EU Corporate Governance Initiatives
How EU's Eighth Directive compares to SOX
How SOX has evolved with respect to IT security management

17.1 Introduction

In this chapter we will initially explore the various methods of doing business. Thereafter, we will discuss the nature of a public business corporation, its method of raising capital, corporate governance, the recent scandals concerning corporate securities, and the controversial law that has been enacted to correct the abuses. A major aspect of the law concerns the role of information technology in insuring that appropriate controls are put in place to prevent fraudulent practices. Before we discuss the laws affecting securities we will review basic legal concepts in order to have a more complete understanding of the problems and issues addressed by the laws. Thereafter, we will discuss the meaning of a "security," the major provisions of the Sarbanes–Oxley Act, and one of the most important aspects of the law, namely, Section 404 mandate of Management Assessment of Internal Controls [1,5]. We will then conclude with a discussion of the international implications of the act upon non-U.S. companies that enter or are part of the U.S. capital markets.

17.2 Methods of Doing Business

17.2.1 Sole Proprietorship

There are a number of ways in which a person may commence and operate a business. Historically, the most natural method is for an individual to open a store to sell products or operate a service business such as plumbing, electrical, or carpentry. It is the simplest method, which traces its roots back thousands of years. It is still the most common form of enterprise because there are almost no governmental regulations other than licensing if certain skills are to be used. It is cheap to form and may be sold or transferred without consent of any other person. Profits and losses may be declared on one's individual tax return. The problem with an individual business (known as a *sole proprietorship*) is that an individual risks his or her money and may be subject to loss of all of one's personal assets should the business cause a person to suffer significant losses. Of course, all profits, if any, also accrue to that individual. An individual using a business name, such as Mary's Boutique, usually is required to file with the local country registry a certificate of doing business under an assumed name.

17.2.2 Partnership

Another form of business that a person may undertake that has been common for hundreds of years is to form a *partnership* whereby two or more persons legally come together to form and operate a business in the hopes of making a profit. Depending on the laws of the particular locality, a written agreement is not necessary, although clearly advisable. The percentage of ownership for purposes of determining profits and losses is dependent on the agreement of the partners. There are generally no taxes due and payable by the partnership, although a partnership tax return may be required to be filed. The taxes, if any, are paid by the individual partners with respect to their individual shares of the profits or losses of the partnership. The problem with a partnership is that each of the partners may be fully responsible for the debts incurred by the partnership. Thus, for example, if there are three persons who form a partnership and the partnership incurs losses in the business, it is possible for one individual partner to be fully liable for all of the losses if the partnership assets and the remaining partners' assets are insufficient to pay for the business losses. Partnerships operating under an assumed name may also be required to file a certificate indicating the names and addresses of the partnership and the name to be used by them.

17.2.3 Limited Partnership (LP)

A third method of doing business that came into being within the last four decades is to form a *limited partnership*. It also is a legal partnership whereby there must be at least one *general partner* who assumes full liability for the debts of the partnership in the event of losses that partnership assets cannot cover. The *limited partners* are persons who invest money or other assets in the business enterprise but whose liability is limited to the amount invested. The advantage, of course, to the limited partners is that they are free from worry that creditors could seek to go after their individual assets should the partnership and general partner assets be insufficient to cover the losses of the enterprise. A limited partnership must be permitted by law, must be in writing and signed by each of the parties designating their partnership status, and then must be filed with the state. The partners are taxed on their profits gained from the partnership. The problem with a limited partnership is that the limited partners have little say or control over the day-to-day operations of the partnership. They are merely investors hoping for a profitable investment. A corporation may be either the general partner or a limited partner.

17.2.4 Limited Liability Partnership (LLP)

A fourth method of doing business is also in the form of a partnership but does not require a general partner to have unlimited liability; rather the *limited liability company* ("LLP") permits all of the partners to be limited partners thus avoiding liability of the partners beyond their capital investment in the partnership. This form of partnership generally is permitted to be used only by certain professionals such as attorneys and physicians. A formal article of limited liability partnership is required to be filed with the secretary of state of the state where the partnership is located. There may be a minimal liability insurance requirement in order to form such partnership.

17.2.5 Limited Liability Company (LLC)

A currently popular method of doing business that has arisen in recent years is the *limited liability company* or LLC. It is an unincorporated business entity whose owners are "members" but who, like an LLP, are not personally liable for the debts and obligations of the company except as to the capital invested in the company. The LLC is taxed in the same manner as a partnership although it may unlikely elect to be taxed as a corporation, i.e., the individuals pay their share of the corporate profits. The LLC is an entity that can sue and be sued in its name, own and sell property, and do almost all things that an individual proprietorship can accomplish. The company is commenced by the filing of articles of organization with the secretary of state in the state where it is located.

17.2.6 Corporation

A *corporation* is a creature of the state (i.e., it is a legal person which is given most of the rights that an individual business person possesses). It may sue or be sued in its name; it may own and sell property; it may transact a legal business of every type and nature that individuals may engage in; and it is taxed on its own earnings, although dividends paid to shareholders are deductible as expenses. Corporations may be family or "closely held" corporations where all of the shares are owned by one or a few persons or it may be a "publicly held" corporation whose shares are sold on stock exchanges. Whereas individual shareholders of close corporations generally operate and fully partake in the overall governance and day-to-day operations of the business enterprise, shareholders in a public corporation have no say in the governance of the corporation except to the extent that they elect the members of the board of directors who oversee the major aspects of the enterprise and who name the officers running the day-to-day operations of the business. There are other types of corporations such as professional corporations (owned by licensed professionals), governmental public corporations including municipal corporations (cities), and Federal Deposit Insurance Corporation (insures bank deposits), and not-for profit corporations, which serve a public purpose such as education, health, religious, or social needs.

17.3 Background of the Sarbanes–Oxley Act

The securities markets, owing to the vast monetary investments made daily in diverse stock exchanges such as the New York Stock Exchange, the London Stock Exchange, and the numerous other exchanges located in capital markets exchanges worldwide, have historically been laden with attempts to perpetrate fraud upon investors. In the past two decades there have been great scandals including the collapse in the early 1990s of the Robert Maxwell financial empire and that of Polly Peck in Great Britain, which led to significant reforms within the nation instigated by the Cadbury, Greenbury, and Hampel Committees' Reports. The United States capital markets, for the past seven decades, has essentially been immune to major corporate scandals due to the enactments of major securities legislation, especially the *Securities Act of 1933* and the *Securities and Exchange Act of 1934*. The Securities and Exchange Commission (SEC) that was created under the legislation, in conjunction with the private organization National Association of Securities Dealers (NASD), and the rules and regulations of the New York Stock Exchange and other exchanges, have been remarkably vigilant in preventing significant corporate malfeasance by determining and punishing persons committing violations of the laws, rules, and regulations.

Notwithstanding the close scrutiny of regulatory agencies, the dot-com boom of the late 1990s and the rise of energy and communication companies led to major scandals that created the need for significant reform of the capital markets. The poster companies for corporate malfeasance, such as Enron, WorldCom, Adelphia, and other scandals led to the passage of the most important securities legislation since the early 1930s securities legislation, namely the *Public Company Accounting Reform and Investor Protection Act of 2002,* much better known as the Sarbanes–Oxley Act (SOX).

17.4 Sarbanes–Oxley Act of 2002

17.4.1 Purpose of Sarbanes–Oxley Act

The purpose of the act was to change the corporate culture and significantly improve the reliability of financial reporting by chief corporate officers (CEOs) and chief financial officers (CFOs) in order to assure investors that decisions to purchase securities would be based upon reliable financial data emanating from corporate officers.

17.4.2 Creation of PCAOB

The act created an independent Public Company Accounting Oversight Board (PCAOB), consisting of five members appointed by the Securities and Exchange Commission (SEC). The duties of the board include the registration of public accounting firms that prepare audit reports for issuers; the conduct of inspections of registered public accounting firms; investigations and disciplinary proceedings, the imposition of sanctions where appropriate on registered public accounting firms; the performance of other duties and functions to ensure high professional standards; and to improve the quality of audits by registered public accounting firms and those persons associated with such firms.

17.4.3 Securities

The definition of a "security" is very broad indeed. It has been defined by the U.S. Securities and Exchange Commission as

> "Any note, stock, treasury stock, bond, debenture, certificate of interest or participation agreement or in any oil, gas, or other mineral royalty or lease, any collateral trust certificate, preorganization certificate or subscription, transferable share, investment contract, voting-trust

certificate, certificate of deposit, for a security, any put, call, straddle, option, or privilege on any security, certificate of deposit, or group or index of securities (including any interest therein or based on the value thereof), or any put, call, straddle, option, or privilege entered into on a national securities exchange relating to foreign currency, or in general, any instrument commonly known as a "security"; or any certificate of interest or participation in, temporary or interim certificate for, receipt for, or warrant or right to subscribe to or purchase, any of the forego-ing; but shall not include currency or any note, draft, bill of exchange, or banker's acceptance which has a maturity at the time of issuance of not exceeding nine months, exclusive of days of grace, or any renewal thereof the maturity of which is likewise limited."

In essence, a security includes any note, stock, bond, preorganization subscrip-tion, and investment contract. An investment contract is any investment of money or property made in expectation of receiving a financial return solely from the efforts of others. Its essential elements are:

- An investment in
- A common enterprise
- Premised on a reasonable expectation of profits
- To be derived from the managerial efforts of others.

17.5 Major Provisions of SOX

17.5.1 Registration and Inspection of Non-U.S. Public Accounting Firms

Section 102(a) of SOX provides: "… it shall be unlawful for any person that is not a registered public accounting firm to prepare or issue, or to participate in the preparation or issuance of, any audit report with respect to any issuer." There is no exception for foreign audit firms. Thus, the statute requires non-US audit firms, whose reports are included in Securities and Exchange Commission (SEC) filings, to register with the newly created Public Company Accounting Oversight Board (PCAOB) by July 19, 2004.

The application for registration with the PCAOB is very extensive. It includes annual fees received for audit and nonaudit services, quality control policies of the firm; a list of all accountants participating in audit reports, criminal or civil disci-plinary proceedings against the firm or person associated with any audit, disputes between the audit firm and the issuer; and other information that the Board may require. A registration by the foreign firm does not relieve it of responsibility for demonstrating its knowledge and experience in applying U.S. Generally Accepted

Accounting Principles (GAAP), PCAOB standards, SEC financial reporting rules, and SEC independence requirements. A grace period for a limited time will be allowed to the foreign firm for the filing of quarterly reports pending the review of an application for registration that has been submitted for PCAOB approval.

PCAOB rules do provide that a non-U.S. registered public accounting firm may request the board to rely upon a non-U.S. inspection by an appropriate non-U.S. regulator by submitting a written statement signed by an authorized partner or officer of the firm. The statement may be made by postal or electronic mail. The board's decision to permit such reliance will be based on its evaluation of the adequacy and integrity of the system, the independence of the system from the auditing profession, its source of funding, transparency, and its historical performance.

17.5.2 Auditor Independence: Prohibition of Nonaudit Services

Section 201(a) of SOX states that it shall be unlawful for a registered accounting firm that performs an audit of an issuer's financial statements to provide certain categories of services. The reasons for the prohibition are premised on the following principles: an auditor cannot function in the role of management; an auditor cannot audit his or her own work; and an auditor cannot serve in an advocacy role for his or her client. The categories of services prohibited are [2]:

1. Bookkeeping or other services relating to the accounting services or financial statements of the audit client
2. Financial information systems design and implementation
3. Appraisal or valuation services, fairness opinions, or contribution-in-kind reports
4. Actuarial services
5. Internal audit outsourcing services
6. Management functions or human resources
7. Broker or dealer, investment adviser, or investment banking services; legal services and expert services unrelated to the audit
8. Any other service that the PCAOB determines by regulation is impermissible

Section 201(g-h) specifies nonaudit services that are prohibited and those services which are permitted subject to approval of the audit committee. Section 202(i) requires the audit committee to preapprove allowable nonaudit services with exceptions. Section 203(j) establishes a mandatory 5-year rotation of the lead and concurring partner. Section 204(k) requires the auditor report to be furnished timely to the audit committee. Section 206(l) concerns certain conflict of interest provisions. Section 206(l) prohibits an accounting firm from performing an audit for a registrant if the chief executive officer, controller, chief financial officer, chief accounting officer, or person employed in an equivalent position was employed by that registered independent public accounting firm and participated in any capacity in the audit of that issuer for a 1-year period prior to the initiation of the audit.

These provisions have particular impact upon the international community. With respect to partner rotation, the difficulty in certain emerging countries is that there may be a lack of qualified auditors conversant in U.S. GAAP and U.S. GAAS (Generally Accepted Auditing Principles and Generally Accepted Auditing Standards) requirements. The SEC, taking into account of the difficulty, has determined that the rotation requirement applies only to partners at the issuer or parent level and shall apply to the lead partner at the issuer's subsidiary whose revenues exceed 20% or more of the parent's consolidated assets or revenues. Further, with respect to the cooling-off 1-year period of employment, the Act shall apply to lead partners who provide more than 10 hours of audit, review or attest services.

17.5.3 Audit Committee Makeup

Section 301 concerns the makeup of public company audit committees. The act prohibits U.S. securities exchanges and associations from listing any security of an issuer not in compliance with the section's provisions. It includes the requirement that the audit committee of an issuer, acting as a committee of the board of directors, shall be responsible for the appointment and supervision of any registered public accounting firm with respect to the preparation or issuance of an audit report or related work. The said registered firm is to report directly to the audit committee. Each member of the audit committee shall be a member of the board of directors and shall be independent therein. The member of the audit committee may not accept any consulting, advisory, or other fee from the issuer or be an affiliated person of the issuer or a subsidiary thereof. The audit committee is to establish procedures for the receipt, retention, and treatment of complaints received by the issuer concerning its internal accounting controls or auditing matters and to maintain the confidentiality of such submissions.

It is critical that the audit committee be truly independent of the issuer and not be subject to overriding influence by the remaining members of the board of directors or from the corporate officers. The latter, especially, may not be members of the audit committee. The selected registered accounting firm must be free to report any discrepancies concerning internal accounting controls to the committee, which must thereafter take action to correct the deficiencies and to report its findings to the full board for appropriate action. Complaints received by the committee or by the designated registered accounting firm must remain confidential. Any attempts of retaliation against whistleblowers will make the issuer subject to criminal and/or civil penalties.

17.5.4 Certifications by Principal Executive and Financial Officers

Section 302 concerns corporate responsibility for financial reports. It mandates that the principal executive officer(s) and principal financial officer(s) certify in each submitted annual or quarterly report that each of the said officers have reviewed the report; based on each officer's knowledge, the report does not state any untrue statement or material fact or omission; the said report, based on each officer's knowledge, fairly represents in all material respects the financial condition of the issuer; the said officers are responsible for establishing and maintaining internal controls designed to ensure that material information is made known to them; they have reviewed the issuer's internal control within the 90 days prior to the report; and the signing officers have disclosed to the issuer's auditors and audit committee all significant deficiencies in the internal controls and any fraud involving management or other employees having a role in the internal controls. Note that an issuer that reincorporates or transfers offices to a non-U.S. state shall remain subject to the act.

It is imperative that the chief corporate officers have internal controls in place to detect significant errors in reporting. It will be much more difficult for corporate officers facing criminal charges and civil suits to raise the defense of due diligence and lack of knowledge of wrongful activities without clear proof that they have assured the promulgation and integrity of the internal controls instituted and supervised by them. In complex organizations, each major subunit should have a system of internal controls that are integrated into the whole. Careful documentation is essential in illustrating the degree to which the senior officers making the certification have complied with statutory and regulatory standards. The role of information technology (IT) discussed at length in the following text is particularly relevant in this context.

17.5.5 Off Balance Sheet Transactions

Section 401 concerns the disclosure of off-balance-sheet transactions. It states that each annual and quarterly financial report required to be filed with the SEC "shall disclose all material off-balance-sheet transactions, arrangements, obligations (including contingent obligations), and other relationships of the issuer with unconsolidated entities or other persons" that may affect the issuer's financial condition, resources, or other significant components of revenues.

The SEC issued Regulation G in 2002 concerning the use of non-GAAP financial measures. The regulation is particularly applicable to non-U.S. registrants. In essence, the registrant must not exclude charges or liabilities that required cash settlements, other than measures before interest and taxes, and earnings before interest, taxes, depreciation, and amortization. A non-GAAP performance measure may not eliminate or smooth over items alleged to be nonrecurring, infrequent or unusual when they reasonably may recur within 2 years or have occurred in the past 2 years. The registrant may not use titles or descriptions of non-GAAP financial measures that are the same or confusingly similar to titles or descriptions used for GAAP measures. The essence of the regulation is to avoid concealment of financial measures that would be revealed by use of GAAP financial measures.

17.5.6 Conflict of Interest Provisions

Section 402 relates to conflict of interest provisions. With minor exceptions, such as housing assistance as part of the executive's compensation, personal loans given by a publicly held issuer to any director or executive officer are expressly prohibited after the Act's date of enactment, whether they be directly or indirectly made, or through a subsidiary. They include the extension, maintenance, or arrangement of credit. A "director" is "any director of a corporation or any person performing similar functions with respect to any organization, whether incorporated or unincorporated." The definition appears to include advisory and emeritus directors. "Executive officer" includes the issuer's president, a vice president in charge of a principal business unit, administration or finance, or other officer having a policy making function. Prior extensions of credit maintained by the issuer prior to the enactment of the statute are grandfathered (i.e., not within the statute provided that they are not later materially modified).

The statute appears to be self-explanatory by prohibiting personal loans in any form. It does not include loans that are made primarily for the issuer's business purposes. It includes extension of credit, which may take numerous forms. Among the forms that may lead to a violation of Section 402 and which should be avoided are personal uses of company credit cards, signing bonuses that are to be repaid upon early cessation of employment, loans for home purchases and tuition, and loans from a Section 401(k) (retirement plan). Not affected are payments for travel and comparable expenses for the issuer's business, business use of a credit card and vehicle, relocation expenses, and loans from the employee's annuity or other form provided they are not from the issuer.

17.5.7 Working Papers

Section 106(a) subjects "any foreign public accounting firm that prepares or furnishes an audit report with respect to any issuer" to the rules and regulations of SOX "in the same manner and to the same extent as a public accounting firm that is organized and operates under the laws of the United States or any state." The PCAOB may also determine that the non-U.S. public accounting firm that plays a substantial role in the preparation of reports be also subject to the Act. The effect of SOX upon the international community goes beyond that of internal controls but also includes external controls. The concern of the U.S. government is not only over auditing to uncover Enron-type investments offshore but also the export of end products to forbidden areas.

Of critical importance and most controversial of the Act's requirements is Section 106(b) concerning the production of audit work papers. Article 106(b) requires a non-U.S. public accounting firm, which issues an opinion or other material services relied upon by a U.S. registered public accounting firm in issuing all or part of any audit report or opinion within the report, consent to access to its working papers with respect to any investigation by the PCAOB or SEC, and to consent to jurisdiction to the courts of the U.S. The said statutory provision appears to violate the contrary provisions and prohibitions of the European Union (EU) national professional secrecy laws. Many of the EU member states provide that working papers may only be given to a court therein, which provision may not be waived. In France, Article L225-240 of the French Commercial Code requires secrecy by auditors. French authorities may be granted access to secrecy as to working papers. Finland has a similar provision. In Denmark and Belgium, the unauthorized handing over of working papers of a client is a criminal offense. Nevertheless, Article 47 of Directive 2006/43/EC on statutory audits of annual accounts and consolidated accounts specifically permits member states to allow transfer of audit working papers on the basis of reciprocity at the request of competent authorities of third countries, provided they relate to audits of companies which have issued securities in that country or form part of a group that issues statutory consolidated accounts therein.

Unless there are regulatory prohibitions in the home state, the auditor must document all significant findings, issues, or actions taken to address the particular problems such as complex or unusual transactions, accounting estimates, uncertainties, and management assumptions. Additional documentation should be made when there are misstatements or omissions in financial statements, audit adjustments, disagreements among management team members concerning final conclusions on significant accounting or auditing matters, and significant difficulties concerning the application of auditing procedures or changes in the level of audit risk. The audit work papers are to be retained for a period of 7 years from the date the auditor's report is made a part of the company's financial statements. Project managers of companies should cooperate with external auditors and comply with their work paper formats. Failure to comply and the deliberate falsification of destruction of work papers may lead to criminal prosecution in the United States.

17.5.8 Material Changes

Section 409 of SOX concerns real time issuer disclosures. It provides that "Each issuer reporting under Section 13(a) or 15(d) shall disclose to the public on a rapid and current basis such additional information concerning material changes in the financial condition or operations of the issuer, in plain English, which may include trend and qualitative information and graphic presentations, as the Commission determines, by rule, is necessary or useful for the protection of investors and in the public interest." Thus, business must be aware of and provide expeditiously the communication of material events. Failure to do so may create serious regulatory problems.

17.6 Management Assessment of Internal Controls and IT Compliance

Section 404(a) of SOX, Management Assessment of Internal Controls, is the most discussed part of the Act. It provides that the PCAOB shall prescribe rules requiring each annual report filed under the Securities Exchange Act of 1934 "contain an internal control report, which shall [1,5]:

(1) State the responsibility of management for establishing and maintaining an adequate internal control structure and procedures for financial reporting; and

(2) Contain an assessment, as of the end of the most recent fiscal year of the issuer, of the effectiveness of the internal control structure and procedures of the issuer for financial reporting." [2]

The internal control assessment mandates that the registered public accounting firm which prepares or issues the audit report must attest and report on the assessment made by the issuer's management. Although the section appears to be mainly targeted to auditing firms and management, the issue arose concerning the extent to which there should be required documentation and testing for information technology (IT) internal controls especially as to their application to program development and changes, computer operations, and access to programs and data. The SEC opined that, with respect to financial reporting, it expects management to document and test general and appropriate application-level controls so as to assure that the financial information generated from the company's application systems can be reasonably relied upon. The company's finance and IT departments should work together to assure that IT controls are properly in place. The SEC said that it would not decide which such controls should be included because "Section 404 is not a one-size-fits-all approach to assessing controls." [5]

17.6.1 PCAOB and SEC Standards

In December 2003 the PCAOB adopted an auditing standard known as AS 1. It requires international auditors' reports to state that they are in compliance with the standards of the PCAOB. It is no longer appropriate or necessary to state that the auditors' reports are in compliance with generally accepted auditing standards. The SEC issued an interpretation of the requirement. In it, the SEC makes it clear that AS 1 does not supersede any of the applicable rules or regulations of the Commission but rather means that a report of an independent accountant must comply with both SEC and PCAOB rules and guidance. Registered public accounting firms must comply with the more restrictive of the rules and regulations of the SEC and the PCAOB. The issue that has arisen was whether the SEC would permit non-US issuers to file reports in compliance with both U.S. GAAS and home country auditing standards. PCAOB rules now require that the entire audit must comply with its standards.

It appears that Section 404 not only applies to a firm's internal control structure but also applies to export controls with respect to end users and end uses; destinations (e.g., Cuba, Iran, North Korea); Commerce Control List determinations;

screening of entities involved in the transaction; hardware, software, and technology controls; re-exports; and release of U.S.-origin technology to foreign nationals. There are significant criminal and civil penalties for the failure to comply with regulatory requirements. For example, Section 404 of the Act requires that the company document every internal and external process that affects corporate earnings [1]. It has been estimated that such costs would exceed $4.6 million for companies with over $5 billion in revenues, but medium-size companies would incur approximately $2 million for compliance. The provisions of SOX clearly intend to apply to non-U.S. companies that have a substantial presence in the United States, especially if their securities are listed in U.S. stock exchanges. The allegedly onerous provisions of the act and its lack of exceptions for companies otherwise regulated by foreign governments have caused significant outcries by the affected companies. They have threatened to delist or will refuse to be listed in U.S. exchanges unless exceptions are granted to them.

17.7 IT Compliance

IT governance is a major aspect of the responsibility of senior officers and members of the board of directors as part of the overall strategies and objectives of the organization. It enables the enterprise to receive, analyze, and incorporate complex data in order to maximize benefits, opportunities, and enable it to compete effectively with other enterprises. In order to accomplish its governance it is necessary that there be a strong IT control environment. The controls are of two key categories, namely, to *prevent* lapses and to *detect* errors and irregularities. The changes should be auditable, authorized, and investigated if they are unauthorized.[1]

There are a number of methodologies that may be utilized to comply with Section 404(a) [5]. The most utilized and is herein suggested is the COSO Internal Control Framework. In October, 1985, the National Commission on Fraudulent Financial Reporting ("Treadway Commission") was formed to study and suggest the implementation of internal control programs. In its initial report of 1987, it encouraged the joining of sponsoring organizations to provide guidance on internal controls. The Committee of Sponsoring Organizations of the Treadway Commission (COSO) was begun. The CPA firm of Coopers & Lybrand was called upon to prepare and issue a report concerning an integrated framework of internal controls. The report was issued in 1992, the key elements of which are summarized hereinafter.

Generally, when IT controls exist within a company, the three major areas of control are:

1. Executive management
2. Business process
3. IT services

Executive Management: SOX, Section 302 and especially Section 404 make senior management responsible for "establishing and maintaining an adequate internal control structure and procedures for financial reporting." Especially in a complex organization, management must set forth the policies and decide how and what resources are to be allocated throughout the organization to assure effective statutory compliance. IT is at the center of maintaining the integrity of reporting all of the complex elements of financial reporting.

Business Process: The business entity sets in place the processes by which value is created and delivered to the entity's stakeholders.

IT Services: It enables the organization to deliver the inputs and outputs of the business processes by its role in network management, database management, storage management, facilities management, and security administration [3].

According to COSO, IT is responsible for:

- Understanding the organization's internal control program and its financial reporting process
- Mapping the IT environment that supports internal control and the financial reporting process
- Identifying risks in the IT systems
- Designing and implementing controls designed to minimize these risks
- Documenting and testing IT systems controls
- Ensuring that IT controls are updated
- Monitoring IT controls for effective operation over time
- Participating in the SOX management office

COSO's five essential elements of effective controls are:

1. *Control environment:* It is the basis for internal control. The factors thereof are integrity, ethical values, management's philosophy and operating style, the assignment of authority and responsibility by management, and the attention and supervision by the board of directors.
2. *Risk assessment:* There is a need to assess the internal and external risks that all companies need to address. The assessment identifies and analyses relevant risks, particularly special risks, to the achievement of company objectives.
3. *Control activities:* They concern the policies and procedures that ensure the carrying out management's directives. They address risks at all levels of the company and include approvals, authorizations, verifications, reconciliations, operating performance, security of assets, and segregation of duties [4].
4. *Information and communication:* Important and pertinent information has to be identified and communicated so that they may be carried out. They include external events, internally generated data, the roles of all persons

within the system, the ability to communicate upstream to management, and communication with all stakeholders.

5. *Monitoring:* It is the process of monitoring internal systems and the quality of performance over time. It is ongoing and includes regular management and supervisory activities.

Companies should use information systems' technology to assist in the internal control compliance. There are two major information systems' organizations that have published guidelines for executives to assess their internal controls: the IT Governance Institute (ITGI) and the Information Systems Audit and Control Association (ISACA). The Treadway Commission indicated that it was not necessary for management to assess all general IT controls but only those relevant to financial reporting. If a company uses proprietary IT frameworks, such as the COSO framework, as a guide for that portion of the assessment report, management should apply reasonable judgment as to the impact that IT systems have on internal control over financial reporting.

Inasmuch as there is no definitive "bright line" guidance to what constitutes effective internal controls, it is proposed that the above-stated COSO guidelines serve as a basis for compliance. The PCAOB adopted, on May 24, 2007, its most recent rule pursuant to this section of the act, Auditing Standard No. 5: An Audit of Internal Control Over Financial Reporting that Is Integrated with an Audit of Financial Statements. The purpose of effective internal control is to identify material weaknesses that may exist and which would impede the reliability of financial reporting and the preparation of financial statements for external purposes. The audit is to make a risk assessment including the determination of significant accounts and disclosures and relevant assertions, the selection of controls to test, and the evidence necessary for a given control.

The audit is to address the risk of fraud, particularly the controls over significant, unusual transactions, especially those that result in late or unusual journal entries. Other fraud assessments concern related party transactions, significant management estimates, journal entries and adjustments, and controls that mitigate incentives for management to falsify financial results. A top-down approach is to be made, starting at the financial statement level and going down to significant accounts and disclosures and their relevant assertions. The auditor is to test the design effectiveness of controls, the operating effectiveness of a control, the relationship of risk to the evidence to be obtained, evaluate identified deficiencies, and form an opinion on the effectiveness of internal control over financial reporting.

17.7.1 CobiT 4.1 Framework

Under the guidance of the IT Governance Institute, Control Objectives for Information and related Technology ("CobiT") presents a framework for good practices based mainly on control in order to optimize IT-enabled investments and provide a mechanism for the determination of erroneous actions. It seeks to provide a link to business requirements, organize IT activities into corporate processes, identify the major IT resources, and identify the management of control objectives. It posits a methodology to measure the achievement and responsibilities of business and IT process owners. The projected users of CobiT are executive management, business management, IT management, and auditors. It divides IT into four domains and 34 processes

There are four domains or elements of the CobiT framework:

1. *Plan and Organize.* This concerns the strategy, tactics, and identification of how ITR can aid in the achievement of business objectives. It seeks to answers questions concerning the alignment of IT and business strategy; whether there has been optimum utilization of resources; whether the organization understands IT objectives; whether IT risks are understood and managed; and whether the quality of IT systems are appropriate for the particular business enterprise.
2. *Acquire and Implement.* This element concerns the identification, development or acquisition, and implementation of IT solutions with the view of meeting business objectives.
3. *Deliver and Support.* IT services are to be delivered in accordance with business priorities, costs optimized, security managed, and a workforce that is able to use the IT systems productively and effectively.
4. *Monitor and Evaluate.* The fourth domain of the framework is the assessment of IT services on a regular basis to determine their effectiveness, regulatory compliance, maintenance of confidentiality and security, as well as integration to meet the business goals of the business concern.

17.7.2 IT Processes: Plan and Organize

The Plan and Organize domain covers the use of information and technology, and how best it can be used in a company to help achieve the company's goals and objectives. It also highlights the organizational and infrastructural form IT is to take in order to achieve the optimal results and to generate the most benefits from the use of IT. The following table lists the IT processes contained in the Planning and Organization domain.[2]

CobiT-proposed Plan and Organize tasks are:

PO1: Define a Strategic IT Plan and Direction
PO2: Define the Information Architecture
PO3: Determine Technological Direction
PO4: Define the IT Processes, Organization, and Relationships
PO5: Manage the IT Investment

PO6: Communicate Management Aims and Direction
PO7: Manage IT Human Resources
PO8: Manage Quality
PO9: Assess and Manage IT Risks
PO10: Manage Projects

17.7.3 IT Processes: *Acquire and Implement*

The Acquire and Implement domain covers identifying IT requirements, acquiring the technology, and implementing it within the company's current business processes. This domain also addresses the development of a maintenance plan that a company should adopt in order to prolong the life of an IT system and its components. The following table lists the IT processes contained in the Acquire and Implement domain.

CobiT proposed Acquire and Implement tasks are:

AI1: Identify Automated Solutions
AI2: Acquire and Maintain Application Software
AI3: Acquire and Maintain Technology Infrastructure
AI4: Enable Operation and Use
AI5: Procure IT Resources
AI6: Manage Changes
AI7: Install and Accredit Solutions and Changes

17.7.4 IT Processes: *Deliver and Support*

The Deliver and Support domain focuses on the delivery aspects of the information technology. It covers areas such as the execution of the applications within the IT system and its results, as well as the support processes that enable the effective and efficient execution of these IT systems. These support processes include security issues and training. The following table lists the IT processes contained in the Deliver and Support domain [3,4].

CobiT-proposed Deliver and Support tasks are:

DS1: Define and Manage Service Levels
DS2: Manage Third-Party Services
DS3: Manage Performance and Capacity
DS4: Ensure Continuous Service
DS5: Ensure Systems Security
DS6: Identify and Allocate Costs
DS7: Educate and Train Users
DS8: Manage Service Desk and Incidents

DS9: Manage the Configuration
DS10: Manage Problems
DS11: Manage Data
DS12: Manage the Physical Environment
DS13: Manage Operations

17.7.5 IT Processes: Monitor and Evaluate

The Monitor and Evaluate domain deals with a company's strategy in assessing the needs of the company and whether or not the current IT system still meets the objectives for which it was designed and the controls necessary to comply with regulatory requirements. Monitoring also covers the issue of an independent assessment of the effectiveness of IT system in its ability to meet business objectives and the company's control processes by internal and external auditors. The following table lists the IT processes contained in the Monitor and Evaluate domain.

CobiT-proposed Monitor and Evaluate tasks are:

ME1: Monitor and Evaluate IT Processes
ME2: Monitor and Evaluate Internal Control
ME3: Ensure Regulatory Compliance
ME4: Provide IT Governance

17.7.6 Integrating COSO and CobiT

The major accounting firms have suggested a number of mechanisms for SOX compliance, some of which have already been noted:

1. A company must have an independent audit committee on its board of directors which, in turn, selects a registered accounting firm to perform the appropriate assessment of internal controls as well as to perform its audit obligations without interference from the board, senior officers, or conflict of interest considerations. Management must play a major role in the implementation of internal controls.

2. A principals-based rather than a rules-based approach should be undertaken by management. A "rules-based approach" is one that is very detailed that attempts ab initio to ascertain possible infractions and unethical practices in order to promote regulations to deal with them. This approach results in the setting forth of numerous regulations, examples, and guidance based on the statute. A "principles-based approach" differs substantially. It seeks to understand the underlying objective of the statute to provide guidance concerning how it is to be implemented. Rather than providing specific guidance or rules for all conceivable situations, it seeks to create a roadmap

of guidance that explains the objective to be achieved and some common examples of implementation.

3. The SEC, pursuant to Section 108(d) of SOX, recommended that a principles-based approach ("objectives-oriented") should have the following characteristics: (1) that it be based on an improved and consistently applied conceptual framework; (2) that it clearly states the accounting objective of the standard; (3) that it be detailed and have a structure so that the standard can be made operational and applied on a consistent basis; (4) it minimizes the use of exceptions from the standard; and (5) avoids bright-line percentage tests that would permit technical observance of the standard while evading the its intent. It cites the SEC's reaffirmation of the evolutionary shift of the Financial Accounting Standards Board (FASB) to objectives-oriented standards.

4. There should be effective internal controls over internet security systems. These systems play a major role in integrating compliance under SOX. Companies have spent close to $2 billion presently on security management. The CobIT and ITGI systems can be customized to a company's needs and can be used for authentication, password management, input validation, logging, data storage, monitoring controls, application development and other related purposes [3].

5. A risk management system program should be in place that is understood and implemented by the board and audit committee at the company.

6, The internal control system should be companywide including out-of-country divisions to prevent lack of adherence because information is hidden in one part of the company, such as the finance department, and unknown and available to other departments.

17.7.7 Internal Controls for Small Business

Historically, small firms have generally been permitted to exercise compliance with statutory standards in a more relaxed way. Thus, under the Securities Act of 1933, the SEC has exempted small firms from the strict dictates of the statute and from its regulations. Small firms have expressed their dismay concerning the potential costs of compliance with SOX. The SEC acknowledges that the costs and burdens of assessing and complying with the reporting requirements on internal control over financial reporting may create a disproportionate burden on the firms. Thus, in its Staff Statement on Management Report of 2005, it created the Securities and Exchange Commission Advisory Committee on Smaller Public Companies to consider such costs and burdens. It also requested and received compliance with COSO to establish and develop additional guidance on applying its framework for internal control to smaller companies. Pending revision and relaxation of SOX requirements for smaller entities, the requirements recited throughout this chapter must also be observed.

17.8 International Responses

International responses have been rather mixed. Nearly half (44%) of executive management felt that SOX and the regulations issued by the Securities and Exchange Commission (SEC) would have little effect while 43% held the opposite view. The major complaints concerned the "noisy withdrawal statute" and the executive certification requirements. As a result of European complaints, a few of the regulations have been relaxed as to foreign companies and non-U.S. lawyers practicing primarily abroad. Nevertheless, European countries and, more particularly, the companies located there, are rebelling against the U.S. requirements. Specifically, there is increasing resentment at the pressure, costs, legal exposure, and possible violation of European law by attempting compliance with SOX.

Thus, companies are considering delisting or not listing their securities on U.S. stock exchanges. Inasmuch as there are some 470 non-U.S. companies listed on U.S. exchanges with a total capitalization of $3.8 trillion, the costs of compliance in some cases exceed $30–40 million as estimated by BASF, the German chemicals producer. Rank Entertainment Group and British Telecom are considering delisting even though SOX required statutory compliance where there are 300 or more shareholders in the U.S. Fugro, a Netherlands-based engineering consulting firm, with a turnover of $1.2 billion (one third in the United States) said that SOX ended any hopes that the company would list its securities in the United States. The chairman of the International Corporate Governance Network and a senior adviser to Morgan Stanley said that SOX would cause Europe to become a haven for global public offerings. In addition, whereas a company had to be listed in order to gain access to U.S. capital markets, today, with the deregulation of global markets, the need to have a U.S. exchange presence is less attractive.

The EU lodged a series of complaints with respect to the promulgation and enforcement of SOX. The overall complaint was the extraterritoriality provisions of the statute, which was reminiscent of the bitterness caused by the extraterritorial enforcement of the U.S. antitrust laws during the 1950s–1970s. Among the complaints by EU finance ministers were the U.S. authorities' compulsion of access to the audit papers, including working papers; the SEC's grant of only a 30-day comment period for its impending regulations; and the subjecting of European audit firms to double oversight by both European member states and by the U.S. If there is a reference to another auditor's report by the principal auditor, then that other auditor's report must also be included in the filing.

The EU finance ministers' additional complaint, coupled with a threat, concerned the need for foreign firms to register with the PCAOB. The EU said that it already has established equivalent registration requirements for all member states, and that compelling these firms to register with the PCAOB would be unnecessarily duplicative and expensive. Thus, it called for mutual recognition and equivalence of registration or else the EU may not be able to avoid reciprocity of member states, which may require U.S. firms to similarly register with the 25 member states in which they may provide auditing services. Furthermore, the costs for registration by small EU auditing firms would be heavy and would exceed that of domestic U.S. firms.

The EU further noted that the PCAOB rules conflict directly with EU and national laws of member states. There were a number of examples given to illustrate the conflict of laws difficulty. In a memorandum to the SEC Chairman, the EU asked for an exemption under Section 106(c) of SOX claiming that the PCAOB's proposal is "ineffective," "unnecessary," "disproportionate in that it involves significant costs of registration for EU audit firms with a relatively small number of U.S. issuers," likely to cause distortions of the market for audit services …, " and is "prejudicial to future EU policy making on audit issues."

Some criticisms were more temperate. The U.K. banking industry, while recognizing the right and goal of the United States to restore investor confidence by measures such as SOX, nevertheless expressed its concern over regulations on companies that are already subject to equivalent or superior measures in their home states. The complaint is not only that of duplication but also may involve compliance with conflicting regulations. It also respected U.S. regulations concerning raising capital in the United States from domestic and foreign sources, but the United States should not hold itself as being the sole determinant of such rules when other governmental authorities are equally competent to assure appropriate regulatory regulations. Specifically, the U.K. banking industry has suggested compromise concerning Sections 301, 302, 401, and 402 of SOX.

With respect to Section 301, concerning the composition of audit committees, the EU published a report concerning the Comparative Study of Corporate Governance Codes of member states and found the U.K.'s Combined Code to be widely adhered to and, though voluntary, compliance is a requirement under its Listing Rules of the Financial Services Authority. Among the standards discussed are the auditing standards and accounting issues. The United Kingdom, particularly after Enron and other debacles in the United States and its own corporate scandals, has evolved standards that negate the need for enforcement of SOX standards. With respect to Section 302, certification of accounts, the concern is that of duplication, ambiguity, and possible conflict with U.K. requirements. Under the U.K. Combined Code, the Board of Directors has specific responsibility to maintain a sound system of internal controls to safeguard shareholders' investments and company assets. At a minimum, an annual review by directors is mandated, and a report to the shareholders is required. There are also additional proposals for further requirements of directors' duties and extension of obligations to auditors with possible criminal penalties for noncompliance.

In regard to Section 401 rules concerning disclosures of off-balance-sheet transactions, the problem is that accounting and disclosure rules differ considerably between U.S. and U.K. GAAP. Whereas U.S. GAAP rules are detailed and require compliance to the letter of the rules, the U.K. GAAP looks to the principles and substance rather than to the legal form. The United Kingdom requires that in the examination of a transaction "all its aspects and implications should be identified and greater weight given to those more likely to have a commercial effect in practice. A group of series of transactions that achieves or is designed to achieve an overall commercial effect should be viewed as a whole." The substance of a quasi-subsidiary's transactions of an entity should also be reported in consolidated financial statements. Section 402 rules forbid loans to directors and employees with the exception of loans made or maintained by depository institutions subject to Federal Reserve Board restrictions, a restriction not extended to foreign entities. It is the view of the U.K. Bankers' Association that such failure is anticompetitive.

Not all commentators abroad have written or espoused highly negative commentaries concerning SOX. One commentator suggested that SOX is compelling European governments, legislators, and regulators to modernize their long overdue overhauling of oversights structures of accountants and corporate governance. SOX has facilitated the efforts of EU Commissioners to modernize market supervision, accounting oversight, and corporate governance. Fritz Bolkenstein, the EU Commissioner for Internal Market and Taxation, stated that the EU was faced with the choice of either engaging in a major dispute with the U.S., as exemplified by the debate over the Iraq War, or to find a constructive way of moving forward to the benefit of both arenas while considering the different traditions and culture. The choice of the latter was exacerbated by the Parmalat fraud and its complicity by the several professions. The need for corporate governance reform is evidenced by the EU's new Corporate Governance Action Plan. Neither area can ignore the demands and needs of the other. Of all capital raised by EU equity issuers, 15% was from U.S. investors; purchases and sales of foreign securities by U.S. investors rose from $53 billion in 1980 to $6.6 trillion in 2003, while foreign investors bought and sold $30.9 trillion U.S. securities (up from $198 billion in 1980).

Bolkestein noted the enormous task of the EU in created a single financial market among the now 25 member states, each of which has its own internal laws and regulations. The problem has been exacerbated by the adoption of SOX with its sizeable complex rules. His suggested solution is to engage in a constructive financial markets dialogue with U.S. regulators to address EU concerns. He expressed his growing impatience with the U.S. especially as the EU–U.S. conflict was not raised under the World Trade Organization's General Agreement on Trade in Services (GATS). Thus, there is a need for cooperation on three fronts: (1) cooperation daily or weekly concerning financial services and markets regulatory issues; (2) convergence on common principles and understandings rather than an identical approach but with the same goal of investor protection (the convergence on International Accounting Standards and U.S. GAAP is an example of such cooperation); and (3) regulatory equivalence rather than one standard as promulgated by the United States, whether it concerns auditing, disclosure standards, market stability, or other such issues. The need for cooperation is immense, given the volume of transaction and peoples involved on both continents.

17.9 Advantages to SOX Compliance

Although there have been significant complaints concerning compliance by foreign companies with SOX, nevertheless, it appears that it is advantageous for these companies to conform to the stringent rules of the act. The main advantage is the greater ease in seeking public financing. The full transparent disclosure appears to assuage any lingering doubts about a company's financial well-being. Compliant public and voluntarily compliant companies appear to have a competitive advantage over noncompliant companies that remain private so that SOX is not applicable. Some one-fourth of private companies, mainly larger companies, have voluntarily adopted SOX best practices in order to attract public financing and position themselves for the issuance of future IPOs or for possible mergers with publicly financed companies. The large majority of private companies, nevertheless, oppose SOX mainly because of the cost of compliance and because of its alleged impediment to profitable growth.

17.10 Foreign Whistleblowers and SOX

SOX provides protection to whistleblowers. Specifically, it provides in Section 301(4) that each audit committee is to establish procedures for "(A) the receipt, retention, treatment of complaints received by the issuer regarding accounting, internal accounting controls, or auditing matters; and (B) the confidential, anonymous submission by employees of the issuer of concerns regarding questionable accounting or auditing matters." The problem is that the information provided may concern data concerning other employees which, in turn, may violate the EU privacy laws. The SEC has refused to grant foreign companies exemption from this statutory requirement. Item 8.1 of SOX's registration form provides that companies agree to provide information at any time in the future. Such agreement may violate the EU statute. Are foreign whistleblowers protected by SOX? The answer appears to be "No!" The laws, regulations, and court decisions of the country where the whistle blowing takes place would apply to the issues at hand.

17.10.1 Working Papers

The provision of Article 106(b) requiring access to working papers flies in the face of contrary provisions and prohibitions with EU national professional secrecy laws. Many of the EU member states provide that working papers may only be given to their courts, a provision that may not be waived. In France, Article L225-240 of the French Commercial Code requires secrecy by auditors, but access may be granted access to French authorities. Finland has a similar provision. In Denmark and Belgium, the unauthorized handing over of working papers of a client is a criminal offense.

There are strict limitations to the collection, use, and disclosure of personal information. In a French court decision on November 21, 2005, Group McDonald's France was denied a request by the company to put into place a procedure for certain high-level employees to voluntarily and anonymously report on alleged wrongful behavior by coworkers. The La Commission nationale de l'informatique et es libertes (the French Data Protection Authority or CNIL) stated that, although the SOX requirement was not per se invalid, nevertheless, employers would have to comply with eleven guidelines or limitations. The difficulty is that the SOX provision appears to conflict with the French Data Protection Act of January 6, 1978 as amended and the EU Directive on Data Protection.

17.11 Reconciling SOX and European Conflicting Standards

Although European companies and regulators have bitterly complained about the extraterritoriality of SOX's provisions, nevertheless, there are significant attempts to reconcile their differences. The need for reconciliation is evident by the degree of cross-border investments both to and from the United States to Europe. Among the efforts at a not unfriendly reconciliation are the U.S.–EU Financial Markets Regulatory Dialogue, which is an informal discussion of U.S. and EU regulatory approaches, developments, and timetables. It brings together experts from the Federal Reserve and their counterparts of the European Commission, particularly with respect to banking operations. It has been estimated that, as of September 30, 2003, there were 34 U.S. banking organizations in the EU with third-party assets of over $747 billion; the sums are much greater today. There were 68 EU banking organizations operating in the United States with third-party banking assets of $937 billion. The regulatory dialogue has served to diffuse tensions concerning SOX between the two entities.

A major effort that was well received in EU capitals is that of the former chairman of the U.S. Securities and Exchange Commission, William H. Donaldson, who expressed his and the SEC's commitment to engaging in a constructive dialogue to assure friendly cooperation in an endeavor to safeguard the integrity of corporate governance. He noted that, although SOX addressed corporate malfeasance that occurred among U.S. enterprises, nevertheless, Europe has had its own series of major corporate scandals, which include Parmalat, Vivendi, Hoolinger, Ahold, Adecco, TV Azteca, Royal Dutch Shell, Seibu, China Aviation, and other scandals. Thus, it is in the best interests of both the United States. and the EU to restore shareholder confidence in the integrity of the marketplace. There is a need for global cooperation to raise standards in all of the many markets on a worldwide basis. Although acknowledging the complaints of the rise in cost of capital as a result of SOX, it should be noted that the costs come with major benefits. Inasmuch as nearly half of all of the world's equity shares, by market capitalization, are traded in the United States, non-U.S. investors have approximately $4.5 trillion invested in U.S. securities.

Donaldson emphasized that the United States, under SOX, enables a registered company to signal to others that it is committed to the highest audit reporting and governance standards. Nevertheless, he assured European regulators that the United States is fully committed to working together to address the legitimate complaints of European regulators. Thus, the SEC has taken a number of steps to avoid have companies engaged in unnecessary and costly duplication of reporting standards. SOX requires that all members of audit committees be independent directors. The issue arose that German corporate governance have dual board systems that require corporate audit committees to include a labor representative. Inasmuch as SEC rules hold that employees of an issuer are not "independent," there was an inherent conflict between SOX and German regulations. After a dialogue between the SEC and the EU, the former was given assurance that labor representatives in issuer audit committees are independent and, accordingly, the SEC provided an exception to its prior position.

Two other examples of U.S. and EU cooperation are the exemption for companies publishing financial information outside the U.S. that were not in accord with U.S. GAAP and the accommodation made to foreign issuers with respect to the information requested by the U.S. Public Company Accounting Oversight Board (PCAOB) that may violate foreign privacy laws and blocking statutes. Thus, the PCAOB is engaging in a collaborative approach to reconcile its oversight role with the laws and regulations governing foreign issuers. Other accommodations include the extension of deadlines for filing requirements, reconciliation of reporting standards, and other efforts.

17.12 EU Corporate Governance Initiatives

Among the reasons for EU opposition to SOX is its own attempts to deal with European corporate scandals. In 2003, reacting to both U.S. and comparable behavior by a number of European-based companies, the EU Commission developed the program "Modernizing Company Law and Enhancing Corporate Governance in the European Union—A Plan to Move Forward." It proposed the enhancement of corporate governance structure. In a company's annual corporate governance statement, listed companies should state the key elements of their corporate governance structure, which should include the operation of their shareholder meetings and key powers, the composition of the board and its committees, the shareholders possessing major holdings and voting rights, material transactions with other related parties, and the existence and nature of a risk management system. Shareholders' rights are to be strengthened by being granted access to information by electronic means, the right to vote in absentia and by electronic means, and the establishment of real shareholder democracy.

The board of directors should be modernized by removal from voting, in favor of nonexecutive or supervisory directors, those board members with conflicts of interest, such as remuneration of directors and supervision of audit accounts; the creation of a one-tier board structure with executive and nonexecutive members, or a two-tier structure with managing directors and supervisory directors; granting a special investigation right to shareholders to ask a court to investigate the affairs of a company; imposition of a directors' disqualification for misleading financial and other misconduct; and the development of a wrongful trading rule that would hold directors personally responsible for a company's failure and due to the conduct or lack of action.

Groups and pyramids of companies would be compelled to provide complete information and disclosure regarding their structure and intragroup relations, as well as better financial and nonfinancial information. In the Annex to the EU Plan, it described the specific steps and timetables for member state actions and preferred types of initiatives. There were Short-Term (2003-2005) steps, Medium-Term steps (2006-2008), and Long-Term (2009 and thereafter).

17.13 E.U.'s Eighth Directive

The enactment of the Eighth Directive[3] by the European Union,[4] however, appears to have lessened the intensity of the anguish over restrictive provisions of SOX inasmuch as the directive appears to contain many articles that emulate SOX. A brief comparison of SOX and the E.U.'s Eighth Directive illustrates the remarkable similarities as well as the differences between the two enactments.

> *Similarities.* The major issues confronting potential registrants concern the sizeable costs, disclosures, and conflicts that may arise by their compliance with either the requirements of SOX or the E.U. Directive or with both entities. It becomes less clear that the SOX requirements are more onerous than those requirements that are now mandated by the E.U. The similarities are evident: registration requirements for auditors and audit firms; the requirement of ethical behavior, independence, and objectivity;
>
> *Dissimilarities.* Unlike the centralization of responsibility in the PCAOB in the United States, the E.U. has left the responsibility of compliance with the member states. Theoretically, the E.U. Commission could enforce compliance by instituting an action against a non-compliant Member State but it is clear that registration and all other mandates are to be carried out by the current 27 Member States. Major differences between SOX and the EU 8th Directive and major audit requirements are provided in Table 17.1.

Table 17.1 U.S.-E.U. Audit Requirements

	U.S. Sarbanes–Oxley Act	*EU Eighth Directive*
Purposes	Protect investors by informative, accurate, independent audits	Harmonization of statutory audit requirements by member states
Oversight	Public Company Accounting Oversight Board (PCAOB)	Member states to create oversight system for statutory auditors
Registration	Every accounting firm engaging in auditing for covered entity must register with PCAOB	Member States must set up system for approval and registration of statutory auditors and audit firms
Ethical requirements, quality control, and independence	PCAOB sets standards; registered firms to maintain work papers for 7 years, second-partner review, auditor's testing of internal control structure	Member states ensure compliance with professional ethical standards, independence , rotation of key partners after 7 years
Approval and education requirements	Left to states to specify educational requirements but each state requires university training and practical training	Member states to require educational and testing, university or equivalent level schooling and practical training
Inspections of registered accounting firms	PCAOB conducts annual inspections for firms auditing over 100 issuers and triennially of 100 or less issuers	Member states assure compliance with international auditing standards as published in EU's official journal
Public company audit committees	Audit committee of board of directors selects auditor and is independent of board	Shareholders select statutory auditors/firm but Member states may provide other methods

Continued

Table 17.1   U.S.-E.U. Audit Requirements (*Continued*)

	U.S. Sarbanes–Oxley Act	*EU Eighth Directive*
Required signatures of audit report	CEO and CFO certify review of report, that it does not contain false information, and is accurate in all material respects	Audit report signed by at least the statutory auditor who conducted audit on behalf of audit firm. Signature may be kept confidential
Investigations and disciplinary proceedings	PCAOB investigates and imposes penalties; may inspect books and records of audit firm; can suspend firm and may refer for criminal prosecution	Member state to promulgate effective system of investigations for detect, correction, and prevention of improper audits and may impose penalties
Confidentiality	PCAOB to keep all documents, information, and board deliberation confidential with exceptions to governmental authorities	Member states are to ensure confidentiality of all information with exceptions for enforcement and discipline
Disclosure of annual reports	Annual and quarterly reports are public through SEC's EDGAR system	Member states ensure auditors publish detailed statutory audits annually
International Applications	Foreign public accounting firms subject to SOX as domestic firms and must furnish work papers on demand	Member states determine approval of non-EU Member states auditor and may impose reciprocity requirements
Foreign application and cooperation with third countries	Cooperation by treaty but affected foreign firm must consent to cooperation	Cooperation is permitted by member states with detailed conditions

Table 17.1   U.S.-E.U. Audit Requirements (*Continued*)

	U.S. Sarbanes–Oxley Act	*EU Eighth Directive*
Accounting standards	PCAOB may recognize accounting principles by a standard setting body funded in part by SOX	All statutory audits to be carried out in accordance with international auditing standards
Report	SEC and Comptroller General to conduct study of auditing	EU Commission is to present report of impact of Directive
Language	English	Language of member state

17.14 Planning IT Management for SOX: Delayed SOX Impact

By now many people, especially in the information security field, have heard of the Enron scandal and start understanding the Sarbanes–Oxley Act of 2002 (SOX). Nobody any longer needed to read Eichenwald's lengthy book, or any other books on similar scandals, to know more about Enron. People just started developing their own stories about Enron. There is indeed great good that came from the Enron accounting scandal, originating at SOX but leading to other new corporate and information security governance trends resulting from SOX evolution. Trying to ignore current media reports about the greed of CEOs who attempted to plan to take full advantage of Obama's bailout of more than $800 billion, I am still hopeful that SOX would scare those greedy executives from allocating taxpayers' bailout assistance money to their private jets and luxury life for CEOs and their relatives.

The jury is still out on Citigroup, which has just accepted $45 billion in taxpayer funds to keep itself alive. Nevertheless, Citigroup planned to spend $50 million on a new corporate jet, a French-made Dassault Falcon 7X, as reported in the *New York Post*.

The big three auto CEOs "flew to the nation's capital in private luxurious jets" to make their case to Washington that the auto industry is running out of cash and needs $25 billion in taxpayer money to avoid bankruptcy.

President Obama promised to impose more restrictions on future bailout money to prevent it from being used for such things as Wall Street bonuses. Obama explained, before a meeting with Congressional leaders at the White House, that there has been a lack of accountability and transparency in how we are managing some of these programs to stabilize the financial system. There have been reports that John Thain, the former Merrill Lynch & Co. chief executive officer, spent $1.2

million redecorating his downtown Manhattan office last year as the company was firing employees.

Thain just lately oversaw the sale of Merrill Lynch to Bank of America. Merrill's $15.4 billion fourth-quarter loss forced Bank of America to seek additional aid from the U.S. government, which agreed to provide $20 billion in capital and $118 billion in asset guarantees.

Despite SOX, which is obviously related but not directly related to those scandals, corporate arrogance, executive inattention, and bad intentions, CFO greed, pervasive conflict of interest, and accountants' malicious games, all seem to continue. Enron's fiasco is an example of accountants' and lawyers' malicious games. This has involved the United States Securities and Exchange Commission's approval of an aggressive, and obviously inappropriate to its uses by Enron, form of accounting by Enron called "mark to market," coupled with a series of CFO-owned limited partnerships that were used to divest significant quantities of Enron debt and, in stealthy ways, vest it back to Enron itself. Enron's accounting firm, Arthur Anderson, was indebted to its client for significant fees from accounting and consulting services in order to create additional conflicts of interest. And, blindly, any complaints from whistleblowers had to be dismissed by senior Enron management. And at times of impasses, every intelligent bit of information is destroyed when all documents are shredded according to the Anderson rule of not retaining accounting work papers, and despite U.S. Supreme Court assertion that such an activity is simply criminal.

Following Enron, Congress faced a chain of other companies that had to be indicted for fraud. These include HeathSouth, Adelphia, Tyco, WorldComm, Quest Communications, and Global Crossing. In each of these cases, it is alleged that senior management participated in events that led to the misstatement of earnings and the deception of investors.

The Sarbanes–Oxley Act imposes significant accounting and control requirements on U.S. publicly owned companies (and probably on foreign companies which are either traded on U.S. exchanges or which make up a significant part of a U.S. company's financial reporting). Thus, the new law, which was signed on July 30, 2002, directly addresses the Enron scandal by, for example, establishing records retention requirements for audit papers, creating a new oversight board for accounting firms auditing publicly traded companies (PCAOB), mandating auditor independence, mandating corporate responsibility and accountability at publicly traded companies, reducing conflicts of interests of financial analysts, providing protections for whistleblowers, and imposing new criminal penalties relating to fraud, conspiracy, and interfering with investigations.

In all of this, the most important concept related to SOX is the assurance of financial information reporting. The relationship to SOX of information security is that this latter aims at enhancing the accuracy, the availability, the reliability, and the integrity of financial information. How can we, therefore, entrust SOX and motivate public agencies to comply with the totality of the standard?

Section 302 states that the chief executive officer (CEO) and chief financial officer (CFO) must personally certify that financial reports are accurate and complete. They must also assess and report on the effectiveness of internal controls around financial reporting.[3] This section clearly places responsibility for accurate financial reporting on the highest level of corporate management. CEOs and CFOs now face the potential for criminal fraud liability.[4] It is noteworthy that Section 302 does not specifically list which internal controls must be assessed.

Section 404 states that a corporation must assess the effectiveness of its internal controls and report this assessment annually to the SEC. The assessment must also be reviewed and judged by an outside auditing firm. [1]

The impact of Section 404 is substantial in that a large amount of resources are needed for compliance. A comprehensive review of all internal controls related to financial reporting may be difficult and lengthy. SOX obviously cannot be achieved without effective information security. There are many security standards and best practices that may be of great assistance to SOX implementations. NIST provide many standards that are very valuable in security planning and security auditing. Examples are FIPS 199, FIPS 200, NIST SP 800-18, NIST SP 800-53, etc. The ISO 27001, ISO 27002 (same as ISO 17799), BS 25999, and many other international security standards may also be very useful [4].

The Institute of Internal Auditors has published a presentation; the SANS Institute, and the United States General Accounting Office also provide a great literature that may be a good source of financial information assurance. The Community Emergency Response Team (CERT) programs also provide assistance to respond to emergency situations in the business communities.

17.15 Conclusion

The impact of SOX on foreign registrants has been mixed. The positive aspects noted by foreign registrants include the restoration of investor confidence in the light of the major corporate scandals both in the United States and abroad; the need for effective internal controls; and the effect on corporate governance; improved vigilance by boards of directors who previously were too often passive; the requirement of financial experts on audit committees; the uniformity of standards for corporations and their subsidiaries; the active dialogue and engagement of advisers; the compelling of companies to reexamine their internal auditing and other financial practices; and the creation of a governmental board to oversee auditing by accounting firms. The negative aspects have been the need for alleged extraordinary effort and cost to comply with the statute; the compelling of restatement of earnings; the great increase in insurance costs for board insurance; and the failure to recognize the auditing standards of foreign companies that are equal to or were greater than that provided by SOX.

17.16 Review Questions

1. How are NIST and ISO IT standards related to SOX?
2. Define the legal methods of doing business. Explain the main differences.
3. Explain what Sarbanes–Oxley Act of 2002 is, and how it all started.
4. Explain major provisions of SOX and give examples.
5. Explain how IT compliance works and give examples.
6. Explain how the international community responded to SOX. Distinguish among main areas of opinion in Europe.
7. Explain major advantages to SOX compliance.
8. Explain how to reconcile SOX and European Conflicting Standards. Give examples as needed.
9. Discuss the EU Corporate Governance Initiatives. Any known standards?
10. Explain how the EU's Eighth Directive compares to SOX.
11. Explain how SOX is currently evolving with respect to IT security management [2].
12. Do any of Obama's financial bailouts have anything to do with SOX deficiencies? Explain.

17.17 Workshops

Workshop 1

Consider a public agency that is created by the government to audit public agencies with budgets higher than $50 million to certify them against SOX. You are hired by the government to write a comprehensive policy that incorporates SOX in such a way that if the agency is internally audited and certified against its own policy it is automatically compliant with SOX. Produce an audit methodology that is cost-effective in asserting an organization's compliance with SOX.

Workshop 2

Develop a risk methodology for the purpose of mitigating risks associated with SOX. Apply your methodology in determining when public agencies have to initiate their SOX compliance projects. How often the agency needs to check for SOX compliance and under what conditions SOX compliance become an emergency?

Endnotes

1. See Dan Swanson, *Keeping Up Your SOX Compliance and Turning IT into a High Performer by Improving Change Control,* Tripwire, Inc. (2006).
2. Wikipedia, http://en.wikipedia.org/wiki/COBIT.

3. *Directive 2006/43/EC of the European Parliament and of the Council of 17 May 2006 on statutory audits of annual accounts and consolidated accounts.* The directive replaced the Eighth Council Directive 84/253/EEC of April 10, 1984 that concerned the approval of persons responsible for carrying out the statutory audits of accounting documents.
4. The European Union is composed of 27 member states as of 2007. They are as follows in the order of accession: the initial six states (Belgium, France, Italy, Luxembourg, Netherlands, and West Germany), followed by three added states (Denmark, Ireland, and the United Kingdom), Greece, Portugal, Spain, Austria, Finland, Sweden, Cyprus, Czech Republic, Estonia, Hungary, Latvia, Lithuania, Malta, Poland, Slovakia, Slovenia, and, as of January 1, 2007, Bulgaria and Romania. Other potential future member states who are in accession negotiations, candidate country, or potential candidate countries are Croatia, Turkey, Republic of Macedonia, Albania, Bosnia and Herzegovina, Montenegro, and Serbia. http://en.wikipedia.org/wiki/List_of_European_Union_member_states_by_accession.

References

1. American Institute of Certified Public Accountants, Inc, SOX Section 404: Responding to an Adverse Report—A Checklist for the Audit Committee, New York, 2005, http://www.aicpa.org/Audcommctr/spotlight/SOX_Section_404.htm, By AICPA Staff.
2. Sabet, R. V., The Real Deal with Sarbanes–Oxley: Perspectives for the Security Manager 2004, https://www.vericept.com/Downloads/NewsArticles/TheRealDealWithSarbanesOxley3_04.pdf.
3. SECURITY AND IDENTITY Novell: Business White Paper, Security and Identity: A Winning Approach to Sarbanes–Oxley Compliance: How Integrated IT Controls and Monitoring Help Organizations Succeed in Controlling the Cost of Compliance, http://www.novell.com/collateral/4621384/4621384.pdf.
4. Swanson, D, *Keeping Up Your SOX Compliance and Turning IT into a High Performance by Improving Change Control*, Tripwire, Inc., 2006.
5. The Institute of Internal Auditors, *Sarbanes–Oxley Section 404: A guide for management by internal controls practitioners*, 2nd edition, January 2008.

Chapter 18

Cyberterrorism and Homeland Security

Learning Objectives

After reading this chapter, students are expected to achieve an understanding of:

Security economic intelligence and how it works
What homeland security is
How cyberterrorism is covered in the literature
The purposes and types of terrorism
The means used to accomplish terrorist activities
The forms of cyberattacks
How real the danger of cyberterrorism is
The benefits perpetrators hope to gain from cyberterrorism
How we are combating cyberterrorism
How the FBI sees cyberterrorism
How legislative enactments and proposed programs work
What U.S. criminal statutes affect the Internet
What statutes and executive orders concerned with cyberterrorism
  exist
What international initiatives exist
How individual European state approaches to security and counter-
  terrorism vary

18.1 Introduction

Technological advances have brought significant benefits to society, but there have always been negative aspects too. The Internet is a recent technological innovation that has transformed the lives of people as much as the revolution initiated by the Gutenberg press. It has made knowledge accessible to a degree never previously experienced: at one's fingertips sitting at home or in an office. Nevertheless, it is also associated with dangers that may be minor in nature or have the potential of causing death or serious injury to the population on a universal basis. Computer systems globally have become interconnected and, as a result, have become much more vulnerable to attack. The fears regarding vulnerability appeared to have been borne out by the terrorist attacks on the New York World Trade Center on September 11, 2001, which led to extensive media coverage concerning the possibility of not only physical attacks but also possible widespread virtual attacks. Among the fears is the possibility that critical infrastructures now relying on the Internet, including energy, finance, transportation, and other essential services, may become subject to terrorist attacks.[1] The United States has taken the potential dangers seriously. On December 1, 2006, it warned of the possible threat by al-Qaeda to the U.S. online stock market and banking services.[2]

The Internet is bringing us closer and closer, but at a great price. Our security is the price. The international community is seized of the urgent need to secure cyberspace, as is clear from the multiplicity of security standards and national schemes interpreting them beyond borders: ISO 15408, ISO 17799, and ISO 27001.

Some countries, including the Security Big Six (SB6), are equipped with security books and may feel relatively safe, but this sense of security is misplaced as long as they share their networks with entities of less security.

The standards impose security best practices and system specifications for the development of information security management systems. Partners beyond borders have to be secure as well for all entities connected to the partnership to remain secure. Unfortunately, there is no way to verify the continuous security of partners without periodic security auditing and certification; members who do not comply should be expelled from the partnership. This concept also applies to cyberspace or the electronic society. In order to protect our society from cybercrimes and cyberterrorism, we need to impose strict security policies and enforce them in a cooperative manner.

18.2 Security Economic Intelligence

Security Economic Intelligence (SEI) mainly addresses organizations and countries that crave for up-to-date security information to make the best security decisions, in terms of disaster recovery planning, business continuity, and homeland security, in a framework of a defined security strategy. Unfortunately, while this concept is very well defined for all SB6 countries (the United States, Canada, the United Kingdom, France, Germany, and the Netherlands), the rest of the world is still lagging behind and has no feasible way to know more or to even assemble the resources to process the security knowledge they seek and act upon. Reasons for failure of the SEI concept in non-SB6 countries include the following:

Lack of sharing for useful security knowledge
Imposed security standards
Imposed security certifications
Nonexportability of useful security solutions
Infeasibility of acting uninformed, that is, acting without information

While the purpose of global computing and Internet power is to share useful knowledge, it seems wrong that the most useful knowledge of all, that is, the security knowledge without which these technologies will be of no use, cannot be shared by all. One sees, instead, endless security standards and certifications that have become barriers for those who cannot afford it, such as many of the non-SB6 countries, which continue to lag behind.

Moreover, the SB6 countries do not export their security solutions and do not share their security economic intelligence with non-SB6 countries in which security economic intelligence is not available, except perhaps with a few friendly nations. Without security economic intelligence, however, the only alternative is to act uninformed, that is, act without information. Unfortunately, uninformed security decisions may do more harm than good.

While economic intelligence relates more to foreign economic resources, activities, and policies, including the production, distribution, and consumption of goods and services, labor, finance, taxation, commerce, trade, and other aspects of the international economic system, we mainly target that intelligence that cope with security resources in terms of data, information, and knowledge, activities, technology, and infrastructure needed to provide for the security of the country. The security intelligence [3] sought will aid in developing and implementing a security strategy that sets strategic directives and strategic, functional, and operational plans for the following main goals:

Business continuity
Disaster recovery
Homeland security

> Strategy is the great work of the organization. In situations of life or death, it is the Tao of survival or extinction. Its study cannot be neglected.
>
> **Sub Tzu [7]**

Figure 18.1 Phases for the development of a national security strategy.

We do not intend to study how to use security economic intelligence in developing a security strategy for a nation or its organizations, as this is beyond the scope of this chapter; we emphasize the fact that this new concept is at the core of any national security strategy, and it also remains a sequential supportive process for all phases of the security strategy, as shown in Figure 18.1.

18.2.1 Imposed Infeasibility of Security

Even if you have all the time and money in the world to read the great mass of security literature, conform to the never-ending list of standards, buy the best from the endless collection of security solutions on the market, and obtain the security certifications [6] needed to satisfy partners' requirements, government requirements, and local, regional, and international standards, your security cannot be guaranteed.

Because of all the imposed infeasibility constraints we described earlier, as shown in Figure 18.2, it will be very difficult for a non-SB6 country to afford the cost of devising implementable strategies to protect its infrastructures, businesses, and national security. There are simply too many security standards (infosyssec,

Figure 18.2 Imposed infeasibility of security.

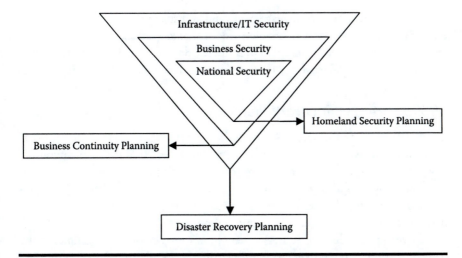

Figure 18.3   Implementable security strategic components.

2007) to conform to, too many security certifications to comply with and, obviously, too many security controls to implement for adequate security.

In addition to the imposed infeasibility constraints, progress toward the ultimate goal of global computing and sharing of computing and information resources across borders is being slowed down by the new cyberspace laws, which are slowly populating but start refraining the still slow flow of productive Internet. Of course, the bad Internet (use for crimes, terrorism, porn, and so on) is already beyond our sense of command.

Let us delineate our insecurity and depict a simple plan (Figure 18.3) that will meet obvious security needs, something that all countries, including non-SB6 countries, can apply.

18.2.2 Business Continuity Planning

Business continuity is the ability of an organization to respond to disaster or business disruption through the timely detection of the disruption event, the accurate measurement of risks and business losses, and the efficient resumption of business operations.

The National Fire Protection Association (NFPA), defined business continuity as follows [4]:

> Business Continuity is an ongoing process supported by senior management and funded to ensure that the necessary steps are taken to identify the impact of potential losses, maintain viable recovery strategies, recovery plans, and continuity of services (NFPA 1600, 2007).

This definition requires that management fund and support the business continuity effort. Business continuity is an ongoing process that keeps track of all possible losses and their impacts on the organization. It is also responsible for maintaining viable safeguards capable of an effective and quick recovery and continuity of business services.

18.2.3 Disaster Recovery Planning

Disaster recovery is the activity of resuming computing operations after a disaster such as floods, severe storms, or geologic incidents. Restoring the computing environment is often achieved through the duplication of computing operations. Disaster recovery is also concerned with routine off-site backup that IT functions migrate to in case a disaster occurs. as well as procedures for activating vital information systems [5] in a safer computing environment.

The quality of a disaster recovery system is measured by the organization's ability to recover information systems quickly after a disaster. While a good disaster recovery system allows the organization to have its computing operations running immediately after the occurrence of the disaster, with a poor disaster recovery system the organization may take several days, or forever, to restore its computing environment.

The scope of the design of a disaster recovery plan depends on many factors, including the type of the incident, data affected, and business losses. The recovery from a disaster attempts to reestablish a computing environment configuration that can produce acceptable business operating conditions.

The World Trade Center in New York was attacked on September 11, 2001, and a large number of businesses in New York, the United States, and in the world were affected. Recoveries from a disaster of such magnitude have been slow and very costly. Some businesses have never recovered from this disaster until today. The literature [4] reports that the cost of business interruptions for the World Trade Center attacks reached between $35 billion and $70 billion.

The undesired incident may be something as simple as a faulty connection or as serious as a disaster, which could be an attack such as arson or an act of God such as an earthquake or tornado. In the case of a big fire that has burned up the infrastructure, a local redundancy system may not be effective, and an immediate continuation of business will not be possible. Instead, the disaster recovery plan should be capable of rebuilding the necessary components and installing them to restore acceptable conditions for resuming business operations.

An organization's computing environment is becoming larger, more complex, and increasingly more integrated. It is very rare that a piece of information, at an information resource, anywhere in the computing environment, can be compromised without affecting other areas of the computing environment [1]. Direct financial losses in one area of the computing environment can rapidly propagate from one functional unit to another functional unit. Indirect financial losses can travel from one unit to another through discontented customers and their complaints.

18.3 Homeland Security

Homeland security refers to the general national effort by federal, state, and local agencies to protect the territory of the United States from hazards both internal and external, natural and man-made. Homeland security is officially defined by the National Strategy for Homeland Security [7] as follows:

> A concerted national effort to prevent terrorist attacks within the United States, reduce America's vulnerability to terrorism, and minimize the damage and recover from attacks that do occur. White House [8,9].

While it had been used only in limited policy circles before, the term has now gained more use in the United States following 9/11. While it is probably more concerned with emergency preparedness and response for both terrorism and natural disasters, the homeland security scope is defined by the U.S. government to consist of the following:

Domestic intelligence activities, largely today within the FBI
Critical infrastructure protection
Border security, including both land and maritime
Transportation security, including aviation and maritime transportation
Biodefense
Detection of nuclear and radiological materials

A simple model for a country's risk position is the following linear equation:

$$\text{Risk position} = \alpha 1 * \text{SEI position} + \alpha 2 * \text{Unreadiness} + \alpha 3 * \text{Adverse exposure}$$

The SEI position varies from 1 to 5 (a score of 5 is only valid for an SB6 country):

1: Considered an enemy by all SB6 countries, for example, Iran
2: Has no friends among the SB6 countries, for example, many African countries
3: Friendly developing countries, for example, Tunisia
4: Industrialized countries not part of the SB6, for example, Japan
5: One of the SB6 countries

Unreadiness is assessed based on a country's exposure to natural, technological, biological, or man-made threats. This may be measured in terms of a country's weaknesses in terms of homeland security, business continuity, and disaster recovery.
    Unreadiness scores are defined as follows:

1: Considered very weak in all of these: homeland security, business continuity, and disaster recovery

2: Considered weak in all of these: homeland security, business continuity, and disaster recovery

3: Considered weak in one of these: homeland security, business continuity, and disaster recovery

4: Considered strong in homeland security, business continuity, and disaster recovery

5: Considered very weak in all of these: homeland security, business continuity, and disaster recovery

Adverse exposure is measured in terms of the peacefulness of the country. Scores may be defined as follows:

1: Has no enemies and is neutral, for example, the Vatican, Switzerland.

2: Has no enemies but is not neutral, for example, many developing countries.

3: Not in any war, for example, many developing countries.

4: In a war but not considered a terrorist country, for example, the United States, the United Kingdom, Poland.

5: Considered a terrorist country by many countries, for example, North Korea, Iran, Syria.

We next propose some metrics that may be useful in estimating a country's risk position.

18.4 Cyberterrorism in the Literature

18.4.1 Definitions of Cyberterrorism

In our discussion, we will also include *cybercrime* or *computer crime* and *computer-enabled crime* because there are distinct links between terrorism and cybercrime.[3] *Computer crime* aims either to target computer systems by means of hacking, dissemination of viruses, and/or denial of service attacks, whereas *computer-enabled* crimes are those that focus on the use of computers to commit fraud and engage in child pornography or other crimes against other persons or entities.[4] In recent years, terrorists have come to the realization that the use of computers to cause havoc and economic disruptions may be more effective than isolated violent acts, which, though damaging, are limited in overall effectiveness against political establishments. Computer crimes have the potential to be far more effective in disrupting national priorities. Often, foreign terrorists are also simultaneously engaged in drug trafficking in order to gain financing and harm purchasers of the illegal substances.[5]

Terrorism is the threat or use of force or violence to compel another person, group, or nation to succumb to the will of the person or group making the threat. *Cyberterrorism* may be defined as an attack on a person's or, more commonly, on information technology networks, generally through the Internet, in order to bring about annoying or serious harm or disruption to accomplish the terrorist's agenda. It has been defined by the U.S. Federal Bureau of Investigation as "a criminal act perpetrated by the use of computers and telecommunications capabilities, resulting in violence, destruction and/or disruption of services, where the intended purpose is to create fear by causing confusion and uncertainty within a given population, with the goal of influencing a government or population to conform to a particular political, social or ideological agenda."[6]

The major differences between terrorism and cyberterrorism are the degrees to which cyberterrorists are able to conceal their identity and to operate on a global basis. Terrorists are usually individuals who act collectively to advance their causes within a particular territory. Law enforcement agencies generally are able to eventually uncover and arrest the perpetrators. Cyberterrorists may operate anywhere in the world and can conceal their identities far more effectively, often with the cooperation of rogue states or through inability of local law enforcement agencies to act effectively. The damage caused by cyberterrorists may take place thousands of miles away from the physical location of the attacker, thereby effectively safeguarding them from arrest.

Cyberterrorism is more than a virus that creates a mild degree of annoyance such as a denial of service; it seeks to cause physical violence or significant financial harm. Targets may include power plants, military installations, the banking industry, air traffic control centers, utility systems, and other major centers affecting the lives and well-being of many persons and companies.[7] The attacks may be "effects-based," that is, the cyber attacks succeed in creating fear similar to that produced by traditional terrorism; or they may be "intent-based," whereby the perpetrators seek to press their political, often religious-based, agenda to cause a government or its inhabitants to alter their views or actions or to cause serious harm to a nation or its peoples.

18.4.2 Purposes and Types of Terrorism

The act of terrorism takes many forms depending on the motivation of the perpetrator. The motives may include the following:

Economic gain. The activity may be inspired by economic gain. From time immemorial, persons have used threats or actions to receive money or other economic benefits. Extortion (blackmail) is the use of threats to coerce an individual or business to pay money to prevent embarrassing disclosures. Examples include the demand that money be paid in exchange for not divulging an adulterous affair, a prior criminal record, or a company's poor financial status, or other "secrets." Economic gain may also take the form of corporate espionage, which consists of spying to gain access to trade secrets or other valuable information, to cause competitive brand defacement, or as an act of revenge by disgruntled employees.

The economic impact of attacks by cybercriminals and cyberterrorists is difficult to gauge because affected firms, especially banks, are extremely hesitant to reveal that their security systems were compromised. Another factor is the inability to quantify the extent of losses, as measured by the costs of protecting the systems, the hours spent on such protection both directly and indirectly, business interruption leading to loss of revenue and worker productivity, loss of value of trade secrets or other important information, loss of reputation or damage to a firm's brand, and other less quantifiable costs. Other factors that make revelation of computer-enabled losses include the effect on a company's stock and credit markets and bond rating firms, the possibility of litigation owing to managerial negligence, possible liability for revelation of private data as exemplified by recent announcements of theft of computers and computer data with thousands or millions of private data including social security numbers, fear of loss of jobs by security personnel, and the possible alerting to attackers of the vulnerability of a company's systems.[8]

Estimates of the monetary cost of computer crime vary substantially due to the factors just cited. Projected costs of computer crime within the United States, as reported by the Computer Security Institute (CSI) and the Federal Bureau of Investigation (FBI), ranged from the low $100 million from 1997 to 1999 to $265.3 million in 2000, $377.8 million in 2001, $455.8 million in 2002, and $201.8 million in 2003.[9] The losses were due mainly to theft of proprietary information and denial of service. Worldwide, the costs of viruses, worms, and other forms of attacks are very significant. The annual financial impact of major virus attacks were projected as being $12.5 billion in 2003 and $226 billion for all forms of digital attacks.[10]

Political terrorism. Nations have used political terrorism to coerce a nation or its leaders into either doing or not doing something. Such threats are legion, and include Hitler's threat to the president of Czechoslovakia that the country would be militarily destroyed unless his demands were conceded and the killing of the Archduke Ferdinand in Sarajevo that precipitated the First World War. The current conflict in the Middle East and in sub-Sahara Africa are examples of such terror.

Religious terrorism. Conflict among the major religions of the world, including sects within the particular religion, has been a major source of violence. The means used by extremist groups to attempt to cause nations and its inhabitants to conform to a particular orthodox ideology or to achieve other religious or national goals, including death and injury to persons and property and, presently, cyberterrorism. Examples of such extremist groups include Hezbollah (Party of God), the Harkat-ul-Mujahideen in Pakistan, the now-disbanded Irish Republican Army, and the al-Qaeda under the leadership of Osama bin Laden; such groups are responsible for terrorist activities in regions ranging from Europe and the United States to Africa and Southeast Asia. Even within a religion, there has been historical animosity among various segments, such as the Sunni-Shia conflict within Iraq and the many denominations of Christianity. The countries that appear to harbor and encourage terrorist activities are generally autocratic nations such as those belonging to the so-called "axis of evil" (U.S. President Bush's claim) of Iraq, Iran, and North Korea. Afghanistan (until its current political reformation), Cuba, and the Sudan are also nations that allegedly have sponsored or supported terrorist activities. Terrorist actions have taken place globally from Germany, Chechnya, Egypt, and France to Algeria, Yemen, Somalia, and the Philippines.

18.4.3 Means Used to Accomplish Terrorist Activities

Until the advent of the computer and the creation of the World Wide Web, the means used were either verbal threats or the use of physical means such as explosives, weaponry, and other methods of violence. The current threats include the use of biological and chemical weapons and the looming possibility of small-scale nuclear devices. Our discussion is limited to the threat and use of cyberterrorism, that is, attacks on computers designed to destroy or hinder computer operations, and the theft of data, including highly secret government data, business secrets, and other important data.

Physical security is related to cyber security; thus, it is important to protect not only against viruses and other Internet access but also against physical access to servers and networks. System vulnerabilities emanate from the ease of access to computers worldwide via the Internet, the methods available to damage or destroy computers, the interdependence of computers both domestically and worldwide, and the globalization and dependence on computers by national infrastructures.[11]

There are three methods of attack that may be employed against computer systems: (1) *physical attack* against computer facilities and transmission lines (this can be accomplished by the use of conventional weapons to destroy or seriously injure computers and their terminals); (2) *electronic attack* by use of electromagnetic high energy or electromagnetic pulses to overload computer circuitry or microwave radio transmission; and (3) *computer network attack*, usually with a malicious code to take advantage of a software's weakness. The latter form of attack is usually employed by hackers, who enjoy the challenge of attacking computer protection devices or gaining access to identities of users of programs or Web sites for financial gain.[12]

As in other forms of terrorism, cyberterrorism encompasses diverse forms and motives. In developed countries, the use of computers is at the core of a nation's infrastructure. A breakdown of computers can render a nation almost helpless, as witnessed by the near hysteria associated with the so-called Y2K nonevent. Had the alleged breakdown of computers occurred at the turn of the new millennium, there was a distinct possibility that massive shortages in the production and distribution of products and services would have occurred until the problem was fixed, or businesses would have had to revert to former modes of operation. Attempts to create havoc among national and global computers occur daily. Significant attacks that result in extensive damage to computers take place, often even with disabling software.

18.4.4 Forms of Cyberattacks and Terrorism

The types of attacks that may be conducted against computers and computer networks include the following:

■ Posting of graffiti on Web sites, which is essentially harmless but annoying to computer users.
■ Attacks by hackers who demonstrate the vulnerabilities of computers to outside attacks for reasons of pride in their capabilities to disable or affect computers.
■ Criminal behavior, generally in the form of stealing passwords to gain access to bank accounts, credit cards, and the like in order to commit fraud and theft.
■ Terrorist attacks to disable computers, gain entry into national security sites and data, cause havoc to a nation's economic structure, and other motivations.[13]
■ Radio frequency (RF) weapons, which are a series of smooth radio waves causing the target to generate heat and burn up.
■ Transient electromagnetic device (TEDs), characterized by emission of a large burst of energy that targets a large spectrum of space. It can be the size of a briefcase, van, or a large satellite dish.
■ Electromagnetic bomb/pulse weapon, which involves the creation of an electromagnetic pulse, that is, an electromagnetic shock wave that creates an enormous current many times that of a lightning strike.
■ TEMPEST monitoring devices.
■ Computer viruses, logic bombs, and Trojan horses.
■ Denial of service (zombie) attack send an overload of e-mails to the target system, causing the system to crash.[14]

Attacks may be:

■ *Structured* — Instituted at a precise time, as, for example, at noon on a given day at a particular facility, thereby creating substantial chaos and confusion. Consider the shutdown of a railway system at a given time.
■ *Sequenced* — Attacks continue at specific time intervals designated by the attacker.
■ *Layered* — These are similar to a sequenced attack but involve a variety of targets at different intervals.[15]

Hackers use a variety of means to further their agenda. Among the means are the following:

- *Virus* — A piece of code attached to a program that becomes active when the program is activated.
- *Worm* — A separate program that replicates itself on computers without changing the underlying or other programs.
- *Trojan horse* — A program fragment that appears to be a worm or a virus and permits the hacker to gain access to the system.
- *Logic bomb* — A type of trojan horse that remains dormant until conditions arise for its activation.
- *Trap doors* — These permit a programmer to access the user's software without the user being aware of the access. The U.S. Federal Bureau of Investigations has for years sought legal permission from Congress to use such programs. There have been indications that usage has been obtained without legal authorization.
- *Chipping* — These are similar to trap doors but remain dormant until access is desired.
- *Denial of service* — The hacker sends almost innumerable requests for information, which causes computer systems to shut down.[16]

18.4.5 How Real Is the Danger?

The difficulty for the United States and other developed nations is their increasing reliance upon information technology for their everyday activities, from running communications systems to energy plants. Obviously, countries such as Afghanistan, with little developed infrastructure, are far less affected by possible attacks on computers than the developed and developing nations. The U.S. government alone anticipated spending some $45 billion on information technology in the year 2002 for its operations.[17] Until the present time, the terrorism threat has emanated from physical attacks, such as the World Trade Center plane attacks, the bombings that have taken place in a number of countries such as, for example, in Bali in Indonesia, in Israel, and previously in Northern Ireland. The present fears of attack include possible chemical, biological, and nuclear attacks. Physical attacks are generally spectacular, as is evident from the television and other media coverage reporting the events. Although the chances of an individual being injured or killed in such attacks are extremely remote, nevertheless, the publicity given to them have caused many people to become somewhat unreasonably frightened by the possibility of becoming victims.[18]

There are disadvantages to using nuclear, biological, and chemical ("nbc") means of attack. Among the problems are the methodologies of dispersal, the requirements on site use, and the limited effects that even a successful operation would entail,[19] all of which militate against their extensive use. Nuclear attacks require governmental cooperation, extensive knowledge, and access to components of the nuclear bomb. It is extremely difficult to accomplish the manufacturing of such weapons without the United States, with its remarkable intelligence-gathering system, becoming aware of and taking steps to thwart such efforts. Thus, the possibility of cyberattacks becomes more apparent.

Rather than attack and kill or injure a relatively small number of people (World Trade Center excepted), a cyberattack has the potential of crippling entire governmental or private corporate systems, thereby causing much confusion and fear, and perhaps a significant number of injuries or casualties. For example, consider the computer systems that operate a city's traffic lights. The chaos in a city like New York would be considerable. Traffic would come to a halt in many areas, which would make the delivery of essential products and services and the movement of emergency vehicles difficult. Critically ill patients may not be able to get to a hospital in time; trucks delivering food and other essential goods may be prevented from making their rounds; and theater and other entertainment facilities would experience major losses. If a subway or other train facility were to be shut down, even temporarily, students could not get to school and millions of employees would have no means of transportation to perform their daily chores. It is arguable that a cyberattack would have a much more devastating effect than a bomb that kills or maims scores of people. People can adjust to bombs, but the closing of entire governmental systems has the potential of causing much more damage.[20]

Critical infrastructure systems are significantly vulnerable to cyberattacks. According to a 2005 report by the President's Information Technology Committee (PITAC), such systems are highly vulnerable to both physical attacks and cyberattacks and, in fact, there have been numerous attempts directed against governmental, financial services, manufacturing, and power infrastructures.[21] Although such systems have redundant backup systems, nevertheless, especially in the light of the Katrina disaster, it is questionable whether disaster can be averted in the future, especially as cyberterrorists and terrorists in general acquire greater sophistication in advanced attack methodologies. It appears from captured documents that groups such as al-Qaeda have recruited scientists and other highly educated personnel to gain the expertise to wreak significant havoc upon targets.[22] It has been reported that Osama bin Laden, although not having explored such possibilities in the past, has now suggested that his group has the expertise to use computer technology as a weapon. Is a "digital Pearl Harbor" in the making, as a U.S. cyberterrorism, Richard Clarke, suggested?[23] There have been globally about 237 million security attacks in the first six months of 2005 targeting government agencies (54 million), manufacturing (36 million), financial services (34 million), and healthcare (17 million). The United States was the primary target with 12 million attacks, with New Zealand and China a distant second and third.[24]

It should be noted that there are scholars who allege that cyberterrorism is a misnomer in that what is claimed to be cyberterrorism is in reality hacking or information warfare. They claim that there is little evidence or even fear that there would be any significant physical harm to the population at large, although this may change in the future with technological advances. They further allege that the threat of cyberterrorism has been overhyped in order to sell newspapers.[25] They claim is that cyberterrorism is a myth, as evidenced by the fact that no person has yet been killed. They allege that although it is conceivable that a person could be seriously hurt or may die from a cyberattack, nevertheless, terrorists, intent on causing maximum injury, would find it far easier to use physical means to inflict such damage, such as explosive devices or poisons, than to attempt to do so by cyber means.

Another claim by some naysayers is that it gives an excuse to governments to curb civil liberties.[26] Other commentators fear that cybercrime and cyberterrorism may lead to loss of privacy and freedom of communication inasmuch as governments will demand curbs on Internet speech and probe alleged suspected communications in the name of protecting the public.[27] Another aspect of the debate is, Who is to control the Internet? The issue has been raised at the recent Tunis Meeting of the World Summit on Information Society, where it was suggested that the United Nations, rather than the U.S.-based Internet Corporation for Assigned Names and Numbers (ICANN) should be entrusted with the registration of domain names.[28]

Cyberterrorism has been the center of a U.S. federal government request for $4.5 billion for infrastructure security. Although cybersecurity is a serious problem, the problem to worry about in the United States is cybercrime. There is little evidence that the U.S. Department of Defense, the FBI, or the CIA can be damaged by alleged cyberterrorists. Less protected targets in private hands, such as power grids, dams, and water systems, may be more vulnerable due to their use of supervisory control and data acquisition systems (SCADA); nevertheless, it is highly unlikely that a terrorist can cause significant damage to these systems.[29] Attacks on computer systems may also have direct or indirect benefits. One scholar has noted that such attacks help strengthen protection against future catastrophic attacks.[30] In an endeavor to protect the U.S. Internet infrastructure, the government has created a United States Computer Emergency Readiness Team (US-CERT), which links to the National Cyber Alert System and promotes efforts to protect against attacks to technical, governments, nontechnical, and control system users.[31]

18.4.6 Advantages Cyberterrorism Brings to Its Perpetrators

There are many advantages that persons or groups who target the global community, and individual countries, gain. Today, the cost of purchasing advanced computer systems is extremely low. Almost anyone can afford to buy sophisticated computers for well under $1000. The purchase of computers does not cause a governmental alert system to go into operation. If a person cannot afford a computer, there are other means of obtaining access, even in the poorest countries, such as libraries and cybercafés. There is no suspicion associated with such purchases, unlike purchases of chemical and biological agents, which would attract the attention of investigative agencies. Another advantage is relative anonymity. Digital signals are virtually anonymous and can emanate from any part of the globe. A virus planted into a program can instantaneously be disseminated globally and cause severe damage before a counterattack can be mounted.

The Internet began as a U.S. government project to enable global communication, especially among the military organizations stationed in various countries in Europe and Asia. Terrorists can utilize the Internet using the same methodology initially envisioned for the military. They can communicate, download materials, send coded messages, and schedule cyber meetings. Although it is theoretically possible to monitor messages to and from these groups, nevertheless, it would be extraordinarily difficult for a government to know which computer of the tens of millions of computers are being utilized; to decipher the coded messages; and to have enough translators to read and understand the messages even if they were not encoded.

The goals of cyberterrorists include the destruction of computer programs and operating systems; access to confidential economic and research and development information from corporations; invasion of privacy of individuals, as well as secret government data; a virtual shutdown of corporate activity; and often, crash systems to expose their vulnerabilities, especially those of prominent U.S. companies such as Microsoft. The threat to corporations is especially acute inasmuch as corporations may lose their trade secrets, confidential customer lists, and intellectual property (patents, copyrights, trademarks).

18.4.7 Where We Are in Combating Cyberterrorism

The United States has a number of secret and not-so-secret efforts to combat cyberterrorism, such as Project Echelon, which is an agreement between the United States, the United Kingdom, Canada, Australia, and New Zealand. Each of these nations agrees to share information captured via communications satellites that monitor millions of messages an hour using voice recognition and other means to ascertain keywords in a multitude of languages in order to identify possible cyberterrorist and other related and unrelated criminal activities.[32]

18.5 Cyberterrorism in the Real World: The FBI Perspective

There is a lot of confusion about terrorism, cyberterrorism, and homeland security, and we now invite the main source of knowledge in this field to educate us and our readers. We provide a Congressional testimony by Keith Lourdeau, before the Senate Judiciary Subcommittee on Terrorism, Technology, and Homeland Security on February 24, 2004 [2]. This section presents very articulated definitions of cyberterrorism and sheds unique light on how to combat it, at least in the United States. We present this testimony without major rephrasing or modification.

As in any other country, the U.S. economy has become more and more dependent on computers and the Internet. New digital vulnerabilities make our networked systems potential targets for an increasing number of attackers and terrorists. The director of the FBI has established new priorities: protecting the United States from terrorist attack is its top priority, and protecting the United States against cyber-based attacks and high-technology crimes is its third priority. In the United States, the FBI's Cyber Division's top priority is designated "counterterrorism-related computer intrusions."

Lately the United States has been the target of increasingly lethal terrorist attacks that highlight the potential vulnerability of our networked systems. These attacks were carried out by terrorists wanting to harm U.S. interests in order to advance their cause. Keith Lourdeau confirms that our networked systems are still inviting targets for terrorists due to the potential for large-scale impact to the nation. The vulnerabilities of our networked systems arise from a number of sources, such as easy accessibility to those systems via the Internet; harmful tools that are widely available to anyone with a computer and a modem; the globalization of our nation's infrastructures, increasing their exposure to potential harm; and the interdependencies of networked systems, making attack consequences harder to predict and perhaps more severe.

Coordinated attacks by cyber terrorists on multiple regions in the country could have a national impact. The most elaborate boundary control programs of firewalls, intrusion detection, and virus filtering are not capable of stopping malicious attacks when the attackers gain physical access to servers, networks, or sensitive information. Given the current U.S. security position, terrorist groups are increasingly adopting the power of modern communications technology for planning, recruiting, propaganda purposes, enhancing communications, command and control, fund raising and funds transfer, information gathering, and the like. According to Lourdeau, mere terrorist use of information technology is not regarded as cyberterrorism; the true threat of cyberterrorism will be realized when all the factors that constitute a terrorist attack, coupled with the use of the Internet, are met.

Cyberterrorism is a criminal act perpetrated by the use of computers and tele-communications capabilities, resulting in violence, destruction, and disruption of services, the purpose being to create fear by causing confusion and uncertainty within a given population with the goal of influencing a government or population to conform to a particular political, social, or ideological agenda.

To date, cyber attacks by terrorists, or persons affiliated with them, have largely been limited to relatively unsophisticated efforts such as the e-mail bombing of ideological foes or the publication of threatening content. However, increasing technical competency in these groups is resulting in an emerging capability for network-based attacks. Terrorist groups have proved themselves capable of carrying out acts of violence against our nation on a large scale. The more familiar they become with computers and their potential as a viable weapon against us, the more likely they will try to acquire the skills necessary to carry out a cyberterrorist event.

The FBI assesses the cyberterrorism threat to the United States to be rapidly expanding, as the number of actors with the ability to utilize computers for illegal, harmful, and possibly devastating purposes is on the rise. Terrorist groups have shown a clear interest in developing basic hacking tools, and the FBI predicts that terrorist groups will either develop or hire hackers, particularly for the purpose of complementing large physical attacks with cyber attacks.

Lourdeau states that if a terrorist lacked the technical sophistication to conduct a computer attack and chose to recruit a hacker, the potential damage would be increased if that hacker were an insider. Insider attacks originate from a variety of motivations (e.g., financial gain, personal grievances, revenge, recruitment, or coercion). He adds that it is not necessarily the motivation that makes insiders dangerous, but the fact that they may have unfiltered access to sensitive computer systems that can place public safety at risk. Moreover, there is an increasing concern over the prevalent trend to outsource, even to foreign conglomerates, services that were previously handled domestically.

There is no doubt that attacks against regional targets could have a significant effect on computer networks, while coordinated attacks on multiple regions could have a national impact with severe consequences. Lourdeau worries that there are numerous control systems whose destruction would have a far-reaching effect. He believes that large-scale distribution systems, such as those involving natural gas, oil, electric power, and water, tend to use automated supervisory and data acquisition (SCADA) systems for administration. SCADA systems tend to have both cyber and physical vulnerabilities. Poor computer security, lack of encryption, and poor enforcement of user privileges lead to risks to SCADA systems. Poor physical controls can make the disruption of the SCADA system a realistic possibility.

Lourdeau asserts that a major method used in preventing cyberterrorism is the sharing of intelligence information. The FBI routinely passes intelligence received in active investigations or developed through research to the intelligence community. Throughout the FBI field offices, special agents serve on cyber task forces with other agencies.

Cyber programs are unique in nature. However, taking proactive investigative measures with tools such as honey pots/nets and undercover operations enhances our ability to prevent a cyberterrorist attack. The FBI has undertaken the following initiatives to combat cyberterrorism: cyber task forces, public/private alliances, international cyber investigative support, mobile cyber assistance teams, cyber action teams, cyber investigators training, a cyber intelligence center, and cyber tactical analytical case support. These programs provide a strategic framework and program management tool for all FBI computer intrusion investigations.

The Computer Intrusion program provides administrative and operational support and guidance to the field offices investigating computer intrusions, assists other FBI programs that have a computer dimension, and coordinates computer intrusion investigations by various criminal investigative and intelligence components of the federal government.

The Special Technologies and Applications program supports FBI counterterrorism computer intrusion-related investigations with all necessary equipment and technical investigative tools.

The Cyber International Investigative program enables international cyber investigative efforts through coordination with FBI Headquarters Office of International Operations, legal attaché offices, and foreign law enforcement agencies.

The Cyber Specialized Training Program coordinates with the Engineering Research Facility, Laboratory Division, Training Division, National White Collar Crime Center, private industry, academia, and others to deliver training to FBI cyber squads, task forces, international law enforcement officers, and others.

In the event of a cyberterrorist attack, the FBI will conduct an intense postincident investigation to determine the source, including the motive and purpose of the attack. In the digital age, data collection in such an investigation can be extremely difficult. The computer industry is also conducting research and development involving basic security, such as developing cryptographic hardware that will serve to filter attempts to introduce malicious code or to stop unauthorized activity. Continued research in these areas will only serve to assist the FBI in its work against cyberterrorism.

While the following two incidents were not cyberterrorism, they are a worrisome indication of the ability of individuals to gain access to our networked systems and the possible damage that can result.

In 1996, an individual used simple explosive devices to destroy the master terminal of a hydroelectric dam in Oregon. Although there was no impact on the dam's structure, this simple attack completely disabled the dam's power-generating turbines and forced a switch to manual control. A coordinated attack on a region's infrastructure systems (e.g., the SCADA systems that control Washington D.C.'s electric power, natural gas, and water supply) would have a profound effect on the nation's sense of security. This incident demonstrates how minimal sophistication and material can subvert a SCADA system.

In 1997, a juvenile accessed the Generation Digital Loop Carrier System operated by NYNEX. Several commands were sent that disrupted the telephone service to the Federal Aviation Administration Tower at the Worcester Airport, to the Worcester Airport Fire Department, and to other related entities such as airport security, the weather service, and various private airfreight companies. As a result of this disruption, the main radio transmitter and the circuit that enabled aircraft to send an electronic signal to activate the runway lights on approach were disabled. This same individual then accessed the loop carrier system for customers in and around Rutland, Massachusetts, and sent commands that disabled the telephone service, including the 911 service, throughout the Rutland area.

On May 3, 2003, an e-mail was sent to the National Science Foundation's (NSF) Network Operations Center that read, "I've hacked into the server of your South Pole Research Station. Pay me off, or I will sell the station's data to another country and tell the world how vulnerable you are." The e-mail contained data only found on the NSF's computer systems, proving that this was no hoax. NSF personnel immediately shut down the compromised servers. During May, the temperature at the South Pole can go down to –70°F; aircrafts cannot land there until November due to the harsh weather conditions. The compromised computer systems controlled the life support systems for the 50 scientists "wintering over" at the South Pole Station.

According to a Congressional testimony by Lourdeau before the Senate Judiciary Subcommittee on Terrorism, Technology, and Homeland Security on February 24, 2004, the unique complexity of protecting our nation's networked systems is a daunting task [2]. The key to prevention is effective attack warnings and the education of the owners and operators of those systems. The protection of our networked systems is a shared responsibility, and requires partnership between the private sector, state and local law enforcement agencies, U.S. federal law enforcement agencies, the Department of Homeland Security, and the intelligence community, both domestic and foreign. The FBI encourages international cooperation to help manage this increasingly global problem.

This testimony also asserts that defending against a cyber attack also requires the integration of operational, physical, communication, and personnel security measures. This involves a full range of precautions such as installing effective passwords, firewall protection, avoidance of unprotected and unnecessarily opened entry points, installation of default configuration and passwords, minimization of server placement in unprotected areas, and vigilance against disgruntled employees. System administrators must be both vigilant and serious about cyber security.

18.6 U.S. Legislative Enactments and Proposed Programs

There have been a number of proposed programs that attempt to remedy the dangers posed by persons seeking to threaten society. Among them is the very controversial program Carnivore, which is an electronic surveillance program that is a part of a surveillance package known as DragonWare Suite.[33] The program, known within the FBI as DCS-1000, can read millions of e-mails per second, look for key words or phrases, review banking and Web browsing activities of individuals, and examine the frequency of usage, time spent, and other critical data. A tapping device at the ISP's access point accomplishes this without impacting the ISP. The data is then filtered in accordance with a court order authorizing its usage and is maintained subject to the order. In this manner, suspected terrorist operations are tapped into revelations of possible unlawful activities. Of course, the program assumes the usage of ISPs and the ability to decipher coded and uuencoded messages. Thus, if the terrorists use manual rather than electronic transmissions, the program will not be useful. Nevertheless, the need to communicate globally among terrorist networks makes usage of Carnivore and other eavesdropping devices useful to law enforcement agencies.

From a U.S. military perspective, the duty of combating cyberterrorism has been entrusted to the Strategic Command's Joint Task Force-Global Network

Operations (JFT-GNO), which directs the operation and Global Information Grid on behalf of the U.S. Department of Defense (DoD). The goals include the department's role in waging war, intelligence gathering, and business missions. In accordance with its mission, it seeks to achieve assured system and network availability, assured information protection, and assured information delivery. It operates through Theater NetOps Centers. This is done by integrating GNO capabilities into the operations of all DoD computers, networks, and systems used by DoD combatant commands, services, and agencies.

18.7 U.S. Criminal Statutes Affecting the Internet

18.7.1 Fraud Statutes

Countries, especially the United States, have enacted a number of statutes to regulate and set ground rules for civil and criminal conduct. Among the laws enacted in the United States that may pertain directly or indirectly to computer technology are statutes concerning fraud, in particular, fraudulent activities affecting the Internet. They are as follows:

The *Access Device Fraud Act of 1984*, as amended, makes it a crime by "whoever … knowingly and with intent to defraud produces, uses or traffics in one or more counterfeit access devices" in interstate commerce.[34] The act also forbids production, trafficking in, or control or custody of, or possession of device-making equipment with intent to defraud.[35] The act protects computer passwords. Possession of counterfeit and/or unauthorized access devices or device-making equipment may violate the act.

An "access device" is defined as "any card, plate, code, account number or other means of account access that can be used, alone or in conjunction with another access device, to obtain money, goods, services, or anything of value, or that can be used to initiate a transfer of funds (other than a transfer originated solely by paper instrument)." A "counterfeit access device" is "any access device that is counterfeit, fictitious, altered, or forged, or an identifiable component of an access device or a counterfeit access device."[36] Credit cards obtained from issuing companies by means of false applications with intent to defraud are subject to the statute. The following case illustrates the application of the act to cellular telephones.

The *Computer Fraud and Abuse Act of 1986* is the leading statute governing computer crime. Its basic provisions are set forth in the endnotes.[37] In essence, it makes it a crime punishable by up to 20 years in prison to unlawfully access a computer to obtain secret or restricted data from the government, financial institutions, or to use data wrongfully obtained to perpetrate fraud, and other unlawful purposes.

Wire Fraud.[38] The statute reads as follows:

> Whoever, having devised or intending to devise any scheme or artifice to defraud, or for obtaining money or property by means of false or fraudulent pretenses, representations, or promises, transmits or causes to be transmitted by means of wire, radio, or television communication in interstate or foreign commerce, any writings, signs, signals, pictures, or sounds for the purpose of executing such scheme or artifice, shall be fined not more than $1000 or imprisoned not more than five years, or both. If the violation affects a financial institution, such person shall be fined not more than $1,000,000 or imprisoned not more than 30 years, or both...

To prove wire or mail fraud, it is necessary for the prosecution to show "(1) a scheme to defraud be means of false pretenses; (2) the defendant's knowing and willing participation in the scheme with the intent to defraud; and (3) the use of interstate wire or mail communications in furtherance of the scheme."[39] Is "confidential information" considered to be property under the statute? At least one court has stated that "Where such information is obtained — thus depriving the rightful owner of its property rights — through dishonest or deceitful means, the wire and mail fraud statutes may be violated...[M]ere access to the confidential information us insufficient...."[40]

Identity Theft and Assumption Deterrence Act.[41] This act, passed in 1998, makes it a felony for a person who "(7) knowingly transfers or uses, without lawful authority, a means of identification of another person with the intent to commit, or to aid or abet, any unlawful activity that constitutes a violation of Federal law, or that constitutes a felony under any applicable State or local law." Imprisonment up to 20 years may be imposed for serious offenses, such as facilitating a drug trafficking offense, or an offense involving a crime of violence. "Means of identification" refers to any name or number used to identify an individual, including a name, Social Security number, driver's license, unique electronic identification number, telecommunication identifying information or access device, and other such identifying manifestations [Section 28(d)]. Interestingly, the attempt or conspiracy to commit the crime is made subject to the same penalties as the commission of the act.

18.7.2 Other Applicable Statutes

The Racketeer Influenced and Corrupt Organizations Act (RICO).[42] The purpose of this act is "to seek the eradication of organized crime in the United States by strengthening the legal tools in the evidence-gathering process, by establishing new penal prohibitions, and by providing enhanced sanctions and new remedies to deal with the unlawful activities of those in organized crime." Few laws are as controversial as RICO. Originally aimed at prosecuting members of organized crime, the statute has been used and abused, especially civilly, to prosecute or sue otherwise legitimate organizations.

It is unlawful for any person to receive or conspire to receive income, directly or indirectly, derived from a pattern of racketeering activity or through the collection of an unlawful debt. In order for the statute to be applicable, a *pattern of racketeering activity* must be alleged and proved. To constitute a pattern, at least two acts of racketeering activity within 10 years must be established. "Racketeering activity" has a long definition that includes violent offenses, dealing in obscene matter, many types of fraud, transmission of gambling information, criminal infringement of intellectual property, and numerous other offenses affecting interstate commerce.[43]

The criminal penalties include fines, imprisonment of up to 20 years (life if the racketeering activity has a maximum penalty of life imprisonment), temporary restraining orders and injunctions, and forfeiture of profits and property derived from the racketeering activity. Forfeiture of property includes real and personal, tangible and intangible property. Civil remedies that can be imposed include divestiture of any interest in the forbidden enterprise, reasonable restrictions on the future activities and investments in the same or similar enterprise, and the dissolution of the enterprise.[44] What gives the statute greater enforceability is the provision that any person who is injured as a result of the prohibited activities may sue the offending persons and recover triple damages plus costs and reasonable attorney's fee. It is this latter provision that may be seriously abused inasmuch as many lawful enterprises have engaged in conduct (often unwittingly through overaggressive agents and employees) that come within the act's prohibitions.

Wire and Electronic Communications Interception and Interception of Oral Communication.[45] This statute prohibits the interception of any wire, oral, or electronic communication; interference with radio transmissions; the use of devices to intercept oral communications without consent, and the disclosure thereof. There are numerous exceptions, including the interception of radio communications available to the general public; persons affiliated with the Federal Communications Commission in the normal course of employment; where the person is a party to the communication or has given prior consent, unless the interception is to commit a criminal or tortious act; electronic surveillance for foreign intelligence operations; and other such purposes. Also applicable is the prohibition of unlawful access to stored communications (18 U.S.C. Section 2701). According to the Congressional findings annexed to the statute, the act seeks both to permit interception, under court order and supervision, of wire or oral communications made in the commission of crimes and also to protect the privacy of innocent persons from unwarranted intrusions.

Unlawful Access to Stored Communications.[46] The statute provides:

"(a) Offense. …[W]hoever—

1. Intentionally accesses without authorization a facility through which an electronic communication service is provided; or

2. Intentionally exceeds an authorization to access that facility; and thereby obtains, alters, or prevents authorized access to a wire or electronic communication while it is in electronic storage in such system shall be punished as provided in subsection (b) of this section."

Exceptions to liability are given to providers of a wire or electronic communication service, the user of the service with respect to a communication of, or intended for, that user; and law enforcement officers who have obtained authorization. Under the statute, a governmental entity may require a provider of electronic communication service to disclose the contents of an electronic communication in electronic storage for a period of up to 180 days pursuant to a warrant issued by a federal or state court [Section 2703]. Punishment ranges from a maximum of only 6 months to 2 years depending on whether the offense was committed for a commercial advantage and whether the offense was a first or subsequent offense.[47]

The foregoing fraud statutes have both criminal and civil in nature. Thus, although governmental enforcement generally is for the most egregious acts, private enforcement is the mainstay of the statutes. Thus, permitting the victims of fraud to institute a lawsuit quite often is the most effective means of preventing and penalizing fraudulent activities. The elements of proof in establishing a case are much easier in a court of law; whereas to convict a person for a crime, it is necessary to prove the essential elements of an offense beyond a reasonable doubt, in a civil case it is only necessary to establish the elements of the offense by a fair preponderance of the evidence, a much lower standard. In nonterrorist fraudulent hacking activities, civil enforcement may be the best alternative.[48]

18.8 Statutes and Executive Orders Concerned with Cyberterrorism

18.8.1 The USA Patriot Act of 2001

The passage of the awkwardly titled "United and Strengthening America by Providing Appropriate Tools Required to Intercept and Obstruct Terrorism Act of 2001" (The "USA Patriot Act")[49] is a milestone in U.S. legislation. Its scope is extraordinarily broad and encompasses numerous areas of activity within the nation. At 342 pages in length, the statute, by its unique provisions and in amending more than 15 other statutes, has raised significant concerns especially among members of the legal community, who perceive it as one of the broadest attacks on civil liberties ever enacted.[50] The statute was passed on October 25, 2001, and signed into law a day later, a little over a month after the World Trade Center collapse. It was subject to almost no debate.[51] It raised the scepter of Orwellian fears[52] in the name of national security against terrorism. Organizations such as the

American Civil Liberties Union (ACLU) and the Electronic Frontier Foundation (EFF)[53] have inveighed against some of the provisions of the act.

The perceived problems addressing the nation at the time of the attacks included the inability of the CIA to share information with the FBI concerning two suspected terrorists prior to 9/11; the lack of sufficient probable cause for the FBI to procure a search warrant of a suspected terrorist who had enrolled in flight simulation training for jumbo jets; the inability to monitor financial records of suspect transactions; the perceived need of immigration reform to ensure that student and visitors' visas are properly administered and supervised; and the extensive use of electronic transmissions by terrorists in the planning and execution of their activities.[54]

18.8.2 *Summary of Provisions*

Title II of the Patriot Act, entitled "Enhanced Surveillance Procedures," amended the Foreign Intelligence Surveillance Act of 1978 (FISA),[55] which was concerned with wiretapping and foreign intelligence surveillance. FISA permits the wiretapping of aliens and U.S. citizens where there is probable cause to believe that the persons being investigated are members of a terrorist group or agents of a foreign power. The statute is specifically aimed at foreign groups or persons involved in data related to actual or potential attacks, sabotage, clandestine intelligence activities, and information concerning national defense or the conduct of foreign affairs.[56] Title II permits domestic law enforcement authorities to share foreign intelligence and counterintelligence information with the CIA, including grand jury data and electronic, wire, and oral interception information, all without a court order. Thus, any law enforcement authority may now share information concerning foreign intelligence or counterintelligence with the CIA. If the information is obtained by the U.S. Department of Justice, it must be expeditiously revealed to the CIA. Prior to the statute, the FBI and the CIA were given specific spheres of intelligence gathering and were not permitted to share the said data. Thus, the relatively clear demarcation of domestic and foreign intelligence gathering has been significantly blurred by the act.[57]

Grand jury proceedings historically have been secret for good reason. If the grand jury does not indict (charge) the persons under investigation for a crime, the revelation of testimony therein could seriously compromise the integrity of the purported accused. Also, persons giving testimony would be less likely to reveal information if the identity of persons who appeared before the grand jury and the extent of the statements made became known. Judges are permitted to unseal grand jury testimony when circumstances mandate such a step, especially where the defendant would be seriously prejudiced without the knowledge of what had taken place.[58] The Patriot Act, however, permits grand jury disclosure without a court order with respect to matters concerning "foreign intelligence or counterintelligence ... or foreign intelligence information ... to any federal law enforcement, intelligence, protective, immigration, national defense, or national security official in order to assist the official receiving that information in the performance of his official duties."[59]

Other provisions of questionable constitutional validity are the act's provisions concerning the issuance of search warrants. The Constitution provides, in the Fourth Amendment thereof, that the person, home, papers, and effects of U.S. citizens may not be unreasonably searched and seized and that search warrants for their search may not be issued except upon a showing of probable cause supported by an oath or affirmation describing the place to be searched and the persons or articles to be seized. The Patriot Act authorizes a federal court judge to delay issuance of a search warrant if the immediate notice thereof may have an adverse effect, or other special circumstances. The role of judges in supervising telephone and Internet surveillance is limited. A warrant may be issued without the necessity of law enforcement officers naming the place or person to be searched within the United States.[60] The issuance of a court order warrant for a pen register or a trap and trace device within the United States is mandated under the act merely upon a statement by a government official that the information to be seized may be relevant to an ongoing criminal investigation.[61]

With respect to searches and seizures conducted against U.S. persons abroad, the so-called "foreign intelligence exception to the warrant requirement" applies. The exception provides that the said search will not violate the Fourth Amendment provided that the purpose of the search concerns foreign intelligence rather than criminal prosecutions. The Constitution does not protect searches and seizures pertaining to foreign persons where the search is conducted abroad.[62] U.S. courts have permitted almost unlimited freedom for governmental agents to conduct foreign intelligence operations without regard to constitutional restraints. In *United States v. Bin Laden*,[63] the federal district court ruled that the foreign intelligence exception was applicable to electronic and physical searches of U.S. persons abroad without the need of a court-issued search warrant. The Patriot Act confirms the rule and further permits law enforcement authorities to divulge the contents of the communication that was intercepted to national security and other governmental officials.[64]

18.8.3 Immigration Restrictions

Title IV of the Patriot Act is concerned with "Protecting the Border" and is composed of two subtitle, namely, "Subtitle A-Protecting the Northern Border" and "Subtitle B-Enhanced Immigration Provisions." It is the latter subtitle that raises fundamental constitutional and international law questions. Section 411, "Definitions Relating to Terrorism," gives very broad definitions of the terms "terrorist activity" and "engage in terrorist activity." In doing so, aliens residents of the U.S. are subject to deportation for a wide range of unlawful activities that, at best, are tangentially related to terrorism in the ordinary meaning of the word.[65] The Immigration and Nationality Act was amended to expand the definitions of "terrorist activity" to include persons using any type of "weapons," including firearms, while engaged in unlawful activity.[66] The activity may have nothing to do with terrorism as previously understood by the definition thereof. A person may be engaged in terrorist activity by aiding an alleged terrorist by providing food or housing even if the person aiding the alleged terrorist in unaware of the activity of such a person.[67]

Section 412 of the act amends the Immigration and Nationality Act to permit a legal alien residing in the United States to be detained indefinitely when the Attorney General has reasonable grounds to believe that the alien is a terrorist. The alien may be detained without charge of a crime for a period of 7 days.[68] The Attorney General may certify the alien as a terrorist, thereby permitting custody of the alien for a period up to 6 months.[69] It appears that the provision flies in the face of the Fifth Amendment to the U.S. Constitution of due process ("no person shall... be deprived of life, liberty, or property, without due process of law").[70] A bedrock of U.S. constitutional law is the writ of habeas corpus[71] and judicial review.

18.8.4 Civil Liberty Implications

The Patriot Act has raised issues of civil liberties to a degree almost without precedent in enacted legislation. On the one hand, a few scholars[72] assume, if not hope, that the government will not abuse the broad discretion permitted to it under the enactment. On the other hand, almost all commentators, some of whom are cited in the footnotes, agree that the statute is fraught with significant constitutional difficulties. The essential arguments of civil libertarians outlined herein are:

- The massively long statute was enacted almost without debate shortly after the 9/11 World Trade Center incident at a time when the Senate was concerned with anthrax contamination that was then plaguing the body.
- The curtailment of civil liberties were not necessary, especially because the incidents concerning Japanese Americans in World War II illustrate the evil innate in isolating U.S. citizens due to unfounded suspicion of lack of loyalty.[73]
- It has not been demonstrated that the enforcement of civil liberties was the cause of the 9/11 attacks.
- The government is able to spy on Americans without proof or need to show that he or she suspected of a crime.
- The government may conduct pen/trap and wiretap searches without the need of a court order and without reporting the findings of the searches.
- The government may subpoena detailed records of U.S. persons without court review.
- The definition of terrorism was greatly expanded to include persons not traditionally includable in the definition.
- The government may seek DNA samples for a database that is not restricted to persons accused of terrorism.
- U.S. foreign intelligence agencies may spy on Americans abroad without the need for court approval.

- The clear demarcation between the domestic spying agency (FBI) and the foreign intelligence agency (CIA) has been virtually eliminated.[74]

18.8.5 Banking Provisions

Title III of the Patriot Act, entitled "International Money Laundering Abatement and Anti-Terrorist Financing Act of 2001," reflects the Congressional findings that some $600 billion annually or between 2% and 5% of the global gross domestic product annually constitutes money laundering that allegedly provides the financial fuel for criminal activities.[75] The goals of the legislation are to improve U.S. capabilities of preventing and detecting international money laundering schemes and the financing of terrorism, and prosecuting those responsible for such activities; subjecting foreign institutions and jurisdictions to special scrutiny; and ensuring the forfeiture of assets in connection with alleged antiterrorist efforts.[76] The Secretary of the Treasury is required by the Patriot Act to issue regulations governing money laundering. The ostensible purpose of the regulations is to prevent the dissemination of monies throughout the world for terrorist activities.

The Secretary issued regulations on April 29, 2002, for so-called TierOne Entities, which entities already had control systems governing them under the Bank Secrecy Act.[77] Regulations for so-called TierTwo entities that were not previously governed by the statute were deferred on October 24, 2002.[78] The regulations provide in part that financial institutions are to verify all new account applicants, maintain records concerning the verification, and consult lists of alleged terrorists or terrorists' organizations to ascertain whether the applicant is connected to them.[79] In addition, special emphasis is given to the recommendations of the Secretary concerning the most effective method of requiring foreign nationals to provide comparable information as well as requiring them to obtain social security numbers or tax identification numbers as a condition of opening accounts with domestic institutions.[80]

18.8.6 President Bush's Executive Order

An equally controversial post 9/11 governmental decree is the Executive Order issued by President George Bush on November 13, 2001, which established military tribunals for alleged terrorists.[81] The Order permits trials of these so-called terrorists before secret tribunals outside the United States. Trials to date have taken place in Guantanamo Naval Base in Cuba. The rules of evidence and other procedural protections afforded by the U.S. Constitution for U.S. nationals were substantially diminished. Many inmates at the Naval Base were imprisoned without resort to legal representations and tried in secret as permitted by the Order. Whether the U.S. Constitution or basic legal protections recognized internationally were violated has been seriously questioned.[82] It appears that the lessons derived from the wrongful removal of U.S. citizens of Japanese descent during World War

II were forgotten. The former racist treatment of African Americans and persons of Japanese origin have been replaced by treatment accorded to Arab Americans.

Lest it appear that the Bush Administration has set the limits of restrictions on personal freedom with the passage of the Patriot Act, it should be noted that the Pentagon has proposed a "Total Information Awareness" project that would create "a virtual centralized grand database" of bank records, medical records, credit card purchases, academic, and other records for retrieval by the FBI and others. Attorney General John Ashcroft has proposed amendments to the Patriot Act that would computerize genetic information without court order or consent and to wiretap citizens for 2 weeks before seeking the approval of a court.[83]

18.8.7 Privacy Rights versus Security Measures

A number of trade-offs that have been suggested and also demanded by governmental officials. The difficulty is that the demands for increased powers of surveillance come into inevitable conflict with First and, more particularly, Fourth Amendment protections of the U.S. Constitution. The extent to which governmental agencies lawfully or surreptitiously invade the privacy of individuals and groups is really unknown except to those persons privy to their usage. When Secretary of State Colin Powell addressed the U.S. Security Council in early February 2003, he revealed, somewhat reluctantly, the extent to which the U.S. government was able to monitor messages among military officials.[84]

18.8.8 The U.S. Antiterrorism Assistance Program

The Department of State was given the responsibility, pursuant to President Bush's February 2003 National Strategy for Combating Terrorism, for developing methodologies to coordinate national and international strategies to prevent and defeat terrorist aggressions. Accordingly, the State Department has been using its Antiterrorism Assistance Program (ATA), created in 1983, to serve as a tool for providing training, equipment, technology, and other resources to other partnering nations to deter, capture, and punish terrorists. ATA has trained some 52,300 students from 146 countries since the program's inception. Among the current initiatives are the Trans-Sahara Counterterrorism Initiative that seeks to strengthen the capabilities of Algeria, Morocco, Tunisia, Mauritania, Mali, Niger, Chad, Senegal, and Nigeria in combating terrorism. Other initiatives include that of developing a regional strategy in the Caribbean, providing assistance to the Ukraine, Haiti, Arabian Gulf Peninsula, Central Asia, Afghanistan, Colombia, Indonesia, Kenya, Pakistan, and the Philippines.[85]

There are also special training programs concerning cyberterrorism, weapons of mass destruction, mobile antiterrorism, "fly away" programs given in foreign countries, an International Law Enforcement Academy, Interdicting Terrorist Organizations, Advanced Explosive Incident Countermeasures, Underwater

Explosive Incident Countermeasures, and detection of fraudulent documents. The programs appear to have had considerable success in the training of security personnel in thwarting almost all terrorist incidents.[86]

18.9 International Initiatives

The European Union. The European Union (E.U.) issued a Council Regulation[87] concerning restrictive measures directed against certain persons and entities with a view to combating terrorism. The regulation, which binds all members of the European Union, freezes funds of persons who knowingly and intentionally participate in acts of terrorism or in preparation thereof. The act of terrorism is broadly defined so as to include the commission of acts that cause death or harm to "the fundamental political, constitutional, economic, or social structure of a country...." The Council of the E.U. is to maintain a registry of the names of people and groups who assist in the commission of terrorist acts. The financial institutions are to provide financial information concerning the accounts of the same persons or groups so as to permit the member states to take appropriate action against them. The accounts may be frozen, with the possible exception of funds to be used for humanitarian purposes. Each member state is to cooperate with the other member states in collecting and sharing data with a view toward criminally prosecuting persons engaged in terrorist activities.[88]

The E.U. has created the Critical Information Infrastructure Research Coordination Office, which is intended to ascertain from member states how their infrastructures are being protected from possible cyberattacks. With such data, vulnerabilities can be detected and security measures suggested to avert destructive consequences.

The Council of Europe. The Council of Europe adopted a *Convention on Cybercrime* on November 23, 2001, effective July 2004, in Strasbourg in order to adopt a common criminal policy for the protection of society against cybercrime.[89] The major concerns, as expressed in the Preamble, include the significant changes brought about due to recent developments in the digitalization, convergence, and globalization of computer networks and the commission of criminal offenses with respect thereto. Accordingly, the measures that are to be taken at the national level are: (1) adoption of substantive criminal laws to address offenses against the confidentiality, integrity, and availability of computer data and systems—included are laws against illegal access, illegal interception, data interference, system interference, and misuse of devices; (2) computer-related offenses—computer-related forgery and computer-related fraud; and (3) content-related offenses—offenses related to child pornography and offenses related to infringements of copyright and related rights.

The G8[90] Ten-Point Action Plan. Ministers at the G8 agreed on December 11, 1997, that a ten-point action plan was to be undertaken in order to combat existing cybercrime and as the groundwork for the 21st century.[91] Obviously, although referring to cybercrime, the steps announced clearly apply to cyberterrorism, which was not a significant issue in the pre-9/11 world at the time of the proposal.[92] The plan calls for the following action to be taken by member states:

- Use our established network of knowledgeable personnel to ensure a timely, effective response to transnational high-tech cases and designate a point of contact who is available on a 24-hour basis.
- Take appropriate steps to ensure that a sufficient number of trained and equipped law enforcement personnel are allocated to the task of combating high-tech crime and assisting law enforcement agencies of other states.
- Review our legal systems to ensure they appropriately criminalize abuses of telecommunications and computer systems and promote the investigation of high-tech crimes.
- Consider issues raised by high-tech crimes, where relevant, when negotiating mutual assistance agreements or arrangements.
- Continue to examine and develop workable solutions regarding the preservation of evidence prior to the execution of a request for mutual assistance; transborder searches; and computer searches of data where the location of that data is unknown.
- Develop expedited procedures for obtaining traffic data from all communications carriers in the chain of a communication and to study ways to expedite the passing of this data internationally.
- Work jointly with industry to ensure that new technologies facilitate our effort to combat high-tech crime by preserving and collecting critical evidence.
- Ensure that we can, in urgent and appropriate cases, accept and respond to mutual assistance requests relating to high-tech crime by expedited but reliable means of communications, including voice, fax, or e-mail, with written confirmation to follow where required.
- Encourage internationally recognized standards-making bodies in the fields of telecommunications and information technologies to continue providing the public and private sectors with standards for reliable and secure telecommunications and data processing technologies.
- Develop and employ compatible forensic standards for retrieving and authenticating electronic data for use in criminal investigations and prosecutions.

NATO. The North Atlantic Treaty Organization on the day following the September 11 attack agreed that "an armed attack against one or more of them … shall be considered an attack against them all and … each of them … will assist the Party or Parties so attacked by … such action as it deems necessary, including the use of armed force, to restore and maintain the security of the North Atlantic area." Among the measures to be taken against terrorists are intelligence sharing and cooperation, providing assistance to the member states and other states who may be subject to terrorist threats or acts, increasing security for facilities for member states, providing for overflight clearance of military flights in connection with terrorism, providing access to ports and airfields including for refueling, and using of NATO military forces in the war against terrorism.[93]

OECD.[94] The Organization of Economic Cooperation and Development issued *Guidelines for the Security of Information Systems and Networks: Towards a Culture of Security*, on July 25, 2002.[95] Among the aims of the guidelines are the promotion and foundation of a culture of security among the member states, the raising of awareness concerning the risks and means necessary to address them, ethical issues, and the promotion of cooperation and information sharing. Accordingly, nine principles were proposed addressing the aims of the OECD:

■ *Awareness*—Participants should be aware of the need for security of information systems and networks and what they can do to enhance security.
■ *Responsibility*—All participants are responsible for the security of information systems and networks.
■ *Response*—Participants should act in a timely and cooperative manner to prevent, detect, and respond to security incidents.
■ *Ethics*—Participants should respect the legitimate interests of others.
■ *Democracy*—The security of information systems and networks should be compatible with essential values of a democratic society.
■ *Risk assessment*—Participants should conduct risk assessments.
■ *Security design and implementation*—Participants should incorporate security as an essential element of information systems and networks.
■ *Security management*—Participants should adopt a comprehensive approach to security management.
■ *Reassessment*—Participants should review and reassess the security of information systems and networks, and make appropriate modifications to security policies, practices, measures, and procedures.

Governments of member states are to provide leadership in the development of a culture of security. Specifically, governments are to "develop national policy on information and security and ensure cross-border cooperation to promote a global culture of security."[96] Governments are to enact a comprehensive set of laws and regulations concerning substantive cybercrimes and ensure cross-border cooperation. They are to identify cybercrime units and points of contacts and establish institutions such as CERTS (Computer Emergency Response Teams) that exchange threat and vulnerability assessments. They also should create closer cooperation with businesses with respect to information security and combating cybercrime.

Governments should also develop and conduct outreach and other programs to foster security concerns among inhabitants. They include education and training, make known the resources available, develop best practices, give support for research and development, and build partnerships with local participants. Awareness campaigns should be established that inform participants of the risks inherent in information systems and networks, security failures that can cause harm to systems and networks, potential harm from interconnectivity and interdependency, good practices to ensure safety of systems, the importance of developing security goals to prevent threats, and other related measures. Governments and businesses must address risk assessment, security design and implementation, security management, and reassessment of information systems and networks. Users of information systems also have the responsibility to ensure that the principles stated earlier are carried out in order to secure a safe and responsible global system.[97]

18.10 Individual European State Approaches to Security and Counterterrorism[98]

A number of countries in Western Europe have developed safeguards against terrorism, especially cyberterrorism. Whereas, in the United States, coordination of efforts is centered on one department, the Department of Homeland Security, in Europe, the tasks of providing protection from terrorist and related attacks are distributed among a number of agencies.

18.10.1 The United Kingdom

The United Kingdom (the U.K.) or Great Britain[99] is not a stranger to terrorist violence, having witnessed a number of bombings, the most recent being the July 2005 London rail system; past killings including that of Lord Mountbatten by the Irish Republican Army and those due to the Irish National Liberation Army terrorists. Among the enactments designed to counter such acts, Parliament passed the United Kingdom's *Prevention of Terrorism Act of 1984*, which gave extensive authority to the executive to detain, arrest, and punish suspected terrorists, and further gave police authorities additional powers to ensure the security of travelers to and from the United Kingdom. In addition, it enacted the "Regulation of Investigatory Powers Act" on October 5, 2000, which allows the government access to e-mail and other electronic data. It also created a special division in the National Criminal Intelligence Service to investigate electronic crime. In April 2004, it revealed a new comprehensive, cross-departmental Counterterrorism Strategy (CONTEST) that concerns four "P" areas, namely, *prevent* (ascertain the causes of terrorism), *pursue* (terrorists are to be identified and their efforts impeded), *protect* (especially critical infrastructures), and *prepare* (be ready to respond to terrorist attacks).

The responsibility for maintenance of security is shared by various governmental departments and agencies. They include the Cabinet and ministerial Cabinet committees and subcommittees, which have overall supervision and responsibility for counterterrorism strategies; the Ministries of Justice of the individuals components of the United Kingdom; and intelligence services, including the Security Service (M15), the Secret Intelligence Service (SIS or M16), and the foreign intelligence service. Other agencies providing protection are the British Transport Police with respect to railway systems, the Civil Nuclear Constabulary with respect to nuclear facilities, 43 regional police departments, and the military.[100] The principal challenges facing the United Kingdom are the strengthening of border controls and transport security, protection of the critical national infrastructure and countering chemical, biological, radiological, and nuclear (CBRN) threats, and improving its response to emergencies especially with respect to CBRN materials. It has passed the *Civil Contingencies Act* in 2004, giving the government powers to declare a state of emergency and to temporarily suspend civil rights during such crises.[101]

18.10.2 France

France too does not possess a central agency comparable to the U.S. Department of Homeland Security. Similar to the United Kingdom, responsibility for combating terrorism in all its forms is shared among various ministries. In essence, terrorism and cyberterrorism are treated as law enforcement matters. Due to its long history of terrorism emanating from separatist groups of Algerian, Basque, and Corsican backgrounds, as well as a major incident involving al-Qaeda that killed French naval personnel in Pakistan, France has devoted significant resources to combating terrorism. The French system is highly centralized, with major roles given to the Ministries of Interior and Defense in the effort. The Ministry of Interior has the responsibility of providing civil protection, while the Council for Internal Security, led by the prime minister and Ministers of the Interior, Justice, Defense, Economy, and Finance, determines policy and priority of measures. France is divided into 90 departments or administrative regions, each led by a prefect responsible to the central government.[102]

France is concerned more with maintaining order than with civil liberties when threats are made to the public order. Thus, in 1986, French law provided that judicial and police authorities be given special powers, including the ordering of wiretaps and surveillance as well as preventive detention of suspects up to 6 days without filing charges. If a threat is imminent, a system called Vigipirate can be activated on two levels by the president without legislative approval. The first level, or "simple" level, provides for calling up reserves, enlisting rescue personnel, and sending police to sensitive areas such as power plants, embassies, airports, trains and train stations, and fuel facilities. The president may also institute a second level called "reinforced," as the September 11, 2001 attack of the New York World Trade Center, whereby she/he can summon the military, police forces, and other security personnel to guard against national attacks.

There are also contingent plans for chemical, biological, and radiological attacks, including calling upon all health services personnel in the event of such emergencies. Similar to the United Kingdom and other nations, France has cooperated with the United States in permitting U.S. customs officials to join with French personnel to examine cargo containers for possible mass destruction weaponry and for illicit drugs. France is an integral part of the E.U. and has joined with other E.U. members in strengthening police and judicial functions. Its present concerns are the rise of Islamic terrorism and immigration. France's Minister of the Interior, Nicholas Sarkozy, caused a major outcry among Islamic groups and civil libertarians when he made it clear that imams who preach hatred and violence would be expelled from France. Places of worship will be investigated to ascertain whether radical and terrorist ideologies and activities were taking place within their houses of worship.[103]

18.10.3 Germany

Germany has a federal system of government, with a central government and 16 semi-autonomous states. Similar to the United Kingdom and France, Germany has had its share of terrorist incidents, especially those attributed to the Red Army Faction from the 1970s to the 1990s. The 9/11 outrage in New York caused the nation to become more vigilant in protecting its infrastructure and its population. As in France, the responsibility of providing protection against terrorism is shared among a number of ministries, namely, Interior, Justice, Defense, Foreign Affairs, and Finance. Other governmental departments also play a role. The major entities in uncovering and protecting against terrorist activities are entrusted to the Federal Intelligence Service under the Federal Chancellery, the Federal Bureau for the Protection of the Constitution under the Ministry of the Interior, and the Military Counterintelligence Service under the Ministry of Defense. Law Enforcement obligations are entrusted to the Federal Bureau of Criminal Investigation, the Federal Border Guard, and the Federal Public Prosecutor General.[104]

After 9/11, the German authorities became increasingly concerned about radical Islamic groups that promote terrorism. Inasmuch as three of the hijackers lived in Hamburg and in parts of Germany, the nation began questioning its liberal asylum policies and its strong commitment to civil rights. Accordingly, it enacted two measures in the legal, law enforcement, financial, and security areas. These include the revocation of immunity of religious groups and charities from investigation or surveillance; the prosecution of terrorists in Germany even if the acts were committed abroad; the curtailment of the entry and residence of terrorists within Germany; and the strengthening of border and aviation security. Germany has undertaken the identification and elimination of terrorist cells, including the use of profiling. It has prosecuted a number of members of terrorist cells, and has taken measures to survey and seize terrorist financing. A new immigration law now makes deportation easier and naturalization more difficult.[105]

18.10.4 Italy

Italy also experienced terrorism at the hands of the Red Brigades, which committed numerous violent acts during the 1970s and 1980s. It also has had perennial problems with the Mafia in Sicily, and its ship and airport have been scenes of violent behavior. Like all member states of the E.U., Italy has cooperated in promulgating E.U. antiterrorist measures, especially since 9/11. The efforts are led by government officials headed by the Council of Ministers and the prime minister as the supreme decision-making body. The Minister of the Interior is in charge of antiterrorist efforts as well as border control, public order, and security. The Public Security Department within the ministry is in charge of the national police force, while the Civil Liberty and Immigration Department promulgates immigration and asylum policy. Other ministries also participating in sharing responsibility include the Defense Ministry, the Health Ministry, the Infrastructure and Transport Ministry, and the Economics and Finance Ministry. There are other departments within these ministries that have specific responsibilities for the safety and welfare of the citizens of the state.[106]

Law enforcement and intelligence gathering is accomplished by the country's (national) state police and are assisted by prefects at the provincial level. In addition, the Italian military corps or carabinieri also carry out police duties. It has an elite counterterrorist unit, gathers intelligence, and investigates terrorist organizations. Italy's main intelligence and security services are carried out by the Military Intelligence and Security Service under the Ministry of Defense. It has counterespionage and counterintelligence duties, mainly with respect to military matters. The Democratic Intelligence and Security Service, under the Department of the Interior, is responsible for intelligence and security tasks with respect to possible subversion of the state.[107]

18.10.5 Spain

Islamist terrorism became a reality on March 11, 2004 when bombs exploded on four commuter trains killing 192 persons. It also has had decades long problems with Basque extremists. Accordingly, it has significantly increased funding and surveillance with a focus on Islamic extremists. There are some 1000 officers assigned to counterterrorist units with the Ministry of the Interior. It has joined bilaterally with France to form investigative teams to fight terrorism. The responsibility for measures of security, emergency preparedness, and response, and related activities lies within the said Ministry. Spain has a National Police Corps promoting security within the nation as well as paramilitary units, the Civil Guard, in more remote areas of the country.[108]

18.10.6 Tunisia

Tunisia, which had its own terrorist bombing incident, has taken steps to avert cyberterrorism. At the close of the 20th century, it created a "Micro-CERT" unit that specializes in Internet security. Its objectives included generating awareness of security issues in policymakers and technical staff, helping monitor critical infrastructures, and creating a task force on IT security. In January 2003, the council of ministers, headed by the president, created a national agency specializing in

Internet security. It introduced mandatory and periodic security audits, and created a body of auditors in the field. Other laws were also passed regarding the protection of privacy and security, electronic signature and e-commerce, cybercrime, and consumer protection and intellectual property rights.[109]

In February 2004, Tunisia promulgated an "original" law on computer security that obligated all public companies (all public and sensitive private companies) to conduct periodic security audits by certified auditors of their information systems. All incidents involving hacking, viruses, and other security incidents are to be reported to the agency, whose reports are to kept confidential. A National Agency for Computer Security was created under the Ministry of Communication Technologies. Within the agency is a Computer Emergency Response Team of the Tunisian Coordination Center (CERT/TCC), which disseminates information on vulnerabilities and attacks as well as sending awareness materials thousands of voluntary subscribers. It creates awareness of the potential hazards by organizing conferences and workshops, setting up booths at national and regional exhibitions, press releases, and developing materials for dissemination. It has a Watch-center that monitors cyberspace security and seeks to detect potential threats. It is also constructing a National Disaster-Recovery Center in the event of a serious cyberattack. The agency has professional training programs and academic master's degree programs, and cooperates with other national and international agencies.[110]

18.11 Other International Efforts

Virtually all countries have enacted legislation making it a crime to unlawfully intrude into another person's computer without authorization. Among the numerous country statutes are the following:

- Mexico—Article 211(1)–211(7) of the *Mexican Federal Penal Code* proscribes copying, modifying, destroying, or damaging information, databases, or computer or information systems.
- Chile—*Law on Automated Data Processing Crimes, No. 19.223*, makes it a crime for a person to "maliciously and makes unusable a system of information processing or its parts or components, or prevents or modifies its operation... [or who] attempts illegally to use, or to know the information contained in an information processing system... [or who] maliciously alters, damages, or destroys the data contained in a system of information processing... [or who] maliciously reveals or spreads the data contained in an IS...."
- China—Its *Computer Information Network and Internet Security, Protection and Management Regulations* are aimed mainly at state security. It prohibits the use of the Internet to harm national security or disclose state secrets or harm state interests or those of citizens. Information that incites resistance to or overthrow of the country's Constitution, laws, or administrative regulations

by use of the Internet is prohibited. Its provisions are extensive and forbid even the use of computer networks or network resources without prior approval.

■ India—The *Information Technology Act, 2000*, specifies computer offenses that are outlawed, including tampering with computers, unauthorized access, damaging or destroying data therein, publishing obscenity, and disclosing private information without consent.

Countries that may not have specific legislation address to cybercrimes, nevertheless, either have pending legislation specifically addressing cybercrime or have analogous legislation that achieves the same ends. Statutes include those that make damage to property punishable or prohibit invasion of privacy. Examples of these statutes include Panama's Criminal Code and Venezuela's Law on the Protection of the Privacy of Communications.[111]

There are a number of international conventions that proscribe terrorist activities. A few of the more important conventions are the *International Convention Against the Taking of Hostages*; the *1963 Convention of the Offences and Certain Acts Committed on Board Aircraft (The Tokyo Convention)*; the *1973 Convention on the Prevention and Punishment of Crimes Against Internationally Protected Persons, Including Diplomatic Agents (The New York Convention)*; and the *1979 International Convention Against the Taking of Hostages*.

18.12 Summary

Future of Cyberterrorism. With the seismic technological changes taking place on an almost daily basis, it is difficult to foresee in the distant future what steps are to be taken to lessen the dangers of cyberterrorism or criminal attacks on computer-based systems. It does appear that, contrary to the opinions expressed by some observers, the threat of significant harm to the populace is real and that there is increasing need for a global united effort to cooperate and share intelligence, stay current with the latest technologies and vulnerabilities, and to enlist the aid of experts to combat the efforts of unscrupulous persons seeking to undermine and harm societies for their political, economic, and religious gains.[112]

Legislation is almost always enacted in response to perceived needs of the various constituencies. Except in exceptional circumstances in authoritarian countries, laws are almost never passed for illegitimate purposes. Nevertheless, events and unusual circumstances may lead to statutes that ultimately may be more harmful than the problem the statutes seek to address. The Patriot Act may be such a statute. Leaving the enforcement to the goodwill and integrity of governmental officials may be fraught with constitutional dangers. It will be seen in the future whether the U.S. Supreme Court will uphold all or part of the statute and whether the curtailment of citizens' rights are justified under the circumstances the nation finds itself in.

18.13 Review Questions

1. Explain how security economic intelligence works, using an example.
2. Explain how to implement cost-effective homeland security. Give an example.
3. Explain the danger of known types of terrorism and how to fight them.
4. Explain the known means used to perform terrorist activities.
5. Identify and give examples of all known forms of cyberattacks.
6. Explain how real is the danger coming from cyberterrorism. Give examples.
7. Identify the advantages perpetrators think they can gain from cyberterrorism, and give examples.
8. Explain how to combat cyberterrorism, and give examples.
9. Explain how to combat cyberterrorism. Give a taxonomy.
10. Explain how the FBI sees cyberterrorism. What are the major differences from what is reported in the literature?
11. Explain how legislative enactments and proposed programs work in the United States.
12. Explain how individual European state approaches to security and counterterrorism are different from the ones we have in the United States.

18.14 Workshops

Workshop 1

I always worry about those containers getting into the homeland and we can only x-ray and check the contents for only 5%–10% of them. Do you see any concepts discussed in this chapter that we can apply to solve this problem? Also, can you think of any strict steps or a cost-effective methodology that we can propose to Homeland Security to mitigate risks associated with the search of inbound containers? Hint: Can we use trusted international private agencies abroad that should certify the security of containers before they are loaded and also on their way to our ports?

Workshop 2

Develop a taxonomy of cyberterrorism based on the congressional testimony delivered by Keith Lourdeau before the Senate Judiciary Subcommittee on Terrorism, Technology, and Homeland Security on February 24, 2004. Notice the differences in views between the existing literature and the real world represented by the FBI. Can you tone up this taxonomy to bridge the gaps between the views of scholars and practitioners?

Endnotes

1. Examples include the railroad and train explosions in Spain and England in recent years.
2. BBC News, *US Warns of Al-Qaeda Cyber Threat* (December 1, 2006), http://news.bbc.co.uk/1/hi/world/Americas/6197446.stm.
3. For a discussion, see John Rollins and Clay Wilson, *Terrorist Capabilities for Cyberattack: Overview and Policy Issues*, Congressional Research Service (October 20, 2005), 12-14.
4. Brian C. Lewis, *Prevention of Computer Crime Amidst International Anarchy*, 41 Am. Crim. L. Rev. 1353 (Summer, 2004).
5. Rollins and Wilson, *supra*, at 12–13.
6. Keith Lourdeau, Deputy Assistant Director, Cyber Division, FBI, testimony before the Senate Judiciary Subcommittee on Terrorism, Technology, and Homeland Security, February 24, 2004.
7. Bitpipe (August 24, 2006), http://www.bitpipe.com/tlist/Cyberterrorism.html.
8. For a detailed examination of the topic including the data stated in this article, see Brian Cashell, William D. Jackson, Mark Jickling, and Baird Webel, *The Economic Impact of Cyber-Attacks*, Congressional Research Service (April 1, 2004).
9. *Id.* at 6–8. The survey may be found at http://www.gocsi.com.
10. *Id.* at 9–10. The sources for the two studies were Computer Economics Inc., *Security Issues: Virus Costs Are Rising Again*,(September 2003), http://www.computereconomics.com and Mi2g, *Frequently Asked Questions: SIPS and EVEDA, v1.00* (February 6, 2004), http://www.mi2g.co.uk.
11. Lourdreau, *op. cit.*
12. Clay Wilson, *Computer Attack and Cyberterrorism: Vulnerabilities and Policy Issues for Congress*, Congressional Research Service (April 1, 2005).
13. See Jacqueline Ann Carberry, *Terrorism: A Global Phenomenon Mandating a Unified International Response*, 6 Ind. J. Global Leg. Stud. 685 (Spring 1999) and Yonah Alexander, *Terrorism in the Twenty-First Century: Threats and Responses*, 12 DePaul Bus. L.J. 59 (Fall, 1999/Spring, 2000).
14. Information Warfare, *Cyberterrorism*, http://ntrg.cs.tcd.ie/undergrad/4ba2.02/infowar/terrorism.html.
15. Susan W. Brenner and Marc D. Goodman, *In Defense of Cyberterrorism: An Argument for Anticipating Cyber-Attacks*, 2002 U. Ill. J.L. Tech. & Pol'y 1 (Spring, 2001), pp. 14–24.
16. Jason Barkham, *Information Warfare and International Law on the Use of Force*, 34 N.Y.U. J. Int'l L. & Pol. 57 (Fall 2001), pp. 62-64.
17. The President's Management Agenda, August 2001.
18. Brenner and Goodman, *op. cit.*
19. The recent anthrax use in the United States, the infection of salad with salmonella bacteria by disciples of Bhagwan Shree Rajneesh, and the subway attack in Japan in 1995 by members of the Aum Shinrikyo cult caused relatively few casualties.
20. Brenner and Goodman, *op. cit.* pp. 13–20.
21. The President's Information Technology Advisory Committee, *Cyber Security: A Crisis of Prioritization*, Report to the President (February 2005), p. 25, http://www.nitrd.gov/pitac/reports/20050301_cybersecurity/cybersecurity.pdf, cited in Rollins and Wilson, *supra* at 5.

22. Anthony Davis, The Afghan files: Al-Qaeda documents from Kabul, *Jane's Intelligence Review* (February 1, 2002), cited in *id.* at 9.

23. Vicki Spencer, *Cyber Terrorism: Mass Destruction or Mass Disruption?*, http://www.crime-research.org/library/mi2g.htm. See also, Religioscope, *Al-Qaeda Disrupted But Retains Vast Network* (June 28, 2002), http://www.religioscope.com/articles/2002/006_queda.htm.

24. *Id.* at 10.

25. BBC News, *Cyber Terrorism "Overhyped"* (14 March, 2003). The article cited a panel of security and technology experts at the CeBIT technology fair.

26. The Guardian, *Cyber Hype* (December 5, 2002), http://technology.guardian.co.uk/online/story/0,3605,853535,00.html.

27. Global Internet Policy Initiative, *Protecting Privacy and Freedom of Communication in the Fight against Cybercrime,* http: www.internetpolicy.net, Southeast Europe Cybersecurity Conference, Sofia, Bulgaria (September 8–9, 2003).

28. There are numerous references to the World Summit. including the following: WISeKey, WSIS World summit on the Information Society, http:/www.wisekey.com/wsis/WSIShomepage.htm; United Nations Press Release PI/1677 (September 20, 2005), http:www.un.org/News/docs/2005/pi1677.doc.htm.; and Declan McCullagh, *Global Web: An Internet Governance Run-Down,* http://news.zdnet.co.uk/internet/0,1000000097,39237328,00.htm.

29. Joshua Green, The Myth of Cyberterrorism, *Washington Monthly* (November 2002), http://www.washingtonmonthly.com/features/2001/0211.green.html.

30. *Immunizing the Internet, or: How I Learned to Stop Worrying and Love the Worm,* 119 Harv. L. Rev. 2442 (June 2006).

31. See government Web site at http:www.us-cert.gov.

32. Information Warfare, *op. cit.* Possible criticisms of the project include claims that among the captured data are trade secrets and other personal data that are shared with national corporate entities.

33. For a discussion of the Carnivore program and its proposed usage by the FBI, see John Lewis, *Carnivore—The FBI's Internet Surveillance System: Is it a Rampaging E-Mailsaurus Rex Devouring Your Constitutional Rights?,* 23 Whittier L. Rev. 317 (Winter, 2001).

34. 18 U.S.C. Section 1029(a)(1).

35. 18 U.S.S. Section 1029(a)(4).

36. 18 U.S.C. Section 1029(e)(1)(2).

37. "Section 1030. Fraud and related activity in connection with computers:

Whoever—having knowingly accessed a computer without authorization or exceeding authorized access, and by means of such conduct having obtained information that has been determined by the United States Government pursuant to an Executive order or statute to require protection against unauthorized disclosure for reasons of national defense or foreign relations, or any restricted data…with reason to believe that such information so obtained could be used to the injury of the United States, or to the advantage of any foreign nation willfully communicates, delivers, transmits, or causes to be communicated, delivered, or transmitted, or attempts to communicate, deliver, transmit or cause to be communicated, delivered, or transmitted the same to any person not entitled to receive it, or willfully retains the same and fails to deliver it to the officer or employee if the United States entitled to receive it intentionally accesses a computer without authorization or exceeds authorized access, and thereby obtains— information contained in a financial record of a financial institution, or of a card issuer...or contained in a file of a consumer reporting agency on a consumer... information from any department or agency of the United States; or information from any protected computer if the conduct involved an interstate or foreign communication; intentionally, without authorization to access any nonpublic computer of a department or agency of the United States, accesses such a computer of that department or agency that is used exclusively for the use of the government... knowingly and with intent to defraud, accesses a protected computer without authorization, or exceeds authorized access, and by means of such conduct furthers the intended fraud and obtains anything of value, unless the object of the fraud and the thing obtained consists only of the use of the computer and the value of such use is not more than $5000 in any 1-year period; (A) knowingly causes the transmission of a program, information, code, or command, and as a result of such conduct, intentionally causes damage without authorization, to a protected computer; (B) intentionally access a protected computer without authorization, and as a result of such conduct, recklessly causes damage; or intentionally accesses a protected computer without authorization, and as a result of such conduct, causes damage; knowingly and with intent to defraud traffics...in any password or similar information through which a computer may be accessed without authorization, if—such trafficking affects interstate of foreign commerce; or such computer is used by of for the Government of the United States; with intent to extort from any person, firm, association, educational institution, financial institution, government entity, or other legal entity, any money or other thing of value, transmits in interstate or foreign commerce any communication containing any threat to cause damage to a protected computer." Punishment for conviction of any of the above offenses range from a fine/ or imprisonment, depending on the offense, of 1–20 years.

38. 18 U.S.C. Section 1343.
39. *U.S. v. Martin*, 228 F.3d 1 (1st Cir. 2000); *U.S. v. Serrano*, 870 F.2d 1, 6 (1st Cir. 1989); and *U.S. v. Montminy*, 936 F.2d 626, 627 (1st Cir. 1991).
40. *U.S. v. Martin, id.*
41. 18 U.S.C. Section 1028.
42. 18 U.S.C. Section 1028.
43. Section 1961.
44. Section 1963.
45. 18 U.S.C. Section 2511.
46. 18 U.S.C. Section 2701.
47. The above statutory materials are taken from Roy J. Girasa, *Cyberlaw: National and International Perspectives,* Prentice Hall, 2002.
48. For a discussion of civil enforcement, see Michael L. Rustad, *Private Enforcement of Cybercrime on the Electronic Frontier,* 11 S. Cal. Interdis. L.J. 63 (Winter, 2001).
49. Pub. L. No. 107-56, 115 Stat. 272 (2001).
50. There are literally several hundred law review articles and almost innumerable other references, some of which can be accessed by reference to LEXIS-NEXIS and other reference sources. A few of the articles will be cited in the discussion herein. The statute is so offensive to perceived beliefs of civil libertarians that the American Civil Liberties Union took out a full-page advertisement in the *New York Times,* setting forth the deprivation of liberties that the act allegedly legitimizes. *New York Times*, February 25, 2003, p. A11.
51. The U.S. Senate debated the proposed statute for 1 day.

52. See *TomPaine.com* for its claim in an article "George Bush Channels George Orwell," that President Bush's war on terrorism and the creation of a homeland security apparatus is in keeping with Orwell's *1984* views of the movement toward a totalitarian society.

53. Electronic Frontier Foundation, *USAPA Sunset Provisions Could Leave Congress in the Dark,* wysiwyg://14/http://www.eff.org//Privacy/...s/20011212_eee_usapa_sunset_analysis.html. The report concerns the sunset provisions of the USA Patriot Act, which provides for the expiration of the statute on December 31, 2005, with respect to a number of surveillance provisions of the act. It concludes as follows: "The EFF remains deeply troubled that Congress has passed such sweeping reductions on the right of Americans to be free from overarching government surveillance. Yet having done so, it is imperative that Congress fulfill the promise of the Sunset provisions by requiring and, where possible, sharing with the American people basic information about how these broad powers are being used."

54. Michael T. McCarthy, *USA Patriot Act,* 39 Harv. J. on Legis. 435 (Summer, 2002) at pp. 437–439.

55. FISA, 50 U.S.C. 1801–1863 (1994 & Supp. V 1999).

56. Section 1801(e) of FISA.

57. For a discussion, see Jennifer C. Evans, *Hijacking Civil Liberties: The USA Patriot Act of 2001,* 33 Loy. U. Chi. L.J. 933 (Summer, 2002), at pp. 944–958 and 967–973.

58. For a discussion of this topic, see Sara Sun Beale and James E. Felman, *Responses to the September 11 Attacks: The Consequences of Enlisting Federal Grand Juries in the War on Terrorism: Assessing the USA Patriot's Act's Changes to Grand Jury Secrecy,* 24 Harv. J.L. & Pub. Pol'y 699 (Spring, 2002).

59. *Id.* at pp. 708–709. The section referred to is 203(a)(1).

60. Section 216(a) of the Patriot Act.

61. A pen register records or decodes electronic or other impulses that identify numbers that are dialed or transmitted telephonically. See Evans, *op. cit.* at pp. 971–973.

62. *United States v. Verdugo-Urquidez,* 494 U.S, 259 (1990).

63. 126 F. Supp.2d 264 (S.D.N.Y. 2000).

64. For a discussion, see Carrie Truehart, *United States v. Bin Laden and the Foreign Intelligence Exception to the Warrant Requirement for Searches of "United States Persons" Abroad,* 82 B.U.L. Rev. 555 (April 2002).

65. 22 U.S.C. Section 2656(d)(2) defines "terrorism" as "premeditated, politically motivated violence perpetrated against noncombatant targets by substantial groups or clandestine agents."

66. USA Patriot Act, section 411(a)(1)(F) states:

"(iv) ENGAGE IN TERRORIST ACTIVITY DEFINED-

As used in this chapter, the term 'engage in terrorist activity' means, in an individual capacity or as a member of an organization-

to commit or to incite to commit, under circumstances indicating an intention to cause death or serious bodily injury, a terrorist activity;

to prepare or plan a terrorist activity;

to gather information on potential targets for terrorist activity;

to solicit funds or other things of value for-

(aa) a terrorist activity

(bb) a terrorist organization described in clause (vi)(I) or (vi)(II); or (cc) a terrorist organization described in clause (vi)(III), unless the solicitor can demonstrate that he did not know, and should not reasonably have known, that the solicitation would further the organization's terrorist activity;

to solicit any individual [to engage in the forbidden conduct or for membership in a terrorist organization]

to commit an act that the actor knows, or reasonably should know, affords material support, including a safe house, transportation, communications, funds, transfer of funds or other material benefit, false documentation or identification, weapons (including chemical, biological, or radiological weapons), explosives, or training-[for terrorist activity or to a terrorist organization]."

67. For a discussion, see Joshua D. Zelman, *International Terrorism: Recent Developments: Recent Developments in International Law: Anti-Terrorism Legislation-Part TWO: The Impact and Consequences,* 11 J. Transnat'l L. & Pol'y 421 (Spring, 2002) at pp. 422-424.

68. Section 412(a) of the Patriot Act amending the Immigration and Nationality Act, 8 U.S.C. sections 1101 et seq. so as to read:

"(5) COMMENCEMENT OF PROCEEDINGS- the Attorney General shall place an alien detained under paragraph (1) in removal proceedings, or shall charge the alien with a criminal offense, not later than 7 days after the commencement of such detention. If the requirement of the preceding sentence is not satisfies, the Attorney General shall release the alien."

69. *Id.*

"LIMITATION OF INDEFINITE DETENTION-An alien detained solely under paragraph (1) who has not been removed under section 241(a)(1)(A), and whose removal is unlikely in the reasonably foreseeable future, may be detained for additional periods of up to six months only if the release of the alien will threaten the national security of the United States or the safety of the community or any person."

70. For a discussion of sections 411 and 412 of the USA Patriot Act, see Joshua D. Zelman, *Focus on: International Terrorism: Recent Developments: Recent Developments in International Law: Anti-Terrorism Legislation-Part Two: The Impact and Consequences,* 11 J. Transnat'l L. & Pol'y 421 (Spring, 2002).

71. Article I, Section 9 clause 2 provides: "The Privilege of the Writ of Habeas Corpus shall not be suspended, unless when in Cases of Rebellion or Invasion the public Safety may require it."

72. For example, see McCarthy *op. cit.*.

73. Korematsu v. United States, 323 U.S. 214 (1944), in which the U.S. Supreme Court (6-3) upheld the removal from the West Coast and the internment of U.S. Japanese citizens and residents based on the war powers of Congress and the president. Justice Black said he could not reject the findings of the military authority, which had been given the responsibility of protecting the shores of the United States during World War II, that the imposition of a mere curfew was insufficient to protect against an unascertained number of disloyal Japanese citizens and residents. Korematsu was an American-born citizen of Japanese parents who was gainfully employed and who had a non-Japanese girlfriend. In an attempt to avoid detention, he had facial surgery performed and claimed he was a Mexican-American. He was convicted and sentenced to prison, but was paroled and sent to a Japanese internment camp. In his dissent, Justice Murphy stated that the military order of removal constituted "a far more subtle blow to liberty than the promulgation of the order itself. A military order, however

unconstitutional, is not apt to last longer than the military emergency. Even during that period a succeeding commander may revoke it all. But once a judicial opinion rationalizes such an order to show it conforms to the Constitution, or rather rationalizes the Constitution to show the Constitution sanctions such an order, the Court for all time has validated the principle of racial discrimination in criminal procedure and of transplanting American citizens...."

74. The Congressional war powers referred to in the opinion are found in Article I, section 8 of the Constitution, which gives Congress the powers to "To declare War;" "to raise and support Armies, but no Appropriation of Money to that Use shall be for a longer Term than two Years;" "To provide and maintain a Navy;" "to make Rules for the Government and Regulation of the land and naval Forces;" "to provide for calling forth the Militia to execute the laws of the Union, suppress Insurrections and repel Invasions;" and "To provide for organizing, arming, and disciplining, the Militia and for governing such Part of them as may be employed in the Service of the United States...." For a commentary of the Congressional powers in war, see Laurence H. Tribe, *American Constitutional Law,* 2d ed., Mineola, N.Y.: The Foundation Press, Inc., 1988, section 5–16. Anthony Lewis, in his column entitled "Marbury v. Madison v. Ashcroft," observed that courts have "disappointed us" in actual or threatened wartime by succumbing to executive claims of national security as illustrated in the *Korematsu* case. The present war on terrorism he fears, may lead to judicial abdication of the protection of visiting or permanent aliens within the United States. In *Marbury,* courts were given the right to declare what the law is in relation to the Constitution. He quotes Justice William J. Brennan Jr., who observed in a lecture in Jerusalem that punitive actions in connection with alleged threats to national security were "so baseless that they would be comical if not for the serious hardship they cause." Lewis reminds us that courts should respect governmental claims of terrorist and other threats to national security, but their greatest duty is "as guardians of freedom." *New York Times,* February 24, 2003, p. A17.

Electronic Frontier Foundation, *EFF Analysis of the Provisions of the USA Patriot Act That Relate to Online Activities (Oct. 31, 2001),* http://www.eff.org/Privacy/Surveillance/T...as/20011031_eff_usa_patriot_analysis.html.

75. Section 302(a) of the Patriot Act.
76. Section 302(b) of the Patriot Act.
77. 31 U.S.C. Section 5211 et seq.
78. It was decided on October 25, 2002, that there would be a final delay apparently for specific regulations directed to the manifold TierTwo entities to be issued thereafter. For a discussion, see William W. Weiner and Hope K. Plasha, *Anti-Terrorism Law Imposes Duties: Lenders and Others Must Stay on Alert for "Restricted Parties,"* New York Law Journal, Nov. 25, 2002, Vo. 228, p. s1, col. 1.
79. Section 326(a)(1)(2) of the Patriot Act.
80. Section 326(b) of the Patriot Act.
81. One author, Melissa K. Mathews, in criticizing the breadth of the President's new emergency powers, traced the history of the expansion of presidential prerogatives in *Restoring the Imperial Presidency: An Examination of President's New Emergency Powers,* 23 Hamline J. Pub. L. & Pol'y 455 (Spring 2002).
82. See Lori Sachs, *September 11, 2001: The Constitution during Crisis: A New Perspective,* 29 Fordham Urb. L.J. 1715 (April 2002) and the citations stated therein.

83. William Safire, Privacy Invasion Curtailed, *New York Times*, February 13, 2003, p. A41.

84. Some of the other known programs available to governmental authorities include Echelon, which not only intercepts large masses of data from e-mails, facsimiles, and the like, filters them, and compares the data with its "dictionary" of words and phrases in a variety of languages, in order to alert reviewers to messages of import to surveillance personnel; "TEMPEST" (Transient Electromagnetic Pulse Emanation Standard), which retrieves and reconstructs data retrieved from a digital device. *Id.* at pp. 333–335.

85. U.S. Department of State, *The Antiterrorism Assistance Program: Report to Congress for Fiscal Year 2005.*

86. *Id.*

87. No. 2580/2001 dated December 27, 2001.

88. Joshua D. Zelman, *Recent Developments in International Law: Anti-Terrorism Legislation – Part One: An Overview*, 11 J. Transnat'l L. & Pol'y 183 (Fall, 2001) at pp. 192–196.

89. The Council of Europe is Europe's oldest political organization, founded in 1949, and includes 46 countries (21 from Central and Eastern Europe) with observer status to the Holy See, United States, Canada, Japan, and Mexico. Its major concerns are the defense of human rights, promulgation of parliamentary democracy, the development of programs of shared values, and economic reforms. It consists of a Committee of Ministers of all member states, a Parliamentary Assembly, a Congress of Local and Regional Authorities, and a Secretariat.

90. The G8 nations consist of the United Kingdom, Canada, France, Germany, Italy, Japan, Russia, and the United States.

91. The cybercrimes being addressed by the G8 nations were pedophilia, drug-trafficking, money-laundering, electronic fraud such as theft of credit card numbers, and computerized piracy, and industrial and state espionage.

92. *Alte Neuigkeiten: G8 Action Plan Computer Crime*, http://www.fitug.de/debate/9803/msg00047.html.

93. *Id.* at pp. 197–199.

94. The OECD came into existence on December 14, 1960, and came into force on 30 September, 1961. Its purpose was the promotion of policies designed:
"To achieve the highest sustainable economic growth and employment and a rising standards of living in Member countries, while maintaining financial stability, and thus to contribute to the development of the world economy;
To contribute to sound economic expansion in Member as well as non-member countries in the process of economic development; and
To contribute to the expansion of world trade on a multilateral, non-discriminatory basis in accordance with international obligations."
The original membership consisted of 20 countries, mainly from Western Europe, but it was expanded to include 10 additional countries. Membership includes the United States, Canada, Australia and New Zealand, Japan, Korea, and several Eastern European nations.

95. The guidelines were adopted as a recommendation of the OECD Council in its 1037th session.

96. OECD Directorate for Science, Technology and Industry, *Implementation Plan for the OECD Guidelines for the Security of Information Systems and Networks: Towards a Culture of Security*, DSTI/ICCP/REG(2003)5/REV1 at 3.
97. *Id.* at 4–6.
98. Data for this section are taken primarily from Kristin Archick, Carl Ek, Paul Gallis, Francis T. Miko, and Steven Woehrel, *European Approaches to Homeland Security and Counterterrorism*, Congressional Research Service (July 24, 2006).
99. The United Kingdom consists of England, Scotland, Wales, and Northern Ireland.
100. *Supra*, note 29 at 39–41.
101. *Id.* at 46–47.
102. *Id.* at 9–10.
103. M. Sarkozy, *Veut Expulser les Imams "Radicaus,"* Le Monde, July 17–19, 2005, at 2, cited in *id.* at 14.
104. *Id.* at 16–18.
105. *Id.* at 20–21.
106. *Id.* at 24–25.
107. *Id.* at 25–27.
108. *Id.* at 32–35.
109. The discussion on Tunisia is taken from Pr Nabil Sahli, Ministry of Communication Technologies, *Insights into the Tunisian Experience and Strategy in the Establishment of National Watch, Warning and Incident Response Capabilities,*
110. *Id.*
111. *Id.*, Appendix for a list of countries and the statutes forbidding cybercrimes or analogous legislation.
112. See, for example, Barry C. Collin, *The Future of CyberTerrorism: Where the Physical and Virtual Worlds Collide,* at the 11th Annual International Symposium on Criminal Justice Issues, http://afgen.com/terrorism1.html.

References

1. ARC (1992). Advanced RISC Computing Specification: ARC Specification. 1991, 1992 MIPS Technology Inc.—Printed. Mountain View, California 94039–7311 USA, http://www.netbsd.org/docs/Hardware/Machines/ARC/riscspec.pdf.
2. Congressional Testimony, Testimony of Keith Lourdeau, Deputy Assistant Director, Cyber Division, FBI, Before the Senate Judiciary Subcommittee on Terrorism, Technology, and Homeland Security, February 24, 2004: http://www.fbi.gov/congress/congress04/lourdeau022404.htm.
3. CSARS. (2006). SIRC Releases 2005–06 Annual Report/ Security Intelligence Review Committee [visited URL: 07/10/2007] http://www.sirc-csars.gc.ca/pdfs/ar_2005-2006-eng.pdf.
4. NFPA 1600. (2007). Standard on Disaster/Emergency Management and Business Continuity Programs. NFPA, 1 Batterymarch Park, Quincy, MA 02169-7471 (International Codes and Standards Organization). 2007 Edition. [visited URL: 07/10/2007] http://www.nfpa.org/assets/files/pdf/nfpa1600.pdf.

5. Oscar Pastor, Joao Falcao e Cunha. (2005). Advanced Information Systems Engineering (CAiSE 2005), in Porto, Portugal in June 2005. Springer Eds. (Óscar Pastor, João Falcão e Cunha—Computers—2005–584 pages).

6. Schneier Bruce. (2007). Security and Security Technology (a blog covering). [visited URL: 07/10/2007] http://www.schneier.com/papers.html and http://www.schneier.com/blog/archives/2006/07/security_certif.html.

7. Sun Tzu (By Lionel Giles, M. A.) (1910). On the Art of War: The Oldest Military Treatise in the World. Translated from the Chinese by Lionel Giles, M.A. (1910). [Visited URL: 07/10/2007] http://Www.Chinapage.Com/Sunzi-E.Html.

8. White House. (2002). The National Strategy For Homeland Security: Office of Homeland Security. USA, July 2002. [visited URL: 07/10/2007] http://www.whitehouse.gov/homeland/book/nat_strat_hls.pdf.

9. White House. (2006).The National Security Strategy. USA, March 2006. [visited URL: 07/10/2007] http://www.whitehouse.gov/nsc/nss/2006/nss2006.pdf.

Index

X

X-scan, 440

Z

Zone Definitions (ZD), 206